AF230105

Miscellaneous Essays and Lays of Ancient Rome

MISCELLANEOUS ESSAYS AND LAYS OF ANCIENT ROME

THOMAS BABINGTON MACAULAY

COSIMO CLASSICS

NEW YORK

Miscellaneous Essays and Lays of Ancient Rome
© 2005 Cosimo, Inc.
All rights reserved. No part of this book may be used or reproduced in
any manner whatsoever without prior written permission except in the
case of brief quotations embodied in critical articles or reviews.
For information, address:

Cosimo, P.O. Box 416
Old Chelsea Station
New York, NY 10113-0416

or visit our website at:
www.cosimobooks.com

Miscellaneous Essays and Lays of Ancient Rome originally published by E.P.
Dutton & Company in 1860.

Library of Congress Cataloging-in-Publication Data
A catalog record for this book is available from the Library of Congress

Cover design by www.wiselephant.com

ISBN: 1-59605-098-5

INTRODUCTION[1]

By T. F. ELLIS

Lord Macaulay always looked forward to a publication of his miscellaneous works, either by himself or by those who should represent him after his death. And latterly he expressly reserved, whenever the arrangements as to copyright made it necessary, the right of such publication.

The collection which is here published comprehends some of the earliest and some of the latest works which he composed. He was born on October 25, 1800; commenced residence at Trinity College, Cambridge, in October 1818; was elected Craven University Scholar in 1821; graduated as B.A. in 1822; was elected Fellow of the college in October 1824; was called to the Bar in February 1826, when he joined the Northern Circuit; and was elected member for Calne in 1830. After this last event, he did not long continue to practise at the Bar. He went to India in 1834, whence he returned in June 1838. He was elected member for Edinburgh in 1839, and lost this seat in July 1847: and this (though he was afterwards again elected for that city in July 1852, without being a candidate) may be considered as the last instance of his taking an active part in the contests of public life. These few dates are mentioned for the purpose of enabling the reader to assign the articles, now and previously published, to the principal periods into which the author's life may be divided.

The admirers of his later works will probably be interested by watching the gradual formation of his style, and will notice in his earlier productions, vigorous and clear as their language always was, the occurrence of faults against which he afterwards most anxiously guarded himself. A much greater interest will undoubtedly be felt in tracing the date and development of his opinions.

[1] From the original edition of 1860.

The articles published in Knight's *Quarterly Magazine* were contributed during the author's residence at college as B.A. It may be remarked that the first two of these exhibit the earnestness with which he already endeavoured to represent to himself and to others the scenes and persons of past times as in actual existence. Of the Dialogue between Milton and Cowley he spoke, many years after its publication, as that one of his works which he remembered with most satisfaction. The article on Mitford's *Greece* he did not himself value so highly as others thought it deserved. This article, at any rate, contains the first distinct enunciation of his views as to the office of an historian, views afterwards more fully set forth in his Essay upon History, in the *Edinburgh Review*. From the protest, in the last-mentioned essay, against the conventional notions respecting the majesty of history might perhaps have been anticipated something like the third chapter of the *History of England*. It may be amusing to notice that in the article on Mitford appears the first sketch of the New Zealander, afterwards filled up in a passage in the review of Mrs. Austin's translation of Ranke, a passage which at one time was the subject of allusion, two or three times a week, in speeches and leading articles. In this, too, appear, perhaps for the first time, the author's views on the representative system. These he retained to the very last; they are brought forward repeatedly in the articles published in this collection and elsewhere, and in his speeches in parliament; and they coincide with the opinions expressed in the letter to an American correspondent, which was so often cited in the late debate on the Reform Bill.

Some explanation appears to be necessary as to the publication of the three articles which stand at the end of the previous volume.[1]

In 1828 Mr. James Mill, the author of the *History of British India*, reprinted some essays which he had contributed to the Supplement to the *Encyclopædia Britannica*, and among these was an Essay on Government. The method of inquiry and reasoning adopted in this essay appeared to Macaulay to be essentially wrong. He entertained a very strong conviction that the only sound foundation for a theory of government must be laid in careful and copious historical induction; and he believed that Mr. Mill's work rested upon a vicious reasoning *a priori*. Upon this point he felt the more earnestly,

---

[1] Macaulay's.

owing to his own passion for historical research, and to his devout admiration of Bacon, whose works he was at that time studying with intense attention. There can, however, be little doubt that he was also provoked by the pretensions of some members of a sect which then commonly went by the name of Benthamites, or Utilitarians. This sect included many of his contemporaries, who had quitted Cambridge at about the same time with him. It had succeeded, in some measure, to the sect of the Byronians, whom he has described in the review of Moore's *Life of Lord Byron*, who discarded their neckcloths, and fixed little models of sculls on the sand-glasses by which they regulated the boiling of their eggs for breakfast. The members of these sects, and of many others that have succeeded, have probably long ago learned to smile at the temporary humours. But Macaulay, himself a sincere admirer of Bentham, was irritated by what he considered the unwarranted tone assumed by several of the class of Utilitarians. "We apprehend," he said, "that many of them are persons who, having read little or nothing, are delighted to be rescued from the sense of their own inferiority by some teacher who assures them that the studies which they have neglected are of no value, puts five or six phrases into their mouths, lends them an odd number of the *Westminster Review*, and in a month transforms them into philosophers;" and he spoke of them as "smatterers, whose attainments just suffice to elevate them from the insignificance of dunces to the dignity of bores, and to spread dismay among their pious aunts and grandmothers." The sect, of course, like other sects, comprehended some pretenders, and these the most arrogant and intolerant among its members. He, however, went so far as to apply the following language to the majority: "As to the greater part of the sect, it is, we apprehend, of little consequence what they study or under whom. It would be more amusing, to be sure, and more reputable, if they would take up the old republican cant and declaim about Brutus and Timoleon, the duty of killing tyrants and the blessedness of dying for liberty. But, on the whole, they might have chosen worse. They may as well be Utilitarians as jockeys or dandies. And, though quibbling about self-interest and motives, and objects of desire, and the greatest happiness of the greatest number, is but a poor employment for a grown man, it certainly hurts the health less than hard drinking and the fortune less than high play; it is not much more laughable than phrenology, and is immeasurably more humane than cock-fighting."

Macaulay inserted in the *Edinburgh Review* of March 1829, an article upon Mr. Mill's essay. He attacked the method with much vehemence; and, to the end of his life, he never saw any ground for believing that in this he had gone too far. But before long he felt that he had not spoken of the author of the essay with the respect due to so eminent a man. In 1833, he described Mr. Mill, during the debate on the India Bill of that year, as a "gentleman, extremely well acquainted with the affairs of our Eastern Empire, a most valuable servant of the Company, and the author of a history of India which, though certainly not free from faults, is, I think, on the whole, the greatest historical work which has appeared in our language since that of Gibbon."

Almost immediately upon the appearance of the article in the *Edinburgh Review*, an article was published in the *Westminster Review*. It was untruly attributed, in the newspapers of the day, to Mr. Bentham himself. Macaulay's answer to this appeared in the *Edinburgh Review*, June 1829. He wrote the answer under the belief that he was answering Mr. Bentham, and was undeceived in time only to add the postscript. The author of the article in the *Westminster Review* had not perceived that the question raised was not as to the truth or falsehood of the result at which Mr. Mill had arrived, but as to the soundness or unsoundness of the method which he pursued; a misunderstanding at which Macaulay, while he supposed the article to be the work of Mr. Bentham, expressed much surprise. The controversy soon became principally a dispute as to the theory which was commonly known by the name of The Greatest Happiness Principle. Another article in the *Westminster Review* followed; and a surrejoinder by Macaulay in the *Edinburgh Review* of October, 1829. Macaulay was irritated at what he conceived to be either extreme dulness or gross unfairness on the part of his unknown antagonist, and struck as hard as he could, and he struck very hard indeed.

The ethical question thus raised was afterwards discussed by Sir James Mackintosh, in the Dissertation contributed by him to the seventh edition of the *Encyclopædia Britannica*. Sir James Mackintosh notices the part taken in the controversy by Macaulay in the following words: "A writer of consummate ability, who has failed in little but the respect due to the abilities and character of his opponents, has given too much countenance to the abuse and confusion of language exemplified in the well-known verse of Pope,—

"'Modes of self-love the Passions we may call.'

'We know,' says he, 'no universal proposition respecting human nature which is true but one—that men always act from self-interest.' It is manifest from the sequel that the writer is not the dupe of the confusion; but many of his readers may be so. If, indeed, the word *self-interest* could with propriety be used for the gratification of every prevalent desire, he has clearly shown that this change in the signification of terms would be of no advantage to the doctrine which he controverts. It would make as many sorts of self-interest as there are appetites, and it is irreconcilably at variance with the system of association proposed by Mr. Mill. The admirable writer whose language has occasioned this illustration, who at an early age has mastered every species of composition, will doubtless hold fast to simplicity, which survives all the fashions of deviation from it, and which a man of genius so fertile has few temptations to forsake."

When Macaulay selected for publication certain articles of the *Edinburgh Review*, he resolved not to publish any of the three essays in question; for which he assigned the following reason:—

" The author has been strongly urged to insert three papers on the Utilitarian Philosophy, which, when they first appeared, attracted some notice, but which are not in the American editions. He has, however, determined to omit these papers, not because he is disposed to retract a single doctrine which they contain, but because he is unwilling to offer what might be regarded as an affront to the memory of one from whose opinions he still widely dissents, but to whose talents and virtues he admits that he formerly did not do justice. Serious as are the faults of the Essay on Government, a critic, while noticing these faults, should have abstained from using contemptuous language respecting the historian of British India. It ought to be known that Mr. Mill had the generosity, not only to forgive, but to forget the unbecoming acrimony with which he had been assailed, and was, when his valuable life closed, on terms of cordial friendship with his assailant."

Under these circumstances, considerable doubt has been felt as to the propriety of republishing the three essays in the present collection.   But it has been determined, not without much hesitation, that they should appear.   It is felt that no disrespect is shown to the memory of Mr. Mill, when the publication is accompanied by so full an apology for the tone adopted towards him; and Mr. Mill himself would have been the last to wish for the suppression of opinions on the ground that they were in express antagonism to his own.   The grave has now closed upon the assailant as well as the assailed.   On the other hand, it cannot but be desirable that opinions which the author retained to the last, on important questions in politics and morals, should be before the public.

Some of the poems now collected have already appeared in print; others are supplied by the recollection of friends.   The first two are published on account of their having been composed in the author's childhood.   In the poems, as well as in the prose works, will be occasionally found thoughts and expressions which have afterwards been adopted in later productions.

With the Early and Miscellaneous Verse collected by T. F. Ellis in 1860 are here included " The Lays of Ancient Rome " and other poems, thus completing the edition of Macaulay in Everyman's Library, in seven volumes, viz.—History of England, Critical and Historical Essays, Speeches, Miscellaneous Writings and Lays of Ancient Rome.

The following are the works of Thomas Babington Macaulay:—

Pompeii (prize poem), 1819; Evening (prize poem), 1821; Lays of Ancient Rome (1842); Ivry and the Armada (*Quarterly Magazine*), added to Edition of 1848; Critical and Historical Essays (*Edinburgh Review*), 1843.

The Essays originally appeared as follows:—

Milton, August 1825; Machiavelli, March 1827; Hallam's " Constitutional History," September 1828; Southey's " Colloquies," January 1830; R. Montgomery's Poems, April 1830; Civil Disabilities of Jews, January 1831; Byron, June 1831; Croker's " Boswell," September 1831; Pilgrim's Progress, December 1831: Hampden, December 1831; Burleigh, April 1832; War of Succession in Spain, January 1833; Horace Walpole, October 1833; Lord Chatham, January 1834; Mackintosh's " History of Revolution," July 1835; Bacon, July 1837; Sir William Temple, October 1838; " Gladstone on Church and State," April 1839; Clive, January 1840; Ranke's " History of the Popes," October 1840; Comic Dramatists, January 1841; Lord Holland, July 1841; Warren Hastings, October 1841; Frederick the Great, April 1842; Madame D'Arblay, January 1843; Addison, July 1843; Lord Chatham (2nd Art.), October 1844.

History of England, vols. i. and ii., 1848; vols. iii. and iv., 1855; vol.

v., Ed. Lady Trevelyan, 1861; Ed. 8 vols., 1858-62 (Life by Dean Milman); Ed. 4 vols., People's Edition, with Life by Dean Milman, 1863-4; Inaugural Address (Glasgow), 1849; Speeches corrected by himself, 1854 (unauthorised version, 1853, by Vizetelly); Miscellaneous Writings, 2 vols., 1860 (Ed. T. F. Ellis). These include poems, lives (Encyclopædia Britannica, 8th ed.), and contributions to *Quarterly Magazine*, and the following from *Edinburgh Review*:

Dryden, January 1828; History, May 1828; Mill on Government, March 1829; Westminster Reviewer's Defence of Mill, June 1829; Utilitarian Theory of Government, October 1829; Sadler's "Law of Population," July 1830; Sadler's "Refutation Refuted," January 1831; Mirabeau, July 1832; Barère, April 1844.

Complete Works (Ed. Lady Trevelyan), 8 vols., 1866.

BOOKS OF REFERENCE

Sir G. O. Trevelyan: *The Life and Letters of Lord Macaulay* (2 vols. 8vo., 1876, 2nd ed. with additions, 1877, subsequent editions 1878 and 1881).

J. Cotter Morison: *Macaulay [English Men of Letters]*, (1882).

Mark Pattison: Art. "Macaulay" in *Encyclopædia Britannica*.

Leslie Stephen: *Hours in a Library* [new ed. 1892], ii. 243-376.
Art. "Macaulay" in *Dictionary of National Biography*.

Frederick Harrison: *Macaulay's Place in Literature* (1894).
Studies in Early Victorian Literature, chap. iii. (1895).

G. Saintsbury: *Corrected Impressions*, chaps. ix. x. (1895).
A History of Nineteenth Century Literature, pp. 224-232 (1896).

P. Oursel: *Les Essais de Lord Macaulay* (1882).

D. H. Macgregor: *Lord Macaulay* (1901).

Sir R. C. Jebb: *Macaulay* (1900).

F. C. Montague: *Macaulay's Essays* (3 vols. 1901).

CONTENTS

MISCELLANEOUS ESSAYS—

                                                   PAGE

History. (May 1828) 1

John Dryden. (January 1828) 39

Mirabeau. (July 1832) 77

Barère. (April 1844) 103

Francis Atterbury. (December 1853) 182

John Bunyan. (May 1854) 195

Oliver Goldsmith. (February 1856) 208

Samuel Johnson. (December 1856) 222

Dante. (January 1824) 255

Petrarch. (April 1824) 272

A Conversation between Mr. Abraham Cowley and Mr. John
    Milton, touching the Great Civil War. (August 1824) . 285

Some Account of the Great Lawsuit between the Parishes of St.
    Dennis and St. George in the Water. (April 1824) . . 303

On the Athenian Orators. (August 1824) 311

A Prophetic Account of a Grand National Epic Poem, to be entitled
    "The Wellingtoniad," and to be Published A.D. 2824.
    (November 1824) 323

William Pitt. (January 1859) 332

On the Royal Society of Literature. (June 1823) . . . 386

Scenes from "Athenian Revels." (January 1824) . . . 392

LAYS OF ANCIENT ROME—

Introduction 405

Horatius 418

The Battle of the Lake Regillus 435

Virginia 459

The Prophecy of Capys 472

Ivry 483

The Armada 486

MISCELLANEOUS POEMS, ETC.—

Epitaph on Henry Martyn. (1812) 489

Lines to the Memory of Pitt. (1813) 489

A Radical War Song. (1820) 490

The Battle of Moncontour. (1824) 492

The Battle of Naseby, by Obadiah Bind-their-kings-in-chains-and-
    their-nobles-with-links-of-iron, Serjeant in Ireton's Regiment.
    (1824) 493

Sermon in a Churchyard. (1825) 495

PAGE

Translation of a Poem by Arnault. (1826) 498
Dies Iræ. (1826) 499
The Marriage of Tirzah and Ahirad. (1827) 500
The Country Clergyman's Trip to Cambridge.   An Election Ballad.
    (1827) 514
Song. (1827) 517
Political Georgics. (March 1828) 518
The Deliverance of Vienna. (1828) 520
The Last Buccaneer. (1839) 524
Epitaph on a Jacobite. (1845) 525
Lines Written in August, 1847 526

MACAULAY'S MISCELLANEOUS ESSAYS

HISTORY [1]

To write history respectably—that is, to abbreviate despatches, and make extracts from speeches, to intersperse in due proportion epithets of praise and abhorrence, to draw up antithetical characters of great men, setting forth how many contradictory virtues and vices they united, and abounding in *withs* and *withouts*—all this is very easy. But to be a really great historian is perhaps the rarest of intellectual distinctions. Many scientific works are, in their kind, absolutely perfect. There are poems which we should be inclined to designate as faultless, or as disfigured only by blemishes which pass unnoticed in the general blaze of excellence. There are speeches, some speeches of Demosthenes particularly, in which it would be impossible to alter a word without altering it for the worse. But we are acquainted with no history which approaches to our notion of what a history ought to be—with no history which does not widely depart, either on the right hand or on the left, from the exact line.

The cause may easily be assigned. This province of literature is a debatable land. It lies on the confines of two distinct territories. It is under the jurisdiction of two hostile powers; and, like other districts similarly situated, it is ill defined, ill cultivated, and ill regulated. Instead of being equally shared between its two rulers, the Reason and the Imagination, it falls alternately under the sole and absolute dominion of each. It is sometimes fiction. It is sometimes theory.

History, it has been said, is philosophy teaching by examples. Unhappily, what the philosophy gains in soundness and depth the examples generally lose in vividness. A perfect historian must possess an imagination sufficiently powerful to make his narrative affecting and picturesque. Yet he must control it so

---

[1] *The Romance of History. England.* By Henry Neele. London, 1828.

absolutely as to content himself with the materials which he finds, and to refrain from supplying deficiencies by additions of his own. He must be a profound and ingenious reasoner. Yet he must possess sufficient self-command to abstain from casting his facts in the mould of his hypothesis. Those who can justly estimate these almost insuperable difficulties will not think it strange that every writer should have failed, either in the narrative or in the speculative department of history.

It may be laid down as a general rule, though subject to considerable qualifications and exceptions, that history begins in novel and ends in essay. Of the romantic historians Herodotus is the earliest and the best. His animation, his simple-hearted tenderness, his wonderful talent for description and dialogue, and the pure sweet flow of his language, place him at the head of narrators. He reminds us of a delightful child. There is a grace beyond the reach of affectation in his awkwardness, a malice in his innocence, an intelligence in his nonsense, an insinuating eloquence in his lisp. We know of no writer who makes such interest for himself and his book in the heart of the reader. At the distance of three-and-twenty centuries, we feel for him the same sort of pitying fondness which Fontaine and Gay are said to have inspired in society. He has written an incomparable book. He has written something better perhaps than the best history; but he has not written a good history; he is, from the first to the last chapter, an inventor. We do not here refer merely to those gross fictions with which he has been reproached by the critics of later times. We speak of that colouring which is equally diffused over his whole narrative, and which perpetually leaves the most sagacious reader in doubt what to reject and what to receive. The most authentic parts of his work bear the same relation to his wildest legends which Henry the Fifth bears to the Tempest. There was an expedition undertaken by Xerxes against Greece; and there was an invasion of France. There was a battle at Platæa; and there was a battle at Agincourt. Cambridge and Exeter, the Constable and the Dauphin, were persons as real as Demaratus and Pausanias. The harangue of the Archbishop on the Salic Law and the Book of Numbers differs much less from the orations which have in all ages proceeded from the right reverend bench than the speeches of Mardonius and Artabanus from those which were delivered at the council-board of Susa. Shakspeare gives us enumerations of armies, and returns of killed and wounded, which are not, we suspect, much less accurate than those of

Herodotus. There are passages in Herodotus nearly as long as acts of Shakspeare, in which everything is told dramatically, and in which the narrative serves only the purpose of stage-directions. It is possible, no doubt, that the substance of some real conversations may have been reported to the historian. But events which, if they ever happened, happened in ages and nations so remote that the particulars could never have been known to him, are related with the greatest minuteness of detail. We have all that Candaules said to Gyges, and all that passed between Astyages and Harpagus. We are, therefore, unable to judge whether, in the account which he gives of transactions respecting which he might possibly have been well informed, we can trust to anything beyond the naked outline; whether, for example, the answer of Gelon to the ambassadors of the Grecian confederacy, or the expressions which passed between Aristides and Themistocles at their famous interview, have been correctly transmitted to us. The great events are, no doubt, faithfully related. So, probably, are many of the slighter circumstances; but which of them it is impossible to ascertain. The fictions are so much like the facts, and the facts so much like the fictions, that, with respect to many most interesting particulars, our belief is neither given nor withheld, but remains in an uneasy and interminable state of abeyance. We know that there is truth; but we cannot exactly decide where it lies.

The faults of Herodotus are the faults of a simple and imaginative mind. Children and servants are remarkably Herodotean in their style of narration. They tell everything dramatically. Their *says hes* and *says shes* are proverbial. Every person who has had to settle their disputes knows that, even when they have no intention to deceive, their reports of conversation always require to be carefully sifted. If an educated man were giving an account of the late change of administration, he would say —" Lord Goderich resigned; and the King, in consequence, sent for the Duke of Wellington." A porter tells the story as if he had been hid behind the curtains of the royal bed at Windsor: " So Lord Goderich says, ' I cannot manage this business; I must go out.' So the King says,—says he, ' Well, then, I must send for the Duke of Wellington—that's all.' " This is in the very manner of the father of history.

Herodotus wrote as it was natural that he should write. He wrote for a nation susceptible, curious, lively, insatiably desirous of novelty and excitement; for a nation in which the fine arts had attained their highest excellence, but in which philosophy was still in its infancy. His countrymen had but recently begun to cultivate prose composition. Public transactions had generally been recorded in verse. The first historians might, therefore, indulge without fear of censure in the licence allowed to their predecessors the bards. Books were few. The events of former times were learned from tradition and from popular ballads; the manners of foreign countries from the reports of travellers. It is well known that the mystery which overhangs what is distant, either in space or time, frequently prevents us from censuring as unnatural what we perceive to be impossible. We stare at a dragoon who has killed three French cuirassiers, as a prodigy; yet we read, without the least disgust, how Godfrey slew his thousands, and Rinaldo his ten thousands. Within the last hundred years, stories about China and Bantam, which ought not to have imposed on an old nurse, were gravely laid down as foundations of political theories by eminent philosophers. What the time of the Crusades is to us, the generation of Crœsus and Solon was to the Greeks of the time of Herodotus. Babylon was to them what Pekin was to the French academicians of the last century.

For such a people was the book of Herodotus composed; and, if we may trust to a report, not sanctioned indeed by writers of high authority, but in itself not improbable, it was composed, not to be read, but to be heard. It was not to the slow circulation of a few copies, which the rich only could possess, that the aspiring author looked for his reward. The great Olympian festival,—the solemnity which collected multitudes, proud of the Grecian name, from the wildest mountains of Doris, and the remotest colonies of Italy and Libya,—was to witness his triumph. The interest of the narrative, and the beauty of the style, were aided by the imposing effect of recitation,—by the splendour of the spectacle,—by the powerful influence of sympathy. A critic who could have asked for authorities in the midst of such a scene must have been of a cold and sceptical nature; and few such critics were there. As was the historian, such were the auditors,—inquisitive, credulous, easily moved by religious awe or patriotic enthusiasm. They were the very men to hear with delight of strange beasts, and birds, and trees,—of dwarfs, and giants, and cannibals—of gods, whose very names it was impiety to utter,—of ancient dynasties, which had left behind them monuments surpassing all the works of later times, —of towns like provinces,—of rivers like seas,—of stupendous walls, and temples, and pyramids,—of the rites which the Magi performed at daybreak on the tops of the mountains,—of the secrets inscribed on the eternal obelisks of Memphis. With equal delight they would have listened to the graceful romances of their own country. They now heard of the exact accomplishment of obscure predictions, of the punishment of crimes over which the justice of heaven had seemed to slumber,—of dreams, omens, warnings from the dead,—of princesses, for whom noble suitors contended in every generous exercise of strength and skill,—of infants, strangely preserved from the dagger of the assassin, to fulfil high destinies.

As the narrative approached their own times, the interest became still more absorbing. The chronicler had now to tell the story of that great conflict from which Europe dates its intellectual and political supremacy,—a story which, even at this distance of time, is the most marvellous and the most touching in the annals of the human race,—a story abounding with all that is wild and wonderful, with all that is pathetic and animating; with the gigantic caprices of infinite wealth and despotic power—with the mightier miracles of wisdom, of virtue, and of courage. He told them of rivers dried up in a day,—of provinces famished for a meal,—of a passage for ships hewn through the mountains,—of a road for armies spread upon the waves,—of monarchies and commonwealths swept away,—of anxiety, of terror, of confusion, of despair!—and then of proud and stubborn hearts tried in that extremity of evil, and not found wanting,—of resistance long maintained against desperate odds,—of lives dearly sold, when resistance could be maintained no more,—of signal deliverance, and of unsparing revenge. Whatever gave a stronger air of reality to a narrative so well calculated to inflame the passions, and to flatter national pride, was certain to be favourably received.

Between the time at which Herodotus is said to have composed his history, and the close of the Peloponnesian war, about forty years elapsed,—forty years, crowded with great military and political events. The circumstances of that period produced a great effect on the Grecian character; and nowhere was this effect so remarkable as in the illustrious democracy of Athens. An Athenian, indeed, even in the time of Herodotus, would scarcely have written a book so romantic and garrulous as that of Herodotus. As civilisation advanced, the citizens of that famous republic became still less visionary, and still less simple-hearted. They aspired to know where their ancestors had been content to doubt; they began to doubt where their ancestors had thought it their duty to believe. Aristophanes is fond of alluding to this change in the temper of his countrymen. The father and son, in the Clouds, are evidently representatives of the generations to which they respectively belonged. Nothing more clearly illustrates the nature of this moral revolution than the change which passed upon tragedy. The wild sublimity of Æschylus became the scoff of every young Phidippides. Lectures on abstruse points of philosophy, the fine distinctions of casuistry, and the dazzling fence of rhetoric, were substituted for poetry. The language lost something of that infantine sweetness which had characterised it. It became less like the ancient Tuscan, and more like the modern French.

The fashionable logic of the Greeks was, indeed, far from strict. Logic never can be strict where books are scarce, and where information is conveyed orally. We are all aware how frequently fallacies, which, when set down on paper, are at once detected, pass for unanswerable arguments when dexterously and volubly urged in Parliament, at the bar, or in private conversation. The reason is evident. We cannot inspect them closely enough to perceive their inaccuracy. We cannot readily compare them with each other. We lose sight of one part of the subject before another, which ought to be received in connection with it, comes before us; and as there is no immutable record of what has been admitted and of what has been denied, direct contradictions pass muster with little difficulty. Almost all the education of a Greek consisted in talking and listening. His opinions on government were picked up in the debates of the assembly. If he wished to study metaphysics, instead of shutting himself up with a book, he walked down to the market-place to look for a sophist. So completely were men formed to these habits, that even writing acquired a conversational air. The philosophers adopted the form of dialogue, as the most natural mode of communicating knowledge. Their reasonings have the merits and the defects which belong to that species of composition, and are characterised rather by quickness and subtlety than by depth and precision. Truth is exhibited in parts, and by glimpses. Innumerable clever hints are given; but no sound and durable system is erected. The *argumentum ad hominem*, a kind of argument most efficacious in debate, but utterly useless for the investigation of general principles, is among their favourite resources. Hence, though nothing can be more admirable than the skill which Socrates displays in the conversations which

Plato has reported or invented, his victories, for the most part,
seem to us unprofitable.   A trophy is set up; but no new province
is added to the dominions of the human mind.

Still, where thousands of keen and ready intellects were constantly employed in speculating on the qualities of actions and
on the principles of government, it was impossible that history
should retain its whole character.   It became less gossiping and
less picturesque; but much more accurate, and somewhat more
scientific.

The history of Thucydides differs from that of Herodotus as
a portrait differs from the representation of an imaginary scene;
as the Burke or Fox of Reynolds differs from his Ugolino or his
Beaufort.   In the former case, the archetype is given: in the
latter it is created.   The faculties which are required for the
latter purpose are of a higher and rarer order than those which
suffice for the former, and indeed necessarily comprise them.
He who is able to paint what he sees with the eye of the mind
will surely be able to paint what he sees with the eye of the body.
He who can invent a story, and tell it well, will also be able to
tell, in an interesting manner, a story which he has not invented.
If, in practice, some of the best writers of fiction have been
among the worst writers of history, it has been because one of
their talents had merged in another so completely that it could
not be severed; because, having long been habituated to invent
and narrate at the same time, they found it impossible to narrate
without inventing.

Some capricious and discontented artists have affected to consider portrait-painting as unworthy of a man of genius.   Some
critics have spoken in the same contemptuous manner of history.
Johnson puts the case thus: The historian tells either what is
false or what is true: in the former case he is no historian: in
the latter he has no opportunity for displaying his abilities: for
truth is one: and all who tell the truth must tell it alike.

It is not difficult to elude both the horns of this dilemma.
We will recur to the analogous art of portrait painting.   Any
man with eyes and hands may be taught to take a likeness.   The
process, up to a certain point, is merely mechanical.   If this
were all, a man of talents might justly despise the occupation.
But we could mention portraits which are resemblances,—but
not mere resemblances; faithful,—but much more than faithful;
portraits which condense into one point of time, and exhibit, at
a single glance, the whole history of turbid and eventful lives—
in which the eye seems to scrutinise us, and the mouth to com-

mand us—in which the brow menaces, and the lip almost quivers with scorn—in which every wrinkle is a comment on some important transaction. The account which Thucydides has given of the retreat from Syracuse is, among narratives, what Vandyke's Lord Strafford is among paintings.

Diversity, it is said, implies error: truth is one, and admits of no degrees. We answer, that this principle holds good only in abstract reasonings. When we talk of the truth of imitation in the fine arts, we mean an imperfect and a graduated truth. No picture is exactly like the original; nor is a picture good in proportion as it is like the original. When Sir Thomas Lawrence paints a handsome peeress, he does not contemplate her through a powerful microscope, and transfer to the canvas the pores of the skin, the blood-vessels of the eye, and all the other beauties which Gulliver discovered in the Brobdignaggian maids of honour. If he were to do this, the effect would not merely be unpleasant, but, unless the scale of the picture were proportionably enlarged, would be absolutely *false*. And, after all, a microscope of greater power than that which he had employed would convict him of innumerable omissions. The same may be said of history. Perfectly and absolutely true it cannot be: for, to be perfectly and absolutely true, it ought to record *all* the slightest particulars of the slightest transactions—all the things done and all the words uttered during the time of which it treats. The omission of any circumstance, however insignificant, would be a defect. If history were written thus, the Bodleian Library would not contain the occurrences of a week. What is told in the fullest and most accurate annals bears an infinitely small proportion to what is suppressed. The difference between the copious work of Clarendon and the account of the civil wars in the abridgment of Goldsmith vanishes when compared with the immense mass of facts respecting which both are equally silent.

No picture, then, and no history, can present us with the whole truth: but those are the best pictures and the best histories which exhibit such parts of the truth as most nearly produce the effect of the whole. He who is deficient in the art of selection may, by showing nothing but the truth, produce all the effect of the grossest falsehood. It perpetually happens that one writer tells less truth than another, merely because he tells more truths. In the imitative arts we constantly see this. There are lines in the human face, and objects in landscape, which stand in such relations to each other, that they ought either to be all introduced into a painting together or all omitted together. A sketch into which none of them enters may be excellent; but, if some are given and others left out, though there are more points of likeness, there is less likeness. An outline scrawled with a pen, which seizes the marked features of a countenance, will give a much stronger idea of it than a bad painting in oils. Yet the worst painting in oils that ever hung at Somerset House resembles the original in many more particulars. A bust of white marble may give an excellent idea of a blooming face. Colour the lips and cheeks of the bust, leaving the hair and eyes unaltered, and the similarity, instead of being more striking, will be less so.

History has its foreground and its background: and it is principally in the management of its perspective that one artist differs from another. Some events must be represented on a large scale, others diminished; the great majority will be lost in the dimness of the horizon; and a general idea of their joint effect will be given by a few slight touches.

In this respect no writer has ever equalled Thucydides. He was a perfect master of the art of gradual diminution. His history is sometimes as concise as a chronological chart; yet it is always perspicuous. It is sometimes as minute as one of Lovelace's letters; yet it is never prolix. He never fails to contract and to expand it in the right place.

Thucydides borrowed from Herodotus the practice of putting speeches of his own into the mouths of his characters. In Herodotus this usage is scarcely censurable. It is of a piece with his whole manner. But it is altogether incongruous in the work of his successor, and violates, not only the accuracy of history, but the decencies of fiction. When once we enter into the spirit of Herodotus, we find no inconsistency. The conventional probability of his drama is preserved from the beginning to the end. The deliberate orations, and the familiar dialogues, are in strict keeping with each other. But the speeches of Thucydides are neither preceded nor followed by anything with which they harmonise. They give to the whole book something of the grotesque character of those Chinese pleasure-grounds in which perpendicular rocks of granite start up in the midst of a soft green plain. Invention is shocking where truth is in such close juxtaposition with it.

Thucydides honestly tells us that some of these discourses are purely fictitious. He may have reported the substance of others correctly, but it is clear from the internal evidence that he has preserved no more than the substance. His own peculiar habits of thought and expression are everywhere discernible. Individual and national peculiarities are seldom to be traced in the sentiments, and never in the diction. The oratory of the Corinthians and Thebans is not less Attic, either in matter or in manner, than that of the Athenians. The style of Cleon is as pure, as austere, as terse, and as significant, as that of Pericles.

In spite of this great fault, it must be allowed that Thucydides has surpassed all his rivals in the art of historical narration, in the art of producing an effect on the imagination, by skilful selection and disposition, without indulging in the licence of invention. But narration, though an important part of the business of a historian, is not the whole. To append a moral to a work of fiction is either useless or superfluous. A fiction may give a more impressive effect to what is already known; but it can teach nothing new. If it presents to us characters and trains of events to which our experience furnishes us with nothing similar, instead of deriving instruction from it, we pronounce it unnatural. We do not form our opinions from it; but we try it by our preconceived opinions. Fiction, therefore, is essentially imitative. Its merit consists in its resemblance to a model with which we are already familiar, or to which at least we can instantly refer. Hence it is that the anecdotes which interest us most strongly in authentic narrative are offensive when introduced into novels; that what is called the romantic part of history is in fact the least romantic. It is delightful as history, because it contradicts our previous notions of human nature, and of the connection of causes and effects. It is, on that very account, shocking and incongruous in fiction. In fiction, the principles are given, to find the facts: in history, the facts are given, to find the principles; and the writer who does not explain the phenomena as well as state them, performs only one half of his office. Facts are the mere dross of history. It is from the abstract truth which interpenetrates them, and lies latent among them like gold in the ore, that the mass derives its whole value: and the precious particles are generally combined with the baser in such a manner that the separation is a task of the utmost difficulty.

Here Thucydides is deficient: the deficiency, indeed, is not discreditable to him. It was the inevitable effect of circumstances. It was in the nature of things necessary that, in some part of its progress through political science, the human mind should reach that point which it attained in his time. Knowledge advances by steps, and not by leaps. The axioms of an English debating club would have been startling and mysterious paradoxes to the most enlightened statesmen of Athens. But it would be as absurd to speak contemptuously of the Athenian on this account as to ridicule Strabo for not having given us an account of Chili, or to talk of Ptolemy as we talk of Sir Richard Phillips. Still, when we wish for solid geographical information, we must prefer the solemn coxcombry of Pinkerton to the noble work of Strabo. If we wanted instruction respecting the solar system, we should consult the silliest girl from a boarding-school rather than Ptolemy.

Thucydides was undoubtedly a sagacious and reflecting man. This clearly appears from the ability with which he discusses practical questions. But the talent of deciding on the circumstances of a particular case is often possessed in the highest perfection by persons destitute of the power of generalisation. Men skilled in the military tactics of civilised nations have been amazed at the far-sightedness and penetration which a Mohawk displays in concerting his stratagems, or in discerning those of his enemies. In England, no class possesses so much of that peculiar ability which is required for constructing ingenious schemes, and for obviating remote difficulties, as the thieves and the thief-takers. Women have more of this dexterity than men. Lawyers have more of it than statesmen: statesmen have more of it than philosophers. Monk had more of it than Harrington and all his club. Walpole had more of it than Adam Smith or Beccaria. Indeed, the species of discipline by which this dexterity is acquired tends to contract the mind, and to render it incapable of abstract reasoning.

The Grecian statesmen of the age of Thucydides were distinguished by their practical sagacity, their insight into motives, their skill in devising means for the attainment of their ends. A state of society in which the rich were constantly planning the oppression of the poor, and the poor the spoliation of the rich, in which the ties of party had superseded those of country, in which revolutions and counter-revolutions were events of daily occurrence, was naturally prolific in desperate and crafty political adventurers. This was the very school in which men were likely to acquire the dissimulation of Mazarin, the judicious temerity of Richelieu, the penetration, the exquisite tact, the almost instinctive presentiment of approaching events which gave so much authority to the counsel of Shaftesbury, that " it was as if a man had inquired of the oracle of God." In this school Thucydides studied; and his wisdom is that which such a school would naturally afford. He judges better of circumstances than of principles. The more a question is narrowed, the better he reasons upon it. His work suggests many most important considerations respecting the first principles of government and morals, the growth of factions, the organisation of armies, and the mutual relations of communities. Yet all his general observations on these subjects are very superficial. His most judicious remarks differ from the remarks of a really philosophical historian, as a sum correctly cast up by a bookkeeper from a general expression discovered by an algebraist. The former is useful only in a single transaction; the latter may be applied to an infinite number of cases.

This opinion will, we fear, be considered as heterodox. For, not to speak of the illusion which the sight of a Greek type, or the sound of a Greek diphthong, often produces, there are some peculiarities in the manner of Thucydides which in no small degree have tended to secure to him the reputation of profundity. His book is evidently the book of a man and a statesman; and in this respect presents a remarkable contrast to the delightful childishness of Herodotus. Throughout it there is an air of matured power, of grave and melancholy reflection, of impartiality and habitual self-command. His feelings are rarely indulged, and speedily repressed. Vulgar prejudices of every kind, and particularly vulgar superstitions, he treats with a cold and sober disdain peculiar to himself. His style is weighty, condensed, antithetical, and not unfrequently obscure. But, when we look at his political philosophy, without regard to these circumstances, we find him to have been, what indeed it would have been a miracle if he had not been, simply an Athenian of the fifth century before Christ.

Xenophon is commonly placed, but we think without much reason, in the same rank with Herodotus and Thucydides. He resembles them, indeed, in the purity and sweetness of his style; but in spirit he rather resembles that later school of historians whose works seem to be fables composed for a moral, and who, in their eagerness to give us warnings and examples, forget to give us men and women. The Life of Cyrus, whether we look upon it as a history or as a romance, seems to us a very wretched performance. The Expedition of the Ten Thousand, and the History of Grecian Affairs, are certainly pleasant reading; but they indicate no great power of mind. In truth, Xenophon, though his taste was elegant, his disposition amiable, and his intercourse with the world extensive, had, we suspect, rather a weak head. Such was evidently the opinion of that extraordinary man to whom he early attached himself, and for whose memory he entertained an idolatrous veneration. He came in only for the milk with which Socrates nourished his babes in philosophy. A few saws of morality, and a few of the simplest doctrines of natural religion, were enough for the good young man. The strong meat, the bold speculations on physical and metaphysical science, were reserved for auditors of a different description. Even the lawless habits of a captain of mercenary troops could not change the tendency which the character of Xenophon early acquired. To the last, he seems to have retained a sort of heathen Puritanism. The sentiments of piety and virtue which abound in his works are those of a well-meaning man, somewhat timid and narrow-minded, devout from constitution rather than from rational conviction. He was as superstitious as Herodotus, but in a way far more offensive. The very peculiarities which charm us in an infant, the toothless mumbling, the stammering, the tottering, the helplessness, the causeless tears and laughter, are disgusting in old age. In the same manner, the absurdity which precedes a period of general intelligence is often pleasing; that which follows it is contemptible. The nonsense of Herodotus is that of a baby. The nonsense of Xenophon is that of a dotard. His stories about dreams, omens, and prophecies, present a strange contrast to the passages in which the shrewd and incredulous Thucydides mentions the popular superstitions. It is not quite clear that Xenophon was honest in his credulity; his fanaticism was in some degree politic. He would have made an excellent member of the Apostolic Camarilla. An alarmist by nature, an aristocrat by party, he carried to an unreasonable excess his horror of popular turbulence. The quiet atrocity of Sparta did not shock him in the same manner; for he hated tumult more than crimes. He was desirous to find restraints which might curb the passions of the multitude; and he absurdly fancied that he had found them in a religion without evidence or sanction, precepts or example, in a frigid system of Theophilanthropy, supported by nursery tales.

Polybius and Arrian have given us authentic accounts of facts; and here their merit ends. They were not men of comprehensive minds; they had not the art of telling a story in an interesting manner. They have in consequence been thrown into the shade by writers who, though less studious of truth than themselves,

understood far better the art of producing effect,—by Livy and
Quintus Curtius.

Yet Polybius and Arrian deserve high praise when compared
with the writers of that school of which Plutarch may be considered as the head. For the historians of this class we must
confess that we entertain a peculiar aversion. They seem to
have been pedants, who, though destitute of those valuable
qualities which are frequently found in conjunction with
pedantry, thought themselves great philosophers and great
politicians. They not only mislead their readers in every page,
as to particular facts, but they appear to have altogether mis-
conceived the whole character of the times of which they write.
They were inhabitants of an empire bounded by the Atlantic
Ocean and the Euphrates, by the ice of Scythia and the sands
of Mauritania; composed of nations whose manners, whose
languages, whose religion, whose countenances and complexions,
were widely different; governed by one mighty despotism, which
had risen on the ruins of a thousand commonwealths and
kingdoms. Of liberty, such as it is in small democracies, of
patriotism, such as it is in small independent communities of any
kind, they had, and they could have, no experimental knowledge.
But they had read of men who exerted themselves in the cause of
their country with an energy unknown in later times, who had
violated the dearest of domestic charities, or voluntarily devoted
themselves to death for the public good; and they wondered at
the degeneracy of their contemporaries. It never occurred to
them that the feelings which they so greatly admired sprung
from local and occasional causes; that they will always grow up
spontaneously in small societies; and that, in large empires,
though they may be forced into existence for a short time by
peculiar circumstances, they cannot be general or permanent.
It is impossible that any man should feel for a fortress on a
remote frontier as he feels for his own house; that he should
grieve for a defeat in which ten thousand people whom he never
saw have fallen as he grieves for a defeat which has half unpeopled the street in which he lives; that he should leave his
home for a military expedition in order to preserve the balance
of power, as cheerfully as he would leave it to repel invaders who
had begun to burn all the corn-fields in his neighbourhood.

The writers of whom we speak should have considered this.
They should have considered that in patriotism, such as it existed
amongst the Greeks, there was nothing essentially and eternally
good; that an exclusive attachment to a particular society,

though a natural, and, under certain restrictions, a most useful sentiment, implies no extraordinary attainments in wisdom or virtue; that, where it has existed in an intense degree, it has turned states into gangs of robbers whom their mutual fidelity has rendered more dangerous, has given a character of peculiar atrocity to war, and has generated that worst of all political evils, the tyranny of nations over nations.

Enthusiastically attached to the name of liberty, these historians troubled themselves little about its definition. The Spartans, tormented by ten thousand absurd restraints, unable to please themselves in the choice of their wives, their suppers, or their company, compelled to assume a peculiar manner, and to talk in a peculiar style, gloried in their liberty. The aristocracy of Rome repeatedly made liberty a plea for cutting off the favourites of the people. In almost all the little commonwealths of antiquity, liberty was used as a pretext for measures directed against everything which makes liberty valuable, for measures which stifled discussion, corrupted the administration of justice, and discouraged the accumulation of property. The writers, whose works we are considering, confounded the sound with the substance, and the means with the end. Their imaginations were inflamed by mystery. They conceived of liberty as monks conceive of love, as cockneys conceive of the happiness and innocence of rural life, as novel-reading sempstresses conceive of Almack's and Grosvenor Square, accomplished Marquesses and handsome colonels of the Guards. In the relation of events, and the delineation of characters, they have paid little attention to facts, to the costume of the times of which they pretend to treat, or to the general principles of human nature. They have been faithful only to their own puerile and extravagant doctrines. Generals and statesmen are metamorphosed into magnanimous coxcombs, from whose fulsome virtues we turn away with disgust. The fine sayings and exploits of their heroes remind us of the insufferable perfections of Sir Charles Grandison, and affect us with a nausea similar to that which we feel when an actor, in one of Morton's or Kotzebue's plays, lays his hand on his heart, advances to the ground-lights, and mouths a moral sentence for the edification of the gods.

These writers, men who knew not what it was to have a country, men who had never enjoyed political rights, brought into fashion an offensive cant about patriotism and zeal for freedom. What the English Puritans did for the language of Christianity, what Scuderi did for the language of love, they did

for the language of public spirit. By habitual exaggeration
they made it mean. By monotonous emphasis they made it
feeble. They abused it till it became scarcely possible to use
it with effect.

Their ordinary rules of morality are deduced from extreme
cases. The common regimen which they prescribe for society
is made up of those desperate remedies which only its most
desperate distempers require. They look with peculiar complacency on actions which even those who approve them consider as exceptions to laws of almost universal application—
which bear so close an affinity to the most atrocious crimes that,
even where it may be unjust to censure them, it is unsafe to
praise them. It is not strange, therefore, that some flagitious
instances of perfidy and cruelty should have been passed un-
challenged in such company, that grave moralists, with no personal interest at stake, should have extolled, in the highest
terms, deeds of which the atrocity appalled even the infuriated
factions in whose cause they were perpetrated. The part which
Timoleon took in the assassination of his brother shocked many
of his own partisans. The recollection of it preyed long on his
own mind. But it was reserved for historians who lived some
centuries later to discover that his conduct was a glorious display of virtue, and to lament that, from the frailty of human
nature, a man who could perform so great an exploit could
repent of it.

The writings of these men, and of their modern imitators,
have produced effects which deserve some notice. The English
have been so long accustomed to political speculation, and have
enjoyed so large a measure of practical liberty, that such works
have produced little effect on their minds. We have classical
associations and great names of our own which we can confidently oppose to the most splendid of ancient times. Senate
has not to our ears a sound so venerable as Parliament. We
respect the Great Charter more than the laws of Solon. The
Capitol and the Forum impress us with less awe than our own
Westminster Hall and Westminster Abbey, the place where the
great men of twenty generations have contended, the place
where they sleep together! The list of warriors and statesmen
by whom our constitution was founded or preserved, from De
Montfort down to Fox, may well stand a comparison with the
Fasti of Rome. The dying thanksgiving of Sidney is as noble
as the libation which Thrasea poured to Liberating Jove: and
we think with far less pleasure of Cato tearing out his entrails

than of Russell saying, as he turned away from his wife, that
the bitterness of death was past. Even those parts of our
history over which, on some accounts, we would gladly throw a
veil may be proudly opposed to those on which the moralists of
antiquity loved most to dwell. The enemy of English liberty
was not murdered by men whom he had pardoned and loaded
with benefits. He was not stabbed in the back by those who
smiled and cringed before his face. He was vanquished on fields
of stricken battle; he was arraigned, sentenced, and executed
in the face of heaven and earth. Our liberty is neither Greek
nor Roman; but essentially English. It has a character of its
own,—a character which has taken a tinge from the sentiments
of the chivalrous ages, and which accords with the peculiarities
of our manners and of our insular situation. It has a language,
too, of its own, and a language singularly idiomatic, full of
meaning to ourselves, scarcely intelligible to strangers.

Here, therefore, the effect of books such as those which we
have been considering has been harmless. They have, indeed,
given currency to many very erroneous opinions with respect to
ancient history. They have heated the imaginations of boys.
They have misled the judgment and corrupted the taste of some
men of letters, such as Akenside and Sir William Jones. But
on persons engaged in public affairs they have had very little
influence. The foundations of our constitution were laid by
men who knew nothing of the Greeks but that they denied the
orthodox procession and cheated the Crusaders; and nothing of
Rome, but that the Pope lived there. Those who followed, contented themselves with improving on the original plan. They
found models at home and therefore they did not look for them
abroad. But, when enlightened men on the Continent began to
think about political reformation, having no patterns before
their eyes in their domestic history, they naturally had recourse
to those remains of antiquity, the study of which is considered
throughout Europe as an important part of education. The
historians of whom we have been speaking had been members of
large communities, and subjects of absolute sovereigns. Hence
it is, as we have already said, that they commit such gross
errors in speaking of the little republics of antiquity. Their
works were now read in the spirit in which they had been
written. They were read by men placed in circumstances closely
resembling their own, unacquainted with the real nature of
liberty, but inclined to believe everything good which could be
told respecting it. How powerfully these books impressed these

speculative reformers is well known to all who have paid any attention to the French literature of the last century. But, perhaps, the writer on whom they produced the greatest effect was Vittorio Alfieri. In some of his plays, particularly in Virginia, Timoleon, and Brutus the Younger, he has even caricatured the extravagance of his masters.

It was not strange that the blind, thus led by the blind, should stumble. The transactions of the French Revolution, in some measure, took their character from these works. Without the assistance of these works, indeed, a revolution would have taken place,—a revolution productive of much good and much evil, tremendous but shortlived, evil dearly purchased, but durable good. But it would not have been exactly such a revolution. The style, the accessories, would have been in many respects different. There would have been less of bombast in language, less of affectation in manner, less of solemn trifling and ostentatious simplicity. The acts of legislative assemblies, and the correspondence of diplomatists, would not have been disgraced by rants worthy only of a college declamation. The government of a great and polished nation would not have rendered itself ridiculous by attempting to revive the usages of a world which had long passed away, or rather of a world which had never existed except in the description of a fantastic school of writers. These second-hand imitations resembled the originals about as much as the classical feast with which the Doctor in Peregrine Pickle turned the stomachs of all his guests resembled one of the suppers of Lucullus in the Hall of Apollo.

These were mere follies. But the spirit excited by these writers produced more serious effects. The greater part of the crimes which disgraced the revolution sprung indeed from the relaxation of law, from popular ignorance, from the remembrance of past oppression, from the fear of foreign conquest, from rapacity, from ambition, from party-spirit. But many atrocious proceedings must, doubtless, be ascribed to heated imagination, to perverted principle, to a distaste for what was vulgar in morals, and a passion for what was startling and dubious. Mr. Burke has touched on this subject with great felicity of expression: " The gradation of their republic," says he, " is laid in moral paradoxes. All those instances to be found in history, whether real or fabulous, of a doubtful public spirit, at which morality is perplexed, reason is staggered, and from which affrighted nature recoils, are their chosen and almost sole examples for the instruction of their youth." This evil, we believe, is to be directly ascribed to the influence of the historians whom we have mentioned, and their modern imitators.

Livy had some faults in common with these writers. But on the whole he must be considered as forming a class by himself: no historian with whom we are acquainted has shown so complete an indifference to truth. He seems to have cared only about the picturesque effect of his book, and the honour of his country. On the other hand, we do not know, in the whole range of literature, an instance of a bad thing so well done. The painting of the narrative is beyond description vivid and graceful. The abundance of interesting sentiments and splendid imagery in the speeches is almost miraculous. His mind is a soil which is never over-teemed, a fountain which never seems to trickle. It pours forth profusely; yet it gives no sign of exhaustion. It was probably to this exuberance of thought and language, always fresh, always sweet, always pure, no sooner yielded than repaired, that the critics applied that expression which has been so much discussed *lactea ubertas*.

All the merits and all the defects of Livy take a colouring from the character of his nation. He was a writer peculiarly Roman; the proud citizen of a commonwealth which had indeed lost the reality of liberty, but which still sacredly preserved its forms—in fact, the subject of an arbitrary prince, but in his own estimation one of the masters of the world, with a hundred kings below him, and only the gods above him. He, therefore, looked back on former times with feelings far different from those which were naturally entertained by his Greek contemporaries, and which at a later period became general among men of letters throughout the Roman Empire. He contemplated the past with interest and delight, not because it furnished a contrast to the present, but because it had led to the present. He recurred to it, not to lose in proud recollections the sense of national degradation, but to trace the progress of national glory. It is true that his veneration for antiquity produced on him some of the effects which it produced on those who arrived at it by a very different road. He has something of their exaggeration, something of their cant, something of their fondness for anomalies and *lusus naturæ* in morality. Yet even here we perceive a difference. They talk rapturously of patriotism and liberty in the abstract. He does not seem to think any country but Rome deserving of love; nor is it for liberty as liberty, but for liberty as a part of the Roman institutions, that he is zealous.

Of the concise and elegant accounts of the campaigns of Cæsar little can be said. They are incomparable models for military despatches. But histories they are not, and do not pretend to be.

The ancient critics placed Sallust in the same rank with Livy; and unquestionably the small portion of his works which has come down to us is calculated to give a high opinion of his talents. But his style is not very pleasant: and his most powerful work, the account of the Conspiracy of Catiline, has rather the air of a clever party pamphlet than that of a history. It abounds with strange inconsistencies, which, unexplained as they are, necessarily excite doubts as to the fairness of the narrative. It is true, that many circumstances now forgotten may have been familiar to his contemporaries, and may have rendered passages clear to them which to us appear dubious and perplexing. But a great historian should remember that he writes for distant generations, for men who will perceive the apparent contradictions, and will possess no means of reconciling them. We can only vindicate the fidelity of Sallust at the expense of his skill. But in fact all the information which we have from contemporaries respecting this famous plot is liable to the same objection, and is read by discerning men with the same incredulity. It is all on one side. No answer has reached our times. Yet on the showing of the accusers the accused seem entitled to acquittal. Catiline, we are told, intrigued with a Vestal virgin, and murdered his own son. His house was a den of gamblers and debauchees. No young man could cross his threshold without danger to his fortune and reputation. Yet this is the man with whom Cicero was willing to coalesce in a contest for the first magistracy of the republic; and whom he described, long after the fatal termination of the conspiracy, as an accomplished hypocrite, by whom he had himself been deceived, and who had acted with consummate skill the character of a good citizen and a good friend. We are told that the plot was the most wicked and desperate ever known, and, almost in the same breath, that the great body of the people, and many of the nobles, favoured it; that the richest citizens of Rome were eager for the spoliation of all property, and its highest functionaries for the destruction of all order; that Crassus, Cæsar, the Prætor Lentulus, one of the consuls of the year, one of the consuls elect, were proved or suspected to be engaged in a scheme for subverting institutions to which they owed the highest honours, and introducing universal anarchy.

We are told that a government, which knew all this, suffered the conspirator, whose rank, talents, and courage rendered him most dangerous, to quit Rome without molestation. We are told that bondmen and gladiators were to be armed against the citizens. Yet we find that Catiline rejected the slaves who crowded to enlist in his army, lest, as Sallust himself expresses it, " he should seem to identify their cause with that of the citizens." Finally, we are told that the magistrate, who was universally allowed to have saved all classes of his countrymen from conflagration and massacre, rendered himself so unpopular by his conduct that a marked insult was offered to him at the expiration of his office, and a severe punishment inflicted on him shortly after.

Sallust tells us, what, indeed, the letters and speeches of Cicero sufficiently prove, that some persons consider the shocking and atrocious parts of the plot as mere inventions of the government, designed to excuse its unconstitutional measures. We must confess ourselves to be of that opinion. There was, undoubtedly, a strong party desirous to change the administration. While Pompey held the command of an army, they could not effect their purpose without preparing means for repelling force, if necessary, by force. In all this there is nothing different from the ordinary practice of Roman factions. The other charges brought against the conspirators are so inconsistent and improbable that we give no credit whatever to them. If our readers think this scepticism unreasonable, let them turn to the contemporary accounts of the Popish plot. Let them look over the votes of Parliament, and the speeches of the king; the charges of Scroggs, and the harangues of the managers employed against Strafford. A person who should form his judgment from these pieces alone would believe that London was set on fire by the Papists, and that Sir Edmondbury Godfrey was murdered for his religion. Yet these stories are now altogether exploded. They have been abandoned by statesmen to aldermen, by aldermen to clergymen, by clergymen to old women, and by old women to Sir Harcourt Lees.

Of the Latin historians, Tacitus was certainly the greatest. His style, indeed, is not only faulty in itself, but is, in some respects, peculiarly unfit for historical composition. He carries his love of effect far beyond the limits of moderation. He tells a fine story finely, but he cannot tell a plain story plainly. He stimulates till stimulants lose their power. Thucydides, as we have already observed, relates ordinary transactions with the unpretending clearness and succinctness of a gazette. His great powers of painting he reserves for events of which the slightest details are interesting. The simplicity of the setting gives additional lustre to the brilliants. There are passages in the narrative of Tacitus superior to the best which can be quoted from Thucydides. But they are not enchased and relieved with the same skill. They are far more striking when extracted from the body of the work to which they belong than when they occur in their place, and are read in connection with what precedes and follows.

In the delineation of character, Tacitus is unrivalled among historians, and has very few superiors among dramatists and novelists. By the delineation of character, we do not mean the practice of drawing up epigrammatic catalogues of good and bad qualities, and appending them to the names of eminent men. No writer, indeed, has done this more skilfully than Tacitus; but this is not his peculiar glory. All the persons who occupy a large space in his works have an individuality of character which seems to pervade all their words and actions. We know them as if we had lived with them. Claudius, Nero, Otho, both the Agrippinas, are masterpieces. But Tiberius is a still higher miracle of art. The historian undertook to make us intimately acquainted with a man singularly dark and inscrutable,—with a man whose real disposition long remained swathed up in intricate folds of factitious virtues, and over whose actions the hypocrisy of his youth, and the seclusion of his old age, threw a singular mystery. He was to exhibit the specious qualities of the tyrant in a light which might render them transparent, and enable us at once to perceive the covering and the vices which it concealed. He was to trace the gradations by which the first magistrate of a republic, a senator mingling freely in debate, a noble associating with his brother nobles, was transformed into an Asiatic sultan; he was to exhibit a character, distinguished by courage, self-command, and profound policy, yet defiled by all

> " th' extravagancy
> And crazy ribaldry of fancy."

He was to mark the gradual effect of advancing age and approaching death on this strange compound of strength and weakness; to exhibit the old sovereign of the world sinking into a dotage which, though it rendered his appetites eccentric, and his temper savage, never impaired the powers of his stern and penetrating mind — conscious of failing strength, raging with

capricious sensuality, yet to the last the keenest of observers,
the most artful of dissemblers, and the most terrible of masters.
The task was one of extreme difficulty. The execution is
almost perfect.

The talent which is required to write history thus bears a
considerable affinity to the talent of a great dramatist. There
is one obvious distinction. The dramatist creates; the historian
only disposes. The difference is not in the mode of execution,
but in the mode of conception. Shakspeare is guided by a
model which exists in his imagination; Tacitus, by a model
furnished from without. Hamlet is to Tiberius what the
Laocoon is to the Newton of Roubilliac.

In this part of his art Tacitus certainly had neither equal nor
second among the ancient historians. Herodotus, though he
wrote in a dramatic form, had little of dramatic genius. The
frequent dialogues which he introduces give vivacity and movement to the narrative, but are not strikingly characteristic.
Xenophon is fond of telling his readers, at considerable length,
what he thought of the persons whose adventures he relates.
But he does not show them the men, and enable them to judge
for themselves. The heroes of Livy are the most insipid of all
beings, real or imaginary, the heroes of Plutarch always excepted. Indeed, the manner of Plutarch in this respect reminds
us of the cookery of those continental inns, the horror of English
travellers, in which a certain nondescript broth is kept constantly
boiling, and copiously poured, without distinction, over every
dish as it comes up to table. Thucydides, though at a wide
interval, comes next to Tacitus. His Pericles, his Nicias, his
Cleon, his Brasidas, are happily discriminated. The lines are
few, the colouring faint: but the general air and expression is
caught.

We begin, like the priest in Don Quixote's library, to be tired
with taking down books one after another for separate judgment,
and feel inclined to pass sentence on them in masses. We shall
therefore, instead of pointing out the defects and merits of the
different modern historians, state generally in what particulars
they have surpassed their predecessors, and in what we conceive
them to have failed.

They have certainly been, in one sense, far more strict in their
adherence to truth than most of the Greek and Roman writers.
They do not think themselves entitled to render their narrative interesting by introducing descriptions, conversations, and
harangues which have no existence but in their own imagina-

tion. This improvement was gradually introduced. History commenced among the modern nations of Europe, as it had commenced among the Greeks, in romance. Froissart was our Herodotus. Italy was to Europe what Athens was to Greece. In Italy, therefore, a more accurate and manly mode of narration was early introduced. Machiavelli and Guicciardini, in imitation of Livy and Thucydides, composed speeches for their historical personages. But, as the classical enthusiasm which distinguished the age of Lorenzo and Leo gradually subsided, this absurd practice was abandoned. In France, we fear it still, in some degree, keeps its ground. In our own country, a writer who should venture on it would be laughed to scorn. Whether the historians of the last two centuries tell more truth than those of antiquity, may perhaps be doubted. But it is quite certain that they tell fewer falsehoods.

In the philosophy of history, the moderns have very far surpassed the ancients. It is not, indeed, strange that the Greeks and Romans should not have carried the science of government, or any other experimental science, so far as it has been carried in our time; for the experimental sciences are generally in a state of progression. They were better understood in the seventeenth century than in the sixteenth, and in the eighteenth century than in the seventeenth. But this constant improvement, this natural growth of knowledge, will not altogether account for the immense superiority of the modern writers. The difference is a difference not in degree, but of kind. It is not merely that new principles have been discovered, but that new faculties seem to be exerted. It is not that at one time the human intellect should have made but small progress, and at another time have advanced far: but that at one time it should have been stationary, and at another time constantly proceeding. In taste and imagination, in the graces of style, in the arts of persuasion, in the magnificence of public works, the ancients were at least our equals. They reasoned as justly as ourselves on subjects which required pure demonstration. But in the moral sciences they made scarcely any advance. During the long period which elapsed between the fifth century before the Christian era and the fifth century after it, little perceptible progress was made. All the metaphysical discoveries of all the philosophers, from the time of Socrates to the northern invasion, are not to be compared in importance with those which have been made in England every fifty years since the time of Elizabeth. There is not the least reason to believe that the principles of government, legislation, and political economy, were better understood in the time of Augustus Cæsar than in the time of Pericles. In our own country, the sound doctrines of trade and jurisprudence have been, within the lifetime of a single generation, dimly hinted, boldly propounded, defended, systematised, adopted by all reflecting men of all parties, quoted in legislative assemblies, incorporated into laws and treaties.

To what is this change to be attributed? Partly, no doubt, to the discovery of printing, a discovery which has not only diffused knowledge widely, but, as we have already observed, has also introduced into reasoning a precision unknown in those ancient communities, in which information was, for the most part, conveyed orally. There was, we suspect, another cause, less obvious, but still more powerful.

The spirit of the two most famous nations of antiquity was remarkably exclusive. In the time of Homer the Greeks had not begun to consider themselves as a distinct race. They still looked with something of childish wonder and awe on the riches and wisdom of Sidon and Egypt. From what causes, and by what gradations, their feelings underwent a change, it is not easy to determine. Their history, from the Trojan to the Persian war, is covered with an obscurity broken only by dim and scattered gleams of truth. But it is certain that a great alteration took place. They regarded themselves as a separate people. They had common religious rites, and common principles of public law, in which foreigners had no part. In all their political systems, monarchical, aristocratical, and democratical there was a strong family likeness. After the retreat of Xerxes and the fall of Mardonius, national pride rendered the separation between the Greeks and the barbarians complete. The conquerors considered themselves men of a superior breed, men who, in their intercourse with neighbouring nations, were to teach, and not to learn. They looked for nothing out of themselves. They borrowed nothing. They translated nothing. We cannot call to mind a single expression of any Greek writer earlier than the age of Augustus, indicating an opinion that anything worth reading could be written in any language except his own. The feelings which sprung from national glory were not altogether extinguished by national degradation. They were fondly cherished through ages of slavery and shame. The literature of Rome herself was regarded with contempt by those who had fled before her arms, and who bowed beneath her fasces. Voltaire says, in one of his six thousand pamphlets, that he was the first person who told the French that England had produced eminent men besides the Duke of Marlborough. Down to a very late period, the Greeks seem to have stood in need of similar information with respect to their masters. With Paulus Æmilius, Sylla, and Cæsar, they were well acquainted. But the notions which they entertained respecting Cicero and Virgil were, probably, not unlike those which Boileau may have formed about Shakspeare. Dionysius lived in the most splendid age of Latin poetry and eloquence. He was a critic, and, after the manner of his age, an able critic. He studied the language of Rome, associated with its learned men, and compiled its history. Yet he seems to have thought its literature valuable only for the purpose of illustrating its antiquities. His reading appears to have been confined to its public records, and to a few old annalists. Once, and but once, if we remember rightly, he quotes Ennius, to solve a question of etymology. He has written much on the art of oratory: yet he has not mentioned the name of Cicero.

The Romans submitted to the pretensions of a race which they despised. Their epic poet, while he claimed for them pre-eminence in the arts of government and war, acknowledged their inferiority in taste, eloquence, and science. Men of letters affected to understand the Greek language better than their own. Pomponius preferred the honour of becoming an Athenian, by intellectual naturalisation, to all the distinctions which were to be acquired in the political contests of Rome. His great friend composed Greek poems and memoirs. It is well known that Petrarch considered that beautiful language in which his sonnets are written as a barbarous jargon, and intrusted his fame to those wretched Latin hexameters which, during the last four centuries, have scarcely found four readers. Many eminent Romans appear to have felt the same contempt for their native tongue as compared with the Greek. The prejudice continued to a very late period. Julian was as partial to the Greek lan-guage as Frederic the Great to the French: and it seems that he could not express himself with elegance in the dialect of the state which he ruled.

Even those Latin writers who did not carry this affectation so far looked on Greece as the only fount of knowledge. From Greece they derived the measures of their poetry, and, indeed, all of poetry that can be imported. From Greece they borrowed the principles and the vocabulary of their philosophy. To the literature of other nations they do not seem to have paid the slightest attention. The sacred books of the Hebrews, for example, books which, considered merely as human compositions, are invaluable to the critic, the antiquarian, and the philosopher, seem to have been utterly unnoticed by them. The peculiarities of Judaism, and the rapid growth of Christianity, attracted their notice. They made war against the Jews. They made laws against the Christians. But they never opened the books of Moses. Juvenal quotes the Pentateuch with censure. The author of the treatise on " the Sublime " quotes it with praise: but both of them quote it erroneously. When we consider what sublime poetry, what curious history, what striking and peculiar views of the Divine nature and of the social duties of men, are to be found in the Jewish scriptures, when we consider that two sects on which the attention of the government was constantly fixed appealed to those scriptures as the rule of their faith and practice, this indifference is astonishing. The fact seems to be, that the Greeks admired only themselves, and that the Romans admired only themselves and the Greeks. Literary men turned away with disgust from modes of thought and expression so widely different from all that they had been accustomed to admire. The effect was narrowness and sameness of thought. Their minds, if we may so express ourselves, bred in and in, and were accordingly cursed with barrenness and degeneracy. No extraneous beauty or vigour was engrafted on the decaying stock. By an exclusive attention to one class of phenomena, by an exclusive taste for one species of excellence, the human intellect was stunted. Occasional coincidences were turned into general rules. Prejudices were confounded with instincts. On man, as he was found in a particular state of society—on government, as it had existed in a particular corner of the world, many just observations were made; but of man as man, or government as government, little was known. Philosophy remained stationary. Slight changes, sometimes for the worse and sometimes for the better, were made in the superstructure. But nobody thought of examining the foundations.

The vast despotism of the Cæsars, gradually effacing all national peculiarities, and assimilating the remotest provinces of the empire to each other, augmented the evil. At the close of the third century after Christ, the prospects of mankind were fearfully dreary. A system of etiquette, as pompously frivolous as that of the Escurial, had been established. A sovereign almost invisible; a crowd of dignitaries minutely distinguished by badges and titles; rhetoricians who said nothing but what had been said ten thousand times; schools in which nothing was taught but what had been known for ages: such was the machinery provided for the government and instruction of the most enlightened part of the human race. That great community was then in danger of experiencing a calamity far more terrible than any of the quick, inflammatory, destroying maladies to which nations are liable,—a tottering, drivelling, paralytic longevity, the immortality of the Struldbrugs, a Chinese civilisation. It would be easy to indicate many points of resemblance between the subjects of Diocletian and the people of that Celestial Empire, where, during many centuries, nothing has been learned or unlearned; where government, where education, where the whole system of life, is a ceremony; where knowledge forgets to increase and multiply, and, like the talent buried in the earth, or the pound wrapped up in the napkin, experiences neither waste nor augmentation.

The torpor was broken by two great revolutions, the one moral, the other political, the one from within, the other from without. The victory of Christianity over Paganism, considered with relation to this subject only, was of great importance. It overthrew the old system of morals; and with it much of the old system of metaphysics. It furnished the orator with new topics of declamation, and the logician with new points of controversy. Above all, it introduced a new principle, of which the operation was constantly felt in every part of society. It stirred the stagnant mass from the inmost depths. It excited all the passions of a stormy democracy in the quiet and listless population of an overgrown empire. The fear of heresy did what the sense of oppression could not do; it changed men, accustomed to be turned over like sheep from tyrant to tyrant, into devoted partisans and obstinate rebels. The tones of an eloquence which had been silent for ages resounded from the pulpit of Gregory. A spirit which had been extinguished on the plains of Philippi revived in Athanasius and Ambrose.

Yet even this remedy was not sufficiently violent for the disease. It did not prevent the empire of Constantinople from relapsing, after a short paroxysm of excitement, into a state of stupefaction, to which history furnishes scarcely any parallel. We there find that a polished society, a society in which a most intricate and elaborate system of jurisprudence was established, in which the arts of luxury were well understood, in which the works of the great ancient writers were preserved and studied, existed for nearly a thousand years without making one great discovery in science, or producing one book which is read by any but curious inquirers. There were tumults, too, and controversies, and wars in abundance: and these things, bad as they are in themselves, have generally been favourable to the progress of the intellect. But here they tormented without stimulating. The waters were troubled; but no healing influence descended. The agitations resembled the grinnings and writhings of a galvanised corpse, not the struggles of an athletic man.

From this miserable state the Western Empire was saved by the fiercest and most destroying visitation with which God has ever chastened his creatures—the invasion of the Northern nations. Such a cure was required for such a distemper. The fire of London, it has been observed, was a blessing. It burned down the city; but it burned out the plague The same may be said of the tremendous devastation of the Roman dominions. It annihilated the noisome recesses in which lurked the seeds of great moral maladies; it cleared an atmosphere fatal to the health and vigour of the human mind. It cost Europe a thousand years of barbarism to escape the fate of China.

At length the terrible purification was accomplished; and the second civilisation of mankind commenced, under circumstances which afforded a strong security that it would never retrograde and never pause. Europe was now a great federal community. Her numerous states were united by the easy ties of international law and a common religion. Their institutions, their languages, their manners, their tastes in literature, their modes of education, were widely different. Their connection was close enough to allow of mutual observation and improvement, yet not so close as to destroy the idioms of national opinion and feeling.

The balance of moral and intellectual influence thus established between the nations of Europe is far more important than the balance of political power. Indeed, we are inclined to think that the latter is valuable principally because it tends to maintain the former. The civilised world has thus been preserved from a uniformity of character fatal to all improvement. Every part of it has been illuminated with light reflected from every other. Competition has produced activity where monopoly would have produced sluggishness. The number of experiments in moral science which the speculator has an opportunity of witnessing has been increased beyond all calculation. Society and human nature, instead of being seen in a single point of view, are presented to him under ten thousand different aspects. By observing the manners of surrounding nations, by studying their literature, by comparing it with that of his own country and of the ancient republics, he is enabled to correct those errors into which the most acute men must fall when they reason from a single species to a genus. He learns to distinguish what is local from what is universal: what is transitory from what is eternal; to discriminate between exceptions and rules; to trace the operation of disturbing causes; to separate those general principles which are always true and everywhere applicable from the accidental circumstances with which, in every community, they are blended, and with which, in an isolated community, they are confounded by the most philosophical mind.

Hence it is that, in generalisation, the writers of modern times have far surpassed those of antiquity. The historians of our own country are unequalled in depth and precision of reason; and, even in the works of our mere compilers, we often meet with speculations beyond the reach of Thucydides or Tacitus.

But it must, at the same time, be admitted that they have characteristic faults, so closely connected with their characteristic merits, and of such magnitude, that it may well be doubted whether, on the whole, this department of literature has gained or lost during the last two-and-twenty centuries.

The best historians of later times have been seduced from truth, not by their imagination, but by their reason. They far excel their predecessors in the art of deducing general principles from facts. But unhappily they have fallen into the error of distorting facts to suit general principles. They arrive at a theory from looking at some of the phenomena; and the remaining phenomena they strain or curtail to suit the theory. For this purpose it is not necessary that they should assert what is absolutely false; for all questions in morals and politics are questions of comparison and degree. Any proposition which does not involve a contradiction in terms may by possibility be true; and if all the circumstances which raise a probability in its favour be stated and enforced, and those which lead to an opposite conclusion be omitted or lightly passed over, it may appear to be demonstrated. In every human character and transaction there is a mixture of good and evil: a little exaggeration, a little suppression, a judicious use of epithets, a watchful and searching scepticism with respect to the evidence

on one side, a convenient credulity with respect to every report
or tradition on the other, may easily make a saint of Laud, or
a tyrant of Henry the Fourth.

This species of misrepresentation abounds in the most valuable
works of modern historians. Herodotus tells his story like a
slovenly witness, who, heated by partialities and prejudices,
unacquainted with the established rules of evidence, and un-
instructed as to the obligations of his oath, confounds what he
imagines with what he has seen and heard, and brings out facts,
reports, conjectures, and fancies, in one mass. Hume is an
accomplished advocate. Without positively asserting much
more than he can prove, he gives prominence to all the circumstances which support his case; he glides lightly over those
which are unfavourable to it; his own witnesses are applauded
and encouraged; the statements which seem to throw discredit
on them are controverted; the contradictions into which they
fall are explained away; a clear and connected abstract of their
evidence is given. Everything that is offered on the other side
is scrutinised with the utmost severity; every suspicious circumstance is a ground for comment and invective; what cannot
be denied is extenuated, or passed by without notice; concessions even are sometimes made: but this insidious candour only
increases the effect of the vast mass of sophistry.

We have mentioned Hume as the ablest and most popular
writer of his class; but the charge which we have brought
against him is one to which all our most distinguished historians
are in some degree obnoxious. Gibbon, in particular, deserves
very severe censure. Of all the numerous culprits, however,
none is more deeply guilty than Mr. Mitford. We willingly acknowledge the obligations which are due to his talents and industry. The modern historians of Greece had been in the habit
of writing as if the world had learned nothing new during the
last sixteen hundred years. Instead of illustrating the events
which they narrated by the philosophy of a more enlightened
age, they judged of antiquity by itself alone. They seemed to
think that notions, long driven from every other corner of
literature, had a prescriptive right to occupy this last fastness.
They considered all the ancient historians as equally authentic.
They scarcely made any distinction between him who related
events at which he had himself been present and him who five
hundred years after composed a philosophic romance for a
society which had in the interval undergone a complete change.
It was all Greek, and all true! The centuries which separated

Plutarch from Thucydides seemed as nothing to men who lived in an age so remote. The distance of time produced an error similar to that which is sometimes produced by distance of place. There are many good ladies who think that all the people in India live together, and who charge a friend setting out for Calcutta with kind messages to Bombay. To Rollin and Barthelemi, in the same manner, all the classics were contemporaries.

Mr. Mitford certainly introduced great improvements; he showed us that men who wrote in Greek and Latin sometimes told lies; he showed us that ancient history might be related in such a manner as to furnish not only allusions to schoolboys, but important lessons to statesmen. From that love of theatrical effect and high-flown sentiment which had poisoned almost every other work on the same subject his book is perfectly free. But his passion for a theory as false, and far more ungenerous, led him substantially to violate truth in every page. Statements unfavourable to democracy are made with unhesitating confidence, and with the utmost bitterness of language. Every charge brought against a monarch or an aristocracy is sifted with the utmost care. If it cannot be denied, some palliating supposition is suggested; or we are at least reminded that some circumstances now unknown *may* have justified what at present appears unjustifiable. Two events are reported by the same author in the same sentence; their truth rests on the same testimony; but the one supports the darling hypothesis, and the other seems inconsistent with it. The one is taken, and the other is left.

The practice of distorting narrative into a conformity with theory is a vice not so unfavourable as at first sight it may appear to the interests of political science. We have compared the writers who indulge in it to advocates; and we may add, that their conflicting fallacies, like those of advocates, correct each other. It has always been held, in the most enlightened nations, that a tribunal will decide a judicial question most fairly when it has heard two able men argue, as unfairly as possible, on the two opposite sides of it; and we are inclined to think that this opinion is just. Sometimes, it is true, superior eloquence and dexterity will make the worse appear the better reason; but it is at least certain that the judge will be compelled to contemplate the case under two different aspects. It is certain that no important consideration will altogether escape notice.

This is at present the state of history. The poet laureate

appears for the Church of England, Lingard for the Church of Rome. Brodie has moved to set aside the verdicts obtained by Hume; and the cause in which Mitford succeeded is, we understand, about to be reheard. In the midst of these disputes, however, history proper, if we may use the term, is disappearing. The high, grave, impartial summing up of Thucydides is nowhere to be found.

While our historians are practising all the arts of controversy, they miserably neglect the art of narration, the art of interesting the affections and presenting pictures to the imagination. That a writer may produce these effects without violating truth is sufficiently proved by many excellent biographical works. The immense popularity which well-written books of this kind have acquired deserves the serious consideration of historians. Voltaire's *Charles the Twelfth*, Marmontel's *Memoirs*, Boswell's *Life of Johnson*, Southey's account of Nelson, are perused with delight by the most frivolous and indolent. Whenever any tolerable book of the same description makes its appearance, the circulating libraries are mobbed; the book societies are in commotion; the new novel lies uncut; the magazines and newspapers fill their columns with extracts. In the meantime histories of great empires, written by men of eminent ability, lie unread on the shelves of ostentatious libraries.

The writers of history seem to entertain an aristocratical contempt for the writers of memoirs. They think it beneath the dignity of men who describe the revolutions of nations to dwell on the details which constitute the charm of biography. They have imposed on themselves a code of conventional decencies as absurd as that which has been the bane of the French drama. The most characteristic and interesting circumstances are omitted or softened down, because, as we are told, they are too trivial for the majesty of history. The majesty of history seems to resemble the majesty of the poor King of Spain, who died a martyr to ceremony because the proper dignitaries were not at hand to render him assistance.

That history would be more amusing if this etiquette were relaxed will, we suppose, be acknowledged. But would it be less dignified or less useful? What do we mean when we say that one past event is important and another insignificant? No past event has any intrinsic importance. The knowledge of it is valuable only as it leads us to form just calculations with respect to the future. A history which does not serve this purpose, though it may be filled with battles, treaties, and commotions, is as useless as the series of turnpike tickets collected by Sir Matthew Mite.

Let us suppose that Lord Clarendon, instead of filling hundreds of folio pages with copies of state papers, in which the same assertions and contradictions are repeated till the reader is over-powered with weariness, had condescended to be the Boswell of the Long Parliament.   Let us suppose that he had exhibited to us the wise and lofty self-government of Hampden, leading while he seemed to follow, and propounding unanswerable arguments in the strongest forms with the modest air of an inquirer anxious for information; the delusions which misled the noble spirit of Vane; the coarse fanaticism which concealed the yet loftier genius of Cromwell, destined to control a mutinous army and a factious people, to abase the flag of Holland, to arrest the victorious arms of Sweden, and to hold the balance firm between the rival monarchies of France and Spain.   Let us suppose that he had made his Cavaliers and Roundheads talk in their own style; that he had reported some of the ribaldry of Rupert's pages, and some of the cant of Harrison and Fleetwood.   Would not his work in that case have been more interesting?   Would it not have been more accurate?

A history in which every particular incident may be true may on the whole be false.   The circumstances which have most influence on the happiness of mankind, the changes of manners and morals, the transition of communities from poverty to wealth, from knowledge to ignorance, from ferocity to humanity—these are, for the most part, noiseless revolutions.   Their progress is rarely indicated by what historians are pleased to call important events.   They are not achieved by armies, or enacted by senates.   They are sanctioned by no treaties, and recorded in no archives.   They are carried on in every school, in every church, behind ten thousand counters, at ten thousand firesides. The upper current of society presents no certain criterion by which we can judge of the direction in which the under-current flows.   We read of defeats and victories.   But we know that nations may be miserable amidst victories and prosperous amidst defeats.   We read of the fall of wise ministers and of the rise of profligate favourites.   But we must remember how small a proportion the good or evil effected by a single statesman can bear to the good or evil of a great social system.

Bishop Watson compares a geologist to a gnat mounted on an elephant, and laying down theories as to the whole internal structure of the vast animal, from the phenomena of the hide.

The comparison is unjust to the geologists; but is very applicable to those historians who write as if the body politic were homogeneous, who look only on the surface of affairs, and never think of the mighty and various organisation which lies deep below.

In the works of such writers as these, England, at the close of the Seven Years' War, is in the highest state of prosperity: at the close of the American war she is in a miserable and degraded condition; as if the people were not on the whole as rich, as well governed, and as well educated at the latter period as at the former. We have read books called Histories of England, under the reign of George the Second, in which the rise of Methodism is not even mentioned. A hundred years hence this breed of authors will, we hope, be extinct. If it should still exist, the late ministerial interregnum will be described in terms which will seem to imply that all government was at an end; that the social contract was annulled; and that the hand of every man was against his neighbour, until the wisdom and virtue of the new cabinet educed order out of the chaos of anarchy. We are quite certain that misconceptions as gross prevail at this moment respecting many important parts of our annals.

The effect of historical reading is analogous, in many respects, to that produced by foreign travel. The student, like the tourist, is transported into a new state of society. He sees new fashions. He hears new modes of expression. His mind is enlarged by contemplating the wide diversities of laws, of morals, and of manners. But men may travel far, and return with minds as contracted as if they had never stirred from their own market-town. In the same manner, men may know the dates of many battles and the genealogies of many royal houses, and yet be no wiser. Most people look at past times as princes look at foreign countries. More than one illustrious stranger has landed on our island amidst the shouts of a mob, has dined with the king, has hunted with the master of the stag-hounds, has seen the guards reviewed, and a knight of the garter installed, has cantered along Regent Street, has visited Saint Paul's, and noted down its dimensions; and has then departed, thinking that he has seen England. He has, in fact, seen a few public buildings, public men, and public ceremonies. But of the vast and complex system of society, of the fine shades of national character, of the practical operation of government and laws, he knows nothing. He who would understand these things rightly must not confine his observations to palaces and solemn days.

He must see ordinary men as they appear in their ordinary business and in their ordinary pleasures. He must mingle in the crowds of the exchange and the coffee-house. He must obtain admittance to the convivial table and the domestic hearth. He must bear with vulgar expressions. He must not shrink from exploring even the retreats of misery. He who wishes to understand the condition of mankind in former ages must proceed on the same principle. If he attends only to public transactions, to wars, congresses, and debates, his studies will be as unprofitable as the travels of those imperial, royal, and serene sovereigns who form their judgment of our island from having gone in state to a few fine sights, and from having held formal conferences with a few great officers.

The perfect historian is he in whose work the character and spirit of an age is exhibited in miniature. He relates no fact, he attributes no expression to his characters, which is not authenticated by sufficient testimony. But, by judicious selection, rejection, and arrangement, he gives to truth those attractions which have been usurped by fiction. In his narrative a due subordination is observed: some transactions are prominent; others retire. But the scale on which he represents them is increased or diminished, not according to the dignity of the persons concerned in them, but according to the degree in which they elucidate the condition of society and the nature of man. He shows us the court, the camp, and the senate. But he shows us also the nation. He considers no anecdote, no peculiarity of manner, no familiar saying, as too insignficant for his notice which is not too insignificant to illustrate the operation of laws, of religion, and of education, and to mark the progress of the human mind. Men will not merely be described, but will be made intimately known to us. The changes of manners will be indicated, not merely by a few general phrases or a few extracts from statistical documents, but by appropriate images presented in every line.

If a man, such as we are supposing, should write the history of England, he would assuredly not omit the battles, the sieges, the negotiations, the seditions, the ministerial changes. But with these he would intersperse the details which are the charm of historical romances. At Lincoln Cathedral there is a beautiful painted window, which was made by an apprentice out of the pieces of glass which had been rejected by his master. It is so far superior to every other in the church that, according to the tradition, the vanquished artist killed himself from mortification.

Sir Walter Scott, in the same manner, has used those fragments of truth which historians have scornfully thrown behind them in a manner which may well excite their envy. He has constructed out of their gleanings works which, even considered as histories, are scarcely less valuable than theirs. But a truly great historian would reclaim those materials which the novelist has appropriated. The history of the government, and the history of the people, would be exhibited in that mode in which alone they can be exhibited justly, in inseparable conjunction and intermixture. We should not then have to look for the wars and votes of the Puritans in Clarendon, and for their phraseology in Old Mortality; for one half of King James in Hume, and for the other half in the Fortunes of Nigel.

The early part of our imaginary history would be rich with colouring from romance, ballad, and chronicle. We should find ourselves in the company of knights such as those of Froissart, and of pilgrims such as those who rode with Chaucer from the Tabard. Society would be shown from the highest to the lowest, —from the royal cloth of state to the den of the outlaw; from the throne of the legate to the chimney-corner where the begging friar regaled himself. Palmers, minstrels, crusaders, — the stately monastery, with the good cheer in its refectory and the high-mass in its chapel,—the manor-house, with its hunting and hawking,—the tournament, with the heralds and ladies, the trumpets and the cloth of gold,—would give truth and life to the representation. We should perceive, in a thousand slight touches, the importance of the privileged burgher, and the fierce and haughty spirit which swelled under the collar of the degraded villain. The revival of letters would not merely be described in a few magnificent periods. We should discern, in innumerable particulars, the fermentation of mind, the eager appetite for knowledge, which distinguished the sixteenth from the fifteenth century. In the Reformation we should see, not merely a schism which changed the ecclesiastical constitution of England and the mutual relations of the European powers, but a moral war which raged in every family, which set the father against the son, and the son against the father, the mother against the daughter, and the daughter against the mother. Henry would be painted with the skill of Tacitus. We should have the change of his character from his profuse and joyous youth to his savage and imperious old age. We would perceive the gradual progress of selfish and tyrannical passions in a mind not naturally insensible or ungenerous; and to the last we should detect some remains of that open and noble temper which endeared him to a people whom he oppressed, struggling with the hardness of despotism and the irritability of disease. We should see Elizabeth in all her weakness and in all her strength, surrounded by the handsome favourites whom she never trusted, and the wise old statesmen whom she never dismissed, uniting in herself the most contradictory qualities of both her parents,—the coquetry, the caprice, the petty malice of Anne,—the haughty and resolute spirit of Henry. We have no hesitation in saying that a great artist might produce a portrait of this remarkable woman at least as striking as that in the novel of Kenilworth, without employing a single trait not authenticated by ample testimony. In the meantime, we should see arts cultivated, wealth accumulated, the conveniences of life improved. We should see the keeps, where nobles, insecure themselves, spread insecurity around them, gradually giving place to the halls of peaceful opulence, to the oriels of Longleat, and the stately pinnacles of Burleigh. We should see towns extended, deserts cultivated, the hamlets of fishermen turned into wealthy havens, the meal of the peasant improved, and his hut more commodiously furnished. We should see those opinions and feelings which produced the great struggle against the House of Stuart slowly growing up in the bosom of private families, before they manifested themselves in parliamentary debates. Then would come the civil war. Those skirmishes on which Clarendon dwells so minutely would be told, as Thucydides would have told them, with perspicuous conciseness. They are merely connecting links. But the great characteristics of the age, the loyal enthusiasm of the brave English gentry, the fierce licentiousness of the swearing, dicing, drunken reprobates, whose excesses disgraced the royal cause,—the austerity of the Presbyterian Sabbaths in the city, the extravagance of the independent preachers in the camp, the precise garb, the severe countenance, the petty scruples, the affected accent, the absurd names and phrases which marked the Puritans,—the valour, the policy, the public spirit, which lurked beneath these ungraceful disguises,—the dreams of the raving Fifth-monarchy-man, the dreams, scarcely less wild, of the philosophic republican, all these would enter into the representation, and render it at once more exact and more striking.

The instruction derived from history thus written would be of a vivid and practical character. It would be received by the imagination as well as by the reason. It would be not merely

traced on the mind, but branded into it. Many truths, too,
would be learned, which can be learned in no other manner. As
the history of states is generally written, the greatest and most
momentous revolutions seem to come upon them like supernatural inflictions, without warning or cause. But the fact is,
that such revolutions are almost always the consequences of
moral changes, which have gradually passed on the mass of the
community, and which originally proceed far before their progress is indicated by any public measure. An intimate knowledge of the domestic history of nations is therefore absolutely
necessary to the prognosis of political events. A narrative,
defective in this respect, is as useless as a medical treatise which
should pass by all the symptoms attendant on the early stage of
a disease and mention only what occurs when the patient is
beyond the reach of remedies.

A historian, such as we have been attempting to describe,
would indeed be an intellectual prodigy. In his mind, powers
scarcely compatible with each other must be tempered into an
exquisite harmony. We shall sooner see another Shakspeare or
another Homer. The highest excellence to which any single
faculty can be brought would be less surprising than such a
happy and delicate combination of qualities. Yet the contemplation of imaginary models is not an unpleasant or useless employment of the mind. It cannot indeed produce perfection; but it
produces improvement and nourishes that generous and liberal
fastidiousness which is not inconsistent with the strongest
sensibility to merit, and which, while it exalts our conceptions
of the art, does not render us unjust to the artist.

JOHN DRYDEN [1]

(JANUARY 1828)

THE public voice has assigned to Dryden the first place in the
second rank of our poets,—no mean station in a table of intellectual precedency so rich in illustrious names. It is allowed
that, even of the few who were his superiors in genius, none has
exercised a more extensive or permanent influence on the national
habits of thought and expression. His life was commensurate

---

[1] *The Poetical Works of John Dryden.* In 2 vols. University Edition.
London, 1826.

with the period during which a great revolution in the public taste was effected; and in that revolution he played the part of Cromwell. By unscrupulously taking the lead in its wildest excesses, he obtained the absolute guidance of it. By trampling on laws, he acquired the authority of a legislator. By signalising himself as the most daring and irreverent of rebels, he raised himself to the dignity of a recognised prince. He commenced his career by the most frantic outrages. He terminated it in the repose of established sovereignty,—the author of a new code, the root of a new dynasty.

Of Dryden, however, as of almost every man who has been distinguished either in the literary or in the political world, it may be said that the course which he pursued, and the effect which he produced, depended less on his personal qualities than on the circumstances in which he was placed. Those who have read history with discrimination know the fallacy of those panegyrics and invectives which represent individuals as effecting great moral and intellectual revolutions, subverting established systems, and imprinting a new character on their age. The difference between one man and another is by no means so great as the superstitious crowd supposes. But the same feelings which in ancient Rome produced the apotheosis of a popular emperor, and in modern Rome the canonisation of a devout prelate, lead men to cherish an illusion which furnishes them with something to adore. By a law of association, from the operation of which even minds the most strictly regulated by reason are not wholly exempt, misery disposes us to hatred, and happiness to love, although there may be no person to whom our misery or our happiness can be ascribed. The peevishness of an invalid vents itself even on those who alleviate his pain. The good humour of a man elated by success often displays itself towards enemies. In the same manner, the feelings of pleasure and admiration, to which the contemplation of great events gives birth, make an object where they do not find it. Thus, nations descend to the absurdities of Egyptian idolatry, and worship stocks and reptiles—Sacheverells and Wilkeses. They even fall prostrate before a deity to which they have themselves given the form which commands their veneration, and which, unless fashioned by them, would have remained a shapeless block. They persuade themselves that they are the creatures of what they have themselves created. For, in fact, it is the age that forms the man, not the man that forms the age. Great minds do indeed re-act on the society which has made them what they are; but they only pay with interest what they have received. We extol Bacon, and sneer at Aquinas. But, if their situations had been changed, Bacon might have been the Angelical Doctor, the most subtle Aristotelian of the schools; the Dominican might have led forth the sciences from their house of bondage. If Luther had been born in the tenth century, he would have effected no reformation. If he had never been born at all, it is evident that the sixteenth century could not have elasped without a great schism in the church. Voltaire, in the days of Louis the Fourteenth, would probably have been, like most of the literary men of that time, a zealous Jansenist, eminent among the defenders of efficacious grace, a bitter assailant of the lax morality of the Jesuits and the unreasonable decisions of the Sorbonne. If Pascal had entered on his literary career when intelligence was more general, and abuses at the same time more flagrant, when the church was polluted by the Iscariot Dubois, the court disgraced by the orgies of Canillac, and the nation sacrificed to the juggles of Law, if he had lived to see a dynasty of harlots, an empty treasury and a crowded harem, an army formidable only to those whom it should have protected, a priesthood just religious enough to be intolerant, he might possibly, like every man of genius in France, have imbibed extravagant prejudices against monarchy and Christianity. The wit which blasted the sophisms of Escobar —the impassioned eloquence which defended the sisters of Port Royal—the intellectual hardihood which was not beaten down even by Papal authority—might have raised him to the Patriarchate of the Philosophical Church. It was long disputed whether the honour of inventing the method of Fluxions belonged to Newton or to Leibnitz. It is now generally allowed that these great men made the same discovery at the same time. Mathematical science, indeed, had then reached such a point that, if neither of them had ever existed, the principle must inevitably have occurred to some person within a few years. So in our own time the doctrine of rent, now universally received by political economists, was propounded, almost at the same moment, by two writers unconnected with each other. Preceding speculators had long been blundering round about it; and it could not possibly have been missed much longer by the most heedless inquirer. We are inclined to think that, with respect to every great addition which has been made to the stock of human knowledge, the case has been similar; that without Copernicus we should have been Copernicans,—that without

Columbus, America would have been discovered,—that without Locke we should have possessed a just theory of the origin of human ideas. Society indeed has its great men and its little men, as the earth has its mountains and its valleys. But the inequalities of intellect, like the inequalities of the surface of our globe, bear so small a proportion to the mass, that, in calculating its great revolutions, they may safely be neglected. The sun illuminates the hills, while it is still below the horizon, and truth is discovered by the highest minds a little before it becomes manifest to the multitude. This is the extent of their superiority. They are the first to catch and reflect a light, which, without their assistance, must, in a short time, be visible to those who lie far beneath them.

The same remark will apply equally to the fine arts. The laws on which depend the progress and decline of poetry, painting, and sculpture, operate with little less certainty than those which regulate the periodical returns of heat and cold, of fertility and barrenness. Those who seem to lead the public taste are, in general, merely outrunning it in the direction which it is spontaneously pursuing. Without a just apprehension of the laws to which we have alluded, the merits and defects of Dryden can be but imperfectly understood. We will, therefore, state what we conceive them to be.

The ages in which the masterpieces of imagination have been produced have by no means been those in which taste has been most correct. It seems that the creative faculty, and the critical faculty, cannot exist together in their highest perfection. The causes of this phenomenon it is not difficult to assign.

It is true that the man who is best able to take a machine to pieces, and who most clearly comprehends the manner in which all its wheels and springs conduce to its general effect, will be the man most competent to form another machine of similar power. In all the branches of physical and moral science which admit of perfect analysis, he who can resolve will be able to combine. But the analysis which criticism can effect of poetry is necessarily imperfect. One element must for ever elude its researches; and that is the very element by which poetry is poetry. In the description of nature, for example, a judicious reader will easily detect an incongruous image. But he will find it impossible to explain in what consists the art of a writer who, in a few words, brings some spot before him so vividly that he shall know it as if he had lived there from childhood; while another, employing the same materials, the same verdure, the same water, and the same flowers, committing no inaccuracy, introducing nothing which can be positively pronounced superfluous, omitting nothing which can be positively pronounced necessary, shall produce no more effect than an advertisement of a capital residence and a desirable pleasure-ground. To take another example: the great features of the character of Hotspur are obvious to the most superficial reader. We at once perceive that his courage is splendid, his thirst of glory intense, his animal spirits high, his temper careless, arbitrary, and petulant; that he indulges his own humour without caring whose feelings he may wound, or whose enmity he may provoke, by his levity. Thus far criticism will go. But something is still wanting. A man might have all those qualities, and every other quality which the most minute examiner can introduce into his catalogue of the virtues and faults of Hotspur, and yet he would not be· Hotspur. Almost everything that we have said of him applies equally to Falconbridge. Yet in the mouth of Falconbridge most of his speeches would seem out of place. In real life this perpetually occurs. We are sensible of wide differences between men whom, if we were required to describe them, we should describe in almost the same terms. If we were attempting to draw elaborate characters of them, we should scarcely be able to point out any strong distinction; yet we approach them with feelings altogether dissimilar. We cannot conceive of them as using the expressions or the gestures of each other. Let us suppose that a zoologist should attempt to give an account of some animal, a porcupine for instance, to people who had never seen it. The porcupine, he might say, is of the class mammalia, and the order glires. There are whiskers on its face; it is two feet long; it has four toes before, five behind, two fore teeth, and eight grinders. Its body is covered with hair and quills. And, when all this has been said, would any one of the auditors have formed a just idea of a porcupine? Would any two of them have formed the same idea? There might exist innumerable races of animals, possessing all the characteristics which have been mentioned, yet altogether unlike to each other. What the description of our naturalist is to a real porcupine, the remarks of criticism are to the images of poetry. What it so imperfectly decomposes it cannot perfectly reconstruct. It is evidently as impossible to produce an Othello or a Macbeth by reversing an analytical process so defective, as it would be for an anatomist to form a living man out of the fragments of his dissecting-room. In both cases the vital principle eludes the finest instruments,

and vanishes in the very instant in which its seat is touched.
Hence those who, trusting to their critical skill, attempt to write
poems give us, not images of things, but catalogues of qualities.
Their characters are allegories—not good men and bad men, but
cardinal virtues and deadly sins.   We seem to have fallen among
the acquaintances of our old friend Christian: sometimes we
meet Mistrust and Timorous; sometimes Mr. Hate-good and
Mr. Love-lust; and then again Prudence, Piety, and Charity.

That critical discernment is not sufficient to make men poets
is generally allowed.   Why it should keep them from becoming
poets is not perhaps equally evident; but the fact is, that poetry
requires not an examining but a believing frame of mind.   Those
feel it most, and write it best, who forget that it is a work of art;
to whom its imitations, like the realities from which they are
taken, are subjects, not for connoisseurship, but for tears and
laughter, resentment and affection; who are too much under the
influence of the illusion to admire the genius which has produced
it; who are too much frightened for Ulysses in the cave of Poly-
phemus to care whether the pun about Outis be good or bad;
who forget that such a person as Shakspeare ever existed, while
they weep and curse with Lear.   It is by giving faith to the
creations of the imagination that a man becomes a poet.   It is
by treating those creations as deceptions, and by resolving them,
as nearly as possible, into their elements, that he becomes a
critic.   In the moment in which the skill of the artist is perceived, the spell of the art is broken.

These considerations account for the absurdities into which the
greatest writers have fallen, when they have attempted to give
general rules for composition, or to pronounce judgment on the
works of others.   They are unaccustomed to analyse what they
feel; they, therefore, perpetually refer their emotions to causes
which have not in the slightest degree tended to produce them.
They feel pleasure in reading a book.   They never consider that
this pleasure may be the effect of ideas which some unmeaning
expression, striking on the first link of a chain of associations,
may have called up in their own minds—that they have themselves furnished to the author the beauties which they admire.

Cervantes is the delight of all classes of readers.   Every
schoolboy thumbs to pieces the most wretched translations of
his romance, and knows the lantern jaws of the Knight Errant,
and the broad cheeks of the Squire, as well as the faces of his own
playfellows.   The most experienced and fastidious judges are
amazed at the perfection of that art which extracts inextin-

guishable laughter from the greatest of human calamities without once violating the reverence due to it; at that discriminating
delicacy of touch which makes a character exquisitely ridiculous,
without impairing its worth, its grace, or its dignity. In Don
Quixote are several dissertations on the principles of poetic
and dramatic writing. No passages in the whole work exhibit
stronger marks of labour and attention; and no passages in any
work with which we are acquainted are more worthless and
puerile. In our time they would scarcely obtain admittance
into the literary department of the *Morning Post*. Every
reader of the Divine Comedy must be struck by the veneration
which Dante expresses for writers far inferior to himself. He
will not lift up his eyes from the ground in the presence of
Brunetto, all whose works are not worth the worst of his own
hundred cantos. He does not venture to walk in the same line
with the bombastic Statius. His admiration of Virgil is absolute idolatry. If, indeed, it had been excited by the elegant,
splendid, and harmonious diction of the Roman poet, it would
not have been altogether unreasonable; but it is rather as an
authority on all points of philosophy, than as a work of imagination, that he values the Æneid. The most trivial passages he
regards as oracles of the highest authority, and of the most
recondite meaning. He describes his conductor as the sea of all
wisdom—the sun which heals every disordered sight. As he
judged of Virgil, the Italians of the fourteenth century judged of
him; they were proud of him; they praised him; they struck
medals bearing his head; they quarrelled for the honour of possessing his remains; they maintained professors to expound his
writings. But what they admired was not that mighty imagination which called a new world into existence, and made all its
sights and sounds familiar to the eye and ear of the mind. They
said little of those awful and lovely creations on which later
critics delight to dwell—Farinata lifting his haughty and tranquil
brow from his couch of everlasting fire—the lion-like repose of
Sordello—or the light which shone from the celestial smile of
Beatrice. They extolled their great poet for his smattering of
ancient literature and history; for his logic and his divinity;
for his absurd physics, and his more absurd metaphysics; for
everything but that in which he pre-eminently excelled. Like
the fool in the story, who ruined his dwelling by digging for gold,
which, as he had dreamed, was concealed under its foundations,
they laid waste one of the noblest works of human genius, by
seeking in it for buried treasures of wisdom which existed only in

their own wild reveries. The finest passages were little valued till they had been debased into some monstrous allegory. Louder applause was given to the lecture on fate and free-will, or to the ridiculous astronomical theories, than to those tremendous lines which disclose the secrets of the tower of hunger, or to that half-told tale of guilty love, so passionate and so full of tears.

We do not mean to say that the contemporaries of Dante read with less emotion than their descendants of Ugolino groping among the wasted corpses of his children, or of Francesca starting at the tremulous kiss and dropping the fatal volume. Far from it. We believe that they admired these things less than ourselves, but that they felt them more. We should perhaps say that they felt them too much to admire them. The progress of a nation from barbarism to civilisation produces a change similar to that which takes place during the progress of an individual from infancy to mature age. What man does not remember with regret the first time that he read Robinson Crusoe? Then, indeed, he was unable to appreciate the powers of the writer; or, rather, he neither knew nor cared whether the book had a writer at all. He probably thought it not half so fine as some rant of Macpherson about dark-browed Foldath, and white-bosomed Strinadona. He now values Fingal and Temora only as showing with how little evidence a story may be believed, and with how little merit a book may be popular. Of the romance of Defoe he entertains the highest opinion. He perceives the hand of a master in ten thousand touches which formerly he passed by without notice. But, though he understands the merits of the narrative better than formerly, he is far less interested by it. Xury, and Friday, and pretty Poll, the boat with the shoulder-of-mutton sail, and the canoe which could not be brought down to the water edge, the tent with its hedge and ladders, the preserve of kids, and the den where the old goat died, can never again be to him the realities which they were. The days when his favourite volume set him upon making wheel-barrows and chairs, upon digging caves and fencing huts in the garden, can never return. Such is the law of our nature. Our judgment ripens; our imagination decays. We cannot at once enjoy the flowers of the spring of life and the fruits of its autumn, the pleasures of close investigation and those of agreeable error. We cannot sit at once in the front of the stage and behind the scenes. We cannot be under the illusion of the spectacle, while we are watching the movements of the ropes and pulleys which dispose it.

The chapter in which Fielding describes the behaviour of Partridge at the theatre affords so complete an illustration of our proposition that we cannot refrain from quoting some parts of it.

" Partridge gave that credit to Mr. Garrick which he had denied to Jones, and fell into so violent a trembling that his knees knocked against each other. Jones asked him what was the matter, and whether he was afraid of the warrior upon the stage?—' O, la, sir,' said he, ' I perceive now it is what you told me. I am not afraid of anything, for I know it is but a play; and if it was really a ghost, it could do one no harm at such a distance and in so much company; and yet, if I was frightened, I am not the only person.'—' Why, who,' cries Jones, ' dost thou take to be such a coward here besides thyself? '—' Nay, you may call me a coward if you will; but if that little man there upon the stage is not frightened, I never saw any man frightened in my life.' . . . He sat with his eyes fixed partly on the ghost and partly on Hamlet, and with his mouth open; the same passions which succeeded each other in Hamlet, succeeding likewise in him. . . .

" Little more worth remembering occurred during the play, at the end of which Jones asked him which of the players he liked best? To this he answered, with some appearance of indignation at the question, ' The King, without doubt.'—' Indeed, Mr. Partridge,' says Mrs. Miller, ' you are not of the same opinion with the town; for they are all agreed that Hamlet is acted by the best player who was ever on the stage.'—' He the best player! ' cries Partridge, with a contemptuous sneer; ' why I could act as well as he myself. I am sure if I had seen a ghost, I should have looked in the very same manner, and done just as he did. And then to be sure, in that scene, as you called it, between him and his mother, where you told me he acted so fine, why any man, that is, any good man, that had such a mother, would have done exactly the same. I know you are only joking with me; but indeed, madam, though I never was at a play in London, yet I have seen acting before in the country, and the King for my money; he speaks all his words distinctly, and half as loud again as the other. Anybody may see he is an actor.' "

In this excellent passage Partridge is represented as a very bad theatrical critic. But none of those who laugh at him possess the tithe of his sensibility to theatrical excellence.   He admires in the wrong place; but he trembles in the right place. It is indeed because he is so much excited by the acting of Garrick that he ranks him below the strutting, mouthing performer, who personates the King.   So, we have heard it said that, in some parts of Spain and Portugal, an actor who should represent a depraved character finely, instead of calling down the applauses of the audience, is hissed and pelted without mercy.   It would be the same in England, if we, for one moment, thought that Shylock or Iago was standing before us.   While the dramatic art was in its infancy at Athens, it produced similar effects on the ardent and imaginative spectators.   It is said that they blamed Æschylus for frightening them into fits with his Furies.   Herodotus tell us that, when Phrynichus produced his tragedy on the fall of Miletus, they fined him in a penalty of a thousand drachmas for torturing their feelings by so pathetic an exhibition.   They did not regard him as a great artist, but merely as a man who had given them pain.   When they woke from the distressing illusion, they treated the author of it as they would have treated a messenger who should have brought them fatal and alarming tidings which turned out to be false. In the same manner a child screams with terror at the sight of a person in an ugly mask.   He has perhaps seen the mask put on.   But his imagination is too strong for his reason; and he entreats that it may be taken off.

We should act in the same manner if the grief and horror produced in us by works of the imagination amounted to real torture.   But in us these emotions are comparatively languid. They rarely affect our appetite or our sleep.   They leave us sufficiently at ease to trace them to their causes, and to estimate the powers which produce them.   Our attention is speedily diverted from the images which call forth our tears to the art by which those images have been selected and combined.   We applaud the genius of the writer.   We applaud our own sagacity and sensibility; and we are comforted.

Yet, though we think that in the progress of nations towards refinement the reasoning powers are improved at the expense of the imagination, we acknowledge that to this rule there are many apparent exceptions.   We are not, however, quite satisfied that they are more than apparent.   Men reasoned better, for example, in the time of Elizabeth than in the time of Egbert; and they also wrote better poetry.   But we must distinguish between poetry as a mental act, and poetry as a species of composition. If we take it in the latter sense, its excellence depends not solely on the vigour of the imagination, but partly also on the instruments which the imagination employs. Within certain limits, therefore, poetry may be improving while the poetical faculty is decaying. The vividness of the picture presented to the reader is not necessarily proportioned to the vividness of the prototype which exists in the mind of the writer. In the other arts we see this clearly. Should a man, gifted by nature with all the genius of Canova, attempt to carve a statue without instruction as to the management of his chisel, or attention to the anatomy of the human body, he would produce something compared with which the Highlander at the door of a snuff shop would deserve admiration. If an uninitiated Raphael were to attempt a painting, it would be a mere daub; indeed, the connoisseurs say that the early works of Raphael are little better. Yet, who can attribute this to want of imagination? Who can doubt that the youth of that great artist was passed amidst an ideal world of beautiful and majestic forms? Or, who will attribute the difference which appears between his first rude essays and his magnificent Transfiguration to a change in the constitution of his mind? In poetry, as in painting and sculpture, it is necessary that the imitator should be well acquainted with that which he undertakes to imitate, and expert in the mechanical part of his art. Genius will not furnish him with a vocabulary: it will not teach him what word most exactly corresponds to his idea, and will most fully convey it to others: it will not make him a great descriptive poet, till he has looked with attention on the face of nature; or a great dramatist, till he has felt and witnessed much of the influence of the passions. Information and experience are, therefore, necessary; not for the purpose of strengthening the imagination, which is never so strong as in people incapable of reasoning— savages, children, madmen, and dreamers; but for the purpose of enabling the artist to communicate his conceptions to others.

In a barbarous age the imagination exercises a despotic power. So strong is the perception of what is unreal that it often overpowers all the passions of the mind and all the sensations of the body. At first, indeed, the phantasm remains undivulged, a hidden treasure, a wordless poetry, an invisible painting, a silent music, a dream of which the pains and pleasures exist to the dreamer alone, a bitterness which the heart only knoweth, a joy with which a stranger intermeddleth not. The machinery, by which ideas are to be conveyed from one person to another, is as yet rude and defective.   Between mind and mind there is a great gulf.   The imitative arts do not exist, or are in their lowest state.   But the actions of men amply prove that the faculty which gives birth to those arts is morbidly active.   It is not yet the inspiration of poets and sculptors; but it is the amusement of the day, the terror of the night, the fertile source of wild superstitions.   It turns the clouds into gigantic shapes, and the winds into doleful voices.   The belief which springs from it is more absolute and undoubting than any which can be derived from evidence.   It resembles the faith which we repose in our own sensations.   Thus, the Arab, when covered with wounds, saw nothing but the dark eyes and the green kerchief of a beckoning Houri.   The Northern warrior laughed in the pangs of death when he thought of the mead of Valhalla.

The first works of the imagination are, as we have said, poor and rude, not from the want of genius, but from the want of materials.   Phidias could have done nothing with an old tree and a fish-bone, or Homer with the language of New Holland.

Yet the effect of these early performances, imperfect as they must necessarily be, is immense.   All deficiencies are supplied by the susceptibility of those to whom they are addressed.   We all know what pleasure a wooden doll, which may be bought for sixpence, will afford to a little girl.   She will require no other company.   She will nurse it, dress it, and talk to it all day.   No grown-up man takes half so much delight in one of the incomparable babies of Chantrey.   In the same manner savages are more affected by the rude compositions of their bards than nations more advanced in civilisation by the greatest masterpieces of poetry.

In process of time the instruments by which the imagination works are brought to perfection.   Men have not more imagination than their rude ancestors.   We strongly suspect that they have much less.   But they produce better works of imagination.   Thus, up to a certain period, the diminution of the poetical powers is far more than compensated by the improvement of all the appliances and means of which those powers stand in need. Then comes the short period of splendid and consummate excellence.   And then, from causes against which it is pain to struggle, poetry begins to decline.   The progress of language, which was at first favourable, becomes fatal to it, and, instead of compensating for the decay of the imagination, accelerates that decay, and renders it more obvious.   When the adventurer in the Arabian tale anointed one of his eyes with the contents of the magical box, all the riches of the earth, however widely dispersed, however sacredly concealed, became visible to him. But, when he tried the experiment on both eyes, he was struck with blindness. What the enchanted elixir was to the sight of the body, language is to the sight of the imagination. At first it calls up a world of glorious illusions; but, when it becomes too copious, it altogether destroys the visual power.

As the development of the mind proceeds, symbols, instead of being employed to convey images, are substituted for them. Civilised men think as they trade, not in kind, but by means of a circulating medium. In these circumstances the sciences improve rapidly, and criticism among the rest; but poetry, in the highest sense of the word, disappears. Then comes the dotage of the fine arts, a second childhood, as feeble as the former, and far more hopeless. This is the age of critical poetry, of poetry by courtesy, of poetry to which the memory, the judgment, and the wit contribute far more than the imagination. We readily allow that many works of this description are excellent: we will not contend with those who think them more valuable than the great poems of an earlier period. We only maintain that they belong to a different species of composition, and are produced by a different faculty.

It is some consolation to reflect that this critical school of poetry improves as the science of criticism improves; and that the science of criticism, like every other science, is constantly tending towards perfection. As experiments are multiplied, principles are better understood.

In some countries, in our own for example, there has been an interval between the downfall of the creative school and the rise of the critical, a period during which imagination has been in its decrepitude, and taste in its infancy. Such a revolutionary interregnum as this will be deformed by every species of extravagance.

The first victory of good taste is over the bombast and conceits which deform such times as these. But criticism is still in a very imperfect state. What is accidental is for a long time confounded with what is essential. General theories are drawn from detached facts. How many hours the action of a play may be allowed to occupy,—how many similes an Epic Poet may introduce into his first book,—whether a piece, which is acknowledged to have a beginning and an end, may not be without a middle, and other questions as puerile as these, formerly occupied the attention of men of letters in France, and even in this country.

Poets, in such circumstances as these, exhibit all the narrowness and feebleness of the criticism by which their manner has been fashioned. From outrageous absurdity they are preserved indeed by their timidity. But they perpetually sacrifice nature and reason to arbitrary canons of taste. In their eagerness to avoid the *mala prohibita* of a foolish code, they are perpetually rushing on the *mala in se*. Their great predecessors, it is true, were as bad critics as themselves, or perhaps worse, but those predecessors, as we have attempted to show, were inspired by a faculty independent of criticism, and, therefore, wrote well while they judged ill.

In time men begin to take more rational and comprehensive views of literature. The analysis of poetry, which, as we have remarked, must at best be imperfect, approaches nearer and nearer to exactness. The merits of the wonderful models of former times are justly appreciated. The frigid productions of a later age are rated at no more than their proper value. Pleasing and ingenious imitations of the manner of the great masters appear. Poetry has a partial revival, a Saint Martin's Summer, which, after a period of dreariness and decay, agreeably reminds us of the splendour of its June. A second harvest is gathered in; though, growing on a spent soil, it has not the heart of the former. Thus, in the present age, Monti has successfully imitated the style of Dante; and something of the Elizabethan inspiration has been caught by several eminent countrymen of our own. But never will Italy produce another Inferno, or England another Hamlet. We look on the beauties of the modern imitations with feelings similar to those with which we see flowers disposed in vases, to ornament the drawing-rooms of a capital. We doubtless regard them with pleasure, with greater pleasure, perhaps, because, in the midst of a place ungenial to them, they remind us of the distant spots on which they flourish in spontaneous exuberance. But we miss the sap, the freshness, and the bloom. Or, if we may borrow another illustration from Queen Scheherezade, we would compare the writers of this school to the jewellers who were employed to complete the unfinished window of the palace of Aladdin. Whatever skill or cost could do was done. Palace and bazaar were ransacked for precious stones. Yet the artists, with all their dexterity, with all their assiduity, and with all their vast means, were unable to produce anything comparable to the wonders which a spirit of a higher order had wrought in a single night.

The history of every literature with which we are acquainted confirms, we think, the principles which we have laid down. In Greece we see the imaginative school of poetry gradually fading into the critical. Æschylus and Pindar were succeeded by Sophocles, Sophocles by Euripides, Euripides by the Alexandrian versifiers. Of these last, Theocritus alone has left compositions which deserve to be read. The splendour and grotesque fairyland of the Old Comedy, rich with such gorgeous hues, peopled with such fantastic shapes, and vocal alternately with the sweetest peals of music and the loudest bursts of elvish laughter, disappeared for ever. The masterpieces of the New Comedy are known to us by Latin translations of extraordinary merit. From these translations, and from the expressions of the ancient critics, it is clear that the original compositions were distinguished by grace and sweetness, that they sparkled with wit, and abounded with pleasing sentiment; but that the creative power was gone. Julius Cæsar called Terence a half Menander,—a sure proof that Menander was not a quarter Aristophanes.

The literature of the Romans was merely a continuation of the literature of the Greeks. The pupils started from the point at which their masters had, in the course of many generations, arrived. They thus almost wholly missed the period of original invention. The only Latin poets whose writings exhibit much vigour of imagination are Lucretius and Catullus. The Augustan age produced nothing equal to their finer passages.

In France that licensed jester, whose jingling cap and motley coat concealed more genius than ever mustered in the saloon of Ninon or of Madame Géoffrin, was succeeded by writers as decorous and as tiresome as gentlemen ushers.

The poetry of Italy and of Spain has undergone the same change. But nowhere has the revolution been more complete and violent than in England. The same person who, when a boy, had clapped his thrilling hands at the first representation of the Tempest might, without attaining to a marvellous longevity, have lived to read the earlier works of Prior and Addison. The change, we believe, must, sooner or later, have taken place. But its progress was accelerated, and its character modified, by the political occurrences of the times, and particularly by two events, the closing of the theatres under the Commonwealth, and the restoration of the House of Stuart.

We have said that the critical and poetical faculties are not only distinct, but almost incompatible. The state of our literature during the reigns of Elizabeth and James the First is a strong confirmation of this remark. The greatest works of imagination that the world has ever seen were produced at that period. The national taste, in the meantime, was to the last degree detestable. Alliterations, puns, antithetical forms of expression lavishly employed where no corresponding opposition existed between the thoughts expressed, strained allegories, pedantic allusions, everything, in short, quaint and affected, in matter and manner, made up what was then considered as fine writing. The eloquence of the bar, the pulpit, and the council-board, was deformed by conceits which would have disgraced the rhyming shepherds of an Italian academy. The king quibbled on the throne. We might, indeed, console ourselves by reflecting that his majesty was a fool. But the chancellor quibbled in concert from the wool-sack: and the chancellor was Francis Bacon. It is needless to mention Sidney and the whole tribe of Euphuists; for Shakspeare himself, the greatest poet that ever lived, falls into the same fault whenever he means to be particularly fine. While he abandons himself to the impulse of his imagination, his compositions are not only the sweetest and the most sublime, but also the most faultless, that the world has ever seen. But, as soon as his critical powers come into play, he sinks to the level of Cowley; or rather he does ill what Cowley did well. All that is bad in his works is bad elaborately, and of malice aforethought. The only thing wanting to make them perfect was, that he should never have troubled himself with thinking whether they were good or not. Like the angels in Milton, he sinks " with compulsion and laborious flight." His natural tendency is upwards. That he may soar, it is only necessary that he should not struggle to fall. He resembles an American Cacique, who, possessing in unmeasured abundance the metals which in polished societies are esteemed the most precious, was utterly unconscious of their value, and gave up treasures more valuable than the imperial crowns of other countries, to secure some gaudy and far-fetched but worthless bauble, a plated button, or a necklace of coloured glass.

We have attempted to show that, as knowledge is extended and as the reason develops itself, the imitative arts decay. We should, therefore, expect that the corruption of poetry would commence in the educated classes of society. And this, in fact, is almost constantly the case. The few great works of imagination which appear in a critical age are, almost without exception, the works of uneducated men. Thus, at a time when persons of quality translated French romances, and when the universities celebrated royal deaths in verses about tritons and fauns, a preaching tinker produced the *Pilgrim's Progress*. And thus a ploughman startled a generation which had thought Hayley and Beattie great poets, with the adventures of Tam O'Shanter. Even in the latter part of the reign of Elizabeth the fashionable poetry had degenerated. It retained few vestiges of the imagination of earlier times. It had not yet been subjected to the rules of good taste. Affectation had completely tainted madrigals and sonnets. The grotesque conceits and the tuneless numbers of Donne were, in the time of James, the favourite models of composition at Whitehall and at the Temple. But, though the literature of the Court was in its decay, the literature of the people was in its perfection. The Muses had taken sanctuary in the theatres, the haunts of a class whose taste was not better than that of the Right Honourables and singular good Lords who admired metaphysical love-verses, but whose imagination retained all its freshness and vigour; whose censure and approbation might be erroneously bestowed, but whose tears and laughter was never in the wrong. The infection which had tainted lyric and didactic poetry had but slightly and partially touched the drama. While the noble and the learned were comparing eyes to burning-glasses, and tears to terrestrial globes, coyness to an enthymeme, absence to a pair of compasses, and an unrequited passion to the fortieth remainder-man in an entail, Juliet leaning from the balcony, and Miranda smiling over the chess-board, sent home many spectators, as kind and simple-hearted as the master and mistress of Fletcher's *Ralpho*, to cry themselves to sleep.

No species of fiction is so delightful to us as the old English drama. Even its inferior productions possess a charm not to be found in any other kind of poetry. It is the most lucid mirror that ever was held up to nature. The creations of the great dramatists of Athens produce the effect of magnificent sculptures, conceived by a mighty imagination, polished with the utmost delicacy, embodying ideas of ineffable majesty and beauty, but cold, pale, and rigid, with no bloom on the cheek, and no speculation in the eye. In all the draperies, the figures, and the faces, in the lovers and the tyrants, the Bacchanals and the Furies, there is the same marble chillness and deadness. Most of the characters of the French stage resemble the waxen gentlemen and ladies in the window of a perfumer, rouged, curled, and bedizened, but fixed in such stiff attitudes, and staring with eyes expressive of such utter unmeaningness, that they cannot produce an illusion for a single moment. In the English plays alone is to be found the warmth, the mellowness, and the reality of painting. We know the minds of the men and women, as we know the faces of the men and women of Vandyke.

The excellence of these works is in a great measure the result of two peculiarities, which the critics of the French school consider as defects—from the mixture of tragedy and comedy, and from the length and extent of the action. The former is necessary to render the drama a just representation of a world in which the laughers and the weepers are perpetually jostling each other,—in which every event has its serious and ludicrous side. The latter enables us to form an intimate acquaintance with characters with which we could not possibly become familiar during the few hours to which the unities restrict the poet. In this respect, the works of Shakspeare, in particular, are miracles of art. In a piece, which may be read aloud in three hours, we see a character gradually unfold all its recesses to us. We see it change with the change of circumstances. The petulant youth rises into the politic and warlike sovereign. The profuse and courteous philanthropist sours into a hater and scorner of his kind. The tyrant is altered, by the chastening of affliction, into a pensive moralist. The veteran general, distinguished by coolness, sagacity, and self-command, sinks under a conflict between love strong as death, and jealousy cruel as the grave. The brave and loyal subject passes, step by step, to the extremities of human depravity. We trace his progress, from the first dawnings of unlawful ambition to the cynical melancholy of his impenitent remorse. Nothing is omitted: nothing is crowded. Great as are the changes, narrow as is the compass within which they are exhibited, they shock us as little as the gradual alterations of those familiar faces which we see every evening and every morning. The magical skill of the poet resembles that of the Dervise in the Spectator, who condensed all the events of seven years into the single moment during which the king held his head under the water.

It is deserving of remark, that, at the time of which we speak, the plays even of men not eminently distinguished by genius,—such, for example, as Jonson,—were far superior to the best works of imagination in other departments. Therefore, though we conceive that, from causes which we have already investigated, our poetry must necessarily have declined, we think that, unless its fate had been accelerated by external attacks, it might have enjoyed an euthanasia, that genius might have been kept alive by the drama till its place could, in some degree, be supplied by taste,—that there would have been scarcely any interval between the age of sublime invention and that of agreeable imitation. The works of Shakspeare, which were not appreciated with any degree of justice before the middle of the eighteenth century, might then have been the recognised standards of excellence during the latter part of the seventeenth; and he and the great Elizabethan writers might have been almost immediately succeeded by a generation of poets similar to those who adorn our own times.

But the Puritans drove imagination from its last asylum. They prohibited theatrical representations, and stigmatised the whole race of dramatists as enemies of morality and religion. Much that is objectionable may be found in the writers whom they reprobated; but whether they took the best measures for stopping the evil appears to us very doubtful, and must, we think, have appeared doubtful to themselves, when, after the lapse of a few years, they saw the unclean spirit whom they had cast out return to his old haunts, with seven others fouler than himself.

By the extinction of the drama, the fashionable school of poetry,—a school without truth of sentiment or harmony of versification,—without the powers of an earlier, or the correctness of a later age,—was left to enjoy undisputed ascendency. A vicious ingenuity, a morbid quickness to perceive resemblances and analogies between things apparently heterogeneous, constituted almost its only claim to admiration. Suckling was dead. Milton was absorbed in political and theological controversy. If Waller differed from the Cowleian sect of writers, he differed for the worse. He had as little poetry as they, and much less wit; nor is the languor of his verses less offensive than the ruggedness of theirs. In Denham alone the faint dawn of a better manner was discernible.

But, low as was the state of our poetry during the civil war and the Protectorate, a still deeper fall was at hand. Hitherto our literature had been idiomatic. In mind as in situation we had been islanders. The revolutions in our taste, like the revolutions in our government, had been settled without the interference of strangers. Had this state of things continued, the same just principles of reasoning which, about this time, were applied with unprecedented success to every part of philosophy would soon have conducted our ancestors to a sounder code of

criticism. There were already strong signs of improvement.
Our prose had at length worked itself clear from those quaint
conceits which still deformed almost every metrical composition.
The parliamentary debates, and the diplomatic correspondence
of that eventful period, had contributed much to this reform.
In such bustling times, it was absolutely necessary to speak and
write to the purpose. The absurdities of Puritanism had, perhaps, done more. At the time when that odious style, which
deforms the writings of Hall and of Lord Bacon, was almost
universal, had appeared that stupendous work, the English
Bible,—a book which, if everything else in our language should
perish, would alone suffice to show the whole extent of its
beauty and power. The respect which the translators felt for
the original prevented them from adding any of the hideous
decorations then in fashion. The groundwork of the version,
indeed, was of an earlier age. The familiarity with which the
Puritans, on almost every occasion, used the Scriptural phrases
was no doubt very ridiculous; but it produced good effects. It
was a cant; but it drove out a cant far more offensive.

The highest kind of poetry is, in a great measure, independent
of those circumstances which regulate the style of composition
in prose. But with that inferior species of poetry which suc-
ceeds to it the case is widely different. In a few years, the
good sense and good taste which had weeded out affectation
from moral and political treatises would, in the natural course
of things, have effected a similar reform in the sonnet and the
ode. The rigour of the victorious sectaries had relaxed. A
dominant religion is never ascetic. The Government connived
at theatrical representations. The influence of Shakspeare was
once more felt. But darker days were approaching. A foreign
yoke was to be imposed on our literature. Charles, surrounded
by the companions of his long exile, returned to govern a nation
which ought never to have cast him out or never to have
received him back. Every year which he had passed among
strangers had rendered him more unfit to rule his countrymen.
In France he had seen the refractory magistracy humbled, and
royal prerogative, though exercised by a foreign priest in the
name of a child, victorious over all opposition. This spectacle
naturally gratified a prince to whose family the opposition of
Parliaments had been so fatal. Politeness was his solitary good
quality. The insults which he had suffered in Scotland had
taught him to prize it. The effeminacy and apathy of his disposition fitted him to excel in it. The elegance and vivacity of

the French manners fascinated him. With the political maxims and the social habits of his favourite people, he adopted their taste in composition, and, when seated on the throne, soon rendered it fashionable, partly by direct patronage, but still more by that contemptible policy, which, for a time, made England the last of the nations, and raised Louis the Fourteenth to a height of power and fame, such as no French sovereign had ever before attained.

It was to please Charles that rhyme was first introduced into our plays. Thus, a rising blow, which would at any time have been mortal, was dealt to the English Drama, then just recovering from its languishing condition. Two detestable manners, the indigenous and the imported, were now in a state of alternate conflict and amalgamation. The bombastic meanness of the new style was blended with the ingenious absurdity of the old; and the mixture produced something which the world had never before seen, and which, we hope, it will never see again,—something, by the side of which the worst nonsense of all other ages appears to advantage—something, which those who have attempted to caricature it have, against their will, been forced to flatter—of which the tragedy of Bayes is a very favourable specimen. What Lord Dorset observed to Edward Howard might have been addressed to almost all his contemporaries—

> " As skilful divers to the bottom fall
> Swifter than those who cannot swim at all;
> So, in this way of writing without thinking,
> Thou hast a strange alacrity in sinking."

From this reproach some clever men of the world must be excepted, and among them Dorset himself. Though by no means great poets, or even good versifiers, they always wrote with meaning, and sometimes with wit. Nothing indeed more strongly shows to what a miserable state literature had fallen than the immense superiority which the occasional rhymes, carelessly thrown on paper by men of this class, possess over the elaborate productions of almost all the professed authors. The reigning taste was so bad that the success of a writer was in inverse proportion to his labour, and to his desire of excellence. An exception must be made for Butler, who had as much wit and learning as Cowley, and who knew, what Cowley never knew, how to use them. A great command of good homely English distinguishes him still more from the other writers of the time. As for Gondibert, those may criticise it who can read it. Imagination was extinct. Taste was depraved. Poetry, driven from palaces, colleges, and theatres, had found an asylum in the obscure dwelling where a Great Man, born out of due season, in disgrace, penury, pain, and blindness, still kept uncontaminated a character and a genius worthy of a better age.

Everything about Milton is wonderful; but nothing is so wonderful as that, in an age so unfavourable to poetry, he should have produced the greatest of modern epic poems. We are not sure that this is not in some degree to be attributed to his want of sight. The imagination is notoriously most active when the external world is shut out. In sleep its illusions are perfect. They produce all the effect of realities. In darkness its visions are always more distinct than in the light. Every person who amuses himself with what is called building castles in the air must have experienced this. We know artists who, before they attempt to draw a face from memory, close their eyes, that they may recall a more perfect image of the features and the expression. We are therefore inclined to believe that the genius of Milton may have been preserved from the influence of times so unfavourable to it by his infirmity. Be this as it may, his works at first enjoyed a very small share of popularity. To be neglected by his contemporaries was the penalty which he paid for surpassing them. His great poem was not generally studied or admired till writers far inferior to him had, by obsequiously cringing to the public taste, acquired sufficient favour to reform it.

Of these, Dryden was the most eminent. Amidst the crowd of authors who, during the earlier years of Charles the Second, courted notoriety by every species of absurdity and affectation, he speedily became conspicuous. No man exercised so much influence on the age. The reason is obvious. On no man did the age exercise so much influence. He was perhaps the greatest of those whom we have designated as the critical poets; and his literary career exhibited, on a reduced scale, the whole history of the school to which he belonged,—the rudeness and extravagance of its infancy,—the propriety, the grace, the dignified good sense, the temperate splendour of its maturity. His imagination was torpid, till it was awakened by his judgment. He began with quaint parallels and empty mouthing. He gradually acquired the energy of the satirist, the gravity of the moralist, the rapture of the lyric poet. The revolution through which English literature has been passing, from the time of Cowley to that of Scott, may be seen in miniature within the compass of his volumes.

His life divides itself into two parts. There is some debatable ground on the common frontier; but the line may be drawn with tolerable accuracy. The year 1678 is that on which we should be inclined to fix as the date of a great change in his manner. During the preceding period appeared some of his courtly panegyrics—his Annus Mirabilis, and most of his plays; indeed, all his rhyming tragedies. To the subsequent period belong his best dramas,—All for Love, the Spanish Friar, and Sebastian,—his satires, his translations, his didactic poems, his fables, and his odes.

Of the small pieces which were presented to chancellors and princes it would scarcely be fair to speak. The greatest advantage which the Fine Arts derive from the extension of knowledge is, that the patronage of individuals becomes unnecessary. Some writers still affect to regret the age of patronage. None but bad writers have reason to regret it. It is always an age of general ignorance. Where ten thousand readers are eager for the appearance of a book, a small contribution from each makes up a splendid remuneration for the author. Where literature is a luxury, confined to few, each of them must pay high. If the Empress Catherine, for example, wanted an epic poem, she must have wholly supported the poet;—just as, in a remote country village, a man who wants a mutton chop is sometimes forced to take the whole sheep;—a thing which never happens where the demand is large. But men who pay largely for the gratification of their taste will expect to have it united with some gratification to their vanity. Flattery is carried to a shameless extent; and the habit of flattery almost inevitably introduces a false taste into composition. Its language is made up of hyperbolical commonplaces,—offensive from their triteness,—still more offensive from their extravagance. In no school is the trick of overstepping the modesty of nature so speedily acquired. The writer, accustomed to find exaggeration acceptable and necessary on one subject, uses it on all. It is not strange, therefore, that the early panegyrical verses of Dryden should be made up of meanness and bombast. They abound with the conceits which his immediate predecessors had brought into fashion. But his language and his versification were already far superior to theirs.

The Annus Mirabilis shows great command of expression, and a fine ear for heroic rhyme. Here its merits end. Not only has it no claim to be called poetry, but it seems to be the work of a man who could never, by any possibility, write poetry. Its affected similes are the best part of it. Gaudy weeds present a more encouraging spectacle than utter barrenness. There is scarcely a single stanza in this long work to which the imagination seems to have contributed anything. It is produced, not by creation, but by construction. It is made up, not of pictures, but of inferences. We will give a single instance, and certainly a favourable instance,—a quatrain which Johnson has praised. Dryden is describing the sea-fight with the Dutch—

> " Amidst whole heaps of spices lights a ball;
> And now their odours armed against them fly.
> Some preciously by shattered porcelain fall,
> And some by aromatic splinters die."

The poet should place his readers, as nearly as possible, in the situation of the sufferers or the spectators. His narration ought to produce feelings similar to those which would be excited by the event itself. Is this the case here? Who, in a sea-fight, ever thought of the price of the china which beats out the brains of a sailor; or of the odour of the splinter which shatters his leg? It is not by an act of the imagination, at once calling up the scene before the interior eye, but by painful meditation,—by turning the subject round and round,—by tracing out facts into remote consequences,—that these incongruous topics are intro- duced into the description. Homer, it is true, perpetually uses epithets which are not peculiarly appropriate. Achilles is the swift-footed, when he is sitting still. Ulysses is the much- enduring, when he has nothing to endure. Every spear casts a long shadow, every ox has crooked horns, and every woman a high bosom, though these particulars may be quite beside the purpose. In our old ballads a similar practice prevails. The gold is always red, and the ladies always gay, though nothing whatever may depend on the hue of the gold, or the temper of the ladies. But these adjectives are mere customary additions. They merge in the substantives to which they are attached. If they at all colour the idea, it is with a tinge so slight as in no respect to alter the general effect. In the passage which we have quoted from Dryden the case is very different. *Preciously* and *aromatic* divert our whole attention to themselves, and dissolve the image of the battle in a moment. The whole poem reminds us of Lucan, and of the worst parts of Lucan,—the sea-fight in the Bay of Marseilles, for example. The description of the two fleets during the night is perhaps the only passage which ought to be exempted from this censure. If it was from the Annus Mirabilis that Milton formed his opinion, when he pronounced Dryden a good rhymer but no poet, he certainly judged correctly.

But Dryden was, as we have said, one of those writers in whom the period of imagination does not precede, but follow, the period of observation and reflection.

His plays, his rhyming plays in particular, are admirable subjects for those who wish to study the morbid anatomy of the drama. He was utterly destitute of the power of exhibiting real human beings. Even in the far inferior talent of composing characters out of those elements into which the imperfect process of our reason can resolve them, he was very deficient. His men are not even good personifications; they are not well-assorted assemblages of qualities. Now and then, indeed, he seizes a very coarse and marked distinction, and gives us, not a likeness, but a strong caricature, in which a single peculiarity is protruded, and everything else neglected; like the Marquis of Granby at an inn-door, whom we know by nothing but his baldness; or Wilkes, who is Wilkes only in his squint. These are the best specimens of his skill. For most of his pictures seem, like Turkey carpets, to have been expressly designed not to resemble anything in the heavens above, in the earth beneath, or in the waters under the earth.

The latter manner he practises most frequently in his tragedies, the former in his comedies. The comic characters are, without mixture, loathsome and despicable. The men of Etherege and Vanbrugh are bad enough. Those of Smollett are perhaps worse. But they do not approach to the Celadons, the Wild-bloods, the Woodalls, and the Rhodophils of Dryden. The vices of these last are set off by a certain fierce hard impudence, to which we know nothing comparable. Their love is the appetite of beasts; their friendship the confederacy of knaves. The ladies seem to have been expressly created to form helps meet for such gentlemen. In deceiving and insulting their old fathers they do not perhaps exceed the licence which, by immemorial prescription, has been allowed to heroines. But they also cheat at cards, rob strong boxes, put up their favours to auction, betray their friends, abuse their rivals in the style of Billingsgate, and invite their lovers in the language of the Piazza. These, it must be remembered, are not the valets and waiting-women, the Mascarilles and Nerines, but the recognised heroes and heroines who appear as the representatives of good society, and who, at the end of the fifth act, marry and live very happily ever after. The sensuality, baseness, and malice of their natures is unredeemed by any quality of a different description,—by any touch of kindness,—or even by any honest burst of hearty hatred and revenge. We are in a world where there is no humanity, no veracity, no sense of shame,—a world for which any good-natured man would gladly take in exchange the society of Milton's devils. But as soon as we enter the regions of Tragedy, we find a great change. There is no lack of fine sentiment there. Metastasio is surpassed in his own department. Scuderi is out-scuderied. We are introduced to people whose proceedings we can trace to no motive,—of whose feelings we can form no more idea than of a sixth sense. We have left a race of creatures, whose love is as delicate and affectionate as the passion which an alderman feels for a turtle. We find ourselves among beings, whose love is a purely disinterested emotion,—a loyalty extending to passive obedience,—a religion, like that of the Quietists, unsupported by any sanction of hope or fear. We see nothing but despotism without power, and sacrifices without compensation.

We will give a few instances. In Aurengzebe, Arimant, governor of Agra, falls in love with his prisoner Indamora. She rejects his suit with scorn; but assures him that she shall make great use of her power over him. He threatens to be angry. She answers, very coolly:

> " Do not: your anger, like your love, is vain:
> Whene'er I please, you must be pleased again.
> Knowing what power I have your will to bend,
> I'll use it; for I need just such a friend."

This is no idle menace. She soon brings a letter addressed to his rival,—orders him to read it,—asks him whether he thinks it sufficiently tender,—and finally commands him to carry it himself. Such tyranny as this, it may be thought, would justify resistance. Arimant does indeed venture to remonstrate:—

> " This fatal paper rather let me tear,
> Than, like Bellerophon, my sentence bear."

The answer of the lady is incomparable:—

> " You may; but 'twill not be your best advice;
> 'Twill only give me pains of writing twice.
> You know you must obey me, soon or late.
> Why should you vainly struggle with your fate? "

Poor Arimant seems to be of the same opinion. He mutters something about fate and free-will, and walks off with the billet-doux.

In the Indian Emperor, Montezuma presents Almeria with a

garland as a token of his love, and offers to make her his queen.
She replies:—

> " I take this garland, not as given by you;
> But as my merit's and my beauty's due;
> As for the crown which you, my slave, possess,
> To share it with you would but make me less."

In return for such proofs of tenderness as these, her admirer consents to murder his two sons and a benefactor to whom he feels the warmest gratitude. Lyndaraxa, in the Conquest of Granada, assumes the same lofty tone with Abdelmelech. He complains that she smiles upon his rival.

> " *Lynd.* And when did I my power so far resign,
> That you should regulate each look of mine?
> *Abdel.* Then, when you gave your love, you gave that power.
> *Lynd.* 'Twas during pleasure—'tis revoked this hour.
> *Abdel.* I'll hate you, and this visit is my last.
> *Lynd.* Do, if you can: you know I hold you fast."

That these passages violate all historical propriety, that sentiments to which nothing similar was ever even affected except by the cavaliers of Europe, are transferred to Mexico and Agra, is a light accusation. We have no objection to a conventional world, an Illyrian puritan, or a Bohemian seaport. While the faces are good, we care little about the background. Sir Joshua Reynolds says that the curtains and hangings in an historical painting ought to be, not velvet or cotton, but merely drapery. The same principle should be applied to poetry and romance. The truth of character is the first object; the truth of place and time is to be considered only in the second place. Puff himself could tell the actor to turn out his toes, and remind him that Keeper Hatton was a great dancer. We wish that, in our own time, a writer of a very different order from Puff had not too often forgotten human nature in the niceties of upholstery, millinery, and cookery.

We blame Dryden, not because the persons of his dramas are not Moors or Americans, but because they are not men and women;—not because love, such as he represents it, could not exist in a harem or in a wigwam, but because it could not exist anywhere. As is the love of his heroes, such are all their other emotions. All their qualities, their courage, their generosity, their pride, are on the same colossal scale. Justice and prudence are virtues which can exist only in a moderate degree, and which change their nature and their name if pushed to excess. Of justice and prudence, therefore, Dryden leaves his favourites destitute. He did not care to give them what he could not give without measure. The tyrants and ruffians are merely the heroes altered by a few touches, similar to those which transformed the honest face of Sir Roger de Coverley into the Saracen's head. Through the grin and frown the original features are still perceptible.

It is in the tragi-comedies that these absurdities strike us most. The two races of men, or rather the angels and the baboons, are there presented to us together. We meet in one scene with nothing but gross, selfish, unblushing, lying libertines of both sexes, who, as a punishment, we suppose, for their depravity, are condemned to talk nothing but prose. But, as soon as we meet with people who speak in verse, we know that we are in society which would have enraptured the Cathos and Madelon of Molière, in society for which Oroondates would have too little of the lover, and Clelia too much of the coquette.

As Dryden was unable to render his plays interesting by means of that which is the peculiar and appropriate excellence of the drama, it was necessary that he should find some substitute for it. In his comedies he supplied its place, sometimes by wit, but more frequently by intrigue, by disguises, mistakes of persons, dialogues at cross purposes, hairbreadth escapes, perplexing concealments, and surprising disclosures. He thus succeeded at least in making these pieces very amusing.

In his tragedies he trusted, and not altogether without reason, to his diction and his versification. It was on this account, in all probability, that he so eagerly adopted, and so reluctantly abandoned, the practice of rhyming in his plays. What is unnatural appears less unnatural in that species of verse than in lines which approach more nearly to common conversation; and in the management of the heroic couplet Dryden has never been equalled. It is unnecessary to urge any arguments against a fashion now universally condemned. But it is worthy of observation that, though Dryden was deficient in that talent which blank verse exhibits to the greatest advantage, and was certainly the best writer of heroic rhyme in our language, yet the plays which have, from the time of their first appearance, been considered as his best, are in blank verse. No experiment can be more decisive.

It must be allowed that the worst even of the rhyming tragedies contains good description and magnificent rhetoric. But, even when we forget that they are plays, and, passing by their dramatic improprieties, consider them with reference to the language, we are perpetually disgusted by passages which it is difficult to conceive how any author could have written, or any audience have tolerated, rants in which the raving violence of the manner forms a strange contrast with the abject tameness of the thought. The author laid the whole fault on the audience, and declared that, when he wrote them, he considered them bad enough to please. This defence is unworthy of a man of genius, and, after all, is no defence. Otway pleased without rant; and so might Dryden have done, if he had possessed the powers of Otway. The fact is, that he had a tendency to bombast, which, though subsequently corrected by time and thought, was never wholly removed, and which showed itself in performances not designed to please the rude mob of the theatre.

Some indulgent critics have represented this failing as an indication of genius, as the profusion of unlimited wealth, the wantonness of exuberant vigour. To us it seems to bear a nearer affinity to the tawdriness of poverty, or the spasms and convulsions of weakness. Dryden surely had not more imagination than Homer, Dante, or Milton, who never fall into this vice. The swelling diction of Æschylus and Isaiah resembles that of Almanzor and Maximin no more than the tumidity of a muscle resembles the tumidity of a boil. The former is symptomatic of health and strength, the latter of debility and disease. If ever Shakspeare rants, it is not when his imagination is hurrying him along, but when he is hurrying his imagination along,—when his mind is for a moment jaded,—when, as was said of Euripides, he resembles a lion, who excites his own fury by lashing himself with his tail. What happened to Shakspeare from the occasional suspension of his powers happened to Dryden from constant impotence. He, like his confederate Lee, had judgment enough to appreciate the great poets of the preceding age, but not judgment enough to shun competition with them. He felt and admired their wild and daring sublimity. That it belonged to another age than that in which he lived and required other talents than those which he possessed, that, in aspiring to emulate it, he was wasting, in a hopeless attempt, powers which might render him pre-eminent in a different career, was a lesson which he did not learn till late. As those knavish enthusiasts, the French prophets, courted inspiration by mimicking the writhings, swoonings, and gaspings which they considered as its symptoms, he attempted, by affected fits of poetical fury, to bring on a real paroxysm; and, like them, he got nothing but his distortions for his pains.

Horace very happily compares those who, in his time, imitated Pindar to the youth who attempted to fly to heaven on waxen wings, and who experienced so fatal and ignominious a fall. His own admirable good sense preserved him from this error, and taught him to cultivate a style in which excellence was within his reach. Dryden had not the same self-knowledge. He saw that the greatest poets were never so successful as when they rushed beyond the ordinary bounds, and that some inexplicable good fortune preserved them from tripping even when they staggered on the brink of nonsense. He did not perceive that they were guided and sustained by a power denied to himself. They wrote from the dictation of the imagination; and they found a response in the imaginations of others. He, on the contrary, sat down to work himself, by reflection and argument, into a deliberate wildness, a rational frenzy.

In looking over the admirable designs which accompany the Faust, we have always been much struck by one which represents the wizard and the tempter riding at full speed. The demon sits on his furious horse as heedlessly as if he were reposing on a chair. That he should keep his saddle in such a posture, would seem impossible to any who did not know that he was secure in the privileges of a superhuman nature. The attitude of Faust, on the contrary, is the perfection of horsemanship. Poets of the first order might safely write as desperately as Mephistopheles rode. But Dryden, though admitted to communion with higher spirits, though armed with a portion of their power, and intrusted with some of their secrets, was of another race. What they might securely venture to do, it was madness in him to attempt. It was necessary that taste and critical science should supply his deficiencies.

We will give a few examples. Nothing can be finer than the description of Hector at the Grecian wall:—

ὁ δ ἄρ' ἔσθορε φαίδιμος Ἕκτωρ,
Νυκτὶ θοῇ ἀτάλαντος ὑπώπια· λάμπε δὲ χαλκῷ
Σμερδαλέῳ, τὸν ἕεστο περὶ χροΐ δοιὰ δὲ χερσὶ
Δοῦρ' ἔχεν· οὐκ ἄν τίς μιν ἐρυκάκοι ἀντιβολήσας,
Νόσφι θεῶν, ὅτ' ἐσᾶλτο πύλας· πυρὶ δ' ὄσσε δεδήει.—
'Αυτίκα δ'οἱ μὲν τεῖχος ὑπέρβασαν, οἱ δὲ κατ' αὐτὰς
Ποιητὰς ἐσέχυντο πύλας· Δαναιοὶ δ ἐφόβηθεν
Νῆας ἀνὰ γλαφυράς· ὅμαδος δ' ἀλίαστος ἐτύχθη.

What daring expressions! Yet how significant! How picturesque! Hector seems to rise up in his strength and fury. The gloom of night in his frown,—the fire burning in his eyes,—

the javelins and the blazing armour,—the mighty rush through
the gates and down the battlements,—the trampling and the
infinite roar of the multitude,—everything is with us; everything
is real.

Dryden has described a very similar event in Maximin, and
has done his best to be sublime, as follows:—

> " There with a forest of their darts he strove,
> And stood like Capaneus defying Jove;
> With his broad sword the boldest beating down,
> Till Fate grew pale, lest he should win the town,
> And turn'd the iron leaves of its dark book
> To make new dooms, or mend what it mistook."

How exquisite is the imagery of the fairy-songs in the
Tempest and the Midsummer Night's Dream; Ariel riding
through the twilight on the bat, or sucking in the bells of
flowers with the bee; or the little bower-women of Titania,
driving the spiders from the couch of the Queen! Dryden truly
said, that—

> " Shakspeare's magic could not copied be;
> Within that circle none durst walk but he."

It would have been well if he had not himself dared to step
within the enchanted line, and drawn on himself a fate similar
to that which, according to the old superstition, punished such
presumptuous interference. The following lines are parts of
the song of his fairies:—

> " Merry, merry, merry, we sail from the East,
> Half-tippled at a rainbow feast.
> In the bright moonshine, while winds whistle loud,
> Tivy, tivy, tivy, we mount and we fly,
> All racking along in a downy white cloud;
> And lest our leap from the sky prove too far,
> We slide on the back of a new falling star,
> And drop from above
> In a jelly of love."

These are very favourable instances. Those who wish for a
bad one may read the dying speeches of Maximin, and may
compare them with the last scenes of Othello and Lear.

If Dryden had died before the expiration of the first of the
periods into which we have divided his literary life, he would
have left a reputation, at best, little higher than that of Lee or
Davenant. He would have been known only to men of letters;
and by them he would have been mentioned as a writer who
threw away, on subjects which he was incompetent to treat,
powers which, judiciously employed, might have raised him to
eminence; whose diction and whose numbers had sometimes

very high merit, but all whose works were blemished by a false taste, and by errors or gross negligence. A few of his prologues and epilogues might perhaps still have been remembered and quoted. In these little pieces he early showed all the powers which afterwards rendered him the greatest of modern satirists. But, during the latter part of his life, he gradually abandoned the drama. His plays appeared at longer intervals. He renounced rhyme in tragedy. His language became less turgid— his characters less exaggerated. He did not indeed produce correct representations of human nature; but he ceased to daub such monstrous chimeras as those which abound in his earlier pieces. Here and there passages occur worthy of the best ages of the British stage. The style which the drama requires changes with every change of character and situation. He who can vary his manner to suit the variation is the great dramatist; but he who excels in one manner only will, when that manner happens to be appropriate, appear to be a great dramatist; as the hands of a watch which does not go point right once in the twelve hours. Sometimes there is a scene of solemn debate. This a mere rhetorician may write as well as the greatest tragedian that ever lived. We confess that to us the speech of Sempronius in Cato seems very nearly as good as Shakspeare could have made it. But when the senate breaks up, and we find that the lovers and their mistresses, the hero, the villain, and the deputy-villain, all continue to harangue in the same style, we perceive the difference between a man who can write a play and a man who can write a speech. In the same manner, wit, a talent for description, or a talent for narration, may, for a time, pass for dramatic genius. Dryden was an incomparable reasoner in verse. He was conscious of his power; he was proud of it; and the authors of the Rehearsal justly charged him with abusing it. His warriors and princesses are fond of discussing points of amorous casuistry, such as would have delighted a Parliament of Love. They frequently go still deeper, and speculate on philosophical necessity and the origin of evil.

There were, however, some occasions which absolutely required this peculiar talent. Then Dryden was indeed at home. All his best scenes are of this description. They are all between men; for the heroes of Dryden, like many other gentlemen, can never talk sense when ladies are in company. They are all intended to exhibit the empire of reason over violent passion. We have two interlocutors, the one eager and impassioned, the other high, cool, and judicious. The composed and rational character gradually acquires the ascendency. His fierce companion is first inflamed to rage by his reproaches, then overawed by his equanimity, convinced by his arguments, and soothed by his persuasions. This is the case in the scene between Hector and Troilus, in that between Antony and Ventidius, and in that between Sebastian and Dorax. Nothing of the same kind in Shakspeare is equal to them, except the quarrel between Brutus and Cassius, which is worth them all three.

Some years before his death, Dryden altogether ceased to write for the stage. He had turned his powers in a new direction, with success the most splendid and decisive. His taste had gradually awakened his creative faculties. The first rank in poetry was beyond his reach; but he challenged and secured the most honourable place in the second. His imagination resembled the wings of an ostrich; it enabled him to run, though not to soar. When he attempted the highest flights, he became ridiculous; but, while he remained in a lower region, he outstripped all competitors.

All his natural and all his acquired powers fitted him to found a good critical school of poetry. Indeed he carried his reforms too far for his age. After his death our literature retrograded; and a century was necessary to bring it back to the point at which he left it. The general soundness and healthfulness of his mental constitution, his information, of vast superficies, though of small volume, his wit scarcely inferior to that of the most distinguished followers of Donne, his eloquence, grave, deliberate, and commanding, could not save him from disgraceful failure as a rival of Shakspeare, but raised him far above the level of Boileau. His command of language was immense. With him died the secret of the old poetical diction of England, —the art of producing rich effects by familiar words. In the following century it was as completely lost as the Gothic method of painting glass, and was but poorly supplied by the laborious and tesselated imitations of Mason and Gray. On the other hand, he was the first writer under whose skilful management the scientific vocabulary fell into natural and pleasing verse. In this department, he succeeded as completely as his contemporary Gibbons succeeded in the similar enterprise of carving the most delicate flowers from heart of oak. The toughest and most knotty parts of language became ductile at his touch. His versification, in the same manner, while it gave the first model of that neatness and precision which the following generation esteemed so highly, exhibited at the same time the last examples of nobleness, freedom, variety of pause, and cadence. His tragedies in rhyme, however worthless in themselves, had at least served the purpose of nonsense-verses; they had taught him all the arts of melody which the heroic couplet admits. For bombast, his prevailing vice, his new subjects gave little opportunity; his better taste gradually discarded it.

He possessed, as we have said, in a pre-eminent degree the power of reasoning in verse; and this power was now peculiarly useful to him. His logic is by no means uniformly sound. On points of criticism, he always reasons ingeniously; and when he is disposed to be honest, correctly. But the theological and political questions which he undertook to treat in verse were precisely those which he understood least. His arguments, therefore, are often worthless. But the manner in which they are stated is beyond all praise. The style is transparent. The topics follow each other in the happiest order. The objections are drawn up in such a manner that the whole fire of the reply may be brought to bear on them. The circumlocutions which are substituted for technical phrases are clear, neat, and exact. The illustrations at once adorn and elucidate the reasoning. The sparkling epigrams of Cowley, and the simple garrulity of the burlesque poets of Italy, are alternately employed, in the happiest manner, to give effect to what is obvious or clearness to what is obscure.

His literary creed was catholic, even to latitudinarianism; not from any want of acuteness, but from a disposition to be easily satisfied. He was quick to discern the smallest glimpse of merit; he was indulgent even to gross improprieties, when accompanied by any redeeming talent. When he said a severe thing, it was to serve a temporary purpose,—to support an argument, or to tease a rival. Never was so able a critic so free from fastidiousness. He loved the old poets, especially Shakspeare. He admired the ingenuity which Donne and Cowley had so wildly abused. He did justice, amidst the general silence, to the memory of Milton. He praised to the skies the school-boy lines of Addison. Always looking on the fair side of every object, he admired extravagance on account of the invention which he supposed it to indicate; he excused affectation in favour of wit; he tolerated even tameness for the sake of the correctness which was its concomitant.

It was probably to this turn of mind, rather than to the more disgraceful causes which Johnson has assigned, that we are to attribute the exaggeration which disfigures the panegyrics of

Dryden. No writer, it must be owned, has carried the flattery of dedication to a greater length. But this was not, we suspect, merely interested servility: it was the overflowing of a mind singularly disposed to admiration,—of a mind which diminished vices, and magnified virtues and obligations. The most adulatory of his addresses is that in which he dedicates the State of Innocence to Mary of Modena. Johnson thinks it strange that any man should use such language without self-detestation. But he has not remarked that to the very same work is prefixed an eulogium on Milton, which certainly could not have been acceptable at the Court of Charles the Second. Many years later, when Whig principles were in a great measure triumphant, Sprat refused to admit a monument of John Phillips into Westminster Abbey—because, in the epitaph, the name of Milton incidentally occurred. The walls of his church, he declared, should not be polluted by the name of a republican! Dryden was attached, both by principle and interest, to the Court. But nothing could deaden his sensibility to excellence. We are unwilling to accuse him severely, because the same disposition, which prompted him to pay so generous a tribute to the memory of a poet whom his patrons detested, hurried him into extravagance when he described a princess distinguished by the splendour of her beauty and the graciousness of her manners.

This is an amiable temper; but it is not the temper of great men. Where there is elevation of character, there will be fastidiousness. It is only in novels and on tombstones that we meet with people who are indulgent to the faults of others, and unmerciful to their own; and Dryden, at all events, was not one of these paragons. His charity was extended most liberally to others; but it certainly began at home. In taste he was by no means deficient. His critical works are, beyond all comparison, superior to any which had, till then, appeared in England. They were generally intended as apologies for his own poems, rather than as expositions of general principles; he, therefore, often attempts to deceive the reader by sophistry which could scarcely have deceived himself. His dicta are the dicta, not of a judge, but of an advocate:—often of an advocate in an unsound cause. Yet, in the very act of misrepresenting the laws of composition, he shows how well he understands them. But he was perpetually acting against his better knowledge. His sins were sins against light. He trusted that what was bad would be pardoned for the sake of what was good. What was good, he took no pains to make better. He was not, like most persons who rise to eminence, dissatisfied even with his best productions.   He had set up no unattainable standard of perfection, the contemplation of which might at once improve and mortify him.   His path was not attended by an unapproachable mirage of excellence, for ever receding, and for ever pursued.   He was not disgusted by the negligence of others; and he extended the same toleration to himself.   His mind was of a slovenly character,—fond of splendour, but indifferent to neatness.   Hence most of his writings exhibit the sluttish magnificence of a Russian noble, all vermin and diamonds, dirty linen and inestimable sables.   Those faults which spring from affectation, time and thought in a great measure removed from his poems.   But his carelessness he retained to the last.   If towards the close of his life he less frequently went wrong from negligence, it was only because long habits of composition rendered it more easy to go right.   In his best pieces we find false rhymes,—triplets, in which the third line appears to be a mere intruder, and, while it breaks the music, adds nothing to the meaning,—gigantic Alexandrines of fourteen and sixteen syllables, and truncated verses for which he never troubled himself to find a termination or a partner.

Such are the beauties and the faults which may be found in profusion throughout the later works of Dryden.   A more just and complete estimate of his natural and acquired powers,—of the merits of his style and of its blemishes,—may be formed from the Hind and Panther than from any of his other writings. As a didactic poem, it is far superior to the Religio Laici.   The satirical parts, particularly the character of Burnet, are scarcely inferior to the best passages in Absalom and Achitophel.   There are, moreover, occasional touches of a tenderness which affects us more, because it is decent, rational, and manly, and reminds us of the best scenes in his tragedies.   His versification sinks and swells in happy unison with the subject; and his wealth of language seems to be unlimited.   Yet, the carelessness with which he has constructed his plot, and the innumerable inconsistencies into which he is every moment falling, detract much from the pleasure which such various excellence affords.

In Absalom and Achitophel he hit upon a new and rich vein, which he worked with signal success.   The ancient satirists were the subjects of a despotic government.   They were compelled to abstain from political topics, and to confine their attention to the frailties of private life.   They might, indeed, sometimes venture to take liberties with public men,

" Quorum Flaminia tegitur cinis atque Latina."

Thus Juvenal immortalised the obsequious senators who met to decide the fate of the memorable turbot. His fourth satire frequently reminds us of the great political poem of Dryden; but it was not written till Domitian had fallen: and it wants something of the peculiar flavour which belongs to contemporary invective alone. His anger has stood so long that, though the body is not impaired, the effervescence, the first cream, is gone. Boileau lay under similar restraints; and, if he had been free from all restraints, would have been no match for our countryman.

The advantages which Dryden derived from the nature of his subject he improved to the very utmost. His manner is almost perfect. The style of Horace and Boileau is fit only for light subjects. The Frenchman did indeed attempt to turn the theological reasonings of the Provincial Letters into verse, but with very indifferent success. The glitter of Pope is gold. The ardour of Persius is without brilliancy. Magnificent versification and ingenious combinations rarely harmonise with the expression of deep feeling. In Juvenal and Dryden alone we have the sparkle and the heat together. Those great satirists succeeded in communicating the fervour of their feelings to materials the most incombustible, and kindled the whole mass into a blaze, at once dazzling and destructive. We cannot, indeed, think, without regret, of the part which so eminent a writer as Dryden took in the disputes of that period. There was, no doubt, madness and wickedness on both sides. But there was liberty on the one, and despotism on the other. On this point, however, we will not dwell. At Talavera the English and French troops for a moment suspended their conflict, to drink of a stream which flowed between them. The shells were passed across from enemy to enemy without apprehension or molestation. We, in the same manner, would rather assist our political adversaries to drink with us of that fountain of intellectual pleasure, which should be the common refreshment of both parties, than disturb and pollute it with the havoc of unseasonable hostilities.

Macflecnoe is inferior to Absalom and Achitophel only in the subject. In the execution it is even superior. But the greatest work of Dryden was the last, the Ode on Saint Cecilia's Day. It is the masterpiece of the second class of poetry, and ranks but just below the great models of the first. It reminds us of the Pedasus of Achilles—

ὃς. καὶ θνητὸς ἐὼν, ἕπεθ ἵπποις ἀθανάτοισι.

By comparing it with the impotent ravings of the heroic tragedies we may measure the progress which the mind of Dryden had made. He had learned to avoid a too audacious competition with higher natures, to keep at a distance from the verge of bombast or nonsense, to venture on no expression which did not convey a distinct idea to his own mind. There is none of that " darkness visible " of style which he had formerly affected, and in which the greatest poets only can succeed. Everything is definite, significant, and picturesque. His early writings re-sembled the gigantic works of those Chinese gardeners who attempt to rival nature herself, to form cataracts of terrific height and sound, to raise precipitous ridges of mountains, and to imitate in artificial plantations the vastness and the gloom of some primeval forest. This manner he abandoned; nor did he ever adopt the Dutch taste which Pope affected, the trim parterres, and the rectangular walks. He rather resembled our Kents and Browns, who, imitating the great features of landscape without emulating them, consulting the genius of the place, assisting nature and carefully disguising their art, produced, not a Chamouni or a Niagara, but a Stowe or a Hagley.

We are, on the whole, inclined to regret that Dryden did not accomplish his purpose of writing an epic poem. It certainly would not have been a work of the highest rank. It would not have rivalled the Iliad, the Odyssey, or the Paradise Lost; but it would have been superior to the productions of Apollonius, Lucan, or Statius, and not inferior to the Jerusalem Delivered. It would probably have been a vigorous narrative, animated with something of the spirit of the old romances, enriched with much splendid description, and interspersed with fine declama-tions and disquisitions. The danger of Dryden would have been from aiming too high; from dwelling too much, for example, on his angels of kingdoms, and attempting a competition with that great writer who in his own time had so incomparably succeeded in representing to us the sights and sounds of another world. To Milton, and to Milton alone, belonged the secrets of the great deep, the beach of sulphur, the ocean of fire, the palaces of the fallen dominations, glimmering through the everlasting shade, the silent wilderness of verdure and fragrance where armed angels kept watch over the sleep of the first lovers, the portico of diamond, the sea of jasper, the sapphire pavement empurpled with celestial roses, and the infinite ranks of the Cherubim, blazing with adamant and gold. The council, the tournament, the procession, the crowded cathedral, the camp, the guard-room, the chase, were the proper scenes for Dryden.

But we have not space to pass in review all the works which Dryden wrote. We, therefore, will not speculate longer on those which he might possibly have written. He may, on the whole, be pronounced to have been a man possessed of splendid talents, which he often abused, and of a sound judgment, the admonitions of which he often neglected; a man who succeeded only in an inferior department of his art, but who, in that department, succeeded pre-eminently; and who with a more independent spirit, a more anxious desire of excellence, and more respect for himself, would, in his own walk, have attained to absolute perfection.

MIRABEAU [1]

(JULY 1832)

THIS is a very amusing and a very instructive book: but even if it were less amusing and less instructive, it would still be interesting as a relic of a wise and virtuous man. M. Dumont was one of those persons, the care of whose fame belongs in an especial manner to mankind. For he was one of those persons who have, for the sake of mankind, neglected the care of their own fame. In his walk through life there was no obtrusiveness, no pushing, no elbowing, none of the little arts which bring forward little men. With every right to the head of the board, he took the lowest room, and well deserved to be greeted with— Friend, go up higher. Though no man was more capable of achieving for himself a separate and independent renown, he attached himself to others; he laboured to raise their fame; he was content to receive as his share of the reward the mere over-flowings which redounded from the full measure of their glory. Not that he was of a servile and idolatrous habit of mind:— not that he was one of the tribe of Boswells,—those literary Gibeonites, born to be hewers of wood and drawers of water to the higher intellectual castes. Possessed of talents and acquire-

---

[1] *Souvenirs sur Mirabeau, et sur les deux Premières Assemblées Législatives.* Par Etienne Dumont, de Genève: ouvrage posthume publié par M. J. L. Duval, Membre du Conseil Représentatif du Canton du Genève. 8vo. Paris: 1832.

ments which made him great, he wished only to be useful.   In
the prime of manhood, at the very time of life at which ambitious
men are most ambitious, he was not solicitous to proclaim that
he furnished information, arguments, and eloquence to Mirabeau.
In his later years he was perfectly willing that his renown should
merge in that of Mr. Bentham.

The services which M. Dumont has rendered to society can be
fully appreciated only by those who have studied Mr. Bentham's
works, both in their rude and in their finished state.   The difference both for show and for use is as great as the difference
between a lump of golden ore and a rouleau of sovereigns fresh
from the mint.   Of Mr. Bentham we would at all times speak
with the reverence which is due to a great original thinker, and
to a sincere and ardent friend of the human race.   If a few
weaknesses were mingled with his eminent virtues,—if a few
errors insinuated themselves among the many valuable truths
which he taught,—this is assuredly no time for noticing those
weaknesses or those errors in an unkind or sarcastic spirit.   A
great man has gone from among us, full of years, of good works,
and of deserved honours.   In some of the highest departments
in which the human intellect can exert itself he has not left his
equal or his second behind him.   From his contemporaries he
has had, according to the usual lot, more or less than justice.
He has had blind flatterers and blind detractors—flatterers who
could see nothing but perfection in his style, detractors who could
see nothing but nonsense in his matter.   He will now have
judges.   Posterity will pronounce its calm and impartial decision; and that decision will, we firmly believe, place in the same
rank with Galileo, and with Locke, the man who found jurisprudence a gibberish and left it a science.   Never was there a
literary partnership so fortunate as that of Mr. Bentham and
M. Dumont.   The raw material which Mr. Bentham furnished
was most precious; but it was unmarketable.   He was, assuredly,
at once a great logician and a great rhetorician.   But the effect
of his logic was injured by a vicious arrangement, and the effect
of his rhetoric by a vicious style.   His mind was vigorous, comprehensive, subtile, fertile of arguments, fertile of illustrations.
But he spoke in an unknown tongue; and, that the congregation
might be edified, it was necessary that some brother having the
gift of interpretation should expound the invaluable jargon.
His oracles were of high import; but they were traced on leaves
and flung loose to the wind.   So negligent was he of the arts of
selection, distribution, and compression, that to persons who

formed their judgment of him from his works in their undigested
state he seemed to be the least systematic of all philosophers.
The truth is, that his opinions formed a system, which, whether
sound or unsound, is more exact, more entire, and more consistent with itself than any other. Yet to superficial readers of
his works in their original form, and indeed to all readers of those
works who did not bring great industry and great acuteness to
the study, he seemed to be a man of a quick and ingenious but
ill-regulated mind,—who saw truth only by glimpses,—who
threw out many striking hints, but who had never thought of
combining his doctrines in one harmonious whole.

M. Dumont was admirably qualified to supply what was wanting in Mr. Bentham. In the qualities in which the French writers
surpass those of all other nations—neatness, clearness, precision,
condensation—he surpassed all French writers. If M. Dumont
had never been born, Mr. Bentham would still have been a very
great man. But he would have been great to himself alone.
The fertility of his mind would have resembled the fertility of
those vast American wildernesses in which blossoms and decays
a rich but unprofitable vegetation, " wherewith the reaper
filleth not his hand, neither he that bindeth up the sheaves his
bosom." It would have been with his discoveries as it has been
with the " Century of Inventions." His speculations on laws
would have been of no more practical use than Lord Worcester's
speculations on steam-engines. Some generations hence, perhaps, when legislation had found its Watt, an antiquarian might
have published to the world the curious fact that, in the reign of
George the Third, there had been a man called Bentham, who had
given hints of many discoveries made since his time, and who had
really, for his age, taken a most philosophical view of the principles of jurisprudence.

Many persons have attempted to interpret between this powerful mind and the public. But, in our opinion, M. Dumont alone
has succeeded. It is remarkable that, in foreign countries,
where Mr. Bentham's works are known solely through the
medium of the French version, his merit is almost universally
acknowledged. Even those who are most decidedly opposed
to his political opinions—the very chiefs of the Holy Alliance—
have publicly testified their respect for him. In England, on
the contrary, many persons who certainly entertained no prejudice against him on political grounds were long in the habit
of mentioning him contemptuously. Indeed, what was said of
Bacon's philosophy may be said of Bentham's. It was in little

repute among us, till judgments in its favour came from beyond sea, and convinced us, to our shame, that we had been abusing and laughing at one of the greatest men of the age.

M. Dumont might easily have found employments more gratifying to personal vanity than that of arranging works not his own. But he could have found no employment more useful or more truly honourable. The book before us, hastily written as it is, contains abundant proof, if proof were needed, that he did not become an editor because he wanted the talents which would have made him eminent as a writer.

Persons who hold democratical opinions, and who have been accustomed to consider M. Dumont as one of their party, have been surprised and mortified to learn that he speaks with very little respect of the French Revolution and of its authors. Some zealous Tories have naturally expressed great satisfaction at finding their doctrines, in some respects, confirmed by the testimony of an unwilling witness. The date of the work, we think, explains everything. If it had been written ten years earlier, or twenty years later, it would have been very different from what it is. It was written, neither during the first excitement of the Revolution, nor at that later period when the practical good produced by the Revolution had become manifest to the most prejudiced observers; but in those wretched times when the enthusiasm had abated, and the solid advantages were not yet fully seen. It was written in the year 1799,—a year in which the most sanguine friend of liberty might well feel some misgivings as to the effects of what the National Assembly had done. The evils which attend every great change had been severely felt. The benefit was still to come. The price—a heavy price—had been paid. The thing purchased had not yet been delivered. Europe was swarming with French exiles. The fleets and armies of the second coalition were victorious. Within France, the reign of terror was over; but the reign of law had not commenced. There had been, indeed, during three or four years, a written Constitution, by which rights were defined and checks provided. But these rights had been repeatedly violated; and these checks had proved utterly inefficient. The laws which had been framed to secure the distinct authority of the executive magistrates and of the legislative assemblies—the freedom of election— the freedom of debate—the freedom of the press—the personal freedom of citizens—were a dead letter. The ordinary mode in which the Republic was governed was by *coups d'état*. On one occasion, the legislative councils were placed under miltary restraint by the directors. Then, again, directors were deposed by the legislative councils. Elections were set aside by the executive authority. Ship-loads of writers and speakers were sent, without a legal trial, to die of fever in Guiana. France, in short, was in that state in which revolutions, effected by violence, almost always leave a nation. The habit of obedience had been lost. The spell of prescription had been broken. Those associations on which, far more than on any arguments about property and order, the authority of magistrates rests, had completely passed away. The power of the government consisted merely in the physical force which it could bring to its support. Moral force it had none. It was itself a government sprung from a recent convulsion. Its own fundamental maxim was, that rebellion might be justifiable. Its own existence proved that rebellion might be successful. The people had been accustomed, during several years, to offer resistance to the constituted authorities on the slightest provocation, and to see the constituted authorities yield to that resistance. The whole political world was " without form and void "—an incessant whirl of hostile atoms, which, every moment, formed some new combination. The only man who could fix the agitated elements of society in a stable form was following a wild vision of glory and empire through the Syrian deserts. The time was not yet come, when

> " Confusion heard his voice; and wild uproar
> Stood ruled: "

when, out of the chaos into which the old society had been resolved, were to rise a new dynasty, a new peerage, a new church, and a new code.

The dying words of Madame Roland, " O Liberty! how many crimes are committed in thy name! " were at that time echoed by many of the most upright and benevolent of mankind. M. Guizot has, in one of his admirable pamphlets, happily and justly described M. Lainé as " an honest and liberal man, discouraged by the Revolution." This description, at the time when M. Dumont's Memoirs were written, would have applied to almost every honest and liberal man in Europe; and would, beyond all doubt, have applied to M. Dumont himself. To that fanatical worship of the all-wise and all-good people, which had been common a few years before, had succeeded an uneasy suspicion that the follies and vices of the people would frustrate all attempts to serve them. The wild and joyous exultation, with which the meeting of the States-General and the fall of the Bastile had been hailed, had passed away.   In its place was dejection, and a gloomy distrust of suspicious appearances.   The philosophers and philanthropists had reigned.   And what had their reign produced?   Philosophy had brought with it mummeries as absurd as any which had been practised by the most superstitious zealot of the darkest age.   Philanthropy had brought with it crimes as horrible as the massacre of Saint Bartholomew.   This was the emancipation of the human mind.   These were the fruits of the great victory of reason over prejudice.   France had rejected the faith of Pascal and Descartes as a nursery fable, that a courtezan might be her idol, and a madman her priest.   She had asserted her freedom against Louis, that she might bow down before Robespierre.   For a time men thought that all the boasted wisdom of the eighteenth century was folly; and that those hopes of great political and social ameliorations which had been cherished by Voltaire and Condorcet were utterly delusive.

Under the influence of these feelings, M. Dumont has gone so far as to say that the writings of Mr. Burke on the French Revolution, though disfigured by exaggeration, and though containing doctrines subversive of all public liberty, had been, on the whole, justified by events, and had probably saved Europe from great disasters.   That such a man as the friend and fellow-labourer of Mr. Bentham should have expressed such an opinion is a circumstance which well deserves the consideration of uncharitable politicians.   These Memoirs have not convinced us that the French Revolution was not a great blessing to mankind.   But they have convinced us that very great indulgence is due to those who, while the Revolution was actually taking place, regarded it with unmixed aversion and horror.   We can perceive where their error lay.   We can perceive that the evil was temporary, and the good durable.   But we cannot be sure that, if our lot had been cast in their times, we should not, like them, have been discouraged and disgusted—that we should not, like them, have seen, in that great victory of the French people, only insanity and crime.

It is curious to observe how some men are applauded, and others reviled, for merely being what all their neighbours are,—for merely going passively down the stream of events,—for merely representing the opinions and passions of a whole generation.   The friends of popular government ordinarily speak with extreme severity of Mr. Pitt, and with respect and tenderness of Mr. Canning. Yet the whole difference, we suspect, consisted merely in this,—that Mr. Pitt died in 1806, and Mr. Canning in 1827. During the years which were common to the public life of both, Mr. Canning was assuredly not a more liberal statesman than his patron. The truth is that Mr. Pitt began his political life at the end of the American War, when the nation was suffering from the effects of corruption. He closed it in the midst of the calamities produced by the French Revolution, when the nation was still strongly impressed with the horrors of anarchy. He changed, undoubtedly. In his youth he had brought in reform bills. In his manhood he brought in gagging bills. But the change, though lamentable, was, in our opinion, perfectly natural, and might have been perfectly honest. He changed with the great body of his countrymen. Mr. Canning, on the other hand, entered into public life when Europe was in dread of the Jacobins. He closed his public life when Europe was suffering under the tyranny of the Holy Alliance. He, too, changed with the nation. As the crimes of the Jacobins had turned the master into something very like a Tory, the events which followed the Congress of Vienna turned the pupil into something very like a Whig.

So much are men the creatures of circumstances. We see that, if M. Dumont had died in 1799, he would have died, to use the new cant word, a decided " Conservative." If Mr. Pitt had lived in 1832, it is our firm belief that he would have been a decided Reformer.

The judgment passed by M. Dumont in this work on the French Revolution must be taken with considerable allowances. It resembles a criticism on a play of which only the first act has been performed, or on a building from which the scaffolding has not yet been taken down. We have no doubt that, if the excellent author had revised these Memoirs thirty years after the time at which they were written, he would have seen reason to omit a few passages, and to add many qualifications and explanations.

He would not probably have been inclined to retract the censures, just, though severe, which he has passed on the ignorance, the presumption, and the pedantry, of the National Assembly. But he would have admitted that, in spite of those faults, perhaps even by reason of those faults, that Assembly had conferred inestimable benefits on mankind. It is clear that, among the French of that day, political knowledge was absolutely in its infancy. It would indeed have been strange if it had attained maturity in the time of censors, of *lettres-de-cachet*, and of beds of justice.   The electors did not know how to elect. The representatives did not know how to deliberate.   M. Dumont taught the constituent body of Montreuil how to perform their functions, and found them apt to learn.   He afterwards tried, in concert with Mirabeau, to instruct the National Assembly in that admirable system of Parliamentary tactics which has been long established in the English House of Commons, and which has made the House of Commons, in spite of all the defects in its composition, the best and fairest debating society in the world.   But these accomplished legislators, though quite as ignorant as the mob of Montreuil, proved much less docile, and cried out that they did not want to go to school to the English. Their debates consisted of endless successions of trashy pamphlets, all beginning with something about the original compact of society, man in the hunting state, and other such foolery.   They sometimes diversified and enlivened these long readings by a little rioting.   They bawled; they hooted; they shook their fists.   They kept no order among themselves.   They were insulted with impunity by the crowd which filled their galleries. They gave long and solemn consideration to trifles.   They hurried through the most important resolutions with fearful expedition.   They wasted months in quibbling about the words of that false and childish Declaration of Rights on which they professed to found their new constitution, and which was at irreconcilable variance with every clause of that constitution. They annihilated in a single night privileges, many of which partook of the nature of property, and ought therefore to have been most delicately handled.

They are called the Constituent Assembly.   Never was a name less appropriate.   They were not constituent, but the very reverse of constituent.   They constituted nothing that stood or that deserved to last.   They had not, and they could not possibly have, the information or the habits of mind which are necessary for the framing of that most exquisite of all machines—a government.   The metaphysical cant with which they prefaced their constitution has long been the scoff of all parties.   Their constitution itself,—that constitution which they described as absolutely perfect, and to which they predicted immortality,—disappeared in a few months, and left no trace behind it.   They were great only in the work of destruction.

The glory of the National Assembly is this, that they were in truth, what Mr. Burke called them in austere irony, the ablest architects of ruin that ever the world saw. They were utterly incompetent to perform any work which required a discriminating eye and a skilful hand. But the work which was then to be done was a work of devastation. They had to deal with abuses so horrible and so deeply rooted that the highest political wisdom could scarcely have produced greater good to mankind than was produced by their fierce and senseless temerity. Demolition is undoubtedly a vulgar task; the highest glory of the statesman is to construct. But there is a time for everything, —a time to set up, and a time to pull down. The talents of revolutionary leaders and those of the legislator have equally their use and their season. It is the natural, the almost universal, law, that the age of insurrections and proscriptions shall precede the age of good government, of temperate liberty, and liberal order.

And how should it be otherwise? It is not in swaddling-bands that we learn to walk. It is not in the dark that we learn to distinguish colours. It is not under oppression that we learn how to use freedom. The ordinary sophism by which misrule is defended is, when truly stated, this:—The people must continue in slavery, because slavery has generated in them all the vices of slaves. Because they are ignorant, they must remain under a power which has made and which keeps them ignorant. Because they have been made ferocious by misgovernment, they must be misgoverned for ever. If the system under which they live were so mild and liberal that under its operation they had become humane and enlightened, it would be safe to venture on a change. But, as this system has destroyed morality, and prevented the development of the intellect,—as it has turned men, who might under different training have formed a virtuous and happy community, into savage and stupid wild beasts,—therefore it ought to last for ever. The English Revolution, it is said, was truly a glorious Revolution. Practical evils were redressed; no excesses were committed; no sweeping confiscations took place; the authority of the laws was scarcely for a moment suspended; the fullest and freest discussion was tolerated in Parliament; the nation showed, by the calm and temperate manner in which it asserted its liberty, that it was fit to enjoy liberty. The French Revolution was, on the other hand, the most horrible event recorded in history, —all madness and wickedness,—absurdity in theory, and atrocity in practice. What folly and injustice in the revolutionary laws! What grotesque affectation in the revolutionary ceremonies! What fanaticism! What licentiousness! What cruelty! Anacharsis Clootz and Marat,—feasts of the Supreme Being, and marriages of the Loire—trees of liberty, and heads dancing on pikes—the whole forms a kind of infernal farce, made up of everything ridiculous, and everything frightful. This it is to give freedom to those who have neither wisdom nor virtue.

It is not only by bad men interested in the defence of abuses that arguments like these have been urged against all schemes of political improvement. Some of the highest and purest of human beings conceived such scorn and aversion for the follies and crimes of the French Revolution that they recanted, in the moment of triumph, those liberal opinions to which they had clung in defiance of persecution. And, if we inquire why it was that they began to doubt whether liberty were a blessing, we shall find that it was only because events had proved, in the clearest manner, that liberty is the parent of virtue and of order. They ceased to abhor tyranny merely because it had been signally shown that the effect of tyranny on the hearts and understandings of men is more demoralising and more stupifying than had ever been imagined by the most zealous friend of popular rights. The truth is, that a stronger argument against the old monarchy of France may be drawn from the *noyades* and the *fusillades* than from the Bastile and the *Parc-aux-cerfs*. We believe it to be a rule without an exception, that the violence of a revolution corresponds to the degree of misgovernment which has produced that revolution. Why was the French Revolution so bloody and destructive? Why was our revolution of 1641 comparatively mild? Why was our revolution of 1688 milder still? Why was the American Revolution, considered as an internal movement, the mildest of all? There is an obvious and complete solution of the problem. The English under James the First and Charles the First were less oppressed than the French under Louis the Fifteenth and Louis the Sixteenth. The English were less oppressed after the Restoration than before the great Rebellion. And America under George the Third was less oppressed than England under the Stuarts. The reaction was exactly proportioned to the pressure,—the vengeance to the provocation.

When Mr. Burke was reminded in his later years of the zeal which he had displayed in the cause of the Americans, he vindicated himself from the charge of inconsistency by contrasting the wisdom and moderation of the Colonial insurgents of 1776 with the fanaticism and wickedness of the Jacobins of 1792. He was in fact bringing an argument *a fortiori* against himself. The circumstances on which he rested his vindication fully proved that the old government of France stood in far more need of a complete change than the old government of America. The difference between Washington and Robespierre, —the difference between Franklin and Barère,—the difference between the destruction of a few barrels of tea and the confiscation of thousands of square miles,—the difference between the tarring and feathering of a tax-gatherer and the massacres of September,—measure the difference between the government of America under the rule of England and the government of France under the rule of the Bourbons.

Louis the Sixteenth made great voluntary concessions to his people; and they sent him to the scaffold. Charles the Tenth violated the fundamental laws of the state, established a despotism, and butchered his subjects for not submitting quietly to that despotism. He failed in his wicked attempt. He was at the mercy of those whom he had injured. The pavements of Paris were still heaped up in barricades;—the hospitals were still full of the wounded;—the dead were still unburied;—a thousand families were in mourning;—a hundred thousand citizens were in arms. The crime was recent;—the life of the criminal was in the hands of the sufferers;—and they touched not one hair of his head. In the first revolution, victims were sent to death by scores for the most trifling acts proved by the lowest testimony, before the most partial tribunals. After the second revolution, those ministers who had signed the ordinances, those ministers, whose guilt, as it was of the foulest kind, was proved by the clearest evidence,—were punished only with imprisonment. In the first revolution, property was attacked. In the second, it was held sacred. Both revolutions, it is true, left the public mind of France in an unsettled state. Both revolutions were followed by insurrectionary movements. But, after the first revolution, the insurgents were almost always stronger than the law; and, since the second revolution, the law has invariably been found stronger than the insurgents. There is, indeed, much in the present state of France which may well excite the uneasiness of those who desire to see her free, happy, powerful, and secure. Yet, if we compare the present state of France with the state in which she was forty years ago, how vast a change for the better has taken place. How little effect, for example, during the first revolution, would the sentence of a

judicial body have produced on an armed and victorious party!
If, after the 10th of August, or after the proscription of the
Gironde, or after the 9th of Thermidor, or after the carnage of
Vendémiaire, or after the arrests of Fructidor, any tribunal had
decided against the conquerors in favour of the conquered, with
what contempt, with what derision, would its award have been
received! The judges would have lost their heads, or would
have been sent to die in some unwholesome colony. The fate
of the victim whom they had endeavoured to save would only
have been made darker and more hopeless by their interference.
We have lately seen a signal proof that, in France, the law is
now stronger than the sword. We have seen a government, in
the very moment of triumph and revenge, submitting itself to
the authority of a court of law. A just and independent sentence
has been pronounced—a sentence worthy of the ancient renown
of that magistracy to which belong the noblest recollections of
French history—which, in an age of persecutors, produced
L'Hôpital,—which, in an age of courtiers, produced D'Aguesseau,
—which, in an age of wickedness and madness, exhibited to
mankind a pattern of every virtue in the life and in the death
of Malesherbes. The respectful manner in which that sentence
has been received is alone sufficient to show how widely the
French of this generation differ from their fathers. And how
is the difference to be explained?   The race, the soil, the climate,
are the same. If those dull, honest Englishmen, who explain
the events of 1793 and 1794 by saying that the French are
naturally frivolous and cruel, were in the right, why is the
guillotine now standing idle? Not surely for want of Carlists,
of aristocrats, of people guilty of incivism, of people suspected
of being suspicious characters. Is not the true explanation this,
that the Frenchman of 1832 has been far better governed than
the Frenchman of 1789,—that his soul has never been galled by
the oppressive privileges of a separate caste,—that he has been
in some degree accustomed to discuss political questions, and to
perform political functions,—that he has lived for seventeen or
eighteen years under institutions which, however defective, have
yet been far superior to any institutions that had before existed
in France?

As the second French Revolution has been far milder than
the first, so that great change which has just been effected in
England has been milder even than the second French Revolution,—milder than any revolution recorded in history. Some
orators have described the reform of the House of Commons as

a revolution. Others have denied the propriety of the term.
The question, though in seeming merely a question of definition,
suggests much curious and interesting matter for reflection.   If
we look at the magnitude of the reform, it may well be called
a revolution. If we look at the means by which it has been
effected, it is merely an Act of Parliament, regularly brought in,
read, committed, and passed. In the whole history of England,
there is no prouder circumstance than this,—that a change,
which could not, in any other age, or in any other country,
have been effected without physical violence, should here have
been effected by the force of reason, and under the forms of
law. The work of three civil wars has been accomplished by
three sessions of Parliament. An ancient and deeply rooted
system of abuses has been fiercely attacked and stubbornly
defended. It has fallen; and not one sword has been drawn;
not one estate has been confiscated; not one family has been
forced to emigrate. The bank has kept its credit. The funds
have kept their price. Every man has gone forth to his work
and to his labour till the evening. During the fiercest excitement of the contest,—during the first fortnight of that immortal
May,—there was not one moment at which any sanguinary act
committed on the person of any of the most unpopular men in
England would not have filled the country with horror and
indignation.

And now that the victory is won, has it been abused? An
immense mass of power has been transferred from an oligarchy
to the nation. Are the members of the vanquished oligarchy
insecure? Does the nation seem disposed to play the tyrant?
Are not those who, in any other state of society, would have
been visited with the severest vengeance of the triumphant
party,—would have been pining in dungeons, or flying to foreign
countries,—still enjoying their possessions and their honours,
still taking part as freely as ever in public affairs? Two years
ago they were dominant. They are now vanquished. Yet the
whole people would regard with horror any man who should
dare to propose any vindictive measure. So common is this
feeling,—so much is it a matter of course among us,—that many
of our readers will scarcely understand what we see to admire
in it.

To what are we to attribute the unparalleled moderation and
humanity which the English people had displayed at this great
conjuncture? The answer is plain. This moderation, this
humanity, are the fruits of a hundred and fifty years of liberty.

During many generations we have had legislative assemblies which, however defective their constitution might be, have always contained many members chosen by the people, and many others eager to obtain the approbation of the people:—assemblies in which perfect freedom of debate was allowed;—assemblies in which the smallest minority had a fair hearing; assemblies in which abuses, even when they were not redressed, were at least exposed. For many generations we have had the trial by jury, the Habeas Corpus Act, the freedom of the press, the right of meeting to discuss public affairs, the right of petitioning the legislature. A vast portion of the population has long been accustomed to the exercise of political functions, and has been thoroughly seasoned to political excitement. In most other countries there is no middle course between absolute submission and open rebellion. In England there has always been for centuries a constitutional opposition. Thus our institutions had been so good that they had educated us into a capacity for better institutions. There is not a large town in the kingdom which does not contain better materials for a legislature than all France could furnish in 1789. There is not a spouting-club at any pot-house in London in which the rules of debate are not better understood, and more strictly observed, than in the Constituent Assembly. There is scarcely a Political Union which could not frame in half an hour a declaration of rights superior to that which occupied the collective wisdom of France for several months.

It would be impossible even to glance at all the causes of the French Revolution within the limits to which we must confine ourselves. One thing is clear. The government, the aristocracy, and the church were rewarded after their works. They reaped that which they had sown. They found the nation such as they had made it. That the people had become possessed of irresistible power before they had attained the slightest knowledge of the art of government—that practical questions of vast moment were left to be solved by men to whom politics had been only matter of theory—that a legislature was composed of persons who were scarcely fit to compose a debating society—that the whole nation was ready to lend an ear to any flatterer who appealed to its cupidity, to its fears, or to its thirst for vengeance—all this was the effect of misrule, obstinately continued in defiance of solemn warnings, and of the visible signs of an approaching retribution.

Even while the monarchy seemed to be in its highest and

most palmy state, the causes of that great destruction had already begun to operate. They may be distinctly traced even under the reign of Louis the Fourteenth. That reign is the time to which the Ultra-Royalists refer as the Golden Age of France. It was in truth one of those periods which shine with an unnatural and delusive splendour, and which are rapidly followed by gloom and decay.

Concerning Louis the Fourteenth himself, the world seeems at last to have formed a correct judgment. He was not a great general; he was not a great statesman; but he was, in one sense of the words, a great king. Never was there so consummate a master of what our James the First would have called kingcraft,—of all those arts which most advantageously display the merits of a prince, and most completely hide his defects. Though his internal administration was bad,—though the military triumphs which gave splendour to the early part of his reign were not achieved by himself,—though his later years were crowded with defeats and humiliations,—though he was so ignorant that he scarcely understood the Latin of his mass-book, —though he fell under the control of a cunning Jesuit and of a more cunning old woman,—he succeeded in passing himself off on his people as a being above humanity. And this is the more extraordinary because he did not seclude himself from the public gaze like those Oriental despots whose faces are never seen, and whose very names it is a crime to pronounce lightly. It has been said that no man is a hero to his valet;—and all the world saw as much of Louis the Fourteenth as his valet could see. Five hundred people assembled to see him shave and put on his breeches in the morning. He then kneeled down at the side of his bed, and said his prayer while the whole assembly awaited the end in solemn silence—the ecclesiastics on their knees, and the laymen with their hats before their faces. He walked about his gardens with a train of two hundred courtiers at his heels. All Versailles came to see him dine and sup. He was put to bed at night in the midst of a crowd as great as that which had met to see him rise in the morning. He took his very emetics in state, and vomited majestically in the presence of all the *grandes* and *petites entrées*. Yet, though he constantly exposed himself to the public gaze in situations in which it is scarcely possible for any man to preserve much personal dignity, he to the last impressed those who surrounded him with the deepest awe and reverence. The illusion which he produced on his worshippers can be compared only to those illusions to which lovers are proverbially subject during the season of courtship. It was an illusion which affected even the senses. The contemporaries of Louis thought him tall. Voltaire, who might have seen him, and who had lived with some of the most distinguished members of his court, speaks repeatedly of his majestic stature. Yet it is as certain as any fact can be that he was rather below than above the middle size. He had, it seems, a way of holding himself, a way of walking, a way of swelling his chest and rearing his head, which deceived the eyes of the multitude. Eighty years after his death, the royal cemetery was violated by the revolutionists, his coffin was opened; his body was dragged out; and it appeared that the prince, whose majestic figure had been so long and loudly extolled, was in truth a little man.[1] That fine expression of Juvenal is singularly applicable, both in its literal and in its metaphorical sense, to Louis the Fourteenth:

> " Mors sola fatetur
> Quantula sint hominum corpuscula."

His person and his government have had the same fate. He had the art of making both appear grand and august, in spite of the clearest evidence that both were below the ordinary standard. Death and time have exposed both the deceptions. The body of the great king has been measured more justly than it was measured by the courtiers who were afraid to look above his shoe-tie. His public character has been scrutinised by men free from the hopes and fears of Boileau and Molière. In the grave, the most majestic of princes is only five feet eight. In history, the hero and the politician dwindles into a vain and feeble tyrant,—the slave of priests and women—little in war, —little in government,—little in everything but the art of simulating greatness.

He left to his infant successor a famished and miserable people, a beaten and humbled army, provinces turned into deserts by misgovernment and persecution, factions dividing the court, a schism raging in the church, an immense debt, an empty treasury, immeasurable palaces, an innumerable household, inestimable jewels and furniture. All the sap and nutriment of the state seemed to have been drawn to feed one bloated and

---

[1] Even M. de Chateaubriand, to whom we should have thought all the Bourbons would have seemed at least six feet high, admits this fact. " C'est une erreur," says he in his strange memoirs of the Duke of Berri, " de croire que Louis XIV. étoit d'une haute stature. Une cuirasse qui nous reste de lui, et les exhumations de St. Denys. n'ont laissé sur ce point aucun doute."

unwholesome excrescence. The nation was withered. The court was morbidly flourishing. Yet it does not appear that the associations which attached the people to the monarchy had lost strength during his reign. He had neglected or sacrificed their dearest interests; but he had struck their imaginations. The very things which ought to have made him most unpopular —the prodigies of luxury and magnificence with which his per-son was surrounded, while, beyond the inclosure of his parks, nothing was to be seen but starvation and despair,—seemed to increase the respectful attachment which his subjects felt for him. That governments exist only for the good of the people appears to be the most obvious and simple of all truths. Yet history proves that it is one of the most recondite. We can scarcely wonder that it should be so seldom present to the minds of rulers, when we see how slowly, and through how much suffering, nations arrive at the knowledge of it.

There was indeed one Frenchman who had discovered those principles which it now seems impossible to miss,—that the many are not made for the use of one,—that the truly good government is not that which concentrates magnificence in a court, but that which diffuses happiness among a people,—that a king who gains victory after victory, and adds province to province, may deserve, not the admiration, but the abhorrence and contempt of mankind. These were the doctrines which Fénélon taught. Considered as an epic poem, Telemachus can scarcely be placed above Glover's Leonidas or Wilkie's Epigoniad. Considered as a treatise on politics and morals, it abounds with errors of detail; and the truths which it inculcates seem trite to a modern reader. But, if we compare the spirit in which it is written with the spirit which pervades the rest of the French literature of that age, we shall perceive that, though in appearance trite, it was in truth one of the most original works that have ever appeared. The fundamental principles of Fénélon's political morality, the tests by which he judged of institutions and of men, were absolutely new to his countrymen. He had taught them indeed, with the happiest effect, to his royal pupil. But how incomprehensible they were to most people, we learn from Saint Simon. That amusing writer tells us, as a thing almost incredible, that the Duke of Burgundy declared it to be his opinion that kings existed for the good of the people, and not the people for the good of kings. Saint Simon is delighted with the benevolence of this saying; but startled by its novelty and terrified by its boldness. Indeed he distinctly says that it was not safe to repeat the sentiment in the court of Louis.   Saint Simon was, of all the members of that court, the least courtly. He was as nearly an oppositionist as any man of his time.   His disposition was proud, bitter, and cynical.   In religion he was a Jansenist; in politics, a less hearty royalist than most of his neighbours.   His opinions and his temper had preserved him from the illusions which the demeanour of Louis produced on others.   He neither loved nor respected the king.   Yet even this man,—one of the most liberal men in France,—was struck dumb with astonishment at hearing the fundamental axiom of all government propounded,—an axiom which, in our time, nobody in England or France would dispute,—which the stoutest Tory takes for granted as much as the fiercest Radical, and concerning which the Carlist would agree with the most republican deputy of the " extreme left."   No person will do justice to Fénélon, who does not constantly keep in mind that Telemachus was written in an age and nation in which bold and independent thinkers stared to hear that twenty millions of human beings did not exist for the gratification of one.   That work is commonly considered as a school-book, very fit for children, because its style is easy and its morality blameless, but unworthy of the attention of statesmen and philosophers.   We can distinguish in it, if we are not greatly mistaken, the first faint dawn of a long and splendid day of intellectual light,—the dim promise of a great deliverance,—the undeveloped germ of the charter and of the code.

What mighty interests were staked on the life of the Duke of Burgundy! and how different an aspect might the history of France have borne if he had attained the age of his grandfather or of his son;—if he had been permitted to show how much could be done for humanity by the highest virtue in the highest fortune!   There is scarcely anything in history more remarkable than the descriptions which remain to us of that extraordinary man.   The fierce and impetuous temper which he showed in early youth,—the complete change which a judicious education produced in his character,—his fervid piety,—his large benevolence,—the strictness with which he judged himself,—the liberality with which he judged others,—the fortitude with which alone, in the whole court, he stood up against the commands of Louis, when a religious scruple was concerned,—the charity with which alone, in the whole court, he defended the profligate Orleans against calumniators,—his great projects for the good of the people,—his activity in business,—his taste for letters,—

his strong domestic attachments,—even the ungraceful person and the shy and awkward manner which concealed from the eyes of the sneering courtiers of his grandfather so many rare endowments,—make his character the most interesting that is to be found in the annals of his house. He had resolved, if he came to the throne, to disperse that ostentatious court, which was supported at an expense ruinous to the nation,—to preserve peace,—to correct the abuses which were found in every part of the system of revenue,—to abolish or modify oppressive privileges,—to reform the administration of justice,—to revive the institution of the States-General. If he had ruled over France during forty or fifty years, that great movement of the human mind, which no government could have arrested, which bad government only rendered more violent, would, we are inclined to think, have been conducted, by peaceable means to a happy termination.

Disease and sorrow removed from the world that wisdom and virtue of which it was not worthy. During two generations France was ruled by men who, with all the vices of Louis the Fourteenth, had none of the art by which that magnificent prince passed off his vices for virtues. The people had now to see tyranny naked. That foul Duessa was stripped of her gorgeous ornaments. She had always been hideous; but a strange enchantment had made her seem fair and glorious in the eyes of her willing slaves. The spell was now broken; the deformity was made manifest; and the lovers, lately so happy and so proud, turned away loathing and horror-struck.

First came the Regency. The strictness with which Louis had, towards the close of his life, exacted from those around him an outward attention to religious duties, produced an effect similar to that which the rigour of the Puritans had produced in England. It was the boast of Madame de Maintenon, in the time of her greatness, that devotion had become the fashion. A fashion indeed it was; and, like a fashion, it passed away. The austerity of the tyrant's old age had injured the morality of the higher orders more than even the licentiousness of his youth. Not only had he not reformed their vices, but, by forcing them to be hypocrites, he had shaken their belief in virtue. They had found it so easy to perform the grimace of piety that it was natural for them to consider all piety as grimace. The times were changed. Pensions, regiments, and abbeys, were no longer to be obtained by regular confession and severe penance: and the obsequious courtiers, who had kept Lent like monks of

La Trappe, and who had turned up the whites of their eyes at
the edifying parts of sermons preached before the king, aspired
to the title of *roué* as ardently as they had aspired to that of
dévot ; and went, during Passion Week, to the revels of the
Palais Royal as readily as they had formerly repaired to the
sermons of Massillon.

The Regent was in many respects the facsimile of our Charles
the Second.   Like Charles, he was a good-natured man, utterly
destitute of sensibility.   Like Charles, he had good natural
talents, which a deplorable indolence rendered useless to the
state.   Like Charles, he thought all men corrupted and interested, and yet did not dislike them for being so.   His opinion
of human nature was Gulliver's; but he did not regard human
nature with Gulliver's horror.   He thought that he and his
fellow-creatures were Yahoos; and he thought a Yahoo a very
agreeable kind of animal.   No princes were ever more social
than Charles and Philip of Orleans: yet no princes ever had
less capacity for friendship.   The tempers of these clever cynics
were so easy, and their minds so languid, that habit supplied in
them the place of affection, and made them the tools of people
for whom they cared not one straw.   In love, both were mere
sensualists without delicacy or tenderness.   In politics, both
were utterly careless of faith and of national honour.   Charles
shut up the Exchequer.   Philip patronised the System.   The
councils of Charles were swayed by the gold of Barillon; the
councils of Philip by the gold of Walpole.   Charles for private
objects made war on Holland, the natural ally of England.
Philip for private objects made war on the Spanish branch of
the house of Bourbon, the natural ally, indeed the creature of
France.   Even in trifling circumstances the parallel might be
carried on.   Both these princes were fond of experimental philosophy, and passed in the laboratory much time which would
have been more advantageously passed at the council-table.
Both were more strongly attached to their female relatives than
to any other human being; and in both cases it was suspected
that this attachment was not perfectly innocent.   In personal
courage, and in all the virtues which are connected with personal
courage, the Regent was indisputably superior to Charles.
Indeed Charles but narrowly escaped the stain of cowardice.
Philip was eminently brave, and, like most brave men, was
generally open and sincere.   Charles added dissimulation to his
other vices.

The administration of the Regent was scarcely less pernicious, and infinitely more scandalous, than that of the deceased monarch. It was by magnificent public works, and by wars conducted on a gigantic scale, that Louis had brought distress on his people. The Regent aggravated that distress by frauds of which a lame duck on the stock-exchange would have been ashamed. France, even while suffering under the most severe calamities, had reverenced the conqueror. She despised the swindler.

When Orleans and the wretched Dubois had disappeared, the power passed to the Duke of Bourbon; a prince degraded in the public eye by the infamously lucrative part which he had taken in the juggles of the System, and by the humility with which he bore the caprices of a loose and imperious woman. It seemed to be decreed that every branch of the royal family should successively incur the abhorrence and contempt of the nation.

Between the fall of the Duke of Bourbon and the death of Fleury, a few years of frugal and moderate government intervened. Then recommenced the downward progress of the monarchy. Profligacy in the court, extravagance in the finances, schism in the church, faction in the Parliaments, unjust war terminated by ignominious peace,—all that indicates and all that produces the ruin of great empires, make up the history of that miserable period. Abroad, the French were beaten and humbled everywhere, by land and by sea, on the Elbe and on the Rhine, in Asia, and in America. At home, they were turned over from vizier to vizier, and from sultana to sultana, till they had reached that point beneath which there was no lower abyss of infamy,—till the yoke of Maupeou had made them pine for Choiseul,—till Madame du Barri had taught them to regret Madame de Pompadour.

But unpopular as the monarchy had become, the aristocracy was more unpopular still; and not without reason. The tyranny of an individual is far more supportable than the tyranny of a caste. The old privileges were galling and hateful to the new wealth and the new knowledge. Everything indicated the approach of no common revolution,—of a revolution destined to change, not merely the form of government, but the distribution of property and the whole social system,—of a revolution the effects of which were to be felt at every fireside in France,—of a new Jaquerie, in which the victory was to remain with *Jaques bonhomme*. In the van of the movement were the moneyed men and the men of letters,—the wounded pride of wealth, and the wounded pride of intellect. An immense multitude, made ignorant and cruel by oppression, was raging in the rear.

We greatly doubt whether any course which could have been pursued by Louis the Sixteenth could have averted a great convulsion.   But we are sure that, if there was such a course, it was the course recommended by M. Turgot.   The church and the aristocracy, with that blindness to danger, that incapacity of believing that anything can be except what has been, which the long possession of power seldom fails to generate, mocked at the counsel which might have saved them.   They would not have reform; and they had revolution.   They would not pay a small contribution in place of the odious corvées; and they lived to see their castles demolished, and their lands sold to strangers.   They would not endure Turgot; and they were forced to endure Robespierre.

Then the rulers of France, as if smitten with judicial blindness, plunged headlong into the American war.   They thus committed at once two great errors.   They encouraged the spirit of revolution.   They augmented at the same time those public burdens, the pressure of which is generally the immediate cause of revolutions.   The event of the war carried to the height the enthusiasm of speculative democrats.   The financial difficulties produced by the war carried to the height the discontent of that larger body of people who cared little about theories, and much about taxes.

The meeting of the States-General was the signal for the explosion of all the hoarded passions of a century.   In that assembly there were undoubtedly very able men.   But they had no practical knowledge of the art of government.   All the great English revolutions have been conducted by practical statesmen.   The French Revolution was conducted by mere speculators.   Our constitution has never been so far behind the age as to have become an object of aversion to the people.   The English revolutions have therefore been undertaken for the purpose of defending, correcting, and restoring,—never for the mere purpose of destroying.   Our countrymen have always, even in times of the greatest excitement, spoken reverently of the form of government under which they lived, and attacked only what they regarded as its corruptions.   In the very act of innovating they have constantly appealed to ancient prescription; they have seldom looked abroad for models; they have seldom troubled themselves with Utopian theories; they have not been anxious to prove that liberty is a natural right of men; they have been content to regard it as the lawful birthright of Englishmen. Their social contract is no fiction. It is still extant on the original parchment, sealed with wax which was affixed at Runnymede, and attested by the lordly names of the Marischals and Fitzherberts. No general arguments about the original equality of men, no fine stories out of Plutarch and Cornelius Nepos, have ever affected them so much as their own familiar words,—Magna Charta,—Habeas Corpus,—Trial by Jury,—Bill of Rights. This part of our national character has undoubtedly its disadvantages. An Englishman too often reasons on politics in the spirit rather of a lawyer than of a philosopher. There is too often something narrow, something exclusive, something Jewish, if we may use the word, in his love of freedom. He is disposed to consider popular rights as the special heritage of the chosen race to which he belongs. He is inclined rather to repel than to encourage the alien proselyte who aspires to a share of his privileges. Very different was the spirit of the Constituent Assembly. They had none of our narrowness; but they had none of our practical skill in the management of affairs. They did not understand how to regulate the order of their own debates; and they thought themselves able to legislate for the whole world. All the past was loathsome to them. All their agreeable associations were connected with the future. Hopes were to them all that recollections are to us. In the institutions of their country they found nothing to love or to admire. As far back as they could look, they saw only the tyranny of one class and the degradation of another,—Frank and Gaul, knight and villein, gentleman and *roturier*. They hated the monarchy, the church, the nobility. They cared nothing for the States or the Parliament. It was long the fashion to ascribe all the follies which they committed to the writings of the philosophers. We believe that it was misrule, and nothing but misrule, that put the sting into those writings. It is not true that the French abandoned experience for theories. They took up with theories because they had no experience of good government. It was because they had no charter that they ranted about the original contract. As soon as tolerable institutions were given to them, they began to look to those institutions. In 1830 their rallying cry was *Vive la Charte*. In 1789 they had nothing but theories round which to rally. They had seen social distinctions only in a bad form; and it was therefore natural that they should be deluded by sophisms about the equality of men. They had experienced so much evil from the sovereignty of kings that they might be excused for lending a ready ear to those who preached, in an exaggerated form, the doctrine of the sovereignty of the people.

The English, content with their own national recollections and names, have never sought for models in the institutions of Greece or Rome. The French, having nothing in their own history to which they could look back with pleasure, had recourse to the history of the great ancient commonwealths: they drew their notions of those commonwealths, not from contemporary writers, but from romances written by pedantic moralists long after the extinction of public liberty. They neglected Thucydides for Plutarch. Blind themselves, they took blind guides. They had no experience of freedom; and they took their opinions concerning it from men who had no more experience of it than themselves, and whose imaginations, inflamed by mystery and privation, exaggerated the unknown enjoyment;—from men who raved about patriotism without having ever had a country, and eulogised tyrannicide while crouching before tyrants. The maxim which the French legislators learned in this school was, that political liberty is an end, and not a means; that it is not merely valuable as the great safeguard of order, of property, and of morality, but that it is in itself a high and exquisite happiness to which order, property, and morality ought without one scruple to be sacrificed. The lessons which may be learned from ancient history are indeed most useful and important; but they were not likely to be learned by men who, in all their rhapsodies about the Athenian democracy, seemed utterly to forget that in that democracy there were ten slaves to one citizen; and who constantly decorated their invectives against the aristocrats with panegyrics on Brutus and Cato,—two aristocrats, fiercer, prouder, and more exclusive, than any that emigrated with the Count of Artois.

We have never met with so vivid and interesting a picture of the National Assembly as that which M. Dumont has set before us. His Mirabeau, in particular, is incomparable. All the former Mirabeaus were daubs in comparison. Some were merely painted from the imagination—others were gross caricatures: this is the very individual, neither god nor demon, but a man— a Frenchman—a Frenchman of the eighteenth century, with great talents, with strong passions, depraved by bad education, surrounded by temptations of every kind,—made desperate at one time by disgrace, and then again intoxicated by fame. All his opposite and seemingly inconsistent qualities are in this representation so blended together as to make up a harmonious and natural whole. Till now, Mirabeau was to us, and, we believe, to most readers of history, not a man, but a string of antitheses. Henceforth he will be a real human being, a remarkable and eccentric being indeed, but perfectly conceivable.

He was fond, M. Dumont tells us, of giving odd compound nicknames. Thus, M. de Lafayette was Grandison-Cromwell; the King of Prussia was Alaric-Cottin; D'Espremenil was Crispin-Catiline. We think that Mirabeau himself might be described, after his own fashion, as a Wilkes-Chatham. He had Wilkes's sensuality, Wilkes's levity, Wilkes's insensibility to shame. Like Wilkes, he had brought on himself the censure even of men of pleasure by the peculiar grossness of his immorality, and by the obscenity of his writings. Like Wilkes, he was heedless, not only of the laws of morality, but of the laws of honour. Yet he affected, like Wilkes, to unite the character of the demagogue to that of the fine gentleman. Like Wilkes, he conciliated, by his good-humour and his high spirits, the regard of many who despised his character. Like Wilkes, he was hideously ugly; like Wilkes, he made a jest of his own ugliness; and, like Wilkes, he was, in spite of his ugliness, very attentive to his dress, and very successful in affairs of gallantry.

Resembling Wilkes in the lower and grosser parts of his character, he had, in his higher qualities, some affinity to Chatham. His eloquence, as far as we can judge of it, bore no inconsiderable resemblance to that of the great English minister. He was not eminently successful in long set speeches. He was not, on the other hand, a close and ready debater. Sudden bursts, which seemed to be the effect of inspiration—short sentences which came like lightning, dazzling, burning, striking down everything before them—sentences which, spoken at critical moments, decided the fate of great questions—sentences which at once became proverbs—sentences which everybody still knows by heart—in these chiefly lay the oratorical power both of Chatham and of Mirabeau. There have been far greater speakers, and far greater statesmen, than either of them; but we doubt whether any men have, in modern times, exercised such vast personal influence over stormy and divided assemblies. The power of both was as much moral as intellectual. In true dignity of character, in private and public virtue, it may seem absurd to institute any comparison between them; but they had the same haughtiness and vehemence of temper. In their language and manner there was a disdainful self-confidence, an imperiousness, a fierceness of passion, before which all common minds quailed. Even Murray and Charles Townshend, though intellectually not inferior to Chatham, were always cowed by him. Barnave, in the same manner, though the best debater in the National Assembly, flinched before the energy of Mirabeau. Men, except in bad novels, are not all good or all evil. It can scarcely be denied that the virtue of Lord Chatham was a little theatrical. On the other hand there was in Mirabeau, not indeed anything deserving the name of virtue, but that imperfect substitute for virtue which is found in almost all superior minds,—a sensibility to the beautiful and the good, which sometimes amounted to sincere enthusiasm; and which, mingled with the desire of admiration, sometimes gave to his character a lustre resembling the lustre of true goodness,—as the " faded splendour wan " which lingered round the fallen archangel resembled the exceeding brightness of those spirits who had kept their first estate.

There are several other admirable portraits of eminent men in these Memoirs. That of Sieyes in particular, and that of Talleyrand, are masterpieces, full of life and expression. But nothing in the book has interested us more than the view which M. Dumont has presented to us, unostentatiously, and, we may say, unconsciously, of his own character. The sturdy rectitude, the large charity, the good-nature, the modesty, the independent spirit, the ardent philanthropy, the unaffected indifference to money and to fame, make up a character which, while it has nothing unnatural, seems to us to approach nearer to perfection than any of the Grandisons and Allworthys of fiction. The work is not indeed precisely such a work as we had anticipated —it is more lively, more picturesque, more amusing than we had promised ourselves; and it is, on the other hand, less profound and philosophic. But, if it is not, in all respects, such as might have been expected from the intellect of M. Dumont, it is assuredly such as might have been expected from his heart.

BARÈRE [1]

(April 1844)

THIS book has more than one title to our serious attention. It is an appeal, solemnly made to posterity by a man who played a conspicuous part in great events, and who represents himself as deeply aggrieved by the rash and malevolent censure of his contemporaries. To such an appeal we shall always give ready audience. We can perform no duty more useful to society, or more agreeable to our own feelings, than that of making, as far as our power extends, reparation to the slandered and persecuted benefactors of mankind. We therefore promptly took into our consideration this copious apology for the life of Bertrand Barère. We have made up our minds; and we now purpose to do him, by the blessing of God, full and signal justice. It is to be observed that the appellant in this case does not come into court alone. He is attended to the bar of public opinion by two compurgators who occupy highly honourable stations. One of these is M. David of Angers, member of the institute, an eminent sculptor, and, if we have been rightly informed, a favourite pupil, though not a kinsman, of the painter who bore the same name. The other, to whom we owe the biographical preface, is M. Hippolyte Carnot, member of the Chamber of Deputies, and son of the celebrated Director. In the judgment of M. David and of M. Hippolyte Carnot, Barère was a deserving and an ill-used man—a man who, though by no means faultless, must yet, when due allowance is made for the force of circumstances and the infirmity of human nature, be considered as on the whole entitled to our esteem. It will be for the public to determine, after a full hearing, whether the editors have, by thus connecting their names with that of Barère, raised his character or lowered their own.

We are not conscious that, when we opened this book, we were under the influence of any feeling likely to pervert our judgment. Undoubtedly we had long entertained a most unfavourable opinion of Barère: but to this opinion we were not

---

[1] *Memoires de Bertrand Barère;* publiés par MM. Hippolyte Carnot, Membre de la Chambre des Députés, et David d'Angers, Membre de l'Institut: précédés d'une Notice Historique par H. Carnot. 4 tomes. Paris: 1843.

tied by any passion or by any interest. Our dislike was a reasonable dislike, and might have been removed by reason. Indeed our expectation was, that these Memoirs would in some measure clear Barère's fame. That he could vindicate himself from all the charges which had been brought against him, we knew to be impossible; and his editors admit that he has not done so. But we thought it highly probable that some grave accusations would be refuted, and that many offences to which he would have been forced to plead guilty would be greatly extenuated. We were not disposed to be severe. We were fully aware that temptations such as those to which the members of the Convention and of the Committee of Public Safety were exposed must try severely the strength of the firmest virtue. Indeed our inclination has always been to regard with an indulgence, which to some rigid moralists appears excessive, those faults into which gentle and noble spirits are sometimes hurried by the excitement of conflict, by the maddening influence of sympathy, and by ill-regulated zeal for a public cause.

With such feelings we read this book, and compared it with other accounts of the events in which Barère bore a part. It is now our duty to express the opinion to which this investigation has led us.

Our opinion then is this: that Barère approached nearer than any person mentioned in history or fiction, whether man or devil, to the idea of consummate and universal depravity. In him the qualities which are the proper objects of hatred, and the qualities which are the proper objects of contempt, preserve an exquisite and absolute harmony. In almost every particular sort of wickedness he has had rivals. His sensuality was immoderate; but this was a failing common to him with many great and amiable men. There have been many men as cowardly as he, some as cruel, a few as mean, a few as impudent. There may also have been as great liars, though we never met with them or read of them. But when we put everything together, sensuality, poltroonery, baseness, effrontery, mendacity, barbarity, the result is something which in a novel we should condemn as caricature, and to which, we venture to say, no parallel can be found in history.

It would be grossly unjust, we acknowledge, to try a man situated as Barère was by a severe standard. Nor have we done so. We have formed our opinion of him, by comparing him, not with politicians of stainless character, not with Chancellor D'Aguesseau, or General Washington, or Mr. Wilberforce, or Earl Grey, but with his own colleagues of the Mountain. That party included a considerable number of the worst men that ever lived; but we see in it nothing like Barère. Compared with him, Fouché seems honest; Billaud seems humane; Hébert seems to rise into dignity. Every other chief of a party, says M. Hippolyte Carnot, has found apologists: one set of men exalts the Girondists; another set justifies Danton; a third deifies Robespierre: but Barère has remained without a defender. We venture to suggest a very simple solution of this phenomenon. All the other chiefs of parties had some good qualities; and Barère had none. The genius, courage, patriotism, and humanity of the Girondist statesmen more than atoned for what was culpable in their conduct, and should have protected them from the insult of being compared with such a thing as Barère. Danton and Robespierre were indeed bad men; but in both of them some important parts of the mind remained sound. Danton was brave and resolute, fond of pleasure, of power, and of distinction, with vehement passions, with lax principles, but with some kind and manly feelings, capable of great crimes, but capable also of friendship and of compassion. He, therefore, naturally finds admirers among persons of bold and sanguine dispositions. Robespierre was a vain, envious, and suspicious man, with a hard heart, weak nerves, and a gloomy temper. But we cannot with truth deny that he was, in the vulgar sense of the word, disinterested, that his private life was correct, or that he was sincerely zealous for his own system of politics and morals. He, therefore, naturally finds admirers among honest but moody and bitter democrats. If no class has taken the reputation of Barère under its patronage, the reason is plain: Barère had not a single virtue, nor even the semblance of one.

It is true that he was not, as far as we are able to judge, originally of a savage disposition; but this circumstance seems to us only to aggravate his guilt. There are some unhappy men constitutionally prone to the darker passions, men all whose blood is gall, and to whom bitter words and harsh actions are as natural as snarling and biting to a ferocious dog. To come into the world with this wretched mental disease is a greater calamity than to be born blind or deaf. A man who, having such a temper, keeps it in subjection, and constrains himself to behave habitually with justice and humanity towards those who are in his power, seems to us worthy of the highest admiration. There have been instances of this self-command; and they are

among the most signal triumphs of philosophy and religion.
On the other hand, a man who, having been blessed by nature
with a bland disposition, gradually brings himself to inflict
misery on his fellow-creatures with indifference, with satisfaction, and at length with a hideous rapture, deserves to be regarded as a portent of wickedness; and such a man was Barère.
The history of his downward progress is full of instruction.
Weakness, cowardice, and fickleness were born with him; the
best quality which he received from nature was a good temper.
These, it is true, are not very promising materials; yet, out of
materials as unpromising, high sentiments of piety and of honour
have sometimes made martyrs and heroes. Rigid principles
often do for feeble minds what stays do for feeble bodies. But
Barère had no principles at all. His character was equally
destitute of natural and of acquired strength. Neither in the
commerce of life, nor in books, did we ever become acquainted
with any mind so unstable, so utterly destitute of tone, so
incapable of independent thought and earnest preference, so
ready to take impressions and so ready to lose them. He resembled those creepers which must lean on something, and
which, as soon as their prop is removed, fall down in utter helplessness. He could no more stand up, erect and self-supported,
in any cause, than the ivy can rear itself like the oak, or the
wild vine shoot to heaven like the cedar of Lebanon. It is
barely possible that, under good guidance and in favourable circumstances, such a man might have slipped through life without
discredit. But the unseaworthy craft, which even in still water
would have been in danger of going down from its own rotten-
ness, was launched on a raging ocean, amidst a storm in which
a whole armada of gallant ships was cast away. The weakest
and most servile of human beings found himself on a sudden an
actor in a Revolution which convulsed the whole civilised world.
At first he fell under the influence of humane and moderate
men, and talked the language of humanity and moderation.
But he soon found himself surrounded by fierce and resolute
spirits, scared by no danger and restrained by no scruple. He
had to choose whether he would be their victim or their accom-
plice. His choice was soon made. He tasted blood, and felt
no loathing; he tasted it again, and liked it well. Cruelty became with him, first a habit, then a passion, at last a madness.
So complete and rapid was the degeneracy of his nature, that
within a very few months after the time when he had passed for
a good-natured man, he had brought himself to look on the

despair and misery of his fellow-creatures with a glee resembling that of the fiends whom Dante saw watching the pool of seething pitch in Malebolge. He had many associates in guilt; but he distinguished himself from them all by the Bacchanalian exultation which he seemed to feel in the work of death. He was drunk with innocent and noble blood, laughed and shouted as he butchered, and howled strange songs and reeled in strange dances amidst the carnage. Then came a sudden and violent turn of fortune. The miserable man was hurled down from the height of power to hopeless ruin and infamy. The shock sobered him at once. The fumes of his horrible intoxication passed away. But he was now so irrecoverably depraved that the discipline of adversity only drove him further into wickedness. Ferocious vices, of which he had never been suspected, had been developed in him by power. Another class of vices, less hateful perhaps, but more despicable, was now developed in him by poverty and disgrace. Having appalled the whole world by great crimes perpetrated under the pretence of zeal for liberty, he became the meanest of all the tools of despotism. It is not easy to settle the order of precedence among his vices, but we are inclined to think that his baseness was, on the whole, a rarer and more marvellous thing than his cruelty.

This is the view which we have long taken of Barère's character; but, till we read these Memoirs, we held our opinion with the diffidence which becomes a judge who has only heard one side. The case seemed strong, and in parts unanswerable: yet we did not know what the accused party might have to say for himself; and, not being much inclined to take our fellow-creatures either for angels of light or for angels of darkness, we could not but feel some suspicion that his offences had been exaggerated. That suspicion is now at an end. The vindication is before us. It occupies four volumes. It was the work of forty years. It would be absurd to suppose that it does not refute every serious charge which admitted of refutation. How many serious charges, then, are here refuted? Not a single one. Most of the imputations which have been thrown on Barère he does not even notice. In such cases, of course, judgment must go against him by default. The fact is, that nothing can be more meagre and uninteresting than his account of the great public transactions in which he was engaged. He gives us hardly a word of new information respecting the proceedings of the Committee of Public Safety; and, by way of compensation, tells us long stories about things which happened before he emerged from

obscurity, and after he had again sunk into it.   Nor is this the
worst.   As soon as he ceases to write trifles, he begins to write
lies; and such lies!   A man who has never been within the
tropics does not know what a thunderstorm means; a man who
has never looked on Niagara has but a faint idea of a cataract;
and he who has not read Barère's Memoirs may be said not
to know what it is to lie.   Among the numerous classes which
make up the great genus *Mendacium*, the *Mendacium Vas-
conicum*, or Gascon lie, has, during some centuries, been highly
esteemed as peculiarly circumstantial and peculiarly impudent;
and, among the *Mendacia Vasconica*, the *Mendacium Barerianum*
is, without doubt, the finest species.   It is indeed a superb
variety, and quite throws into the shade some *Mendacia* which
we were used to regard with admiration.   The *Mendacium
Wraxallianum*, for example, though by no means to be despised,
will not sustain the comparison for a moment.   Seriously, we
think that M. Hippolyte Carnot is much to blame in this matter.
We can hardly suppose him to be worse read than ourselves in
the history of the Convention, a history which must interest
him deeply, not only as a Frenchman, but also as a son.   He
must, therefore, be perfectly aware that many of the most important statements which these volumes contain are falsehoods,
such as Corneille's Dorante, or Molière's Scapin, or Colin d'Harle-
ville's Monsieur de Crac would have been ashamed to utter.
We are far, indeed, from holding M. Hippolyte Carnot answerable
for Barère's want of veracity; but M. Hippolyte Carnot has
arranged these Memoirs, has introduced them to the world by
a laudatory preface, has described them as documents of great
historical value, and has illustrated them by notes.   We cannot
but think that, by acting thus, he contracted some obligations
of which he does not seem to have been at all aware; and that
he ought not to have suffered any monstrous fiction to go forth
under the sanction of his name, without adding a line at the
foot of the page for the purpose of cautioning the reader.

We will content ourselves at present with pointing out two
instances of Barère's wilful and deliberate mendacity; namely,
his account of the death of Marie Antoinette, and his account
of the death of the Girondists.   His account of the death of
Marie Antoinette is as follows: "Robespierre in his turn proposed that the members of the Capet family should be banished,
and that Marie Antoinette should be brought to trial before the
Revolutionary Tribunal.   He would have been better employed
in concerting military measures which might have repaired our

disasters in Belgium, and might have arrested the progress of the enemies of the Revolution in the west."—(Vol. ii. p. 312.)

Now, it is notorious that Marie Antoinette was sent before the Revolutionary Tribunal, not at Robespierre's instance, but in direct opposition to Robespierre's wishes. We will cite a single authority, which is quite decisive. Bonaparte, who had no conceivable motive to disguise the truth, who had the best opportunities of knowing the truth, and who, after his marriage with the Archduchess, naturally felt an interest in the fate of his wife's kinswomen, distinctly affirmed that Robespierre opposed the trying of the Queen.[1] Who, then, was the person who really did propose that the Capet family should be banished, and that Marie Antoinette should be tried? Full information will be found in the *Moniteur*.[2] From that valuable record it appears that, on the first of August 1793, an orator, deputed by the Committee of Public Safety, addressed the Convention in a long and elaborate discourse. He asked, in passionate language how it happened that the enemies of the Republic still continued to hope for success. " Is it," he cried, " because we have too long forgotten the crimes of the Austrian woman? Is it because we have shown so strange an indulgence to the race of our ancient tyrants? It is time that this unwise apathy should cease; it is time to extirpate from the soil of the Republic the last roots of royalty. As for the children of Louis the conspirator, they are hostages for the Republic. The charge of their maintenance shall be reduced to what is necessary for the food and keep of two individuals. The public treasure shall no longer be lavished on creatures who have too long been considered as privileged. But behind them lurks a woman who has been the cause of all the disasters of France, and whose share in every project adverse to the revolution has long been known. National justice claims its rights over her. It is to the tribunal appointed for the trial of conspirators that she ought to be sent. It is only by striking the Austrian woman that you can make Francis and George, Charles and William, sensible of the crimes which their ministers and their armies have committed." The speaker concluded by moving that Marie Antoinette should be brought to judgment, and should, for that end, be forthwith transferred to the Conciergerie; and that all the members of the house of Capet, with the exception of those who were under the sword of the law, and of the two

---

[1] O'Meara's *Voice from St. Helena*, ii. 170.
[2] *Moniteur*, 2nd, 7th, and 9th of August 1793.

children of Louis, should be banished from the French territory. The motion was carried without debate.

Now, who was the person who made this speech and this motion? It was Barère himself. It is clear, then, that Barère attributed his own mean insolence and barbarity to one who, whatever his crimes may have been, was in this matter innocent. The only question remaining is, whether Barère was misled by his memory, or wrote a deliberate falsehood.

We are convinced that he wrote a deliberate falsehood. His memory is described by his editors as remarkably good, and must have been bad indeed if he could not remember such a fact as this. It is true that the number of murders in which he subsequently bore a part was so great that he might well confound one with another, that he might well forget what part of the daily hecatomb was consigned to death by himself, and what part by his colleagues. But two circumstances make it quite incredible that the share which he took in the death of Marie Antoinette should have escaped his recollection. She was one of his earliest victims. She was one of his most illustrious victims. The most hardened assassin remembers the first time that he shed blood; and the widow of Louis was no ordinary sufferer. If the question had been about some milliner, butchered for hiding in her garret her brother who had let drop a word against the Jacobin Club—if the question had been about some old nun, dragged to death for having mumbled what were called fanatical words over her beads—Barère's memory might well have deceived him. It would be as unreasonable to expect him to remember all the wretches whom he slew as all the pinches of snuff that he took. But, though Barère murdered many hundreds of human beings, he murdered only one Queen. That he, a small country lawyer, who, a few years before, would have thought himself honoured by a glance or a word from the daughter of so many Cæsars, should call her the Austrian woman, should send her from jail to jail, should deliver her over to the executioner, was surely a great event in his life. Whether he had reason to be proud of it or ashamed of it, is a question on which we may perhaps differ from his editors; but they will admit, we think, that he could not have forgotten it.

We, therefore, confidently charge Barère with having written a deliberate falsehood; and we have no hesitation in saying that we never, in the course of any historical researches that we have happened to make, fell in with a falsehood so audacious, except only the falsehood which we are about to expose.

Of the proceeding against the Girondists, Barère speaks with just severity. He calls it an atrocious injustice perpetrated against the legislators of the republic. He complains that distinguished deputies, who ought to have been readmitted to their seats in the Convention, were sent to the scaffold as conspirators. The day, he exclaims, was a day of mourning for France. It mutilated the national representation; it weakened the sacred principle, that the delegates of the people were inviolable. He protests that he had no share in the guilt. "I have had," he says, "the patience to go through the *Moniteur*, extracting all the charges brought against deputies, and all the decrees for arresting and impeaching deputies. Nowhere will you find my name. I never brought a charge against any of my colleagues, or made a report against any, or drew up an impeachment against any."[1]

Now, we affirm that this is a lie. We affirm that Barère himself took the lead in the proceedings of the Convention against the Girondists. We affirm that he, on the twenty-eighth of July 1793, proposed a decree for bringing nine Girondist deputies to trial, and for putting to death sixteen other Girondist deputies without any trial at all. We affirm that, when the accused deputies had been brought to trial, and when some apprehension arose that their eloquence might produce an effect even on the Revolutionary Tribunal, Barère did, on the 8th of Brumaire, second a motion for a decree authorising the tribunal to decide without hearing out the defence; and, for the truth of every one of these things so affirmed by us, we appeal to the very *Moniteur* to which Barère has dared to appeal.[2]

What M. Hippolyte Carnot, knowing, as he must know, that this book contains such falsehoods as those which we have exposed, can have meant, when he described it as a valuable addition to our stock of historical information, passes our comprehension. When a man is not ashamed to tell lies about events which took place before hundreds of witnesses, and which are recorded in well-known and accessible books, what credit can we give to his account of things done in corners? No historian who does not wish to be laughed at will ever cite the unsupported authority of Barère as sufficient to prove any fact whatever. The only thing, as far as we can see, on which these volumes throw any light, is the exceeding baseness of the author.

---

[1] Vol. ii. 407.

[2] *Moniteur*, 31st of July 1793, and Nonidi, first Decade of Brumaire, in the year 2.

So much for the veracity of the Memoirs.   In a literary point of view, they are beneath criticism.   They are as shallow, flippant, and affected, as Barère's oratory in the Convention. They are also, what his oratory in the Convention was not, utterly insipid.   In fact, they are the mere dregs and rinsings of a bottle of which even the first froth was but of very questionable flavour.

We will now try to present our readers with a sketch of this man's life.   We shall, of course, make very sparing use indeed of his own Memoirs; and never without distrust, except where they are confirmed by other evidence.

Bertrand Barère was born in the year 1755, at Tarbes in Gascony.   His father was the proprietor of a small estate at Vieuzac, in the beautiful vale of Argelès.   Bertrand always loved to be called Barère de Vieuzac, and flattered himself with the hope that, by the help of this feudal addition to his name, he might pass for a gentleman.   He was educated for the bar at Toulouse, the seat of one of the most celebrated parliaments of the kingdom, practised as an advocate with considerable success, and wrote some small pieces, which he sent to the principal literary societies in the south of France.   Among provincial towns, Toulouse seems to have been remarkably rich in indifferent versifiers and critics.   It gloried especially in one venerable institution, called the Academy of the Floral Games.   This body held every year a grand meeting which was a subject of intense interest to the whole city, and at which flowers of gold and silver were given as prizes for odes, for idyls, and for something that was called eloquence.   These bounties produced of course the ordinary effect of bounties, and turned people who might have been thriving attorneys and useful apothecaries into small wits and bad poets.   Barère does not appear to have been so lucky as to obtain any of these precious flowers; but one of his performances was mentioned with honour.   At Montauban he was more fortunate. The academy of that town bestowed on him several prizes, one for a panegyric on Louis the Twelfth, in which the blessings of monarchy and the loyalty of the French nation were set forth; and another for a panegyric on poor Franc de Pompignan, in which, as may easily be supposed, the philosophy of the eighteenth century was sharply assailed.   Then Barère found an old stone inscribed with three Latin words, and wrote a dissertation upon it, which procured him a seat in a learned Assembly, called the Toulouse Academy of Sciences, Inscriptions, and Polite Literature.   At length the doors of the Academy of

the Floral Games were opened to so much merit.   Barère, in his
thirty-third year, took his seat as one of that illustrious brotherhood, and made an inaugural oration which was greatly admired.
He apologises for recounting these triumphs of his youthful
genius.   We own that we cannot blame him for dwelling long on
the least disgraceful portion of his existence.   To send in declamations for prizes offered by provincial academies is indeed no
very useful or dignified employment for a bearded man; but it
would have been well if Barère had always been so employed.

In 1785 he married a young lady of considerable fortune.
Whether she was in other respects qualified to make a home
happy, is a point respecting which we are imperfectly informed.
In a little work, entitled *Melancholy Pages*, which was written
in 1797, Barère avers that his marriage was one of mere conveni-
ence, that at the altar his heart was heavy with sorrowful fore-
bodings, that he turned pale as he pronounced the solemn " Yes,"
that unbidden tears rolled down his cheeks, that his mother
shared his presentiment, and that the evil omen was accomplished.
" My marriage," he says, " was one of the most unhappy of
marriages."   So romantic a tale, told by so noted a liar, did not
command our belief.   We were, therefore, not much surprised to
discover that, in his Memoirs, he calls his wife a most amiable
woman, and declares that, after he had been united to her six
years, he found her as amiable as ever.   He complains, indeed,
that she was too much attached to royalty and to the old superstition; but he assures us that his respect for her virtues induced
him to tolerate her prejudices.   Now Barère, at the time of his
marriage, was himself a Royalist and a Catholic.   He had gained
one prize by flattering the Throne, and another by defending the
Church.   It is hardly possible, therefore, that disputes about
politics or religion should have embittered his domestic life till
some time after he became a husband.   Our own guess is, that
his wife was, as he says, a virtuous and amiable woman, and that
she did her best to make him happy during some years.   It
seems clear that, when circumstances developed the latent
atrocity of his character, she could no longer endure him, refused
to see him, and sent back his letters unopened.   Then it was, we
imagine, that he invented the fable about his distress on his
wedding day.

In 1788 Barère paid his first visit to Paris, attended reviews,
heard Laharpe at the Lycæum, and Condorcet at the Academy
of Sciences, stared at the envoys of Tippoo Sahib, saw the Royal
Family dine at Versailles, and kept a journal in which he noted

down adventures and speculations. Some parts of this journal are printed in the first volume of the work before us, and are certainly most characteristic. The worst vices of the writer had not yet shown themselves; but the weakness which was the parent of those vices appears in every line. His levity, his inconsistency, his servility, were already what they were to the last. All his opinions, all his feelings, spin round and round like a weathercock in a whirlwind. Nay, the very impressions which he receives through his senses are not the same two days together. He sees Louis the Sixteenth, and is so much blinded by loyalty as to find his Majesty handsome. " I fixed my eyes," he says, " with a lively curiosity on his fine countenance, which I thought open and noble." The next time that the king appears all is altered. His Majesty's eyes are without the smallest expression; he has a vulgar laugh which seems like idiocy, an ignoble figure, an awkward gait, and the look of a big boy ill brought up. It is the same with more important questions. Barère is for the parliaments on the Monday and against the parliaments on the Tuesday, for feudality in the morning and against feudality in the afternoon. One day he admires the English constitution; then he shudders to think that, in the struggles by which that constitution had been obtained, the barbarous islanders had murdered a king, and gives the preference to the constitution of Bearn. Bearn, he says, has a sublime constitution, a beautiful constitution. There the nobility and clergy meet in one house, and the Commons in another. If the houses differ, the King has the casting vote. A few weeks later we find him raving against the principles of this sublime and beautiful constitution. To admit deputies of the nobility and clergy into the legislature is, he says, neither more nor less than to admit enemies of the nation into the legislature.

In this state of mind, without one settled purpose or opinion, the slave of the last word, royalist, aristocrat, democrat, according to the prevailing sentiment of the coffee-house or drawing-room into which he had just looked, did Barère enter into public life. The States-General had been summoned. Barère went down to his own province, was there elected one of the representatives of the Third Estate, and returned to Paris in May 1789.

A great crisis, often predicted, had at last arrived. In no country, we conceive, have intellectual freedom and political servitude existed together so long as in France, during the seventy or eighty years which preceded the last convocation of the Orders. Ancient abuses and new theories flourished in equal vigour side by side. The people, having no constitutional means of checking even the most flagitious misgovernment, were indemnified for oppression by being suffered to luxuriate in anarchical speculation, and to deny or ridicule every principle on which the institutions of the State reposed. Neither those who attribute the downfall of the old French institutions to the public grievances, nor those who attribute it to the doctrines of the philosophers, appear to us to have taken into their view more than one half of the subject. Grievances as heavy have often been endured without producing a revolution; doctrines as bold have often been propounded without producing a revolution. The question, whether the French nation was alienated from its old polity by the follies and vices of the Viziers and Sultanas who pillaged and disgraced it, or by the writings of Voltaire and Rousseau, seems to us as idle as the question whether it was fire or gunpowder that blew up the mills at Hounslow. Neither cause would have sufficed alone. Tyranny may last through ages where discussion is suppressed. Discussion may safely be left free by rulers who act on popular principles. But combine a press like that of London with a government like that of St. Petersburg; and the inevitable effect will be an explosion that will shake the world. So it was in France. Despotism and Licence, mingling in unblessed union, engendered that mighty Revolution in which the lineaments of both parents were strangely blended. The long gestation was accomplished; and Europe saw, with mixed hope and terror, that agonising travail and that portentous birth.

Among the crowd of legislators which at this conjuncture poured from all the provinces of France into Paris, Barère made no contemptible figure. The opinions which he for the moment professed were popular, yet not extreme. His character was fair; his personal advantages are said to have been considerable; and, from the portrait which is prefixed to these Memoirs, and which represents him as he appeared in the Convention, we should judge that his features must have been strikingly handsome, though we think that we can read in them cowardice and meanness very legibly written by the hand of God. His conversation was lively and easy; his manners remarkably good for a country lawyer. Women of rank and wit said that he was the only man who, on his first arrival from a remote province, had that indescribable air which it was supposed that Paris alone could give. His eloquence, indeed, was by no means so much admired in the capital as it had been by the ingenious academicians of Montauban and Toulouse. His style was thought very bad; and very bad, if a foreigner may venture to judge, it continued to the last. It would, however, be unjust to deny that he had some talents for speaking and writing. His rhetoric, though deformed by every imaginable fault of taste, from bombast down to buffoonery, was not wholly without force and vivacity. He had also one quality which, in active life, often gives fourth-rate men an advantage over first-rate men. Whatever he could do, he could do without effort, at any moment, in any abundance, and on any side of any question. There was, indeed, a perfect harmony between his moral character and his intellectual character. His temper was that of a slave; his abilities were exactly those which qualified him to be a useful slave. Of thinking to purpose, he was utterly incapable; but he had wonderful readiness in arranging and expressing thoughts furnished by others.

In the National Assembly he had no opportunity of displaying the full extent either of his talents or of his vices. He was indeed eclipsed by much abler men. He went, as was his habit, with the stream, spoke occasionally with some success, and edited a journal called the *Point du Jour*, in which the debates of the Assembly were reported.

He at first ranked by no means among the violent reformers. He was not friendly to that new division of the French territory which was among the most important changes introduced by the Revolution, and was especially unwilling to see his native province dismembered. He was entrusted with the task of framing Reports on the Woods and Forests. Louis was exceedingly anxious about this matter; for his majesty was a keen sportsman, and would much rather have gone without the Veto, or the prerogative of making peace and war, than without his hunting and shooting. Gentlemen of the royal household were sent to Barère, in order to intercede for the deer and pheasants. Nor was this intercession unsuccessful. The reports were so drawn that Barère was afterwards accused of having dishonestly sacrificed the interests of the public to the tastes of the court. To one of these reports he had the inconceivable folly and bad taste to prefix a punning motto from Virgil, fit only for such essays as he had been in the habit of composing for the Floral Games—

" Si canimus sylvas, sylvæ sint Consule dignæ."

This literary foppery was one of the few things in which he was consistent. Royalist or Girondist, Jacobin or Imperialist, he was always a Trissotin.

As the monarchical party became weaker and weaker, Barère gradually estranged himself more and more from it, and drew closer and closer to the republicans. It would seem that, during this transition, he was for a time closely connected with the family of Orleans. It is certain that he was entrusted with the guardianship of the celebrated Pamela, afterwards Lady Edward Fitzgerald; and it was asserted that he received during some years a pension of twelve thousand francs from the Palais Royal.

At the end of September 1791, the labours of the National Assembly terminated, and those of the first and last Legislative Assembly commenced.

It had been enacted that no member of the National Assembly should sit in the Legislative Assembly; a preposterous and mischievous regulation, to which the disasters which followed must in part be ascribed. In England, what would be thought of a Parliament which did not contain one single person who had ever sat in parliament before? Yet it may safely be affirmed that the number of Englishmen who, never having taken any share in public affairs, are yet well qualified, by knowledge and observation, to be members of the legislature is at least a hundred times as great as the number of Frenchmen who were so qualified in 1791. How, indeed, should it have been otherwise? In England, centuries of representative government have made all educated people in some measure statesmen. In France the National Assembly had probably been composed of as good materials as were then to be found. It had undoubtedly removed a vast mass of abuses; some of its members had read and thought much about theories of government; and others had shown great oratorical talents. But that kind of skill which is required for the constructing, launching, and steering of a polity was lamentably wanting; for it is a kind of skill to which practice contributes more than books. Books are indeed useful to the politician, as they are useful to the navigator and to the surgeon. But the real navigator is formed on the waves; the real surgeon is formed at bedsides; and the conflicts of free states are the real school of constitutional statesmen. The National Assembly had, however, now served an apprenticeship of two laborious and eventful years. It had, indeed, by no means finished its education; but it was no longer, as on the day when it met, altogether rude to political functions. Its later proceedings contain abundant proof that the members had profited by their experience. Beyond all doubt there was not in France any equal number of persons possessing in an equal degree the qualities necessary for the judicious direction of public affairs; and, just at this moment, these legislators, misled by a childish wish to display their own disinterestedness, deserted the duties which they had half learned, and which nobody else had learned at all, and left their hall to a second crowd of novices, who had still to master the first rudiments of political business. When Barère wrote his Memoirs, the absurdity of this self-denying ordinance had been proved by events, and was, we believe, acknowledged by all parties. He accordingly, with his usual mendacity, speaks of it in terms implying that he had opposed it. There was, he tells us, no good citizen who did not regret this fatal vote. Nay, all wise men, he says, wished the National Assembly to continue its sittings as the first Legislative Assembly. But no attention was paid to the wishes of the enlightened friends of liberty; and the generous but fatal suicide was perpetrated. Now the fact is, that Barère, far from opposing this ill-advised measure, was one of those who most eagerly supported it; that he described it from the tribune as wise and magnanimous; that he assigned, as his reasons for taking this view, some of those phrases in which orators of his class delight, and which, on all men who have the smallest insight into politics, produce an effect very similar to that of ipecacuanha. "Those," he said, "who have framed a constitution for their country are, so to speak, out of the pale of that social state of which they are the authors; for creative power is not in the same sphere with that which it has created."

M. Hippolyte Carnot has noticed this untruth, and attributes it to mere forgetfulness. We leave it to him to reconcile his very charitable supposition with what he elsewhere says of the remarkable excellence of Barère's memory.

Many members of the National Assembly were indemnified for the sacrifice of legislative power by appointments in various departments of the public service. Of these fortunate persons Barère was one. A high Court of Appeal had just been instituted. This court was to sit at Paris: but its jurisdiction was to extend over the whole realm; and the departments were to choose the judges. Barère was nominated by the department of the Upper Pyrenees, and took his seat in the Palace of Justice. He asserts, and our readers may, if they choose, believe, that it was about this time in contemplation to make him Minister of the Interior, and that in order to avoid so grave a responsibility,

he obtained permission to pay a visit to his native place.   It is
certain that he left Paris early in the year 1792, and passed some
months in the south of France.

In the meantime, it became clear that the constitution of 1791
would not work.   It was, indeed, not to be expected that a constitution new both in its principles and its details would at first
work easily.   Had the chief magistrate enjoyed the entire confidence of the people, had he performed his part with the utmost
zeal, fidelity, and ability—had the representative body included
all the wisest statesmen of France, the difficulties might still have
been found insuperable.   But, in fact, the experiment was made
under every disadvantage.   The King, very naturally, hated the
constitution.   In the Legislative Assembly were men of genius
and men of good intentions, but not a single man of experience.
Nevertheless, if France had been suffered to settle her own affairs
without foreign interference, it is possible that the calamities
which followed might have been averted.   The King, who, with
many good qualities, was sluggish and sensual, might have found
compensation for his lost prerogatives in his immense civil list,
in his palaces and hunting grounds, in soups, Perigord pies, and
champagne.   The people, finding themselves secure in the enjoyment of the valuable reforms which the National Assembly had,
in the midst of all its errors, effected, would not have been easily
excited by demagogues to acts of atrocity; or, if acts of atrocity
had been committed, those acts would probably have produced
a speedy and violent reaction.   Had tolerable quiet been preserved during a few years, the constitution of 1791 might perhaps
have taken root, might have gradually acquired the strength
which time alone can give, and might, with some modifications
which were undoubtedly needed, have lasted down to the present
time.   The European coalition against the Revolution extinguished all hope of such a result.   The deposition of Louis was,
in our opinion, the necessary consequence of that coalition.   The
question was now no longer, whether the King should have an
absolute Veto or a suspensive Veto, whether there should be one
chamber or two chambers, whether the members of the representative body should be re-eligible or not; but whether France
should belong to the French.   The independence of the nation,
the integrity of the territory, were at stake; and we must say
plainly that we cordially approve of the conduct of those Frenchmen who, at that conjuncture, resolved, like our own Blake, to
play the men for their country, under whatever form of government their country might fall.

It seems to us clear that the war with the Continental coalition was, on the side of France, at first a defensive war, and therefore a just war. It was not a war for small objects, or against despicable enemies. On the event were staked all the dearest interests of the French people. Foremost among the threatening powers appeared two great and martial monarchies, either of which, situated as France then was, might be regarded as a formidable assailant. It is evident that, under such circumstances, the French could not, without extreme imprudence, entrust the supreme administration of their affairs to any person whose attachment to the national cause admitted of doubt. Now, it is no reproach to the memory of Louis to say that he was not attached to the national cause. Had he been so, he would have been something more than man. He had held absolute power, not by usurpation, but by the accident of birth, and by the ancient polity of the kingdom. That power he had, on the whole, used with lenity. He had meant well by his people. He had been willing to make to them, of his own mere motion, concessions such as scarcely any other sovereign has ever made except under duress. He had paid the penalty of faults not his own, of the haughtiness and ambition of some of his predecessors, of the dissoluteness and baseness of others. He had been vanquished, taken captive, led in triumph, put in ward. He had escaped; he had been caught; he had been dragged back like a runaway galley-slave to the oar. He was still a state prisoner. His quiet was broken by daily affronts and lampoons. Accustomed from the cradle to be treated with profound reverence, he was now forced to command his feelings, while men who, a few months before, had been hackney writers or country attorneys, sat in his presence with covered heads, and addressed him in the easy tone of equality. Conscious of fair intentions, sensible of hard usage, he doubtless detested the Revolution; and, while charged with the conduct of the war against the confederates, pined in secret for the sight of the German eagles and the sound of the German drums. We do not blame him for this. But can we blame those who, being resolved to defend the work of the National Assembly against the interference of strangers, were not disposed to have him at their head in the fearful struggle which was approaching? We have nothing to say in defence or extenuation of the insolence, injustice, and cruelty with which, after the victory of the republicans, he and his family were treated. But this we say, that the French had only one alternative, to deprive him of the powers of first magistrate, or to ground their arms and submit patiently to foreign dictation. The events of the tenth of August sprang inevitably from the league of Pilnitz. The King's palace was stormed; his guards were slaughtered. He was suspended from his regal functions; and the Legislative Assembly invited the nation to elect an extraordinary Convention, with the full powers which the conjuncture required. To this Convention the members of the National Assembly were eligible; and Barère was chosen by his own department.

The Convention met on the 21st of September 1792. The first proceedings were unanimous. Royalty was abolished by acclamation. No objections were made to this great change; and no reasons were assigned for it. For certainly we cannot honour with the name of reasons such apophthegms, as that kings are in the moral world what monsters are in the physical world; and that the history of kings is the martyrology of nations. But, though the discussion was worthy only of a debating club of schoolboys, the resolution to which the Convention came seems to have been that which sound policy dictated. In saying this, we do not mean to express an opinion that a republic is, either in the abstract the best form of government, or is, under ordinary circumstances, the form of government best suited to the French people. Our own opinion is, that the best governments which have ever existed in the world have been limited monarchies; and that France, in particular, has never enjoyed so much prosperity and freedom as under a limited monarchy. Nevertheless, we approve of the vote of the Convention which abolished kingly government. The interference of foreign powers had brought on a crisis which made extraordinary measures necessary. Hereditary monarchy may be, and we believe that it is, a very useful institution in a country like France. And masts are very useful parts of a ship. But, if the ship is on her beam-ends, it may be necessary to cut the masts away. When once she has righted, she may come safe into port under jury rigging, and there be completely repaired. But, in the meantime, she must be hacked with unsparing hand, lest that which, under ordinary circumstances, is an essential part of her fabric should, in her extreme distress, sink her to the bottom. Even so there are political emergencies in which it is necessary that governments should be mutilated of their fair proportions for a time, lest they be cast away for ever; and with such an emergency the Convention had to deal. The first object of a good Frenchman should have been to save

France from the fate of Poland. The first requisite of a government was entire devotion to the national cause. That requisite was wanting in Louis; and such a want, at such a moment, could not be supplied by any public or private virtues. If the king were set aside, the abolition of kingship necessarily followed. In the state in which the public mind then was, it would have been idle to think of doing what our ancestors did in 1688, and what the French Chamber of Deputies did in 1830. Such an attempt would have failed amidst universal derision and execration. It would have disgusted all zealous men of all opinions; and there were then few men who were not zealous. Parties fatigued by long conflict, and instructed by the severe discipline of that school in which alone mankind will learn, are disposed to listen to the voice of a mediator. But when they are in their first heady youth, devoid of experience, fresh for exertion, flushed with hope, burning with animosity, they agree only in spurning out of their way the daysman who strives to take his stand between them and to lay his hand upon them both. Such was in 1792 the state of France. On one side was the great name of the heir of Hugh Capet, the thirty-third king of the third race; on the other side was the great name of the republic. There was no rallying point save these two. It was necessary to make a choice; and those, in our opinion, judged well who, waiving for the moment all subordinate questions, preferred independence to subjugation, and the natal soil to the emigrant camp.

As to the abolition of royalty, and as to the vigorous prosecution of the war, the whole Convention seemed to be united as one man. But a deep and broad gulf separated the representative body into two great parties.

On one side were those statesmen who are called, from the name of the department which some of them represented, the Girondists, and, from the name of one of their most conspicuous leaders, the Brissotines. In activity and practical ability, Brissot and Gensonné were the most conspicuous among them. In parliamentary eloquence, no Frenchman of that time can be considered as equal to Vergniaud. In a foreign country, and after the lapse of half a century, some parts of his speeches are still read with mournful admiration. No man, we are inclined to believe, ever rose so rapidly to such a height of oratorical excellence. His whole public life lasted barely two years. This is a circumstance which distinguishes him from our own greatest speakers, Fox, Burke, Pitt, Sheridan, Windham, Canning.

Which of these celebrated men would now be remembered as an orator, if he had died two years after he first took his seat in the House of Commons? Condorcet brought to the Girondist party a different kind of strength. The public regarded him with justice as an eminent mathematician, and, with less reason, as a great master of ethical and political science; the philosophers considered him as their chief, as the rightful heir, by intellectual descent and by solemn adoption, of their deceased sovereign D'Alembert. In the same ranks were found Guadet, Isnard, Barbaroux, Buzot, Louvet, too well known as the author of a very ingenious and very licentious romance, and more honourably distinguished by the generosity with which he pleaded for the unfortunate, and by the intrepidity with which he defied the wicked and powerful. Two persons whose talents were not brilliant, but who enjoyed a high reputation for probity and public spirit, Pétion and Roland, lent the whole weight of their names to the Girondist connection. The wife of Roland brought to the deliberations of her husband's friends masculine courage and force of thought, tempered by womanly grace and vivacity. Nor was the splendour of a great military reputation wanting to this celebrated party. Dumourier, then victorious over the foreign invaders, and at the height of popular favour, must be reckoned among the allies of the Gironde.

The errors of the Brissotines were undoubtedly neither few nor small; but, when we fairly compare their conduct with the conduct of any other party which acted or suffered during the French Revolution, we are forced to admit their superiority in every quality except that single quality which in such times prevails over every other, decision. They were zealous for the great social reform which had been effected by the National Assembly; and they were right. For, though that reform was, in some respects, carried too far, it was a blessing well worth even the fearful price which has been paid for it. They were resolved to maintain the independence of their country against foreign invaders; and they were right. For the heaviest of all yokes is the yoke of the stranger. They thought that, if Louis remained at their head, they could not carry on with the requisite energy the conflict against the European coalition. They therefore concurred in establishing a republican government; and here, again, they were right. For, in that struggle for life and death, it would have been madness to trust a hostile or even a half hearted leader.

Thus far they went along with the revolutionary movement.

At this point they stopped; and, in our judgment, they were right in stopping, as they had been right in moving. For great ends, and under extraordinary circumstances, they had concurred in measures which, together with much good, had necessarily produced much evil; which had unsettled the public mind; which had taken away from government the sanction of prescription; which had loosened the very foundations of property and law. They thought that it was now their duty to prop what it had recently been their duty to batter. They loved liberty, but liberty associated with order, with justice, with mercy, and with civilisation. They were republicans; but they were desirous to adorn their republic with all that had given grace and dignity to the fallen monarchy. They hoped that the humanity, the courtesy, the taste, which had done much in old times to mitigate the slavery of France would now lend additional charms to her freedom. They saw with horror crimes exceeding in atrocity those which had disgraced the infuriated religious factions of the sixteenth century, perpetrated in the name of reason and philanthropy. They demanded, with eloquent vehemence, that the authors of the lawless massacre, which, just before the meeting of the Convention, had been committed in the prisons of Paris, should be brought to condign punishment. They treated with just contempt the pleas which have been set up for that great crime. They admitted that the public danger was pressing; but they denied that it justified a violation of those principles of morality on which all society rests. The independence and honour of France were indeed to be vindicated, but to be vindicated by triumphs and not by murders.

Opposed to the Girondists was a party which, having been long execrated throughout the civilised world, has of late—such is the ebb and flow of opinion—found not only apologists, but even eulogists. We are not disposed to deny that some members of the Mountain were sincere and public spirited men. But even the best of them, Carnot, for example, and Cambon, were far too unscrupulous as to the means which they employed for the purpose of attaining great ends. In the train of these enthusiasts followed a crowd, composed of all who, from sensual, sordid, or malignant motives, wished for a period of boundless licence.

When the Convention met, the majority was with the Girondists, and Barère was with the majority. On the King's trial, indeed, he quitted the party with which he ordinarily acted, voted with the Mountain, and spoke against the prisoner with a violence such as few members even of the Mountain showed.

The conduct of the leading Girondists on that occasion was little to their honour. Of cruelty, indeed, we fully acquit them; but it is impossible to acquit them of criminal irresolution and disingenuousness. They were far, indeed, from thirsting for the blood of Louis: on the contrary, they were most desirous to protect him. But they were afraid that, if they went straight forward to their object, the sincerity of their attachment to republican institutions would be suspected. They wished to save the King's life, and yet to obtain all the credit of having been regicides. Accordingly, they traced out for themselves a crooked course, by which they hoped to attain both their objects. They first voted the King guilty. They then voted for referring the question respecting his fate to the whole body of the people. Defeated in this attempt to rescue him, they reluctantly, and with ill-suppressed shame and concern, voted for the capital sentence. Then they made a last attempt in his favour, and voted for respiting the execution. These zigzag politics produced the effect which any man conversant with public affairs might have foreseen. The Girondists, instead of attaining both their ends, failed of both. The Mountain justly charged them with having attempted to save the King by underhand means. Their own consciences told them, with equal justice, that their hands had been dipped in the blood of the most inoffensive and most unfortunate of men. The direct path was here, as usual, the path not only of honour, but of safety. The principle on which the Girondists stood as a party was, that the season for revolutionary violence was over, and that the reign of law and order ought now to commence. But the proceeding against the King was clearly revolutionary in its nature. It was not in conformity with the laws. The only plea for it was, that all ordinary rules of jurisprudence and morality were suspended by the extreme public danger. This was the very plea which the Mountain urged in defence of the massacre of September, and to which, when so urged, the Girondists refused to listen. They therefore, by voting for the death of the King, conceded to the Mountain the chief point at issue between the two parties. Had they given a manful vote against the capital sentence, the regicides would have been in a minority. It is probable that there would have been an immediate appeal to force. The Girondists might have been victorious. In the worst event, they would have fallen with unblemished honour. Thus much is certain, that their boldness and honesty could not possibly have produced a worse effect than was actually produced by their timidity and their stratagems.

Barère, as we have said, sided with the Mountain on this occasion. He voted against the appeal to the people and against the respite. His demeanour and his language also were widely different from those of the Girondists. Their hearts were heavy, and their deportment was that of men oppressed by sorrow. It was Vergniaud's duty to proclaim the result of the roll-call. His face was pale, and he trembled with emotion, as in a low and broken voice he announced that Louis was condemned to death. Barère had not, it is true, yet attained to full perfection in the art of mingling jests and conceits with words of death; but he already gave promise of his future excellence in this high department of Jacobin oratory. He concluded his speech with a sentence worthy of his head and heart. " The tree of liberty," he said, " as an ancient author remarks, flourishes when it is watered with the blood of all classes of tyrants." M. Hippolyte Carnot has quoted this passage in order, as we suppose, to do honour to his hero. We wish that a note had been added to inform us from what ancient author Barère quoted. In the course of our own small reading among the Greek and Latin writers, we have not happened to fall in with trees of liberty and watering-pots full of blood; nor can we, such is our ignorance of classical antiquity, even imagine an Attic or Roman orator employing imagery of that sort. In plain words, when Barère talked about an ancient author, he was lying, as he generally was when he asserted any fact, great or small. Why he lied on this occasion we cannot guess, unless indeed it was to keep his hand in.

It is not improbable that, but for the one circumstance, Barère would, like most of those with whom he ordinarily acted, have voted for the appeal to the people and for the respite. But, just before the commencement of the trial, papers had been discovered which proved that, while a member of the National Assembly, he had been in communication with the Court respecting his Reports on the Woods and Forests. He was acquitted of all criminality by the Convention; but the fiercer Republicans considered him as a tool of the fallen monarch; and this reproach was long repeated in the journal of Marat, and in the speeches at the Jacobin club. It was natural that a man like Barère should, under such circumstances, try to distinguish himself among the crowd of regicides by peculiar ferocity. It was because he had been a royalist that he was one of the foremost in shedding blood.

The King was no more. The leading Girondists had, by their conduct towards him, lowered their character in the eyes both of friends and foes. They still, however, maintained the contest against the Mountain, called for vengeance on the assassins of September, and protested against the anarchical and sanguinary doctrines of Marat. For a time they seemed likely to prevail. As publicists and orators, they had no rivals in the Convention. They had with them, beyond all doubt, the great majority both of the deputies and of the French nation. These advantages, it should seem, ought to have decided the event of the struggle. But the opposite party had compensating advantages of a different kind. The chiefs of the Mountain, though not eminently distinguished by eloquence or knowledge, had great audacity, activity, and determination. The Convention and France were against them; but the mob of Paris, the clubs of Paris, and the municipal government of Paris, were on their side.

The policy of the Jacobins, in this situation, was to subject France to an aristocracy infinitely worse than that aristocracy which had emigrated with the Count of Artois—to an aristocracy not of birth, not of wealth, not of education, but of mere locality. They would not hear of privileged orders; but they wished to have a privileged city. That twenty-five millions of Frenchmen should be ruled by a hundred thousand gentlemen and clergymen was insufferable; but that twenty-five millions of Frenchmen should be ruled by a hundred thousand Parisians was as it should be. The qualification of a member of the new oligarchy was simply that he should live near the hall where the Convention met, and should be able to squeeze himself daily into the gallery during a debate, and now and then to attend with a pike for the purpose of blockading the doors. It was quite agreeable to the maxims of the Mountain that a score of draymen from Santerre's brewery, or of devils from Hébert's printing-house, should be permitted to drown the voices of men commissioned to speak the sense of such cities as Marseilles, Bordeaux, and Lyons; and that a rabble of half-naked porters from the Faubourg St. Antoine should have power to annul decrees for which the representatives of fifty or sixty departments had voted. It was necessary to find some pretext for so odious and absurd a tyranny. Such a pretext was found. To the old phrases of liberty and equality were added the sonorous watchwords, unity and indivisability. A new crime was in-

vented, and called by the name of federalism.   The object of
the Girondists, it was asserted, was to break up the great nation
into little independent commonwealths, bound together only by
a league like that which connects the Swiss Cantons or the
United States of America.   The great obstacle in the way of
this pernicious design was the influence of Paris.   To strengthen
the influence of Paris ought therefore to be the chief object of
every patriot.

The accusation brought against the leaders of the Girondist
party was a mere calumny.   They were undoubtedly desirous
to prevent the capital from domineering over the republic, and
would gladly have seen the Convention removed for a time to
some provincial town, or placed under the protection of a trusty
guard, which might have overawed the Parisian mob; but there
is not the slightest reason to suspect them of any design against
the unity of the state.   Barère, however, really was a federalist,
and, we are inclined to believe, the only federalist in the Convention.   As far as a man so unstable and servile can be said
to have felt any preference for any form of government, he felt
a preference for federal government.   He was born under the
Pyrenees; he was a Gascon of the Gascons, one of a people
strongly distinguished by intellectual and moral character, by
manners, by modes of speech, by accent, and by physiognomy,
from the French of the Seine and of the Loire; and he had
many of the peculiarities of the race to which he belonged.
When he first left his own province he had attained his thirty-
fourth year, and had acquired a high local reputation for eloquence and literature.   He had then visited Paris for the first
time.   He had found himself in a new world.   His feelings were
those of a banished man.   It is clear also that he had been by
no means without his share of the small disappointments and
humiliations so often experienced by men of letters who, elated
by provincial applause, venture to display their powers before
the fastidious critics of a capital.   On the other hand, whenever
he revisited the mountains among which he had been born, he
found himself an object of general admiration.   His dislike of
Paris, and his partiality to his native district, were therefore as
strong and durable as any sentiments of a mind like his could be.
He long continued to maintain that the ascendency of one great
city was the bane of France; that the superiority of taste and
intelligence which it was the fashion to ascribe to the inhabitants
of that city were wholly imaginary; and that the nation would
never enjoy a really good government till the Alsatian people,

the Breton people, the people of Bearn, the people of Provence, should have each an independent existence, and laws suited to its own tastes and habits. These communities he proposed to unite by a tie similar to that which binds together the grave Puritans of Connecticut and the dissolute slave-drivers of New Orleans. To Paris he was unwilling to grant even the rank which Washington holds in the United States. He thought it desirable that the congress of the French federation should have no fixed place of meeting, but should sit sometimes at Rouen, sometimes at Bordeaux, sometimes at his own Toulouse.

Animated by such feelings, he was, till the close of May 1793, a Girondist, if not an ultra-Girondist. He exclaimed against those impure and bloodthirsty men who wished to make the public danger a pretext for cruelty and rapine. " Peril," he said, " could be no excuse for crime. It is when the wind blows hard, and the waves run high, that the anchor is most needed; it is when a revolution is raging, that the great laws of morality are most necessary to the safety of a state." Of Marat he spoke with abhorrence and contempt; of the municipal authorities of Paris with just severity. He loudly complained that there were Frenchmen who paid to the Mountain that homage which was due to the Convention alone. When the establishment of the Revolutionary Tribunal was first proposed, he joined himself to Vergniaud and Buzot, who strongly objected to that odious measure. " It cannot be," exclaimed Barère, " that men really attached to liberty will imitate the most frightful excesses of despotism ! " He proved to the Convention, after his fashion, out of Sallust, that such arbitrary courts may indeed, for a time, be severe only on real criminals, but must inevitably degenerate into instruments of private cupidity and revenge. When, on the tenth of March, the worst part of the population of Paris made the first unsuccessful attempt to destroy the Girondists, Barère eagerly called for vigorous measures of repression and punishment. On the second of April, another attempt of the Jacobins of Paris to usurp supreme dominion over the republic was brought to the knowledge of the Convention; and again Barère spoke with warmth against the new tyranny which afflicted France, and declared that the people of the departments would never crouch beneath the tyranny of one ambitious city. He even proposed a resolution to the effect that the Convention would exert against the demagogues of the capital the same energy which had been exerted against the tyrant Louis. We

E

are assured that, in private as in public, he at this time uniformly spoke with strong aversion of the Mountain.

His apparent zeal for the cause of humanity and order had its reward. Early in April came the tidings of Dumourier's defection. This was a heavy blow to the Girondists. Dumourier was their general. His victories had thrown a lustre on the whole party; his army, it had been hoped, would, in the worst event, protect the deputies of the nation against the ragged pikemen of the garrets of Paris. He was now a deserter and an exile; and those who had lately placed their chief reliance on his support were compelled to join with their deadliest enemies in execrating his treason. At this perilous conjuncture, it was resolved to appoint a Committee of Public Safety, and to arm that committee with powers, small indeed when compared with those which it afterwards drew to itself, but still great and formidable. The moderate party, regarding Barère as a representative of their feelings and opinions, elected him a member. In his new situation he soon began to make himself useful. He brought to the deliberations of the Committee, not indeed the knowledge or the ability of a great statesman, but a tongue and a pen which, if others would only supply ideas, never paused for want of words. His mind was a mere organ of communication between other minds. It originated nothing; it retained nothing; but it transmitted everything. The post assigned to him by his colleagues was not really of the highest importance; but it was prominent, and drew the attention of all Europe. When a great measure was to be brought forward, when an account was to be rendered of an important event, he was generally the mouthpiece of the administration. He was therefore not unnaturally considered, by persons who lived at a distance from the seat of government, and above all by foreigners, who, while the war raged, knew France only from journals, as the head of that administration of which, in truth, he was only the secretary and the spokesman. The author of the History of Europe, in our own Annual Registers, appears to have been completely under this delusion.

The conflict between the hostile parties was meanwhile fast approaching to a crisis. The temper of Paris grew daily fiercer and fiercer. Delegates appointed by thirty-five of the forty-eight wards of the city appeared at the bar of the Convention, and demanded that Vergniaud, Brissot, Guadet, Gensonné, Barbaroux, Buzot, Pétion, Louvet, and many other deputies, should be expelled. This demand was disapproved by at least

three-fourths of the Assembly, and, when known in the department-
ments, called forth a general cry of indignation. Bordeaux
declared that it would stand by its representatives, and would,
if necessary, defend them by the sword against the tyranny of
Paris. Lyons and Marseilles were animated by a similar spirit.
These manifestations of public opinion gave courage to the
majority of the Convention. Thanks were voted to the people
of Bordeaux for their patriotic declaration; and a commission
consisting of twelve members was appointed for the purpose of
investigating the conduct of the municipal authorities of Paris,
and was empowered to place under arrest such persons as should
appear to have been concerned in any plot against the authority
of the Convention. This measure was adopted on the motion of
Barère.

A few days of stormy excitement and profound anxiety
followed; and then came the crash. On the thirty-first of May
the mob of Paris rose; the palace of the Tuileries was besieged by
a vast array of pikes; the majority of the deputies, after vain
struggles and remonstrances, yielded to violence, and suffered
the Mountain to carry a decree for the suspension and arrest of
the deputies whom the wards of the capital had accused.

During this contest, Barère had been tossed backwards and
forwards between the two raging factions. His feelings, languid
and unsteady as they always were, drew him to the Girondists;
but he was awed by the vigour and determination of the Mountain. At one moment he held high and firm language, complained that the Convention was not free, and protested against
the validity of any vote passed under coercion. At another
moment he proposed to conciliate the Parisians by abolishing
that commission of twelve which he had himself proposed only
a few days before; and himself drew up a paper condemning the
very measures which had been adopted at his own instance, and
eulogising the public spirit of the insurgents. To do him justice,
it was not without some symptoms of shame that he read this
document from the tribune, where he had so often expressed
very different sentiments. It is said that, at some passages, he
was even seen to blush. It may have been so; he was still in
his novitiate of infamy.

Some days later he proposed that hostages for the personal
safety of the accused deputies should be sent to the departments,
and offered to be himself one of those hostages. Nor do we in
the least doubt that the offer was sincere. He would, we firmly
believe, have thought himself far safer at Bordeaux or Marseilles

than at Paris. His proposition, however, was not carried into effect; and he remained in the power of the victorious Mountain.

This was the great crisis of his life. Hitherto he had done nothing inexpiable, nothing which marked him out as a much worse man than most of his colleagues in the Convention. His voice had generally been on the side of moderate measures. Had he bravely cast in his lot with the Girondists, and suffered with them, he would, like them, have had a not dishonourable place in history. Had he, like the great body of deputies who meant well, but who had not the courage to expose themselves to martyrdom, crouched quietly under the dominion of the triumphant minority, and suffered every motion of Robespierre and Billaud to pass unopposed, he would have incurred no peculiar ignominy. But it is probable that this course was not open to him. He had been too prominent among the adversaries of the Mountain to be admitted to quarter without making some atonement. It was necessary that, if he hoped to find pardon from his new lords, he should not be merely a silent and passive slave. What passed in private between him and them cannot be accurately related; but the result was soon apparent. The Committee of Public Safety was renewed. Several of the fiercest of the dominant faction, Couthon for example, and Saint Just, were substituted for more moderate politicians; but Barère was suffered to retain his seat at the Board.

The indulgence with which he was treated excited the murmurs of some stern and ardent zealots. Marat, in the very last words that he wrote, words not published till the dagger of Charlotte Corday had avenged France and mankind, complained that a man who had no principles, who was always on the side of the strongest, who had been a royalist, and who was ready, in case of a turn of fortune, to be a royalist again, should be entrusted with an important share in the administration.[1] But the chiefs of the Mountain judged more correctly. They knew, indeed, as well as Marat, that Barère was a man utterly without faith or steadiness; that, if he could be said to have any political leaning, his leaning was not towards them; that he felt for the Girondist party that faint and wavering sort of preference of which alone his nature was susceptible; and that, if he had been at liberty to make his choice, he would rather have murdered Robespierre and Danton than Vergniaud and Gensonné. But they justly appreciated that levity which made him incapable

[1] See the *Publiciste* of the 14th July 1793. Marat was stabbed on the evening of the 13th.

alike of earnest love and of earnest hatred, and that meanness which made it necessary to him to have a master. In truth, what the planters of Carolina and Louisiana say of black men with flat noses and woolly hair was strictly true of Barère. The curse of Canaan was upon him. He was born a slave. Baseness was an instinct in him. The impulse which drove him from a party in adversity to a party in prosperity was as irresistible as that which drives the cuckoo and the swallow towards the sun when the dark and cold months are approaching. The law which doomed him to be the humble attendant of stronger spirits resembled the law which binds the pilot-fish to the shark. " Ken ye," said a shrewd Scotch lord, who was asked his opinion of James the First—" Ken ye a John Ape? If I have Jacko by the collar, I can make him bite you; but, if you have Jacko, you can make him bite me." Just such a creature was Barère. In the hands of the Girondists he would have been eager to proscribe the Jacobins; he was just as ready, in the gripe of the Jacobins, to proscribe the Girondists. On the fidelity of such a man the heads of the Mountain could not, of course, reckon; but they valued their conquest as the very easy and not very delicate lover in Congreve's lively song valued the conquest of a prostitute of a different kind. Barère was, like Chloe, false and common; but he was, like Chloe, constant while possessed; and they asked no more. They needed a service which he was perfectly competent to perform. Destitute as he was of all the talents both of an active and of a speculative statesman, he could with great facility draw up a report, or make a speech on any subject and on any side. If other people would furnish facts and thoughts, he could always furnish phrases; and this talent was absolutely at the command of his owners for the time being. Nor had he excited any angry passion among those to whom he had hitherto been opposed. They felt no more hatred to him than they felt to the horses which dragged the cannon of the Duke of Brunswick and of the Prince of Saxe-Coburg. The horses had only done according to their kind, and would, if they fell into the hands of the French, drag with equal vigour and equal docility the guns of the republic, and therefore ought not merely to be spared, but to be well fed and curried. So was it with Barère. He was of a nature so low, that it might be doubted whether he could properly be an object of the hostility of reasonable beings. He had not been an enemy; he was not now a friend. But he had been an annoyance; and he would now be a help.

But, though the heads of the Mountain pardoned this man, and admitted him into partnership with themselves, it was not without exacting pledges such as made it impossible for him, false and fickle as he was, ever again to find admission into the ranks which he had deserted. That was truly a terrible sacrament by which they admitted the apostate into their communion. They demanded of him that he should himself take the most prominent part in murdering his old friends. To refuse was as much as his life was worth. But what is life worth when it is only one long agony of remorse and shame? These, however, are feelings of which it is idle to talk, when we are considering the conduct of such a man as Barère. He undertook the task, mounted the tribune, and told the Convention that the time was come for taking the stern attitude of justice, and for striking at all conspirators without distinction. He then moved that Buzot, Barbaroux, Pétion, and thirteen other deputies, should be placed out of the pale of the law, or, in other words, beheaded without a trial; and that Vergniaud, Guadet, Gensonné, and six others, should be impeached. The motion was carried without debate.

We have already seen with what effrontery Barère has denied, in these Memoirs, that he took any part against the Girondists. This denial, we think, was the only thing wanting to make his infamy complete. The most impudent of all lies was a fit companion for the foulest of all murders.

Barère, however, had not yet earned his pardon. The Jacobin party contained one gang which, even in that party, was pre-eminent in every mean and every savage vice; a gang so low-minded and so inhuman that, compared with them, Robespierre might be called magnanimous and merciful. Of these wretches Hébert was perhaps the best representative. His favourite amusement was to torment and insult the miserable remains of that great family which, having ruled France during eight hundred years, had now become an object of pity to the humblest artisan or peasant. The influence of this man, and of men like him, induced the Committee of Public Safety to determine that Marie Antoinette should be sent to the scaffold. Barère was again summoned to his duty. Only four days after he had proposed the decrees against the Girondist deputies, he again mounted the tribune, in order to move that the Queen should be brought before the Revolutionary Tribunal. He was improving fast in the society of his new allies. When he asked for the heads of Vergniaud and Pétion he had spoken like a

man who had some slight sense of his own guilt and degradation: he had said little; and that little had not been violent.
The office of expatiating on the guilt of his old friends he had
left to Saint Just. Very different was Barère's second appearance in the character of an accuser. He now cried out for blood
in the eager tones of the true and burning thirst, and raved
against the Austrian woman with the virulence natural to a
coward who finds himself at liberty to outrage that which he
has feared and envied. We have already exposed the shameless
mendacity with which, in these Memoirs, he attempts to throw
the blame of his own guilt on the guiltless.

On the day on which the fallen Queen was dragged, already
more than half dead, to her doom, Barère regaled Robespierre
and some other Jacobins at a tavern. Robespierre's acceptance
of the invitation caused some surprise to those who knew how
long and how bitterly it was his nature to hate. "Robespierre
of the party!" muttered Saint Just. "Barère is the only man
whom Robespierre has forgiven." We have an account of this
singular repast from one of the guests. Robespierre condemned
the senseless brutality with which Hébert had conducted the
proceedings against the Austrian woman, and, in talking on that
subject, became so much excited that he broke his plate in the
violence of his gesticulation. Barère exclaimed that the guillotine had cut a diplomatic knot which it might have been difficult
to untie. In the intervals between the Beaune and the Champagne, between the ragout of thrushes and the partridge with
truffles, he fervently preached his new political creed. "The
vessel of the revolution," he said, "can float into port only on
waves of blood. We must begin with the members of the
National Assembly and of the Legislative Assembly. That
rubbish must be swept away."

As he talked at table he talked in the Convention. His
peculiar style of oratory was now formed. It was not altogether
without ingenuity and liveliness. But in any other age or
country it would have been thought unfit for the deliberations
of a grave assembly, and still more unfit for state papers. It
might, perhaps, succeed at a meeting of a Protestant Association
in Exeter Hall, at a Repeal dinner in Ireland, after men had well
drunk, or in an American oration on the fourth of July. No
legislative body would now endure it. But in France, during the
reign of the Convention, the old laws of composition were held
in as much contempt as the old government or the old creed.
Correct and noble diction belonged, like the etiquette of Ver-

sailles and the solemnities of Notre Dame, to an age which had passed away. Just as a swarm of ephemeral constitutions, democratic, directorial, and consular, sprang from the decay of the ancient monarchy; just as a swarm of new superstitions, the worship of the Goddess of Reason, and the fooleries of the Theophilanthropists, sprang from the decay of the ancient Church; even so, out of the decay of the ancient French eloquence sprang new fashions of eloquence, for the understanding of which new grammars and dictionaries were necessary. The same innovating spirit which altered the common phrases of salutation, which turned hundreds of Johns and Peters into Scævolas and Aristogitons, and which expelled Sunday and Monday, January and February, Lady-day and Christmas, from the calendar, in order to substitute Decadi and Primidi, Nivose and Pluviose, Feasts of Opinion and Feasts of the Supreme Being, changed all the forms of official correspondence. For the calm, guarded, and sternly courteous language which governments had long been accustomed to employ, were substituted puns, interjections, Ossianic rants, rhetoric worthy only of a schoolboy, scurrility worthy only of a fishwife. Of the phraseology which was now thought to be peculiarly well suited to a report or a manifesto Barère had a greater command than any man of his time, and, during the short and sharp paroxysm of the revolutionary delirium, passed for a great orator. When the fit was over, he was considered as what he really was, a man of quick apprehension and fluent elocution, with no originality, with little information, and with a taste as bad as his heart. His Reports were popularly called Carmagnoles. A few months ago we should have had some difficulty in conveying to an English reader an exact notion of the state papers to which this appellation was given. Fortunately a noble and distinguished person, whom her Majesty's Ministers have thought qualified to fill the most important post in the empire, has made our task easy. Whoever has read Lord Ellenborough's proclamations is able to form a complete idea of a Carmagnole.

The effect which Barère's discourses at one time produced is not to be wholly attributed to the perversion of the national taste. The occasions on which he rose were frequently such as would have secured to the worst speaker a favourable hearing. When any military advantage had been gained, he was generally deputed by the Committee of Public Safety to announce the good news. The hall resounded with applause as he mounted the tribune, holding the despatches in his hand. Deputies and strangers listened with delight while he told them that victory was the order of the day; that the guineas of Pitt had been vainly lavished to hire machines six feet high, carrying guns; that the flight of the English leopard deserved to be celebrated by Tyrtæus; and that the saltpetre dug out of the cellars of Paris had been turned into thunder, which would crush the Titan brethren, George and Francis.

Meanwhile the trial of the accused Girondists, who were under arrest in Paris, came on. They flattered themselves with a vain hope of escape. They placed some reliance on their innocence, and some reliance on their eloquence. They thought that shame would suffice to restrain any man, however violent and cruel, from publicly committing the flagrant iniquity of condemning them to death. The Revolutionary Tribunal was new to its functions. No member of the Convention had yet been executed; and it was probable that the boldest Jacobin would shrink from being the first to violate the sanctity which was supposed to belong to the representatives of the people.

The proceedings lasted some days. Gensonné and Brissot defended themselves with great ability and presence of mind against the vile Hébert and Chaumette, who appeared as accusers. The eloquent voice of Vergniaud was heard for the last time. He pleaded his own cause and that of his friends, with such force of reason and elevation of sentiment that a murmur of pity and admiration rose from the audience. Nay, the court itself, not yet accustomed to riot in daily carnage, showed signs of emotion. The sitting was adjourned; and a rumour went forth that there would be an acquittal. The Jacobins met, breathing vengeance. Robespierre undertook to be their organ. He rose on the following day in the Convention, and proposed a decree of such atrocity that even among the acts of that year it can hardly be paralleled. By this decree the tribunal was empowered to cut short the defence of the prisoners, to pronounce the case clear, and to pass immediate judgment. One deputy made a faint opposition. Barère instantly sprang up to support Robespierre —Barère, the federalist; Barère, the author of that Commission of Twelve which was among the chief causes of the hatred borne by Paris to the Girondists; Barère, who in these Memoirs denies that he ever took any part against the Girondists; Barère, who has the effrontery to declare that he greatly loved and esteemed Vergniaud. The decree was passed; and the tribunal, without suffering the prisoners to conclude what they had to say, pronounced them guilty.

The following day was the saddest in the sad history of the Revolution. The sufferers were so innocent, so brave, so eloquent, so accomplished, so young. Some of them were graceful and handsome youths of six or seven and twenty. Vergniaud and Gensonné were little more than thirty. They had been only a few months engaged in public affairs. In a few months the fame of their genius had filled Europe; and they were to die for no crime but this, that they had wished to combine order, justice, and mercy with freedom. Their great fault was want of courage. We mean want of political courage—of that courage which is proof to clamour and obloquy, and which meets great emergencies by daring and decisive measures. Alas! they had but too good an opportunity of proving that they did not want courage to endure with manly cheerfulness the worst that could be inflicted by such tyrants as Saint Just, and such slaves as Barère.

They were not the only victims of the noble cause. Madame Roland followed them to the scaffold with a spirit as heroic as their own. Her husband was in a safe hiding-place, but could not bear to survive her. His body was found on the high road near Rouen. He had fallen on his sword. Condorcet swallowed opium. At Bordeaux the steel fell on the necks of the bold and quick-witted Guadet and of Barbaroux, the chief of those enthusiasts from the Rhone whose valour, in the great crisis of the tenth of August, had turned back the tide of battle from the Louvre to the Tuileries. In a field near the Garonne was found all that the wolves had left of Pétion, once honoured, greatly indeed beyond his deserts, as the model of republican virtue. We are far from regarding even the best of the Girondists with unmixed admiration; but history owes to them this honourable testimony, that, being free to choose whether they would be oppressors or victims, they deliberately and firmly resolved rather to suffer injustice than to inflict it.

And now began that strange period known by the name of the Reign of Terror. The Jacobins had prevailed. This was their hour, and the power of darkness. The Convention was subjugated and reduced to profound silence on the highest questions of state. The sovereignty passed to the Committee of Public Safety. To the edicts framed by that Committee the representative assembly did not venture to offer even the species of opposition which the ancient parliament had frequently offered to the mandates of the ancient kings. Six persons held the chief power in the small cabinet which now domineered over France— Robespierre, Saint Just, Couthon, Collot, Billaud, and Barère.

To some of these men, and of those who adhered to them, it is due to say that the fanaticism which had emancipated them from the restraints of justice and compassion had emancipated them also from the dominion of vulgar cupidity and of vulgar fear; that, while hardly knowing where to find an assignat of a few francs to pay for a dinner, they expended with strict integrity the immense revenue which they collected by every art of rapine; and that they were ready, in support of their cause, to mount the scaffold with as much indifference as they showed when they signed the death-warrants of aristocrats and priests. But no great party can be composed of such materials as these. It is the inevitable law that such zealots as we have described shall collect around them a multitude of slaves, of cowards, and of libertines, whose savage tempers and licentious appetites, withheld only by the dread of law and magistracy from the worst excesses, are called into full activity by the hope of immunity. A faction which, from whatever motive, relaxes the great laws of morality is certain to be joined by the most immoral part of the community. This has been repeatedly proved in religious wars. The war of the Holy Sepulchre, the Albigensian war, the Huguenot war, the Thirty Years' war, all originated in pious zeal. That zeal inflamed the champions of the Church to such a point that they regarded all generosity to the vanquished as a sinful weakness. The infidel, the heretic, was to be run down like a mad dog. No outrage committed by the Catholic warrior on the miscreant enemy could deserve punishment. As soon as it was known that boundless licence was thus given to barbarity and dissoluteness, thousands of wretches who cared nothing for the sacred cause, but who were eager to be exempted from the police of peaceful cities, and the discipline of well-governed camps, flocked to the standard of the faith. The men who had set up that standard were sincere, chaste, regardless of lucre, and perhaps, where only themselves were concerned, not unforgiving; but round that standard were assembled such gangs of rogues, ravishers, plunderers, and ferocious bravoes, as were scarcely ever found under the flag of any state engaged in a mere temporal quarrel. In a very similar way was the Jacobin party composed. There was a small nucleus of enthusiasts; round that nucleus was gathered a vast mass of ignoble depravity; and in all that mass there was nothing so depraved and so ignoble as Barère.

Then came those days when the most barbarous of all codes was administered by the most barbarous of all tribunals; when no man could greet his neighbours, or say his prayers, or dress his hair, without danger of committing a capital crime; when spies lurked in every corner; when the guillotine was long and hard at work every morning; when the jails were filled as close as the hold of a slave-ship; when the gutters ran foaming with blood into the Seine; when it was death to be great-niece of a captain of the royal guards, or half-brother of a doctor of the Sorbonne, to express a doubt whether assignats would not fall, to hint that the English had been victorious in the action of the first of June, to have a copy of one of Burke's pamphlets locked up in a desk, to laugh at a Jacobin for taking the name of Cassius or Timoleon, or to call the Fifth Sansculottide by its old superstitious name of St. Matthew's Day. While the daily waggon-loads of victims were carried to their doom through the streets of Paris, the Proconsuls whom the sovereign Committee had sent forth to the departments revelled in an extravagance of cruelty unknown even in the capital. The knife of the deadly machine rose and fell too slow for their work of slaughter. Long rows of captives were mowed down with grapeshot. Holes were made in the bottom of crowded barges. Lyons was turned into a desert. At Arras even the cruel mercy of a speedy death was denied to the prisoners. All down the Loire, from Saumur to the sea, great flocks of crows and kites feasted on naked corpses, twined together in hideous embraces. No mercy was shown to sex or age. The number of young lads and of girls of seventeen who were murdered by that execrable government is to be reckoned by hundreds. Babies torn from the breast were tossed from pike to pike along the Jacobin ranks. One champion of liberty had his pockets well stuffed with ears. Another swaggered about with the finger of a little child in his hat. A few months had sufficed to degrade France below the level of New Zealand.

It is absurd to say that any amount of public danger can justify a system like this, we do not say on Christian principles, we do not say on the principles of a high morality, but even on principles of Machiavellian policy. It is true that great emergencies call for activity and vigilance; it is true that they justify severity which, in ordinary times, would deserve the name of cruelty. But indiscriminate severity can never, under any circumstances, be useful. It is plain that the whole efficacy of punishment depends on the care with which the guilty are distinguished. Punishment which strikes the guilty and the innocent promiscuously, operates merely like a pestilence or a

great convulsion of nature, and has no more tendency to prevent
offences than the cholera, or an earthquake like that of Lisbon,
would have. The energy for which the Jacobin administration
is praised was merely the energy of the Malay who maddens
himself with opium, draws his knife, and runs amuck through
the streets, slashing right and left at friends and foes. Such
has never been the energy of truly great rulers; of Elizabeth,
for example, of Oliver, or of Frederick. They were not, indeed,
scrupulous. But, had they been less scrupulous than they were,
the strength and amplitude of their minds would have preserved
them from crimes such as those which the small men of the
Committee of Public Safety took for daring strokes of policy.
The great Queen who so long held her own against foreign and
domestic enemies, against temporal and spiritual arms; the
great Protector who governed with more than regal power, in
despite both of royalists and republicans; the great King who,
with a beaten army and an exhausted treasury, defended his
little dominions to the last against the united efforts of Russia,
Austria, and France; with what scorn would they have heard
that it was impossible for them to strike a salutary terror into
the disaffected without sending school-boys and school-girls to
death by cart-loads and boat-loads!

The popular notion is, we believe, that the leading Terrorists
were wicked men, but, at the same time, great men. We can
see nothing great about them but their wickedness. That their
policy was daringly original is a vulgar error. Their policy is
as old as the oldest accounts which we have of human misgovernment. It seemed new in France and in the eighteenth
century only because it had been long disused, for excellent
reasons, by the enlightened part of mankind. But it has always
prevailed, and still prevails, in savage and half-savage nations,
and is the chief cause which prevents such nations from making
advances towards civilisation. Thousands of deys, of beys, of
pachas, of rajahs, of nabobs, have shown themselves as great
masters of statecraft as the members of the Committee of Public
Safety. Djezzar, we imagine, was superior to any of them in
their new line. In fact, there is not a petty tyrant in Asia or
Africa so dull or so unlearned as not to be fully qualified for
the business of Jacobin police and Jacobin finance. To behead
people by scores without caring whether they are guilty or
innocent; to wring money out of the rich by the help of jailers
and executioners; to rob the public creditor, and to put him to
death if he remonstrates; to take loaves by force out of the

bakers' shops; to clothe and mount soldiers by seizing on one man's wool and linen, and on another man's horses and saddles, without compensation; is of all modes of governing the simplest and most obvious. Of its morality we at present say nothing. But surely it requires no capacity beyond that of a barbarian or a child. By means like those which we have described, the Committee of Public Safety undoubtedly succeeded, for a short time, in enforcing profound submission, and in raising immense funds. But to enforce submission by butchery, and to raise funds by spoliation, is not statesmanship. The real statesman is he who, in troubled times, keeps down the turbulent without unnecessarily harassing the well-affected; and who, when great pecuniary resources are needed, provides for the public exigencies without violating the security of property and drying up the sources of future prosperity. Such a statesman, we are confident, might, in 1793, have preserved the independence of France without shedding a drop of innocent blood, without plundering a single warehouse. Unhappily, the Republic was subject to men who were mere demagogues and in no sense statesmen. They could declaim at a club. They could lead a rabble to mischief. But they had no skill to conduct the affairs of an empire. The want of skill they supplied for a time by atrocity and blind violence. For legislative ability, fiscal ability, military ability, diplomatic ability, they had one substitute, the guillotine. Indeed their exceeding ignorance, and the barrenness of their invention, are the best excuse for their murders and robberies. We really believe that they would not have cut so many throats, and picked so many pockets, if they had known how to govern in any other way.

That under their administration the war against the European Coalition was successfully conducted is true. But that war had been successfully conducted before their elevation, and continued to be successfully conducted after their fall. Terror was not the order of the day when Brussels opened its gates to Dumourier. Terror had ceased to be the order of the day when Piedmont and Lombardy were conquered by Bonaparte. The truth is, that France was saved, not by the Committee of Public Safety, but by the energy, patriotism, and valour of the French people. Those high qualities were victorious in spite of the incapacity of rulers whose administration was a tissue, not merely of crimes, but of blunders.

We have not time to tell how the leaders of the savage faction at length began to avenge mankind on each other: how the

craven Hébert was dragged wailing and trembling to his doom;
how the nobler Danton, moved by a late repentance, strove in
vain to repair the evil which he had wrought, and half redeemed
the great crime of September by manfully encountering death
in the cause of mercy.

Our business is with Barère. In all those things he was not
only consenting, but eagerly and joyously forward. Not merely
was he one of the guilty administration. He was the man to
whom was especially assigned the office of proposing and defending outrages on justice and humanity, and of furnishing to
atrocious schemes an appropriate garb of atrocious rodomon-
tade. Barère first proclaimed from the tribune of the Convention that terror must be the order of the day. It was by Barère
that the Revolutionary Tribunal of Paris was provided with the
aid of a public accuser worthy of such a court, the infamous
Fouquier Tinville. It was Barère who, when one of the old
members of the National Assembly had been absolved by the
Revolutionary Tribunal, gave orders that a fresh jury should be
summoned. " Acquit one of the National Assembly! " he cried.
" The Tribunal is turning against the Revolution." It is unnecessary to say that the prisoner's head was soon in the basket.
It was Barère who moved that the city of Lyons should be
destroyed. " Let the plough," he cried from the tribune, " pass
over her. Let her name cease to exist. The rebels are conquered; but are they all exterminated? No weakness. No
mercy. Let every one be smitten. Two words will suffice to
tell the whole. Lyons made war on liberty; Lyons is no more."
When Toulon was taken Barère came forward to announce the
event. " The conquest," said the apostate Brissotine, " won by
the Mountain over the Brissotines must be commemorated by a
mark set on the place where Toulon once stood. The national
thunder must crush the house of every trader in the town.
When Camille Desmoulins, long distinguished among the republicans by zeal and ability, dared to raise his eloquent voice
against the Reign of Terror, and to point out the close analogy
between the government which then oppressed France and the
government of the worst of the Cæsars, Barère rose to complain
of the weak compassion which tried to revive the hopes of the
aristocracy. " Whoever," he said, " is nobly born is a man to
be suspected. Every priest, every frequenter of the old court,
every lawyer, every banker, is a man to be suspected. Every
person who grumbles at the course which the Revolution takes
is a man to be suspected. There are whole castes already tried

and condemned. There are callings which carry their doom with them. There are relations of blood which the law regards with an evil eye. Republicans of France! " yelled the renegade Girondist, the old enemy of the Mountain—" Republicans of France! the Brissotines led you by gentle means to slavery. The Mountain leads you by strong measures to freedom. Oh! who can count the evils which a false compassion may produce? " When the friends of Danton mustered courage to express a wish that the Convention would at least hear him in his own defence before it sent him to certain death, the voice of Barère was the loudest in opposition to their prayer. When the crimes of Lebon, one of the worst, if not the very worst, of the vicegerents of the Committee of Public Safety, had so maddened the people of the Department of the North that they resorted to the desperate expedient of imploring the protection of the Convention, Barère pleaded the cause of the accused tyrant, and threatened the petitioners with the utmost vengeance of the government. " These charges," he said, " have been suggested by wily aristocrats. The man who crushes the enemies of the people, though he may be hurried by his zeal into some excesses, can never be a proper object of censure. The proceedings of Lebon may have been a little harsh as to form." One of the small irregularities thus gently censured was this: Lebon kept a wretched man a quarter of an hour under the knife of the guillotine, in order to torment him, by reading to him, before he was despatched, a letter, the contents of which were supposed to be such as would aggravate even the bitterness of death. " But what," proceeded Barère, " is not permitted to the hatred of a republican against aristocracy? How many generous sentiments atone for what may perhaps seem acrimonious in the prosecution of public enemies? Revolutionary measures are always to be spoken of with respect. Liberty is a virgin whose veil it is not lawful to lift."

After this, it would be idle to dwell on facts which would indeed, of themselves, suffice to render a name infamous, but which make no perceptible addition to the great infamy of Barère. It would be idle, for example, to relate how he, a man of letters, a member of an Academy of Inscriptions, was foremost in that war against learning, art, and history which disgraced the Jacobin government; how he recommended a general conflagration of libraries; how he proclaimed that all records of events anterior to the Revolution ought to be destroyed; how he laid waste the Abbey of St. Denis, pulled down monuments consecrated by the veneration of ages, and scattered on the wind the dust of ancient kings. He was, in truth, seldom so well employed as when he turned for a moment from making war on the living to make war on the dead.

Equally idle would it be to dilate on his sensual excesses. That in Barère as in the whole breed of Neros, Caligulas, and Domitians whom he resembled, voluptuousness was mingled with cruelty; that he withdrew, twice in every decade, from the work of blood, to the smiling gardens of Clichy, and there forgot public cares in the madness of wine and in the arms of courtesans, has often been repeated. M. Hippolyte Carnot does not altogether deny the truth of these stories, but justly observes that Barère's dissipation was not carried to such a point as to interfere with his industry. Nothing can be more true. Barère was by no means so much addicted to debauchery as to neglect the work of murder. It was his boast that, even during his hours of recreation, he cut out work for the Revolutionary Tribunal. To those who expressed a fear that his exertions would hurt his health, he gaily answered that he was less busy than they thought. " The guillotine," he said, " does all; the guillotine governs." For ourselves, we are much more disposed to look indulgently on the pleasures which he allowed to himself than on the pain which he inflicted on his neighbours.

> " Atque utinam his potius nugis tota illa dedisset
> Tempora sævitiæ, claras quibus abstulit urbi
> Illustresque animas, impune ac vindice nullo."

An immoderate appetite for sensual gratifications is undoubtedly a blemish on the fame of Henry the Fourth, of Lord Somers, of Mr. Fox. But the vices of honest men are the virtues of Barère.

And now Barère had become a really cruel man. It was from mere pusillanimity that he had perpetrated his first great crimes. But the whole history of our race proves that the taste for the misery of others is a taste which minds not naturally ferocious may too easily acquire, and which, when once acquired, is as strong as any of the propensities with which we are born. A very few months had sufficed to bring this man into a state of mind in which images of despair, wailing, and death had an exhilarating effect on him, and inspired him as wine and love inspire men of free and joyous natures. The cart creaking under its daily freight of victims, ancient men and lads, and fair young girls, the binding of the hands, the thrusting of the

head out of the little national sash-window, the crash of the
axe, the pool of blood beneath the scaffold, the heads rolling by
scores in the panier—these things were to him what Lalage and
a cask of Falernian were to Horace, what Rosette and a bottle
of iced champagne are to De Béranger. As soon as he began
to speak of slaughter his heart seemed to be enlarged, and his
fancy to become unusually fertile of conceits and gasconades.
Robespierre, Saint Just, and Billaud, whose barbarity was the
effect of earnest and gloomy hatred, were, in his view, men who
made a toil of a pleasure. Cruelty was no such melancholy
business, to be gone about with an austere brow and a whining
tone; it was a recreation, fitly accompanied by singing and
laughing.   In truth, Robespierre and Barère might be well compared to the two renowned hangmen of Louis the Eleventh.
They were alike insensible of pity, alike bent on havoc.   But,
while they murdered, one of them frowned and canted, the
other grinned and joked. For our own part, we prefer *Jean
qui pleure* to *Jean qui rit.*

In the midst of the funeral gloom which overhung Paris, a
gaiety stranger and more ghastly than the horrors of the prison
and the scaffold distinguished the dwelling of Barère. Every
morning a crowd of suitors assembled to implore his protection.
He came forth in his rich dressing-gown, went round the ante-
chamber, dispensed smiles and promises among the obsequious
crowd, addressed himself with peculiar animation to every handsome woman who appeared in the circle, and complimented her
in the florid style of Gascony on the bloom of her cheeks and the
lustre of her eyes.   When he had enjoyed the fear and anxiety of
his suppliants he dismissed them, and flung all their memorials
unread into the fire. This was the best way, he conceived, to
prevent arrears of business from accumulating. Here he was
only an imitator. Cardinal Dubois had been in the habit of
clearing his table of papers in the same way. Nor was this the
only point in which we could point out a resemblance between
the worst statesman of the monarchy and the worst statesman
of the republic.

Of Barère's peculiar vein of pleasantry a notion may be
formed from an anecdote which one of his intimate associates,
a juror of the revolutionary tribunal, has related. A courtesan
who bore a conspicuous part in the orgies of Clichy implored
Barère to use his power against a head-dress which did not suit
her style of face, and which a rival beauty was trying to bring
into fashion. One of the magistrates of the capital was sum-

moned and received the necessary orders.   Aristocracy, Barère said, was again rearing its front.   These new wigs were counter-revolutionary.   He had reason to know that they were made out of the long fair hair of handsome aristocrats who had died by the national chopper.   Every lady who adorned herself with the relics of criminals might justly be suspected of incivism.   This ridiculous lie imposed on the authorities of Paris.   Female citizens were solemnly warned against the obnoxious ringlets, and were left to choose between their head-dresses and their heads.   Barère's delight at the success of this facetious fiction was quite extravagant: he could not tell the story without going into such convulsions of laughter as made his hearers hope that he was about to choke.   There was something peculiarly tickling and exhilarating to his mind in this grotesque combination of the frivolous with the horrible, of false locks and curling-irons with spouting arteries and reeking hatchets.

But, though Barère succeeded in earning the honourable nick-names of the Witling of Terror, and the Anacreon of the Guillo-tine, there was one place where it was long remembered to his disadvantage that he had, for a time, talked the language of humanity and moderation.   That place was the Jacobin club. Even after he had borne the chief part in the massacre of the Girondists, in the murder of the Queen, in the destruction of Lyons, he durst not show himself within that sacred precinct. At one meeting of the society, a member complained that the committee to which the supreme direction of affairs was en-trusted, after all the changes which had been made, still con-tained one man who was not trustworthy.   Robespierre, whose influence over the Jacobins was boundless, undertook the defence of his colleague, owned there was some ground for what had been said, but spoke highly of Barère's industry and aptitude for business.   This seasonable interposition silenced the accuser; but it was long before the neophyte could venture to appear at the club.

At length a masterpiece of wickedness, unique, we think, even among Barère's great achievements, obtained his full pardon even from that rigid conclave.   The insupportable tyranny of the Committee of Public Safety had at length brought the minds of men, and even of women, into a fierce and hard temper, which defied or welcomed death.   The life which might be any morning taken away, in consequence of the whisper of a private enemy, seemed of little value.   It was something to die after smiting one of the oppressors; it was something to bequeath to the surviving tyrants a terror not inferior to that which they had themselves inspired. Human nature, hunted and worried to the utmost, now turned furiously to bay. Fouquier Tinville was afraid to walk the streets; a pistol was snapped at Collot D'Herbois; a young girl, animated apparently by the spirit of Charlotte Corday, attempted to obtain an interview with Robespierre. Suspicions arose; she was searched; and two knives were found about her. She was questioned, and spoke of the Jacobin domination with resolute scorn and aversion. It is unnecessary to say that she was sent to the guillotine. Barère declared from the tribune that the cause of these attempts was evident. Pitt and his guineas had done the whole. The English Government had organised a vast system of murder, had armed the hand of Charlotte Corday, and had now, by similar means, attacked two of the most eminent friends of liberty in France. It is needless to say that these imputations were, not only false, but destitute of all show of truth. Nay, they were demonstrably absurd: for the assassins to whom Barère referred rushed on certain death, a sure proof that they were not hirelings. The whole wealth of England would not have bribed any sane person to do what Charlotte Corday did. But, when we consider her as an enthusiast, her conduct is perfectly natural. Even those French writers who are childish enough to believe that the English Government contrived the infernal machine and strangled the Emperor Paul have fully acquitted Mr. Pitt of all share in the death of Marat and in the attempt on Robespierre. Yet on calumnies so futile as those which we have mentioned did Barère ground a motion at which all Christendom stood aghast. He proposed a decree that no quarter should be given to any English or Hanoverian soldier.[1] His Carmagnole was worthy of the proposition with which it concluded. " That one Englishman should be spared, that for the slaves of George, for the

[1] M. Hippolyte Carnot does his best to excuse this decree. His abuse of England is merely laughable. England has managed to deal with enemies of a very different sort from either himself or his hero. One disgraceful blunder, however, we think it right to notice.

M. Hippolyte Carnot asserts that a motion similar to that of Barère was made in the English Parliament by the late Lord Fitzwilliam. This assertion is false. We defy M. Hippolyte Carnot to state the date and terms of the motion of which he speaks. We do not accuse him of intentional misrepresentation; but we confidently accuse him of extreme ignorance and temerity. Our readers will be amused to learn on what authority he has ventured to publish such a fable. He quotes, not the Journals of the Lords, not the Parliamentary Debates, but a ranting message of the Executive Directory to the Five Hundred, a message, too, the whole meaning of which he has utterly misunderstood.

human machines of York, the vocabulary of our armies should contain such a word as generosity, this is what the National Convention cannot endure. War to the death against every English soldier. If last year, at Dunkirk, quarter had been refused to them when they asked it on their knees, if our troops had exterminated them all, instead of suffering them to infest our fortresses by their presence, the English government would not have renewed its attack on our frontiers this year. It is only the dead man who never comes back. What is this moral pestilence which has introduced into our armies false ideas of humanity? That the English were to be treated with indulgence was the philanthropic notion of the Brissotines; it was the patriotic practice of Dumourier. But humanity consists in exterminating our enemies. No mercy to the execrable Englishman. Such are the sentiments of the true Frenchman; for he knows that he belongs to a nation revolutionary as nature, powerful as freedom, ardent as the saltpetre which she has just torn from the entrails of the earth. Soldiers of liberty, when victory places Englishmen at your mercy, strike! None of them must return to the servile soil of Great Britain; none must pollute the free soil of France."

The Convention, thoroughly tamed and silenced, acquiesced in Barère's motion without debate. And now at last the doors of the Jacobin Club were thrown open to the disciple who had surpassed his masters. He was admitted a member by acclamation, and was soon selected to preside.

For a time he was not without hope that his decree would be carried into full effect. Intelligence arrived from the seat of war of a sharp contest between some French and English troops, in which the Republicans had the advantage, and in which no prisoners had been made. Such things happen occasionally in all wars. Barère, however, attributed the ferocity of this combat to his darling decree, and entertained the Convention with another Carmagnole.

" The Republicans," he said, " saw a division in red uniform at a distance. The red-coats are attacked with the bayonet. Not one of them escapes the blows of the Republicans. All the red-coats have been killed. No mercy, no indulgence, has been shown towards the villains. Not an Englishman whom the Republicans could reach is now living. How many prisoners should you guess that we have made? One single prisoner is the result of this great day."

And now this bad man's craving for blood had become insatiable. The more he quaffed, the more he thirsted. He had begun with the English; but soon he came down with a proposition for new massacres. " All the troops," he said, " of the coalesced tyrants in garrison at Condé, Valenciennes, Le Quesnoy, and Landrecies, ought to be put to the sword unless they surrender at discretion in twenty-four hours. The English, of course, will be admitted to no capitulation whatever. With the English we have no treaty but death. As to the rest, surrender at discretion in twenty-four hours, or death, these are our conditions. If the slaves resist, let them feel the edge of the sword." And then he waxed facetious. " On these terms the Republic is willing to give them a lesson in the art of war." At that jest, some hearers, worthy of such a speaker, set up a laugh. Then he became serious again. " Let the enemy perish," he cried, " I have already said it from this tribune. It is only the dead man who never comes back. Kings will not conspire against us in the grave. Armies will not fight against us when they are annihilated. Let our war with them be a war of extermination. What pity is due to slaves whom the Emperor leads to war under the cane; whom the King of Prussia beats to the shambles with the flat of the sword; and whom the Duke of York makes drunk with rum and gin? " And at the rum and gin the Mountain and the galleries laughed again.

If Barère had been able to effect his purpose, it is difficult to estimate the extent of the calamity which he would have brought on the human race. No government, however averse to cruelty, could, in justice to its own subjects, have given quarter to enemies who gave none. Retaliation would have been, not merely justifiable, but a sacred duty. It would have been necessary for Howe and Nelson to make every French sailor whom they took walk the plank. England has no peculiar reason to dread the introduction of such a system. On the contrary, the operation of Barère's new law of war would have been more unfavourable to his countrymen than to ours; for we believe that, from the beginning to the end of the war, there never was a time at which the number of French prisoners in England was not greater than the number of English prisoners in France; and so, we apprehend, it will be in all wars while England retains her maritime superiority. Had the murderous decree of the Convention been in force from 1794 to 1815, we are satisfied that, for every Englishman slain by the French, at least three Frenchmen would have been put to the sword by the English. It is, therefore, not as Englishmen, but as members of the great society of mankind, that we speak with indignation and horror of the change which Barère attempted to introduce. The mere slaughter would have been the smallest part of the evil. The butchering of a single unarmed man in cold blood, under an act of the legislature, would have produced more evil than the carnage of ten such fields as Albuera. Public law would have been subverted from the foundations; national enmities would have been inflamed to a degree of rage which happily it is not easy for us to conceive; cordial peace would have been impossible. The moral character of the European nations would have been rapidly and deeply corrupted; for in all countries those men whose calling is to put their lives in jeopardy for the defence of the public weal enjoy high consideration, and are considered as the best arbitrators on points of honour and manly bearing. With the standard of morality established in the military profession the general standard of morality must to a great extent sink or rise. It is, therefore, a fortunate circumstance that, during a long course of years, respect for the weak and clemency towards the vanquished have been considered as qualities not less essential to the accomplished soldier than personal courage. How long would this continue to be the case, if the slaying of prisoners were a part of the daily duty of the warrior? What man of kind and generous nature would, under such a system, willingly bear arms? Who, that was compelled to bear arms, would long continue kind and generous? And is it not certain that, if barbarity towards the helpless became the characteristic of military men, the taint must rapidly spread to civil and to domestic life, and must show itself in all the dealings of the strong with the weak, of husbands with wives, of employers with workmen, of creditors with debtors?

But, thank God, Barère's decree was a mere dead letter. It was to be executed by men very different from those who, in the interior of France, were the instruments of the Committee of Public Safety, who prated at Jacobin Clubs, and ran to Fouquier Tinville with charges of incivism against women whom they could not seduce, and bankers from whom they could not extort money. The warriors who, under Hoche, had guarded the walls of Dunkirk, and who, under Kléber had made good the defence of the wood of Monceaux, shrank with horror from an office more degrading than that of the hangman. "The Convention," said an officer to his men, "has sent orders that all the English prisoners shall be shot." "We will not shoot them," answered a stout-hearted sergeant. "Send them to the Convention. If the deputies take pleasure in killing a prisoner, they may kill him themselves, and eat him too, like savages as they are." This was the sentiment of the whole army. Bonaparte, who thoroughly understood war, who at Jaffa and elsewhere gave ample proof that he was not unwilling to strain the laws of war to their utmost rigour, and whose hatred of England amounted to a folly, always spoke of Barère's decree with loathing, and boasted that the army had refused to obey the Convention.

Such disobedience on the part of any other class of citizens would have been instantly punished by wholesale massacre; but the Committee of Public Safety was aware that the discipline which had tamed the unwarlike population of the fields and cities might not answer in camps. To fling people by scores out of a boat, and, when they catch hold of it, to chop off their fingers with a hatchet, is undoubtedly a very agreeable pastime for a thoroughbred Jacobin, when the sufferers are as at Nantes, old confessors, young girls, or women with child. But such sport might prove a little dangerous if tried upon grim ranks of grenadiers, marked with the scars of Hondschoote, and singed by the smoke of Fleurus.

Barère, however, found some consolation. If he could not succeed in murdering the English and the Hanoverians, he was amply indemnified by a new and vast slaughter of his own countrymen and countrywomen. If the defence which has been set up for the members of the Committee of Public Safety had been well founded, if it had been true that they governed with extreme severity only because the republic was in extreme peril, it is clear that the severity would have diminished as the peril diminished. But the fact is, that those cruelties for which the public danger is made a plea became more and more enormous as the danger became less and less, and reached the full height when there was no longer any danger at all. In the autumn of 1793, there was undoubtedly reason to apprehend that France might be unable to maintain the struggle against the European coalition. The enemy was triumphant on the frontiers. More than half the departments disowned the authority of the Convention. But at that time eight or ten necks a day were thought an ample allowance for the guillotine of the capital. In the summer of 1794, Bordeaux, Toulon, Caen, Lyons, Marseilles, had submitted to the ascendency of Paris. The French arms were victorious under the Pyrenees and on the Sambre. Brussels had fallen. Prussia had announced her intention of withdrawing from the contest. The Republic, no longer content with defending her own independence, was beginning to meditate conquest beyond the Alps and the Rhine. She was now more formidable to her neighbours than ever Louis the Fourteenth had been. And now the Revolutionary Tribunal of Paris was not content with forty, fifty, sixty heads in a morning. It was just after a series of victories, which destroyed the whole force of the single argument which has been urged in defence of the system of terror, that the Committee of Public Safety resolved to infuse into that system an energy hitherto unknown. It was proposed to reconstruct the Revolutionary Tribunal, and to collect in the space of two pages the whole revolutionary jurisprudence. Lists of twelve judges and fifty jurors were made out from among the fiercest Jacobins. The substantive law was simply this, that whatever the tribunal should think pernicious to the republic was a capital crime. The law of evidence was simply this, that whatever satisfied the jurors was sufficient proof. The law of procedure was a piece with everything else. There was to be an advocate against the prisoner, and no advocate for him. It was expressly declared that, if the jurors were in any manner convinced of the guilt of the prisoner, they might convict him without hearing a single witness. The only punishment which the court could inflict was death.

Robespierre proposed this decree. When he had read it, a murmur rose from the Convention. The fear which had long restrained the deputies from opposing the Committee was overcome by a stronger fear. Every man felt the knife at his throat. " The decree," said one, " is of grave importance. I move that it be printed and the debate be adjourned. If such a measure were adopted without time for consideration, I would blow my brains out at once." The motion for adjournment was seconded. Then Barère sprang up. " It is impossible," he said, " that there can be any difference of opinion among us as to a law like this, a law so favourable in all respects to patriots; a law which insures the speedy punishment of conspirators. If there is to be an adjournment, I must insist that it shall not be for more than three days." The opposition was overawed; the decree was passed; and, during the six weeks which followed, the havoc was such as has never been known before.

And now the evil was beyond endurance. That timid majority which had for a time supported the Girondists, and which had, after their fall, contented itself with registering in silence the decrees of the Committee of Public Safety, at length drew courage from despair. Leaders of bold and firm character were not wanting, men such as Fouché and Tallien, who, having been long conspicuous among the chiefs of the Mountain, now found that their own lives, or lives still dearer to them than their own, were in extreme peril. Nor could it be longer kept secret that there was a schism in the despotic committee. On one side were Robespierre, Saint Just, and Couthon; on the other, Collot and Billaud. Barère leaned towards these last, but only leaned towards them. As was ever his fashion when a great crisis was at hand, he fawned alternately on both parties, struck alternately at both, and held himself in readiness to chant the praises or to sign the death-warrant of either. In any event his Carmagnole was ready. The tree of liberty, the blood of traitors, the dagger of Brutus, the guineas of perfidious Albion, would do equally well for Billaud and for Robespierre.

The first attack which was made on Robespierre was indirect. An old woman named Catherine Théot, half maniac, half impostor, was protected by him, and exercised a strange influence over his mind; for he was naturally prone to superstition, and, having abjured the faith in which he had been brought up, was looking about for something to believe. Barère drew up a report against Catherine, which contained many facetious conceits, and ended, as might be expected, with a motion for sending her and some other wretched creatures of both sexes to the Revolutionary Tribunal, or, in other words, to death. This report, however, he did not dare to read to the Convention himself. Another member, less timid, was induced to farther the cruel buffoonery; and the real author enjoyed in security the dismay and vexation of Robespierre.

Barère now thought that he had done enough on one side, and that it was time to make his peace with the other. On the seventh of Thermidor, he pronounced in the Convention a panegyric on Robespierre. "That representative of the people," he said, "enjoys a reputation for patriotism, earned by five years of exertion, and by unalterable fidelity to the principles of independence and liberty." On the eighth of Thermidor, it became clear that a decisive struggle was at hand. Robespierre struck the first blow. He mounted the tribune, and uttered a long invective on his opponents. It was moved that his discourse should be printed; and Barère spoke for the printing. The sense of the Convention soon appeared to be the other way; and Barère apologised for his former speech, and implored his colleagues to abstain from disputes which could be agreeable only to Pitt and York. On the next day, the ever-memorable ninth of Thermidor, came the real tug of war. Tallien, bravely taking his life in his hand, led the onset. Billaud followed; and then all that infinite hatred which had long been kept down by terror burst forth, and swept every barrier before it. When at length the voice of Robespierre, drowned by the President's bell, and by shouts of " Down with the tyrant! " had died away in hoarse gasping, Barère rose. He began with timid and doubtful phrases, watched the effect of every word he uttered, and, when the feeling of the Assembly had been unequivocally manifested, declared against Robespierre. But it was not till the people out of doors, and especially the gunners of Paris, had espoused the cause of the Convention, that Barère felt quite at ease. Then he sprang to the tribune, poured forth a Carmagnole about Pisistratus and Catiline, and concluded by moving that the heads of Robespierre and Robespierre's accomplices should be cut off without a trial. The motion was carried. On the following morning the vanquished members of the Committee of Public Safety and their principal adherents suffered death. It was exactly one year since Barère had commenced his career of slaughter by moving the proscription of his old allies the Girondists. We greatly doubt whether any human being has ever succeeded in packing more wickedness into the space of three hundred and sixty-five days.

The ninth of Thermidor is one of the great epochs in the history of Europe. It is true that the three members of the Committee of Public Safety who triumphed were by no means better men than the three who fell. Indeed, we are inclined to think that of these six statesmen the least bad were Robespierre and Saint Just, whose cruelty was the effect of sincere fanaticism operating on narrow understandings and acrimonious tempers. The worst of the six was, beyond all doubt, Barère, who had no faith in any part of the system which he upheld by persecution; who, while he sent his fellow-creatures to death for being the third cousins of royalists, had not in the least made up his mind that a republic was better than a monarchy; who, while he slew his old friends for federalism, was himself far more a federalist than any of them; who had become a murderer merely for his safety, and who continued to be a murderer merely for his pleasure.

The tendency of the vulgar is to embody everything. Some individual is selected, and often selected very injudicially, as the representative of every great movement of the public mind, of every great revolution in human affairs; and on this indi-

vidual are concentrated all the love and all the hatred, all the
admiration and all the contempt, which he ought rightfully to
share with a whole party, a whole sect, a whole nation, a whole
generation.   Perhaps no human being has suffered so much
from this propensity of the multitude as Robespierre.   He is
regarded, not merely as what he was, an envious, malevolent
zealot, but as the incarnation of Terror, as Jacobinism personified.   The truth is, that it was not by him that the system
of terror was carried to the last extreme.   The most horrible
days in the history of the Revolutionary Tribunal of Paris were
those which immediately preceded the ninth of Thermidor.
Robespierre had then ceased to attend the meetings of the
sovereign Commitee; and the direction of affairs was really in
the hands of Billaud, of Collot, and of Barère.

It had never occurred to those three tyrants that, in overthrowing Robespierre, they were overthrowing that system of
terror to which they were more attached than he had ever been.
Their object was to go on slaying even more mercilessly than
before.   But they had misunderstood the nature of the great
crisis which had at last arrived.   The yoke of the Committee
was broken for ever.   The Convention had regained its liberty,
had tried its strength, had vanquished and punished its enemies.
A great reaction had commenced.   Twenty-four hours after
Robespierre had ceased to live, it was moved and carried, amidst
loud bursts of applause, that the sittings of the Revolutionary
Tribunal should be suspended.   Billaud was not at that moment
present.   He entered the hall soon after, learned with indignation what had passed, and moved that the vote should be
rescinded.   But loud cries of " No, no! " rose from those benches
which had lately paid mute obedience to his commands.   Barère
came forward on the same day, and abjured the Convention not
to relax the system of terror.   " Beware, above all things," he
cried, " of that fatal moderation which talks of peace and of
clemency.   Let aristocracy know that here she will find only
enemies sternly bent on vengeance, and judges who have no
pity."   But the day of the Carmagnoles was over: the restraint
of fear had been relaxed; and the hatred with which the nation
regarded the Jacobin dominion broke forth with ungovernable
violence.   Not more strongly did the tide of public opinion run
against the old monarchy and aristocracy, at the time of the
taking of the Bastile, than it now ran against the tyranny of
the Mountain.   From every dungeon the prisoners came forth
as they had gone in, by hundreds.   The decree which forbade

the soldiers of the republic to give quarter to the English was repealed by an unanimous vote, amidst loud acclamations; nor, passed as it was, disobeyed as it was, and rescinded as it was, can it be with justice considered as a blemish on the fame of the French nation. The Jacobin Club was refractory. It was suppressed without resistance. The surviving Girondist deputies, who had concealed themselves from the vengeance of their enemies in caverns and garrets, were readmitted to their seats in the Convention. No day passed without some signal reparation of injustice; no street in Paris was without some trace of the recent change. In the theatre, the bust of Marat was pulled down from its pedestal and broken in pieces, amidst the applause of the audience. His carcase was ejected from the Pantheon. The celebrated picture of his death, which had hung in the hall of the Convention, was removed. The savage inscriptions with which the walls of the city had been covered disappeared; and, in place of death and terror, humanity, the watchword of the new rulers, was everywhere to be seen. In the meantime, the gay spirit of France, recently subdued by oppression, and now elated by the joy of a great deliverance, wantoned in a thousand forms. Art, taste, luxury, revived. Female beauty regained its empire—an empire strengthened by the remembrance of all the tender and all the sublime virtues which women, delicately bred and reputed frivolous, had displayed during the evil days. Refined manners, chivalrous sentiments, followed in the train of love. The dawn of the Arctic summer day after the Arctic winter night, the great unsealing of the waters, the awakening of animal and vegetable life, the sudden softening of the air, the sudden blooming of the flowers, the sudden bursting of old forests into verdure, is but a feeble type of that happiest and most genial of revolutions, the revolution of the ninth of Thermidor.

But, in the midst of the revival of all kind and generous sentiments, there was one portion of the community against which mercy itself seemed to cry out for vengeance. The chiefs of the late government and their tools were now never named but as the men of blood, the drinkers of blood, the cannibals. In some parts of France, where the creatures of the Mountain had acted with peculiar barbarity, the populace took the law into its own hands and meted out justice to the Jacobins with the true Jacobin measure; but at Paris the punishments were inflicted with order and decency, and were few when compared with the number, and lenient when compared with the enormity, of the crimes.   Soon after the ninth of Thermidor, two of the vilest of mankind, Fouquier Tinville, whom Barère had placed at the Revolutionary Tribunal, and Lebon, whom Barère had defended in the Convention, were placed under arrest.   A third miscreant soon shared their fate, Carrier, the tyrant of Nantes.   The trials of these men brought to light horrors surpassing anything that Suetonius and Lampridius have related of the worst Cæsars.   But it was impossible to punish subordinate agents, who, bad as they were, had only acted in accordance with the spirit of the government which they served, and, at the same time, to grant impunity to the heads of the wicked administration.   A cry was raised, both within and without the Convention, for justice on Collot, Billaud, and Barère.

Collot and Billaud, with all their vices, appear to have been men of resolute natures.   They made no submission;   but opposed to the hatred of mankind, at first a fierce resistance, and afterwards a dogged and sullen endurance.   Barère, on the other hand, as soon as he began to understand the real nature of the revolution of Thermidor, attempted to abandon the Mountain, and to obtain admission among his old friends of the moderate party.   He declared everywhere that he had never been in favour of severe measures;   that he was a Girondist;   that he had always condemned and lamented the manner in which the Brissotine deputies had been treated.   He now preached mercy from that tribune from which he had recently preached extermination.   " The time," he said, " has come at which our clemency may be indulged without danger.   We may now safely consider temporary imprisonment as an adequate punishment for political misdemeanours."   It was only a fortnight since, from the same place, he had declaimed against the moderation which dared even to talk of clemency;   it was only a fortnight since he had ceased to send men and women to the guillotine of Paris, at the rate of three hundred a week.   He now wished to make his peace with the moderate party at the expense of the Terrorists, as he had, a year before, made his peace with the Terrorists at the expense of the moderate party.   But he was disappointed.   He had left himself no retreat.   His face, his voice, his rants, his jokes, had become hateful to the Convention.   When he spoke he was interrupted by murmurs.   Bitter reflections were daily cast on his cowardice and perfidy.   On one occasion Carnot rose to give an account of a victory, and so far forgot the gravity of his own character as to indulge in the sort of oratory which Barère had affected on similar

occasions. He was interrupted by cries of "No more Carmagnoles!" "No more of Barère's puns!"

At length, five months after the revolution of Thermidor, the
Convention resolved that a committee of twenty-one members
should be appointed to examine into the conduct of Billaud,
Collot, and Barère. In some weeks the report was made.
From that report we learn that a paper had been discovered,
signed by Barère, and containing a proposition for adding the
last improvement to the system of terror. France was to be
divided into circuits; itinerant revolutionary tribunals, composed of trusty Jacobins, were to move from department
to department; and the guillotine was to travel in their
train.

Barère, in his defence, insisted that no speech or motion which
he had made in the Convention could, without a violation of
the freedom of debate, be treated as a crime. He was asked
how he could resort to such a mode of defence, after putting to
death so many deputies on account of opinions expressed in
the Convention. He had nothing to say, but that it was much
to be regretted that the sound principle had ever been violated.

He arrogated to himself a large share of the merit of the
revolution in Thermidor. The men who had risked their lives
to effect that revolution, and who knew that, if they had failed,
Barère would, in all probability, have moved the decree for be-
heading them without a trial, and have drawn up a proclamation
announcing their guilt and their punishment to all France, were
by no means disposed to acquiesce in his claims. He was reminded that, only forty-eight hours before the decisive conflict,
he had, in the tribune, been profuse of adulation to Robespierre.
His answer to this reproach is worthy of himself. "It was
necessary," he said, "to dissemble. It was necessary to flatter
Robespierre's vanity, and, by panegyric, to impel him to the
attack. This was the motive which induced me to load him
with those praises of which you complain. Who ever blamed
Brutus for dissembling with Tarquin?"

The accused triumvirs had only one chance of escaping
punishment. There was severe distress at that moment among
the working people of the capital. This distress the Jacobins
attributed to the reaction of Thermidor, to the lenity with which
the aristocrats were now treated, and to the measures which
had been adopted against the chiefs of the late administration.
Nothing is too absurd to be believed by a populace which has
not breakfasted, and which does not know how it is to dine.

The rabble of the Faubourg St. Antoine rose, menaced the deputies, and demanded with loud cries the liberation of the persecuted patriots.   But the Convention was no longer such as it had been, when similar means were employed too successfully against the Girondists.   Its spirit was roused.   Its strength had been proved.   Military means were at its command.   The tumult was suppressed: and it was decreed that same evening that Collot, Billaud, and Barère should instantly be removed to a distant place of confinement.

The next day the order of the Convention was executed.   The account which Barère has given of his journey is the most interesting and the most trustworthy part of these Memoirs. There is no witness so infamous that a court of justice will not take his word against himself; and even Barère may be believed when he tells us how much he was hated and despised.

The carriage in which he was to travel passed, surrounded by armed men, along the street of St. Honoré.   A crowd soon gathered round it and increased every moment.   On the long flight of steps before the church of St. Roch stood rows of eager spectators.   It was with difficulty that the coach could make its way through those who hung upon it, hooting, cursing, and striving to burst the doors.   Barère thought his life in danger, and was conducted at his own request to a public office, where he hoped that he might find shelter till the crowd should disperse.   In the meantime, another discussion on his fate took place in the Convention.   It was proposed to deal with him as he had dealt with better men, to put him out of the pale of the law, and to deliver him at once without any trial to the headsman.   But the humanity which, since the ninth of Thermidor, had generally directed the public councils restrained the deputies from taking this course.

It was now night; and the streets gradually became quiet. The clock struck twelve; and Barère, under a strong guard, again set forth on his journey.   He was conducted over the river to the place where the Orleans road branches off from the southern boulevard.   Two travelling carriages stood there.   In one of them was Billaud, attended by two officers; in the other two more officers were waiting to receive Barère.   Collot was already on the road.

At Orleans, a city which had suffered cruelly from the Jacobin tyranny, the three deputies were surrounded by a mob bent on tearing them to pieces.   All the national guards of the neighbourhood were assembled; and this force was not greater than the emergency required; for the multitude pursued the carriages far on the road to Blois.

At Amboise the prisoners learned that Tours was ready to receive them. The stately bridge was occupied by a throng of people, who swore that the men under whose rule the Loire had been choked with corpses should have full personal experience of the nature of a *noyade*. In consequence of this news, the officers who had charge of the criminals made such arrangements that the carriages reached Tours at two in the morning, and drove straight to the post-house. Fresh horses were instantly ordered; and the travellers started again at full gallop. They had, in truth, not a moment to lose; for the alarm had been given; lights were seen in motion; and the yells of a great multitude, disappointed of its revenge, mingled with the sound of the departing wheels.

At Poitiers there was another narrow escape. As the prisoners quitted the post-house, they saw the whole population pouring in fury down the steep declivity on which the city is built. They passed near Niort, but could not venture to enter it. The inhabitants came forth with threatening aspect, and vehemently cried to the postillions to stop; but the postillions urged the horses to full speed, and soon left the town behind. Through such dangers the men of blood were brought in safety to Rochelle.

Oléron was the place of their destination, a dreary island beaten by the raging waves of the Bay of Biscay. The prisoners were confined in the castle; each had a single chamber, at the door of which a guard was placed; and each was allowed the ration of a single soldier. They were not allowed to communicate either with the garrison or with the population of the island; and soon after their arrival they were denied the indulgence of walking on the ramparts. The only place where they were suffered to take exercise was the esplanade where the troops were drilled.

They had not been long in this situation when news came that the Jacobins of Paris had made a last attempt to regain ascendency in the state, that the hall of the Convention had been forced by a furious crowd, that one of the deputies had been murdered and his head fixed on a pike, that the life of the President had been for a time in imminent danger, and that some members of the legislature had not been ashamed to join the rioters. But troops had arrived in time to prevent a massacre. The insurgents had been put to flight; the inhabitants of the disaffected quarters of the capital had been disarmed; the guilty deputies had suffered the just punishment of their treason; and the power of the Mountain was broken for ever. These events strengthened the aversion with which the system of terror and the authors of that system were regarded. One member of the Convention had moved that the three prisoners of Oléron should be put to death; another, that they should be brought back to Paris, and tried by a council of war. These propositions were rejected. But something was conceded to the party which called for severity. A vessel which had been fitted out with great expedition at Rochefort touched at Oléron; and it was announced to Collot and Billaud that they must instantly go on board. They were forthwith conveyed to Guiana, where Collot soon drank himself to death with brandy. Billaud lived many years, shunning his fellow-creatures and shunned by them; and diverted his lonely hours by teaching parrots to talk. Why a distinction was made between Barère and his companions in guilt, neither he nor any other writer, as far as we know, has explained. It does not appear that the distinction was meant to be at all in his favour; for orders soon arrived from Paris that he should be brought to trial for his crimes before the criminal court of the department of the Upper Charente. He was accordingly brought back to the continent, and confined during some months at Saintes, in an old convent which had lately been turned into a jail.

While he lingered here, the reaction which had followed the great crisis of Thermidor met with a temporary check. The friends of the House of Bourbon, presuming on the indulgence with which they had been treated after the fall of Robespierre, not only ventured to avow their opinions with little disguise, but at length took arms against the Convention, and were not put down till much blood had been shed in the streets of Paris. The vigilance of the public authorities was therefore now directed chiefly against the Royalists; and the rigour with which the Jacobins had lately been treated was somewhat relaxed. The Convention, indeed, again resolved that Barère should be sent to Guiana. But this decree was not carried into effect. The prisoner, probably with the connivance of some powerful persons, made his escape from Saintes and fled to Bordeaux, where he remained in concealment during some years. There seems to have been a kind of understanding between him and the government that, as long as he hid himself, he should not be found, but that, if he obtruded himself on the public eye, he must take the consequences of his rashness.

While the constitution of 1795, with its Executive Directory, its Council of Elders, and its Council of Five Hundred, was in operation, he continued to live under the ban of the law. It was in vain that he solicited, even at moments when the politics of the Mountain seemed to be again in the ascendant, a remission of the sentence pronounced by the Convention. Even his fellow-regicides, even the authors of the slaughter of Vendémiaire and of the arrests of Fructidor, were ashamed of him.

About eighteen months after his escape from prison, his name was again brought before the world. In his own province he still retained some of his early popularity. He had, indeed, never been in that province since the downfall of the monarchy. The mountaineers of Gascony were far removed from the seat of government, and were but imperfectly informed of what passed there. They knew that their countryman had played an important part, and that he had on some occasions promoted their local interests; and they stood by him in his adversity and in his disgrace with a constancy which presents a singular contrast to his own abject fickleness. All France was amazed to learn that the department of the Upper Pyrenees had chosen the proscribed tyrant a member of the Council of Five Hundred. The council which, like our House of Commons, was the judge of the election of its own members, refused to admit him. When his name was read from the roll, a cry of indignation rose from the benches. " Which of you," exclaimed one of the members, " would sit by the side of such a monster? " " Not I, not I! " answered a crowd of voices. One deputy declared that he would vacate his seat if the hall were polluted by the presence of such a wretch. The election was declared null on the ground that the person elected was a criminal skulking from justice; and many severe reflections were thrown on the lenity which suffered him to be still at large.

He tried to make his peace with the Directory, by writing a bulky libel on England, entitled, The Liberty of the Seas. He seems to have confidently expected that this work would produce a great effect. He printed three thousand copies, and in order to defray the expense of publication, sold one of his farms for the sum of ten thousand francs. The book came out; but nobody bought it, in consequence, if Barère is to be believed, of the villainy of Mr. Pitt, who bribed the Directory to order the Reviewers not to notice so formidable an attack on the maritime greatness of perfidious Albion.

Barère had been about three years at Bordeaux when he received intelligence that the mob of the town designed him the honour of a visit on the ninth of Thermidor, and would probably administer to him what he had, in his defence of his friend Lebon, described as substantial justice under forms a little harsh. It was necessary for him to disguise himself in clothes such as were worn by the carpenters of the dock. In this garb, with a bundle of wood shavings under his arm, he made his escape into the vineyards which surrounded the city, lurked during some days in a peasant's hut, and, when the dreaded anniversary was over, stole back into the city. A few months later he was again in danger. He now thought that he should be nowhere so safe as in the neighbourhood of Paris. He quitted Bordeaux, hastened undetected through those towns where four years before his life had been in extreme danger, passed through the capital in the morning twilight, when none were in the streets except shop-boys taking down the shutters, and arrived safe at the pleasant village of St. Ouen on the Seine. Here he remained in seclusion during some months. In the meantime Bonaparte returned from Egypt, placed himself at the head of a coalition of discontented parties, covered his designs with the authority of the Elders, drove the Five Hundred out of their hall at the point of the bayonet, and became absolute monarch of France under the name of First Consul.

Barère assures us that these events almost broke his heart; that he could not bear to see France again subject to a master; and that if the representatives had been worthy of that honourable name, they would have arrested the ambitious general who insulted them. These feelings, however, did not prevent him from soliciting the protection of the new government, and from sending to the First Consul a handsome copy of the essay on the Liberty of the Seas.

The policy of Bonaparte was to cover all the past with a general oblivion. He belonged half to the Revolution and half to the reaction. He was an upstart and a sovereign; and had therefore something in common with the Jacobin, and something in common with the Royalist. All, whether Jacobins or Royalists, who were disposed to support his government, were readily received—all, whether Jacobins or Royalists, who showed hostility to his government, were put down and punished. Men who had borne a part in the worst crimes of the Reign of Terror, and men who had fought in the army of Condé, were to be found close together, both in his antechambers and in his dungeons. He decorated Fouché and Maury with the same cross. He sent

Aréna and Georges Cadoudal to the same scaffold. From a government acting on such principles Barère easily obtained the indulgence which the Directory had constantly refused to grant. The sentence passed by the Convention was remitted; and he was allowed to reside at Paris. His pardon, it is true, was not granted in the most honourable form; and he remained, during some time, under the special supervision of the police. He hastened, however, to pay his court at the Luxemburg palace, where Bonaparte then resided, and was honoured with a few dry and careless words by the master of France.

Here begins a new chapter of Barère's history. What passed between him and the Consular government cannot, of course, be so accurately known to us as the speeches and reports which he made in the Convention. It is, however, not difficult, from notorious facts, and from the admissions scattered over these lying Memoirs, to form a tolerably accurate notion of what took place. Bonaparte wanted to buy Barère: Barère wanted to sell himself to Bonaparte. The only question was one of price; and there was an immense interval between what was offered and what was demanded.

Bonaparte, whose vehemence of will, fixedness of purpose, and reliance on his own genius were not only great but extravagant, looked with scorn on the most effeminate and dependent of human minds. He was quite capable of perpetrating crimes under the influence either of ambition or of revenge: but he had no touch of that accursed monomania, that craving for blood and tears, which raged in some of the Jacobin chiefs. To proscribe the Terrorists would have been wholly inconsistent with his policy; but, of all the classes of men whom his comprehensive system included, he liked them the least; and Barère was the worst of them. This wretch had been branded with infamy, first by the Convention, and then by the Council of Five Hundred. The inhabitants of four or five great cities had attempted to tear him limb from limb. Nor were his vices redeemed by eminent talents for administration or legislation. It would be unwise to place in any honourable or important post a man so wicked, so odious, and so little qualified to discharge high political duties. At the same time there was a way in which it seemed likely that he might be of use to the government. The First Consul, as he afterwards acknowledged, greatly overrated Barère's powers as a writer. The effect which the Reports of the Committee of Public Safety had produced by the camp fires of the Republican armies had been great. Napoleon himself, when a young soldier, had been delighted by those compositions, which had much in common with the rhapsodies of his favourite poet, Macpherson. The taste, indeed, of the great warrior and statesman was never very pure.   His bulletins, his general orders, and his proclamations, are sometimes, it is true, masterpieces in their kind; but we too often detect, even in his best writing, traces of Fingal, and of the Carmagnoles.   It is not strange, therefore, that he should have been desirous to secure the aid of Barère's pen.   Nor was this the only kind of assistance which the old member of the Committee of Public Safety might render to the Consular government.   He was likely to find admission into the gloomy dens in which those Jacobins whose constancy was to be overcome by no reverse, or whose crimes admitted of no expiation, hid themselves from the curses of mankind.   No enterprise was too bold or too atrocious for minds crazed by fanaticism, and familiar with misery and death.   The government was anxious to have information of what passed in their secret councils; and no man was better qualified to furnish such information than Barère.

For these reasons the First Consul was disposed to employ Barère as a writer and as a spy.   But Barère—was it possible that he would submit to such a degradation?   Bad as he was, he had played a great part.   He had belonged to that class of criminals who filled the world with the renown of their crimes; he had been one of a cabinet which had ruled France with absolute power, and made war on all Europe with signal success. Nay, he had been, though not the most powerful, yet, with the single exception of Robespierre, the most conspicuous member of that cabinet.   His name had been a household word at Moscow and at Philadelphia, at Edinburgh and at Cadiz.   The blood of the Queen of France, the blood of the greatest orators and philosophers of France was on his hands.   He had spoken; and it had been decreed that the plough should pass over the great city of Lyons.   He had spoken again; and it had been decreed that the streets of Toulon should be razed to the ground.   When depravity is placed so high as his, the hatred which it inspires is mingled with awe.   His place was with great tyrants, with Critias and Sylla, with Eccelino and Borgia; not with hireling scribblers and police runners.

> " Virtue, I grant you, is an empty boast;
> But shall the dignity of vice be lost? "

So sang Pope; and so felt Barère.   When it was proposed to him to publish a journal in defence of the Consular government, rage and shame inspired him for the first and last time with something like courage. He had filled as large a space in the eyes of mankind as Mr. Pitt or General Washington; and he was coolly invited to descend at once to the level of Mr. Lewis Goldsmith. He saw, too, with agonies of envy, that a wide distinction was made between himself and the other statesmen of the Revolution who were summoned to the aid of the government. Those statesmen were required, indeed, to make large sacrifices of principle; but they were not called on to sacrifice what, in the opinion of the vulgar, constitutes personal dignity. They were made tribunes and legislators, ambassadors and counsellors of state, ministers, senators, and consuls. They might reasonably expect to rise with the rising fortunes of their master; and, in truth, many of them were destined to wear the badge of his Legion of Honour and of his order of the Iron Crown; to be arch-chancellors and arch-treasurers, counts, dukes, and princes. Barère, only six years before, had been far more powerful, far more widely renowned, than any of them; and now, while they were thought worthy to represent the majesty of France at foreign courts, while they received crowds of suitors in gilded antechambers, he was to pass his life in measuring paragraphs, and scolding correctors of the press. It was too much. Those lips which had never before been able to fashion themselves to a No, now murmured expostulation and refusal. " I could not " —these are his own words—" abase myself to such a point as to serve the First Consul merely in the capacity of a journalist, while so many insignificant, low, and servile people, such as the Treilhards, the Rœderers, the Lebruns, the Marets, and others whom it is superfluous to name, held the first place in this government of upstarts."

This outbreak of spirit was of short duration. Napoleon was inexorable. It is said indeed that he was, for a moment, half inclined to admit Barère into the Council of State; but the members of that body remonstrated in the strongest terms, and declared that such a nomination would be a disgrace to them all. This plan was therefore relinquished. Thenceforth Barère's only chance of obtaining the patronage of the government was to subdue his pride, to forget that there had been a time when, with three words, he might have had the heads of the three consuls, and to betake himself, humbly and industriously, to the task of composing lampoons on England and panegyrics on Bonaparte.

It has been often asserted, we know not on what grounds,

that Barère was employed by the government not only as a writer, but as a censor of the writings of other men. This imputation he vehemently denies in his Memoirs; but our readers will probably agree with us in thinking that his denial leaves the question exactly where it was.

Thus much is certain, that he was not restrained from exercising the office of censor by any scruple of conscience or honour; for he did accept an office, compared with which that of censor, odious as it is, may be called an august and beneficient magistracy. He began to have what are delicately called relations with the police. We are not sure that we have formed, or that we can convey, an exact notion of the nature of Barère's new calling. It is a calling unknown in our country. It has indeed often happened in England that a plot has been revealed to the government by one of the conspirators. The informer has sometimes been directed to carry it fair towards his accomplices, and to let the evil design come to full maturity. As soon as his work is done, he is generally snatched from the public gaze, and sent to some obscure village or to some remote colony. The use of spies, even to this extent, is in the highest degree unpopular in England; but a political spy by profession is a creature from which our island is as free as it is from wolves. In France the race is well known, and was never more numerous, more greedy, more cunning, or more savage, than under the government of Bonaparte.

Our idea of a gentleman in relations with the Consular and Imperial police may perhaps be incorrect. Such as it is, we will try to convey it to our readers. We image to ourselves a well-dressed person, with a soft voice and affable manners. His opinions are those of the society in which he finds himself, but a little stronger. He often complains, in the language of honest indignation, that what passes in private conversation finds its way strangely to the government, and cautions his associates to take care what they say when they are not sure of their company. As for himself, he owns that he is indiscreet. He can never refrain from speaking his mind; and that is the reason that he is not prefect of a department.

In a gallery of the Palais Royal he overhears two friends talking earnestly about the King and the Count of Artois. He follows them into a coffee-house, sits at the table next to them, calls for his half-dish and his small glass of cognac, takes up a journal, and seems occupied with the news. His neighbours go on talking without restraint, and in the style of persons warmly attached to the exiled family. They depart; and he follows them half round the boulevards till he fairly tracks them to their apartments, and learns their names from the porters. From that day every letter addressed to either of them is sent from the post-office to the police, and opened. Their correspondents become known to the government, and are carefully watched. Six or eight honest families, in different parts of France, find themselves at once under the frown of power without being able to guess what offence they have given. One person is dismissed from a public office; another learns with dismay that his promising son has been turned out of the Polytechnic school.

Next, the indefatigable servant of the state falls in with an old republican, who has not changed with the times, who regrets the red cap and the tree of liberty, who has not unlearned the Thee and Thou, and who still subscribes his letters with " Health and Fraternity." Into the ears of this sturdy politician our friend pours forth a long series of complaints. What evil times! What a change since the days when the Mountain governed France! What is the First Consul but a king under a new name? What is this Legion of Honour but a new aristocracy? The old superstition is reviving with the old tyranny. There is a treaty with the Pope, and a provision for the clergy. Emigrant nobles are returning in crowds, and are better received at the Tuileries than the men of the 10th of August. This cannot last. What is life without liberty? What terrors has death to the true patriot? The old Jacobin catches fire, bestows and receives the fraternal hug, and hints that there will soon be great news, and that the breed of Harmodius and Brutus is not quite extinct. The next day he is close prisoner, and all his papers are in the hands of the government.

To this vocation, a vocation compared with which the life of a beggar, of a pickpocket, of a pimp, is honourable, did Barère now descend. It was his constant practice, as often as he enrolled himself in a new party, to pay his footing with the heads of old friends. He was at first a Royalist; and he made atonement by watering the tree of liberty with the blood of Louis. He was then a Girondist; and he made atonement by murdering Vergniaud and Gensonné. He fawned on Robespierre up to the eighth of Thermidor; and he made atonement by moving, on the ninth, that Robespierre should be beheaded without a trial. He was now enlisted in the service of the new monarchy; and he proceeded to atone for his republican heresies by sending republican throats to the guillotine.

Among his most intimate associates was a Gascon named Demerville, who had been employed in an office of high trust under the Committee of Public Safety. This man was fanatically attached to the Jacobin system of politics, and, in conjunction with other enthusiasts of the same class, formed a design against the First Consul. A hint of this design escaped him in conversation with Barère. Barère carried the intelligence to Lannes, who commanded the Consular Guards. Demerville was arrested, tried, and beheaded; and among the witnesses who appeared against him was his friend Barère.

The account which Barère has given of these transactions is studiously confused and grossly dishonest. We think, however, that we can discern, through much falsehood and much artful obscurity, some truths which he labours to conceal. It is clear to us that the government suspected him of what the Italians call a double treason. It was natural that such a suspicion should attach to him. He had, in times not very remote, zealously preached the Jacobin doctrine, that he who smites a tyrant deserves higher praise than he who saves a citizen. Was it possible that the member of the Committee of Public Safety, the king-killer, the queen-killer, could in earnest mean to deliver his old confederates, his bosom friends, to the executioner, solely because they had planned an act which, if there were any truth in his own Carmagnoles, was in the highest degree virtuous and glorious? Was it not more probable that he was really concerned in the plot, and that the information which he gave was merely intended to lull or to mislead the police? Accordingly, spies were set on the spy. He was ordered to quit Paris, and not to come within twenty leagues till he received further orders. Nay, he ran no small risk of being sent, with some of his old friends, to Madagascar.

He made his peace, however, with the government so far that he was not only permitted, during some years, to live unmolested, but was employed in the lowest sort of political drudgery. In the summer of 1803, while he was preparing to visit the south of France, he received a letter which deserves to be inserted. It was from Duroc, who is well known to have enjoyed a large share of Napoleon's confidence and favour.

" The First Consul, having been informed that Citizen Barère is about to set out for the country, desires that he will stay at Paris.

" Citizen Barère will every week draw up a report on the state of public opinion on the proceedings of the government, and generally on everything which, in his judgment, it will be interesting to the First Consul to learn.

" He may write with perfect freedom.

" He will deliver his reports under seal into General Duroc's own hand, and General Duroc will deliver them to the First Consul. But it is absolutely necessary that nobody should suspect that this species of communication takes place; and, should any such suspicion get abroad, the First Consul will cease to receive the reports of Citizen Barère.

" It will also be proper that Citizen Barère should frequently insert in the journals articles tending to animate the public mind, particularly against the English."

During some years Barère continued to discharge the functions assigned to him by his master. Secret reports, filled with the talk of coffee-houses, were carried by him every week to the Tuileries. His friends assure us that he took especial pains to do all the harm in his power to the returned emigrants. It was not his fault if Napoleon was not apprised of every murmur and every sarcasm which old marquesses who had lost their estates, and old clergymen who had lost their benefices, uttered against the imperial system. M. Hippolyte Carnot, we grieve to say, is so much blinded by party spirit that he seems to reckon this dirty wickedness among his hero's titles to public esteem.

Barère was, at the same time, an indefatigable journalist and pamphleteer. He set up a paper directed against England, and called the *Mémorial Antibritannique*. He planned a work entitled, " France made great and illustrious by Napoleon." When the Imperial government was established, the old regicide made himself conspicuous even among the crowd of flatterers by the peculiar fulsomeness of his adulation. He translated into French a contemptible volume of Italian verses entitled, " The Poetic Crown, composed on the glorious accession of Napoleon the First, by the Shepherds of Arcadia." He commenced a new series of Carmagnoles very different from those which had charmed the Mountain. The title of Emperor of the French, he said, was mean; Napoleon ought to be Emperor of Europe. King of Italy was too humble an appellation; Napoleon's style ought to be King of Kings.

But Barère laboured to small purpose in both his vocations. Neither as a writer nor as a spy was he of much use. He complains bitterly that his paper did not sell. While the *Journal des Débats*, then flourishing under the able management of Geoffroy, had a circulation of at least twenty thousand copies, the *Mémorial Antibritannique* never, in its most prosperous times, had more than fifteen hundred subscribers; and these subscribers were, with scarcely an exception, persons residing far from Paris, probably Gascons, among whom the name of Barère had not yet lost its influence.

A writer who cannot find readers generally attributes the public neglect to any cause rather than to the true one; and Barère was no exception to the general rule. His old hatred to Paris revived in all its fury. That city, he says, has no sympathy with France. No Parisian cares to subscribe to a journal which dwells on the real wants and interests of the country. To a Parisian nothing is so ridiculous as patriotism. The higher classes of the capital have always been devoted to England. A corporal from London is better received among them than a French general. A journal, therefore, which attacks England has no chance of their support.

A much better explanation of the failure of the *Mémorial* was given by Bonaparte at St. Helena. " Barère," said he to Barry O'Meara, " had the reputation of being a man of talent: but I did not find him so. I employed him to write; but he did not display ability. He used many flowers of rhetoric, but no solid argument; nothing but *coglionerie* wrapped up in high-sounding language."

The truth is that, though Barère was a man of quick parts, and could do with ease what he could do at all, he had never been a good writer. In the day of his power he had been in the habit of haranguing an excitable audience on exciting topics. The faults of his style passed uncensured; for it was a time of literary as well as of civil lawlessness, and a patriot was licensed to violate the ordinary rules of composition as well as the ordinary rules of jurisprudence and of social morality. But there had now been a literary as well as a civil reaction. As there was again a throne and a court, a magistracy, a chivalry, and a hierarchy, so was there a revival of classical taste. Honour was again paid to the prose of Pascal and Massillon, and to the verse of Racine and La Fontaine. The oratory which had delighted the galleries of the Convention was not only as much out of date as the language of Villehardouin and Joinville, but was associated in the public mind with images of horror. All the peculiarities of the Anacreon of the guillotine, his words unknown to the Dictionary of the Academy, his conceits and his jokes, his Gascon idioms and his Gascon hyperboles, had become as odious as the cant of the Puritans was in England after the Restoration.

Bonaparte, who had never loved the men of the Reign of Terror, had now ceased to fear them. He was all-powerful and at the height of glory; they were weak and universally abhorred. He was a sovereign; and it is probable that he already meditated a matrimonial alliance with sovereigns. He was naturally unwilling, in his new position, to hold any intercourse with the worst class of Jacobins. Had Barère's literary assistance been important to the government, personal aversion might have yielded to considerations of policy; but there was no motive for keeping terms with a worthless man who had also proved a worthless writer. Bonaparte, therefore, gave loose to his feelings. Barère was not gently dropped, not sent into an honourable retirement, but spurned and scourged away like a troublesome dog. He had been in the habit of sending six copies of his journal on fine paper daily to the Tuileries. Instead of receiving the thanks and praises which he expected, he was drily told that the great man had ordered five copies to be sent back. Still he toiled on; still he cherished a hope that at last Napoleon would relent, and that at last some share in the honours of the state would reward so much assiduity and so much obsequiousness. He was bitterly undeceived. Under the Imperial constitution the electoral colleges of the departments did not possess the right of choosing senators or deputies, but merely that of presenting candidates. From among these candidates the emperor named members of the senate, and the senate named members of the legislative body. The inhabitants of the Upper Pyrenees were still strangely partial to Barère. In the year 1805, they were disposed to present him as a candidate for the senate. On this Napoleon expressed the highest displeasure; and the president of the electoral college was directed to tell the voters, in plain terms, that such a choice would be disgraceful to the department. All thought of naming Barère a candidate for the senate was consequently dropped. But the people of Argelès ventured to name him a candidate for the legislative body. That body was altogether destitute of weight and dignity; it was not permitted to debate; its only function was to vote in silence for whatever the government proposed. It is not easy to understand how any man who had sat in free and powerful deliberative assemblies could condescend to bear a part in such a mummery. Barère, however, was desirous of a place even in this mock legislature; and a place even in this mock legislature was refused to him.   In the whole senate he had not a single vote.

Such treatment was sufficient, it might have been thought, to move the most abject of mankind to resentment.   Still, however, Barère cringed and fawned on.   His letters came weekly to the Tuileries till the year 1807.   At length, while he was actually writing the two hundred and twenty-third of the series, a note was put into his hands.   It was from Duroc, and was much more perspicuous than polite.   Barère was requested to send no more of his Reports to the palace, as the Emperor was too busy to read them.

Contempt, says the Indian proverb, pierces even the shell of the tortoise; and the contempt of the Court was felt to the quick even by the callous heart of Barère.   He had humbled himself to the dust; and he had humbled himself in vain. Having been eminent among the rulers of a great and victorious state, he had stooped to serve a master in the vilest capacities: and he had been told that, even in those capacities, he was not worthy of the pittance which had been disdainfully flung to him.   He was now degraded below the level even of the hire- lings whom the government employed in the most infamous offices.   He stood idle in the market-place, not because he thought any office too infamous, but because none would hire him.

Yet he had reason to think himself fortunate; for, had all that is avowed in these Memoirs been known, he would have received very different tokens of the Imperial displeasure.   We learn from himself that, while publishing daily columns of flattery on Bonaparte, and while carrying weekly budgets of calumny to the Tuileries, he was in close connection with the agents whom the Emperor Alexander, then by no means favour- ably disposed towards France, employed to watch all that passed at Paris; was permitted to read their secret despatches; was consulted by them as to the temper of the public mind and the character of Napoleon; and did his best to persuade them that the government was in a tottering condition, and that the new sovereign was not, as the world supposed, a great statesman and soldier.   Next, Barère, still the flatterer and talebearer of the Imperial Court, connected himself in the same manner with the Spanish envoy.   He owns that with that envoy he had relations which he took the greatest pains to conceal from his own government; that they met twice a day; and that their conversation chiefly turned on the vices of Napoleon, on his designs against Spain, and on the best mode of rendering those designs abortive. In truth, Barère's baseness was unfathomable. In the lowest deeps of shame he found out lower deeps. It is bad to be a sycophant; it is bad to be a spy. But even among sycophants and spies there are degrees of meanness. The vilest sycophant is he who privily slanders the master on whom he fawns; and the vilest spy is he who serves foreigners against the government of his native land.

From 1807 to 1814 Barère lived in obscurity, railing as bitterly as his craven cowardice would permit against the Imperial administration, and coming sometimes unpleasantly across the police. When the Bourbons returned, he, as might have been expected, became a royalist, and wrote a pamphlet setting forth the horrors of the system from which the Restoration had delivered France, and magnifying the wisdom and goodness which had dictated the charter. He who had voted for the death of Louis, he who had moved the decree for the trial of Marie Antoinette, he whose hatred of monarchy had led him to make war even upon the sepulchres of ancient monarchs, assures us, with great complacency, that " in this work monarchical principles and attachment to the House of Bourbon are nobly expressed." By this apostasy he got nothing, not even any additional infamy; for his character was already too black to be blackened.

During the hundred days he again emerged for a very short time into public life; he was chosen by his native district a member of the Chamber of Representatives. But, though that assembly was composed in a great measure of men who regarded the excesses of the Jacobins with indulgence, he found himself an object of general aversion. When the President first informed the Chamber that M. Barère requested a hearing, a deep and indignant murmur ran round the benches. After the battle of Waterloo, Barère proposed that the Chamber should save France from the victorious enemy, by putting forth a proclamation about the pass of Thermopylæ and the Lacedæmonian custom of wearing flowers in times of extreme danger. Whether this composition, if it had then appeared, would have stopped the English and Prussian armies, is a question respecting which we are left to conjecture. The Chamber refused to adopt this last of the Carmagnoles.

The Emperor had abdicated. The Bourbons returned. The Chamber of Representatives, after burlesquing during a few weeks the proceedings of the National Convention, retired with the well-earned character of having been the silliest political assembly that had met in France.   Those dreaming pedants and praters never for a moment comprehended their position.   They could never understand that Europe must be either conciliated or vanquished; that Europe could be conciliated only by the restoration of Louis, and vanquished only by means of a dictatorial power entrusted to Napoleon.   They would not hear of Louis; yet they would not hear of the only measures which could keep him out.   They incurred the enmity of all foreign powers by putting Napoleon at their head; yet they shackled him, thwarted him, quarrelled with him about every trifle, abandoned him on the first reverse.   They then opposed declamations and disquisitions to eight hundred thousand bayonets; played at making a constitution for their country, when it depended on the indulgence of the victor whether they should have a country; and were at last interrupted, in the midst of their babble about the rights of man and the sovereignty of the people, by the soldiers of Wellington and Blucher.

A new Chamber of Deputies was elected, so bitterly hostile to the Revolution that there was no small risk of a new Reign of Terror.   It is just, however, to say that the king, his ministers, and his allies exerted themselves to restrain the violence of the fanatical royalists, and that the punishments inflicted, though in our opinion unjustifiable, were few and lenient when compared with those which were demanded by M. de Labourdonnaye and M. Hyde de Neuville.   We have always heard, and are inclined to believe, that the government was not disposed to treat even the regicides with severity.   But on this point the feeling of the Chamber of Deputies was so strong that it was thought necessary to make some concession.   It was enacted, therefore, that whoever, having voted in January 1793 for the death of Louis the Sixteenth, had in any manner given in an adhesion to the government of Bonaparte during the hundred days should be banished for life from France.   Barère fell within this description.   He had voted for the death of Louis; and he had sat in the Chamber of Representatives during the hundred days.

He accordingly retired to Belgium, and resided there, forgotten by all mankind, till the year 1830.   After the revolution of July he was at liberty to return to France; and he fixed his residence in his native province.   But he was soon involved in a succession of lawsuits with his nearest relations—" three fatal sisters and an ungrateful brother," to use his own words.

Who was in the right is a question about which we have no means of judging, and certainly shall not take Barère's word. The Courts appear to have decided some points in his favour and some against him. The natural inference is, that there were faults on all sides. The result of this litigation was that the old man was reduced to extreme poverty, and was forced to sell his paternal house.

As far as we can judge from the few facts which remain to be mentioned, Barère continued Barère to the last. After his exile he turned Jacobin again, and, when he came back to France, joined the party of the extreme left in railing at Louis Philippe, and at all Louis Philippe's ministers. M. Casimir Périer, M. de Broglie, M. Guizot, and M. Thiers, in particular, are honoured with his abuse; and the King himself is held up to execration as a hypocritical tyrant. Nevertheless, Barère had no scruple about accepting a charitable donation of a thousand francs a year from the privy purse of the sovereign whom he hated and reviled. This pension, together with some small sums occasionally doled out to him by the department of the Interior, on the ground that he was a distressed man of letters, and by the department of Justice, on the ground that he had formerly held a high judicial office, saved him from the necessity of begging his bread. Having survived all his colleagues of the renowned Committee of Public Safety, and almost all his colleagues of the Convention, he died in January 1841. He had attained his eighty-sixth year.

We have now laid before our readers what we believe to be a just account of this man's life. Can it be necessary for us to add anything for the purpose of assisting their judgment of his character? If we were writing about any of his colleagues in the Committee of Public Safety, about Carnot, about Robespierre, or Saint Just, nay, even about Couthon, Collot, or Billaud, we might feel it necessary to go into a full examination of the arguments which have been employed to vindicate or to excuse the system of Terror. We could, we think, show that France was saved from her foreign enemies, not by the system of Terror, but in spite of it; and that the perils which were made the plea of the violent policy of the Mountain were to a great extent created by that very policy. We could, we think, also show that the evils produced by the Jacobin administration did not terminate when it fell; that it bequeathed a long series of calamities to France and to Europe; that public opinion, which had during two generations been constantly becoming more and more favourable to civil and religious freedom, underwent, during the days of Terror, a change of which the traces are still to be distinctly perceived. It was natural that there should be such a change, when men saw that those who called themselves the champions of popular rights had compressed into the space of twelve months more crimes than the Kings of France, Merovingian, Carlovingian, and Capetian, had perpetrated in twelve centuries. Freedom was regarded as a great delusion. Men were willing to submit to the government of hereditary princes, of fortunate soldiers, of nobles, of priests; to any government but that of philosophers and philanthropists. Hence the imperial despotism, with its enslaved press and its silent tribune, its dungeons stronger than the old Bastile, and its tribunals more obsequious than the old parliaments. Hence the restoration of the Bourbons and of the Jesuits, the Chamber of 1815 with its categories of proscription, the revival of the feudal spirit, the encroachments of the clergy, the persecution of the Protestants, the appearance of a new breed of De Montforts and Dominics in the full light of the nineteenth century. Hence the admission of France into the Holy Alliance, and the war waged by the old soldiers of the tricolour against the liberties of Spain. Hence, too, the apprehensions with which, even at the present day, the most temperate plans for widening the narrow basis of the French representation are regarded by those who are especially interested in the security of property and the maintenance of order. Half a century has not sufficed to obliterate the stain which one year of depravity and madness has left on the noblest of causes.

Nothing is more ridiculous than the manner in which writers like M. Hippolyte Carnot defend or excuse the Jacobin administration, while they declaim against the reaction which followed. That the reaction has produced and is still producing much evil, is perfectly true. But what produced the reaction? The spring flies up with a force proportioned to that with which it has been pressed down. The pendulum which is drawn far in one direction swings as far in the other. The joyous madness of intoxication in the evening is followed by languor and nausea on the morrow. And so, in politics, it is the sure law that every excess shall generate its opposite; nor does he deserve the name of a statesman who strikes a great blow without fully calculating the effect of the rebound. But such calculation was infinitely beyond the reach of the authors of the Reign of Terror. Violence, and more violence, blood, and more blood, made up their whole policy. In a few months these poor creatures succeeded in bringing about a reaction, of which none of them saw, and of which none of us may see the close; and, having brought it about, they marvelled at it; they bewailed it; they execrated it; they ascribed it to everything but the real cause—their own immorality and their own profound incapacity for the conduct of great affairs.

These, however, are considerations to which, on the present occasion, it is hardly necessary for us to advert; for, be the defence which has been set up for the Jacobin policy good or bad, it is a defence which cannot avail Barère. From his own life, from his own pen, from his own mouth, we can prove that the part which he took in the work of blood is to be attributed, not even to sincere fanaticism, not even to misdirected and ill-regulated patriotism, but either to cowardice, or to delight in human misery. Will it be pretended that it was from public spirit that he murdered the Girondists? In these very Memoirs he tells us that he always regarded their death as the greatest calamity that could befall France. Will it be pretended that it was from public spirit that he raved for the head of the Austrian woman? In these very Memoirs he tells us that the time spent in attacking her was ill spent, and ought to have been employed in concerting measures of national defence. Will it be pretended that he was induced by sincere and earnest abhorrence of kingly government to butcher the living and to outrage the dead; he who invited Napoleon to take the title of King of Kings, he who assures us that after the Restoration he expressed in noble language his attachment to monarchy, and to the house of Bourbon? Had he been less mean, something might have been said in extenuation of his cruelty. Had he been less cruel, something might have been said in extenuation of his meanness. But for him, regicide and court-spy, for him who patronised Lebon and betrayed Demerville, for him who wantoned alternately in gasconades of Jacobinism and gasconades of servility, what excuse has the largest charity to offer?

We cannot conclude without saying something about two parts of his character, which his biographer appears to consider as deserving of high admiration. Barère, it is admitted, was somewhat fickle; but in two things he was consistent, in his love of Christianity, and in his hatred to England. If this were so, we must say that England is much more beholden to him than Christianity.

It is possible that our inclinations may bias our judgment;

but we think that we do not flatter ourselves when we say that Barère's aversion to our country was a sentiment as deep and constant as his mind was capable of entertaining. The value of this compliment is indeed somewhat diminished by the circumstance that he knew very little about us. His ignorance of our institutions, manners, and history is the less excusable, because, according to his own account, he consorted much, during the peace of Amiens, with Englishmen of note, such as that eminent noblemen Lord Greaten, and that not less eminent philosopher Mr. Mackensie Cœfhis. In spite, however, of his connection with these well-known ornaments of our country, he was so ill-informed about us as to fancy that our government was always laying plans to torment him. If he was hooted at Saintes, probably by people whose relations he had murdered, it was because the cabinet of St. James's had hired the mob. If nobody would read his bad books it was because the cabinet of St. James's had secured the Reviewers. His accounts of Mr. Fox, of Mr. Pitt, of the Duke of Wellington, of Mr. Canning, swarm with blunders surpassing even the ordinary blunders committed by Frenchmen who write about England. Mr. Fox and Mr. Pitt, he tells us, were ministers in two different reigns. Mr. Pitt's sinking fund was instituted in order to enable England to pay subsidies to the powers allied against the French republic. The Duke of Wellington's house in Hyde Park was built by the nation, which twice voted the sum of £200,000 for the purpose. This, however, is exclusive of the cost of the frescoes, which were also paid for out of the public purse. Mr. Canning was the first Englishman whose death Europe had reason to lament; for the death of Lord Ward, a relation, we presume, of Lord Greaten and Mr. Cœfhis, had been an immense benefit to mankind.

Ignorant, however, as Barère was, he knew enough of us to hate us; and we persuade ourselves that, had he known us better, he would have hated us more. The nation which has combined, beyond all example and all hope, the blessings of liberty with those of order, might well be an object of aversion to one who had been false alike to the cause of order and to the cause of liberty. We have had amongst us intemperate zeal for popular rights; we have had amongst us also the intemperance of loyalty. But we have never been shocked by such a spectacle as the Barère of 1794, or as the Barère of 1804. Compared with him, our fiercest demagogues have been gentle; compared with him, our meanest courtiers have been manly. Mix together Thistlewood and Bubb Doddington; and you are still far from having

Barère. The antipathy between him and us is such that neither for the crimes of his earlier nor for those of his later life does our language, rich as it is, furnish us with adequate names. We have found it difficult to relate his history without having perpetual recourse to the French vocabulary of horror, and to the French vocabulary of baseness. It is not easy to give a notion of his conduct in the Convention without using those emphatic terms, *guillotinade, noyade, fusillade, mitraillade*. It is not easy to give a notion of his conduct under the Consulate and the Empire without borrowing such words as *mouchard* and *mouton*.

We therefore like his invectives against us much better than anything else that he has written; and dwell on them, not merely with complacency, but with a feeling akin to gratitude. It was but little that he could do to promote the honour of our country; but that little he did strenuously and constantly. Renegade, traitor, slave, coward, liar, slanderer, murderer, hack writer, police-spy—the one small service which he could render to England was to hate her: and such as he was may all who hate her be!

We cannot say that we contemplate with equal satisfaction that fervent and constant zeal for religion which, according to M. Hippolyte Carnot, distinguished Barère; for, as we think, that whatever brings dishonour on religion is a serious evil, we had, we own, indulged a hope that Barère was an atheist. We now learn, however, that he was at no time even a sceptic, that he adhered to his faith through the whole Revolution, and that he has left several manuscript works on divinity. One of these is a pious treatise, entitled " Of Christianity, and of its Influence." Another consists of meditations on the Psalms, which will doubtless greatly console and edify the Church.

This makes the character complete. Whatsoever things are false, whatsoever things are dishonest, whatsoever things are unjust, whatsoever things are impure, whatsoever things are hateful, whatsoever things are of evil report, if there be any vice, and if there be any infamy, all these things, we knew, were blended in Barère. But one thing was still wanting; and that M. Hippolyte Carnot has supplied. When to such an assemblage of qualities a high profession of piety is added, the effect becomes overpowering. We sink under the contemplation of such exquisite and manifold perfection; and feel, with deep humility, how presumptuous it was in us to think of composing the legend of this beatified athlete of the faith, St. Bertrand of the Carmagnoles.

Something more we had to say about him. But let him go.
We did not seek him out, and will not keep him longer. If those
who call themselves his friends had not forced him on our notice
we should never have vouchsafed to him more than a passing
word of scorn and abhorrence, such as we might fling at his
brethren, Hébert and Fouquier Tinville, and Carrier and Lebon.
We have no pleasure in seeing human nature thus degraded. We
turn with disgust from the filthy and spiteful Yahoos of the
fiction; and the filthiest and most spiteful Yahoo of the fiction
was a noble creature when compared with the Barère of history.
But what is no pleasure M. Hippolyte Carnot has made a duty.
It is no light thing that a man in high and honourable public
trust, a man who, from his connections and position, may not
unnaturally be supposed to speak the sentiments of a large class
of his countrymen, should come forward to demand approbation
for a life black with every sort of wickedness, and unredeemed
by a single virtue. This M. Hippolyte Carnot has done. By
attempting to enshrine this Jacobin carrion, he has forced us to
gibbet it; and we venture to say that, from the eminence of
infamy on which we have placed it, he will not easily take it
down.

FRANCIS ATTERBURY [1]

(December 1853)

FRANCIS ATTERBURY, a man who holds a conspicuous place in
the political, ecclesiastical, and literary history of England, was
born in the year 1662, at Middleton in Buckinghamshire, a parish
of which his father was rector. Francis was educated at Westminster School, and carried thence to Christchurch a stock of
learning which, though really scanty, he through life exhibited
with such judicious ostentation that superficial observers believed
his attainments to be immense. At Oxford, his parts, his taste,
and his bold, contemptuous, and imperious spirit, soon made him
conspicuous. Here he published, at twenty, his first work, a
translation of the noble poem of Absalom and Achitophel into
Latin verse. Neither the style nor the versification of the young
scholar was that of the Augustan age. In English composition
he succeeded much better. In 1687 he distinguished himself

---

[1] From *The Encyclopædia Britannica.*

among many able men who wrote in defence of the Church of
England, then persecuted by James II., and calumniated by
apostates who had for lucre quitted her communion. Among
these apostates none was more active or malignant than Obadiah
Walker, who was master of University College, and who had set
up there, under the royal patronage, a press for printing tracts
against the established religion. In one of these tracts, written
apparently by Walker himself, many aspersions were thrown on
Martin Luther. Atterbury undertook to defend the great Saxon
Reformer, and performed that task in a manner singularly characteristic. Whoever examines his reply to Walker will be struck
by the contrast between the feebleness of those parts which are
argumentative and defensive, and the vigour of those parts which
are rhetorical and aggressive. The Papists were so much galled
by the sarcasms and invectives of the young polemic that they
raised a cry of treason, and accused him of having, by implica-
tion, called King James a Judas.

After the Revolution, Atterbury, though bred in the doctrines
of non-resistance and passive obedience, readily swore fealty to
the new government. In no long time he took holy orders. He
occasionally preached in London with an eloquence which raised
his reputation, and soon had the honour of being appointed one
of the royal chaplains. But he ordinarily resided at Oxford,
where he took an active part in academical business, directed
the classical studies of the undergraduates of his college, and was
the chief adviser and assistant of Dean Aldrich, a divine now
chiefly remembered by his catches, but renowned among his contemporaries as a scholar, a Tory, and a high-churchman. It was
the practice, not a very judicious practice, of Aldrich to employ
the most promising youths of his college in editing Greek and
Latin books. Among the studious and well-disposed lads who
were, unfortunately for themselves, induced to become teachers
of philology when they should have been content to be learners,
was Charles Boyle, son of the Earl of Orrery, and nephew of
Robert Boyle, the great experimental philosopher. The task
assigned to Charles Boyle was to prepare a new edition of one of
the most worthless books in existence. It was a fashion, among
those Greeks and Romans who cultivated rhetoric as an art, to
compose epistles and harangues in the names of eminent men.
Some of these counterfeits are fabricated with such exquisite
taste and skill that it is the highest achievement of criticism to
distinguish them from originals. Others are so feebly and rudely
executed that they can hardly impose on an intelligent school-

boy.   The best specimen which has come down to us is perhaps the oration for Marcellus, such an imitation of Tully's eloquence as Tully would himself have read with wonder and delight.   The worst specimen is perhaps a collection of letters purporting to have been written by that Phalaris who governed Agrigentum more than 500 years before the Christian era.   The evidence, both internal and external, against the genuineness of these letters is overwhelming.   When, in the fifteenth century, they emerged, in company with much that was far more valuable, from their obscurity, they were pronounced spurious by Politian, the greatest scholar of Italy, and by Erasmus, the greatest scholar on our side of the Alps.   In truth, it would be as easy to persuade an educated Englishman that one of Johnson's Ramblers was the work of William Wallace as to persuade a man like Erasmus that a pedantic exercise, composed in the trim and artificial Attic of the time of Julian, was a dispatch written by a crafty and ferocious Dorian, who roasted people alive many years before there existed a volume of prose in the Greek language. But, though Christchurch could boast of many good Latinists, of many good English writers, and of a greater number of clever and fashionable men of the world than belonged to any other academic body, there was not then in the college a single man capable of distinguishing between the infancy and the dotage of Greek literature.   So superficial indeed was the learning of the rulers of this celebrated society that they were charmed by an essay which Sir William Temple published in praise of the ancient writers.   It now seems strange that even the eminent public services, the deserved popularity, and the graceful style of Temple should have saved so silly a performance from universal contempt.   Of the books which he most vehemently eulogised his eulogies proved that he knew nothing.   In fact, he could not read a line of the language in which they were written. Among many other foolish things, he said that the letters of Phalaris were the oldest letters and also the best in the world. Whatever Temple wrote attracted notice.   People who had never heard of the Epistles of Phalaris began to inquire about them.   Aldrich, who knew very little Greek, took the word of Temple who knew none, and desired Boyle to prepare a new edition of these admirable compositions which, having long slept in obscurity, had become on a sudden objects of general interest.

The edition was prepared with the help of Atterbury, who was Boyle's tutor, and of some other members of the college.   It was an edition such as might be expected from people who would stoop to edite such a book. The notes were worthy of the text; the Latin version worthy of the Greek original. The volume would have been forgotten in a month had not a misunderstanding about a manuscript arisen between the young editor and the greatest scholar that had appeared in Europe since the revival of letters, Richard Bentley. The manuscript was in Bentley's keeping. Boyle wished it to be collated. A mischief-making bookseller informed him that Bentley had refused to lend it, which was false, and also that Bentley had spoken contemptuously of the letters attributed to Phalaris, and of the critics who were taken in by such counterfeits, which was perfectly true. Boyle, much provoked, paid, in his preface, a bitterly ironical compliment to Bentley's courtesy. Bentley revenged himself by a short dissertation, in which he proved that the epistles were spurious, and the new edition of them worthless: but he treated Boyle personally with civility as a young gentleman of great hopes, whose love of learning was highly commendable, and who deserved to have had better instructors.

Few things in literary history are more extraordinary than the storm which this little dissertation raised. Bentley had treated Boyle with forbearance; but he had treated Christchurch with contempt; and the Christchurch-men, wherever dispersed, were as much attached to their college as a Scotchman to his country, or a Jesuit to his order. Their influence was great. They were dominant at Oxford, powerful in the Inns of Court and in the College of Physicians, conspicuous in Parliament and in the literary and fashionable circles of London. Their unanimous cry was, that the honour of the college must be vindicated, that the insolent Cambridge pedant must be put down. Poor Boyle was unequal to the task, and disinclined to it. It was, therefore, assigned to his tutor, Atterbury.

The answer to Bentley, which bears the name of Boyle, but which was, in truth, no more the work of Boyle than the letters to which the controversy related were the work of Phalaris, is now read only by the curious, and will in all probability never be reprinted again. But it had its day of noisy popularity. It was to be found, not only in the studies of men of letters, but on the tables of the most brilliant drawing-rooms of Soho Square and Covent Garden. Even the beaus and coquettes of that age, the Wildairs and the Lady Lurewells, the Mirabells and the Millaments, congratulated each other on the way in which the gay young gentleman, whose erudition sate so easily upon him, and who wrote with so much pleasantry and good breeding about the

Attic dialect and the anapæstic measure, Sicilian talents and
Thericlean cups, had bantered the queer prig of a doctor.   Nor
was the applause of the multitude undeserved.   The book is,
indeed, Atterbury's masterpiece, and gives a higher notion of his
powers than any of those works to which he put his name.   That
he was altogether in the wrong on the main question, and on all
the collateral questions springing out of it, that his knowledge
of the language, the literature, and the history of Greece was not
equal to what many freshmen now bring up every year to Cambridge and Oxford, and that some of his blunders seem rather to
deserve a flogging than a refutation, is true; and therefore it is
that his performance is, in the highest degree, interesting and
valuable to a judicious reader.   It is good by reason of its exceeding badness.   It is the most extraordinary instance that exists
of the art of making much show with little substance.   There is
no difficulty, says the steward of Molière's miser, in giving a fine
dinner with plenty of money: the really great cook is he who
can set out a banquet with no money at all.   That Bentley
should have written excellently on ancient chronology and geography, on the development of the Greek language, and the origin
of the Greek drama, is not strange.   But that Atterbury should,
during some years, have been thought to have treated these
subjects much better that Bentley is strange indeed.   It is true
that the champion of Christchurch had all the help which the
most celebrated members of that society could give him.   Smalridge contributed some very good wit; Friend and others some
very bad archæology and philology.   But the greater part of the
volume was entirely Atterbury's: what was not his own was
revised and retouched by him: and the whole bears the mark of
his mind, a mind inexhaustibly rich in all the resources of controversy, and familiar with all the artifices which make falsehood
look like truth, and ignorance like knowledge.   He had little
gold; but he beat that little out to the very thinnest leaf, and
spread it over so vast a surface that to those who judged by a
glance, and who did not resort to balances and tests, the glittering heap of worthless matter which he produced seemed to be an
inestimable treasure of massy bullion.   Such arguments as he
had he placed in the clearest light.   Where he had no arguments,
he resorted to personalities, sometimes serious, generally ludicrous, always clever and cutting.   But, whether he was grave or
merry, whether he reasoned or sneered, his style was always pure,
polished, and easy.

Party spirit then ran high; yet, though Bentley ranked among

Whigs, and Christchurch was a stronghold of Toryism, Whigs joined with Tories in applauding Atterbury's volume. Garth insulted Bentley, and extolled Boyle in lines which are now never quoted except to be laughed at. Swift, in his " Battle of the Books," introduced with much pleasantry Boyle, clad in armour, the gift of all the gods, and directed by Apollo in the form of a human friend, for whose name a blank is left which may easily be filled up. The youth, so accoutred, and so assisted, gains an easy victory over his uncourteous and boastful antagonist. Bentley, meanwhile, was supported by the consciousness of an immeasurable superiority, and encouraged by the voices of the few who were really competent to judge the combat. " No man, he said, justly and nobly, " was ever written down but by himself." He spent two years in preparing a reply, which will never cease to be read and prized while the literature of ancient Greece is studied in any part of the world. This reply proved, not only that the letters ascribed to Phalaris were spurious, but that Atterbury, with all his wit, his eloquence, his skill in controversial fence, was the most audacious pretender that ever wrote about what he did not understand. But to Atterbury this exposure was matter of indifference. He was now engaged in a dispute about matters far more important and exciting than the laws of Zaleucus and the laws of Charondas. The rage of religious factions was extreme. High church and Low church divided the nation. The great majority of the clergy were on the high-church side; the majority of King William's bishops were inclined to latitudinarianism. A dispute arose between the two parties touching the extent of the powers of the Lower House of Convocation. Atterbury thrust himself eagerly into the front rank of the high-churchmen. Those who take a comprehensive and impartial view of his whole career will not be disposed to give him credit for religious real. But it was his nature to be vehement and pugnacious in the cause of every fraternity of which he was a member. He had defended the genuineness of a spurious book simply because Christchurch had put forth an edition of that book; he now stood up for the clergy against the civil power, simply because he was a clergyman, and for the priests against the episcopal order, simply because he was as yet only a priest. He asserted the pretensions of the class to which he belonged in several treatises written with much wit, ingenuity, audacity, and acrimony. In this, as in his first controversy, he was opposed to antagonists whose knowledge of the subject in dispute was far superior to his; but in this, as in his first controversy, he imposed on the multitude by bold assertion, by sarcasm, by declamation, and, above all, by his peculiar knack of exhibiting a little erudition in such a manner as to make it look like a great deal.   Having passed himself off on the world as a greater master of classical learning than Bentley, he now passed himself off as a greater master of ecclesiastical learning than Wake or Gibson.   By the great body of the clergy he was regarded as the ablest and most intrepid tribune that had ever defended their rights against the oligarchy of prelates.   The Lower House of Convocation voted him thanks for his services; the University of Oxford created him a doctor of divinity; and soon after the accession of Anne, while the Tories still had the chief weight in the government, he was promoted to the deanery of Carlisle.

Soon after he had obtained this preferment, the Whig party rose to ascendency in the state.   From that party he could expect no favour.   Six years elapsed before a change of fortune took place.   At length, in the year 1710, the prosecution of Sacheverell produced a formidable explosion of high-church fanaticism.   At such a moment Atterbury could not fail to be conspicuous.   His inordinate zeal for the body to which he belonged, his turbulent and aspiring temper, his rare talents for agitation and for controversy, were again signally displayed. He bore a chief part in framing that artful and eloquent speech which the accused divine pronounced at the bar of the Lords, and which presents a singular contrast to the absurd and scurrilous sermon which had very unwisely been honoured with impeachment.   During the troubled and anxious months which followed the trial, Atterbury was among the most active of those pamphleteers who inflamed the nation against the Whig ministry and the Whig parliament.   When the ministry had been changed and the parliament dissolved, rewards were showered upon him. The Lower House of Convocation elected him prolocutor.   The Queen appointed him Dean of Christchurch on the death of his old friend and patron Aldrich.   The college would have preferred a gentler ruler.   Nevertheless, the new head was received with every mark of honour.   A congratulatory oration in Latin was addressed to him in the magnificent vestibule of the hall; and he in reply professed the warmest attachment to the venerable house in which he had been educated, and paid many gracious compliments to those over whom he was to preside.   But it was not in his nature to be a mild or an equitable governor.   He had left the chapter of Carlisle distracted by quarrels.   He found

Christchurch at peace; but in three months his despotic and contentious temper did at Christchurch what it had done at Carlisle. He was succeeded in both his deaneries by the humane and accomplished Smalridge, who gently complained of the state in which both had been left. " Atterbury goes before, and sets everything on fire. I come after him with a bucket of water." It was said by Atterbury's enemies that he was made a bishop because he was so bad a dean. Under his administration Christchurch was in confusion, scandalous altercations took place, opprobrious words were exchanged; and there was reason to fear that the great Tory college would be ruined by the tyranny of the great Tory doctor. He was soon removed to the bishopric of Rochester, which was then always united with the deanery of Westminster. Still higher dignities seemed to be before him. For, though there were many able men on the episcopal bench, there was none who equalled or approached him in parliamentary talents. Had his party continued in power, it is not improbable that he would have been raised to the archbishopric of Canterbury. The more splendid his prospects, the more reason he had to dread the accession of a family which was well known to be partial to the Whigs. There is every reason to believe that he was one of those politicians who hoped that they might be able, during the life of Anne, to prepare matters in such a way that at her decease there might be little difficulty in setting aside the Act of Settlement and placing the Pretender on the throne. Her sudden death confounded the projects of these conspirators. Atterbury, who wanted no kind of courage, implored his confederates to proclaim James III., and offered to accompany the heralds in lawn sleeves. But he found even the bravest soldiers of his party irresolute, and exclaimed, not, it is said, without interjections which ill became the mouth of a father of the church, that the best of all causes and the most precious of all moments had been pusillanimously thrown away. He acquiesced in what he could not prevent, took the oaths to the House of Hanover, and at the coronation officiated with the outward show of zeal, and did his best to ingratiate himself with the royal family. But his servility was requited with cold contempt. No creature is so revengeful as a proud man who has humbled himself in vain. Atterbury became the most factious and pertinacious of all the opponents of the government. In the House of Lords his oratory, lucid, pointed, lively, and set off with every grace of pronunciation and of gesture, extorted the attention and admiration even of a hostile majority. Some of the most remarkable protests which appear in the journals of the peers were drawn up by him; and in some of the bitterest of those pamphlets which called on the English to stand up for their country against the aliens who had come from beyond the seas to oppress and plunder her, critics easily detected his style. When the rebellion of 1715 broke out, he refused to sign the paper in which the bishops of the province of Canterbury declared their attachment to the Protestant succession. He busied himself in electioneering, especially at Westminster, where, as dean, he possessed great influence; and was, indeed, strongly suspected of having once set on a riotous mob to prevent his Whig fellow-citizens from polling.

After having been long in indirect communication with the exiled family, he, in 1717, began to correspond directly with the Pretender. The first letter of the correspondence is extant. In that letter Atterbury boasts of having, during many years past, neglected no opportunity of serving the Jacobite cause. " My daily prayer," he says, " is that you may have success. May I live to see that day, and live no longer than I do what is in my power to forward it." It is to be remembered that he who wrote thus was a man bound to set to the church of which he was overseer an example of strict probity; that he had repeatedly sworn allegiance to the House of Brunswick; that he had assisted in placing the crown on the head of George I., and that he had abjured James III., " without equivocation or mental reservation, on the true faith of a Christian."

It is agreeable to turn from his public to his private life. His turbulent spirit, wearied with faction and treason, now and then required repose, and found it in domestic endearments, and in the society of the most illustrious of the living and of the dead. Of his wife little is known: but between him and his daughter there was an affection singularly close and tender. The gentleness of his manners when he was in the company of a few friends was such as seemed hardly credible to those who knew him only by his writings and speeches. The charm of his " softer hour " has been commemorated by one of those friends in imperishable verse. Though Atterbury's classical attainments were not great, his taste in English literature was excellent; and his admiration of genius was so strong that it overpowered even his political and religious antipathies. His fondness for Milton, the mortal enemy of the Stuarts and of the church, was such as to many Tories seemed a crime. On the sad night on which Addison was laid in the chapel of Henry VII., the Westminster boys remarked that Atterbury read the

funeral service with a peculiar tenderness and solemnity. The
favourite companions, however, of the great Tory prelate were,
as might have been expected, men whose politics had at least
a tinge of Toryism. He lived on friendly terms with Swift,
Arbuthnot, and Gay. With Prior he had a close intimacy,
which some misunderstanding about public affairs at last dissolved. Pope found in Atterbury, not only a warm admirer,
but a most faithful, fearless, and judicious adviser. The poet
was a frequent guest at the episcopal palace among the elms of
Bromley, and entertained not the slightest suspicion that his
host, now declining in years, confined to an easy chair by gout,
and apparently devoted to literature, was deeply concerned in
criminal and perilous designs against the government.

The spirit of the Jacobites had been cowed by the events of
1715. It revived in 1721. The failure of the South Sea project, the panic in the money market, the downfall of great
commercial houses, the distress from which no part of the
kingdom was exempt, had produced general discontent. It
seemed not improbable that at such a moment an insurrection
might be successful. An insurrection was planned. The streets
of London were to be barricaded; the Tower and the Bank
were to be surprised; King George, his family, and his chief
captains and councillors, were to be arrested; and King James
was to be proclaimed. The design became known to the Duke
of Orleans, regent of France, who was on terms of friendship
with the House of Hanover. He put the English government
on its guard. Some of the chief malcontents were committed
to prison; and among them was Atterbury. No bishop of the
Church of England had been taken into custody since that
memorable day when the applauses and prayers of all London
had followed the seven bishops to the gate of the Tower. The
Opposition entertained some hope that it might be possible to
excite among the people an enthusiasm resembling that of their
fathers, who rushed into the waters of the Thames to implore
the blessing of Sancroft. Pictures of the heroic confessor in his
cell were exhibited at the shop windows. Verses in his praise
were sung about the streets. The restraints by which he was
prevented from communicating with his accomplices were represented as cruelties worthy of the dungeons of the Inquisition.
Strong appeals were made to the priesthood. Would they
tamely permit so gross an insult to be offered to their cloth?
Would they suffer the ablest, the most eloquent member of
their profession, the man who had so often stood up for their

rights against the civil power, to be treated like the vilest of mankind? There was considerable excitement; but it was allayed by a temperate and artful letter to the clergy, the work, in all probability, of Bishop Gibson, who stood high in the favour of Walpole, and shortly after became minister for ecclesiastical affairs.

Atterbury remained in close confinement during some months. He had carried on his correspondence with the exiled family so cautiously that the circumstantial proofs of his guilt, though sufficient to produce entire moral conviction, were not sufficient to justify legal conviction. He could be reached only by a bill of pains and penalties. Such a bill the Whig party, then decidedly predominant in both houses, was quite prepared to support. Many hot-headed members of that party were eager to follow the precedent which had been set in the case of Sir John Fenwick, and to pass an act for cutting off the bishop's head. Cadogan, who commanded the army, a brave soldier, but a headstrong politician, is said to have exclaimed with great vehemence: "Fling him to the lions in the Tower." But the wiser and more humane Walpole was always unwilling to shed blood; and his influence prevailed. When Parliament met, the evidence against the bishop was laid before committees of both houses. Those committees reported that his guilt was proved. In the Commons a resolution, pronouncing him a traitor, was carried by nearly two to one. A bill was then introduced which provided that he should be deprived of his spiritual dignities, that he should be banished for life, and that no British subject should hold any intercourse with him except by the royal permission.

This bill passed the Commons with little difficulty. For the bishop, though invited to defend himself, chose to reserve his defence for the assembly of which he was a member. In the Lords the contest was sharp. The young Duke of Wharton, distinguished by his parts, his dissoluteness, and his versatility, spoke for Atterbury with great effect; and Atterbury's own voice was heard for the last time by that unfriendly audience which had so often listened to him with mingled aversion and delight. He produced few witnesses; nor did those witnesses say much that could be of service to him. Among them was Pope. He was called to prove that, while he was an inmate of the palace at Bromley, the bishop's time was completely occupied by literary and domestic matters, and that no leisure was left for plotting. But Pope, who was quite unaccustomed to speak in public, lost his head, and, as he afterwards owned, though he had only ten words to say, made two or three blunders.

The bill finally passed the Lords by eighty-three votes to forty-three. The bishops, with a single exception, were in the majority. Their conduct drew on them a sharp taunt from Lord Bathurst, a warm friend of Atterbury and a zealous Tory. " The wild Indians," he said, " give no quarter, because they believe that they shall inherit the skill and prowess of every adversary whom they destroy. Perhaps the animosity of the right reverend prelates to their brother may be explained in the same way."

Atterbury took leave of those whom he loved with a dignity and tenderness worthy of a better man. Three fine lines of his favourite poet were often in his mouth:—

> " Some natural tears he dropped, but wiped them soon:
> The world was all before him, where to chuse
> His place of rest, and Providence his guide."

At parting he presented Pope with a Bible, and said, with a disingenuousness of which no man who had studied the Bible to much purpose would have been guilty: " If ever you learn that I have any dealings with the Pretender, I give you leave to say that my punishment is just." Pope at this time really believed the bishop to be an injured man. Arbuthnot seems to have been of the same opinion. Swift, a few months later, ridiculed with great bitterness, in the " Voyage to Laputa," the evidence which had satisfied the two Houses of Parliament. Soon, however, the most partial friends of the banished prelate ceased to assert his innocence, and contented themselves with lamenting and excusing what they could not defend. After a short stay at Brussels, he had taken up his abode at Paris, and had become the leading man among the Jacobite refugees who were assembled there. He was invited to Rome by the Pretender, who then held his mock court under the immediate protection of the Pope. But Atterbury felt that a bishop of the Church of England would be strangely out of place at the Vatican, and declined the invitation. During some months, however, he might flatter himself that he stood high in the good graces of James. The correspondence between the master and the servant was constant. Atterbury's merits were warmly acknowledged; his advice was respectfully received; and he was, as Bolingbroke had been before him, the prime minister of a king without a kingdom. But the new favourite found, as Bolingbroke had found before him, that it was quite as hard to keep the shadow of power under a vagrant and

mendicant prince as to keep the reality of power at Westminster.
Though James had neither territories nor revenues, neither army
nor navy, there was more faction and more intrigue among his
courtiers than among those of his successful rival. Atterbury
soon perceived that his counsels were disregarded, if not distrusted.
His proud spirit was deeply wounded. He quitted Paris, fixed
his residence at Montpellier, gave up politics, and devoted himself entirely to letters. In the sixth year of his exile he had so
severe an illness that his daughter, herself in very delicate health,
determined to run all risks that she might see him once more.
Having obtained a licence from the English Government, she
went by sea to Bordeaux, but landed there in such a state that
she could travel only by boat or in a litter. Her father, in spite
of his infirmities, set out from Montpellier to meet her; and she,
with the impatience which is often the sign of approaching death,
hastened towards him. Those who were about her in vain
implored her to travel slowly. She said that every hour was
precious, that she only wished to see her papa and to die. She
met him at Toulouse, embraced him, received from his hand the
sacred bread and wine, and thanked God that they had passed
one day in each other's society before they parted for ever. She
died that night.

It was some time before even the strong mind of Atterbury
recovered from this cruel blow. As soon as he was himself again
he became eager for action and conflict; for grief, which disposes
gentle natures to retirement, to inaction, and to meditation, only
makes restless spirits more restless. The Pretender, dull and
bigoted as he was, had found out that he had not acted wisely in
parting with one who, though a heretic, was, in abilities and
accomplishments, the foremost man of the Jacobite party. The
bishop was courted back, and was without much difficulty
induced to return to Paris and to become once more the phantom
minister of a phantom monarchy. But his long and troubled
life was drawing to a close. To the last, however, his intellect
retained all its keenness and vigour. He learned, in the ninth
year of his banishment, that he had been accused by Oldmixon,
as dishonest and malignant a scribbler as any that has been saved
from oblivion by the Dunciad, of having, in concert with other
Christchurchmen, garbled Clarendon's History of the Rebellion.
The charge, as respected Atterbury, had not the slightest foundation: for he was not one of the editors of the History, and never
saw it till it was printed. He published a short vindication of
himself, which is a model in its kind, luminous, temperate, and

dignified. A copy of this little work he sent to the Pretender, with a letter singularly eloquent and graceful. It was impossible, the old man said, that he should write anything on such a subject without being reminded of the resemblance between his own fate and that of Clarendon. They were the only two English subjects that had ever been banished from their country and debarred from all communication with their friends by act of parliament. But here the resemblance ended. One of the exiles had been so happy as to bear a chief part in the restoration of the Royal house. All that the other could now do was to die asserting the rights of that house to the last. A few weeks after this letter was written Atterbury died. He had just completed his seventieth year.

His body was brought to England, and laid, with great privacy, under the nave of Westminster Abbey. Only three mourners followed the coffin. No inscription marks the grave. That the epitaph with which Pope honoured the memory of his friend does not appear on the walls of the great national cemetery is no subject of regret: for nothing worse was ever written by Colley Cibber.

Those who wish for more complete information about Atterbury may easily collect it from his sermons and his controversial writings, from the report of the parliamentary proceedings against him, which will be found in the State Trials, from the five volumes of his correspondence, edited by Mr. Nichols, and from the first volume of the Stuart papers, edited by Mr. Glover. A very indulgent but a very interesting account of the bishop's political career will be found in Lord Mahon's valuable History of England.

JOHN BUNYAN [1]

(MAY 1854)

JOHN BUNYAN, the most popular religious writer in the English language, was born at Elstow, about a mile from Bedford, in the year 1628. He may be said to have been born a tinker. The tinkers then formed an hereditary caste, which was held in no high estimation. They were generally vagrants and pilferers, and were often confounded with the gipsies, whom in truth they nearly resembled. Bunyan's father was more respectable than

[1] *Encyclopædia Britannica.*

most of the tribe. He had a fixed residence, and was able to send his son to a village school where reading and writing were taught.

The years of John's boyhood were those during which the puritan spirit was in the highest vigour all over England; and nowhere had that spirit more influence than in Bedfordshire. It is not wonderful, therefore, that a lad to whom nature had given a powerful imagination, and sensibility which amounted to a disease, should have been early haunted by religious terrors. Before he was ten, his sports were interrupted by fits of remorse and despair; and his sleep was disturbed by dreams of fiends trying to fly away with him. As he grew older, his mental conflicts became still more violent. The strong language in which he described them has strangely misled all his biographers except Mr. Southey. It has long been an ordinary practice with pious writers to cite Bunyan as an instance of the supernatural power of divine grace to rescue the human soul from the lowest depths of wickedness. He is called in one book the most notorious of profligates; in another, the brand plucked from the burning. He is designated in Mr. Ivimey's History of the Baptists as the depraved Bunyan, the wicked tinker of Elstow. Mr. Ryland, a man once of great note among the Dissenters, breaks out into the following rhapsody:—" No man of common sense and common integrity can deny that Bunyan was a practical atheist, a worthless contemptible infidel, a vile rebel to God and goodness, a common profligate, a soul-despising, a soul-murder-ing, a soul-damning, thoughtless wretch as could exist on the face of the earth. Now be astonished, O heavens, to eternity! and wonder, O earth and hell! while time endures. Behold this very man become a miracle of mercy, a mirror of wisdom, good-ness, holiness, truth, and love." But whoever takes the trouble to examine the evidence will find that the good men who wrote this had been deceived by a phraseology which, as they had been hearing it and using it all their lives, they ought to have understood better. There cannot be a greater mistake than to infer, from the strong expressions in which a devout man bemoans his exceeding sinfulness, that he has led a worse life than his neighbours. Many excellent persons, whose moral character from boyhood to old age has been free from any stain discernible to their fellow-creatures, have, in their autobiographies and diaries, applied to themselves, and doubtless with sincerity, epithets as severe as could be applied to Titus Oates or Mrs. Brownrigg. It is quite certain that Bunyan was, at eighteen, what, in any but the most austerely puritanical circles, would have been considered as a young man of singular gravity and innocence. Indeed, it may be remarked that he, like many other penitents who, in general terms, acknowledged themselves to have been the worst of mankind, fired up and stood vigorously on his defence, whenever any particular charge was brought against him by others. He declares, it is true, that he had let loose the reins on the neck of his lusts, that he had delighted in all transgressions against the divine law, and that he had been the ringleader of the youth of Elstow in all manner of vice. But, when those who wished him ill accused him of licentious amours, he called on God and the angels to attest his purity. No woman, he said, in heaven, earth, or hell, could charge him with having ever made any improper advances to her. Not only had he been strictly faithful to his wife; but he had even before his marriage been perfectly spotless. It does not appear from his own confessions, or from the railings of his enemies, that he ever was drunk in his life. One bad habit he contracted, that of using profane language; but he tells us that a single reproof cured him so effectually that he never offended again. The worst that can be laid to the charge of this poor youth, whom it has been the fashion to represent as the most desperate of reprobates, as a village Rochester, is that he had a great liking for some diversions, quite harmless in themselves, but condemned by the rigid precisians among whom he lived, and for whose opinion he had a great respect. The four chief sins of which he was guilty were dancing, ringing the bells of the parish church, playing at tipcat, and reading the history of Sir Bevis of Southampton. A rector of the school of Laud would have held such a young man up to the whole parish as a model. But Bunyan's notions of good and evil had been learned in a very different school; and he was made miserable by the conflict between his tastes and his scruples.

When he was about seventeen, the ordinary course of his life was interrupted by an event which gave a lasting colour to his thoughts. He enlisted in the parliamentary army, and served during the decisive campaign of 1645. All that we know of his military career is that, at the siege of Leicester, one of his comrades, who had taken his post, was killed by a shot from the town. Bunyan ever after considered himself as having been saved from death by the special interference of Providence. It may be observed that his imagination was strongly impressed by the glimpse which he had caught of the pomp of war. To the last he loved to draw his illustrations of sacred things from camps and fortresses, from guns, drums, trumpets, flags of truce, and regiments arrayed, each under its own banner. His Greatheart, his Captain Boanerges, and his Captain Credence, are evidently portraits, of which the originals were among those martial saints who fought and expounded in Fairfax's army.

In a few months Bunyan returned home and married. His wife had some pious relations, and brought him as her only portion some pious books. And now his mind, excitable by nature, very imperfectly disciplined by education, and exposed, without any protection, to the infectious virulence of the enthusiasm which was then epidemic in England, began to be fearfully disordered. In outward things he soon became a strict Pharisee. He was constant in attendance at prayers and sermons. His favourite amusements were one after another relinquished, though not without many painful struggles. In the middle of a game at tipcat he paused, and stood staring wildly upwards with his stick in his hand. He had heard a voice asking him whether he would leave his sins and go to heaven, or keep his sins and go to hell; and he had seen an awful countenance frowning on him from the sky. The odious vice of bellringing he renounced; but he still for a time ventured to go to the church tower and look on while others pulled the ropes. But soon the thought struck him that, if he persisted in such wickedness, the steeple would fall on his head; and he fled in terror from the accursed place. To give up dancing on the village green was still harder; and some months elapsed before he had the fortitude to part with this darling sin. When this last sacrifice had been made, he was, even when tried by the maxims of that austere time, faultless. All Elstow talked of him as an eminently pious youth. But his own mind was more unquiet than ever. Having nothing more to do in the way of visible reformation, yet finding in religion no pleasures to supply the place of the juvenile amusements which he had relinquished, he began to apprehend that he lay under some special malediction; and he was tormented by a succession of fantasies which seemed likely to drive him to suicide or to Bedlam.

At one time he took it into his head that all persons of Israelite blood would be saved, and tried to make out that he partook of that blood; but his hopes were speedily destroyed by his father, who seems to have had no ambition to be regarded as a Jew.

At another time Bunyan was disturbed by a strange dilemma: " If I have not faith, I am lost; if I have faith, I can work miracles." He was tempted to cry to the puddles between Elstow and Bedford, " Be ye dry," and to stake his eternal hopes on the event.

Then he took up a notion that the day of grace for Bedford and the neighbouring villages was past: that all who were to be saved in that part of England were already converted; and that he had begun to pray and strive some months too late.

Then he was harassed by doubts whether the Turks were not in the right, and the Christians in the wrong. Then he was troubled by a maniacal impulse which prompted him to pray to the trees, to a broomstick, to the parish bull. As yet, however, he was only entering the Valley of the Shadow of Death. Soon the darkness grew thicker. Hideous forms floated before him. Sounds of cursing and wailing were in his ears. His way ran through stench and fire, close to the mouth of the bottomless pit. He began to be haunted by a strange curiosity about the unpardonable sin, and by a morbid longing to commit it. But the most frightful of all the forms which his disease took was a propensity to utter blasphemy, and especially to renounce his share in the benefits of the redemption. Night and day, in bed, at table, at work, evil spirits, as he imagined, were repeating close to his ear the words, " Sell him, sell him." He struck at the hobgoblins; he pushed them from him; but still they were ever at his side. He cried out in answer to them, hour after hour: " Never, never; not for thousands of worlds; not for thousands." At length, worn out by this long agony, he suffered the fatal words to escape him, " Let him go, if he will." Then his misery became more fearful than ever. He had done what could not be forgiven. He had forfeited his part of the great sacrifice. Like Esau, he had sold his birthright; and there was no longer any place for repentance. " None," he afterwards wrote, " knows the terrors of those days but myself." He has described his sufferings with singular energy, simplicity, and pathos. He envied the brutes; he envied the very stones in the street, and the tiles on the houses. The sun seemed to withhold its light and warmth from him. His body, though cast in a sturdy mould, and though still in the highest vigour of youth, trembled whole days together with the fear of death and judgment. He fancied that this trembling was the sign set on the worst reprobates, the sign which God had put on Cain. The unhappy man's emotion destroyed his power of digestion. He had such pains that he expected to burst asunder like Judas, whom he regarded as his prototype.

Neither the books which Bunyan read, nor the advisers whom he consulted, were likely to do much good in a case like his. His small library had received a most unseasonable addition, the account of the lamentable end of Francis Spira. One ancient man of high repute for piety, whom the sufferer consulted, gave an opinion which might well have produced fatal consequences. " I am afraid," said Bunyan, " that I have committed the sin against the Holy Ghost." "Indeed," said the old fanatic, " I am afraid that you have."

At length the clouds broke; the light became clearer and clearer; and the enthusiast, who had imagined that he was branded with the mark of the first murderer, and destined to the end of the arch traitor, enjoyed peace and a cheerful con-fidence in the mercy of God. Years elapsed, however, before his nerves, which had been so perilously overstrained, recovered their tone. When he had joined a Baptist society at Bedford, and was for the first time admitted to partake of the Eucharist, it was with difficulty that he could refrain from imprecating destruction on his brethren while the cup was passing from hand to hand. After he had been some time a member of the congregation, he began to preach; and his sermons produced a powerful effect. He was indeed illiterate; but he spoke to illiterate men. The severe training through which he had passed had given him such an experimental knowledge of all the modes of religious melancholy as he could never have gathered from books; and his vigorous genius, animated by a fervent spirit of devotion, enabled him, not only to exercise a great influence over the vulgar, but even to extort the half contemptuous admiration of scholars. Yet it was long before he ceased to be tormented by an impulse which urged him to utter words of horrible impiety in the pulpit.

Counter-irritants are of as great use in moral as in physical diseases. It should seem that Bunyan was finally relieved from the internal sufferings which had embittered his life by sharp persecution from without. He had been five years a preacher, when the Restoration put it in the power of the Cavalier gentle-men and clergymen all over the country to oppress the Dis-senters; and of all the Dissenters whose history is known to us, he was perhaps the most hardly treated. In November 1660, he was flung into Bedford gaol; and there he remained, with some intervals of partial and precarious liberty, during twelve years. His persecutors tried to extort from him a promise that he would abstain from preaching; but he was convinced that he was divinely set apart and commissioned to be a teacher of righteousness; and he was fully determined to obey God rather than man. He was brought before several tribunals, laughed at, caressed, reviled, menaced, but in vain. He was facetiously told that he was quite right in thinking that he ought not to hide his gift; but that his real gift was skill in repairing old kettles. He was compared to Alexander the coppersmith. He was told that, if he would give up preaching, he should be instantly liberated. He was warned that, if he persisted in disobeying the law, he would be liable to banishment, and that, if he were found in England after a certain time his neck would be stretched. His answer was, " If you let me out to-day, I will preach again to-morrow." Year after year he lay patiently in a dungeon, compared with which the worst prison now to be found in the island is a palace. His fortitude is the more extraordinary, because his domestic feelings were unusually strong. Indeed, he was considered by his stern brethren as somewhat too fond and indulgent a parent. He had several small children, and among them a daughter who was blind, and whom he loved with peculiar tenderness. He could not, he said, bear even to let the wind blow on her; and now she must suffer cold and hunger; she must beg; she must be beaten; " yet," he added, " I must, I must do it." While he lay in prison he could do nothing in the way of his old trade for the support of his family. He determined, therefore, to take up a new trade. He learned to make long tagged thread laces; and many thousands of these articles were furnished by him to the hawkers. While his hands were thus busied, he had other employment for his mind and his lips. He gave religious instruction to his fellow-captives, and formed from among them a little flock, of which he was himself the pastor. He studied indefatigably the few books which he possessed. His two chief companions were the Bible and Fox's Book of Martyrs. His knowledge of the Bible was such that he might have been called a living concordance; and on the margin of his copy of the Book of Martyrs are still legible the ill spelt lines of doggrel in which he expressed his reverence for the brave sufferers, and his implacable enmity to the mystical Babylon.

At length he began to write; and though it was some time before he discovered where his strength lay, his writings were not unsuccessful. They were coarse, indeed; but they showed a keen mother wit, a great command of the homely mother tongue, an intimate knowledge of the English Bible, and a vast and dearly-bought spiritual experience. They therefore, when the corrector of the press had improved the syntax and the spelling, were well received by the humbler class of Dissenters.

Much of Bunyan's time was spent in controversy. He wrote sharply against the Quakers, whom he seems always to have held in utter abhorrence. It is, however, a remarkable fact that he adopted one of their peculiar fashions: his practice was to write, not November or December, but eleventh month and twelfth month.

He wrote against the liturgy of the Church of England. No two things, according to him, had less affinity than the form of prayer and the spirit of prayer. Those, he said with much point, who have most of the spirit of prayer are all to be found in gaol; and those who have most zeal for the form of prayer are all to be found at the alehouse. The doctrinal articles, on the other hand, he warmly praised, and defended against some Arminian clergymen who had signed them. The most acrimonious of all his works is his answer to Edward Fowler, afterwards Bishop of Gloucester, an excellent man, but not free from the taint of Pelagianism.

Bunyan had also a dispute with some of the chiefs of the sect to which he belonged. He doubtless held with perfect sincerity the distinguishing tenet of that sect; but he did not consider that tenet as one of high importance, and willingly joined in communion with quiet Presbyterians and Independents. The sterner Baptists, therefore, loudly pronounced him a false brother. A controversy arose which long survived the original combatants. In our own time the cause which Bunyan had defended with rude logic and rhetoric against Kiffin and Danvers was pleaded by Robert Hall with an ingenuity and eloquence such as no polemical writer has ever surpassed.

During the years which immediately followed the Restoration, Bunyan's confinement seems to have been strict. But, as the passions of 1660 cooled, as the hatred with which the Puritans had been regarded while their reign was recent gave place to pity, he was less and less harshly treated. The distress of his family, and his own patience, courage, and piety softened the hearts of his persecutors. Like his own Christian in the cage, he found protectors even among the crowd of Vanity Fair. The bishop of the diocese, Dr. Barlow, is said to have interceded for him. At length the prisoner was suffered to pass most of his time beyond the walls of the gaol, on condition, as it should seem, that he remained within the town of Bedford.

He owed his complete liberation to one of the worst acts of one of the worst governments that England has ever seen. In 1671 the Cabal was in power. Charles II. had concluded the treaty by which he bound himself to set up the Roman Catholic religion in England. The first step which he took towards that end was to annul, by an unconstitutional exercise of his prerogative, all the penal statutes against the Roman Catholics; and, in order to disguise his real design, he annulled at the same time the penal statutes against Protestant nonconformists. Bunyan was consequently set at large. In the first warmth of his gratitude he published a tract in which he compared Charles to that humane and generous Persian king who, though not himself blest with the light of the true religion, favoured the chosen people, and permitted them, after years of captivity, to rebuild their beloved temple. To candid men, who consider how much Bunyan had suffered, and how little he could guess the secret designs of the court, the unsuspicious thankfulness with which he accepted the precious boon of freedom will not appear to require any apology.

Before he left his prison he had begun the book which has made his name immortal. The history of that book is remarkable. The author was, as he tells us, writing a treatise, in which he had occasion to speak of the stages of the Christian progress. He compared that progress, as many others had compared it, to a pilgrimage. Soon his quick wit discovered innumerable points of similarity which had escaped his predecessors. Images came crowding on his mind faster than he could put them into words, quagmires and pits, steep hills, dark and horrible glens, soft vales, sunny pastures, a gloomy castle of which the courtyard was strewn with the skulls and bones of murdered prisoners, a town all bustle and splendour, like London on the Lord Mayor's Day, and the narrow path, straight as a rule could make it, running on up hill and down hill, through city and through wilderness, to the Black River and the Shining Gate. He had found out, as most people would have said, by accident, as he would doubtless have said, by the guidance of Providence, where his powers lay. He had no suspicion, indeed, that he was producing a masterpiece. He could not guess what place his allegory would occupy in English literature; for of English literature he knew nothing. Those who suppose him to have studied the Fairy Queen might easily be confuted, if this were the proper place for a detailed examination of the passages in which the two allegories have been thought to resemble each other. The only work of fiction, in all probability, with which he could compare his Pilgrim, was his old favourite, the legend of Sir Bevis of Southampton. He would have thought it a sin to borrow any time from the serious business of his life, from his expositions, his controversies, and his lace tags, for the purpose of amusing himself with what he considered merely as a trifle. It was only, he assures us, at spare moments that he returned to the House Beautiful, the Delectable Mountains, and the Enchanted Ground. He had no assistance. Nobody but himself saw a line, till the whole was complete. He then consulted his pious friends. Some were pleased. Others were much scandalised. It was a vain story, a mere romance, about giants, and lions, and goblins, and warriors, sometimes fighting with monsters and sometimes regaled by fair ladies in stately palaces. The loose atheistical wits at Will's might write such stuff to divert the painted Jezebels of the court: but did it become a minister of the gospel to copy the evil fashions of the world? There had been a time when the cant of such fools would have made Bunyan miserable. But that time was passed; and his mind was now in a firm and healthy state. He saw that, in employing fiction to make truth clear and goodness attractive, he was only following the example which every Christian ought to propose to himself; and he determined to print.

The " Pilgrim's Progress " stole silently into the world. Not a single copy of the first edition is known to be in existence. The year of publication has not been ascertained. It is probable that, during some months, the little volume circulated only among poor and obscure sectaries. But soon the irresistible charm of a book which gratified the imagination of the reader with all the action and scenery of a fairy tale, which exercised his ingenuity by setting him to discover a multitude of curious analogies, which interested his feelings for human beings, frail like himself, and struggling with temptations from within and from without, which every moment drew a smile from him by some stroke of quaint yet simple pleasantry, and nevertheless left on his mind a sentiment of reverence for God and of sympathy for man, began to produce its effect. In puritanical circles, from which plays and novels were strictly excluded, that effect was such as no work of genius, though it were superior to the Iliad, to Don Quixote, or to Othello, can ever produce on a mind accustomed to indulge in literary luxury. In 1678 came forth a second edition with additions; and then the demand became immense.

In the four following years the book was reprinted six times. The eighth edition, which contains the last improvements made by the author, was published in 1682, the ninth in 1684, the tenth in 1685. The help of the engraver had early been called in; and tens of thousands of children looked with terror and delight on execrable copper plates, which represented Christian thrusting his sword into Apollyon, or writhing in the grasp of Giant Despair. In Scotland, and in some of the colonies, the Pilgrim was even more popular than in his native country. Bunyan has told us, with very pardonable vanity, that in New England his dream was the daily subject of the conversation of thousands, and was thought worthy to appear in the most superb binding. He had numerous admirers in Holland, and among the Huguenots of France. With the pleasures, however, he experienced some of the pains of eminence. Knavish booksellers put forth volumes of trash under his name; and envious scribblers maintained it to be impossible that the poor ignorant tinker should really be the author of the book which was called his.

He took the best way to confound both those who counterfeited him and those who slandered him. He continued to work the gold-field which he had discovered, and to draw from it new treasures, not indeed with quite such ease and in quite such abundance as when the precious soil was still virgin, but yet with success which left all competition far behind. In 1684 appeared the second part of the " Pilgrim's Progress." It was soon followed by the " Holy War," which, if the " Pilgrim's Progress " did not exist, would be the best allegory that ever was written.

Bunyan's place in society was now very different from what it had been. There had been a time when many Dissenting ministers, who could talk Latin and read Greek, had affected to treat him with scorn. But his fame and influence now far exceeded theirs. He had so great an authority among the Baptists that he was popularly called Bishop Bunyan. His episcopal visitations were annual. From Bedford he rode every year to London, and preached there to large and attentive congregations. From London he went his circuit through the country, animating the zeal of his brethren, collecting and distributing alms, and making up quarrels. The magistrates seem in general to have given him little trouble. But there is reason to believe that, in the year 1685, he was in some danger of again occupying his old quarters in Bedford gaol. In that year the rash and wicked enterprise of Monmouth gave the Government a pretext for persecuting the Nonconformists; and scarcely one eminent divine of the Presbyterian, Independent, or Baptist persuasion remained unmolested.   Baxter was in prison: Howe was driven into exile: Henry was arrested.   Two eminent Baptists, with whom Bunyan had been engaged in controversy, were in great peril and distress.   Danvers was in danger of being hanged; and Kiffin's grandsons were actually hanged.   The tradition is that, during those evil days, Bunyan was forced to disguise himself as a waggoner, and that he preached to his congregation at Bedford in a smoke-frock, with a cart-whip in his hand.   But soon a great change took place.   James the Second was at open war with the Church, and found it necessary to court the Dissenters. Some of the creatures of the government tried to secure the aid of Bunyan.   They probably knew that he had written in praise of the indulgence of 1672, and therefore hoped that he might be equally pleased with the indulgence of 1687.   But fifteen years of thought, observation, and commerce with the world had made him wiser.   Nor were the cases exactly parallel.   Charles was a professed Protestant: James was a professed Papist.   The object of Charles's indulgence was disguised;   the object of James's indulgence was patent.   Bunyan was not deceived. He exhorted his hearers to prepare themselves by fasting and prayer for the danger which menaced their civil and religious liberties, and refused even to speak to the courtier who came down to remodel the corporation of Bedford, and who, as was supposed, had it in charge to offer some municipal dignity to the Bishop of the Baptists.

Bunyan did not live to see the Revolution.   In the summer of 1688 he undertook to plead the cause of a son with an angry father, and at length prevailed on the old man not to disinherit the young one.   This good work cost the benevolent intercessor his life.   He had to ride through heavy rain.   He came drenched to his lodgings on Snow Hill, was seized with a violent fever, and died in a few days.   He was buried in Bunhill Fields; and the spot where he lies is still regarded by the Nonconformists with a feeling which seems scarcely in harmony with the stern spirit of their theology.   Many Puritans, to whom the respect paid by Roman Catholics to the reliques and tombs of saints seemed childish or sinful, are said to have begged with their dying breath that their coffins might be placed as near as possible to the office of the author of the " Pilgrim's Progress."

The fame of Bunyan during his life, and during the century which followed his death, was indeed great, but was almost entirely confined to religious families of the middle and lower classes. Very seldom was he during that time mentioned with respect by any writer of great literary eminence. Young coupled his prose with the poetry of the wretched D'Urfey. In the Spiritual Quixote, the adventures of Christian are ranked with those of Jack the Giant-Killer and John Hickathrift. Cowper ventured to praise the great allegorist, but did not venture to name him. It is a significant circumstance that, till a recent period, all the numerous editions of the " Pilgrim's Progress " were evidently meant for the cottage and the servants' hall. The paper, the printing, the plates, were all of the meanest description. In general, when the educated minority and the common people differ about the merit of a book, the opinion of the educated minority finally prevails. The " Pilgrim's Progress " is perhaps the only book about which, after the lapse of a hundred years, the educated minority has come over to the opinion of the common people.

The attempts which have been made to improve and to imitate this book are not to be numbered. It has been done into verse: it has been done into modern English. " The Pilgrimage of Tender Conscience," " The Pilgrimage of Good Intent," " The Pilgrimage of Seek Truth," " The Pilgrimage of Theophilus," " The Infant Pilgrim," " The Hindoo Pilgrim," are among the many feeble copies of the great original. But the peculiar glory of Bunyan is that those who most hated his doctrines have tried to borrow the help of his genius. A Catholic version of his parable may be seen with the head of the Virgin in the title-page. On the other hand, those Antinomians for whom his Calvinism is not strong enough may study the pilgrimage of Hephzibah, in which nothing will be found which can be construed into an admission of free agency and universal redemption. But the most extraordinary of all the acts of Vandalism by which a fine work of art was ever defaced was committed so late as the year 1853. It was determined to transform the " Pilgrim's Progress " into a Tractarian book. The task was not easy: for it was necessary to make the two sacraments the most prominent objects in the allegory; and of all Christian theologians, avowed Quakers excepted, Bunyan was the one in whose system the sacraments held the least prominent place. However, the Wicket Gate became a type of Baptism, and the House Beautiful of the Eucharist. The effect of this change is such as assuredly the ingenious person who made it never contemplated. For, as not a single pilgrim passes through the Wicket Gate in infancy, and as Faithful hurries past the House

Beautiful without stopping, the lesson which the fable in its altered shape teaches, is that none but adults ought to be baptised, and that the Eucharist may safely be neglected. Nobody would have discovered from the original " Pilgrim's Progress " that the author was not a Pædobaptist. To turn his book into a book against Pædobaptism was an achievement reserved for an Anglo-Catholic divine. Such blunders must necessarily be committed by every man who mutilates parts of a great work, without taking a comprehensive view of the whole.

OLIVER GOLDSMITH [1]

(FEBRUARY 1856)

OLIVER GOLDSMITH, one of the most pleasing English writers of the eighteenth century. He was of a Protestant and Saxon family which had been long settled in Ireland, and which had, like most other Protestant and Saxon families, been, in troubled times, harassed and put in fear by the native population. His father, Charles Goldsmith, studied in the reign of Queen Anne at the diocesan school of Elphin, became attached to the daughter of the schoolmaster, married her, took orders, and settled at a place called Pallas in the county of Longford. There he with difficulty supported his wife and children on what he could earn, partly as a curate and partly as a farmer.

At Pallas Oliver Goldsmith was born in November 1728. That spot was then, for all practical purposes, almost as remote from the busy and splendid capital in which his later years were passed, as any clearing in Upper Canada or any sheep-walk in Australasia now is. Even at this day those enthusiasts who venture to make a pilgrimage to the birthplace of the poet are forced to perform the latter part of their journey on foot. The hamlet lies far from any high road, on a dreary plain which, in wet weather, is often a lake. The lanes would break any jaunting car to pieces; and there are ruts and sloughs through which the most strongly built wheels cannot be dragged.

While Oliver was still a child, his father was presented to a living worth about £200 a year, in the county of Westmeath. The family accordingly quitted their cottage in the wilderness

<hr>

[1] *Encyclopædia Britannica.*

for a spacious house on a frequented road, near the village of
Lissoy.   Here the boy was taught his letters by a maid-servant,
and was sent in his seventh year to a village school kept by an
old quartermaster on half-pay, who professed to teach nothing
but reading, writing, and arithmetic, but who had an inexhaustible fund of stories about ghosts, banshees, and fairies,
about the great Rapparee chiefs, Baldearg O'Donnell and
galloping Hogan, and about the exploits of Peterborough and
Stanhope, the surprise of Monjuich, and the glorious disaster
of Brihuega.   This man must have been of the Protestant
religion; but he was of the aboriginal race, and not only spoke
the Irish language, but could pour forth unpremeditated Irish
verses.   Oliver early became, and through life continued to be,
a passionate admirer of the Irish music, and especially of the
compositions of Carolan, some of the last notes of whose harp
he heard.   It ought to be added that Oliver, though by birth
one of the Englishry, and though connected by numerous ties
with the Established Church, never showed the least sign of that
contemptuous antipathy with which, in his days, the ruling
minority in Ireland too generally regarded the subject majority.
So far indeed was he from sharing in the opinions and feelings of
the caste to which he belonged, that he conceived an aversion to
the Glorious and Immortal Memory, and, even when George the
Third was on the throne, maintained that nothing but the
restoration of the banished dynasty could save the country.

From the humble academy kept by the old soldier Goldsmith
was removed in his ninth year.   He went to several grammar
schools, and acquired some knowledge of the ancient languages.
His life at this time seems to have been far from happy.   He
had, as appears from the admirable portrait of him at Knowle,
features harsh even to ugliness.   The small-pox had set its
mark on him with more than usual severity.   His stature was
small, and his limbs ill put together.   Among boys little tenderness is shown to personal defects; and the ridicule excited by
poor Oliver's appearance was heightened by a peculiar simplicity
and a disposition to blunder which he retained to the last.   He
became the common butt of boys and masters, was pointed at
as a fright in the playground, and flogged as a dunce in the
school-room.   When he had risen to eminence, those who had
once derided him ransacked their memory for the events of his
early years, and recited repartees and couplets which had
dropped from him, and which, though little noticed at the time,
were supposed, a quarter of a century later, to indicate the

powers which produced the " Vicar of Wakefield " and the " Deserted Village."

In his seventeenth year Oliver went up to Trinity College, Dublin, as a sizar, The sizars paid nothing for food and tuition, and very little for lodging; but they had to perform some menial services from which they have long been relieved. They swept the court: they carried up the dinner to the fellows' table, and changed the plates and poured out the ale of the rulers of the society. Goldsmith was quartered, not alone, in a garret, on the window of which his name, scrawled by himself, is still read with interest.[1] From such garrets many men of less parts than his have made their way to the woolsack or to the episcopal bench. But Goldsmith, while he suffered all the humiliations, threw away all the advantages, of his situation. He neglected the studies of the place, stood low at the examinations, was turned down to the bottom of his class for playing the buffoon in the lecture-room, was severely reprimanded for pumping on a constable, and was caned by a brutal tutor for giving a ball in the attic story of the college to some gay youths and damsels from the city.

While Oliver was leading at Dublin a life divided between squalid distress and squalid dissipation, his father died, leaving a mere pittance. The youth obtained his bachelor's degree, and left the university. During some time the humble dwelling to which his widowed mother had retired was his home. He was now in his twenty-first year; it was necessary that he should do something; and his education seemed to have fitted him to do nothing but to dress himself in guady colours, of which he was as fond as a magpie, to take a hand at cards, to sing Irish airs, to play the flute, to angle in summer, and to tell ghost stories by the fire in winter. He tried five or six professions in turn without success. He applied for ordination; but, as he applied in scarlet clothes, he was speedily turned out of the episcopal palace. He then became tutor in an opulent family, but soon quitted his situation in consequence of a dispute about play. Then he determined to emigrate to America. His relations, with much satisfaction, saw him set out for Cork on a good horse with thirty pounds in his pocket. But in six weeks he came back on a miserable hack, without a penny, and informed

---

[1] The glass on which the name is written has, as we are informed by a writer in *Notes and Queries* (2nd S. ix. p. 91), been inclosed in a frame and deposited in the Manuscript Room of the College Library, where it is still to be seen.

his mother that the ship in which he had taken his passage, having got a fair wind while he was at a party of pleasure, had sailed without him. Then he resolved to study the law. A generous kinsman advanced fifty pounds. With this sum Goldsmith went to Dublin, was enticed into a gaming house, and lost every shilling. He then thought of medicine. A small purse was made up; and in his twenty-fourth year he was sent to Edinburgh. At Edinburgh he passed eighteen months in nominal attendance on lectures, and picked up some superficial information about chemistry and natural history. Thence he went to Leyden, still pretending to study physic. He left that celebrated university, the third university at which he had resided, in his twenty-seventh year, without a degree, with the merest smattering of medical knowledge, and with no property but his clothes and his flute. His flute, however, proved a useful friend. He rambled on foot through Flanders, France, and Switzerland, playing tunes which everywhere set the peasantry dancing, and which often procured for him a supper and a bed. He wandered as far as Italy. His musical performances, indeed, were not to the taste of the Italians; but he contrived to live on the alms which he obtained at the gates of the convents. It should, however, be observed that the stories which he told about this part of his life ought to be received with great caution; for strict veracity was never one of his virtues; and a man who is ordinarily inaccurate in narration is likely to be more than ordinarily inaccurate when he talks about his own travels. Goldsmith, indeed, was so regardless of truth as to assert in print that he was present at a most interesting conversation between Voltaire and Fontenelle, and that this conversation took place at Paris. Now it is certain that Voltaire never was within a hundred leagues of Paris during the whole time which Goldsmith passed on the Continent.

In 1756 the wanderer landed at Dover, without a shilling, without a friend, and without a calling. He had, indeed, if his own unsupported evidence may be trusted, obtained from the University of Padua a doctor's degree; but this dignity proved utterly useless to him. In England his flute was not in request: there were no convents; and he was forced to have recourse to a series of desperate expedients. He turned strolling player; but his face and figure were ill suited to the boards even of the humblest theatre. He pounded drugs and ran about London with phials for charitable chemists. He joined a swarm of beggars, which made its nest in Axe Yard. He was for a time usher of a school, and felt the miseries and humiliations of this situation so keenly that he thought it a promotion to be permitted to earn his bread as a bookseller's hack; but he soon found the new yoke more galling than the old one, and was glad to become an usher again.   He obtained a medical appointment in the service of the East India Company; but the appointment was speedily revoked.   Why it was revoked we are not told. The subject was one on which he never liked to talk.   It is probable that he was incompetent to perform the duties of the place.   Then he presented himself at Surgeon's Hall for examination, as mate to a naval hospital.   Even to so humble a post he was found unequal.   By this time the schoolmaster whom he had served for a morsel of food and the third part of a bed was no more.   Nothing remained but to return to the lowest drudgery of literature.   Goldsmith took a garret in a miserable court, to which he had to climb from the brink of Fleet Ditch by a dizzy ladder of flagstones called Breakneck Steps.   The court and the ascent have long disappeared; but old Londoners will remember both.[1]   Here, at thirty, the unlucky adventurer sat down to toil like a galley slave.

In the succeeding six years he sent to the press some things which have survived and many which have perished.   He produced articles for reviews, magazines, newspapers; children's books which, bound in gilt paper and adorned with hideous woodcuts, appeared in the window of the once far-famed shop at the corner of Saint Paul's Churchyard; "An Inquiry into the State of Polite Learning in Europe," which, though of little or no value, is still reprinted among his works; a " Life of Beau Nash," which is not reprinted, though it well deserves to be so; [2] a superficial and incorrect, but very readable, " History of England," in a series of letters purporting to be addressed by a nobleman to his son; and some very lively and amusing " Sketches of London Society," in a series of letters purporting to be addressed by a Chinese traveller to his friends.   All these works were anonymous; but some of them were well known to

---

[1] A gentleman, who states that he has known the neighbourhood for thirty years, corrects this account, and informs the present publisher that the Breakneck Steps, thirty-two in number, divided into two flights, are still in existence, and that, according to tradition, Goldsmith's house was not on the steps, but was the first house at the head of the court, on the left hand, going from the Old Bailey.   See *Notes and Queries* (2nd S. ix. 280).

[2] Mr. Black has pointed out that this is inaccurate: the life of Nash has been twice reprinted; once in Mr. Prior's edition (vol. iii. p. 249), and once in Mr. Cunningham's edition (vol. iv. p. 35).

be Goldsmith's; and he gradually rose in the estimation of the booksellers for whom he drudged. He was, indeed, emphatically a popular writer. For accurate research or grave disquisition he was not well qualified by nature or by education. He knew nothing accurately: his reading had been desultory; nor had he meditated deeply on what he had read. He had seen much of the world; but he had noticed and retained little more of what he had seen than some grotesque incidents and characters which had happened to strike his fancy. But, though his mind was very scantily stored with materials, he used what materials he had in such a way as to produce a wonderful effect. There have been many greater writers; but perhaps no writer was ever more uniformly agreeable. His style was always pure and easy, and, on proper occasions, pointed and energetic. His narratives were always amusing, his descriptions always picturesque, his humour rich and joyous, yet not without an occasional tinge of amiable sadness. About everything that he wrote, serious or sportive, there was a certain natural grace and decorum, hardly to be expected from a man a great part of whose life had been passed among thieves and beggars, street-walkers and merry andrews, in those squalid dens which are the reproach of great capitals.

As his name gradually became known, the circle of his acquaintance widened. He was introduced to Johnson, who was then considered as the first of living English writers; to Reynolds, the first of English painters; and to Burke, who had not yet entered parliament, but had distinguished himself greatly by his writings and by the eloquence of his conversation. With these eminent men Goldsmith became intimate. In 1763 he was one of the nine original members of that celebrated fraternity which has sometimes been called the Literary Club, but which has always disclaimed that epithet, and still glories in the simple name of The Club.

By this time Goldsmith had quitted his miserable dwelling at the top of Breakneck Steps, and had taken chambers in the more civilised region of the Inns of Court. But he was still often reduced to pitiable shifts. Towards the close of 1764 his rent was so long in arrear that his landlady one morning called in the help of a sheriff's officer. The debtor, in great perplexity, despatched a messenger to Johnson; and Johnson, always friendly, though often surly, sent back the messenger with a guinea, and promised to follow speedily. He came, and found that Goldsmith had changed the guinea, and was railing at the

landlady over a bottle of Madeira. Johnson put the cork into
the bottle, and entreated his friend to consider calmly how
money was to be procured. Goldsmith said that he had a novel
ready for the press. Johnson glanced at the manuscript, saw
that there were good things in it, took it to a bookseller, sold it
for £60, and soon returned with the money. The rent was paid;
and the sheriff's officer withdrew. According to one story,
Goldsmith gave his landlady a sharp reprimand for her treatment of him; according to another, he insisted on her joining
him in a bowl of punch. Both stories are probably true. The
novel which was thus ushered into the world was the " Vicar
of Wakefield."

But, before the " Vicar of Wakefield " appeared in print,
came the great crisis of Goldsmith's literary life. In Christmas
week, 1764, he published a poem, entitled the " Traveller." It
was the first work to which he had put his name; and it at
once raised him to the rank of a legitimate English classic.
The opinion of the most skilful critics was, that nothing finer
had appeared in verse since the fourth book of the " Dunciad."
In one respect the " Traveller " differs from all Goldsmith's other
writings. In general his designs were bad, and his execution
good. In the " Traveller," the execution, though deserving of
much praise, is far inferior to the design. No philosophical
poem, ancient or modern, has a plan so noble, and at the same
time so simple. An English wanderer, seated on a crag among
the Alps, near the point where three great countries meet, looks
down on the boundless prospect, reviews his long pilgrimage,
recalls the varieties of scenery, of climate, of government, of
religion, of national character, which he has observed, and
comes to the conclusion, just or unjust, that our happiness
depends little on political institutions, and much on the temper
and regulation of our own minds.

While the fourth edition of the " Traveller " was on the
counters of the booksellers, the " Vicar of Wakefield " appeared,
and rapidly obtained a popularity which has lasted down to our
own time, and which is likely to last as long as our language.
The fable is indeed one of the worst that ever was constructed.
It wants, not merely that probability which ought to be found
in a tale of common English life, but that consistency which
ought to be found in the wildest fiction about witches, giants,
and fairies. But the earlier chapters have all the sweetness of
pastoral poetry, together with all the vivacity of comedy.
Moses and his spectacles, the vicar and his monogamy, the

sharper and his cosmogony, the squire proving from Aristotle that relatives are related, Olivia preparing herself for the arduous task of converting a rakish lover by studying the controversy between Robinson Crusoe and Friday, the great ladies with their scandal about Sir Tomkyn's amours and Dr. Burdock's verses, and Mr. Burchell with his " Fudge," have caused as much harmless mirth as has ever been caused by matter packed into so small a number of pages. The latter part of the tale is unworthy of the beginning. As we approach the catastrophe, the absurdities lie thicker and thicker; and the gleams of pleasantry become rarer and rarer.

The success which had attended Goldsmith as a novelist emboldened him to try his fortune as a dramatist. He wrote the " Goodnatured Man," a piece which had a worse fate than it deserved. Garrick refused to produce it at Drury Lane. It was acted at Covent Garden in 1768, but was coldly received. The author, however, cleared by his benefit nights, and by the sale of the copyright, no less than £500, five times as much as he had made by the " Traveller " and the " Vicar of Wakefield " together. The plot of the " Goodnatured Man " is, like almost all Goldsmith's plots, very ill constructed. But some passages are exquisitely ludicrous; much more ludicrous, indeed, than suited the taste of the town at that time. A canting, mawkish play, entitled " False Delicacy," had just had an immense run. Sentimentality was all the mode. During some years, more tears were shed at comedies than at tragedies; and a pleasantry which moved the audience to anything more than a grave smile was reprobated as low. It is not strange, therefore, that the very best scene in the " Goodnatured Man," that in which Miss Richland finds her lover attended by the bailiff and the bailiff's follower in full court dresses, should have been mercilessly hissed, and should have been omitted after the first night.

In 1770 appeared the " Deserted Village." In mere diction and versification this celebrated poem is fully equal, perhaps superior, to the " Traveller; " and it is generally preferred to the " Traveller " by that large class of readers who think, with Bayes in the " Rehearsal," that the only use of a plan is to bring in fine things. More discerning judges, however, while they admire the beauty of the details, are shocked by one unpardonable fault which pervades the whole. The fault we mean is not that theory about wealth and luxury which has so often been censured by political economists. The theory is indeed false: but the poem, considered merely as a poem, is not necessarily the worse on that account. The finest poem in the Latin language, indeed the finest didactic poem in any language, was written in defence of the silliest and meanest of all systems of natural and moral philosophy. A poet may easily be pardoned for reasoning ill; but he cannot be pardoned for describing ill, for observing the world in which he lives so carelessly that his portraits bear no resemblance to the originals, for exhibiting as copies from real life monstrous combinations of things which never were and never could be found together. What would be thought of a painter who should mix August and January in one landscape, who should introduce a frozen river into a harvest scene? Would it be a sufficient defence of such a picture to say that every part was exquisitely coloured, that the green hedges, the apple-trees loaded with fruit, the waggons reeling under the yellow sheaves, and the sun-burned reapers wiping their foreheads, were very fine, and that the ice and the boys sliding were also very fine? To such a picture the " Deserted Village " bears a great resemblance. It is made up of incongruous parts. The village in its happy days is a true English village. The village in its decay is an Irish village. The felicity and the misery which Goldsmith has brought close together belong to two different countries; and to two different stages in the progress of society. He had assuredly never seen in his native island such a rural paradise, such a seat of plenty, content, and tranquillity, as his " Auburn." He had assuredly never seen in England all the inhabitants of such a paradise turned out of their homes in one day and forced to emigrate in a body to America. The hamlet he had probably seen in Kent; the ejectment he had probably seen in Munster: but, by joining the two, he has produced something which never was and never will be seen in any part of the world.

In 1773 Goldsmith tried his chance at Covent Garden with a second play, " She Stoops to Conquer." The manager was not without great difficulty induced to bring this piece out. The sentimental comedy still reigned; and Goldsmith's comedies were not sentimental. The " Goodnatured Man " had been too funny to succeed; yet, the mirth of the " Goodnatured Man " was sober when compared with the rich drollery of " She Stoops to Conquer," which is, in truth, an incomparable farce in five acts. On this occasion, however, genius triumphed. Pit, boxes, and galleries, were in a constant roar of laughter. If any bigoted admirer of Kelly and Cumberland ventured to hiss or groan, he was speedily silenced by a general cry of " turn him out," or

" throw him over." Two generations have since confirmed the verdict which was pronounced on that night.

While Goldsmith was writing the " Deserted Village," and " She Stoops to Conquer," he was employed on works of a very different kind, works from which he derived little reputation but much profit. He compiled for the use of schools a " History of Rome," by which he made £300, a " History of England," by which he made £600, a " History of Greece," for which he received £250, a " Natural History," for which the booksellers covenanted to pay him 800 guineas. These works he produced without any elaborate research, by merely selecting, abridging, and translating into his own clear, pure, and flowing language what he found in books well known to the world, but too bulky or too dry for boys and girls. He committed some strange blunders; for he knew nothing with accuracy. Thus in his " History of England," he tells us that Naseby is in Yorkshire; nor did he correct this mistake when the book was reprinted. He was very nearly hoaxed into putting into the " History of Greece " an account of a battle between Alexander the Great and Montezuma. In his " Animated Nature " he relates, with faith and with perfect gravity, all the most absurd lies which he could find in books of travels about gigantic Patagonians, monkeys that preach sermons, nightingales that repeat long conversations. " If he can tell a horse from a cow," said Johnson, " that is the extent of his knowledge of zoology." How little Goldsmith was qualified to write about the physical sciences is sufficiently proved by two anecdotes. He on one occasion denied that the sun is longer in the northern than in the southern signs. It was vain to cite the authority of Maupertuis. " Maupertuis! " he cried, " I understand those matters better than Maupertuis." On another occasion he, in defiance of the evidence of his own senses, maintained obstinately, and even angrily, that he chewed his dinner by moving his upper jaw.

Yet, ignorant as Goldsmith was, few writers have done more to make the first steps in the laborious road to knowledge easy and pleasant. His compilations are widely distinguished from the compilations of ordinary book-makers. He was a great, perhaps an unequalled, master of the arts of selection and condensation. In these respects his histories of Rome and of England, and still more his own abridgments of these histories, well deserve to be studied. In general nothing is less attractive than an epitome: but the epitomes of Goldsmith, even when most concise, are always amusing; and to read them is considered by intelligent children, not as a task, but as a pleasure.

Goldsmith might now be considered as a prosperous man. He had the means of living in comfort, and even in what to one who had so often slept in barns and on bulks must have been luxury. His fame was great and was constantly rising. He lived in what was intellectually far the best society of the kingdom, in a society in which no talent or accomplishment was wanting, and in which the art of conversation was cultivated with splendid success. There probably were never four talkers more admirable in four different ways than Johnson, Burke, Beauclerk, and Garrick; and Goldsmith was on terms of intimacy with all the four. He aspired to share in their colloquial renown; but never was ambition more unfortunate. It may seem strange that a man who wrote with so much perspicuity, vivacity, and grace, should have been, whenever he took a part in conversation, an empty, noisy, blundering rattle. But on this point the evidence is overwhelming. So extraordinary was the contrast between Goldsmith's published works and the silly things which he said, that Horace Walpole described him as an inspired idiot. " Noll," said Garrick, " wrote like an angel, and talked like poor Poll." Chamier declared that it was a hard exercise of faith to believe that so foolish a chatterer could have really written the " Traveller." Even Boswell could say, with contemptuous compassion, that he liked very well to hear honest Goldsmith run on. " Yes, sir," said Johnson, " but he should not like to hear himself." Minds differ as rivers differ. There are transparent and sparkling rivers from which it is delightful to drink as they flow; to such rivers the minds of such men as Burke and Johnson may be compared. But there are rivers of which the water when first drawn is turbid and noisome, but becomes pellucid as crystal, and delicious to the taste, if it be suffered to stand till it has deposited a sediment; and such a river is a type of the mind of Goldsmith. His first thoughts on every subject were confused even to absurdity; but they required only a little time to work themselves clear. When he wrote they had that time; and therefore his readers pronounced him a man of genius: but when he talked he talked nonsense, and made himself the laughing-stock of his hearers. He was painfully sensible of his inferiority in conversation; he felt every failure keenly; yet he had not sufficient judgment and self-command to hold his tongue. His animal spirits and vanity were always impelling him to try to do the one thing which he could not do. After every attempt he felt that he had exposed himself, and writhed with shame and vexation; yet the next moment he began again.

His associates seem to have regarded him with kindness, which, in spite of their admiration of his writings, was not unmixed with contempt. In truth, there was in his character much to love, but very little to respect. His heart was soft even to weakness: he was so generous that he quite forgot to be just: he forgave injuries so readily that he might be said to invite them; and was so liberal to beggars that he had nothing left for his tailor and his butcher. He was vain, sensual, frivolous, profuse, improvident. One vice of a darker shade was imputed to him, envy. But there is not the least reason to believe that this bad passion, though it sometimes made him wince and utter fretful exclamations, ever impelled him to injure by wicked arts the reputation of any of his rivals. The truth probably is, that he was not more envious, but merely less prudent, than his neighbours. His heart was on his lips. All those small jealousies, which are but too common among men of letters, but which a man of letters who is also a man of the world does his best to conceal, Goldsmith avowed with the simplicity of a child. When he was envious, instead of affecting indifference, instead of damning with faint praise, instead of doing injuries slily and in the dark, he told everybody that he was envious. " Do not, pray, do not talk of Johnson in such terms," he said to Boswell; " you harrow up my very soul." George Steevens and Cumberland were men far too cunning to say such a thing. They would have echoed the praises of the man whom they envied, and then have sent to the newspapers anonymous libels upon him. Both what was good and what was bad in Goldsmith's character was to his associates a perfect security that he would never commit such villainy. He was neither ill natured enough, nor long headed enough, to be guilty of any malicious act which required contrivance and disguise.

Goldsmith has sometimes been represented as a man of genius, cruelly treated by the world, and doomed to struggle with difficulties which at last broke his heart. But no representation can be more remote from the truth. He did, indeed, go through much sharp misery before he had done anything considerable in literature. But, after his name had appeared on the title-page of the " Traveller," he had none but himself to blame for his distresses. His average income, during the last seven years of his life, certainly exceeded £400 a year; and £400 a year ranked, among the incomes of that day, at least as high as £800 a year would rank at present. A single man living in the Temple with £400 a year might then be called opulent. Not one in ten of the young gentlemen of good families who were studying the law there had so much. But all the wealth which Lord Clive had brought from Bengal, and Sir Lawrence Dundas from Germany, joined together, would not have sufficed for Goldsmith. He spent twice as much as he had. He wore fine clothes, gave dinners of several courses, paid court to venal beauties. He had also, it should be remembered, to the honour of his heart, though not of his head, a guinea, or five, or ten, according to the state of his purse, ready for any tale of distress, true or false. But it was not in dress or feasting, in promiscuous amours or promiscuous charities, that his chief expense lay. He had been from boyhood a gambler, and at once the most sanguine and the most unskilful of gamblers. For a time he put off the day of inevitable ruin by temporary expedients. He obtained advances from booksellers, by promising to execute works which he never began. But at length this source of supply failed. He owed more than £2000; and he saw no hope of extrication from his embarrassments. His spirits and health gave way. He was attacked by a nervous fever, which he thought himself competent to treat. It would have been happy for him if his medical skill had been appreciated as justly by himself as by others. Notwithstanding the degree which he pretended to have received at Padua, he could procure no patients. "I do not practise," he once said; "I make it a rule to prescribe only for my friends." "Pray, dear Doctor," said Beauclerk, "alter your rule; and prescribe only for your enemies." Goldsmith now, in spite of this excellent advice, prescribed for himself. The remedy aggravated the malady. The sick man was induced to call in real physicians; and they at one time imagined that they had cured the disease. Still his weakness and restlessness continued. He could get no sleep. He could take no food. "You are worse," said one of his medical attendants, "than you should be from the degree of fever which you have. Is your mind at ease?" "No, it is not," were the last recorded words of Oliver Goldsmith. He died on the third of April 1774, in his forty-sixth year. He was laid in the churchyard of the Temple; but the spot was not marked by any inscription, and is now forgotten. The coffin was followed by Burke and Reynolds. Both these great men were sincere mourners. Burke, when he heard of Goldsmith's death, had burst into a flood of tears. Reynolds had been so much moved by the news that he had flung aside his brush and palette for the day.

A short time after Goldsmith's death, a little poem appeared, which will, as long as our language lasts, associate the names of his two illustrious friends with his own. It has already been mentioned that he sometimes felt keenly the sarcasm which his wild blundering talk brought upon him. He was, not long before his last illness, provoked into retaliating. He wisely betook himself to his pen; and at that weapon he proved himself a match for all his assailants together. Within a small compass he drew with a singularly easy and vigorous pencil the characters of nine or ten of his intimate associates. Though this little work did not receive his last touches, it must always be regarded as a masterpiece. It is impossible, however, not to wish that four or five likenesses which have no interest for posterity were wanting to that noble gallery, and that their places were supplied by sketches of Johnson and Gibbon, as happy and vivid as the sketches of Burke and Garrick.

Some of Goldsmith's friends and admirers honoured him with a cenotaph in Westminster Abbey. Nollekens was the sculptor; and Johnson wrote the inscription. It is much to be lamented that Johnson did not leave to posterity a more durable and a more valuable memorial of his friend. A life of Goldsmith would have been an inestimable addition to the Lives of the Poets. No man appreciated Goldsmith's writings more justly than Johnson; no man was better acquainted with Goldsmith's character and habits; and no man was more competent to delineate with truth and spirit the peculiarities of a mind in which great powers were found in company with great weaknesses. But the lists of poets to whose works Johnson was requested by the booksellers to furnish prefaces ended with Lyttleton, who died in 1773. The line seems to have been drawn expressly for the purpose of excluding the person whose portrait would have most fitly closed the series. Goldsmith, however, has been fortunate in his biographers. Within a few years his life has been written by Mr. Prior, by Mr. Washington Irving, and by Mr. Forster. The diligence of Mr. Prior deserves great praise; the style of Mr. Washington Irving is always pleasing; but the highest place must, in justice, be assigned to the eminently interesting work of Mr. Forster.

SAMUEL JOHNSON [1]

(DECEMBER 1856)

SAMUEL JOHNSON, one of the most eminent English writers of the eighteenth century, was the son of Michael Johnson, who was, at the beginning of that century, a magistrate of Lichfield, and a bookseller of great note in the midland counties. Michael's abilities and attainments seem to have been considerable. He was so well acquainted with the contents of the volumes which he exposed to sale, that the country rectors of Staffordshire and Worcestershire thought him an oracle on points of learning. Between him and the clergy, indeed, there was a strong religious and political sympathy. He was a zealous churchman, and, though he had qualified himself for municipal office by taking the oaths to the sovereigns in possession, was to the last a Jacobite in heart. At his house, a house which is still pointed out to every traveller who visits Lichfield, Samual was born on the 18th of September 1709. In the child, the physical, intellectual, and moral peculiarities which afterwards distinguished the man were plainly discernible; great muscular strength accompanied by much awkwardness and many infirmities; great quickness of parts, with a morbid propensity to sloth and procrastination; a kind and generous heart, with a gloomy and irritable temper. He had inherited from his ancestors a scrofulous taint, which it was beyond the power of medicine to remove. His parents were weak enough to believe that the royal touch was a specific for this malady. In his third year he was taken up to London, inspected by the court surgeon, prayed over by the court chaplains, and stroked and presented with a piece of gold by Queen Anne. One of his earliest recollections was that of a stately lady in a diamond stomacher and a long black hood. Her hand was applied in vain. The boy's features, which were originally noble and not irregular, were distorted by his malady. His cheeks were deeply scarred. He lost for a time the sight of one eye; and he saw but very imperfectly with the other. But the force of his mind overcame every impediment. Indolent as he was, he acquired knowledge with such ease and rapidity that at every school to which he was sent he was soon

[1] *Encyclopædia Britannica.*

the best scholar.   From sixteen to eighteen he resided at home,
and was left to his own devices.   He learned much at this time,
though his studies were without guidance and without plan.
He ransacked his father's shelves, dipped into a multitude of
books, read what was interesting, and passed over what was
dull.   An ordinary lad would have acquired little or no useful
knowledge in such a way: but much that was dull to ordinary
lads was interesting to Samuel.   He read little Greek: for his
proficiency in that language was not such that he could take
much pleasure in the masters of Attic poetry and eloquence.
But he had left school a good Latinist; and he soon acquired,
in the large and miscellaneous library of which he now had the
command, an extensive knowledge of Latin literature.   That
Augustan delicacy of taste which is the boast of the great public
schools of England he never possessed.   But he was early
familiar with some classical writers who were quite unknown to
the best scholars in the sixth form at Eton.   He was peculiarly
attracted by the works of the great restorers of learning.   Once,
while searching for some apples, he found a huge folio volume
of Petrarch's works.   The name excited his curiosity; and he
eagerly devoured hundreds of pages.   Indeed, the diction and
versification of his own Latin compositions show that he had
paid at least as much attention to modern copies from the
antique as to the original models.

While he was thus irregularly educating himself, his family
was sinking into hopeless poverty.   Old Michael Johnson was
much better qualified to pore upon books, and to talk about
them, than to trade in them.   His business declined; his debts
increased; it was with difficulty that the daily expenses of his
household were defrayed.   It was out of his power to support
his son at either university; but a wealthy neighbour offered
assistance; and, in reliance on promises which proved to be of
very little value, Samuel was entered at Pembroke College,
Oxford.   When the young scholar presented himself to the
rulers of that society, they were amazed not more by his un-
gainly figure and eccentric manners than by the quantity of
extensive and curious information which he had picked up
during many months of desultory but not unprofitable study.
On the first day of his residence he surprised his teachers by
quoting Macrobius; and one of the most learned among them
declared that he had never known a freshman of equal attainments.

At Oxford, Johnson resided during about three years.   He

was poor, even to raggedness; and his appearance excited a mirth and a pity which were equally intolerable to his haughty spirit. He was driven from the quadrangle of Christ Church by the sneering looks which the members of that aristocratical society cast at the holes in his shoes. Some charitable person placed a new pair at his door; but he spurned them away in a fury. Distress made him, not servile, but reckless and ungovernable. No opulent gentleman commoner, panting for one-and-twenty, could have treated the academical authorities with more gross disrespect. The needy scholar was generally to be seen under the gate of Pembroke, a gate now adorned with his effigy, haranguing a circle of lads, over whom, in spite of his tattered gown and dirty linen, his wit and audacity gave him an undisputed ascendency. In every mutiny against the discipline of the college he was the ringleader. Much was pardoned, however, to a youth so highly distinguished by abilities and acquirements. He had early made himself known by turning Pope's Messiah into Latin verse. The style and rhythm, indeed, were not exactly Virgilian; but the translation found many admirers, and was read with pleasure by Pope himself.

The time drew near at which Johnson would, in the ordinary course of things, have become a Bachelor of Arts: but he was at the end of his resources. Those promises of support on which he had relied had not been kept. His family could do nothing for him. His debts to Oxford tradesmen were small indeed, yet larger than he could pay. In the autumn of 1731, he was under the necessity of quitting the university without a degree. In the following winter his father died. The old man left but a pittance; and of that pittance almost the whole was appropriated to the support of his widow. The property to which Samuel succeeded amounted to no more than twenty pounds.

His life, during the thirty years which followed, was one hard struggle with poverty. The misery of that struggle needed no aggravation, but was aggravated by the sufferings of an unsound body and an unsound mind. Before the young man left the university, his hereditary malady had broken forth in a singularly cruel form. He had become an incurable hypochondriac. He said long after that he had been mad all his life, or at least not perfectly sane; and, in truth, eccentricities less strange than his have often been thought grounds sufficient for absolving felons, and for setting aside wills. His grimaces, his gestures, his mutterings, sometimes diverted and sometimes terrified people who did not know him. At a dinner table he would, in a fit of absence, stoop down and twitch off a lady's shoe. He would amaze a drawing-room by suddenly ejaculating a clause of the Lord's Prayer. He would conceive an unintelligible aversion to a particular alley, and perform a great circuit rather than see the hateful place. He would set his heart on touching every post in the streets through which he walked. If by any chance he missed a post, he would go back a hundred yards and repair the omission. Under the influence of his disease, his senses became morbidly torpid, and his imagination morbidly active. At one time he would stand poring on the town clock without being able to tell the hour. At another, he would distinctly hear his mother, who was many miles off, calling him by his name. But this was not the worst. A deep melancholy took possession of him, and gave a dark tinge to all his views of human nature and of human destiny. Such wretchedness as he endured has driven many men to shoot themselves or drown themselves. But he was under no temptation to commit suicide. He was sick of life; but he was afraid of death; and he shuddered at every sight or sound which reminded him of the inevitable hour. In religion he found but little comfort during his long and frequent fits of dejection; for his religion partook of his own character. The light from heaven shone on him indeed, but not in a direct line, or with its own pure splendour. The rays had to struggle through a disturbing medium; they reached him refracted, dulled and discoloured by the thick gloom which had settled on his soul; and, though they might be sufficiently clear to guide him, were too dim to cheer him.

With such infirmities of body and mind, this celebrated man was left, at two-and-twenty, to fight his way through the world. He remained during about five years in the midland counties. At Lichfield, his birthplace and his early home, he had inherited some friends and acquired others. He was kindly noticed by Henry Hervey, a gay officer of noble family, who happened to be quartered there. Gilbert Walmesley, registrar of the ecclesiastical court of the diocese, a man of distinguished parts, learning, and knowledge of the world, did himself honour by patronising the young adventurer, whose repulsive person, unpolished manners, and squalid garb moved many of the petty aristocracy of the neighbourhood to laughter or to disgust. At Lichfield, however, Johnson could find no way of earning a livelihood. He became usher of a grammar school in Leicestershire; he resided as a humble companion in the house of a country gentleman; but a life of dependence was insupportable to his haughty spirit. He repaired to Birmingham, and there earned a few guineas by literary drudgery. In that town he printed a translation, little noticed at the time, and long forgotten, of a Latin book about Abyssinia. He then put forth proposals for publishing by subscription the poems of Politian, with notes containing a history of modern Latin verse: but subscriptions did not come in; and the volume never appeared.

While leading this vagrant and miserable life, Johnson fell in love. The object of his passion was Mrs. Elizabeth Porter, a widow who had children as old as himself. To ordinary spectators, the lady appeared to be a short, fat, coarse woman, painted half an inch thick, dressed in gaudy colours, and fond of exhibiting provincial airs and graces which were not exactly those of the Queensberrys and Lepels. To Johnson, however, whose passions were strong, whose eyesight was too weak to distinguish ceruse from natural bloom, and who had seldom or never been in the same room with a woman of real fashion, his Titty, as he called her, was the most beautiful, graceful, and accomplished of her sex. That his admiration was unfeigned cannot be doubted; for she was as poor as himself. She accepted, with a readiness which did her little honour, the addresses of a suitor who might have been her son. The marriage, however, in spite of occasional wranglings, proved happier than might have been expected. The lover continued to be under the illusions of the wedding-day till the lady died in her sixty-fourth year. On her monument he placed an inscription extolling the charms of her person and of her manners; and when, long after her decease, he had occasion to mention her, he exclaimed, with a tenderness half ludicrous, half pathetic, " Pretty creature! "

His marriage made it necessary for him to exert himself more strenuously than he had hitherto done. He took a house in the neighbourhood of his native town, and advertised for pupils. But eighteen months passed away; and only three pupils came to his academy. Indeed, his appearance was so strange, and his temper so violent, that his schoolroom must have resembled an ogre's den. Nor was the tawdry painted grandmother whom he called his Titty well qualified to make provision for the comfort of young gentlemen. David Garrick, who was one of the pupils, used, many years later, to throw the best company of London into convulsions of laughter by mimicking the endearments of this extraordinary pair.

At length Johnson, in the twenty-eighth year of his age,

determined to seek his fortune in the capital as a literary adventurer. He set out with a few guineas, three acts of the tragedy of Irene in manuscript, and two or three letters of introduction from his friend Walmesley.

Never, since literature became a calling in England, had it been a less gainful calling than at the time when Johnson took up his residence in London. In the preceding generation a writer of eminent merit was sure to be munificently rewarded by the government. The least that he could expect was a pension or a sinecure place; and, if he showed any aptitude for politics, he might hope to be a member of parliament, a lord of the treasury, an ambassador, a secretary of state. It would be easy, on the other hand, to name several writers of the nineteenth century of whom the least successful has received forty thousand pounds from the booksellers. But Johnson entered on his vocation in the most dreary part of the dreary interval which separated two ages of prosperity. Literature had ceased to flourish under the patronage of the great, and had not begun to flourish under the patronage of the public. One man of letters, indeed, Pope, had acquired by his pen what was then considered as a handsome fortune, and lived on a footing of equality with nobles and ministers of state. But this was a solitary exception. Even an author whose reputation was established, and whose works were popular, such an author as Thomson, whose Seasons were in every library, such an author as Fielding, whose Pasquin had had a greater run than any drama since The Beggar's Opera, was sometimes glad to obtain, by pawning his best coat, the means of dining on tripe at a cookshop underground, where he could wipe his hands, after his greasy meal, on the back of a Newfoundland dog. It is easy, therefore, to imagine what humiliations and privations must have awaited the novice who had still to earn a name. One of the publishers to whom Johnson applied for employment measured with a scornful eye that athletic though uncouth frame, and exclaimed, " You had better get a porter's knot, and carry trunks." Nor was the advice bad; for a porter was likely to be as plentifully fed, and as comfortably lodged, as a poet.

Some time appears to have elapsed before Johnson was able to form any literary connection from which he could expect more than bread for the day which was passing over him. He never forgot the generosity with which Hervey, who was now residing in London, relieved his wants during this time of trial. " Harry Hervey," said the old philosopher many years later, "was a vicious man; but he was very kind to me. If you call a dog Hervey I shall love him." At Hervey's table Johnson sometimes enjoyed feasts which were made more agreeable by contrast. But in general he dined, and thought that he dined well, on sixpenny worth of meat, and a pennyworth of bread, at an alehouse near Drury Lane.

The effect of the privations and sufferings which he endured at this time was discernible to the last in his temper and his deportment. His manners had never been courtly. They now became almost savage. Being frequently under the necessity of wearing shabby coats and dirty shirts, he became a confirmed sloven. Being often very hungry when he sat down to his meals, he contracted a habit of eating with ravenous greediness. Even to the end of his life, and even at the tables of the great, the sight of food affected him as it affects wild beasts and birds of prey. His taste in cookery, formed in subterranean ordinaries and alamode beefshops, was far from delicate. Whenever he was so fortunate as to have near him a hare that had been kept too long, or a meat pie made with rancid butter, he gorged himself with such violence that his veins swelled, and the moisture broke out on his forehead. The affronts which his poverty emboldened stupid and low-minded men to offer to him would have broken a mean spirit into sycophancy, but made him rude even to ferocity. Unhappily the insolence which, while it was defensive, was pardonable, and in some sense respectable, accompanied him into societies where he was treated with courtesy and kindness. He was repeatedly provoked into striking those who had taken liberties with him. All the sufferers, however, were wise enough to abstain from talking about their beatings, except Osborne, the most rapacious and brutal of booksellers, who proclaimed everywhere that he had been knocked down by the huge fellow whom he had hired to puff the Harleian Library.

About a year after Johnson had begun to reside in London, he was fortunate enough to obtain regular employment from Cave, an enterprising and intelligent bookseller, who was proprietor and editor of the "Gentleman's Magazine." That journal, just entering on the ninth year of its long existence, was the only periodical work in the kingdom which then had what would now be called a large circulation. It was, indeed, the chief source of parliamentary intelligence. It was not then safe, even during a recess, to publish an account of the proceedings of either House without some disguise. Cave, how-

ever, ventured to entertain his readers with what he called
"Reports of the Debates of the Senate of Lilliput." France
was Blefuscu; London was Mildendo: pounds were sprugs: the
Duke of Newcastle was the Nardac secretary of State: Lord
Hardwicke was the Hurgo Hickrad: and William Pulteney was
Wingul Pulnub. To write the speeches was, during several
years, the business of Johnson. He was generally furnished
with notes, meagre indeed, and inaccurate, of what had been
said; but sometimes he had to find arguments and eloquence
both for the ministry and for the opposition. He was himself
a Tory, not from rational conviction—for his serious opinion
was that one form of government was just as good or as bad as
another—but from mere passion, such as inflamed the Capulets
against the Montagues, or the Blues of the Roman circus against
the Greens. In his infancy he had heard so much talk about
the villainies of the Whigs, and the dangers of the Church, that
he had become a furious partisan when he could scarcely speak.
Before he was three he had insisted on being taken to hear
Sacheverell preach at Lichfield Cathedral, and had listened to
the sermon with as much respect, and probably with as much
intelligence, as any Staffordshire squire in the congregation.
The work which had been begun in the nursery had been completed by the university. Oxford, when Johnson resided there,
was the most Jacobitical place in England; and Pembroke was
one of the most Jacobitical colleges in Oxford. The prejudices
which he brought up to London were scarcely less absurd than
those of his own Tom Tempest. Charles II. and James II. were
two of the best kings that ever reigned. Laud, a poor creature
who never did, said, or wrote anything indicating more than
the ordinary capacity of an old woman, was a prodigy of parts
and learning over whose tomb Art and Genius still continued to
weep. Hampden deserved no more honourable name than that
of "the zealot of rebellion." Even the ship money, condemned
not less decidedly by Falkland and Clarendon than by the
bitterest Roundheads, Johnson would not pronounce to have
been an unconstitutional impost. Under a government, the
mildest that had ever been known in the world—under a government, which allowed to the people an unprecedented liberty of
speech and action—he fancied that he was a slave; he assailed
the ministry with obloquy which refuted itself, and regretted
the lost freedom and happiness of those golden days in which a
writer who had taken but one-tenth part of the licence allowed
to him would have been pilloried, mangled with the shears,

whipped at the cart's tail, and flung into a noisome dungeon to die. He hated dissenters and stockjobbers, the excise and the army, septennial parliaments, and continental connections. He long had an aversion to the Scotch, an aversion of which he could not remember the commencement, but which, he owned, had probably originated in his abhorrence of the conduct of the nation during the Great Rebellion. It is easy to guess in what manner debates on great party questions were likely to be reported by a man whose judgment was so much disordered by party spirit. A show of fairness was indeed necessary to the prosperity of the Magazine. But Johnson long afterwards owned that, though he had saved appearances, he had taken care that the Whig dogs should not have the best of it; and, in fact, every passage which has lived, every passage which bears the marks of his higher faculties, is put into the mouth of some member of the opposition.

A few weeks after Johnson had entered on these obscure labours, he published a work which at once placed him high among the writers of his age. It is probable that what he had suffered during his first year in London had often reminded him of some parts of that noble poem in which Juvenal had described the misery and degradation of a needy man of letters, lodged among the pigeons' nests in the tottering garrets which overhung the streets of Rome. Pope's admirable imitations of Horace's Satires and Epistles had recently appeared, were in every hand, and were by many readers thought superior to the originals. What Pope had done for Horace, Johnson aspired to do for Juvenal. The enterprise was bold and yet judicious. For between Johnson and Juvenal there was much in common, much more certainly than between Pope and Horace.

Johnson's London appeared without his name in May 1738. He received only ten guineas for this stately and vigorous poem; but the sale was rapid, and the success complete. A second edition was required within a week. Those small critics who are always desirous to lower established reputations ran about proclaiming that the anonymous satirist was superior to Pope in Pope's own peculiar department of literature. It ought to be remembered, to the honour of Pope, that he joined heartily in the applause with which the appearance of a rival genius was welcomed. He made inquiries about the author of London. Such a man, he said, could not long be concealed. The name was soon discovered; and Pope, with great kindness, exerted himself to obtain an academical degree and the mastership of a grammar school for the poor young poet. The attempt failed; and Johnson remained a bookseller's hack.

It does not appear that these two men, the most eminent writer of the generation which was going out, and the most eminent writer of the generation which was coming in, ever saw each other. They lived in very different circles, one surrounded by dukes and earls, the other by starving pamphleteers and index makers. Among Johnson's associates at this time may be mentioned Boyse, who, when his shirts were pledged, scrawled Latin verses sitting up in bed with his arms through two holes in his blanket; who composed very respectable sacred poetry when he was sober; and who was at last run over by a hackney coach when he was drunk: Hoole, surnamed the metaphysical tailor, who, instead of attending to his measures, used to trace geometrical diagrams on the board where he sate cross-legged; and the penitent impostor, George Psalmanazar, who, after poring all day, in a humble lodging, on the folios of Jewish rabbis and Christian fathers, indulged himself at night with literary and theological conversation at an alehouse in the city. But the most remarkable of the persons with whom at this time Johnson consorted was Richard Savage, an earl's son, a shoemaker's apprentice, who had seen life in all its forms, who had feasted among blue ribands in Saint James's Square, and had lain with fifty pounds' weight of iron on his legs in the condemned ward of Newgate. This man had, after many vicissitudes of fortune, sunk at last into abject and hopeless poverty. His pen had failed him. His patrons had been taken away by death, or estranged by the riotous profusion with which he squandered their bounty, and the ungrateful insolence with which he rejected their advice. He now lived by begging. He dined on venison and champagne whenever he had been so fortunate as to borrow a guinea. If his questing had been unsuccessful, he appeased the rage of hunger with some scraps of broken meat, and lay down to rest under the Piazza of Covent Garden in warm weather, and, in cold weather, as near as he could get to the furnace of a glass house. Yet, in his misery, he was still an agreeable companion. He had an inexhaustible store of anecdotes about that gay and brilliant world from which he was now an outcast. He had observed the great men of both parties in hours of careless relaxation, had seen the leaders of opposition without the mask of patriotism, and had heard the prime minister roar with laughter and tell stories not over decent. During some months Savage lived in the closest familiarity with

Johnson; and then the friends parted, not without tears. Johnson remained in London to drudge for Cave. Savage went to the West of England, lived there as he had lived everywhere, and in 1743, died, penniless and heart-broken, in Bristol gaol.

Soon after his death, while the public curiosity was strongly excited about his extraordinary character, and his not less extraordinary adventures, a life of him appeared widely different from the catchpenny lives of eminent men which were then a staple article of manufacture in Grub Street. The style was indeed deficient in ease and variety; and the writer was evidently too partial to the Latin element of our language. But the little work, with all its faults, was a masterpiece. No finer specimen of literary biography existed in any language, living or dead; and a discerning critic might have confidently predicted that the author was destined to be the founder of a new school of English eloquence.

The life of Savage was anonymous; but it was well known in literary circles that Johnson was the writer. During the three years which followed, he produced no important work; but he was not, and indeed could not be, idle. The fame of his abilities and learning continued to grow. Warburton pronounced him a man of parts and genius; and the praise of Warburton was then no light thing. Such was Johnson's reputation that, in 1747, several eminent booksellers combined to employ him in the arduous work of preparing a Dictionary of the English language, in two folio volumes. The sum which they agreed to pay him was only fifteen hundred guineas; and out of this sum he had to pay several poor men of letters who assisted him in the humbler parts of his task.

The prospectus of the Dictionary he addressed to the Earl of Chesterfield. Chesterfield had long been celebrated for the politeness of his manners, the brilliancy of his wit, and the delicacy of his taste. He was acknowledged to be the finest speaker in the House of Lords. He had recently governed Ireland, at a momentous conjuncture, with eminent firmness, wisdom, and humanity; and he had since become Secretary of State. He received Johnson's homage with the most winning affability, and requited it with a few guineas, bestowed doubtless in a very graceful manner, but was by no means desirous to see all his carpets blackened with the London mud, and his soups and wines thrown to right and left over the gowns of fine ladies and the waistcoats of fine gentlemen, by an absent, awkward scholar, who gave strange starts and uttered strange growls, who dressed like a scarecrow, and ate like a cormorant. During some time Johnson continued to call on his patron, but after being repeatedly told by the porter that his lordship was not at home, took the hint, and ceased to present himself at the inhospitable door.

Johnson had flattered himself that he should have completed his Dictionary by the end of 1750; but it was not till 1755 that he at length gave his huge volumes to the world. During the seven years which he passed in the drudgery of penning definitions and marking quotations for transcription, he sought for relaxation in literary labour of a more agreeable kind. In 1749 he published the Vanity of Human Wishes, an excellent imitation of the Tenth Satire of Juvenal. It is in truth not easy to say whether the palm belongs to the ancient or to the modern poet. The couplets in which the fall of Wolsey is described, though lofty and sonorous, are feeble when compared with the wonderful lines which bring before us all Rome in tumult on the day of the fall of Sejanus, the laurels on the doorposts, the white bull stalking towards the Capitol, the statues rolling down from their pedestals, the flatterers of the disgraced minister running to see him dragged with a hook through the streets, and to have a kick at his carcase before it is hurled into the Tiber. It must be owned too that in the concluding passage the Christian moralist has not made the most of his advantages, and has fallen decidedly short of the sublimity of his Pagan model. On the other hand, Juvenal's Hannibal must yield to Johnson's Charles; and Johnson's vigorous and pathetic enumeration of the miseries of a literary life must be allowed to be superior to Juvenal's lamentations over the fate of Demosthenes and Cicero.

For the copyright of the Vanity of Human Wishes Johnson received only fifteen guineas.

A few days after the publication of this poem, his tragedy, begun many years before, was brought on the stage. His pupil, David Garrick, had, in 1741, made his appearance on a humble stage in Goodman's Fields, had at once risen to the first place among actors, and was now, after several years of almost uninterrupted success, manager of Drury Lane Theatre. The relation between him and his old preceptor was of a very singular kind. They repelled each other strongly, and yet attracted each other strongly. Nature had made them of very different clay; and circumstances had fully brought out the natural peculiarities of both. Sudden prosperity had turned Garrick's head. Continued adversity had soured Johnson's temper.

Johnson saw with more envy than became so great a man the villa, the plate, the china, the Brussels carpet, which the little mimic had got by repeating, with grimaces and gesticulations, what wiser men had written; and the exquisitely sensitive vanity of Garrick was galled by the thought that, while all the rest of the world was applauding him, he could obtain from one morose cynic, whose opinion it was impossible to despise, scarcely any compliment not acidulated with scorn. Yet the two Lichfield men had so many early recollections in common, and sympathised with each other on so many points on which they sympathised with nobody else in the vast population of the capital, that, though the master was often provoked by the monkey-like impertinence of the pupil, and the pupil by the bearish rudeness of the master, they remained friends till they were parted by death. Garrick now brought Irene out, with alterations sufficient to displease the author, yet not sufficient to make the piece pleasing to the audience. The public, however, listened with little emotion, but with much civility, to five acts of monotonous declamation. After nine representations the play was withdrawn. It is, indeed, altogether unsuited to the stage, and, even when perused in the closet, will be found hardly worthy of the author. He had not the slightest notion of what blank verse should be. A change in the last syllable of every other line would make the versification of the Vanity of Human Wishes closely resemble the versification of Irene. The poet, however, cleared, by his benefit nights, and by the sale of the copyright of his tragedy, about three hundred pounds, then a great sum in his estimation.

About a year after the representation of Irene, he began to publish a series of short essays on morals, manners, and literature. This species of composition had been brought into fashion by the success of the Tatler, and by the still more brilliant success of the Spectator. A crowd of small writers had vainly attempted to rival Addison. The Lay Monastery, the Censor, the Free-thinker, the Plain Dealer, the Champion, and other works of the same kind, had had their short day. None of them had obtained a permanent place in our literature; and they are now to be found only in the libraries of the curious. At length Johnson undertook the adventure in which so many aspirants had failed. In the thirty-sixth year after the appearance of the last number of the Spectator appeared the first number of the Rambler. From March 1750 to March 1752 this paper continued to come out every Tuesday and Saturday.

From the first the Rambler was enthusiastically admired by a few eminent men. Richardson, when only five numbers had appeared, pronounced it equal, if not superior, to the Spectator. Young and Hartley expressed their approbation not less warmly. Bubb Doddington, among whose many faults indifference to the claims of genius and learning cannot be reckoned, solicited the acquaintance of the writer. In consequence probably of the good offices of Doddington, who was then the confidential adviser of Prince Frederic, two of his Royal Highness's gentlemen carried a gracious message to the printing office, and ordered seven copies for Leicester House. But these overtures seem to have been very coldly received. Johnson had had enough of the patronage of the great to last him all his life, and was not disposed to haunt any other door as he had haunted the door of Chesterfield.

By the public the Rambler was at first very coldly received. Though the price of a number was only twopence, the sale did not amount to five hundred. The profits were therefore very small. But as soon as the flying leaves were collected and reprinted they became popular. The author lived to see thirteen thousand copies spread over England alone. Separate editions were published for the Scotch and Irish markets. A large party pronounced the style perfect, so absolutely perfect that in some essays it would be impossible for the writer himself to alter a single word for the better. Another party, not less numerous, vehemently accused him of having corrupted the purity of the English tongue. The best critics admitted that his diction was too monotonous, too obviously artificial, and now and then turgid even to absurdity. But they did justice to the acuteness of his observations on morals and manners, to the constant precision and frequent brilliancy of his language, to the weighty and magnificent eloquence of many serious passages, and to the solemn yet pleasing humour of some of the lighter papers. On the question of precedence between Addison and Johnson, a question which, seventy years ago, was much disputed, posterity has pronounced a decision from which there is no appeal. Sir Roger, his chaplain and his butler, Will Wimble and Will Honeycomb, the Vision of Mirza, the Journal of the Retired Citizen, the Everlasting Club, the Dunmow Flitch, the Loves of Hilpah and Shalum, the Visit to the Exchange, and the Visit to the Abbey, are known to everybody. But many men and women, even of highly cultivated minds, are unacquainted with Squire Bluster and Mrs. Busy, Quisquilius and Venustulus, the

Allegory of Wit and Learning, the Chronicle of the Revolutions of a Garret, and the sad fate of Aningait and Ajut.

The last Rambler was written in a sad and gloomy hour. Mrs. Johnson had been given over by the physicians. Three days later she died. She left her husband almost broken-hearted. Many people had been suprised to see a man of his genius and learning stooping to every drudgery, and denying himself almost every comfort, for the purpose of supplying a silly, affected old woman with superfluities, which she accepted with but little gratitude. But all his affection had been concentrated on her. He had neither brother nor sister, neither son nor daughter. To him she was beautiful as the Gunnings, and witty as Lady Mary. Her opinion of his writings was more important to him than the voice of the pit of Drury Lane Theatre or the judgment of the Monthly Review. The chief support which had sustained him through the most arduous labour of his life was the hope that she would enjoy the fame and the profit which he anticipated from his Dictionary. She was gone; and in that vast labyrinth of streets, peopled by eight hundred thousand human beings, he was alone. Yet it was necessary for him to set himself, as he expressed it, doggedly to work. After three more laborious years, the Dictionary was at length complete.

It had been generally supposed that this great work would be dedicated to the eloquent and accomplished nobleman to whom the prospectus had been addressed. He well knew the value of such a compliment; and therefore, when the day of publication drew near, he exerted himself to soothe, by a show of zealous and at the same time of delicate and judicious kindness, the pride which he had so cruelly wounded. Since the Ramblers had ceased to appear, the town had been entertained by a journal called the World, to which many men of high rank and fashion contributed. In two successive numbers of the World the Dictionary was, to use the modern phrase, puffed with wonderful skill. The writings of Johnson were warmly praised. It was proposed that he should be invested with the authority of a Dictator, nay, of a Pope, over our language, and that his decisions about the meaning and the spelling of words should be received as final. His two folios, it was said, would of course be bought by everybody who could afford to buy them. It was soon known that these papers were written by Chesterfield. But the just resentment of Johnson was not to be so appeased. In a letter written with singular energy and dignity of thought and language, he repelled the tardy advances of his patron. The

Dictionary came forth without a dedication. In the preface the author truly declared that he owed nothing to the great, and described the difficulties with which he had been left to struggle so forcibly and pathetically that the ablest and most malevolent of all the enemies of his fame, Horne Tooke, never could read that passage without tears.

The public, on this occasion, did Johnson full justice, and something more than justice. The best lexicographer may well be content if his productions are received by the world with cold esteem. But Johnson's Dictionary was hailed with an enthusiasm such as no similar work has ever excited. It was indeed the first dictionary which could be read with pleasure. The definitions show so much acuteness of thought and command of language, and the passages quoted from poets, divines, and philosophers are so skilfully selected, that a leisure hour may always be very agreeably spent in turning over the pages. The faults of the book resolve themselves, for the most part, into one great fault. Johnson was a wretched etymologist. He knew little or nothing of any Teutonic language except English, which indeed, as he wrote it, was scarcely a Teutonic language; and thus he was absolutely at the mercy of Junius and Skinner.

The Dictionary, though it raised Johnson's fame, added nothing to his pecuniary means. The fifteen hundred guineas which the booksellers had agreed to pay him had been advanced and spent before the last sheets issued from the press. It is painful to relate that, twice in the course of the year which followed the publication of this great work, he was arrested and carried to spunging-houses, and that he was twice indebted for his liberty to his excellent friend Richardson. It was still necessary for the man who had been formally saluted by the highest authority as Dictator of the English language to supply his wants by constant toil. He abridged his Dictionary. He proposed to bring out an edition of Shakspeare by subscription; and many subscribers sent in their names and laid down their money; but he soon found the task so little to his taste that he turned to more attractive employments. He contributed many papers to a new monthly journal, which was called the Literary Magazine. Few of these papers have much interest; but among them was the very best thing that he ever wrote, a masterpiece both of reasoning and of satirical pleasantry, the review of Jenyns's Inquiry into the Nature and Origin of Evil.

In the spring of 1758 Johnson put forth the first of a series of essays, entitled the Idler. During two years these essays continued to appear weekly. They were eagerly read, widely circulated, and indeed, impudently pirated, while they were still in the original form, and had a large sale when collected into volumes. The Idler may be described as a second part of the Rambler, somewhat livelier and somewhat weaker than the first part.

While Johnson was busied with his Idlers, his mother, who had accomplished her ninetieth year, died at Lichfield. It was long since he had seen her; but he had not failed to contribute largely, out of his small means, to her comfort. In order to defray the charges of her funeral, and to pay some debts which she had left, he wrote a little book in a single week, and sent off the sheets to the press without reading them over. A hundred pounds were paid him for the copyright; and the purchasers had great cause to be pleased with their bargain; for the book was Rasselas.

The success of Rasselas was great, though such ladies as Miss Lydia Languish must have been grievously disappointed when they found that the new volume from the circulating library was little more than a dissertation on the author's favourite theme, the Vanity of Human Wishes; that the Prince of Abyssinia was without a mistress, and the princess without a lover; and that the story set the hero and the heroine down exactly where it had taken them up. The style was the subject of much eager controversy. The Monthly Review and the Critical Review took different sides. Many readers pronounced the writer a pompous pedant, who would never use a word of two syllables where it was possible to use a word of six, and who could not make a waiting woman relate her adventures without balancing every noun with another noun, and every epithet with another epithet. Another party, not less zealous, cited with delight numerous passages in which weighty meaning was expressed with accuracy and illustrated with splendour. And both the censure and the praise were merited.

About the plan of Rasselas little was said by the critics; and yet the faults of the plan might seem to invite severe criticism. Johnson has frequently blamed Shakspeare for neglecting the proprieties of time and place, and for ascribing to one age or nation the manners and opinions of another. Yet Shakspeare has not sinned in this way more grievously than Johnson. Rasselas and Imlac, Nekayah and Pekuah, are evidently meant to be Abyssinians of the eighteenth century: for the Europe which Imlac describes is the Europe of the eighteenth century;

and the inmates of the Happy Valley talk familiarly of that law of gravitation which Newton discovered, and which was not fully received even at Cambridge till the eighteenth century. What a real company of Abyssinians would have been may be learned from Bruce's Travels. But Johnson, not content with turning filthy savages, ignorant of their letters, and gorged with raw steaks cut from living cows, into philosophers as eloquent and enlightened as himself or his friend Burke, and into ladies as highly accomplished as Mrs. Lennox or Mrs. Sheridan, transferred the whole domestic system of England to Egypt. Into a land of harems, a land of polygamy, a land where women are married without ever being seen, he introduced the flirtations and jealousies of our ball-rooms. In a land where there is boundless liberty of divorce, wedlock is described as the indissoluble compact. " A youth and maiden meeting by chance, or brought together by artifice, exchange glances, reciprocate civilities, go home, and dream of each other. Such," says Rasselas, " is the common process of marriage." Such it may have been, and may still be, in London, but assuredly not at Cairo. A writer who was guilty of such improprieties had little right to blame the poet who made Hector quote Aristotle, and represented Julio Romano as flourishing in the days of the oracle of Delphi.

By such exertions as have been described, Johnson supported himself till the year 1762. In that year a great change in his circumstances took place. He had from a child been an enemy of the reigning dynasty. His Jacobite prejudices had been exhibited with little disguise both in his works and in his conversation. Even in his massy and elaborate Dictionary, he had, with a strange want of taste and judgment, inserted bitter and contumelious reflections on the Whig party. The excise, which was a favourite resource of Whig financiers, he had designated as a hateful tax. He had railed against the commissioners of excise in language so coarse that they had seriously thought of prosecuting him. He had with difficulty been prevented from holding up the Lord Privy Seal by name as an example of the meaning of the word " renegade." A pension he had defined as pay given to a state hireling to betray his country; a pensioner as a slave of state hired by a stipend to obey a master. It seemed unlikely that the author of these definitions would himself be pensioned. But that was a time of wonders. George the Third had ascended the throne; and had, in the course of a few months, disgusted many of the old

friends and conciliated many of the old enemies of his house.
The city was becoming mutinous.   Oxford was becoming loyal.
Cavendishes and Bentincks were murmuring.   Somersets and
Wyndhams were hastening to kiss hands.   The head of the
treasury was now Lord Bute, who was a Tory, and could have
no objection to Johnson's Toryism.   Bute wished to be thought
a patron of men of letters; and Johnson was one of the most
eminent and one of the most needy men of letters in Europe.
A pension of three hundred a year was graciously offered, and
with very little hesitation accepted.

This event produced a change in Johnson's whole way of life.
For the first time since his boyhood he no longer felt the daily
goad urging him to the daily toil.   He was at liberty, after
thirty years of anxiety and drudgery, to indulge his constitutional indolence, to lie in bed till two in the afternoon, and to
sit up talking till four in the morning, without fearing either
the printer's devil or the sheriff's officer.

One laborious task indeed he had bound himself to perform.
He had received large subscriptions for his promised edition of
Shakspeare; he had lived on those subscriptions during some
years: and he could not without disgrace omit to perform his
part of the contract.   His friends repeatedly exhorted him to
make an effort; and he repeatedly resolved to do so.   But,
notwithstanding their exhortations and his resolutions, month
followed month, year followed year, and nothing was done.   He
prayed fervently against his idleness; he determined, as often
as he received the sacrament, that he would no longer doze
away and trifle away his time; but the spell under which he
lay resisted prayer and sacrament.   His private notes at this
time are made up of self-reproaches.   " My indolence," he wrote
on Easter Eve in 1764, " has sunk into grosser sluggishness.   A
kind of strange oblivion has overspread me, so that I know not
what has become of the last year."   Easter 1765 came, and
found him still in the same state.   " My time," he wrote, " has
been unprofitably spent, and seems as a dream that has left
nothing behind   My memory grows confused, and I know not
how the days pass over me."   Happily for his honour, the
charm which held him captive was at length broken by no
gentle or friendly hand.   He had been weak enough to pay
serious attention to a story about a ghost which haunted a
house in Cock Lane, and had actually gone himself with some
of his friends, at one in the morning, to St. John's Church,
Clerkenwell, in the hope of receiving a communication from the

perturbed spirit. But the spirit, though adjured with all solemnity, remained obstinately silent; and it soon appeared that a naughty girl of eleven had been amusing herself by making fools of so many philosophers. Churchill, who, confident in his powers, drunk with popularity, and burning with party spirit, was looking for some man of established fame and Tory politics to insult, celebrated the Cock Lane Ghost in three cantos, nicknamed Johnson Pomposo, asked where the book was which had been so long promised and so liberally paid for, and directly accused the great moralist of cheating. This terrible word proved effectual; and in October 1765 appeared, after a delay of nine years, the new edition of Shakspeare.

This publication saved Johnson's character for honesty, but added nothing to the fame of his abilities and learning. The preface, though it contains some good passages, is not in his best manner. The most valuable notes are those in which he had an opportunity of showing how attentively he had during many years observed human life and human nature. The best specimen is the note on the character of Polonius. Nothing so good is to be found even in Wilhelm Meister's admirable examination of Hamlet. But here praise must end. It would be difficult to name a more slovenly, a more worthless edition of any great classic. The reader may turn over play after play without finding one happy conjectural emendation, or one ingenious and satisfactory explanation of a passage which had baffled preceding commentators. Johnson had, in his prospectus, told the world that he was peculiarly fitted for the task which he had undertaken, because he had, as a lexicographer, been under the necessity of taking a wider view of the English language than any of his predecessors. That his knowledge of our literature was extensive is indisputable. But, unfortunately, he had altogether neglected that very part of our literature with which it is especially desirable that an editor of Shakspeare should be conversant. It is dangerous to assert a negative. Yet little will be risked by the assertion, that in the two folio volumes of the English Dictionary there is not a single passage quoted from any dramatist of the Elizabethan age, except Shakspeare and Ben. Even from Ben the quotations are few. Johnson might easily, in a few months, have made himself well acquainted with every old play that was extant. But it never seems to have occurred to him that this was a necessary preparation for the work which he had undertaken. He would doubtless have admitted that it would be the height of absurdity in a man who was not familiar with the works of Æschylus and Euripides to publish an edition of Sophocles.   Yet he ventured to publish an edition of Shakspeare, without having ever in his life, as far as can be discovered, read a single scene of Massinger, Ford, Decker, Webster, Marlow, Beaumont, or Fletcher.   His detractors were noisy and scurrilous.   Those who most loved and honoured him had little to say in praise of the manner in which he had discharged the duty of a commentator.   He had, however, acquitted himself of a debt which had long lain heavy on his conscience; and he sank back into the repose from which the sting of satire had roused him.   He long continued to live upon the fame which he had already won.   He was honoured by the University of Oxford with a Doctor's degree, by the Royal Academy with a professorship, and by the King with an interview, in which his Majesty most graciously expressed a hope that so excellent a writer would not cease to write.   In the interval, however, between 1765 and 1775 Johnson published only two or three political tracts, the longest of which he could have produced in forty-eight hours, if he had worked as he worked on the life of Savage and on Rasselas.

But, though his pen was now idle, his tongue was active.   The influence exercised by his conversation, directly upon those with whom he lived, and indirectly on the whole literary world, was altogether without a parallel.   His colloquial talents were indeed of the highest order.   He had strong sense, quick discernment, wit, humour, immense knowledge of literature and of life, and an infinite store of curious anecdotes.   As respected style, he spoke far better than he wrote.   Every sentence which dropped from his lips was as correct in structure as the most nicely balanced period of the Rambler.   But in his talk there was no pompous triads, and little more than a fair proportion of words in *osity* and *ation*.   All was simplicity, ease, and vigour.   He uttered his short, weighty, and pointed sentences with a power of voice, and a justness and energy of emphasis, of which the effect was rather increased than diminished by the rollings of his huge form, and by the asthmatic gaspings and puffings in which the peals of his eloquence generally ended.   Nor did the laziness which made him unwilling to sit down to his desk prevent him from giving instruction or entertainment orally.   To discuss questions of taste, of learning, of casuistry, in language so exact and so forcible that it might have been printed without the alteration of a word, was to him no exertion, but a pleasure. He loved, as he said, to fold his legs and have his talk out.

He was ready to bestow the overflowings of his full mind on anybody who would start a subject, on a fellow-passenger in a stage coach, or on the person who sate at the same table with him in an eating-house. But his conversation was nowhere so brilliant and striking as when he was surrounded by a few friends, whose abilities and knowledge enabled them, as he once expressed it, to send him back every ball that he threw. Some of these, in 1764, formed themselves into a club, which gradually became a formidable power in the commonwealth of letters.

The verdicts pronounced by this conclave on new books were speedily known over all London, and were sufficient to sell off a whole edition in a day, or to condemn the sheets to the service of the trunk-maker and the pastry-cook. Nor shall we think this strange when we consider what great and various talents and acquirements met in the little fraternity. Goldsmith was the representative of poetry and light literature, Reynolds of the arts, Burke of political eloquence and political philosophy. There, too, were Gibbon, the greatest historian, and Jones, the greatest linguist, of the age. Garrick brought to the meetings his inexhaustible pleasantry, his incomparable mimicry, and his consummate knowledge of stage effect. Among the most constant attendants were two high-born and high-bred gentlemen, closely bound together by friendship, but of widely different characters and habits; Bennet Langton, distinguished by his skill in Greek literature, by the orthodoxy of his opinions, and by the sanctity of his life; and Topham Beauclerk, renowned for his amours, his knowledge of the gay world, his fastidious taste, and his sarcastic wit. To predominate over such a society was not easy. Yet even over such a society Johnson predominated. Burke might indeed have disputed the supremacy to which others were under the necessity of submitting. But Burke, though not generally a very patient listener, was content to take the second part when Johnson was present; and the club itself, consisting of so many eminent men, is to this day popularly designated as Johnson's Club.

Among the members of this celebrated body was one to whom it has owed the greater part of its celebrity, yet who was regarded with little respect by his brethren, and had not without difficulty obtained a seat among them. This was James Boswell, a young Scotch lawyer, heir to an honourable name and a fair estate. That he was a coxcomb and a bore, weak, vain, pushing, curious, garrulous, was obvious to all who were acquainted with him. That he could not reason, that he had no wit, no humour, no eloquence, is apparent from his writings. And yet his writings are read beyond the Mississippi, and under the Southern Cross, and are likely to be read as long as the English exists, either as a living or as a dead language. Nature had made him a slave and an idolater. His mind resembled those creepers which the botanists call parasites, and which can subsist only by clinging round the stems and imbibing the juices of stronger plants. He must have fastened himself on somebody. He might have fastened himself on Wilkes, and have became the fiercest patriot in the Bill of Rights Society. He might have fastened himself on Whitfield, and have become the loudest field preacher among the Calvinistic Methodists. In a happy hour he fastened himself on Johnson. The pair might seem ill matched. For Johnson had early been prejudiced against Boswell's country. To a man of Johnson's strong understanding and irritable temper, the silly egotism and adulation of Boswell must have been as teasing as the constant buzz of a fly.

Johnson hated to be questioned; and Boswell was eternally catechising him on all kinds of subjects, and sometimes propounded such questions as " What would you do, sir, if you were locked up in a tower with a baby? " Johnson was a water drinker; and Boswell was a wine-bibber, and indeed little better than a habitual sot. It was impossible that there should be perfect harmony between two such companions. Indeed, the great man was sometimes provoked into fits of passion in which he said things which the small man, during a few hours, seriously resented. Every quarrel, however, was soon made up. During twenty years the disciple continued to worship the master: the master continued to scold the disciple, to sneer at him, and to love him. The two friends ordinarily resided at a great distance from each other. Boswell practised in the Parliament House of Edinburgh, and could pay only occasional visits to London. During those visits his chief business was to watch Johnson, to discover all Johnson's habits, to turn the conversation to subjects about which Johnson was likely to say something remarkable, and to fill quarto note books with minutes of what Johnson had said. In this way were gathered the materials out of which was afterwards constructed the most interesting biographical work in the world.

Soon after the club began to exist, Johnson formed a connection less important indeed to his fame, but much more important to his happiness, than his connection with Boswell. Henry Thrale, one of the most opulent brewers in the kingdom, a man of sound and cultivated understanding, rigid principles, and liberal spirit, was married to one of those clever, kind-hearted, engaging, vain, pert young women, who are perpetually doing or saying what is not exactly right, but who, do or say what they may, are always agreeable. In 1765 the Thrales became acquainted with Johnson; and the acquaintance ripened fast into friendship. They were astonished and delighted by the brilliancy of his conversation. They were flattered by finding that a man so widely celebrated preferred their house to any other in London. Even the peculiarities which seemed to unfit him for civilised society, his gesticulations, his rollings, his puffings, his mutterings, the strange way in which he put on his clothes, the ravenous eagerness with which he devoured his dinner, his fits of melancholy, his fits of anger, his frequent rudeness, his occasional ferocity, increased the interest which his new associates took in him. For these things were the cruel marks left behind by a life which had been one long conflict with disease and with adversity. In a vulgar hack writer such oddities would have excited only disgust. But in a man of genius, learning, and virtue their effect was to add pity to admiration and esteem. Johnson soon had an apartment at the brewery in Southwark, and a still more pleasant apartment at the villa of his friends on Streatham Common. A large part of every year he passed in those abodes, abodes which must have seemed magnificent and luxurious indeed, when compared with the dens in which he had generally been lodged. But his chief pleasures were derived from what the astronomer of his Abyssinian tale called " the endearing elegance of female friendship."

Mrs. Thrale rallied him, soothed him, coaxed him, and, if she sometimes provoked him by her flippancy, made ample amends by listening to his reproofs with angelic sweetness of temper. When he was diseased in body and in mind, she was the most tender of nurses. No comfort that wealth could purchase, no contrivance that womanly ingenuity, set to work by womanly compassion, could devise, was wanting to his sick-room. He requited her kindness by an affection pure as the affection of a father, yet delicately tinged with a gallantry, which, though awkward, must have been more flattering than the attentions of a crowd of the fools who gloried in the names, now obsolete, of Buck and Maccaroni. It should seem that a full half of Johnson's life, during about sixteen years, was passed under the roof of the Thrales. He accompanied the family sometimes to Bath, and sometimes to Brighton, once to Wales, and once to Paris. But he had at the same time a house in one of the narrow and gloomy courts on the north of Fleet Street. In the garrets was his library, a large and miscellaneous collection of books, falling to pieces and begrimed with dust. On a lower floor he sometimes, but very rarely, regaled a friend with a plain dinner, a veal pie, or a leg of lamb and spinage, and a rice pudding. Nor was the dwelling uninhabited during his long absences. It was the home of the most extraordinary assemblage of inmates that ever was brought together. At the head of the establishment Johnson had placed an old lady named Williams, whose chief recommendations were her blind-ness and her poverty. But, in spite of her murmurs and re-proaches, he gave an asylum to another lady who was as poor as herself, Mrs. Desmoulins, whose family he had known many years before in Staffordshire. Room was found for the daughter of Mrs. Desmoulins, and for another destitute damsel, who was generally addressed as Miss Carmichael, but whom her generous host called Polly. An old quack doctor named Levett, who bled and dosed coal-heavers and hackney coachmen, and received for fees crusts of bread, bits of bacon, glasses of gin, and some-times a little copper, completed this strange menagerie. All these poor creatures were at constant war with each other, and with Johnson's negro servant Frank. Sometimes, indeed, they transferred their hostilities from the servant to the master, complained that a better table was not kept for them, and railed or maundered till their benefactor was glad to make his escape to Streatham, or to the Mitre Tavern. And yet he, who was generally the haughtiest and most irritable of mankind, who was but too prompt to resent anything which looked like a slight on the part of a purse-proud bookseller, or of a noble and powerful patron, bore patiently from mendicants, who, but for his bounty, must have gone to the workhouse, insults more provoking than those for which he had knocked down Osborne and bidden defiance to Chesterfield. Year after year Mrs. Desmoulins, Polly, and Levett, continued to torment him and to live upon him.

The course of life which has been described was interrupted in Johnson's sixty-fourth year by an important event. He had early read an account of the Hebrides, and had been much interested by learning that there was so near him a land peopled by a race which was still as rude and simple as in the middle ages. A wish to become intimately acquainted with a state of society so utterly unlike all that he had ever seen frequently crossed his mind. But it is not probable that his curiosity would have overcome his habitual sluggishness, and his love of the smoke, the mud, and the cries of London, had not Boswell importuned him to attempt the adventure, and offered to be his squire. At length, in August 1773, Johnson crossed the Highland line, and plunged courageously into what was then considered, by most Englishmen, as a dreary and perilous wilderness. After wandering about two months through the Celtic region, sometimes in rude boats which did not protect him from the rain, and sometimes on small shaggy ponies which could hardly bear his weight, he returned to his old haunts with a mind full of new images and new theories.

During the following year he employed himself in recording his adventures. About the beginning of 1775, his Journey to the Hebrides was published, and was, during some weeks, the chief subject of conversation in all circles in which any attention was paid to literature. The book is still read with pleasure. The narrative · is entertaining; the speculations, whether sound or unsound, are always ingenious; and the style, though too stiff and pompous, is somewhat easier and more graceful than that of his early writings. His prejudice against the Scotch had at length become little more than matter of jest; and whatever remained of the old feeling had been effectually removed by the kind and respectful hospitality with which he had been received in every part of Scotland. It was, of course, not to be expected that an Oxonian Tory should praise the Presbyterian polity and ritual, or that an eye accustomed to the hedgerows and parks of England should not be struck by the bareness of Berwickshire and East Lothian. But even in censure Johnson's tone is not unfriendly. The most enlightened Scotchmen, with Lord Mansfield at their head, were well pleased. But some foolish and ignorant Scotchmen were moved to anger by a little unpalatable truth which was mingled with much eulogy, and assailed him whom they chose to consider as the enemy of their country with libels much more dishonourable to their country than anything that he had ever said or written. They published paragraphs in the newspapers, articles in the magazines, sixpenny pamphlets, five-shilling books. One scribbler abused Johnson for being blear-eyed; another for being a pensioner; a third informed the world that one of the Doctor's uncles had been convicted of felony in Scotland, and had found that there was in that country one tree capable of supporting the weight of an Englishman. Macpherson, whose Fingal had been proved in the Journey to be an impudent forgery, threatened to take vengeance with a cane. The only effect of this threat was that Johnson reiterated the charge of forgery in the most contemptuous terms, and walked about, during some time, with a cudgel, which, if the impostor had not been too wise to encounter it, would assuredly have descended upon him, to borrow the sublime language of his own epic poem, "like a hammer on the red son of the furnace."

Of other assailants Johnson took no notice whatever. He had early resolved never to be drawn into controversy; and he adhered to his resolution with a steadfastness which is the more extraordinary, because he was, both intellectually and morally, of the stuff of which controversalists are made. In conversation, he was a singularly eager, acute, and pertinacious disputant. When at a loss for good reasons, he had recourse to sophistry; and, when heated by altercation, he made unsparing use of sarcasm and invective. But, when he took his pen in his hand, his whole character seemed to be changed. A hundred bad writers misrepresented him and reviled him; but not one of the hundred could boast of having been thought by him worthy of a refutation, or even of a retort. The Kenricks, Campbells, MacNicols, and Hendersons, did their best to annoy him, in the hope that he would give them importance by answering them. But the reader will in vain search his works for any allusion to Kenrick or Campbell, to MacNicol or Henderson. One Scotchman, bent on vindicating the fame of Scotch learning, defied him to the combat in a detestable Latin hexameter.

" Maxime, si tu vis, cupio contendere tecum."

But Johnson took no notice of the challenge. He had learned, both from his own observation and from literary history, in which he was deeply read, that the place of books in the public estimation is fixed, not by what is written about them, but by what is written in them; and that an author whose works are likely to live is very unwise if he stoops to wrangle with detractors whose works are certain to die. He always maintained that fame was a shuttlecock which could be kept up only by being beaten back, as well as beaten forward, and which would soon fall if there were only one battledore. No saying was oftener in his mouth than that fine apophthegm of Bentley, that no man was ever written down but by himself.

Unhappily, a few months after the appearance of the Journey to the Hebrides, Johnson did what none of his envious assailants could have done, and to a certain extent succeeded in writing himself down. The disputes between England and her American colonies had reached a point at which no amicable adjustment was possible. Civil war was evidently impending; and the ministers seem to have thought that the eloquence of Johnson might with advantage be employed to inflame the nation against the opposition here, and against the rebels beyond the Atlantic.

He had already written two or three tracts in defence of the foreign and domestic policy of the government; and those tracts, though hardly worthy of him, were much superior to the crowd of pamphlets which lay on the counters of Almon and Stockdale. But his Taxation No Tyranny was a pitiable failure. The very title was a silly phrase, which can have been recommended to his choice by nothing but a jingling alliteration which he ought to have despised. The arguments were such as boys use in debating societies. The pleasantry was as awkward as the gambols of a hippopotamus. Even Boswell was forced to own that, in this unfortunate piece, he could detect no trace of his master's powers. The general opinion was that the strong faculties which had produced the Dictionary and the Rambler were beginning to feel the effect of time and of disease, and that the old man would best consult his credit by writing no more.

But this was a great mistake. Johnson had failed, not because his mind was less vigorous than when he wrote Rasselas in the evenings of a week, but because he had foolishly chosen, or suffered others to choose for him, a subject such as he would at no time have been competent to treat. He was in no sense a statesman. He never willingly read or thought or talked about affairs of state. He loved biography, literary history, the history of manners; but political history was positively distasteful to him. The question at issue between the colonies and the mother country was a question about which he had really nothing to say. He failed, therefore, as the greatest men must fail when they attempt to do that for which they are unfit; as Burke would have failed if Burke had tried to write comedies like those of Sheridan; as Reynolds would have failed if Reynolds had tried to paint landscapes like those of Wilson.

Happily, Johnson soon had an opportunity of proving most signally that his failure was not to be ascribed to intellectual decay.

On Easter Eve 1777, some persons, deputed by a meeting which consisted of forty of the first booksellers in London, called upon him.   Though he had some scruples about doing business at that season, he received his visitors with much civility.   They came to inform him that a new edition of the English poets, from Cowley downwards, was in contemplation, and to ask him to furnish short biographical prefaces.   He readily undertook the task, a task for which he was pre-eminently qualified.   His knowledge of the literary history of England since the Restoration was unrivalled.   That knowledge he had derived partly from books, and partly from sources which had long been closed; from old Grub Street traditions; from the talk of forgotten poetasters and pamphleteers who had long been lying in parish vaults; from the recollections of such men as Gilbert Walmesley, who had conversed with the wits of Button; Cibber, who had mutilated the plays of two generations of dramatists; Orrery, who had been admitted to the society of Swift; and Savage, who had rendered services of no very honourable kind to Pope. The biographer therefore sate down to his task with a mind full of matter.   He had at first intended to give only a paragraph to every minor poet, and only four or five pages to the greatest name.   But the flood of anecdote and criticism overflowed the narrow channel.   The work, which was originally meant to consist only of a few sheets, swelled into ten volumes, small volumes, it is true, and not closely printed.   The first four appeared in 1779, the remaining six in 1781.

The Lives of the Poets are, on the whole, the best of Johnson's works.   The narratives are as entertaining as any novel.   The remarks on life and on human nature are eminently shrewd and profound.   The criticisms are often excellent, and, even when grossly and provokingly unjust, well deserve to be studied. For, however erroneous they may be, they are never silly.   They are the judgments of a mind trammelled by prejudice and deficient in sensibility, but vigorous and acute.   They therefore generally contain a portion of valuable truth which deserves to be separated from the alloy; and, at the very worst, they mean something, a praise to which much of what is called criticism in our time has no pretensions.

Savage's Life Johnson reprinted nearly as it had appeared in 1744.   Whoever, after reading that life, will turn to the other lives will be struck by the difference of style. Since Johnson had been at ease in his circumstances he had written little and had talked much. When, therefore, he, after the lapse of years, resumed his pen, the mannerism which he had contracted while he was in the constant habit of elaborate composition was less perceptible than formerly; and his diction frequently had a colloquial ease which it had formerly wanted. The improvement may be discerned by a skilful critic in the Journey to the Hebrides, and in the Lives of the Poets is so obvious that it cannot escape the notice of the most careless reader.

Among the lives the best are perhaps those of Cowley, Dryden, and Pope. The very worst is, beyond all doubt, that of Gray.

This great work at once became popular. There was, indeed, much just and much unjust censure: but even those who were loudest in blame were attracted by the book in spite of themselves. Malone computed the gains of the publishers at five or six thousand pounds. But the writer was very poorly remunerated. Intending at first to write very short prefaces, he had stipulated for only two hundred guineas. The booksellers, when they saw how far his performance had surpassed his promise, added only another hundred. Indeed, Johnson, though he did not despise, or affect to despise, money, and though his strong sense and long experience ought to have qualified him to protect his own interests, seems to have been singularly unskilful and unlucky in his literary bargains. He was generally reputed the first English writer of his time. Yet several writers of his time sold their copyrights for sums such as he never ventured to ask. To give a single instance, Robertson received four thousand five hundred pounds for the History of Charles V.; and it is no disrespect to the memory of Robertson to say that the History of Charles V. is both a less valuable and a less amusing book than the Lives of the Poets.

Johnson was now in his seventy-second year. The infirmities of age were coming fast upon him. That inevitable event of which he never thought without horror was brought near to him; and his whole life was darkened by the shadow of death. He had often to pay the cruel price of longevity. Every year he lost what could never be replaced. The strange dependents to whom he had given shelter, and to whom, in spite of their faults, he was strongly attached by habit, dropped off one by one; and, in the silence of his home, he regretted even the noise of their scolding matches. The kind and generous Thrale was no more; and it would have been well if his wife had been laid beside him. But she survived to be the laughing-stock of those who had envied her, and to draw from the eyes of the old man who had loved her beyond anything in the world tears far more bitter than he would have shed over her grave. With some estimable and many agreeable qualities, she was not made to be independent. The control of a mind more steadfast than her own was necessary to her respectability. While she was restrained by her husband, a man of sense and firmness, indulgent to her taste in trifles, but always the undisputed master of his house, her worst offences had been impertinent jokes, white lies, and short fits of pettishness ending in sunny good humour. But he was gone; and she was left an opulent widow of forty, with strong sensibility, volatile fancy, and slender judgment. She soon fell in love with a music-master from Brescia, in whom nobody but herself could discover anything to admire. Her pride, and perhaps some better feelings, struggled hard against this degrading passion. But the struggle irritated her nerves, soured her temper, and at length endangered her health. Conscious that her choice was one which Johnson could not approve, she became desirous to escape from his inspection. Her manner towards him changed. She was sometimes cold and sometimes petulant. She did not conceal her joy when he left Streatham; she never pressed him to return; and, if he came unbidden, she received him in a manner which convinced him that he was no longer a welcome guest. He took the very intelligible hints which she gave. He read, for the last time, a chapter of the Greek Testament in the library which had been formed by himself.

In a solemn and tender prayer he commended the house and its inmates to the Divine protection, and, with emotions which choked his voice and convulsed his powerful frame, left for ever that beloved home for the gloomy and desolate house behind Fleet Street, where the few and evil days which still remained to him were to run out. Here, in June 1783, he had a paralytic stroke, from which, however, he recovered, and which does not appear to have at all impaired his intellectual faculties. But other maladies came thick upon him. His asthma tormented him day and night. Dropsical symptoms made their appearance. While sinking under a complication of diseases, he heard that the woman whose friendship had been the chief happiness of sixteen years of his life had married an

Italian fiddler; that all London was crying shame upon her; and that the newspapers and magazines were filled with allusions to the Ephesian matron, and the two pictures in Hamlet. He vehemently said that he would try to forget her existence. He never uttered her name. Every memorial of her which met his eye he flung into the fire. She meanwhile fled from the laughter and hisses of her countrymen and countrywomen to a land where she was unknown, hastened across Mount Cenis, and learned, while passing a merry Christmas of concerts and lemonade parties at Milan, that the great man with whose name hers is inseparably associated had ceased to exist.

He had, in spite of much mental and much bodily affliction, clung vehemently to life. The feeling described in that fine but gloomy paper which closes the series of his Idlers seemed to grow stronger in him as his last hour drew near. He fancied that he should be able to draw his breath more easily in a southern climate, and would probably have set out for Rome and Naples, but for his fear of the expense of the journey. That expense, indeed, he had the means of defraying; for he had laid up about two thousand pounds, the fruit of labours which had made the fortune of several publishers. But he was unwilling to break in upon this hoard; and he seems to have wished even to keep its existence a secret. Some of his friends hoped that the government might be induced to increase his pension to six hundred pounds a year; but this hope was disappointed; and he resolved to stand one English winter more. That winter was his last. His legs grew weaker; his breath grew shorter; the fatal water gathered fast, in spite of incisions which he, courageous against pain, but timid against death, urged his surgeons to make deeper and deeper. Though the tender care which had mitigated his sufferings during months of sickness at Streatham was withdrawn, he was not left desolate. The ablest physicians and surgeons attended him, and refused to accept fees from him. Burke parted from him with deep emotion. Windham sate much in the sick room, arranged the pillows, and sent his own servant to watch a night by the bed. Frances Burney, whom the old man had cherished with fatherly kindness, stood weeping at the door; while Langton, whose piety eminently qualified him to be an adviser and comforter at such a time, received the last pressure of his friend's hand within.

When at length the moment, dreaded through so many years, came close, the dark cloud passed away from Johnson's mind. His temper became unusually patient and gentle; he ceased to think with terror of death, and of that which lies beyond death; and he spoke much of the mercy of God, and of the propitiation of Christ. In this serene frame of mind he died on the 13th of December 1784. He was laid, a week later, in Westminster Abbey, among the eminent men of whom he had been the historian,—Cowley and Denham, Dryden and Congreve, Gay, Prior, and Addison.

Since his death the popularity of his works—the Lives of the Poets, and, perhaps, the Vanity of Human Wishes, excepted—has greatly diminished. His Dictionary has been altered by editors till it can scarcely be called his. An allusion to his Rambler or his Idler is not readily apprehended in literary circles. The fame even of Rasselas has grown somewhat dim. But, though the celebrity of the writings may have declined, the celebrity of the writer, strange to say, is as great as ever. Boswell's book has done for him more than the best of his own books could do. The memory of other authors is kept alive by their works. But the memory of Johnson keeps many of his works alive. The old philosopher is still among us in the brown coat with the metal buttons and the shirt which ought to be at wash, blinking, puffing, rolling his head, drumming with his fingers, tearing his meat like a tiger, and swallowing his tea in oceans. No human being who has been more than seventy years in the grave is so well known to us. And it is but just to say that our intimate acquaintance with what he would himself have called the anfractuosities of his intellect and of his temper serves only to strengthen our conviction that he was both a great and a good man.

DANTE

(JANUARY 1824)

> " Fairest of stars, last in the train of night,
> If better thou belong not to the dawn,
> Sure pledge of day, that crown'st the smiling morn
> With thy bright circlet."—MILTON.

IN a review of Italian literature, Dante has a double claim to precedency. He was the earliest and the greatest writer of his country. He was the first man who fully descried and exhibited the powers of his native dialect. The Latin tongue, which, under the most favourable circumstances, and in the hands of the greatest masters, had still been poor, feeble, and singularly unpoetical, and which had, in the age of Dante, been debased by the admixture of innumerable barbarous words and idioms, was still cultivated with superstitious veneration, and received, in the last stage of corruption, more honours than it had deserved in the period of its life and vigour. It was the language of the cabinet, of the university, of the church. It was employed by all who aspired to distinction in the higher walks of poetry. In compassion to the ignorance of his mistress, a cavalier might now and then proclaim his passion in Tuscan or Provençal rhymes. The vulgar might occasionally be edified by a pious allegory in the popular jargon. But no writer had conceived it possible that the dialect of peasants and market-women should possess sufficient energy and precision for a majestic and durable work. Dante adventured first. He detected the rich treasures of thought and diction which still lay latent in their ore. He refined them into purity. He burnished them into splendour. He fitted them for every purpose of use and magnificence. And he has thus acquired the glory, not only of producing the finest narrative poem of modern times, but also of creating a language, distinguished by unrivalled melody, and peculiarly capable of furnishing to lofty and passionate thoughts their appropriate garb of severe and concise expression.

To many this may appear a singular panegyric on the Italian tongue. Indeed the great majority of the young gentlemen and young ladies, who, when they are asked whether they read Italian, answer " yes," never go beyond the stories at the end of their grammar, *The Pastor Fido*, or an act of *Artaserse*. They could as soon read a Babylonian brick as a canto of

Dante.   Hence it is a general opinion, among those who know little or nothing of the subject, that this admirable language is adapted only to the effeminate cant of sonnetteers, musicians, and connoisseurs.

The fact is that Dante and Petrarch have been the Oromasdes and Arimanes of Italian literature.   I wish not to detract from the merits of Petrarch.   No one can doubt that his poems exhibit, amidst some imbecility and more affectation, much elegance, ingenuity, and tenderness.   They present us with a mixture which can only be compared to the whimsical concert described by the humorous poet of Modena:

> S' udian gli usignuoli, al primo albore,
> E gli asini cantar versi d'amore.[1]

I am not, however, at present speaking of the intrinsic excellencies of his writings, which I shall take another opportunity to examine, but of the effect which they produced on the literature of Italy.   The florid and luxurious charms of his style enticed the poets and the public from the contemplation of nobler and sterner models.   In truth, though a rude state of society is that in which great original works are most frequently produced, it is also that in which they are worst appreciated. This may appear paradoxical; but it is proved by experience, and is consistent with reason.   To be without any received canons of taste is good for the few who can create, but bad for the many who can only imitate and judge.   Great and active minds cannot remain at rest.   In a cultivated age they are too often contented to move on in the beaten path.   But where no path exists they will make one.   Thus the *Iliad*, the *Odyssey*, the *Divine Comedy*, appeared in dark and half barbarous times: and thus of the few original works which have been produced in more polished ages we owe a large proportion to men in low stations and of uninformed minds.   I will instance, in our own language, the *Pilgrim's Progress* and *Robinson Crusoe*.   Of all the prose works of fiction which we possess, these are, I will not say the best, but the most peculiar, the most unprecedented, the most inimitable.   Had Bunyan and Defoe been educated gentlemen, they would probably have published translations and imitations of French romances " by a person of quality." I am not sure that we should have had " Lear " if Shakspeare had been able to read Sophocles.

But these circumstances, while they foster genius, are un-

---

[1] Tassoni: *Secchia Rapita*, canto i. stanza 6.

favourable to the science of criticism. Men judge by comparison. They are unable to estimate the grandeur of an object when there is no standard by which they can measure it. One of the French philosophers (I beg Gerard's pardon), who accompanied Napoleon to Egypt, tells us that, when he first visited the great Pyramid, he was surprised to see it so diminutive. It stood alone in a boundless plain. There was nothing near it from which he could calculate its magnitude. But when the camp was pitched beside it, and the tents appeared like diminutive specks around its base, he then perceived the immensity of this mightiest work of man. In the same manner, it is not till a crowd of petty writers has sprung up that the merit of the great masterspirits of literature is understood.

We have indeed ample proof that Dante was highly admired in his own and the following age. I wish that we had equal proof that he was admired for his excellencies. But it is a remarkable corroboration of what has been said, that this great man seems to have been utterly unable to appreciate himself. In his treatise *De Vulgari Eloquentia* he talks with satisfaction of what he has done for Italian literature, of the purity and correctness of his style. " *Cependant*," says a favourite [1] writer of mine, " *il n'est ni pur, ni correct, mais il est créateur.*" Considering the difficulties with which Dante had to struggle, we may perhaps be more inclined than the French critic to allow him this praise. Still it is by no means his highest or most peculiar title to applause. It is scarcely necessary to say that those qualities which escaped the notice of the poet himself were not likely to attract the attention of the commentators. The fact is, that, while the public homage was paid to some absurdities with which his works may be justly charged, and to many more which were falsely imputed to them; while lecturers were paid to expound and eulogise his physics, his metaphysics, his theology, all bad of their kind; while annotators laboured to detect allegorical meanings of which the author never dreamed—the great powers of his imagination, and the incomparable force of his style, were neither admired nor imitated. Arimanes had prevailed. The *Divine Comedy* was to that age what St. Paul's Cathedral was to Omai. The poor Otaheitean stared listlessly for a moment at the huge cupola, and ran into a toyshop to play with beads. Italy, too, was charmed with literary trinkets, and played with them for four centuries.

[1] Sismondi: *Littérature du Midi de l'Europe.*

From the time of Petrarch to the appearance of Alfieri's tragedies, we may trace in almost every page of Italian literature the influence of those celebrated sonnets which, from the nature both of their beauties and their faults, were peculiarly unfit to be models for general imitation. Almost all the poets of that period, however different in the degree and quality of their talents, are characterised by great exaggeration, and as a necessary consequence, great coldness of sentiment; by a passion for frivolous and tawdry ornament; and, above all, by an extreme feebleness and diffuseness of style. Tasso, Marino, Guarini, Metastasio, and a crowd of writers of inferior merit and celebrity, were spell-bound in the enchanted gardens of a gaudy and meretricious Alcina, who concealed debility and deformity beneath the deceitful semblance of loveliness and health. Ariosto, the great Ariosto himself, like his own Ruggiero, stooped for a time to linger amidst the magic flowers and fountains, and to caress the gay and painted sorceress. But to him, as to his own Ruggiero, had been given the omnipotent ring and the winged courser, which bore him from the paradise of deception to the regions of light and nature.

The evil of which I speak was not confined to the graver poets. It infected satire, comedy, burlesque. No person can admire more than I do the great masterpieces of wit and humour which Italy has produced. Still I cannot but discern and lament a great deficiency, which is common to them all. I find in them abundance of ingenuity, of droll naïveté, of profound and just reflection, of happy expression. Manners, characters, opinions, are treated with " a most learned spirit of human dealing." But something is still wanting. We read, and we admire, and we yawn. We look in vain for the bacchanalian fury which inspired the comedy of Athens, for the fierce and withering scorn which animates the invectives of Juvenal and Dryden, or even for the compact and pointed diction which adds zest to the verses of Pope and Boileau. There is no enthusiasm, no energy, no condensation, nothing which springs from strong feeling, nothing which tends to excite it. Many fine thoughts and fine expressions reward the toil of reading. Still it is a toil. The " Secchia Rapita," in some points the best poem of its kind, is painfully diffuse and languid. The " Animali Parlanti " of Casti is perfectly intolerable. I admire the dexterity of the plot, and the liberality of the opinions. I admit that it is impossible to turn to a page which does not contain something that deserves to be remembered; but it is at least six times as long as it ought to be. And tne garrulous feebleness of the style is a still greater fault than the length of the work.

It may be thought that I have gone too far in attributing these evils to the influence of the works and the fame of Petrarch. It cannot, however, be doubted that they have arisen, in a great measure, from a neglect of the style of Dante. This is not more proved by the decline of Italian poetry than by its resuscitation. After the lapse of four hundred and fifty years, there appeared a man capable of appreciating and imitating the father of Tuscan literature—Vittorio Alfieri. Like the prince in the nursery tale, he sought and found the sleeping beauty within the recesses which had so long concealed her from mankind. The portal was indeed rusted by time; the dust of ages had accumulated on the hangings; the furniture was of antique fashion; and the gorgeous colour of the embroidery had faded. But the living charms which were well worth all the rest remained in the bloom of eternal youth, and well rewarded the bold adventurer who roused them from their long slumber. In every line of the " Philip " and the " Saul," the greatest poems, I think, of the eighteenth century, we may trace the influence of that mighty genius which has immortalised the ill-starred love of Francesca, and the paternal agonies of Ugolino. Alfieri bequeathed the sovereignty of Italian literature to the author of the " Aristodemus "—a man of genius scarcely inferior to his own, and a still more devoted disciple of the great Florentine. It must be acknowledged that this eminent writer has sometimes pushed too far his idolatry of Dante. To borrow a sprightly illustration from Sir John Denham, he has not only imitated his garb, but borrowed his clothes. He often quotes his phrases; and he has, not very judiciously as it appears to me, imitated his versification. Nevertheless, he has displayed many of the higher excellencies of his master; and his works may justly inspire us with a hope that the Italian language will long flourish under a new literary dynasty, or rather under the legitimate line, which has at length been restored to a throne long occupied by specious usurpers.

The man to whom the literature of his country owes its origin and its revival was born in times singulary adapted to call forth his extraordinary powers. Religious zeal, chivalrous love and honour, democratic liberty, are the three most powerful principles that have ever influenced the character of large masses of men. Each of them singly has often excited the greatest enthusiasm, and produced the most important changes. In the time of Dante all the three, often in amalgamation, generally in conflict, agitated the public mind. The preceding generation had witnessed the wrongs and the revenge of the brave, the accomplished, the unfortunate Emperor Frederic the Second, a poet in an age of schoolmen, a philosopher in an age of monks, a statesman in an age of crusaders. During the whole life of the poet, Italy was experiencing the consequences of the memorable struggle which he had maintained against the Church. The finest works of imagination have always been produced in times of political convulsion, as the richest vineyards and the sweetest flowers always grow on the soil which has been fertilised by the fiery deluge of a volcano. To look no further than the literary history of our own country, can we doubt that Shakespeare was in a great measure produced by the Reformation, and Wordsworth by the French Revolution? Poets often avoid political transactions; they often affect to despise them. But, whether they perceive it or not, they must be influenced by them. As long as their minds have any point of contact with those of their fellow-men, the electric impulse, at whatever distance it may originate, will be circuitously communicated to them.

This will be the case even in large societies, where the division of labour enables many speculative men to observe the face of nature, or to analyse their own minds, at a distance from the seat of political transactions. In the little republic of which Dante was a member the state of things was very different. These small communities are most unmercifully abused by most of our modern professors of the science of government. In such states, they tell us, factions are always most violent: where both parties are cooped up within a narrow space, political differences necessarily produce personal malignity. Every man must be a soldier; every moment may produce a war. No citizen can lie down secure that he shall not be roused by the alarum-bell, to repel or avenge an injury. In such petty quarrels Greece squandered the blood which might have purchased for her the permanent empire of the world, and Italy wasted the energy and the abilities which would have enabled her to defend her independence against the pontiffs and the Cæsars.

All this is true: yet there is still a compensation. Mankind has not derived so much benefit from the empire of Rome as from the city of Athens, nor from the kingdom of France as from the city of Florence. The violence of party feeling may be an evil; but it calls forth that activity of mind which in some states of society it is desirable to produce at any expense. Universal soldiership may be an evil; but where every man is a soldier there will be no standing army. And is it no evil that one man in every fifty should be bred to the trade of slaughter; should live only by destroying and by exposing himself to be destroyed; should fight without enthusiasm and conquer without glory; be sent to a hospital when wounded, and rot on a dunghill when old? Such, over more than two-thirds of Europe, is the fate of soldiers. It was something that the citizen of Milan or Florence fought, not merely in the vague and rhetorical sense in which the words are often used, but in sober truth, for his parents, his children, his lands, his house, his altars. It was something that he marched forth to battle beneath the Carroccio, which had been the object of his childish veneration: that his aged father looked down from the battlements on his exploits; that his friends and his rivals were the witnesses of his glory. If he fell, he was consigned to no venal or heedless guardians. The same day saw him conveyed within the walls which he had defended. His wounds were dressed by his mother; his confession was whispered to the friendly priest who had heard and absolved the follies of his youth; his last sigh was breathed upon the lips of the lady of his love. Surely there is no sword like that which is beaten out of a ploughshare. Surely this state of things was not unmixedly bad; its evils were alleviated by enthusiasm and by tenderness; and it will at least be acknowledged that it was well fitted to nurse poetical genius in an imaginative and observant mind.

Nor did the religious spirit of the age tend less to this result than its political circumstances. Fanaticism is an evil, but it is not the greatest of evils. It is good that a people should be roused by any means from a state of utter torpor; that their minds should be diverted from objects merely sensual, to meditations, however erroneous, on the mysteries of the moral and intellectual world; and from interests which are immediately selfish to those which relate to the past, the future, and the remote. These effects have sometimes been produced by the worst superstitions that ever existed; but the Catholic religion, even in the time of its utmost extravagance and atrocity, never wholly lost the spirit of the Great Teacher, whose precepts form the noblest code, as His conduct furnished the purest example, of moral excellence. It is of all religions the most poetical. The ancient superstitions furnished the fancy with beautiful images, but took no hold on the heart. The doctrines of the reformed churches have most powerfully influenced the feelings and the conduct of men, but have not presented them with visions of sensible beauty and grandeur. The Roman Catholic Church has united to the awful doctrines of the one what Mr. Coleridge calls the " fair humanities " of the other. It has enriched sculpture and painting with the loveliest and most majestic forms. To the Phidian Jupiter it can oppose the Moses of Michael Angelo; and to the voluptuous beauty of the Queen of Cyprus, the serene and pensive loveliness of the Virgin Mother. The legends of its martyrs and its saints may vie in ingenuity and interest with the mythological fables of Greece; its ceremonies and processions were the delight of the vulgar; the huge fabric of secular power with which it was connected attracted the admiration of the statesman. At the same time, it never lost sight of the most solemn and tremendous doctrines of Christianity—the incarnate God, the judgment, the retribution, the eternity of happiness or torment. Thus, while, like the ancient religions, it received incalculable support from policy and ceremony, it never wholly became, like those religions, a merely political and ceremonial institution.

The beginning of the thirteenth century was, as Machiavelli has remarked, the era of a great revival of this extraordinary system. The policy of Innocent, the growth of the inquisition and the mendicant orders, the wars against the Albigenses, the Pagans of the East, and the unfortunate princes of the house of Swabia, agitated Italy during the two following generations. In this point Dante was completely under the influence of his age. He was a man of a turbid and melancholy spirit. In early youth he had entertained a strong and unfortunate passion, which, long after the death of her whom he loved, continued to haunt him. Dissipation, ambition, misfortunes had not effaced it. He was not only a sincere, but a passionate, believer. The crimes and abuses of the Church of Rome were indeed loathsome to him; but to all its doctrines and all its rites he adhered with enthusiastic fondness and veneration; and, at length, driven from his native country, reduced to a situation the most painful to a man of his disposition, condemned to learn by experience that no [1] food is so bitter as the bread of dependence, and no ascent so painful as the staircase

---

[1] " Tu proverai si come sa di sale
  Lo pane altrui, e come é duro calle
  Lo scendere e'l salir per l' altrui scale."
  Paradiso, canto xvii.

of a patron, his wounded spirit took refuge in visionary devotion. Beatrice, the unforgotten object of his early tenderness, was invested by his imagination with glorious and mysterious attributes; she was enthroned among the highest of the celestial hierarchy: Almighty Wisdom had assigned to her the care of the sinful and unhappy wanderer who had loved her with such a perfect love.[1] By a confusion, like that which often takes place in dreams, he has sometimes lost sight of her human nature, and even of her personal existence, and seems to consider her as one of the attributes of the Deity.

But those religious hopes which had released the mind of the sublime enthusiast from the terrors of death had not rendered his speculations on human life more cheerful. This is an inconsistency which may often be observed in men of a similar temperament. He hoped for happiness beyond the grave: but he felt none on earth. It is from this cause, more than from any other, that his description of Heaven is so far inferior to the Hell or the Purgatory. With the passions and miseries of the suffering spirits he feels a strong sympathy. But among the beatified he appears as one who has nothing in common with them, as one who is incapable of comprehending, not only the degree, but the nature of their enjoyment. We think that we see him standing amidst those smiling and radiant spirits with that scowl of unutterable misery on his brow, and that curl of bitter disdain on his lips, which all his portraits have preserved, and which might furnish Chantrey with hints for the head of his projected Satan.

There is no poet whose intellectual and moral character are so closely connected. The great source, as it appears to me, of the power of the *Divine Comedy* is the strong belief with which the story seems to be told. In this respect, the only books which approach to its excellence are *Gulliver's Travels* and *Robinson Crusoe*. The solemnity of his asseverations, the consistency and minuteness of his details, the earnestness with which he labours to make the reader understand the exact shape and size of everything that he describes, give an air of reality to his wildest fictions. I should only weaken this statement by quoting instances of a feeling which pervades the whole work, and to which it owes much of its fascination. This is the real justification of the many passages in his poem which bad critics have condemned as grotesque. I am concerned to see

---

[1] " L'amico mio, e non della ventura."
Inferno, canto ii.

that Mr. Cary, to whom Dante owes more than ever poet owed
to translator, has sanctioned an accusation utterly unworthy
of his abilities. "His solicitude," says that gentleman, "to
define all his images in such a manner as to bring them within
the circle of our vision, and to subject them to the power of the
pencil, renders him little better than grotesque, where Milton
has since taught us to expect sublimity." It is true that Dante
has never shrunk from embodying his conceptions in deter-
minate words, that he has even given measures and numbers,
where Milton would have left his images to float undefined in a
gorgeous haze of language. Both were right. Milton did not
profess to have been in heaven or hell. He might therefore
reasonably confine himself to magnificent generalities. Far
different was the office of the lonely traveller, who had wandered
through the nations of the dead. Had he described the abode
of the rejected spirits in language resembling the splendid lines
of the English poet, had he told us of—

> An universe of death, which God by curse
> Created evil, for evil only good,
> Where all life dies, death lives, and Nature breeds
> Perverse all monstrous, all prodigious things,
> Abominable, unutterable, and worse
> Than fables yet have feigned, or fear conceived,
> Gorgons, and hydras, and chimæras dire—

this would doubtless have been noble writing. But where would
have been that strong impression of reality, which, in accordance
with his plan, it should have been his great object to produce?
It was absolutely necessary for him to delineate accurately "all
monstrous, all prodigious things," to utter what might to others
appear "unutterable," to relate with the air of truth what
fables had never feigned, to embody what fear had never conceived. And I will frankly confess that the vague sublimity of
Milton affects me less than these reviled details of Dante. We
read Milton; and we know that we are reading a great poet.
When we read Dante, the poet vanishes. We are listening to
the man who had returned from "the valley of the dolorous
abyss;"[1] we seem to see the dilated eye of horror, to hear the
shuddering accents with which he tells his fearful tale. Considered in this light, the narratives are exactly what they should
be, definite in themselves, but suggesting to the mind ideas of
awful and indefinite wonder. They are made up of the images of
the earth: they are told in the language of the earth. Yet the

---

[1] "La valle d'abisso doloroso."—*Inferno*, canto iv.

whole effect is, beyond expression, wild and unearthly. The fact is, that supernatural beings, as long as they are considered merely with reference to their own nature, excite our feelings very feebly. It is when the great gulf which separates them from us is passed, when we suspect some strange and undefinable relation between the laws of the visible and the invisible world, that they rouse, perhaps, the strongest emotions of which our nature is capable. How many children, and how many men, are afraid of ghosts, who are not afraid of God! And this, because, though they entertain a much stronger conviction of the existence of a deity than of the reality of apparitions, they have no apprehension that he will manifest himself to them in any sensible manner. While this is the case, to describe superhuman beings in the language, and to attribute to them the actions, of humanity may be grotesque, unphilosophical, inconsistent; but it will be the only mode of working upon the feelings of men, and, therefore, the only mode suited for poetry. Shakspeare understood this well, as he understood everything that belonged to his art. Who does not sympathise with the rapture of Ariel, flying after sunset on the wings of the bat, or sucking in the cups of flowers with the bee? Who does not shudder at the caldron of Macbeth? Where is the philosopher who is not moved when he thinks of the strange connection between the infernal spirits and " the sow's blood that hath eaten her nine farrow? " But this difficult task of representing supernatural beings to our minds, in a manner which shall be neither unintelligible to our intellects nor wholly inconsistent with our ideas of their nature, has never been so well performed as by Dante. I will refer to three instances, which are, perhaps, the most striking: the description of the transformations of the serpents and the robbers, in the twenty-fifth canto of the *Inferno,* the passage concerning Nimrod, in the thirty-first canto of the same part, and the magnificent procession in the twenty-ninth canto of the *Purgatorio.*

The metaphors and comparisons of Dante harmonise admirably with that air of strong reality of which I have spoken. They have a very peculiar character. He is perhaps the only poet whose writings would become much less intelligible if all illustrations of this sort were expunged. His similes are frequently rather those of a traveller than of a poet. He employs them not to display his ingenuity by fanciful analogies, not to delight the reader by affording him a distant and passing glimpse of beautiful images remote from the path in which he is proceeding, but to give an exact idea of the objects which he is describing, by comparing them with others generally known. The boiling pitch in Malebolge was like that in the Venetian arsenal; the mound on which he travelled along the banks of Phlegethon was like that between Ghent and Bruges, but not so large; the cavities where the Simoniacal prelates are confined resemble the fonts in the Church of John at Florence. Every reader of Dante will recall many other illustrations of this description, which add to the appearance of sincerity and earnestness from which the narrative derives so much of its interest.

Many of his comparisons, again, are intended to give an exact idea of his feelings under particular circumstances. The delicate shades of grief, of fear, of anger, are rarely discriminated with sufficient accuracy in the language of the most refined nations. A rude dialect never abounds in nice distinctions of this kind. Dante therefore employs the most accurate and infinitely the most poetical mode of marking the precise state of his mind. Every person who has experienced the bewildering effect of sudden bad tidings—the stupefaction, the vague doubt of the truth of our own perceptions which they produce—will understand the following simile: " I was as he is who dreameth his own harm, who, dreaming, wishes that it may be all a dream, so that he desires that which is as though it were not." This is only one out of a hundred equally striking and expressive similitudes. The comparisons of Homer and Milton are magnificent digressions. It scarcely injures their effect to detach them from the work. Those of Dante are very different. They derive their beauty from the context, and reflect beauty upon it. His embroidery cannot be taken out without spoiling the whole web. I cannot dismiss this part of the subject without advising every person who can muster sufficient Italian to read the simile of the sheep, in the third canto of the *Purgatorio*. I think it the most perfect passage of the kind in the world, the most imaginative, the most picturesque, and the most sweetly expressed.

No person can have attended to the *Divine Comedy* without observing how little impression the forms of the external world appear to have made on the mind of Dante. His temper and his situation had led him to fix his observation almost exclusively on human nature. The exquisite opening of the eighth [1] canto

[1] I cannot help observing that Gray's imitation of that noble line

" Che paia 'lgiorna pianger che si muore,"—

is one of the most striking instances of injudicious plagiarism with which I of the *Purgatorio* affords a strong instance of this. He leaves to others the earth, the ocean, and the sky. His business is with man. To other writers, evening may be the season of dews and stars and radiant clouds. To Dante it is the hour of fond recollection and passionate devotion, the hour which melts the heart of the mariner and kindles the love of the pilgrim, the hour when the toll of the bell seems to mourn for another day which is gone and will return no more.

The feeling of the present age has taken a direction diametrically opposite. The magnificence of the physical world, and its influence upon the human mind, have been the favourite themes of our most eminent poets. The herd of bluestocking ladies and sonneteering gentlemen seem to consider a strong sensibility to the " splendour of the grass, the glory of the flower," as an ingredient absolutely indispensable in the formation of a poetical mind. They treat with contempt all writers who are unfortunately

nec ponere lucum
Artifices, nec rus saturum laudare.

The orthodox poetical creed is more Catholic. The noblest earthly objects of the contemplation of man is man himself. The universe, and all its fair and glorious forms, are indeed included in the wide empire of the imagination; but she has placed her home and her sanctuary amidst the inexhaustible varieties and the impenetrable mysteries of the mind.

In tutte parti impera, e quivi regge;
Quivi è la sua cittade, e l'alto seggio.[1]

" Othello " is perhaps the greatest work in the world. From what does it derive its power? From the clouds? From the ocean? From the mountains? Or from love strong as death, and jealousy cruel as the grave? What is it that we go forth to see in " Hamlet "? Is it a reed shaken with the wind? A small celandine? A bed of daffodils? Or is it to contemplate a mighty and wayward mind laid bare before us to the inmost

am acquainted. Dante did not put this strong personification at the beginning of his description. The imagination of the reader is so well prepared for it by the previous lines, that it appears perfectly natural and pathetic. Placed as Gray has placed it, neither preceded nor followed by anything that harmonises with it, it becomes a frigid conceit. Woe to the unskilful rider who ventures on the horses of Achilles!

οἱ δ' ἀλεγεινοὶ
ἀνδράσι γε θνητοῖσι δαμήμεναι ἠδ' ὀχέεσθαι,
ἄλλῳ γ' ἢ 'Αχιλῆϊ τὸν ἀθανάτη τέκε μήτηρ.

[1] *Inferno*, canto i.

recesses? It may perhaps be doubted whether the lakes and the hills are better fitted for the education of a poet than the dusky streets of a huge capital. Indeed who is not tired to death with pure description of scenery? Is it not the fact, that external objects never strongly excite our feelings but when they are contemplated in reference to man, as illustrating his destiny, or as influencing his character? The most beautiful object in the world, it will be allowed, is a beautiful woman. But who that can analyse his feelings is not sensible that she owes her fascination less to grace of outline and delicacy of colour, than to a thousand associations which, often unperceived by ourselves, connect those qualities with the source of our existence, with the nourishment of our infancy, with the passions of our youth, with the hopes of our age—with elegance, with vivacity, with tenderness, with the strongest of natural instincts, with the dearest of social ties?

To those who think thus, the insensibility of the Florentine poet to the beauties of nature will not appear an unpardonable deficiency. On mankind no writer, with the exception of Shakspeare, has looked with a more penetrating eye. I have said that his poetical character had derived a tinge from his peculiar temper. It is on the sterner and darker passions that he delights to dwell. All love excepting the half-mystic passion which he still felt for his buried Beatrice, had palled on the fierce and restless exile. The sad story of Rimini is almost a single exception. I know not whether it has been remarked, that, in one point, misanthropy seems to have affected his mind, as it did that of Swift. Nauseous and revolting images seem to have had a fascination for his mind; and he repeatedly places before his readers, with all the energy of his incomparable style, the most loathsome objects of the sewer and the dissecting-room.

There is another peculiarity in the poem of Dante, which, I think, deserves notice. Ancient mythology has hardly ever been successfully interwoven with modern poetry. One class of writers have introduced the fabulous deities merely as allegorical representatives of love, wine, or wisdom. This necessarily renders their works tame and cold. We may sometimes admire their ingenuity; but with what interest can we read of beings of whose personal existence the writer does not suffer us to entertain, for a moment, even a conventional belief? Even Spenser's allegory is scarcely tolerable, till we contrive to forget that Una signifies innocence, and consider her merely as an oppressed lady under the protection of a generous knight.

Those writers who have, more judiciously, attempted to preserve the personality of the classical divinities have failed from a different cause. They have been imitators, and imitators at a disadvantage. Euripides and Catullus believed in Bacchus and Cybele as little as we do. But they lived among men who did. Their imaginations, if not their opinions, took the colour of the age. Hence the glorious inspiration of the Bacchæ and the Atys. Our minds are formed by circumstances: and I do not believe that it would be in the power of the greatest modern poet to lash himself up to a degree of enthusiasm adequate to the production of such works.

Dante, alone among the poets of later times, has been, in this respect, neither an allegorist nor an imitator; and, consequently, he alone has introduced the ancient fictions with effect. His Minos, his Charon, his Pluto, are absolutely terrific. Nothing can be more beautiful or original than the use which he has made of the River of Lethe. He has never assigned to his mythological characters any functions inconsistent with the creed of the Catholic Church. He has related nothing concerning them which a good Christian of that age might not believe possible. On this account there is nothing in these passages that appears puerile or pedantic. On the contrary, this singular use of classical names suggests to the mind a vague and awful idea of some mysterious revelation, anterior to all recorded history, of which the dispersed fragments might have been retained amidst the impostures and superstitions of later religions. Indeed the mythology of the *Divine Comedy* is of the elder and more colossal mould. It breathes the spirit of Homer and Æschylus, not of Ovid and Claudian.

This is the more extraordinary, since Dante seems to have been utterly ignorant of the Greek language; and his favourite Latin models could only have served to mislead him. Indeed, it is impossible not to remark his admiration of writers far inferior to himself; and, in particular, his idolatry of Virgil, who, elegant and splendid as he is, has no pretensions to the depth and originality of mind which characterise his Tuscan worshipper. In truth it may be laid down as an almost universal rule that good poets are bad critics. Their minds are under the tyranny of ten thousand associations imperceptible to others. The worst writer may easily happen to touch a spring which is connected in their minds with a long succession of beautiful images. They are like the gigantic slaves of Aladdin, gifted with matchless power, but bound by spells so mighty that when a child whom they could have crushed touched a talisman, of whose secret he was ignorant, they immediately became his vassals. It has more than once happened to me to see minds, graceful and majestic as the Titania of Shakspeare, bewitched by the charms of an ass's head, bestowing on it the fondest caresses, and crowning it with the sweetest flowers. I need only mention the poems attributed to Ossian. They are utterly worthless, except as an edifying instance of the success of a story without evidence, and of a book without merit. They are a chaos of words which present no image, of images which have no archetype: they are without form and void; and darkness is upon the face of them. Yet how many men of genius have panegyrised and imitated them!

The style of Dante is, if not his highest, perhaps his most peculiar excellence. I know nothing with which it can be compared. The noblest models of Greek composition must yield to it. His words are the fewest and the best which it is possible to use. The first expression in which he clothes his thoughts is always so energetic and comprehensive that amplification would only injure the effect. There is probably no writer in any language who has presented so many strong pictures to the mind. Yet there is probably no writer equally concise. This perfection of style is the principal merit of the *Paradiso*, which, as I have already remarked, is by no means equal in other respects to the two preceding parts of the poem. The force and felicity of the diction, however, irresistibly attract the reader through the theological lectures and the sketches of ecclesiastical biography, with which this division of the work too much abounds. It may seem almost absurd to quote particular specimens of an excellence which is diffused over all his hundred cantos. I will, however, instance the third canto of the *Inferno*, and the sixth of the *Purgatorio*, as passages incomparable in their kind. The merit of the latter is, perhaps, rather oratorical than poetical; nor can I recollect anything in the great Athenian speeches which equals it in force of invective and bitterness of sarcasm. I have heard the most eloquent statesman of the age remark that, next to Demosthenes, Dante is the writer who ought to be most attentively studied by every man who desires to attain oratorical eminence.

But it is time to close this feeble and rambling critique. I cannot refrain, however, from saying a few words upon the translations of the *Divine Comedy*. Boyd's is as tedious and languid as the original is rapid and forcible. The strange measure which he has chosen, and, for aught I know, invented, is most unfit for such a work. Translations ought never to be written in a verse which requires much command of rhyme. The stanza becomes a bed of Procrustes; and the thoughts of the unfortunate author are alternately racked and curtailed to fit their new receptacle. The abrupt and yet consecutive style of Dante suffers more than that of any other poet by a version diffuse in style, and divided into paragraphs, for they deserve no other name, of equal length.

Nothing can be said in favour of Hayley's attempt, but that it is better than Boyd's. His mind was a tolerable specimen of filigree work—rather elegant, and very feeble. All that can be said for his best works is that they are neat. All that can be said against his worst is that they are stupid. He might have translated Metastasio tolerably. But he was utterly unable to do justice to the

> rime e aspre e chiocce,
> Come si converrebbe al tristo buco.[1]

I turn with pleasure from these wretched performances to Mr. Cary's translation. It is a work which well deserves a separate discussion, and on which, if this article were not already too long, I could dwell with great pleasure. At present I will only say that there is no other version in the world, as far as I know, so faithful, yet that there is no other version which so fully proves that the translator is himself a man of poetical genius. Those who are ignorant of the Italian language should read it to become acquainted with the *Divine Comedy*. Those who are most intimate with Italian literature should read it for its original merits: and I believe that they will find it difficult to determine whether the author deserves most praise for his intimacy with the language of Dante, or for his extraordinary mastery over his own.

[1] *Inferno*, canto xxxii.

PETRARCH

"Et vos, o lauri, carpam, et te, proxima myrte,
Sic positæ quoniam suaves miscetis odores."
VIRGIL.

IT would not be easy to name a writer whose celebrity, when both its extent and its duration are taken into the account, can be considered as equal to that of Petrarch. Four centuries and a half have elapsed since his death. Yet still the inhabitants of every nation throughout the western world are as familiar with his character and his adventures as with the most illustrious names, and the most recent anecdotes, of their own literary history. This is indeed a rare distinction. His detractors must acknowledge that it could not have been acquired by a poet destitute of merit. His admirers will scarcely maintain that the unassisted merit of Petrarch could have raised him to that eminence which has not yet been attained by Shakspeare, Milton, or Dante—that eminence, of which perhaps no modern writer, excepting himself and Cervantes, has long retained possession—an European reputation.

It is not difficult to discover some of the causes to which this great man has owed a celebrity, which I cannot but think disproportioned to his real claims on the admiration of mankind. In the first place, he is an egotist. Egotism in conversation is universally abhorred. Lovers, and, I believe, lovers alone, pardon it in each other. No services, no talents, no powers of pleasing, render it endurable. Gratitude, admiration, interest, fear, scarcely prevent those who are condemned to listen to it from indicating their disgust and fatigue. The childless uncle, the powerful patron can scarcely extort this compliance. We leave the inside of the mail in a storm, and mount the box, rather than hear the history of our companion. The chaplain bites his lips in the presence of the archbishop. The midshipman yawns at the table of the First Lord. Yet, from whatever cause, this practice, the pest of conversation, gives to writing a zest which nothing else can impart. Rousseau made the boldest experiment of this kind; and it fully succeeded. In our own time Lord Byron, by a series of attempts of the same nature, made himself the object of general interest and admiration. Wordsworth wrote with egotism more intense, but less obvious; and he has been rewarded with a sect of worshippers, comparatively small in number, but far more enthusiastic in their devotion. It is needless to multiply instances. Even now all the walks of literature are infested with mendicants for fame, who attempt to excite our interest by exhibiting all the distortions of their intellects, and stripping the covering from all the putrid sores of their feelings. Nor are there wanting many who push their imitation of the beggars whom they resemble a step further, and who find it easier to extort a pittance from the spectator, by simulating deformity and debility from which they are exempt, than by such honest labour as their health and strength enable them to perform. In the meantime the credulous public pities and pampers a nuisance which requires only the treadmill and the whip. This art, often successful when employed by dunces, gives irresistible fascination to works which possess intrinsic merit. We are always desirous to know something of the character and situation of those whose writings we have perused with pleasure. The passages in which Milton has alluded to his own circumstances are perhaps read more frequently, and with more interest, than any other lines in his poems. It is amusing to observe with what labour critics have attempted to glean from the poems of Homer, some hints as to his situation and feelings. According to one hypothesis, he intended to describe himself under the name of Demodocus. Others maintain that he was the identical Phemius whose life Ulysses spared. This propensity of the human mind explains, I think, in a great degree, the extensive popularity of a poet whose works are little else than the expression of his personal feelings.

In the second place, Petrarch was not only an egotist, but an amatory egotist. The hopes and fears, the joys and sorrows, which he described, were derived from the passion which of all passions exerts the widest influence, and which of all passions borrows most from the imagination. He had also another immense advantage. He was the first eminent amatory poet who appeared after the great convulsion which had changed, not only the political, but the moral, state of the world. The Greeks, who, in their public institutions and their literary tastes, were diametrically opposed to the oriental nations, bore a considerable resemblance to those nations in their domestic habits. Like them, they despised the intellects and immured the persons of their women; and it was among the least of the frightful evils to which this pernicious system gave birth, that all the accomplishments of mind, and all the fascinations of manner, which, in a highly cultivated age, will generally be necessary to attach men to their female associates, were monopolised by the Phrynes and the Lamais. The indispensable ingredients of honourable and chivalrous love were nowhere to be found united. The matrons and their daughters confined in the harem—insipid, uneducated, ignorant of all but the mechanical arts, scarcely seen till they were married—could rarely excite interest; while their brilliant rivals, half Graces, half Harpies, elegant and informed, but fickle and rapacious, could never inspire respect.

The state of society in Rome was, in this point, far happier; and the Latin literature partook of the superiority. The Roman poets have decidedly surpassed those of Greece in the delineation of the passion of love. There is no subject which they have treated with so much success. Ovid, Catullus, Tibullus, Horace, and Propertius, in spite of all their faults, must be allowed to rank high in this department of the art. To these I would add my favourite Plautus; who, though he took his plots from Greece, found, I suspect, the originals of his enchanting female characters at Rome.

Still many evils remained: and, in the decline of the great empire, all that was pernicious in its domestic institutions appeared more strongly. Under the influence of governments at once dependent and tyrannical, which purchased, by cringing to their enemies, the power of trampling on their subjects, the Romans sunk into the lowest state of effeminacy and debasement. Falsehood, cowardice, sloth, conscious and unrepining degradation, formed the national character. Such a character is totally incompatible with the stronger passions. Love, in particular, which, in the modern sense of the word, implies protection and devotion on the one side, confidence on the other, respect and fidelity on both, could not exist among the sluggish and heartless slaves who cringed around the thrones of Honorius and Augustulus. At this period the great renovation commenced. The warriors of the north, destitute as they were of knowledge and humanity, brought with them, from their forests and marshes, those qualities without which humanity is a weakness and knowledge a curse—energy—independence—the dread of shame—the contempt of danger. It would be most interesting to examine the manner in which the admixture of the savage conquerors and the effeminate slaves, after many generations of darkness and agitation, produced the modern European character;—to trace back, from the first conflict to the final amalgamation, the operation of that mysterious alchemy which, from hostile and worthless elements, has extracted the pure gold of human nature—to analyse the mass, and to determine the proportion in which the ingredients are mingled. But I will confine myself to the subject to which I have more particularly referred. The nature of the passion of love had undergone a complete change. It still retained, indeed, the fanciful and voluptuous character which it had possessed among the southern nations of antiquity. But it was tinged with the superstitious veneration with which the northern warriors had been accustomed to regard women. Devotion and war had imparted to it their most solemn and animating feelings. It was sanctified by the blessings of the Church, and decorated with the wreaths of the tournament. Venus, as in the ancient fable, was again rising above the dark and tempestuous waves which had so long covered her beauty. But she rose not now, as of old, in exposed and luxurious loveliness. She still wore the cestus of her ancient witchcraft; but the diadem of Juno was on her brow, and the ægis of Pallas in her hand. Love might, in fact, be called a new passion; and it is not astonishing that the first poet of eminence who wholly devoted his genius to this theme should have excited an extraordinary sensation. He may be compared to an adventurer who accidentally lands in a rich and unknown island; and who, though he may only set up an ill-shaped cross upon the shore, acquires possession of its treasures, and gives it his name. The claim of Petrarch was indeed somewhat like that of Amerigo Vespucci to the continent which should have derived its appellation from Columbus. The Provençal poets were unquestionably the masters of the Florentine. But they wrote in an age which could not appreciate their merits; and their imitator lived at the very period when composition in the vernacular language began to attract general attention. Petrarch was in literature what a Valentine is in love. The public preferred him, not because his merits were of a transcendent order, but because he was the first person whom they saw after they awoke from their long sleep.

Nor did Petrarch gain less by comparison with his immediate successors than with those who had preceded him. Till more than a century after his death Italy produced no poet who could be compared to him. This decay of genius is doubtless to be ascribed, in a great measure, to the influence which his own works had exercised upon the literature of his country. Yet it

has conduced much to his fame. Nothing is more favourable
to the reputation of a writer than to be succeeded by a race
inferior to himself; and it is an advantage, from obvious causes,
much more frequently enjoyed by those who corrupt the
national taste than by those who improve it.

Another cause has co-operated with those which I have mentioned to spread the renown of Petrarch. I mean the interest
which is inspired by the events of his life—an interest which
must have been strongly felt by his contemporaries, since, after
an interval of five hundred years, no critic can be wholly exempt
from its influence. Among the great men to whom we owe the
resuscitation of science he deserves the foremost place; and his
enthusiastic attachment to this great cause constitutes his most
just and splendid title to the gratitude of posterity. He was
the votary of literature. He loved it with a perfect love. He
worshipped it with an almost fanatical devotion. He was the
missionary, who proclaimed its discoveries to distant countries,
the pilgrim, who travelled far and wide to collect its reliques,
the hermit, who retired to seclusion to meditate on its beauties,
the champion, who fought its battles, the conqueror, who, in
more than a metaphorical sense, led barbarism and ignorance
in triumph, and received in the Capitol the laurel which his
magnificent victory had earned.

Nothing can be conceived more noble or affecting than that
ceremony. The superb palaces and porticoes, by which had
rolled the ivory chariots of Marius and Cæsar, had long mouldered
into dust. The laurelled fasces, the golden eagles, the shouting
legions, the captives and the pictured cities, were indeed wanting
to his victorious procession. The sceptre had passed away from
Rome. But she still retained the mightier influence of an intellectual empire, and was now to confer the prouder reward of
an intellectual triumph. To the man who had extended the
dominion of her ancient language, who had erected the trophies
of philosophy and imagination in the haunts of ignorance and
ferocity, whose captives were the heart of admiring nations
enchained by the influence of his song, whose spoils were the
treasures of ancient genius rescued from obscurity and decay,
the Eternal City offered the just and glorious tribute of her
gratitude. Amidst the ruined monuments of ancient and the
infant erections of modern art, he who had restored the broken
link between the two ages of human civilisation was crowned
with the wreath which he had deserved from the moderns who
owed to him their refinement—from the ancients who owed to

him their fame. Never was a coronation so august witnessed by Westminster or by Rheims.

When we turn from this glorious spectacle to the private chamber of the poet; when we contemplate the struggle of passion and virtue, the eye dimmed, the cheek furrowed, by the tears of sinful and hopeless desire; when we reflect on the whole history of his attachment, from the gay fantasy of his youth to the lingering despair of his age, pity and affection mingle with our admiration. Even after death had placed the last seal on his misery, we see him devoting to the cause of the human mind all the strength and energy which love and sorrow had spared. He lived the apostle of literature; he fell its martyr:—he was found dead with his head reclined on a book.

Those who have studied the life and writings of Petrarch with attention, will perhaps be inclined to make some deductions from this panegyric. It cannot be denied that his merits were disfigured by a most unpleasant affectation. His zeal for literature communicated a tinge of pedantry to all his feelings and opinions. His love was the love of a sonnetteer; his patriotism was the patriotism of an antiquarian. The interest with which we contemplate the works, and study the history, of those who, in former ages, have occupied our country, arises from the associations which connect them with the community in which are comprised all the objects of our affection and our hope. In the mind of Petrarch these feelings were reversed. He loved Italy, because it abounded with the monuments of the ancient masters of the world. His native city, the fair and glorious Florence, the modern Athens, then in all the bloom and strength of its youth, could not obtain, from the most distinguished of its citizens, any portion of that passionate homage which he paid to the decrepitude of Rome. These and many other blemishes, though they must in candour be acknowledged, can but in a very slight degree diminish the glory of his career. For my own part, I look upon it with so much fondness and pleasure that I feel reluctant to turn from it to the consideration of his works, which I by no means contemplate with equal admiration.

Nevertheless, I think highly of the poetical powers of Petrarch. He did not possess, indeed, the art of strongly presenting sensible objects to the imagination;—and this is the more remarkable, because the talent of which I speak is that which peculiarly distinguishes the Italian poets. In the *Divine Comedy* it is displayed in its highest perfection. It characterises almost every celebrated poem in the language. Perhaps this is to be attributed to the circumstance, that painting and sculpture had attained a high degree of excellence in Italy before poetry had been extensively cultivated. Men were debarred from books, but accustomed from childhood to contemplate the admirable works of art, which, even in the thirteenth century, Italy began to produce. Hence their imaginations received so strong a bias that, even in their writings, a taste for graphic delineation is discernible. The progress of things in England has been in all respects different. The consequence is, that English historical pictures are poems on canvas; while Italian poems are pictures painted to the mind by means of words. Of this national characteristic the writings of Petrarch are almost totally destitute. His sonnets indeed, from their subject and nature, and his Latin poems, from the restraints which always shackle one who writes in a dead language, cannot fairly be received in evidence. But his " Triumphs " absolutely required the exercise of this talent, and exhibit no indications of it.

Genius, however, he certainly possessed, and genius of a high order. His ardent, tender, and magnificent turn of thought, his brilliant fancy, his command of expression, at once forcible and elegant, must be acknowledged. Nature meant him for the prince of lyric writers. But by one fatal present she deprived her other gifts of half their value. He would have been a much greater poet had he been a less clever man. His ingenuity was the bane of his mind. He abandoned the noble and natural style, in which he might have excelled, for the conceits which he produced with a facility at once admirable and disgusting. His muse, like the Roman lady in Livy, was tempted by gaudy ornaments to betray the fastnesses of her strength, and, like her, was crushed beneath the glittering bribes which had seduced her.

The paucity of his thoughts is very remarkable. It is impossible to look without amazement on a mind so fertile in combinations, yet so barren of images. His amatory poetry is wholly made up of a very few topics, disposed in so many orders, and exhibited in so many lights, that it reminds us of those arithmetical problems about permutations, which so much astonish the unlearned. The French cook, who boasted that he could make fifteen different dishes out of a nettle-top, was not a greater master of his art. The mind of Petrarch was a kaleidoscope. At every turn it presents us with new forms, always fantastic, occasionally beautiful; and we can scarcely believe that all these varieties have been produced by the same worthless fragments of glass. The sameness of his images is, indeed, in some degree, to be attributed to the sameness of his subject. It would be unreasonable to expect perpetual variety from so many hundred compositions, all of the same length, all in the same measure, and all addressed to the same insipid and heartless coquette. I cannot but suspect also that the perverted taste, which is the blemish of his amatory verses, was to be attributed to the influence of Laura, who, probably, like most critics of her sex, preferred a gaudy to a majestic style. Be this as it may, he no sooner changes his subject than he changes his manner. When he speaks of the wrongs and degradation of Italy, devastated by foreign invaders, and but feebly defended by her pusillanimous children, the effeminate lisp of the sonnetteer is exchanged for a cry, wild, and solemn, and piercing as that which proclaimed " Sleep no more " to the bloody house of Cawdor. " Italy seems not to feel her sufferings," exclaims her impassioned poet; " decrepit, sluggish, and languid, will she sleep for ever? Will there be none to awake her? Oh that I had my hands twisted in her hair! " [1]

Nor is it with less energy that he denounces against the Mahometan Babylon the vengeance of Europe and of Christ. His magnificent enumeration of the ancient exploits of the Greeks must always excite admiration, and cannot be perused without the deepest interest, at a time when the wise and good, bitterly disappointed in so many other countries, are looking with breathless anxiety towards the natal land of liberty, the field of Marathon, and the deadly pass where the Lion of Lacedæmon turned to bay.[2]

His poems on religious subjects also deserve the highest commendation. At the head of these must be placed the " Ode to the Virgin." It is, perhaps, the finest hymn in the world. His devout veneration receives an exquisitely poetical character from the delicate perception of the sex and the loveliness of his idol, which we may easily trace throughout the whole composition.

I could dwell with pleasure on these and similar parts of the

---

[1] " Che suoi guai non par che senta;
    Vecchia, oziosa, e lenta.
    Dormirà sempre, e non fia chi la svegli?
    Le man l' avess' io avvolte entro e capegli."
Canzone xi.

[2] " Maratona, e le mortali strette
    Che difese il LEON con poca gente."
Canzone v.

writings of Petrarch; but I must return to his amatory poetry: to that he entrusted his fame; and to that he has principally owed it.

The prevailing defect of his best compositions on this subject is the universal brilliancy with which they are lighted up. The natural language of the passions is, indeed, often figurative and fantastic; and with none is this more the case than with that of love. Still there is a limit. The feelings should, indeed, have their ornamental garb; but, like an elegant woman, they should be neither muffled nor exposed. The drapery should be so arranged, as at once to answer the purposes of modest conceal-ment and judicious display. The decorations should sometimes be employed to hide a defect, and sometimes to heighten a beauty; but never to conceal, much less to distort, the charms to which they are subsidiary. The love of Petrarch, on the contrary, arrays itself like a foppish savage, whose nose is bored with a golden ring, whose skin is painted with grotesque forms and dazzling colours, and whose ears are drawn down his shoulders by the weight of jewels. It is a rule, without any exception, in all kinds of composition, that the principal idea, the predominant feeling, should never be confounded with the accompanying decorations. It should generally be distin-guished from them by greater simplicity of expression; as we recognise Napoleon in the pictures of his battles, amidst a crowd of embroidered coats and plumes, by his grey cloak and his hat without a feather. In the verses of Petrarch it is generally impossible to say what thought is meant to be prominent. All is equally elaborate. The chief wears the same gorgeous and degrading livery with his retinue, and obtains only his share of the indifferent stare which we bestow upon them in common. The poems have no strong lights and shades, no background, no foreground; they are like the illuminated figures in an oriental manuscript, plenty of rich tints and no perspective. Such are the faults of the most celebrated of these compositions. Of those which are universally acknowledged to be bad it is scarcely possible to speak with patience. Yet they have much in common with their splendid companions. They differ from them, as a May-day procession of chimneysweepers differs from the Field of Cloth of Gold. They have the gaudiness but not the wealth. His muse belongs to that numerous class of females who have no objection to be dirty, while they can be tawdry. When his brilliant conceits are exhausted, he supplies their place with metaphysical quibbles, forced antitheses, bad puns, and execrable charades. In his fifth sonnet he may, I think, be said to have sounded the lowest chasm of the Bathos. Upon the whole, that piece may be safely pronounced to be the worst attempt at poetry, and the worst attempt at wit, in the world.

A strong proof of the truth of these criticisms is, that almost all the sonnets produce exactly the same effect on the mind of the reader. They relate to all the various moods of a lover, from joy to despair: yet they are perused, as far as my experience and observation have gone, with exactly the same feeling. The fact is, that in none of them are the passion and the ingenuity mixed in just proportions. There is not enough sentiment to dilute the condiments which are employed to season it. The repast which he sets before us resembles the Spanish entertainment in Dryden's *Mock Astrologer*, at which the relish of all the dishes and sauces was overpowered by the common flavour of spice. Fish, flesh, fowl, everything at table tasted of nothing but red pepper.

The writings of Petrarch may indeed suffer undeservedly from one cause to which I must allude. His imitators have so much familiarised the ear of Italy and of Europe to the favourite topics of amorous flattery and lamentation, that we can scarcely think them original when we find them in the first author; and, even when our understandings have convinced us that they were new to him, they are still old to us. This has been the fate of many of the finest passages of the most eminent writers. It is melancholy to trace a noble thought from stage to stage of its profanation; to see it transferred from the first illustrious wearer to his lacqueys, turned, and turned again, and at last hung on a scarecrow. Petrarch has really suffered much from this cause. Yet that he should have so suffered is a sufficient proof that his excellences were not of the highest order. A line may be stolen; but the pervading spirit of a great poet is not to be surreptitiously obtained by a plagiarist. The continued imitation of twenty-five centuries has left Homer as it found him. If every simile and every turn of Dante had been copied ten thousand times, the *Divine Comedy* would have retained all its freshness. It was easy for the porter in Farquhar to pass for Beau Clincher, by borrowing his lace and his pulvilio. It would have been more difficult to enact Sir Harry Wildair.

Before I quit this subject I must defend Petrarch from one accusation which is in the present day frequently brought against him. His sonnets are pronounced by a large sect of critics not to possess certain qualities which they maintain to be indispensable to sonnets, with as much confidence, and as much reason, as their prototypes of old insisted on the unities of the drama. I am an exoteric, utterly unable to explain the mysteries of this new poetical faith. I only know that it is a faith, which except a man do keep pure and undefiled, without doubt he shall be called a blockhead. I cannot, however, refrain from asking what is the particular virtue which belongs to fourteen as distinguished from all other numbers. Does it arise from its being a multiple of seven? Has this principle any reference to the sabbatical ordinance? Or is it to the order of rhymes that these singular properties are attached? Unhappily the sonnets of Shakespeare differ as much in this respect from those of Petrarch, as from a Spenserian or an octave stanza. Away with this unmeaning jargon! We have pulled down the old regime of criticism. I trust that we shall never tolerate the equally pedantic and irrational despotism, which some of the revolutionary leaders would erect upon its ruins. We have not dethroned Aristotle and Bossu for this.

These sonnet-fanciers would do well to reflect that, though the style of Petrarch may not suit the standard of perfection which they have chosen, they lie under great obligations to these very poems, that, but for Petrarch the measure, concerning which they legislate so judiciously, would probably never have attracted notice; and that to him they owe the pleasure of admiring, and the glory of composing, pieces, which seem to have been produced by Master Slender, with the assistance of his man Simple.

I cannot conclude these remarks without making a few observations on the Latin writings of Petrarch. It appears that, both by himself and by his contemporaries, these were far more highly valued than his compositions in the vernacular language. Posterity, the supreme court of literary appeal, has not only reversed the judgment, but, according to its general practice, reversed it with costs, and condemned the unfortunate works to pay, not only for their own inferiority, but also for the injustice of those who had given them an unmerited preference. And it must be owned that, without making large allowances for the circumstances under which they were produced, we cannot pronounce a very favourable judgment. They must be considered as exotics, transplanted to a foreign climate, and reared in an unfavourable situation; and it would be unreasonable to expect from them the health and the vigour which we find in the indigenous plants around them, or which they might themselves have possessed in their native soil. He has but very imperfectly imitated the style of the Latin authors, and has not compensated for the deficiency by enriching the ancient language with the graces of modern poetry. The splendour and ingenuity, which we admire, even when we condemn it, in his Italian works, is almost totally wanting, and only illuminates with rare and occasional glimpses the dreary obscurity of the African. The eclogues have more animation; but they can only be called poems by courtesy. They have nothing in common with his writings in his native language, except the eternal pun about Laura and Daphne. None of these works would have placed him on a level with Vida or Buchanan. Yet, when we compare him with those who preceded him, when we consider that he went on the forlorn hope of literature, that he was the first who perceived, and the first who attempted to revive, the finer elegancies of the ancient language of the world, we shall perhaps think more highly of him than of those who could never have surpassed his beauties if they had not inherited them.

He has aspired to emulate the philosophical eloquence of Cicero, as well as the poetical majesty of Virgil. His essay on the "Remedies of Good and Evil Fortune" is a singular work in a colloquial form, and a most scholastic style. It seems to be framed upon the model of the Tusculan Questions, with what success those who have read it may easily determine. It consists of a series of dialogues: in each of these a person is introduced who has experienced some happy or some adverse event: he gravely states his case; and a reasoner, or rather Reason personified, confutes him; a task not very difficult, since the disciple defends his position only by pertinaciously repeating it, in almost the same words at the end of every argument of his antagonist. In this manner Petrarch solves an immense variety of cases. Indeed, I doubt whether it would be possible to name any pleasure or any calamity which does not find a place in this dissertation. He gives excellent advice to a man who is in expectation of discovering the philosopher's stone; to another, who has formed a fine aviary; to a third, who is delighted with the tricks of a favourite monkey. His lectures to the unfortunate are equally singular. He seems to imagine that a precedent in point is a sufficient consolation for every form of suffering. "Our town is taken," says one complainant; "So was Troy," replies his comforter. "My wife has eloped," says another; "If it has happened to you once, it happened to

Menelaus twice."   One poor fellow is in great distress at having discovered that his wife's son is none of his.   " It is hard," says he, " that I should have had the expense of bringing up one who is indifferent to me."   " You are a man," returns his monitor, quoting the famous line of Terence; " and nothing that belongs to any other man ought to be indifferent to you."   The physical calamities of life are not omitted; and there is in particular a disquisition on the advantages of having the itch, which, if not convincing, is certainly very amusing.

The invectives on an unfortunate physician, or rather upon the medical science, have more spirit.   Petrarch was thoroughly in earnest on this subject.   And the bitterness of his feelings occasionally produces, in the midst of his classical and scholastic pedantry, a sentence worthy of the second Philippic.   Swift himself might have envied the chapter on the causes of the paleness of physicians.

Of his Latin works the *Epistles* are the most generally known and admired.   As compositions they are certainly superior to his essays.   But their excellence is only comparative.   From so large a collection of letters, written by so eminent a man, during so varied and eventful a life, we should have expected a complete and spirited view of the literature, the manners, and the politics of the age.   A traveller, a poet, a scholar, a lover, a courtier, a recluse, he might have perpetuated, in an imperishable record, the form and pressure of the age and body of the time.   Those who read his correspondence, in the hope of finding such information as this, will be utterly disappointed.   It contains nothing characteristic of the period or of the individual. It is a series, not of letters, but of themes; and, as it is not generally known, might be very safely employed at public schools as a magazine of commonplaces.   Whether he write on politics to the emperor and the doge, or send advice and consolation to a private friend, every line is crowded with examples and quotations, and sounds big with Anaxagoras and Scipio.   Such was the interest excited by the character of Petrarch, and such the admiration which was felt for his epistolary style, that it was with difficulty that his letters reached the place of their destination.

In conclusion, we may pronounce that the works of Petrarch were below both his genius and his celebrity; and that the circumstances under which he wrote were as adverse to the development of his powers as they were favourable to the extension of his fame.

A CONVERSATION BETWEEN MR. ABRAHAM COWLEY AND MR. JOHN MILTON, TOUCHING THE GREAT CIVIL WAR

SET DOWN BY A GENTLEMAN OF THE MIDDLE TEMPLE

[*August* 1824.]

" Referre sermones Deorum et
Magna modis tenuare parvis."
HORACE.

I HAVE thought it good to set down in writing a memorable debate, wherein I was a listener, and two men of pregnant parts and great reputation discoursers; hoping that my friends will not be displeased to have a record both of the strange times through which I have lived, and of the famous men with whom I have conversed. It chanced in the warm and beautiful spring of the year 1665, a little before the saddest summer that ever London saw, that I went to the bowling green at Piccadilly, whither, at that time, the best gentry made continual resorts. There I met Mr. Cowley, who had lately left Barnelms. There was then a house preparing for him at Chertsey; and till it should be finished, he had come up for a short time to London, that he might urge a suit to his Grace of Buckingham touching certain lands of her Majesty's, whereof he requested a lease. I had the honour to be familiarly acquainted with that worthy gentleman and most excellent poet, whose death hath been deplored with as general a consent of all powers that delight in the woods, or in verse, or in love, as was of old that of Daphnis or of Callus.

After some talk, which it is not material to set down at large, concerning his suit and his vexations at the court, where indeed his honesty did him more harm than his parts could do him good, I entreated him to dine with me at my lodging in the Temple, which he most courteously promised. And, that so eminent a guest might not lack a better entertainment than cooks or vintners can provide, I sent to the house of Mr. John Milton, in the Artillery Walk, to beg that he would also be my guest. For, though he had been secretary, first to the Council of State, and, after that, to the Protector, and Mr. Cowley had held the same post under the Lord St. Albans in his banishment, I hoped, notwithstanding, that they would think themselves rather united by their common art than divided by their different factions. And so indeed it proved. For, while we sat at table, they talked freely of many men and things, as well ancient as modern, with much civility. Nay, Mr. Milton, who seldom tasted wine, both because of his singular temperance and because of his gout, did more than once pledge Mr. Cowley, who was indeed no hermit in diet. At last, being heated, Mr. Milton begged that I would open the windows. " Nay," said I, " if you desire fresh air and coolness, what should hinder us, as the evening is fair, from sailing for an hour on the river? " To this they both cheerfully consented; and forth we walked, Mr. Cowley and I leading Mr. Milton between us, to the Temple Stairs. There we took a boat; and thence we were rowed up the river.

The wind was pleasant; the evening fine; the sky, the earth, and the water beautiful to look upon. But Mr. Cowley and I held our peace, and said nothing of the gay sights around us, lest we should too feelingly remind Mr. Milton of his calamity; whereof, however, he needed no monitor: for soon he said, sadly, " Ah, Mr. Cowley, you are a happy man. What would I now give but for one more look at the sun, and the waters, and the gardens of this fair city ! "

" I know not," said Mr. Cowley, " whether we ought not rather to envy you for that which makes you to envy others: and that specially in this place, where all eyes which are not closed in blindness ought to become fountains of tears. What can we look upon which is not a memorial of change and sorrow, of fair things vanished, and evil things done? When I see the gate of Whitehall, and the stately pillars of the Banqueting House, I cannot choose but think of what I have there seen in former days, masques, and pageants, and dances, and smiles, and the waving of graceful heads, and the bounding of delicate feet. And then I turn to thoughts of other things, which even to remember makes me to blush and weep; of the great black scaffold, and the axe and block, which were placed before those very windows; and the voice seems to sound in mine ears, the lawless and terrible voice, which cried out that the head of a king was the head of a traitor. There stands Westminster Hall, which who can look upon, and not tremble to think how time, and change, and death confound the councils of the wise, and beat down the weapons of the mighty? How have I seen it surrounded with tens of thousands of petitioners crying for justice and privilege ! How have I heard it shake with fierce and proud words, which made the hearts of the people burn within them! Then it is blockaded by dragoons, and cleared by pikemen. And they who have conquered their master go forth trembling at the word of their servant. And yet a little while, and the usurper comes forth from it, in his robe of ermine, with the golden staff in one hand and the Bible in the other, amidst the roaring of the guns and the shouting of the people. And yet again a little while, and the doors are thronged with multitudes in black, and the hearse and the plumes come forth; and the tyrant is borne, in more than royal pomp, to a royal sepulchre. A few days more, and his head is fixed to rot on the pinnacles of that very hall where he sat on a throne in his life, and lay in state after his death. When I think on all these things, to look round me makes me sad at heart. True it is that God hath restored to us our old laws, and the rightful line of our kings. Yet, how I know not, but it seems to me that something is wanting—that our court hath not the old gravity, nor our people the old loyalty. These evil times, like the great deluge, have overwhelmed and con-fused all earthly things. And, even as those waters, though at last they abated, yet, as the learned write, destroyed all trace of the garden of Eden, so that its place hath never since been found, so hath this opening of all the flood-gates of political evil effaced all marks of the ancient political paradise."

" Sir, by your favour," said Mr. Milton, " though, from many circumstances both of body and of fortune, I might plead fairer excuses for despondency than yourself, I yet look not so sadly either on the past or on the future. That a deluge hath passed over this our nation, I deny not. But I hold it not to be such a deluge as that of which you speak; but rather a blessed flood, like those of the Nile, which in its overflow doth indeed wash away ancient landmarks, and confound boundaries, and sweep away dwellings, yea, doth give birth to many foul and dangerous reptiles. Yet hence is the fulness of the granary, the beauty of the garden, the nurture of all living things.

" I remember well, Mr. Cowley, what you have said concerning these things in your "Discourse on the Government of Oliver Cromwell," which my friend Elwood read to me last year. Truly, for elegance and rhetoric, that essay is to be compared with the finest tractates of Isocrates and Cicero. But neither that nor any other book, nor any events, which with most men have, more than any book, weight and authority, have altered my opinion, that, of all assemblies that ever were in this world, the best and the most useful was our Long Parliament. I speak not this as wishing to provoke a debate; which neither yet do I decline."

Mr. Cowley was, as I could see, a little nettled. Yet, as he was a man of a kind disposition and a most refined courtesy, he put a force upon himself, and answered with more vehemence and quickness indeed than was his wont, yet not uncivilly. "Surely, Mr. Milton, you speak not as you think. I am indeed one of those who believe that God hath reserved to himself the censure of kings, and that their crimes and oppressions are not to be resisted by the hands of their subjects. Yet can I easily find excuse for the violence of such as are stung to madness by grievous tyranny. But what shall we say for these men? Which of their just demands was not granted? Which even of their cruel and unreasonable requisitions, so as it were not inconsistent with all law and order, was refused? Had they not sent Strafford to the block and Laud to the Tower? Had they not destroyed the courts of the High Commission and the Star Chamber? Had they not reversed the proceedings confirmed by the voices of the judges of England, in the matter of ship-money? Had they not taken from the king his ancient and most lawful power touching the order of knighthood? Had they not provided that, after their dissolution, triennial parliaments should be holden, and that their own power should continue till of their great condescension they should be pleased to resign it themselves? What more could they ask? Was it not enough that they had taken from their king all his oppressive powers, and many that were most salutary? Was it not enough that they had filled his council-board with his enemies, and his prisons with his adherents? Was it not enough that they had raised a furious multitude, to shout and swagger daily under the very windows of his royal palace? Was it not enough that they had taken from him the most blessed prerogative of princely mercy; that, complaining of intolerance themselves, they had denied all toleration to others; that they had urged, against forms, scruples childish as those of any formalist; that they had persecuted the least remnant of the popish rites with the fiercest bitterness of the popish spirit? Must they besides all this have full power to command his armies, and to massacre his friends?

" For military command, it was never known in any monarchy, nay, in any well ordered republic, that it was committed to the debates of a large and unsettled assembly. For their other requisition, that he should give up to their vengeance all who had defended the rights of his crown, his honour must have been ruined if he had complied. Is it not therefore plain that they desired these things only in order that, by refusing, his Majesty might give them a pretence for war?

" Men have often risen up against fraud, against cruelty, against rapine. But when before was it known that concessions were met with importunities, graciousness with insults, the open palm of bounty with the clenched fist of malice? Was it like trusty delegates of the Commons of England, and faithful stewards of their liberty and their wealth, to engage them for such causes in civil war, which both to liberty and to wealth is of all things the most hostile. Evil indeed must be the disease which is not more tolerable than such a medicine. Those who, even to save a nation from tyrants, excite it to civil war do in general but minister to it the same miserable kind of relief wherewith the wizards of Pharaoh mocked the Egyptian. We read that, when Moses had turned their waters into blood, those impious magicians, intending, not benefit to the thirsting people, but vain and emulous ostentation of their own art, did themselves also change into blood the water which the plague had spared. Such sad comfort do those who stir up war minister to the oppressed. But here where was the oppression? What was the favour which had not been granted? What was the evil which had not been removed? What further could they desire?"

" These questions," said Mr. Milton, austerely, " have indeed often deceived the ignorant; but that Mr. Cowley should have been so beguiled, I marvel. You ask what more the parliament could desire? I will answer you in one word, security. What are votes, and statutes, and resolutions? They have no eyes to see, no hands to strike and avenge. They must have some safeguard from without. Many things, therefore, which in themselves were peradventure hurtful, was this parliament constrained to ask, lest otherwise good laws and precious rights should be without defence. Nor did they want a great and signal example of this danger. I need not remind you that, many years before, the two Houses had presented to the king the Petition of Right, wherein were set down all the most valuable privileges of the people of this realm. Did not Charles accept it? Did he not declare it to be law? Was it not as fully enacted as ever were any of those bills of the Long Parliament concerning which you spoke? And were those privileges therefore enjoyed more fully by the people? No: the king did from that time redouble his oppressions as if to avenge himself for the shame of having been compelled to renounce them. Then were our estates laid under shameful impositions, our houses ransacked, our bodies imprisoned. Then was the steel of the hangman blunted with mangling the ears of harmless men. Then our very minds were fettered, and the iron entered into our souls. Then we were compelled to hide our hatred, our sorrow, and our scorn, to laugh with hidden faces at the mummery of Laud, to curse under our breath the tyranny of Wentworth. Of old time it was well and nobly said, by one of our kings, that an Englishman ought to be as free as his thoughts. Our prince reversed the maxim; he strove to make our thoughts as much slaves as ourselves. To sneer at a Romish pageant, to miscall a lord's crest, were crimes for which there was no mercy. These were all the fruits which we gathered from those excellent laws of the former parliament, from these solemn promises of the king. Were we to be deceived again? Were we again to give subsidies, and receive nothing but promises? Were we again to make wholesome statutes, and then leave them to be broken daily and hourly, until the oppressor should have squandered another supply, and should be ready for another perjury? You ask what they could desire which he had not already granted. Let me ask of you another question. What pledge could he give which he had not already violated? From the first year of his reign, whenever he had need of the purses of his Commons to support the revels of Buckingham or the processions of Laud, he had assured them that, as he was a gentleman and a king, he would sacredly preserve their rights. He had pawned those solemn pledges, and pawned them again and again; but when had he redeemed them? ' Upon my faith,' ' Upon my sacred word,' ' Upon the honour of a prince,' came so easily from his lips, and dwelt so short a time on his mind that there were as little to be trusted as the ' By the hilts ' of an Alsatian dicer.

" Therefore it is that I praise this parliament for what else I might have condemned. If what he had granted had been granted graciously and readily, if what he had before promised had been faithfully observed, they could not be defended. It was because he had never yielded the worst abuse without a long struggle, and seldom without a large bribe; it was because he had no sooner disentangled himself from his troubles than he forgot his promises; and, more like a villainous huckster than a great king, kept both the prerogative and the large price which had been paid to him to forego it; it was because of these things that it was necessary and just to bind with forcible restraints one who could be bound neither by law nor honour. Nay, even while he was making those very concessions of which you speak, he betrayed his deadly hatred against the people and their friends. Not only did he, contrary to all that ever was deemed lawful in England, order that members of the Commons House of Parliament should be impeached of high treason at the bar of the Lords; thereby violating both the trial by jury and the privileges of the House; but, not content with breaking the law by his ministers, he went himself armed to assail it. In the birthplace and sanctuary of freedom, in the House itself, nay in the very chair of the speaker, placed for the protection of free speech and privilege, he sat, rolling his eyes round the benches, searching for those whose blood he desired, and singling out his opposers to the slaughter. This most foul outrage fails. Then again for the old arts. Then come gracious messages. Then come courteous speeches. Then is again mortgaged his often forfeited honour. He will never again violate the laws. He will respect their rights as if they were his own. He pledges the dignity of his crown; that crown which had been committed to him for the weal of his people, and which he never named, but that he might the more easily delude and oppress them.

"The power of the sword, I grant you, was not one to be permanently possessed by parliament. Neither did that parliament demand it as a permanent possession. They asked it only for temporary security. Nor can I see on what conditions they could safely make peace with that false and wicked king, save such as would deprive him of all power to injure.

"For civil war, that it is an evil I dispute not. But that it is the greatest of evils, that I stoutly deny. It doth indeed appear to the misjudging to be a worse calamity than bad government, because its miseries are collected together within a short space and time, and may easily at one view be taken in and perceived. But the misfortunes of nations ruled by tyrants, being distributed over many centuries and many places, as they are of greater weight and number, so are they of less display. When the devil of tyranny hath gone into the body politic he departs not but with struggles, and foaming, and great convulsions. Shall he, therefore, vex it for ever, lest, in going out, he for a moment tear and rend it? Truly this argument touching the evils of war would better become my friend Elwood, or some other of the people called Quakers, than a courtier and a cavalier. It applies no more to this war than to all others, as well foreign as domestic, and, in this war, no more to the Houses than to the king; nay, not so much, since he by a little sincerity and moderation might have rendered that needless which their duty to God and man then enforced them to do."

" Pardon me, Mr. Milton," said Mr. Cowley; " I grieve to hear you speak thus of that good king. Most unhappy indeed he was, in that he reigned at a time when the spirit of the then living generation was for freedom, and the precedents of former ages for prerogative. His case was like to that of Christopher Columbus, when he sailed forth on an unknown ocean, and found that the compass, whereby he shaped his course, had shifted from the north pole whereto before it had constantly pointed. So it was with Charles. His compass varied; and therefore he could not tack aright. If he had been an absolute king he would doubtless, like Titus Vespasian, have been called the delight of the human race. If he had been a doge of Venice, or a stadtholder of Holland, he would never have outstepped the laws. But he lived when our government had neither clear definitions nor strong sanctions. Let, therefore, his faults be ascribed to the time. Of his virtues the praise is his own.

" Never was there a more gracious prince, or a more proper gentleman. In every pleasure he was temperate, in conversation mild and grave, in friendship constant, to his servants liberal, to his queen faithful and loving, in battle grave, in sorrow and captivity resolved, in death most Christian and forgiving.

" For his oppressions, let us look at the former history of this realm. James was never accounted a tyrant. Elizabeth is esteemed to have been the mother of her people. Were they less arbitrary? Did they never lay hands on the purses of their subjects but by Act of Parliament? Did they never confine insolent and disobedient men but in due course of law? Was the court of Star Chamber less active? Were the ears of libellers more safe? I pray you, let not King Charles be thus dealt with. It was enough that in his life he was tried for an alleged breach of laws which none ever heard named till they were discovered for his destruction. Let not his fame be treated as was his sacred and anointed body. Let not his memory be tried by principles found out *ex post facto*. Let us not judge by the spirit of one generation a man whose disposition had been formed by the temper and fashion of another."

" Nay, but conceive me, Mr. Cowley," said Mr. Milton; " inasmuch as, at the beginning of his reign, he imitated those who had governed before him, I blame him not. To expect that kings will, of their own free choice, abridge their prerogative, were argument of but slender wisdom. Whatever, therefore, lawless, unjust, or cruel, he either did or permitted during the first years of his reign, I pass by. But for what was done after that he had solemnly given his consent to the Petition of Right, where shall we find defence? Let it be supposed, which yet I concede not, that the tyranny of his father and of Queen Elizabeth had been no less rigorous than was his. But had his father, had that queen, sworn like him, to abstain from those rigours? Had they, like him, for good and valuable consideration, aliened their hurtful prerogatives? Surely not: from whatever excuse you can plead for him he had wholly excluded himself. The borders of countries, we know, are mostly the seats of perpetual wars and tumults. It was the same with the undefined frontiers, which of old separated privilege and prerogative. They were the debatable land of our polity. It was no marvel if, both on the one side and on the other, inroads were often made. But, when treaties have been concluded, spaces measured, lines drawn, landmarks set up, that which before might pass for innocent error or just reprisal becomes robbery, perjury, deadly sin. He knew not, you say, which of his powers were founded on ancient law, and which only on vicious example. But had he not read the Petition of Right? Had not proclamation been made from his throne, *Soit fait comme il est desiré ?*

" For his private virtues they are beside the question. Remember you not," and Mr. Milton smiled, but somewhat sternly, " what Dr. Caius saith in the ' Merry Wives ' of Shakespeare? ' What shall the honest man do in my closet? There is no honest man that shall come in my closet.' Even so say I. There is no good man who shall make us his slaves. If he break his word to his people, is it a sufficient defence that he keeps it to his companions? If he oppress and extort all day, shall he be held blameless because he prayeth at night and morning? If he be insatiable in plunder and revenge, shall we pass it by because in meat and drink he is temperate? If he have lived like a tyrant, shall all be forgotten because he hath died like a martyr?

" He was a man, as I think, who had so much semblance of virtues as might make his vices most dangerous. He was not a tyrant after our wonted English model. The second Richard, the second and fourth Edwards, and the eighth Harry, were men profuse, gay, boisterous; lovers of women and of wine, of no outward sanctity or gravity. Charles was a ruler after the Italian fashion; grave, demure, of a solemn carriage, and a sober diet; as constant at prayers as a priest, as heedless of oaths as an athiest."

Mr. Cowley answered somewhat sharply: " I am sorry, sir, to hear you speak thus. I had hoped that the vehemence of spirit which was caused by these violent times had now abated. Yet, sure, Mr. Milton, whatever you may think of the character of King Charles, you will not still justify his murder? "

" Sir," said Mr. Milton, " I must have been of a hard and strange nature, if the vehemence which was imputed to me in my younger days had not been diminished by the afflictions wherewith it hath pleased Almighty God to chasten my age. I will not now defend all that I may heretofore have written. But this I say, that I perceive not wherefore a king should be exempted from all punishment. Is it just that where most is given least should be required? Or politic that where there is the greatest power to injure there should be no danger to restrain? But, you will say, there is no such law. Such a law there is. There is the law of self-preservation written by God himself on our hearts. There is the primal compact and bond of society, not graven on stone, or sealed with wax, nor put down on parchment, nor set forth in any express form of words by men when of old they came together; but implied in the very act that they so came together, pre-supposed in all subsequent law, not to be repealed by any authority, nor invalidated by being omitted in any code; inasmuch as from thence are all codes and all authority.

" Neither do I well see wherefore you cavaliers, and, indeed, many of us whom you merrily call roundheads, distinguish between those who fought against King Charles, and specially after the second commission given to Sir Thomas Fairfax, and those who condemned him to death. Sure, if his person were inviolable, it was as wicked to lift the sword against it at Naseby as the axe at Whitehall. If his life might justly be taken, why not in course of trial as well as by right of war?

" Thus much in general as touching the right. But, for the execution of King Charles in particular, I will not now undertake to defend it. Death is inflicted, not that the culprit may die, but that the state may be thereby advantaged. And, from all that I know, I think that the death of King Charles hath more hindered than advanced the liberties of England.

" First, he left an heir. He was in captivity. The heir was in freedom. He was odious to the Scots. The heir was favoured by them.   To kill the captive therefore, whereby the heir, in the apprehension of all royalists, became forthwith king—what was it, in truth, but to set their captive free, and to give him besides other great advantages?

" Next, it was a deed most odious to the people, and not only to your party, but to many among ourselves; and, as it is perilous for any government to outrage the public opinion, so was it most perilous for a government which had from that opinion alone its birth, its nurture, and its defence.

" Yet doth not this properly belong to our dispute; nor can these faults be justly charged upon that most renowned parliament.   For, as you know, the high court of justice was not established until the House had been purged of such members as were adverse to the army, and brought wholly under the control of the chief officers."

" And who," said Mr. Cowley, " levied that army?   Who commissioned those officers?   Was not the fate of the Commons as justly deserved as was that of Diomedes, who was devoured by those horses whom he had himself taught to feed on the flesh and blood of men?   How could they hope that others would respect laws which they had themselves insulted; that swords which had been drawn against the prerogatives of the king would be put up at an ordinance of the Commons?   It was believed, of old, that there were some devils easily raised but never to be laid; insomuch that, if a magician called them up, he should be forced to find them always some employment; for, though they would do all his bidding, yet, if he left them but for one moment without some work of evil to perform, they would turn their claws against himself.   Such a fiend is an army. They who evoke it cannot dismiss it.   They are at once its masters and its slaves.   Let them not fail to find for it task after task of blood and rapine.   Let them not leave it for a moment in repose, lest it tear them in pieces.

" Thus was it with that famous assembly.   They formed a force which they could neither govern nor resist.   They made it powerful.   They made it fanatical.   As if military insolence were not of itself sufficiently dangerous, they heightened it with spiritual pride, they encouraged their soldiers to rave from the tops of tubs against the men of Belial, till every trooper thought himself a prophet.   They taught them to abuse popery, till every drummer fancied that he was as infallible as a pope.

" Then it was that religion changed her nature.   She was no longer the parent of arts and letters, of wholesome knowledge, of innocent pleasures, of blessed household smiles. In their place came sour faces, whining voices, the chattering of fools, the yells of madmen. Then men fasted from meat and drink, who fasted not from bribes and blood. Then men frowned at stage-plays, who smiled at massacres. Then men preached against painted faces, who felt no remorse for their own most painted lives. Religion had been a pole-star to light and to guide. It was now more like to that ominous star in the book of the Apocalypse, which fell from heaven upon the fountains and rivers and changed them into wormwood; for even so did it descend from its high and celestial dwelling-place to plague this earth, and to turn into bitterness all that was sweet, and into poison all that was nourishing.

" Therefore it was not strange that such things should follow. They who had closed the barriers of London against the king could not defend them against their own creatures. They who had so stoutly cried for privilege, when that prince, most unadvisedly no doubt, came among them to demand their members, durst not wag their fingers when Oliver filled their hall with soldiers, gave their mace to a corporal, put their keys in his pocket, and drove them forth with base terms, borrowed half from the conventicle and half from the ale-house. Then were we, like the trees of the forest in holy writ, given over to the rule of the bramble; then from the basest of the shrubs came forth the fire which devoured the cedars of Lebanon. We bowed down before a man of mean birth, of ungraceful demeanour, of stammering and most vulgar utterance, of scandalous and notorious hypocrisy. Our laws were made and unmade at his pleasure; the constitution of our parliaments changed by his writ and proclamation; our persons imprisoned; our property plundered; our lands and houses overrun with soldiers; and the great charter itself was but argument for a scurrilous jest; and for all this we may thank that parliament; for never, unless they had so violently shaken the vessel, could such foul dregs have risen to the top."

Then answered Mr. Milton: " What you have now said comprehends so great a number of subjects, that it would require, not an evening's sail on the Thames, but rather a voyage to the Indies, accurately to treat of all: yet, in as few words as I may, I will explain my sense of these matters.

" First, as to the army. An army, as you have well set forth, is always a weapon dangerous to those who use it; yet he who falls among thieves spares not to fire his musquetoon, because he may be slain if it burst in his hand.   Nor must states refrain from defending themselves, lest their defenders should at last turn against them.   Nevertheless, against this danger statesmen should carefully provide; and, that they may do so, they should take especial care that neither the officers nor the soldiers do forget that they are also citizens.   I do believe that the English army would have continued to obey the parliament with all duty, but for one act, which, as it was in intention, in seeming, and in immediate effect, worthy to be compared with the most famous in history, so was it, in its final consequence, most injurious.   I speak of that ordinance called the *self-denying*, and of the new model of the army.   By those measures the Commons gave up the command of their forces into the hands of men who were not of themselves.   Hence, doubtless, derived no small honour to that noble assembly, which sacrificed to the hope of public good the assurance of private advantage. And, as to the conduct of the war, the scheme prospered.   Witness the battle of Naseby, and the memorable exploits of Fairfax in the west.   But thereby the parliament lost that hold on the soldiers and that power to control them, which they retained while every regiment was commanded by their own members. Politicians there be, who would wholly divide the legislative from the executive power.   In the golden age this may have succeeded; in the millennium it may succeed again.   But, where great armies and great taxes are required, there the executive government must always hold a great authority, which authority, that it may not oppress and destroy the legislature, must be in some manner blended with it.   The leaders of foreign mercenaries have always been most dangerous to a country.   The officers of native armies, deprived of the civil privileges of other men, are as much to be feared.   This was the great error of that parliament: and, though an error it were, it was an error generous, virtuous, and more to be deplored than censured.

" Hence came the power of the army and its leaders, and especially of that most famous leader, whom both in our conversation to-day, and in that discourse whereon I before touched, you have, in my poor opinion, far too roughly handled.   Wherefore you speak contemptibly of his parts I know not; but I suspect that you are not free from the error common to studious and speculative men.   Because Oliver was an ungraceful orator, and never said, either in public or private, anything memorable, you will have it that he was of a mean capacity.   Sure this is unjust. Many men have there been ignorant of letters, without wit, without eloquence, who yet had the wisdom to devise, and the courage to perform, that which they lacked language to explain. Such men often, in troubled times, have worked out the deliverance of nations and their own greatness, not by logic, not by rhetoric, but by wariness in success, by calmness in danger, by fierce and stubborn resolution in all adversity. The hearts of men are their books; events are their tutors; great actions are their eloquence: and such an one, in my judgment, was his late Highness, who, if none were to treat his name scornfully now shook not at the sound of it while he lived, would, by very few, be mentioned otherwise than with reverence. His own deeds shall avouch him for a great states-man, a great soldier, a true lover of his country, a merciful and generous conqueror.

" For his faults, let us reflect that they who seem to lead are oftentimes most constrained to follow. They who will mix with men, and especially they who will govern them, must in many things obey them. They who will yield to no such con-ditions may be hermits, but cannot be generals and statesmen. If a man will walk straight forward without turning to the right or the left, he must walk in a desert, and not in Cheapside. Thus was he enforced to do many things which jumped not with his inclination nor made for his honour; because the army, on which alone he could depend for power and life, might not otherwise be contented. And I, for mine own part, marvel less that he sometimes was fain to indulge their violence than that he could so often restrain it.

" In that he dissolved parliament, I praise him. It then was so diminished in numbers, as well by the death as by the exclusion of members, that it was no longer the same assembly; and, if at that time it had made itself perpetual, we should have been governed, not by an English House of Commons, but by a Venetian Council.

" If in his following rule he overstepped the laws, I pity rather than condemn him. He may be compared to that Mæandrius of Samos, of whom Herodotus saith, in his " Thalia," that, wishing to be of all men the most just, he was not able; for after the death of Polycrates he offered freedom to the people; and not till certain of them threatened to call him to a reckoning for what he had formerly done, did he change his purpose, and make himself a tyrant, lest he should be treated as a criminal.

" Such was the case of Oliver. He gave to his country a form of government so free and admirable that, in near six thousand years, human wisdom hath never devised any more excellent contrivance for human happiness. To himself he reserved so little power that it would scarcely have sufficed for his safety, and it is a marvel that it could suffice for his ambition. When, after that, he found that the members of his parliament disputed his right even to that small authority which he had kept, when he might have kept all, then indeed I own that he began to govern by the sword those who would not suffer him to govern by the law.

" But, for the rest, what sovereign was ever more princely in pardoning injuries, in conquering enemies, in extending the dominions and the renown of his people? What sea, what shore did he not mark with imperishable memorials of his friendship or his vengeance? The gold of Spain, the steel of Sweden, the ten thousand sails of Holland, availed nothing against him. While every foreign state trembled at our arms, we sat secure from all assault. War, which often so strangely troubles both husbandry and commerce, never silenced the song of our reapers, or the sound of our looms. Justice was equally administered; God was freely worshipped.

" Now look at that which we have taken in exchange. With the restored king have come over to us vices of every sort, and most the basest and most shameful, lust without love, servitude without loyalty, foulness of speech, dishonesty of dealing, grinning contempt of all things good and generous. The throne is surrounded by men whom the former Charles would have spurned from his footstool. The altar is served by slaves whose knees are supple to every being but God. Rhymers, whose books the hangman should burn, pandars, actors, and buffoons, these drink a health and throw a main with the king; these have stars on their breasts and gold sticks in their hands; these shut out from his presence the best and bravest of those who bled for his house. Even so doth God visit those who know not how to value freedom. He gives them over to the tyranny which they have desired, Ἵνα πάντες ἐπαύρωνται βασιλῆος."

" I will not," said Mr. Cowley, " dispute with you on this argument. But, if it be as you say, how can you maintain that England hath been so greatly advantaged by the rebellion? "

" Understand me rightly, sir," said Mr. Milton. " This nation is not given over to slavery and vice. We tasted indeed the fruits of liberty before they had well ripened.   Their flavour was harsh and bitter; and we turned from them with loathing to the sweeter poisons of servitude.   This is but for a time. England is sleeping on the lap of Dalilah, traitorously chained, but not yet shorn of strength.   Let the cry be once heard—the Philistines be upon thee; and at once that sleep will be broken, and those chains will be as flax in the fire.   The great parliament hath left behind it in our hearts and minds a hatred of tyrants, a just knowledge of our rights, a scorn of vain and deluding names;   and that the revellers of Whitehall shall surely find.   The sun is darkened; but it is only for a moment: it is but an eclipse; though all birds of evil omen have begun to scream, and all ravenous beasts have gone forth to prey, thinking it to be midnight.   Woe to them if they be abroad when the rays again shine forth!

" The king hath judged ill.   Had he been wise he would have remembered that he owed his restoration only to confusions which had wearied us out, and made us eager for repose.   He would have known that the folly and perfidy of a prince would restore to the good old cause many hearts which had been alienated thence by the turbulence of factions; for, if I know aught of history, or of the heart of man, he will soon learn that the last champion of the people was not destroyed when he murdered Vane, nor seduced when he beguiled Fairfax."

Mr. Cowley seemed to me not to take much amiss what Mr. Milton had said touching that thankless court, which had indeed but poorly requited his own good service.   He only said, therefore, " Another rebellion!   Alas!   alas!   Mr. Milton!   If there be no choice but between despotism and anarchy, I prefer despotism."

" Many men," said Mr. Milton, " have floridly and ingeniously compared anarchy and despotism; but they who so amuse themselves do but look at separate parts of that which is truly one great whole.   Each is the cause and the effect of the other; the evils of either are the evils of both.   Thus do states move on in the same eternal cycle, which, from the remotest point, brings them back again to the same sad starting-post: and, till both those who govern and those who obey shall learn and mark this great truth, men can expect little through the future, as they have known little through the past, save vicissitudes of extreme evils, alternately producing and produced.

" When will rulers learn that, where liberty is not, security and order can never be?   We talk of absolute power; but all power hath limits, which, if not fixed by the moderation of the governors, will be fixed by the force of the governed. Sovereigns may send their opposers to dungeons; they may clear out a senate-house with soldiers; they may enlist armies of spies; they may hang scores of the disaffected in chains at every cross road; but what power shall stand in that frightful time when rebellion hath become a less evil than endurance? Who shall dissolve that terrible tribunal, which, in the hearts of the oppressed, denounces against the oppressor the doom of its wild justice? Who shall repeal the law of self-defence? What arms or discipline shall resist the strength of famine and despair? How often were the ancient Cæsars dragged from their golden palaces, stripped of their purple robes, mangled, stoned, defiled with filth, pierced with hooks, hurled into Tiber? How often have the Eastern Sultans perished by the sabres of their own janissaries, or the bow-strings of their own mutes! For no power which is not limited by laws can ever be protected by them. Small, therefore, is the wisdom of those who would fly to servitude as if it were a refuge from commotion; for anarchy is the sure consequence of tyranny. That governments may be safe, nations must be free. Their passions must have an outlet provided, lest they make one.

" When I was at Naples, I went with Signor Manso, a gentleman of excellent parts and breeding, who had been the familiar friend of that famous poet Torquato Tasso, to see the burning mountain Vesuvius. I wondered how the peasants could venture to dwell so fearlessly and cheerfully on its sides, when the lava was flowing from its summit; but Manso smiled, and told me that when the fire descends freely they retreat before it without haste or fear. They can tell how fast it will move, and how far; and they know, moreover, that, though it may work some little damage, it will soon cover the fields over which it hath passed with rich vineyards and sweet flowers. But, when the flames are pent up in the mountain, then it is that they have reason to fear; then it is that the earth sinks and the sea swells; then cities are swallowed up; and their place knoweth them no more. So it is in politics: where the people is most closely restrained, there it gives the greatest shocks to peace and order; therefore would I say to all kings, let your demagogues lead crowds, lest they lead armies; let them bluster, lest they massacre; a little turbulence is, as it were, the rainbow of the state; it shows indeed that there is a passing shower; but it is a pledge that there shall be no deluge."

" This is true," said Mr. Cowley; " yet these admonitions are not less needful to subjects than to sovereigns."

" Surely," said Mr. Milton; " and, that I may end this long debate with a few words in which we shall both agree, I hold that, as freedom is the only safeguard of governments, so are order and moderation generally necessary to preserve freedom. Even the vainest opinions of men are not to be outraged by those who propose to themselves the happiness of men for their end, and who must work with the passions of men for their means. The blind reverence for things ancient is indeed so foolish that it might make a wise man laugh, if it were not also sometimes so mischievous that it would rather make a good man weep. Yet, since it may not be wholly cured it must be discreetly indulged; and therefore those who would amend evil laws should consider rather how much it may be safe to spare, than how much it may be possible to change. Have you not heard that men who have been shut up for many years in dungeons shrink if they see the light, and fall down if their irons be struck off? And so, when nations have long been in the house of bondage, the chains which have crippled them are necessary to support them, the darkness which hath weakened their sight is necessary to preserve it. Therefore release them not too rashly, lest they curse their freedom and pine for their prison.

" I think indeed that the renowned parliament, of which we have talked so much, did show, until it became subject to the soldiers, a singular and admirable moderation, in such times scarcely to be hoped, and most worthy to be an example to all that shall come after. But on this argument I have said enough: and I will therefore only pray to Almighty God that those who shall, in future times, stand forth in defence of our liberties, as well civil as religious, may adorn the good cause by mercy, prudence, and soberness, to the glory of his name and the happiness and honour of the English people."

And so ended that discourse; and not long after we were set on shore again at the Temple Gardens, and there parted company: and the same evening I took notes of what had been said, which I have here more fully set down, from regard both to the fame of the men, and the importance of the subject-matter.

SOME ACCOUNT OF THE GREAT LAWSUIT BETWEEN
  THE PARISHES OF ST. DENNIS AND ST. GEORGE
  IN THE WATER. (April 1824)

The parish of St. Dennis is one of the most pleasant parts of
the county in which it is situated. It is fertile, well wooded,
well watered, and of an excellent air. For many generations the
manor had been holden in tail-male by a worshipful family, who
have always taken precedence of their neighbours at the races
and the sessions.

In ancient times the affairs of this parish were administered
by a court-baron, in which the freeholders were judges; and the
rates were levied by select vestries of the inhabitant householders.
But at length these good customs fell into disuse. The lords of
the manor, indeed, still held courts for form's sake; but they or
their stewards had the whole management of affairs. They
demanded services, duties, and customs to which they had no
just title. Nay, they would often bring actions against their
neighbours for their own private advantage, and then send in
the bill to the parish. No objection was made, during many
years, to these proceedings, so that the rates became heavier
and heavier: nor was any person exempted from these demands,
except the footmen and gamekeepers of the squire and the
rector of the parish. They indeed were never checked in any
excess. They would come to an honest labourer's cottage, eat
his pancakes, tuck his fowls into their pockets, and cane the
poor man himself. If he went up to the great house to complain,
it was hard to get the speech of Sir Lewis; and, indeed, his only
chance of being righted was to coax the squire's pretty house-
keeper, who could do what she pleased with her master. If he
ventured to intrude upon the lord of the manor without this
precaution, he gained nothing by his pains. Sir Lewis, indeed,
would at first receive him with a civil face; for, to give him his due,
he could be a fine gentleman when he pleased. " Good day, my
friend," he would say, " what situation have you in my family ? "
" Bless your honour ! " says the poor fellow, " I am not one of
your honour's servants; I rent a small piece of ground, your
honour." " Then, you dog," quoth the squire, " what do you
mean by coming here? Has a gentleman nothing to do but to

hear the complaints of clowns? Here! Philip, James, Dick, toss this fellow in a blanket; or duck him, and set him in the stocks to dry."

One of these precious lords of the manor enclosed a deer-park; and, in order to stock it, he seized all the pretty pet fawns that his tenants had brought up, without paying them a farthing, or asking their leave. It was a sad day for the parish of St. Dennis. Indeed, I do not believe that all his oppressive exactions and long bills enraged the poor tenants so much as this cruel measure.

Yet for a long time, in spite of all these inconveniences, St. Dennis's was a very pleasant place. The people could not refrain from capering if they heard the sound of a fiddle. And, if they were inclined to be riotous, Sir Lewis had only to send for Punch, or the dancing dogs, and all was quiet again. But this could not last for ever; they began to think more and more of their condition; and, at last, a club of foul-mouthed, good-for-nothing rascals was held at the sign of the Devil, for the purpose of abusing the squire and the parson. The doctor, to own the truth, was old and indolent, extremely fat and greedy. He had not preached a tolerable sermon for a long time. The squire was still worse; so that, partly by truth and partly by falsehood, the club set the whole parish against their superiors. The boys scrawled caricatures of the clergyman upon the church-door, and shot at the landlord with pop-guns as he rode a-hunting. It was even whispered about that the lord of the manor had no right to his estate, and that, if he were compelled to produce the original title-deeds, it would be found that he only held the estate in trust for the inhabitants of the parish.

In the meantime the squire was pressed more and more for money. The parish could pay no more. The rector refused to lend a farthing. The Jews were clamorous for their money; and the landlord had no other resource than to call together the inhabitants of the parish, and to request their assistance. They now attacked him furiously about their grievances, and in-sisted that he should relinquish his oppressive powers. They insisted that his footmen should be kept in order, that the parson should pay his share of the rates, that the children of the parish should be allowed to fish in the trout-stream, and to gather blackberries in the hedges. They at last went so far as to demand that he should acknowledge that he held his estate only in trust for them. His distress compelled him to submit. They, in return, agreed to set him free from his pecuniary difficulties, and to suffer him to inhabit the manor-house; and only annoyed him from time to time by singing impudent ballads under his window.

The neighbouring gentlefolks did not look on these proceedings with much complacency. It is true that Sir Lewis and his ancestors had plagued them with lawsuits, and affronted them at county meetings. Still they preferred the insolence of a gentleman to that of the rabble, and felt some uneasiness lest the example should infect their own tenants.

A large party of them met at the house of Lord Cæsar Germain. Lord Cæsar was the proudest man in the county. His family was very ancient and illustrious, though not particularly opulent. He had invited most of his wealthy neighbours. There was Mrs. Kitty North, the relict of poor Squire Peter, respecting whom the coroner's jury had found a verdict of accidental death, but whose fate had nevertheless excited strange whispers in the neighbourhood. There was Squire Don, the owner of the great West Indian property, who was not so rich as he had formerly been, but still retained his pride, and kept up his customary pomp; so that he had plenty of plate but no breeches. There was Squire Von Blunderbussen, who had succeeded to the estates of his uncle, old Colonel Frederic Von Blunderbussen, of the hussars. The colonel was a very singular old fellow; he used to learn a page of Chambaud's grammar, and to translate *Télémaque*, every morning, and he kept six French masters to teach him to parleyvoo. Nevertheless he was a shrewd clever man, and improved his estate with so much care, sometimes by honest and sometimes by dishonest means, that he left a very pretty property to his nephew.

Lord Cæsar poured out a glass of Tokay for Mrs. Kitty. " Your health, my dear madam, I never saw you look more charming. Pray, what think you of these doings at St. Dennis's? "

" Fine doings, indeed! " interrupted Von Blunderbussen; " I wish that we had my old uncle alive, he would have had had some of them up to the halberts. He knew how to use a cat-o'-nine-tails. If things go on in this way, a gentleman will not be able to horsewhip an impudent farmer, or to say a civil word to a milk-maid."

" Indeed, it's very true, sir," said Mrs. Kitty; " their insolence is intolerable. Look at me, for instance: a poor lone woman! My dear Peter dead! I loved him: so I did; and, when he died, I was so hysterical you cannot think. And now

I cannot lean on the arm of a decent footman, or take a walk with a tall grenadier behind me, just to protect me from audacious vagabonds, but they must have their nauseous suspicions; odious creatures!"

"This must be stopped," replied Lord Cæsar. "We ought to contribute to support my poor brother-in-law against these rascals. I will write to Squire Guelf on this subject by this night's post. His name is always at the head of our county subscriptions."

If the people of St. Dennis's had been angry before, they were well-nigh mad when they heard of this conversation. The whole parish ran to the manor-house. Sir Lewis's Swiss porter shut the door against them; but they broke in and knocked him on the head for his impudence. They then seized the squire, hooted at him, pelted him, ducked him, and carried him to the watch-house. They turned the rector into the street, burnt his wig and band, and sold the church-plate by auction. They put up a painted Jezebel in the pulpit to preach. They scratched out the texts which were written round the church, and scribbled profane scraps of songs and plays in their place. They set the organ playing to pot-house tunes. Instead of being decently asked in church, they were married over a broomstick. But, of all their whims, the use of the new patent steel-traps was the most remarkable.

This trap was constructed on a completely new principle. It consisted of a cleaver hung in a frame like a window; when any poor wretch got in, down it came with a tremendous din, and took off his head in a twinkling. They got the squire into one of these machines. In order to prevent any of his partisans from getting footing in the parish, they placed traps at every corner. It was impossible to walk through the highway at broad noon without tumbling into one or other of them. No man could go about his business in security. Yet so great was the hatred which the inhabitants entertained for the old family, that a few decent, honest people, who begged them to take down the steel-traps, and to put up humane man-traps in their room, were very roughly handled for their good nature.

In the meantime the neighbouring gentry undertook a suit against the parish on the behalf of Sir Lewis's heir, and applied to Squire Guelf for his assistance.

Everybody knows that Squire Guelf is more closely tied up than any gentleman in the shire. He could, therefore, lend them no help; but he referred them to the Vestry of the Parish

of St. George in the Water.   These good people had long borne
a grudge against their neighbours on the other side of the
stream; and some mutual trespasses had lately occurred which
increased their hostility.

There was an honest Irishman, a great favourite among
them, who used to entertain them with raree-shows, and to
exhibit a magic lantern to the children on winter evenings.   He
had gone quite mad upon this subject.   Sometimes he would
call out in the middle of the street, " Take care of that corner,
neighbours; for the love of Heaven, keep clear of that post,
there is a patent steel-trap concealed thereabouts."   Sometimes he would be disturbed by frightful dreams; then he would
get up at dead of night, open his window and cry " fire," till
the parish was roused, and the engines sent for.   The pulpit of
the Parish of St. George seemed likely to fall; I believe that
the only reason was that the parson had grown too fat and
heavy; but nothing would persuade this honest man but that
it was a scheme of the people at St. Dennis's, and that they had
sawed through the pillars in order to break the rector's neck.
Once he went about with a knife in his pocket, and told all the
persons whom he met that it had been sharpened by the knife-
grinder of the next parish to cut their throats.   These extrava-
gancies had a great effect on the people; and the more so
because they were espoused by Squire Guelf's steward, who
was the most influential person in the parish.   He was a very
fair-spoken man, very attentive to the main chance, and the
idol of the old women, because he never played at skittles or
danced with the girls; and, indeed, never took any recreation
but that of drinking on Saturday nights with his friend Harry,
the Scotch pedlar.   His supporters called him Sweet William;
his enemies the Bottomless Pit.

The people of St. Dennis's, however, had their advocates.
There was Frank, the richest farmer in the parish, whose great
grandfather had been knocked on the head many years before,
in a squabble between the parish and a former landlord.   There
was Dick, the merry-andrew, rather light-fingered and riotous,
but a clever droll fellow.   Above all, there was Charley, the
publican, a jolly, fat, honest lad, a great favourite with the
women, who, if he had not been rather too fond of ale and
chuck-farthing, would have been the best fellow in the neighbourhood.

" My boys," said Charley, " this is exceedingly well for Madam
North; not that I would speak uncivilly of her; she put up my

picture in her best room, bless her for it! But, I say, this is very well for her, and for Lord Cæsar, and Squire Don, and Colonel Von; but what affair is it of yours or mine? It is not to be wondered at, that gentlemen should wish to keep poor people out of their own. But it is strange indeed that they should expect the poor themselves to combine against their own interests. If the folks at St. Dennis's should attack us we have the law and our cudgels to protect us. But why, in the name of wonder, are we to attack them? When old Sir Charles, who was lord of the manor formerly, and the parson, who was presented by him to the living, tried to bully the vestry, did not we knock their heads together, and go to meeting to hear Jeremiah Ringletub preach? And did the Squire Don, or the great Sir Lewis, that lived at that time, or the Germains, say a word against us for it? Mind your own business, my lads: law is not to be had for nothing; and we, you may be sure, shall have to pay the whole bill."

Nevertheless the people of St. George's were resolved on law. They cried out most lustily, "Squire Guelf for ever! Sweet William for ever! No steel traps!" Squire Guelf took all the rascally footmen who had worn old Sir Lewis's livery into his service. They were fed in the kitchen on the very best of everything, though they had no settlement. Many people, and the paupers in particular, grumbled at these proceedings. The steward, however, devised a way to keep them quiet.

There had lived in this parish for many years an old gentleman, named Sir Habeas Corpus. He was said by some to be of Saxon, by some of Norman, extraction. Some maintain that he was not born till after the time of Sir Charles, to whom we have before alluded. Others are of opinion that he was a legitimate son of old Lady Magna Charta, although he was long concealed and kept out of his birthright. Certain it is that he was a very benevolent person. Whenever any poor fellow was taken up on grounds which he thought insufficient, he used to attend on his behalf and bail him; and thus he had become so popular, that to take direct measures against him was out of the question.

The steward, accordingly, brought a dozen physicians to examine Sir Habeas. After consultation, they reported that he was in a very bad way, and ought not, on any account, to be allowed to stir out for several months. Fortified with this authority, the parish officers put him to bed, closed his windows, and barred his doors. They paid him every attention, and from time to time issued bulletins of his health. The steward never spoke of him without declaring that he was the best gentleman in the world; but excellent care was taken that he should never stir out of doors.   ·

When this obstacle was removed, the squire and the steward kept the parish in excellent order; flogged this man, sent that man to the stocks, and pushed forward the law-suit with a noble disregard of expense. They were, however, wanting either in skill or in fortune. And everything went against them after their antagonists had begun to employ Solicitor Nap.

Who does not know the name of Solicitor Nap? At what alehouse is not his behaviour discussed? In what print-shop is not his picture seen? Yet how little truth has been said about him! Some people hold that he used to give laudanum by pints to his six clerks for his amusement. Others, whose number has very much increased since he was killed by the gaol distemper, conceive that he was the very model of honour and good-nature. I shall try to tell the truth about him.

He was assuredly an excellent solicitor. In his way he never was surpassed. As soon as the parish began to employ him, their cause took a turn. In a very little time they were successful; and Nap became rich. He now set up for a gentleman; took possession of the old manor-house; got into the commission of the peace, and affected to be on a par with the best of the county. He governed the vestries as absolutely as the old family had done. Yet, to give him his due, he managed things with far more discretion than either Sir Lewis or the rioters who had pulled the lords of the manor down. He kept his servants in tolerable order. He removed the steel traps from the high-ways and the corners of the streets. He still left a few indeed in the more exposed parts of his premises; and set up a board announcing that traps and spring guns were set in his grounds. He brought the poor parson back to the parish; and, though he did not enable him to keep a fine house and a coach as formerly, he settled him in a snug little cottage, and allowed him a pleasant pad-nag. He whitewashed the church again; and put the stocks, which had been much wanted of late, into good repair.

With the neighbouring gentry, however, he was no favourite. He was crafty and litigious. He cared nothing for right, if he could raise a point of law against them. He pounded their cattle, broke their hedges, and seduced their tenants for them. He almost ruined Lord Cæsar with actions, in every one of which he was successful. Von Blunderbussen went to law with him for an alleged trespass, but was cast, and almost ruined by the costs of suit. He next took a fancy to the seat of Squire Don, who was, to say the truth, little better than an idiot. He asked the poor dupe to dinner, and then threatened to have him tossed in a blanket unless he would make over his estates to him. The poor squire signed and sealed a deed by which the property was assigned to Joe, a brother of Nap's, in trust for and to the use of Nap himself. The tenants, however, stood out. They maintained that the estate was entailed, and refused to pay rents to the new landlord; and in this refusal they were stoutly supported by the people in St. George's.

About the same time Nap took it into his head to match with quality, and nothing would serve him but one of the Miss Germains. Lord Cæsar swore like a trooper; but there was no help for it. Nap had twice put executions in his principal residence, and had refused to discharge the latter of the two till he had extorted a bond from his lordship which compelled him to comply, . . .

[END OF THE FIRST PART]

ON THE ATHENIAN ORATORS

" To the famous orators repair,
Those ancient, whose resistless eloquence
Wielded at will that fierce democratie,
Shook the arsenal, and fulmined over Greece
To Macedon and Artaxerxes' throne."

MILTON.

THE celebrity of the great classical writers is confined within no limits, except those which separate civilised from savage man. Their works are the common property of every polished nation. They have furnished subjects for the painter, and models for the poet. In the minds of the educated classes throughout Europe, their names are indissolubly associated with the endearing recollections of childhood, the old school-room, the dog-eared grammar, the first prize, the tears so often shed and so quickly dried. So great is the veneration with which they are regarded, that even the editors and commentators who perform the lowest menial offices to their memory, are considered, like the equerries and chamberlains of sovereign princes, as entitled to a high rank in the table of literary precedence. It is, therefore, somewhat singular that their productions should so rarely have been examined on just and philosophical principles of criticism.

The ancient writers themselves afford us but little assistance. When they particularise, they are commonly trivial: when they would generalise, they become indistinct. An exception must, indeed, be made in favour of Aristotle. Both in analysis and in combination, that great man was without a rival. No philosopher has ever possessed, in an equal degree, the talent either of separating established systems into their primary elements, or of connecting detached phenomena in harmonious systems. He was the great fashioner of the intellectual chaos; he changed its darkness into light, and its discord into order. He brought to literary researches the same vigour and amplitude of mind to which both physical and metaphysical science are so greatly indebted. His fundamental principles of criticism are excellent. To cite only a single instance:—the doctrine which he established, that poetry is an imitative art, when justly understood, is to the critic what the compass is to the navigator. With it he may venture upon the most extensive excursions. Without it he must creep cautiously along the coast, or lose himself in a trackless expanse, and trust, at best, to the guidance of an occasional star. It is a discovery which changes a caprice into a science.

The general propositions of Aristotle are valuable. But the merit of the superstructure bears no proportion to that of the foundation. This is partly to be ascribed to the character of the philosopher, who, though qualified to do all that could be done by the resolving and combining powers of the under-standing, seems not to have possessed much of sensibility or imagination. Partly, also, it may be attributed to the deficiency of materials. The great works of genius which then existed were not either sufficiently numerous or sufficiently varied to enable any man to form a perfect code of literature. To require that a critic should conceive classes of composition which had never existed, and then investigate their principles, would be as unreasonable as the demand of Nebuchadnezzar, who expected his magicians first to tell him his dream and then to interpret it.

With all his deficiencies, Aristotle was the most enlightened and profound critic of antiquity. Dionysius was far from possessing the same exquisite subtilty, or the same vast com-prehension. But he had access to a much greater number of specimens; and he had devoted himself, as it appears, more exclusively to the study of elegant literature. His peculiar judgments are of more value than his general principles. He is only the historian of literature. Aristotle is its philosopher.

Quintilian applied to general literature the same principles by which he had been accustomed to judge of the declamations of his pupils. He looks for nothing but rhetoric, and rhetoric not of the highest order. He speaks coldly of the incomparable works of Æschylus. He admires, beyond expression, those in-exhaustible mines of commonplaces, the plays of Euripides. He bestows a few vague words on the poetical character of Homer. He then proceeds to consider him merely as an orator. An orator Homer doubtless was, and a great orator. But surely nothing is more remarkable, in his admirable works, than the art with which his oratorical powers are made subservient to the purposes of poetry. Nor can I think Quintilian a great critic in his own province. Just as are many of his remarks, beautiful as are many of his illustrations, we can perpetually detect in his thoughts that flavour which the soil of despotism generally communicates to all the fruits of genius. Eloquence was, in his time, little more than a condiment which served to stimulate in a despot the jaded appetite for panegyric, an amusement for the travelled nobles and the blue-stocking matrons of Rome. It is, therefore, with him, rather a sport than a war; it is a contest of foils, not of swords. He appears to think more of the grace of the attitude than of the direction and vigour of the thrust. It must be acknowledged, in justice to Quintilian, that this is an error to which Cicero has too often given the sanction, both of his precept and of his example.

Longinus seems to have had great sensibility, but little discrimination. He gives us eloquent sentences, but no principles. It was happily said that Montesquieu ought to have changed the name of his book from *L'Esprit des Lois* to *L'Esprit sur les Lois*. In the same manner the philosopher of Palmyra ought to have entitled his famous work, not *Longinus on the Sublime*, but *The Sublimities of Longinus*. The origin of the sublime is one of the most curious and interesting subjects of inquiry that can occupy the attention of a critic. In our own country it has been discussed, with great ability, and, I think, with very little success, by Burke and Dugald Stuart. Longinus dispenses himself from all investigations of this nature, by telling his friend Terentianus that he already knows everything that can be said upon the question. It is to be regretted that Terentianus did not impart some of his knowledge to his instructor: for from Longinus we learn only that sublimity means height, or elevation.[1] This name, so commodiously vague, is applied indifferently to the noble prayer of Ajax in the *Iliad*, and to a passage of Plato about the human body, as full of conceits as an ode of Cowley. Having no fixed standard, Longinus is right only by accident. He is rather a fancier than a critic.

Modern writers have been prevented by many causes from supplying the deficiencies of their classical predecessors. At the time of the revival of literature, no man could, without great and painful labour, acquire an accurate and elegant knowledge of the ancient languages. And, unfortunately, those grammatical and philological studies, without which it was impossible to understand the great works of Athenian and Roman genius, have a tendency to contract the views and deaden the sensibility of those who follow them with extreme assiduity. A powerful mind, which has been long employed in such studies, may be compared to the gigantic spirit in the Arabian tale, who was persuaded to contract himself to small dimensions in order to enter within the enchanted vessel, and,

---

[1] Ἀκρότης καὶ ἐξοχή τις λόγων ἐστὶ τὰ ὕψη.

when his prison had been closed upon him, found himself unable to escape from the narrow boundaries to the measure of which he had reduced his stature. When the means have long been the objects of application, they are naturally substituted for the end. It was said, by Eugene of Savoy, that the greatest generals have commonly been those who have been at once raised to command, and introduced to the great operations of war, without being employed in the petty calculations and manœuvres which employ the time of an inferior officer. In literature the principle is equally sound. The great tactics of criticism will, in general, be best understood by those who have not had much practice in drilling syllables and particles.

I remember to have observed among the French Anas a ludicrous instance of this. A scholar, doubtless of great learning, recommends the study of some long Latin treatise, of which I now forget the name, on the religion, manners, government, and language of the early Greeks. " For there," says he, " you will learn everything of importance that is contained in the *Iliad* and *Odyssey*, without the trouble of reading two such tedious books." Alas! it had not occurred to the poor gentleman that all the knowledge to which he attached so much value was useful only as it illustrated the great poems which he despised, and would be as worthless for any other purpose as the mythology of Caffraria, or the vocabulary of Otaheite.

Of those scholars who have disdained to confine themselves to verbal criticism few have been successful. The ancient languages have, generally, a magical influence on their faculties. They were " fools called into a circle by Greek invocations." The *Iliad* and *Æneid* were to them not books but curiosities, or rather reliques. They no more admired those works for their merits than a good Catholic venerates the house of the Virgin at Loretto for its architecture. Whatever was classical was good. Homer was a great poet, and so was Callimachus. The epistles of Cicero were fine, and so were those of Phalaris. Even with respect to questions of evidence they fell into the same error. The authority of all narrations, written in Greek or Latin, was the same with them. It never crossed their minds that the lapse of five hundred years, or the distance of five hundred leagues, could affect the accuracy of a narration; that Livy could be a less veracious historian than Polybius; or that Plutarch could know less about the friends of Xenophon than Xenophon himself. Deceived by the distance of time, they seem to consider all the classics as contemporaries; just as I have known people in England, deceived by the distance of place, take it for granted that all persons who live in India are neighbours, and ask an inhabitant of Bombay about the health of an acquaintance at Calcutta. It is to be hoped that no barbarian deluge will ever again pass over Europe. But should such a calamity happen, it seems not improbable that some future Rollin or Gillies will compile a history of England from Miss Porter's *Scottish Chiefs*, Miss Lee's *Recess*, and Sir Nathaniel Wraxall's *Memoirs*.

It is surely time that ancient literature should be examined in a different manner, without pedantical prepossessions, but with a just allowance, at the same time, for the difference of circumstances and manners. I am far from pretending to the knowledge or ability which such a task would require. All that I mean to offer is a collection of desultory remarks upon a most interesting portion of Greek literature.

It may be doubted whether any compositions which have ever been produced in the world are equally perfect in their kind with the great Athenian orations. Genius is subject to the same laws which regulate the production of cotton and molasses. The supply adjusts itself to the demand. The quantity may be diminished by restrictions, and multiplied by bounties. The singular excellence to which eloquence attained at Athens is to be mainly attributed to the influence which it exerted there. In turbulent times, under a constitution purely democratic, among a people educated exactly to that point at which men are most susceptible of strong and sudden impressions, acute, but not sound reasoners, warm in their feelings, unfixed in their principles, and passionate admirers of fine composition, oratory received such encouragement as it has never since obtained.

The taste and knowledge of the Athenian people was a favourite object of the contemptuous derision of Samuel Johnson; a man who knew nothing of Greek literature beyond the common school-books, and who seems to have brought to what he had read scarcely more than the discernment of a common school-boy. He used to assert, with that arrogant absurdity which, in spite of his great abilities and virtues, renders him, perhaps, the most ridiculous character in literary history, that Demosthenes spoke to a people of brutes; to a barbarous people; that there could have been no civilisation before the invention of printing. Johnson was a keen but a very narrow-minded observer of mankind. He perpetually confounded their general nature with their particular circumstances. He knew London intimately. The sagacity of his remarks on its society is perfectly astonishing. But Fleet Street was the world to him. He saw that Londoners who did not read were profoundly ignorant; and he inferred that a Greek, who had few or no books, must have been as uninformed as one of Mr. Thrale's draymen.

There seems to be, on the contrary, every reason to believe, that, in general intelligence, the Athenian populace far surpassed the lower orders of any community that has ever existed. It must be considered, that to be a citizen was to be a legislator, a soldier, a judge, one upon whose voice might depend the fate of the wealthiest tributary state, of the most eminent public man. The lowest offices, both of agriculture and of trade, were, in common, performed by slaves. The commonwealth supplied its meanest members with the support of life, the opportunity of leisure, and the means of amusement. Books were indeed few; but they were excellent; and they were accurately known. It is not by turning over libraries, but by repeatedly perusing and intently contemplating a few great models, that the mind is best disciplined. A man of letters must now read much that he soon forgets, and much from which he learns nothing worthy to be remembered. The best works employ, in general, but a small portion of his time. Demosthenes is said to have transcribed six times the history of Thucydides. If he had been a young politician of the present age, he might in the same space of time have skimmed innumerable newspapers and pamphlets. I do not condemn that desultory mode of study which the state of things, in our day, renders a matter of necessity. But I may be allowed to doubt whether the changes on which the admirers of modern institutions delight to dwell have improved our condition so much in reality as in appearance. Rumford, it is said, proposed to the Elector of Bavaria a scheme for feeding his soldiers at a much cheaper rate than formerly. His plan was simply to compel them to masticate their food thoroughly. A small quantity, thus eaten, would, according to that famous projector, afford more sustenance than a large meal hastily devoured. I do not know how Rumford's proposition was received; but to the mind, I believe, it will be found more nutritious to digest a page than to devour a volume.

Books, however, were the least part of the education of an Athenian citizen. Let us, for a moment, transport ourselves in thought, to that glorious city.   Let us imagine that we are entering its gates, in the time of its power and glory.   A crowd is assembled round a portico.   All are gazing with delight at the entablature; for Phidias is putting up the frieze.   We turn into another street; a rhapsodist is reciting there: men, women, children are thronging round him: the tears are running down their cheeks: their eyes are fixed: their very breath is still; for he is telling how Priam fell at the feet of Achilles, and kissed those hands—the terrible, the murderous—which had slain so many of his sons.[1]   We enter the public place; there is a ring of youths, all leaning forward, with sparkling eyes, and gestures of expectation.   Socrates is pitted against the famous atheist, from Ionia, and has just brought him to a contradiction in terms.   But we are interrupted.   The herald is crying, " Room for the Prytanes." The general assembly is to meet.   The people are swarming in on every side.   Proclamation is made, " Who wishes to speak? " There is a shout, and a clapping of hands; Pericles is mounting the stand.   Then for a play of Sophocles; and away to sup with Aspasia.   I know of no modern university which has so excellent a system of education.

Knowledge thus acquired and opinions thus formed were, indeed, likely to be, in some respects, defective.   Propositions which are advanced in discourse generally result from a partial view of the question, and cannot be kept under examination long enough to be corrected.   Men of great conversational powers almost universally practise a sort of lively sophistry and exaggeration, which deceives, for the moment, both themselves and their auditors.   Thus we see doctrines, which cannot bear a close inspection, triumph perpetually in drawing-rooms, in debating societies, and even in legislative or judicial assemblies. To the conversational education of the Athenians I am inclined to attribute the great looseness of reasoning which is remarkable in most of their scientific writings.   Even the most illogical of modern writers would stand perfectly aghast at the puerile fallacies which seem to have deluded some of the greatest men of antiquity.   Sir Thomas Lethbridge would stare at the political economy of Xenophon; and the author of *Soirées de Pétersbourg* would be ashamed of some of the metaphysical arguments of Plato.   But the very circumstances which retarded the growth of science were peculiarly favourable to the cultivation of eloquence.   From the early habit of taking a share in animated

---

[1] καὶ κύσε χεῖρας,
δεινὰς, ἀνδροφόνους, αἴ οἱ πολέας κτάνον υἷας.

discussion the intelligent student would derive that readiness of resource, that copiousness of language, and that knowledge of the temper and understanding of an audience, which are far more valuable to an orator than the greatest logical powers.

Horace has prettily compared poems to those paintings of which the effect varies as the spectator changes his stand. The same remark applies with at least equal justice to speeches. They must be read with the temper of those to whom they were addressed, or they must necessarily appear to offend against the laws of taste and reason; as the finest picture, seen in a light different from that for which it was designed, will appear fit only for a sign. This is perpetually forgotten by those who criticise oratory. Because they are reading at leisure, pausing at every line, reconsidering every argument, they forget that the hearers were hurried from point to point too rapidly to detect the fallacies through which they were conducted; that they had no time to disentangle sophisms, or to notice slight inaccuracies of expression; that elaborate excellence, either of reasoning or of language, would have been absolutely thrown away. To recur to the analogy of the sister art, these connoisseurs examine a panorama through a microscope, and quarrel with a scene-painter because he does not give to his work the exquisite finish of Gerard Dow.

Oratory is to be estimated on principles different from those which are applied to other productions. Truth is the object of philosophy and history. Truth is the object even of those works which are peculiarly called works of fiction, but which, in fact, bear the same relation to history which algebra bears to arithmetic. The merit of poetry, in its wildest forms, still consists in its truth, truth conveyed to the understanding, not directly by the words, but circuitously by means of imaginative associations, which serve as its conductors. The object of oratory alone is not truth, but persuasion. The admiration of the multitude does not make Moore a greater poet than Coleridge, or Beattie a greater philosopher than Berkeley. But the criterion of eloquence is different. A speaker who exhausts the whole philosophy of a question, who displays every grace of style, yet produces no effect on his audience, may be a great essayist, a great statesman, a great master of composition; but he is not an orator. If he miss the mark, it makes no difference whether he have taken aim too high or too low.

The effect of the great freedom of the press in England has been, in a great measure, to destroy this distinction, and to leave among us little of what I call oratory proper. Our legislators, our candidates, on great occasions even our advocates, address themselves less to the audience than to the reporters. They think less of the few hearers than of the innumerable readers. At Athens the case was different; there the only object of the speaker was immediate conviction and persuasion. He, therefore, who would justly appreciate the merit of the Grecian orators should place himself, as nearly as possible, in the situation of their auditors: he should divest himself of his modern feelings and acquirements, and make the prejudices and interests of the Athenian citizen his own. He who studies their works in this spirit will find that many of those things which, to an English reader, appear to be blemishes—the frequent violation of those excellent rules of evidence by which our courts of law are regulated, the introduction of extraneous matter, the reference to considerations of political expediency in judicial investigations, the assertions, without proof, the passionate entreaties, the furious invectives—are really proofs of the prudence and address of the speakers. He must not dwell maliciously on arguments or phrases, but acquiesce in his first impressions. It requires repeated perusal and reflection to decide rightly on any other portion of literature. But with respect to works of which the merit depends on their instantaneous effect the most hasty judgment is likely to be best.

The history of eloquence at Athens is remarkable. From a very early period great speakers had flourished there. Pisistratus and Themistocles are said to have owed much of their influence to their talents for debate. We learn, with more certainty, that Pericles was distinguished by extraordinary oratorical powers. The substance of some of his speeches is transmitted to us by Thucydides; and that excellent writer has doubtless faithfully reported the general line of his arguments. But the manner, which in oratory is of at least as much consequence as the matter, was of no importance to his narration. It is evident that he has not attempted to preserve it. Throughout his work, every speech on every subject, whatever may have been the character of the dialect of the speaker, is in exactly the same form. The grave king of Sparta, the furious demagogue of Athens, the general encouraging his army, the captive supplicating for his life, all are represented as speakers in one unvaried style, a style moreover wholly unfit for oratorical purposes. His mode of reasoning is singularly elliptical, in reality most consecutive, yet in appearance often incoherent.

His meaning, in itself sufficiently perplexing, is compressed into the fewest possible words. His great fondness for antithetical expression has not a little conduced to this effect. Every one must have observed how much more the sense is condensed in the verses of Pope and his imitators, who never ventured to continue the same clause from couplet to couplet, than in those of poets who allow themselves that licence. Every artificial division, which is strongly marked, and which frequently recurs, has the same tendency. The natural and perspicuous expression which spontaneously rises to the mind will often refuse to accommodate itself to such a form. It is necessary either to expand it into weakness, or to compress it into almost impenetrable density. The latter is generally the choice of an able man, and was assuredly the choice of Thucydides.

It is scarcely necessary to say that such speeches could never have been delivered. They are perhaps among the most difficult passages in the Greek language, and would probably have been scarcely more intelligible to an Athenian auditor than to a modern reader. Their obscurity was acknowledged by Cicero, who was as intimate with the literature and language of Greece as the most accomplished of its natives, and who seems to have held a respectable rank among the Greek authors. Their difficulty to a modern reader lies, not in the words, but in the reasoning. A dictionary is of far less use in studying them than a clear head and a close attention to the context. They are valuable to the scholar as displaying, beyond almost any other compositions, the powers of the finest of languages: they are valuable to the philosopher as illustrating the morals and manners of a most interesting age; they abound in just thought and energetic expression. But they do not enable us to form any accurate opinion on the merits of the early Greek orators.

Though it cannot be doubted that, before the Persian wars, Athens had produced eminent speakers, yet the period during which eloquence most flourished among the citizens was by no means that of her greatest power and glory. It commenced at the close of the Peloponnesian war. In fact, the steps by which Athenian oratory approached to its finished excellence seem to have been almost contemporaneous with those by which the Athenian character and the Athenian empire sunk to degradation. At the time when the little commonwealth achieved those victories which twenty-five eventful centuries have left un-equalled, eloquence was in its infancy. The deliverers of Greece became its plunderers and oppressors. Unmeasured exaction, atrocious vengeance, the madness of the multitude, the tyranny of the great, filled the Cyclades with tears, and blood, and mourning. The sword unpeopled whole islands in a day. The plough passed over the ruins of famous cities. The imperial republic sent forth her children by thousands to pine in the quarries of Syracuse, or to feed the vultures of Ægospotami. She was at length reduced by famine and slaughter to humble herself before her enemies, and to purchase existence by the sacrifice of her empire and her laws. During these disastrous and gloomy years, oratory was advancing towards its highest excellence. And it was when the moral, the political, and the military character of the people was most utterly degraded, it was when the viceroy of a Macedonian sovereign gave law to Greece, that the courts of Athens witnessed the most splendid contest of eloquence that the world has ever known.

The causes of this phenomenon it is not, I think, difficult to assign. The division of labour operates on the productions of the orator as it does on those of the mechanic. It was remarked by the ancients that the Pentathlete, who divided his attention between several exercises, though he could not vie with a boxer in the use of the cestus, or with one who had confined his attention to running in the contest of the stadium, yet enjoyed far greater general vigour and health than either. It is the same with the mind. The superiority in technical skill is often more than compensated by the inferiority in general intelligence. And this is peculiarly the case in politics. States have always been best governed by men who have taken a wide view of public affairs, and who have rather a general acquaintance with many sciences than a perfect mastery of one. The union of the political and military departments in Greece contributed not a little to the splendour of its early history. After their separation more skilful generals and greater speakers appeared; but the breed of statesmen dwindled and became almost extinct. Themistocles or Pericles would have been no match for Demosthenes in the assembly, or for Iphicrates in the field. But surely they were incomparably better fitted than either for the supreme direction of affairs.

There is indeed a remarkable coincidence between the progress of the art of war, and that of the art of oratory, among the Greeks. They both advanced to perfection by contemporaneous steps, and from similar causes. The early speakers, like the early warriors of Greece, were merely a militia. It was found that in both employments practice and discipline gave superiority.[1]   Each pursuit therefore became first an art, and then a trade.   In proportion as the professors of each became more expert in their particular craft, they became less respectable in their general character.   Their skill had been obtained at too great expense to be employed only from disinterested views.   Thus, the soldiers forgot that they were citizens, and the orators that they were statesmen.   I know not to what Demosthenes and his famous contemporaries can be so justly compared as to those mercenary troops who, in their time, overran Greece; or those who, from similar causes, were some centuries ago the scourge of the Italian republics—perfectly acquainted with every part of their profession, irresistible in the field, powerful to defend or to destroy, but defending without love, and destroying without hatred.   We may despise the characters of these political *Condottieri;* but it is impossible to examine the system of their tactics without being amazed at its perfection.

I had intended to proceed to this examination, and to consider separately the remains of Lysias, of Æschines, of Demosthenes, and of Isocrates, who, though strictly speaking he was rather a pamphleteer than an an orator, deserves, on many accounts, a place in such a disquisition.   The length of my prolegomena and digressions compels me to postpone this part of the subject to another occasion.   A magazine is certainly a delightful invention for a very idle or a very busy man.   He is not compelled to complete his plan or to adhere to his subject.

[1] It has often occurred to me, that to the circumstances mentioned in the text is to be referred one of the most remarkable events in Grecian history; I mean the silent but rapid downfall of the Lacedæmonian power. Soon after the termination of the Peloponnesian war, the strength of Lacedæmon began to decline.   Its military discipline, its social institutions, were the same.   Agesilaus, during whose reign the change took place, was the ablest of its kings.   Yet the Spartan armies were frequently defeated in pitched battles—an occurrence considered impossible in the earlier ages of Greece.   They are allowed to have fought most bravely; yet they were no longer attended by the success to which they had formerly been accustomed.   No solution of these circumstances is offered, as far as I know, by any ancient author.   The real cause, I conceive, was this.   The Lacedæmonians, alone among the Greeks, formed a permanent standing army.   While the citizens of other commonwealths were engaged in agriculture and trade, they had no employment whatever but the study of military discipline.   Hence, during the Persian and Peloponnesian wars, they had that advantage over their neighbours which regular troops always possess over militia.   This advantage they lost, when other states began, at a later period, to employ mercenary forces, who were probably as superior to them in the art of war as they had hitherto been to their antagonists.

He may ramble as far as he is inclined, and stop as soon as
he is tired. No one takes the trouble to recollect his contradictory opinions or his unredeemed pledges. He may be as
superficial, as inconsistent, and as careless as he chooses.
Magazines resemble those little angels, who, according to the
pretty Rabbinical tradition, are generated every morning by
the brook which rolls over the flowers of Paradise, whose life
is a song, who warble till sunset, and then sink back without
regret into nothingness. Such spirits have nothing to do with
the detecting spear of Ithuriel or the victorious sword of Michael.
It is enough for them to please and be forgotten.

A PROPHETIC ACCOUNT OF A GRAND NATIONAL EPIC
    POEM, TO BE ENTITLED " THE WELLINGTONIAD,"
    AND TO BE PUBLISHED A.D. 2824

(NOVEMBER, 1824)

How I became a prophet it is not very important to the reader
to know. Nevertheless I feel all the anxiety which, under
similar circumstances, troubled the sensitive mind of Sidrophel;
and, like him, am eager to vindicate myself from the suspicion
of having practised forbidden arts, or held intercourse with
beings of another world. I solemnly declare, therefore, that I
never saw a ghost, like Lord Lyttleton; consulted a gipsy, like
Josephine; or heard my name pronounced by an absent person,
like Dr. Johnson. Though it is now almost as usual for gentlemen to appear at the moment of their death to their friends as
to call on them during their life, none of my acquaintance have
been so polite as to pay me that customary attention. I have
derived my knowledge neither from the dead nor from the
living; neither from the lines of a hand, nor from the grounds
of a tea-cup; neither from the stars of the firmament, nor from
the fiends of the abyss. I have never, like the Wesley family,
heard " that mighty leading angel," who " drew after him the
third part of heaven's sons," scratching in my cupboard. I
have never been enticed to sign any of those delusive bonds
which have been the ruin of so many poor creatures; and,
having always been an indifferent horseman, I have been careful
not to venture myself on a broomstick.

My insight into futurity, like that of George Fox the quaker, and that of our great and philosophic poet, Lord Byron, is derived from simple presentiment. This is a far less artificial process than those which are employed by some others. Yet my predictions will, I believe, be found more correct than theirs, or, at all events, as Sir Benjamin Backbite says in the play, " more circumstantial."

I prophesy then, that, in the year 2824, according to our present reckoning, a grand national Epic Poem, worthy to be compared with the *Iliad*, the *Æneid*, or the *Jerusalem*, will be published in London.

Men naturally take an interest in the adventures of every eminent writer. I will, therefore, gratify the laudable curiosity, which, on this occasion, will doubtless be universal, by prefixing to my account of the poem a concise memoir of the poet.

Richard Quongti will be born at Westminster on the 1st of July, 2786. He will be the younger son of the younger branch of one of the most respectable families in England. He will be lineally descended from Quongti, the famous Chinese liberal, who, after the failure of the heroic attempt of his party to obtain a constitution from the Emperor Fim Fam, will take refuge in England, in the twenty-third century. Here his descendants will obtain considerable note; and one branch of the family will be raised to the peerage.

Richard, however, though destined to exalt his family to distinction far nobler than any which wealth or titles can bestow, will be born to a very scanty fortune. He will display in his early youth such striking talents as will attract the notice of Viscount Quongti, his third cousin, then secretary of state for the Steam Department. At the expense of this eminent nobleman, he will be sent to prosecute his studies at the university of Tombuctoo. To that illustrious seat of the muses all the ingenuous youth of every country will then be attracted by the high scientific character of Professor Quashaboo, and the eminent literary attainments of Professor Kissey Kickey. In spite of this formidable competition, however, Quongti will acquire the highest honours in every department of knowledge, and will obtain the esteem of his associates by his amiable and unaffected manners. The guardians of the young Duke of Carrington, premier peer of England, and the last remaining scion of the ancient and illustrious house of Smith, will be desirous to secure so able an instructor for their ward. With the duke, Quongti will perform the grand tour, and visit the polished courts of

Sydney and Capetown. After prevailing on his pupil, with great difficulty, to subdue a violent and imprudent passion which he had conceived for a Hottentot lady, of great beauty and accomplishments indeed, but of dubious character, he will travel with him to the United States of America. But that tremendous war which will be fatal to American liberty will, at that time, be raging through the whole federation. At New York the travellers will hear of the final defeat and death of the illustrious champion of freedom, Jonathan Higginbottom, and of the elevation of Ebenezer Hogsflesh to the perpetual Presidency. They will not choose to proceed in a journey which would expose them to the insults of that brutal soldiery, whose cruelty and rapacity will have devastated Mexico and Colombia, and now, at length, enslaved their own country.

On their return to England, A.D. 2810, the death of the duke will compel his preceptor to seek for a subsistence by literary labours. His fame will be raised by many small productions of considerable merit; and he will at last obtain a permanent place in the highest class of writers by his great epic poem.

The celebrated work will become, with unexampled rapidity, a popular favourite. The sale will be so beneficial to the author that, instead of going about the dirty streets on his velocipede, he will be enabled to set up his balloon.

The character of this noble poem will be so finely and justly given in the *Tombuctoo Review* for April 2825, that I cannot refrain from translating the passage. The author will be our poet's old preceptor, Professor Kissey Kickey.

" In pathos, in splendour of language, in sweetness of versification, Mr. Quongti has long been considered as unrivalled. In his exquisite poem on the *Ornithorhynchus Paradoxus* all these qualities are displayed in their greatest perfection. How exquisitely does that work arrest and embody the undefined and vague shadows which flit over an imaginative mind. The cold worldling may not comprehend it; but it will find a response in the bosom of every youthful poet, of every enthusiastic lover, who has seen an *Ornithorhynchus Paradoxus* by moonlight. But we were yet to learn that he possessed the comprehension, the judgment, and the fertility of mind indispensable to the epic poet.

" It is difficult to conceive a plot more perfect than that of the ' Wellingtoniad.' It is most faithful to the manners of the age to which it relates. It preserves exactly all the historical circumstances, and interweaves them most artfully with all the *speciosa miracula* of supernatural agency."

Thus far the learned Professor of Humanity in the University of Tombuctoo. I fear that the critics of our time will form an opinion diametrically opposite as to these very points. Some will, I fear, be disgusted by the machinery, which is derived from the mythology of ancient Greece. I can only say that, in the twenty-ninth century, that machinery will be universally in use among poets; and that Quongti will use it, partly in conformity with the general practice, and partly from a veneration, perhaps excessive, for the great remains of classical antiquity, which will then, as now, be assiduously read by every man of education; though Tom Moore's songs will be forgotten, and only three copies of Lord Bryon's works will exist: one in the possession of King George the Nineteenth, one in the Duke of Carrington's collection, and one in the library of the British Museum. Finally, should any good people be concerned to hear that Pagan fictions will so long retain their influence over literature, let them reflect that, as the Bishop of St. David's says, in his " Proofs of the Inspiration of the Sibylline Verses," read at the last meeting of the Royal Society of Literature, " at all events, a Pagan is not a Papist."

Some readers of the present day may think that Quongti is by no means entitled to the compliments which his negro critic pays him on his adherence to the historical circumstances of the time in which he has chosen his subject; that, where he introduces any trait of our manners, it is in the wrong place, and that he confounds the customs of our age with those of much more remote periods. I can only say that the charge is infinitely more applicable to Homer, Virgil, and Tasso. If, therefore, the reader should detect, in the following abstract of the plot, any little deviation from strict historical accuracy, let him reflect, for a moment, whether Agamemnon would not have found as much to censure in the *Iliad*, Dido in the *Æneid*, or Godfrey in the *Jerusalem*. Let him not suffer his opinions to depend on circumstances which cannot possibly affect the truth or falsehood of the representation. If it be impossible for a single man to kill hundreds in battle, the impossibility is not diminished by distance of time. If it be as certain that Rinaldo never disenchanted a forest in Palestine as it is that the Duke of Wellington never disenchanted the forest of Soignies, can we, as rational men, tolerate the one story and ridicule the other? Of this, at least, I am certain, that whatever excuse we have

for admiring the plots of those famous poems our children will
have for extolling that of the " Wellingtoniad."

I shall proceed to give a sketch of the narrative.   The subject
is " The Reign of the Hundred Days."

BOOK I

The poem commences, in form, with a solemn proposition of
the subject.   Then the muse is invoked to give the poet accurate
information as to the causes of so terrible a commotion.   The
answer to this question, being, it is to be supposed, the joint
production of the poet and the muse, ascribes the event to circumstances which have hitherto eluded all the research of
political writers, namely, the influence of the god Mars, who,
we are told, had some forty years before usurped the conjugal
rights of old Carlo Buonaparte, and given birth to Napoleon.
By his incitement it was that the emperor with his devoted
companions was now on the sea, returning to his ancient
dominions.   The gods were at present, fortunately for the
adventurer, feasting with the Ethiopians, whose entertainments, according to the ancient custom described by Homer,
they annually attended, with the same sort of condescending
gluttony which now carries the cabinet to Guildhall on the 9th
of November.   Neptune was, in consequence, absent, and unable to prevent the enemy of his favourite island from crossing
his element.   Boreas, however, who had his abode on the banks
of the Russian ocean, and who, like Thetis in the *Iliad*, was not
of sufficient quality to have an invitation to Ethiopia, resolves
to destroy the armament which brings war and danger to his
beloved Alexander.   He accordingly raises a storm which is
most powerfully described.   Napoleon bewails the inglorious
fate for which he seems to be reserved.   " Oh! thrice happy,"
says he, " those who were frozen to death at Krasnoi, or
slaughtered at Leipsic.   Oh, Kutusoff, bravest of the Russians,
wherefore was I not permitted to fall by thy victorious sword? "
He then offers a prayer to Æolus, and vows to him a sacrifice of
a black ram.   In consequence, the god recalls his turbulent
subject; the sea is calmed; and the ship anchors in the port of
Frejus.   Napoleon and Bertrand, who is always called the
faithful Bertrand, land to explore the country; Mars meets
them disguised as a lancer of the guard, wearing the cross of the
legion of honour.   He advises them to apply for necessaries of all
kinds to the governor, shows them the way, and disappears
with a strong smell of gunpowder.   Napoleon makes a pathetic

speech, and enters the governor's house. Here he sees hanging
up a fine print of the battle of Austerlitz, himself in the foreground giving his orders. This puts him in high spirits; he
advances and salutes the governor, who receives him most
loyally, gives him an entertainment, and, according to the usage
of all epic hosts, insists after dinner on a full narration of all
that has happened to him since the battle of Leipsic.

BOOK II

Napoleon carries his narrative from the battle of Leipsic to
his abdication. But, as we shall have a great quantity of
fighting on our hands, I think it best to omit the details.

BOOK III

Napoleon describes his sojourn at Elba, and his return; how
he was driven by stress of weather to Sardinia, and fought with
the harpies there; how he was then carried southward to Sicily,
where he generously took on board an English sailor, whom a
man-of-war had unhappily left there, and who was in imminent
danger of being devoured by the Cyclops; how he landed in the
bay of Naples, saw the Sibyl, and descended to Tartarus; how
he held a long and pathetic conversation with Poniatowski,
whom he found wandering unburied on the banks of Styx; how
he swore to give him a splendid funeral; how he had also an
affectionate interview with Desaix; how Moreau and Sir Ralph
Abercrombie fled at the sight of him. He relates that he then
re-embarked, and met with nothing of importance till the commencement of the storm with which the poem opens.

BOOK IV

The scene changes to Paris. Fame, in the garb of an express,
brings intelligence of the landing of Napoleon. The king performs a sacrifice: but the entrails are unfavourable; and the
victim is without a heart. He prepares to encounter the in-
vader. A young captain of the guard, the son of Maria
Antoinette by Apollo, in the shape of a fiddler, rushes in to tell
him that Napoleon is approaching with a vast army. The royal
forces are drawn out for battle. Full catalogues are given of
the regiments on both sides; their colonels, lieutenant-colonels,
and uniform.

BOOK V

The king comes forward and defies Napoleon to single combat.
Napoleon accepts it. Sacrifices are offered. The ground is

measured by Ney and Macdonald.   The combatants advance.
Louis snaps his pistol in vain.   The bullet of Napoleon, on the
contrary, carries off the tip of the king's ear.   Napoleon then
rushes on him sword in hand.   But Louis snatches up a stone,
such as ten men of those degenerate days will be unable to move,
and hurls it at his antagonist.   Mars averts it.   Napoleon then
seizes Louis, and is about to strike a fatal blow, when Bacchus
intervenes, like Venus in the third book of the *Iliad*, bears off
the king in a thick cloud, and seats him in an hotel at Lille, with
a bottle of Maraschino and a basin of soup before him.   Both
armies instantly proclaim Napoleon emperor.

BOOK VI

Neptune, returned from his Ethiopian revels, sees with rage
the events which have taken place in Europe.   He flies to the
cave of Alecto, and drags out the fiend, commanding her to
excite universal hostility against Napoleon.   The Fury repairs
to Lord Castlereagh; and, as, when she visited Turnus, she
assumed the form of an old woman, she here appears in the
kindred shape of Mr. Vansittart, and in an impassioned address
exhorts his lordship to war.   His lordship, like Turnus, treats
this unwonted monitor with great disrespect, tells him that he
is an old doting fool, and advises him to look after the ways and
means, and leave questions of peace and war to his betters.
The Fury then displays all her terrors.   The neat powdered
hair bristles up into snakes; the black stockings appear clotted
with blood; and, brandishing a torch, she announces her name
and mission.   Lord Castlereagh, seized with fury, flies instantly
to the parliament, and recommends war with a torrent of
eloquent invective.   All the members instantly clamour for
vengeance, seize their arms which are hanging round the walls
of the House, and rush forth to prepare for instant hostilities.

BOOK VII

In this book intelligence arrives at London of the flight of the
Duchess d'Angoulême from France.   It is stated that this
heroine, armed from head to foot, defended Bordeaux against
the adherents of Napoleon, and that she fought hand to hand
with Clausel, and beat him down with an enormous stone.
Deserted by her followers, she at last, like Turnus, plunged,
armed as she was, into the Garonne, and swam to an English
ship which lay off the coast.   This intelligence yet more in-
flames the English to war.

L 2

A yet bolder flight than any which has been mentioned
follows. The Duke of Wellington goes to take leave of the
duchess; and a scene passes quite equal to the famous interview of Hector and Andromache. Lord Douro is frightened
at his father's feather, but begs for his epaulette.

BOOK VIII

Neptune, trembling for the event of the war, implores Venus,
who, as the offspring of his element, naturally venerates him,
to procure from Vulcan a deadly sword and a pair of unerring
pistols for the duke. They are accordingly made, and superbly
decorated. The sheath of the sword, like the shield of Achilles,
is carved, in exquisitely fine miniature, with scenes from the
common life of the period; a dance at Almack's, a boxing match
at the Fives-court, a lord mayor's procession, and a man hanging. All these are fully and elegantly described. The duke
thus armed hastens to Brussels.

BOOK IX

The duke is received at Brussels by the King of the Netherlands with great magnificence. He is informed of the approach
of the armies of all the confederate kings. The poet, however,
with a laudable zeal for the glory of his country, completely
passes over the exploits of the Austrians in Italy, and the dis-
cussions of the congress. England and France, Wellington and
Napoleon, almost exclusively occupy his attention. Several
days are spent at Brussels in revelry. The English heroes
astonish their allies by exhibiting splendid games, similar to
those which draw the flower of the British aristocracy to New-
market and Moulsey Hurst, and which will be considered by
our descendants with as much veneration as the Olympian and
Isthmian contests by classical students of the present time. In
the combat of the cestus, Shaw, the life-guardsman, vanquishes
the Prince of Orange, and obtains a bull as a prize. In the
horse-race, the Duke of Wellington and Lord Uxbridge ride
against each other; the duke is victorious, and is rewarded
with twelve opera-girls. On the last day of the festivities, a
splendid dance takes place, at which all the heroes attend.

BOOK X

Mars, seeing the English army thus inactive, hastens to rouse
Napoleon, who, conducted by Night and Silence, unexpectedly
attacks the Prussians. The slaughter is immense. Napoleon

kills many whose histories and families are happily particularised. He slays Herman, the craniologist, who dwelt by the linden-shadowed Elbe, and measured with his eye the skulls of all who walked through the streets of Berlin. Alas! his own skull is now cleft by the Corsican sword. Four pupils of the University of Jena advance together to encounter the emperor; at four blows he destroys them all. Blucher rushes to arrest the devastation; Napoleon strikes him to the ground, and is on the point of killing him, but Gneisenau, Ziethen, Bulow, and all the other heroes of the Prussian army, gather round him, and bear the venerable chief to a distance from the field. The slaughter is continued till night. In the meantime Neptune has despatched Fame to bear the intelligence to the duke, who is dancing at Brussels. The whole army is put in motion. The Duke of Brunswick's horse speaks to admonish him of his danger, but in vain.

BOOK XI

Picton, the Duke of Brunswick, and the Prince of Orange, engage Ney at Quatre Bras. Ney kills the Duke of Brunswick, and strips him, sending his belt to Napoleon. The English fall back on Waterloo. Jupiter calls a council of the gods, and commands that none shall interfere on either side. Mars and Neptune make very eloquent speeches. The battle of Waterloo commences. Napoleon kills Picton and Delancy. Ney engages Ponsonby and kills him. The Prince of Orange is wounded by Soult. Lord Uxbridge flies to check the carnage. He is severely wounded by Napoleon, and only saved by the assistance of Lord Hill. In the meantime the duke makes a tremendous carnage among the French. He encounters General Duhesme and vanquishes him, but spares his life. He kills Toubert, who kept the gaming-house in the Palais Royal, and Maronet, who loved to spend whole nights in drinking champagne. Clerval, who had been hooted from the stage, and had then become a captain in the Imperial Guard, wished that he had still continued to face the more harmless enmity of the Parisian pit. But Larrey, the son of Esculapius, whom his father had instructed in all the secrets of his art, and who was surgeon-general of the French army, embraced the knees of the destroyer, and conjured him not to give death to one whose office it was to give life. The duke raised him, and bade him live.

But we must hasten to the close. Napoleon rushes to

encounter Wellington. Both armies stand in mute amaze. The heroes fire their pistols; that of Napoleon misses, but that of Wellington, formed by the hand of Vulcan, and primed by the Cyclops, wounds the Emperor in the thigh. He flies, and takes refuge among his troops. The flight becomes promiscuous. The arrival of the Prussians, from a motive of patriotism, the poet completely passes over.

BOOK XII

Things are now hastening to the catastrophe. Napoleon flies to London, and, seating himself on the hearth of the regent, embraces the household gods and conjures him, by the venerable age of George III., and by the opening perfections of the Princess Charlotte, to spare him. The prince is inclined to do so; when, looking on his breast, he sees there the belt of the Duke of Brunswick. He instantly draws his sword, and is about to stab the destroyer of his kinsman. Piety and hospitality, however, restrain his hand. He takes a middle course, and condemns Napoleon to be exposed on a desert island. The King of France re-enters Paris; and the poem concludes.

WILLIAM PITT

WILLIAM PITT, the second son of William Pitt, Earl of Chatham, and of Lady Hester Grenville, daughter of Hester, Countess Temple, was born on the 28th of May 1759. The child inherited a name which, at the time of his birth, was the most illustrious in the civilised world, and was pronounced by every Englishman with pride, and by every enemy of England with mingled admiration and terror. During the first year of his life, every month had its illuminations and bonfires, and every wind brought some messenger charged with joyful tidings and hostile standards. In Westphalia the English infantry won a great battle which arrested the armies of Louis the Fifteenth in the midst of a career of conquest: Boscawen defeated one French fleet on the coast of Portugal: Hawke put to flight another in the Bay of Biscay: Johnson took Niagara: Amherst took Ticonderoga: Wolfe died by the most enviable of deaths under the walls of Quebec: Clive destroyed a Dutch armament in the Hoogley, and established the English supremacy in Bengal: Coote routed

Lally at Wandewash, and established the English supremacy in the Carnatic. The nation, while loudly applauding the successful warriors, considered them all, on sea and on land, in Europe, in America, and in Asia, merely as instruments which received their direction from one superior mind. It was the great William Pitt, the great commoner, who had vanquished French marshals in Germany, and French admirals on the Atlantic; who had conquered for his country one great empire on the frozen shores of Ontario, and another under the tropical sun near the mouths of the Ganges. It was not in the nature of things that popularity such as he at this time enjoyed should be permanent. That popularity had lost its gloss before his children were old enough to understand that their father was a great man. He was at length placed in situations in which neither his talents for administration nor his talents for debate appeared to the best advantage. The energy and decision which had eminently fitted him for the direction of war were not needed in time of peace. The lofty and spirit-stirring eloquence, which had made him supreme in the House of Commons, often fell dead on the House of Lords. A cruel malady racked his joints, and left his joints only to fall on his nerves and on his brain. During the closing years of his life, he was odious to the court, and yet was not on cordial terms with the great body of the opposition. Chatham was only the ruin of Pitt, but an awful and majestic ruin, not to be contemplated by any man of sense and feeling without emotions resembling those which are excited by the remains of the Parthenon and of the Colosseum. In one respect the old statesman was eminently happy. Whatever might be the vicissitudes of his public life, he never failed to find peace and love by his own hearth. He loved all his children, and was loved by them; and, of all his children, the one of whom he was fondest and proudest was his second son.

The child's genius and ambition displayed themselves with a rare and almost unnatural precocity. At seven, the interest which he took in grave subjects, the ardour with which he pursued his studies, and the sense and vivacity of his remarks on books and on events, amazed his parents and instructors. One of his sayings of this date was reported to his mother by his tutor. In August 1766, when the world was agitated by the news that Mr. Pitt had become Earl of Chatham, little William exclaimed, " I am glad that I am not the eldest son. I want to speak in the House of Commons like papa." A letter is extant in which Lady Chatham, a woman of considerable abilities, remarked to her lord that their younger son at twelve had left far behind him his elder brother, who was fifteen. " The fineness," she wrote, " of William's mind makes him enjoy with the greatest pleasure what would be above the reach of any other creature of his small age." At fourteen the lad was in intellect a man. Hayley, who met him at Lyme in the summer of 1773, was astonished, delighted, and somewhat over-awed, by hearing wit and wisdom from so young a mouth. The poet, indeed, was afterwards sorry that his shyness had prevented him from submitting the plan of an extensive literary work, which he was then meditating, to the judgment of this extra-ordinary boy. The boy, indeed, had already written a tragedy, bad of course, but not worse than the tragedies of his friend. This piece is still preserved at Chevening, and is in some respects highly curious. There is no love. The whole plot is political; and it is remarkable that the interest, such as it is, turns on a contest about a regency. On one side is a faithful servant of the Crown, on the other an ambitious and unprincipled conspirator. At length the king, who had been missing, re-appears, resumes his power, and rewards the faithful defender of his rights. A reader who should judge only by internal evidence would have no hesitation in pronouncing that the play was written by some Pittite poetaster at the time of the rejoicings for the recovery of George the Third in 1789.

The pleasure with which William's parents observed the rapid development of his intellectual powers was alloyed by appre-hensions about his health. He shot up alarmingly fast; he was often ill, and always weak; and it was feared that it would be impossible to rear a stripling so tall, so slender, and so feeble. Port wine was prescribed by his medical advisers; and it is said that he was, at fourteen, accustomed to take this agreeable physic in quantities which would, in our abstemious age, be thought much more than sufficient for any full-grown man. This regimen, though it would probably have killed ninety-nine boys out of a hundred, seems to have been well suited to the peculiarities of William's constitution; for at fifteen he ceased to be molested by disease, and, though never a strong man, continued, during many years of labour and anxiety, of nights passed in debate and of summers passed in London, to be a tolerably healthy one. It was probably on account of the delicacy of his frame that he was not educated like other boys of the same rank. Almost all the eminent English statesmen and orators to whom he was afterwards opposed or allied, North,

Fox, Shelburne, Windham, Grey, Wellesley, Grenville, Sheridan,
Canning, went through the training of great public schools.
Lord Chatham had himself been a distinguished Etonian; and
it is seldom that a distinguished Etonian forgets his obligations
to Eton. But William's infirmities required a vigilance and
tenderness such as could be found only at home. He was therefore bred under the paternal roof. His studies were super-
intended by a clergyman named Wilson; and those studies,
though often interrupted by illness, were prosecuted with extraordinary success. Before the lad had completed his fifteenth
year, his knowledge both of the ancient languages and of
mathematics was such as very few men of eighteen then carried
up to college. He was therefore sent, towards the close of the
year 1773, to Pembroke Hall, in the university of Cambridge.
So young a student required much more than the ordinary care
which a college tutor bestows on undergraduates. The governor,
to whom the direction of William's academical life was confided,
was a bachelor of arts named Pretyman, who had been senior
wrangler in the preceding year, and who, though not a man of
prepossessing appearance or brilliant parts, was eminently acute
and laborious, a sound scholar, and an excellent geometrician.
At Cambridge, Pretyman was, during more than two years, the
inseparable companion, and indeed almost the only companion,
of his pupil. A close and lasting friendship sprang up between
the pair. The disciple was able, before he completed his twenty-
eighth year, to make his preceptor bishop of Lincoln and dean
of St. Paul's; and the preceptor showed his gratitude by writing
a Life of the disciple, which enjoys the distinction of being the
worst biographical work of its size in the world.

Pitt, till he graduated, had scarcely one acquaintance,
attended chapel regularly morning and evening, dined every
day in hall, and never went to a single evening party. At
seventeen, he was admitted, after the bad fashion of those
times, by right of birth, without any examination, to the degree
of Master of Arts. But he continued during some years to
reside at college, and to apply himself vigorously, under Pretyman's direction, to the studies of the place, while mixing freely
in the best academic society.

The stock of learning which Pitt laid in during this part of
his life was certainly very extraordinary. In fact, it was all
that he ever possessed; for he very early became too busy to
have any spare time for books. The work in which he took the
greatest delight was Newton's Principia. His liking for mathe-

matics, indeed, amounted to a passion, which, in the opinion
of his instructors, themselves distinguished mathematicians,
required to be checked rather than encouraged. The acuteness
and readiness with which he solved problems was pronounced
by one of the ablest of the moderators, who in those days
presided over the disputations in the schools, and conducted
the examinations of the Senate-House, to be unrivalled in the
university. Nor was the youth's proficiency in classical learning less remarkable. In one respect, indeed, he appeared to
disadvantage when compared with even second-rate and third-
rate men from public schools. He had never, while under
Wilson's care, been in the habit of composing in the ancient
languages; and he therefore never acquired that knack of
versification which is sometimes possessed by clever boys whose
knowledge of the language and literature of Greece and Rome
is very superficial. It would have been utterly out of his
power to produce such charming elegiac lines as those in which
Wellesley bade farewell to Eton, or such Virgilian hexameters
as those in which Canning described the pilgrimage to Mecca.
But it may be doubted whether any scholar has ever, at twenty,
had a more solid and profound knowledge of the two great
tongues of the old civilised world. The facility with which he
penetrated the meaning of the most intricate sentences in the
Attic writers astonished veteran critics. He had set his heart
on being intimately acquainted with all the extant poetry of
Greece, and was not satisfied till he had mastered Lycophron's
Cassandra, the most obscure work in the whole range of ancient
literature. This strange rhapsody, the difficulties of which have
perplexed and repelled many excellent scholars, " he read,"
says his preceptor, " with an ease at first sight, which, if I had
not witnessed it, I should have thought beyond the compass of
human intellect."

To modern literature Pitt paid comparatively little attention.
He knew no living language except French; and French he
knew very imperfectly. With a few of the best English writers
he was intimate, particularly with Shakspeare and Milton. The
debate in Pandemonium was, as it well deserved to be, one of
his favourite passages; and his early friends used to talk, long
after his death, of the just emphasis and the melodious cadence
with which they had heard him recite the incomparable speech
of Belial. He had indeed been carefully trained from infancy
in the art of managing his voice, a voice naturally clear and
deep-toned. His father, whose oratory owed no small part of

its effect to that art, had been a most skilful and judicious instructor. At a later period, the wits of Brookes's, irritated by observing, night after night, how powerfully Pitt's sonorous elocution fascinated the rows of country gentlemen, reproached him with having been " taught by his dad on à stool."

His education, indeed, was well adapted to form a great parliamentary speaker. One argument often urged against those classical studies which occupy so large a part of the early life of every gentleman bred in the south of our island is, that they prevent him from acquiring a command of his mother tongue, and that it is not unusual to meet with a youth of excellent parts, who writes Ciceronian Latin prose and Horatian Latin Alcaics, but who would find it impossible to express his thoughts in pure, perspicuous, and forcible English. There may perhaps be some truth in this observation. But the classical studies of Pitt were carried on in a peculiar manner, and had the effect of enriching his English vocabulary, and of making him wonderfully expert in the art of constructing correct English sentences. His practice was to look over a page or two of a Greek or Latin author, to make himself master of the meaning, and then to read the passage straight forward into his own language. This practice, begun under his first teacher Wilson, was continued under Pretyman. It is not strange that a young man of great abilities, who had been exercised daily in this way during ten years, should have acquired an almost unrivalled power of putting his thoughts, without premeditation, into words well selected and well arranged.

Of all the remains of antiquity, the orations were those on which he bestowed the most minute examination. His favourite employment was to compare harangues on opposite sides of the same question, to analyse them, and to observe which of the arguments of the first speaker were refuted by the second, which were evaded, and which were left untouched. Nor was it only in books that he at this time studied the art of parliamentary fencing. When he was at home, he had frequent opportunities of hearing important debates at Westminster; and he heard them, not only with interest and enjoyment, but with a close scientific attention resembling that with which a diligent pupil at Guy's Hospital watches every turn of the hand of a great surgeon through a difficult operation. On one of these occasions, Pitt, a youth whose abilities were as yet known only to his own family and to a small knot of college friends, was introduced on the steps of the throne in the House of Lords to Fox, who was his senior by eleven years, and who was already the greatest debater, and one of the greatest orators, that had appeared in England.   Fox used afterwards to relate that, as the discussion proceeded, Pitt repeatedly turned to him, and said, " But surely, Mr. Fox, that might be met thus; " or, " Yes; but he lays himself open to this retort."   What the particular criticisms were Fox had forgotten; but he said that he was much struck at the time by the precocity of a lad who, through the whole sitting, seemed to be thinking only how all the speeches on both sides could be answered.

One of the young man's visits to the House of Lords was a sad and memorable era in his life.   He had not quite completed his nineteenth year, when, on the 7th of April 1778, he attended his father to Westminster.   A great debate was expected.   It was known that France had recognised the independence of the United States.   The Duke of Richmond was about to declare his opinion that all thought of subjugating those states ought to be relinquished.   Chatham had always maintained that the resistance of the colonies to the mother country was justifiable. But he conceived, very erroneously, that on the day on which their independence should be acknowledged the greatness of England would be at an end.   Though sinking under the weight of years and infirmities, he determined, in spite of the entreaties of his family, to be in his place.   His son supported him to a seat.   The excitement and exertion were too much for the old man.   In the very act of addressing the peers, he fell back in convulsions.   A few weeks later his corpse was borne, with gloomy pomp, from the Painted Chamber to the Abbey.   The favourite child and namesake of the deceased statesman followed the coffin as chief mourner, and saw it deposited in the transept where his own was destined to lie.

His elder brother, now Earl of Chatham, had means suffi- cient, and barely sufficient, to support the dignity of the peerage. The other members of the family were poorly provided for. William had little more than three hundred a year.   It was necessary for him to follow a profession.   He had already begun to eat his terms.   In the spring of 1780 he came of age.   He then quitted Cambridge, was called to the bar, took chambers in Lincoln's Inn, and joined the western circuit.   In the autumn of that year a general election took place; and he offered him- self as a candidate for the university; but he was at the bottom of the poll.   It is said that the grave doctors who then sate, robed in scarlet, on the benches of Golgotha, thought it great presumption in so young a man to solicit so high a distinction. He was, however, at the request of a hereditary friend, the Duke of Rutland, brought into Parliament by Sir James Lowther for the borough of Appleby.

The dangers of the country were at that time such as might well have disturbed even a constant mind. Army after army had been sent in vain against the rebellious colonists of North America. On pitched fields of battle the advantage had been with the disciplined troops of the mother country. But it was not on pitched fields of battle that the event of such a contest could be decided. An armed nation, with hunger and the Atlantic for auxiliaries, was not to be subjugated. Meanwhile the House of Bourbon, humbled to the dust a few years before by the genius and vigour of Chatham, had seized the opportunity of revenge. France and Spain were united against us, and had recently been joined by Holland. The command of the Mediterranean had been for a time lost. The British flag had been scarcely able to maintain itself in the British Channel. The northern powers professed neutrality; but their neutrality had a menacing aspect. In the East, Hyder had descended on the Carnatic, had destroyed the little army of Baillie, and had spread terror even to the ramparts of Fort Saint George. The discontents of Ireland threatened nothing less than civil war. In England the authority of the government had sunk to the lowest point. The King and the House of Commons were alike unpopular. The cry for parliamentary reform was scarcely less loud and vehement than in the autumn of 1830. Formidable associations, headed, not by ordinary demagogues, but by men of high rank, stainless character, and distinguished ability, demanded a revision of the representative system. The populace, emboldened by the impotence and irresolution of the government, had recently broken loose from all restraint, besieged the chambers of the legislature, hustled peers, hunted bishops, attacked the residences of ambassadors, opened prisons, burned and pulled down houses. London had presented during some days the aspect of a city taken by storm; and it had been necessary to form a camp among the trees of Saint James's Park.

In spite of dangers and difficulties abroad and at home, George the Third, with a firmness which had little affinity with virtue or with wisdom, persisted in his determination to put down the American rebels by force of arms; and his ministers submitted their judgment to his. Some of them were probably actuated merely by selfish cupidity; but their chief, Lord North, a man of high honour, amiable temper, winning manners, lively wit, and excellent talents both for business and for debate, must be acquitted of all sordid motives. He remained at a post from which he had long wished and had repeatedly tried to escape, only because he had not sufficient fortitude to resist the entreaties and reproaches of the King, who silenced all arguments by passionately asking whether any gentleman, any man of spirit, could have the heart to desert a kind master in the hour of extremity.

The opposition consisted of two parties which had once been hostile to each other, and which had been very slowly, and, as it soon appeared, very imperfectly reconciled, but which at this conjuncture seemed to act together with cordiality. The larger of these parties consisted of the great body of the Whig aristocracy. Its head was Charles, Marquess of Rockingham, a man of sense and virtue, and in wealth and parliamentary interest equalled by very few of the English nobles, but afflicted with a nervous timidity which prevented him from taking a prominent part in debate. In the House of Commons, the adherents of Rockingham were led by Fox, whose dissipated habits and ruined fortunes were the talk of the whole town, but whose commanding genius, and whose sweet, generous, and affectionate disposition, extorted the admiration and love of those who most lamented the errors of his private life. Burke, superior to Fox in largeness of comprehension, in extent of knowledge, and in splendour of imagination, but less skilled in that kind of logic and in that kind of rhetoric which convince and persuade great assemblies, was willing to be the lieutenant of a young chief who might have been his son.

A smaller section of the opposition was composed of the old followers of Chatham. At their head was William, Earl of Shelburne, distinguished both as a statesman and as a lover of science and letters. With him were leagued Lord Camden, who had formerly held the Great Seal, and whose integrity, ability, and constitutional knowledge commanded the public respect; Barré, an eloquent and acrimonious declaimer; and Dunning, who had long held the first place at the English bar. It was to this party that Pitt was naturally attracted.

On the 26th of February 1781 he made his first speech in favour of Burke's plan of economical reform. Fox stood up at the same moment, but instantly gave way. The lofty yet animated deportment of the young member, his perfect self-possession, the readiness with which he replied to the orators

who had preceded him, the silver tones of his voice, the perfect
structure of his unpremeditated sentences, astonished and
delighted his hearers. Burke, moved even to tears, exclaimed,
" It is not a chip of the old block; it is the old block itself."
" Pitt will be one of the first men in Parliament," said a member
of the opposition to Fox. " He is so already," answered Fox,
in whose nature envy had no place. It is a curious fact, well
remembered by some who were very recently living, that soon
after this debate Pitt's name was put up by Fox at Brookes's.

On two subsequent occasions during that session Pitt addressed the House, and on both fully sustained the reputation
which he had acquired on his first appearance. In the summer,
after the prorogation, he again went the western circuit, held
several briefs, and acquitted himself in such a manner that he
was highly complimented by Buller from the bench, and by
Dunning at the bar.

On the 27th of November the Parliament reassembled. Only
forty-eight hours before had arrived tidings of the surrender of
Cornwallis and his army; and it had consequently been necessary to re-write the royal speech. Every man in the kingdom,
except the King, was now convinced that it was mere madness
to think of conquering the United States. In the debate on the
report of the address, Pitt spoke with even more energy and
brilliancy than on any former occasion. He was warmly applauded by his allies; but it was remarked that no person on
his own side of the house was so loud in eulogy as Henry Dundas,
the Lord Advocate of Scotland, who spoke from the ministerial
ranks. That able and versatile politician distinctly foresaw the
approaching downfall of the government with which he was
connected, and was preparing to make his own escape from the
ruin. From that night dates his connection with Pitt, a connection which soon became a close intimacy, and which lasted
till it was dissolved by death.

About a fortnight later, Pitt spoke in the committee of supply
on the army estimates. Symptoms of dissension had begun to
appear on the Treasury bench. Lord George Germaine, the
Secretary of State who was especially charged with the direction
of the war in America, had held language not easily to be
reconciled with declarations made by the First Lord of the
Treasury. Pitt noticed the discrepancy with much force and
keenness. Lord George and Lord North began to whisper together; and Welbore Ellis, an ancient placeman who had been
drawing salary almost every quarter since the days of Henry

Pelham, bent down between them to put in a word. Such interruptions sometimes discompose veteran speakers. Pitt stopped, and looking at the group, said, with admirable readiness, " I shall wait till Nestor has composed the dispute between Agamemnon and Achilles."

After several defeats, or victories hardly to be distinguished from defeats, the ministry resigned. The King, reluctantly and ungraciously, consented to accept Rockingham as first minister. Fox and Shelburne became Secretaries of State. Lord John Cavendish, one of the most upright and honourable of men, was made Chancellor of the Exchequer. Thurlow, whose abilities and force of character had made him the dictator of the House of Lords, continued to hold the great seal.

To Pitt was offered, through Shelburne, the Vice-Treasurership of Ireland, one of the easiest and most highly paid places in the gift of the Crown; but the offer was, without hesitation, declined. The young statesman had resolved to accept no post which did not entitle him to a seat in the cabinet; and a few days later, he announced that resolution in the House of Commons. It must be remembered that the cabinet was then a much smaller and more select body than at present. We have seen cabinets of sixteen. In the time of our grandfathers a cabinet of ten or eleven was thought inconveniently large. Seven was a usual number. Even Burke, who had taken the lucrative office of Paymaster, was not in the cabinet. Many therefore thought Pitt's declaration indecent. He himself was sorry that he had made it. The words, he said in private, had escaped him in the heat of speaking; and he had no sooner uttered them than he would have given the world to recall them. They, however, did him no harm with the public. The second William Pitt, it was said, had shown that he had inherited the spirit, as well as the genius, of the first. In the son, as in the father, there might perhaps be too much pride; but there was nothing low or sordid. It might be called arrogance in a young barrister, living in chambers on three hundred a year, to refuse a salary of five thousand a year, merely because he did not choose to bind himself to speak or vote for plans which he had no share in framing; but surely such arrogance was not very far removed from virtue.

Pitt gave a general support to the administration of Rockingham, but omitted, in the meantime, no opportunity of courting that Ultra-Whig party which the persecution of Wilkes and the Middlesex election had called into existence, and which the disastrous events of the war, and the triumph of republican principles in America, had made formidable both in numbers and in temper. He supported a motion for shortening the duration of Parliaments. He made a motion for a committee to examine into the state of the representation, and, in the speech by which that motion was introduced, avowed himself the enemy of the close boroughs, the strongholds of that corruption to which he attributed all the calamities of the nation, and which, as he phrased it in one of those exact and sonorous sentences of which he had a boundless command, had grown with the growth of England and strengthened with her strength, but had not diminished with her diminution or decayed with her decay. On this occasion he was supported by Fox. The motion was lost by only twenty votes in a house of more than three hundred members. The reformers never again had so good a division till the year 1831.

The new administration was strong in abilities, and was more popular than any administration which had held office since the first year of George the Third, but was hated by the King, hesitatingly supported by the Parliament, and torn by internal dissensions. The Chancellor was disliked and distrusted by almost all his colleagues. The two Secretaries of State regarded each other with no friendly feeling. The line between their departments had not been traced with precision; and there were consequently jealousies, encroachments, and complaints. It was all that Rockingham could do to keep the peace in his cabinet; and, before the cabinet had existed three months, Rockingham died.

In an instant all was confusion. The adherents of the deceased statesman looked on the Duke of Portland as their chief. The King placed Shelburne at the head of the Treasury. Fox, Lord John Cavendish, and Burke, immediately resigned their offices; and the new prime minister was left to constitute a government out of very defective materials. His own parliamentary talents were great; but he could not be in the place where parliamentary talents were most needed. It was necessary to find some member of the House of Commons who could confront the great orators of the opposition; and Pitt alone had the eloquence and the courage which were required. He was offered the great place of Chancellor of the Exchequer, and he accepted it. He had scarcely completed his twenty-third year.

The Parliament was speedily prorogued. During the recess, a negotiation for peace which had been commenced under

Rockingham was brought to a successful termination. England acknowledged the independence of her revolted colonies; and she ceded to her European enemies some places in the Mediterranean and in the Gulf of Mexico. But the terms which she obtained were quite as advantageous and honourable as the events of the war entitled her to expect, or as she was likely to obtain by persevering in a contest against immense odds. All her vital parts, all the real sources of her power, remained uninjured. She preserved even her dignity; for she ceded to the House of Bourbon only part of what she had won from that house in previous wars. She retained her Indian empire undiminished; and, in spite of the mightiest efforts of two great monarchies, her flag still waved on the rock of Gibraltar. There is not the slightest reason to believe that Fox, if he had remained in office, would have hesitated one moment about concluding a treaty on such conditions. Unhappily that great and most amiable man was, at this crisis, hurried by his passions into an error which made his genius and his virtues, during a long course of years, almost useless to his country.

He saw that the great body of the House of Commons was divided into three parties, his own, that of North, and that of Shelburne; that none of those three parties was large enough to stand alone; that, therefore, unless two of them united, there must be a miserably feeble administration, or, more probably, a rapid succession of miserably feeble administrations, and this at a time when a strong government was essential to the prosperity and respectability of the nation. It was then necessary and right that there should be a coalition. To every possible coalition there were objections. But, of all possible coalitions, that to which there were the fewest objections was undoubtedly a coalition between Shelburne and Fox. It would have been generally applauded by the followers of both. It might have been made without any sacrifice of public principle on the part of either. Unhappily, recent bickerings had left in the mind of Fox a profound dislike and distrust of Shelburne. Pitt attempted to mediate, and was authorised to invite Fox to return to the service of the Crown. " Is Lord Shelburne," said Fox, " to remain prime minister? " Pitt answered in the affirmative. " It is impossible that I can act under him," said Fox. " Then negotiation is at an end," said Pitt; " for I cannot betray him." Thus the two statesmen parted. They were never again in a private room together.

As Fox and his friends would not treat with Shelburne,

nothing remained to them but to treat with North. That fatal coalition which is emphatically called " The Coalition " was formed. Not three quarters of a year had elapsed since Fox and Burke had threatened North with impeachment, and had described him, night after night, as the most arbitrary, the most corrupt, the most incapable of ministers. They now allied themselves with him for the purpose of driving from office a statesman with whom they cannot be said to have differed as to any important question. Nor had they even the prudence and the patience to wait for some occasion on which they might, without inconsistency, have combined with their old enemies in opposition to the government. That nothing might be wanting to the scandal, the great orators who had, during seven years, thundered against the war, determined to join with the authors of that war in passing a vote of censure on the peace.

The Parliament met before Christmas 1782. But it was not till January 1783 that the preliminary treaties were signed. On the 17th of February they were taken into consideration by the House of Commons. There had been, during some days, floating rumours that Fox and North had coalesced; and the debate indicated but too clearly that those rumours were not unfounded. Pitt was suffering from indisposition: he did not rise till his own strength and that of his hearers were exhausted; and he was consequently less successful than on any former occasion. His admirers owned that his speech was feeble and petulant. He so far forgot himself as to advise Sheridan to confine himself to amusing theatrical audiences. This ignoble sarcasm gave Sheridan an opportunity of retorting with great felicity. " After what I have seen and heard to-night," he said, " I really feel strongly tempted to venture on a competition with so great an artist as Ben Jonson, and to bring on the stage a second Angry Boy." On a division, the address proposed by the supporters of the government was rejected by a majority of sixteen.

But Pitt was not a man to be disheartened by a single failure, or to be put down by the most lively repartee. When, a few days later, the opposition proposed a resolution directly censuring the treaties, he spoke with an eloquence, energy, and dignity, which raised his fame and popularity higher than ever. To the coalition of Fox and North he alluded in language which drew forth tumultuous applause from his followers. " If," he said, " this ill-omened and unnatural marriage be not yet consummated, I know of a just and lawful impediment; and, in the name of the public weal, I forbid the banns."

The ministers were again left in a minority, and Shelburne consequently tendered his resignation. It was accepted: but the King struggled long and hard before he submitted to the terms dictated by Fox, whose faults he detested, and whose high spirit and powerful intellect he detested still more. The first place at the board of Treasury was repeatedly offered to Pitt: but the offer, though tempting, was steadfastly declined. The young man, whose judgment was as precocious as his eloquence, saw that his time was coming, but was not come, and was deaf to royal importunities and reproaches. His Majesty, bitterly complaining of Pitt's faintheartedness, tried to break the coalition. Every art of seduction was practised on North, but in vain. During several weeks the country remained without a government. It was not till all devices had failed, and till the aspect of the House of Commons became threatening, that the King gave way. The Duke of Portland was declared First Lord of the Treasury. Thurlow was dismissed. Fox and North became Secretaries of State, with power ostensibly equal. But Fox was the real prime minister.

The year was far advanced before the new arrangements were completed; and nothing very important was done during the remainder of the session. Pitt, now seated on the opposition bench, brought the question of parliamentary reform a second time under the consideration of the Commons. He proposed to add to the House at once a hundred county members and several members for metropolitan districts, and to enact that every borough of which an election committee should report that the majority of voters appeared to be corrupt should lose the franchise. The motion was rejected by 293 votes to 149.

After the prorogation, Pitt visited the Continent for the first and last time. His travelling companion was one of his most intimate friends, a young man of his own age, who had already distinguished himself in Parliament by an engaging natural eloquence, set off by the sweetest and most exquisitely modulated of human voices, and whose affectionate heart, caressing manners, and brilliant wit, made him the most delightful of companions, William Wilberforce. That was the time of Anglomania in France; and at Paris the son of the great Chatham was absolutely hunted by men of letters and women of fashion, and forced, much against his will, into political disputation. One remarkable saying which dropped from him during this tour has been preserved. A French gentleman expressed some surprise at the immense influence which Fox, a man of pleasure, ruined by the dice-box and the turf, exercised over the English nation. " You have not," said Pitt, " been under the wand of the magician."

In November 1783 the Parliament met again. The government had irresistible strength in the House of Commons, and seemed to be scarcely less strong in the House of Lords, but was, in truth, surrounded on every side by dangers. The King was impatiently waiting for the moment at which he could emancipate himself from a yoke which galled him so severely that he had more than once seriously thought of retiring to Hanover; and the King was scarcely more eager for a change than the nation. Fox and North had committed a fatal error. They ought to have known that coalitions between parties which have long been hostile can succeed only when the wish for coalition pervades the lower ranks of both. If the leaders unite before there is any disposition to union among the followers, the probability is that there will be a mutiny in both camps, and that the two revolted armies will make a truce with each other, in order to be revenged on those by whom they think that they have been betrayed. Thus it was in 1783. At the beginning of that eventful year, North had been the recognised head of the old Tory party, which, though for a moment prostrated by the disastrous issue of the American war, was still a great power in the state. To him the clergy, the universities, and that large body of country gentlemen whose rallying cry was " Church and King," had long looked up with respect and confidence. Fox had, on the other hand, been the idol of the Whigs, and of the whole body of Protestant dissenters. The coalition at once alienated the most zealous Tories from North, and the most zealous Whigs from Fox. The University of Oxford, which had marked its approbation of North's orthodoxy by electing him chancellor, the city of London, which had been during two and twenty years at war with the Court, were equally disgusted. Squires and rectors, who had inherited the principles of the cavaliers of the preceding century, could not forgive their old leader for combining with disloyal subjects in order to put a force on the sovereign. The members of the Bill of Rights Society and of the Reform Associations were enraged by learning that their favourite orator now called the great champion of tyranny and corruption his noble friend. Two great multitudes were at once left without any head, and both at once turned their eyes on Pitt. One party saw in him the only man who could rescue the King; the other saw in him the only man who could purify the Parliament. He was supported on one side by Archbishop Markham, the preacher of divine right, and by Jenkinson, the captain of the Prætorian band of the King's friends; on the other side by Jebb and Priestley, Sawbridge and Cartwright, Jack Wilkes and Horne Tooke. On the benches of the House of Commons, however, the ranks of the ministerial majority were unbroken; and that any statesman would venture to brave such a majority was thought impossible. No prince of the Hanoverian line had ever, under any provocation, ventured to appeal from the representative body to the constituent body. The ministers, therefore, notwithstanding the sullen looks and muttered words of displeasure with which their suggestions were received in the closet, notwithstanding the roar of obloquy which was rising louder and louder every day from every corner of the island, thought themselves secure.

Such was their confidence in their strength that, as soon as the Parliament had met, they brought forward a singularly bold and original plan for the government of the British territories in India.   What was proposed was that the whole authority, which till that time had been exercised over those territories by the East India Company, should be transferred to seven commissioners who were to be named by Parliament, and were not to be removable at the pleasure of the Crown.   Earl Fitzwilliam, the most intimate personal friend of Fox, was to be chairman of this board, and the eldest son of North was to be one of the members.

As soon as the outlines of the scheme were known, all the hatred which the coalition had excited burst forth with an astounding explosion.   The question which ought undoubtedly to have been considered as paramount to every other was, whether the proposed change was likely to be beneficial or injurious to the thirty millions of people who were subject to the Company.   But that question cannot be said to have been even seriously discussed.   Burke, who, whether right or wrong in the conclusions to which he came, had at least the merit of looking at the subject in the right point of view, vainly reminded his hearers of that mighty population whose daily rice might depend on a vote of the British Parliament.   He spoke with even more than his wonted power of thought and language, about the desolation of Rohilcund, about the spoliation of Benares, about the evil policy which had suffered the tanks of the Carnatic to go to ruin; but he could scarcely obtain a hearing.   The contending parties, to their shame it must be said, would listen to none but English topics. Out of doors the cry against the ministry was almost universal. Town and country were united. Corporations exclaimed against the violation of the charter of the greatest corporation in the realm. Tories and democrats joined in pronouncing the proposed board an unconstitutional body. It was to consist of Fox's nominees. The effect of his bill was to give, not to the Crown, but to him personally, whether in office or in opposition, an enormous power, a patronage sufficient to counterbalance the patronage of the Treasury and of the Admiralty, and to decide the elections for fifty boroughs. He knew, it was said, that he was hateful alike to King and people; and he had devised a plan which would make him independent of both. Some nicknamed him Cromwell, and some Carlo Khan. Wilberforce, with his usual felicity of expression, and with very unusual bitterness of feeling, described the scheme as the genuine offspring of the coalition, as marked with the features of both its parents, the corruption of one and the violence of the other. In spite of all opposition, however, the bill was supported in every stage by great majorities, was rapidly passed, and was sent up to the Lords. To the general astonishment, when the second reading was moved in the Upper House, the opposition proposed an adjournment, and carried it by eighty-seven votes to seventy-nine. The cause of this strange turn of fortune was soon known. Pitt's cousin, Earl Temple, had been in the royal closet, and had there been authorised to let it be known that His Majesty would consider all who voted for the bill as his enemies. The ignominious commission was performed, and instantly a troop of Lords of the Bedchamber, of Bishops who wished to be translated, and of Scotch peers who wished to be re-elected, made haste to change sides. On a later day, the Lords rejected the bill. Fox and North were immediately directed to send their seals to the palace by their Under Secretaries; and Pitt was appointed First Lord of the Treasury and Chancellor of the Exchequer.

The general opinion was, that there would be an immediate dissolution. But Pitt wisely determined to give the public feeling time to gather strength. On this point he differed from his kinsman Temple. The consequence was, that Temple, who had been appointed one of the Secretaries of State, resigned his office forty-eight hours after he had accepted it, and thus relieved the new government from a great load of unpopularity: for all men of sense and honour, however strong might be their dislike of the India Bill, disapproved of the manner in which that bill had been thrown out. Temple carried away with him the scandal which the best friends of the new government could not but lament. The fame of the young prime minister preserved its whiteness. He could declare with perfect truth that, if unconstitutional machinations had been employed, he had been no party to them.

He was, however, surrounded by difficulties and dangers. In the House of Lords, indeed, he had a majority; nor could any orator of the opposition in that assembly be considered as a match for Thurlow, who was now again Chancellor, or for Camden, who cordially supported the son of his old friend Chatham. But in the other House there was not a single eminent speaker among the official men who sate round Pitt. His most useful assistant was Dundas, who, though he had not eloquence, had sense, knowledge, readiness, and boldness. On the opposite benches was a powerful majority, led by Fox, who was supported by Burke, North, and Sheridan. The heart of the young minister, stout as it was, almost died within him. He could not once close his eyes on the night which followed Temple's resignation. But, whatever his internal emotions might be, his language and deportment indicated nothing but unconquerable firmness and haughty confidence in his own powers. His contest against the House of Commons lasted from the 17th of December 1783 to the 8th of March 1784. In sixteen divisions the opposition triumphed. Again and again the King was requested to dismiss his ministers. But he was determined to go to Germany rather than yield. Pitt's resolution never wavered. The cry of the nation in his favour became vehement and almost furious. Addresses assuring him of public support came up daily from every part of the kingdom. The freedom of the city of London was presented to him in a gold box. He went in state to receive this mark of distinction. He was sumptuously feasted in Grocers' Hall; and the shopkeepers of the Strand and Fleet Street illuminated their houses in his honour. These things could not but produce an effect within the walls of Parliament. The ranks of the majority began to waver; a few passed over to the enemy; some skulked away; many were for capitulating while it was still possible to capitulate with the honours of war. Negotiations were opened with the view of forming an administration on a wide basis, but they had scarcely been opened when they were closed. The opposition demanded, as a preliminary article of the treaty, that Pitt should resign the Treasury; and with this demand Pitt stead-fastly refused to comply. While the contest was raging, the Clerkship of the Pells, a sinecure place for life, worth three thousand a year, and tenable with a seat in the House of Commons, became vacant. The appointment was with the Chancellor of the Exchequer: nobody doubted that he would appoint himself; and nobody could have blamed him if he had done so: for such sinecure offices had always been defended on the ground that they enabled a few men of eminent abilities and small incomes to live without any profession, and to devote themselves to the service of the state. Pitt, in spite of the remonstrances of his friends, gave the Pells to his father's old adherent, Colonel Barré, a man distinguished by talent and eloquence, but poor and afflicted with blindness. By this arrangement a pension which the Rockingham administration had granted to Barré was saved to the public. Never was there a happier stroke of policy. About treaties, wars, expeditions, tariffs, budgets, there will always be room for dispute. The policy which is applauded by half the nation may be condemned by the other half. But pecuniary disinterestedness everybody comprehends. It is a great thing for a man who has only three hundred a year to be able to show that he considers three thousand a year as mere dirt beneath his feet, when compared with the public interest and the public esteem. Pitt had his reward. No minister was ever more rancorously libelled; but even when he was known to be overwhelmed with debt, when millions were passing through his hands, when the wealthiest magnates of the realm were soliciting him for marquisates and garters, his bitterest enemies did not dare to accuse him of touching unlawful gain.

At length the hard fought fight ended. A final remonstrance, drawn up by Burke with admirable skill, was carried on the 8th of March by a single vote in a full House. Had the experiment been repeated, the supporters of the coalition would probably have been in a minority. But the supplies had been voted; the Mutiny Bill had been passed; and the Parliament was dissolved.

The popular constituent bodies all over the country were in general enthusiastic on the side of the new government. A hundred and sixty of the supporters of the coalition lost their seats. The First Lord of the Treasury himself came in at the head of the poll for the University of Cambridge. His young friend, Wilberforce, was elected knight of the great shire of York, in opposition to the whole influence of the Fitzwilliams, Cavendishes, Dundases, and Saviles.   In the midst of such triumphs Pitt completed his twenty-fifth year.   He was now the greatest subject that England had seen during many generations.   He domineered absolutely over the cabinet, and was the favourite at once of the Sovereign, of the Parliament, and the nation.   His father had never been so powerful, nor Walpole, nor Marlborough.

This narrative has now reached a point beyond which a full history of the life of Pitt would be a history of England, or rather of the whole civilised world; and for such a history this is not the proper place.   Here a very slight sketch must suffice; and in that sketch prominence will be given to such points as may enable a reader who is already acquainted with the general course of events to form a just notion of the character of the man on whom so much depended.

If we wish to arrive at a correct judgment of Pitt's merits and defects, we must never forget that he belonged to a peculiar class of statesmen, and that he must be tried by a peculiar standard.   It is not easy to compare him fairly with such men as Ximenes and Sully, Richelieu and Oxenstiern, John De Witt and Warren Hastings.   The means by which these politicians governed great communities were of quite a different kind from those which Pitt was under the necessity of employing.   Some talents, which they had never any opportunity of showing that they possessed, were developed in him to an extraordinary degree.   In some qualities, on the other hand, to which they owe a large part of their fame, he was decidedly their inferior. They transacted business in their closets, or at boards where a few confidential councillors sate.   It was his lot to be born in an age and in a country in which parliamentary government was completely established; his whole training from infancy was such as fitted him to bear a part in parliamentary govern- ment; and from the prime of his manhood to his death, all the powers of his vigorous mind were almost constantly exerted in the work of parliamentary government.   He accordingly became the greatest master of the whole art of parliamentary govern- ment that has ever existed, a greater than Montague or Walpole, a greater than his father Chatham or his rival Fox, a greater than either of his illustrious successors Canning and Peel.

Parliamentary government, like every other contrivance of man, has its advantages and its disadvantages.   On the ad- vantages there is no need to dilate.   The history of England during the hundred and seventy years which have elapsed since the House of Commons became the most powerful body in the state, her immense and still growing prosperity, her freedom, her tranquillity, her greatness in arts, in sciences, and in arms, her maritime ascendency, the marvels of her public credit, her American, her African, her Australian, her Asiatic empires sufficiently prove the excellence of her institutions. But those institutions, though excellent, are assuredly not perfect. Parliamentary government is government by speaking. In such a government, the power of speaking is the most highly prized of all the qualities which a politician can possess; and that power may exist, in the highest degree without judgment, without fortitude, without skill in reading the characters of men or the signs of the times, without any knowledge of the principles of legislation or of political economy, and without any skill in diplomacy or in the administration of war. Nay, it may well happen that those very intellectual qualities which give a peculiar charm to the speeches of a public man may be incompatible with the qualities which would fit him to meet a pressing emergency with promptitude and firmness. It was thus with Charles Townshend. It was thus with Windham. It was a privilege to listen to those accomplished and ingenious orators. But in a perilous crisis they would have been found far inferior in all the qualities of rulers to such a man as Oliver Cromwell, who talked nonsense, or as William the Silent, who did not talk at all. When parliamentary government is established, a Charles Townshend or a Windham will almost always exercise much greater influence than such men as the great Protector of England, or as the founder of the Batavian commonwealth. In such a government, parliamentary talent, though quite distinct from the talents of a good executive or judicial officer, will be a chief qualification for executive and judicial office. From the Book of Dignities a curious list might be made out of Chancellors ignorant of the principles of equity, and First Lords of the Admiralty ignorant of the principles of navigation, of Colonial ministers who could not repeat the names of the Colonies, of Lords of the Treasury who did not know the difference between funded and unfunded debt, and of Secretaries of the India Board who did not know whether the Mahrattas were Mahometans or Hindoos. On these grounds, some persons, incapable of seeing more than one side of a question, have pronounced parliamentary government a positive evil, and have maintained that the administration would be greatly improved if the power, now exercised by a large assembly, were transferred to a single person. Men of sense will probably think the remedy very much worse than the disease, and will be of opinion that there would be small gain in exchanging Charles Townshend and Windham for the Prince of the Peace, or the poor slave and dog Steenie.

Pitt was emphatically the man of parliamentary government, the type of his class, the minion, the child, the spoiled child, of the House of Commons. For the House of Commons he had a hereditary, an infantine love. Through his whole boyhood, the House of Commons was never out of his thoughts, or out of the thoughts of his instructors. Reciting at his father's knee, reading Thucydides and Cicero into English, analysing the great Attic speeches on the Embassy and on the Crown, he was constantly in training for the conflicts of the House of Commons. He was a distinguished member of the House of Commons at twenty-one. The ability which he had displayed in the House of Commons made him the most powerful subject in Europe before he was twenty-five. It would have been happy for himself and for his country if his elevation had been deferred. Eight or ten years, during which he would have had leisure and opportunity for reading and reflection, for foreign travel, for social intercourse and free exchange of thought on equal terms with a great variety of companions, would have supplied what, without any fault on his part, was wanting to his powerful intellect. He had all the knowledge that he could be expected to have; that is to say, all the knowledge that a man can acquire while he is a student at Cambridge, and all the knowledge that a man can acquire when he is First Lord of the Treasury and Chancellor of the Exchequer. But the stock of general information which he brought from college, extraordinary for a boy, was far inferior to what Fox possessed, and beggarly when compared with the massy, the splendid, the various treasures laid up in the large mind of Burke. After Pitt became minister, he had no leisure to learn more than was necessary for the purposes of the day which was passing over him. What was necessary for those purposes such a man could earn with little difficulty. He was surrounded by experienced and able public servants. He could at any moment command their best assistance. From the stores which they produced his vigorous mind rapidly collected the materials for a good parliamentary case: and that was enough. Legislation and administration were with him secondary matters. To the work of framing statutes, of negotiating treaties, of organising fleets and armies, of sending forth expeditions, he gave only the leavings of his time and the dregs of his fine intellect. The strength and sap of his mind were all drawn in a different direction. It was when the House of Commons was to be convinced and persuaded that he put forth all his powers.

Of those powers we must form our estimate chiefly from tradition; for of all the eminent speakers of the last age, Pitt has suffered most from the reporters. Even while he was still living, critics remarked that his eloquence could not be preserved, that he must be heard to be appreciated. They more than once applied to him the sentence in which Tacitus describes the fate of a senator whose rhetoric was admired in the Augustan age: "Haterii canorum illud et profluens cum ipso simul exstinctum est." There is, however, abundant evidence that nature had bestowed on Pitt the talents of a great orator; and those talents had been developed in a very peculiar manner, first by his education, and secondly by the high official position to which he rose early, and in which he passed the greater part of his public life.

At his first appearance in Parliament he showed himself superior to all his contemporaries in command of language. He could pour forth a long succession of round and stately periods, without premeditation, without ever pausing for a word, without ever repeating a word, in a voice of silver clearness, and with a pronunciation so articulate that not a letter was slurred over. He had less amplitude of mind and less richness of imagination than Burke, less ingenuity than Windham, less wit than Sheridan, less perfect mastery of dialectical fence, and less of that highest sort of eloquence which consists of reason and passion fused together, than Fox. Yet the almost unanimous judgment of those who were in the habit of listening to that remarkable race of men placed Pitt, as a speaker, above Burke, above Windham, above Sheridan, and not below Fox. His declamation was copious, polished, and splendid. In power of sarcasm he was probably not surpassed by any speaker, ancient or modern; and of this formidable weapon he made merciless use. In two parts of the oratorical art which are of the highest value to a minister of state he was singularly expert. No man knew better how to be luminous or how to be obscure. When he wished to be understood, he never failed to make himself understood. He could with ease present to his audience, not perhaps an exact or profound, but a clear, popular, and plausible view of the most extensive and complicated subject. Nothing was out of place; nothing was forgotten; minute details, dates, sums of money, were all faithfully preserved in his memory. Even intricate questions of finance, when explained by him, seemed clear to the plainest man among his hearers. On the other hand, when he did not wish to be explicit,—and no man who is at the head of affairs always wishes to be explicit,—he had a marvellous power of saying nothing in language which left on his audience the impression that he had said a great deal. He was at once the only man who could open a budget without notes, and the only man who, as Windham said, could speak that most elaborately evasive and unmeaning of human compositions, a King's speech, without premeditation.

The effect of oratory will always to a great extent depend on the character of the orator. There perhaps never were two speakers whose eloquence had more of what may be called the race, more of the flavour imparted by moral qualities, than Fox and Pitt. The speeches of Fox owe a great part of their charm to that warmth and softness of heart, that sympathy with human suffering, that admiration for everything great and beautiful, and that hatred of cruelty and injustice, which interest and delight us even in the most defective reports. No person, on the other hand, could hear Pitt without perceiving him to be a man of high, intrepid, and commanding spirit, proudly conscious of his own rectitude and of his own intellectual superiority, incapable of the low vices of fear and envy, but too prone to feel and to show disdain. Pride, indeed, pervaded the whole man, was written in the harsh, rigid lines of his face, was marked by the way in which he walked, in which he sate, in which he stood, and, above all, in which he bowed. Such pride, of course, inflicted many wounds. It may confidently be affirmed that there cannot be found, in all the ten thousand invectives written against Fox, a word indicating that his demeanour had ever made a single personal enemy. On the other hand, several men of note who had been partial to Pitt, and who to the last continued to approve his public conduct and to support his administration—Cumberland for example, Boswell, and Matthias—were so much irritated by the contempt with which he treated them, that they complained in print of their wrongs. But his pride, though it made him bitterly disliked by individuals, inspired the great body of his followers in Parliament and throughout the country with respect and confidence. They took him at his own valuation. They saw that his self-esteem was not that of an upstart who was drunk with good luck and with applause, and who, if fortune turned, would sink from arro-

gance into abject humility. It was that of the magnanimous
man so finely described by Aristotle in the Ethics, of the man
who thinks himself worthy of great things, being in truth worthy.
It sprang from a consciousness of great powers and great virtues,
and was never so conspicuously displayed as in the midst of
difficulties and dangers which would have unnerved and bowed
down any ordinary mind. It was closely connected, too, with
an ambition which had no mixture of low cupidity. There was
something noble in the cynical disdain with which the mighty
minister scattered riches and titles to right and left among those
who valued them, while he spurned them out of his own way.
Poor himself, he was surrounded by friends on whom he had
bestowed three thousand, six thousand, ten thousand a year.
Plain Mister himself, he had made more lords than any three
ministers that had preceded him. The garter, for which the
first dukes in the kingdom were contending, was repeatedly
offered to him, and offered in vain.

The correctness of his private life added much to the dignity
of his pubilc character. In the relations of son, brother, uncle,
master, friend, his conduct was exemplary. In the small circle
of his intimate associates, he was amiable, affectionate, even
playful.   They loved him sincerely; they regretted him long;
and they would hardly admit that he who was so kind and gentle
with them could be stern and haughty with others. He indulged,
indeed, somewhat too freely in wine, which he had early been
directed to take as a medicine, and which use had made a necessary of life to him. But it was very seldom that any indication
of undue excess could be detected in his tones or gestures; and,
in truth, two bottles of port were little more to him than two
dishes of tea. He had, when he was first introduced into the
clubs of Saint James's Street, shown a strong taste for play;
but he had the prudence and the resolution to stop before this
taste had acquired the strength of habit. From the passion
which generally exercises the most tyrannical dominion over
the young he possessed an immunity, which is probably to be
ascribed partly to his temperament and partly to his situation.
His constitution was feeble: he was very shy; and he was very
busy. The strictness of his morals furnished such buffoons as
Peter Pindar and Captain Morris with an inexhaustible theme for
merriment of no very delicate kind. But the great body of the
middle class of Englishmen could not see the joke They warmly
praised the young statesman for commanding his passions, and
for covering his frailties, if he had frailties, with decorous

obscurity, and would have been very far indeed from thinking better of him if he had vindicated himself from the taunts of his enemies by taking under his protection a Nancy Parsons or a Marianne Clark.

No part of the immense popularity which Pitt long enjoyed is to be attributed to the eulogies of wits and poets. It might have been naturally expected that a man of genius, of learning, of taste, an orator whose diction was often compared to that of Tully, the representative, too, of a great university, would have taken a peculiar pleasure in befriending eminent writers, to whatever political party they might have belonged. The love of literature had induced Augustus to heap benefits on Pompeians, Somers to be the protector of nonjurors, Harley to make the fortunes of Whigs. But it could not move Pitt to show any favour even to Pittites. He was doubtless right in thinking that, in general, poetry, history, and philosophy, ought to be suffered, like calico and cutlery, to find their proper price in the market, and that to teach men of letters to look habitually to the state for their recompense is bad for the state and bad for letters. Assuredly nothing can be more absurd or mischievous than to waste the public money in bounties for the purpose of inducing people who ought to be weighing out grocery or measuring out drapery to write bad or middling books. But, though the sound rule is that authors should be left to be remunerated by their readers, there will, in every generation, be a few exceptions to this rule. To distinguish these special cases from the mass is an employment well worthy of the faculties of a great and accomplished ruler; and Pitt would assuredly have had little difficulty in finding such cases. While he was in power, the greatest philologist of the age, his own contemporary at Cambridge, was reduced to earn a livelihood by the lowest literary drudgery, and to spend in writing squibs for the *Morning Chronicle* years to which we might have owed an all but perfect text of the whole tragic and comic drama of Athens. The greatest historian of the age, forced by poverty to leave his country, completed his immortal work on the shores of Lake Leman. The political heterodoxy of Porson, and the religious heterodoxy of Gibbon, may perhaps be pleaded in defence of the minister by whom those eminent men were neglected. But there were other cases in which no such excuse could be set up. Scarcely had Pitt obtained possession of unbounded power when an aged writer of the highest eminence, who had made very little by his writings, and who was sinking into the grave under a load of infirmities and sorrows, wanted five or six hundred pounds to enable him, during the winter or two which might still remain to him, to draw his breath more easily in the soft climate of Italy. Not a farthing was to be obtained; and before Christmas the author of the English Dictionary and of the Lives of the Poets had gasped his last in the river fog and coal smoke of Fleet Street. A few months after the death of Johnson appeared the Task, incomparably the best poem that any Englishman then living had produced—a poem, too, which could hardly fail to excite in a well-constituted mind a feeling of esteem and compassion for the poet, a man of genius and virtue, whose means were scanty, and whom the most cruel of all the calamities incident to humanity had made incapable of supporting himself by vigorous and sustained exertion. Nowhere had Chatham been praised with more enthusiasm, or in verse more worthy of the subject, than in the Task. The son of Chatham, however, contented himself with reading and admiring the book, and left the author to starve. The pension which, long after, enabled poor Cowper to close his melancholy life, unmolested by duns and bailiffs, was obtained for him by the strenuous kindness of Lord Spencer. What a contrast between the way in which Pitt acted towards Johnson and the way in which Lord Grey acted towards his political enemy Scott, when Scott, worn out by misfortune and disease, was advised to try the effect of the Italian air! What a contrast between the way in which Pitt acted towards Cowper and the way in which Burke, a poor man and out of place, acted towards Crabbe! Even Dundas, who made no pretensions to literary taste, and was content to be considered as a hard - headed and somewhat coarse man of business, was, when compared with his eloquent and classically educated friend, a Mæcenas or a Leo. Dundas made Burns an exciseman, with seventy pounds a year; and this was more than Pitt, during his long tenure of power, did for the encouragement of letters. Even those who may think that it is, in general, no part of the duty of a government to reward literary merit, will hardly deny that a government, which has much lucrative church preferment in its gift, is bound, in distributing that pre-ferment, not to overlook divines whose writings have rendered great service to the cause of religion. But it seems never to have occurred to Pitt that he lay under any such obligation. All the theological works of all the numerous bishops whom he made and translated are not, when put together, worth fifty pages of the Horæ Paulinæ, of the Natural Theology, or of the

View of the Evidences of Christianity. But on Paley the all-powerful minister never bestowed the smallest benefice. Artists Pitt treated as contemptuously as writers. For painting he did simply nothing. Sculptors, who had been selected to execute monuments voted by Parliament, had to haunt the ante-chambers of the Treasury during many years before they could obtain a farthing from him. One of them, after vainly soliciting the minister for payment during fourteen years, had the courage to present a memorial to the King, and thus obtained tardy and ungracious justice. Architects it was absolutely necessary to employ; and the worst that could be found seem to have been employed. Not a single fine public building of any kind or in any style was erected during his long administration. It may be confidently affirmed that no ruler whose abilities and attainments would bear any comparison with his has ever shown such cold disdain for what is excellent in arts and letters.

His first administration lasted seventeen years. That long period is divided by a strongly marked line into two almost exactly equal parts. The first part ended and the second began in the autumn of 1792. Throughout both parts Pitt displayed in the highest degree the talents of a parliamentary leader. During the first part he was a fortunate, and, in many respects, a skilful administrator. With the difficulties which he had to encounter during the second part he was altogether incapable of contending: but his eloquence and his perfect mastery of the tactics of the House of Commons concealed his incapacity from the multitude.

The eight years which followed the general election of 1784 were as tranquil and prosperous as any eight years in the whole history of England. Neighbouring nations which had lately been in arms against her, and which had flattered themselves that, in losing her American colonies, she had lost a chief source of her wealth and of her power, saw, with wonder and vexation, that she was more wealthy and more powerful than ever. Her trade increased. Her manufactures flourished. Her exchequer was full to overflowing. Very idle apprehensions were generally entertained that the public debt, though much less than a third of the debt which we now bear with ease, would be found too heavy for the strength of the nation. Those apprehensions might not perhaps have been easily quieted by reason. But Pitt quieted them by a juggle. He succeeded in persuading first himself, and then the whole nation, his opponents included, that a new sinking fund, which, so far as it differed from former sinking funds, differed for the worse, would, by virtue of some mysterious power of propagation belonging to money, put into the pocket of the public creditor great sums not taken out of the pocket of the tax-payer. The country, terrified by a danger which was no danger, hailed with delight and boundless confidence a remedy which was no remedy. The minister was almost universally extolled as the greatest of financiers. Meanwhile both the branches of the House of Bourbon found that England was as formidable an antagonist as she had ever been. France had formed a plan for reducing Holland to vassalage. But England interposed, and France receded. Spain interrupted by violence the trade of our merchants with the regions near the Oregon. But England armed, and Spain receded. Within the island there was profound tranquillity. The King was, for the first time, popular. During the twenty-three years which had followed his accession he had not been loved by his subjects. His domestic virtues were acknowledged. But it was generally thought that the good qualities by which he was distinguished in private life were wanting to his political character. As a Sovereign, he was resentful, unforgiving, stubborn, cunning. Under his rule the country had sustained cruel disgraces and disasters; and every one of those disgraces and disasters was imputed to his strong antipathies, and to his perverse obstinacy in the wrong. One statesman after another complained that he had been induced by royal caresses, entreaties, and promises, to undertake the direction of affairs at a difficult conjuncture, and that, as soon as he had, not without sullying his fame and alienating his best friends, served the turn for which he was wanted, his ungrateful master began to intrigue against him, and to canvass against him. Grenville, Rockingham, Chatham, men of widely different characters, but all three upright and high spirited, agreed in thinking that the Prince under whom they had successively held the highest place in the government was one of the most insincere of mankind. His confidence was reposed, they said, not in those known and responsible counsellors to whom he had delivered the seals of office, but in secret advisers who stole up the back stairs into his closet. In Parliament, his ministers, while defending themselves against the attacks of the opposition in front, were perpetually, at his instigation, assailed on the flank or in the rear by a vile band of mercenaries who called themselves his friends. These men constantly, while in possession of lucrative places in his service, spoke and voted against bills which he had authorised the First

Lord of the Treasury or the Secretary of State to bring in.   But from the day on which Pitt was placed at the head of affairs there was an end of secret influence.   His haughty and aspiring spirit was not to be satisfied with the mere show of power.   Any attempt to undermine him at Court, any mutinous movement among his followers in the House of Commons, was certain to be at once put down.   He had only to tender his resignation, and he could dictate his own terms.   For he, and he alone, stood between the King and the Coalition.   He was therefore little less than Mayor of the Palace.   The nation loudly applauded the King for having the wisdom to repose entire confidence in so excellent a minister.   His Majesty's private virtues now began to produce their full effect.   He was generally regarded as the model of a respectable country gentleman, honest, good-natured, sober, religious.   He rose early: he dined temperately: he was strictly faithful to his wife: he never missed church; and at church he never missed a response.   His people heartily prayed that he might long reign over them; and they prayed the more heartily because his virtues were set off to the best advantage by the vices and follies of the Prince of Wales, who lived in close intimacy with the chiefs of the opposition.

How strong this feeling was in the public mind appeared signally on one great occasion.   In the autumn of 1788 the King became insane.   The opposition, eager for office, committed the great indiscretion of asserting that the heir apparent had, by the fundamental laws of England, a right to be Regent with the full powers of royalty.   Pitt, on the other hand, maintained it to be the constitutional doctrine that, when a Sovereign is, by reason of infancy, disease, or absence, incapable of exercising the regal functions, it belongs to the estates of the realm to determine who shall be the vicegerent, and with what portion of the executive authority such vicegerent shall be entrusted.   A long and violent contest followed, in which Pitt was supported by the great body of the people with as much enthusiasm as during the first months of his administration.   Tories with one voice applauded him for defending the sick-bed of a virtuous and unhappy Sovereign against a disloyal faction and an undutiful son.   Not a few Whigs applauded him for asserting the authority of Parliaments and the principles of the Revolution, in opposition to a doctrine which seemed to have too much affinity with the servile theory of indefeasible hereditary right. The middle class, always zealous on the side of decency and the domestic virtues, looked forward with dismay to a reign resembling that of Charles II. The palace, which had now been, during thirty years, the pattern of an English home, would be a public nuisance, a school of profligacy. To the good King's repast of mutton and lemonade, despatched at three o'clock, would succeed midnight banquets, from which the guests would be carried home speechless. To the backgammon board at which the good King played for a little silver with his equerries, would succeed faro tables from which young patricians who had sate down rich would rise up beggars. The drawing-room, from which the frown of the Queen had repelled a whole generation of frail beauties, would now be again what it had been in the days of Barbara Palmer and Louisa de Querouaille. Nay, severely as the public reprobated the Prince's many illicit attachments, his one virtuous attachment was reprobated more severely still. Even in grave and pious circles his Protestant mistresses gave less scandal than his Popish wife. That he must be Regent nobody ventured to deny. But he and his friends were so unpopular that Pitt could, with general approbation, propose to limit the powers of the Regent by restrictions to which it would have been impossible to subject a Prince beloved and trusted by the country. Some interested men, fully expecting a change of administration, went over to the opposition. But the majority, purified by these desertions, closed its ranks, and presented a more firm array than ever to the enemy. In every division Pitt was victorious. When at length, after a stormy interregnum of three months, it was announced, on the very eve of the inauguration of the Regent, that the King was himself again, the nation was wild with delight. On the evening of the day on which His Majesty resumed his functions, a spontaneous illumination, the most general that had ever been seen in England, brightened the whole vast space from Highgate to Tooting, and from Hammersmith to Greenwich. On the day on which he returned thanks in the cathedral of his capital, all the horses and carriages within a hundred miles of London were too few for the multitudes which flocked to see him pass through the streets. A second illumination followed, which was even superior to the first in magnificence. Pitt with difficulty escaped from the tumultuous kindness of an innumerable multitude which insisted on drawing his coach from Saint Paul's Churchyard to Downing Street. This was the moment at which his fame and fortune may be said to have reached the zenith. His influence in the closet was as great as that of Carr or Villiers had been. His dominion over the Parliament was more abso-

lute than that of Walpole or Pelham had been.   He was at the
same time as high in the favour of the populace as ever Wilkes
or Sacheverell had been.   Nothing did more to raise his character than his noble poverty.   It was well known that, if he
had been dismissed from office after more than five years of
boundless power, he would hardly have carried out with him a
sum sufficient to furnish the set of chambers in which, as he
cheerfully declared, he meant to resume the practice of the law.
His admirers, however, were by no means disposed to suffer him
to depend on daily toil for his daily bread.   The voluntary contributions which were awaiting his acceptance in the city of
London alone would have sufficed to make him a rich man.   But
it may be doubted whether his haughty spirit would have
stooped to accept a provision so honourably earned and so
honourably bestowed.

To such a height of power and glory had this extraordinary
man risen at twenty-nine years of age.   And now the tide was
on the turn.   Only ten days after the triumphant procession to
Saint Paul's, the States-General of France, after an interval of
a hundred and seventy-four years, met at Versailles.

The nature of the great Revolution which followed was long
very imperfectly understood in this country.   Burke saw much
further than any of his contemporaries; but whatever his
sagacity descried was refracted and discoloured by his passions
and his imagination.   More than three years elapsed before the
principles of the English administration underwent any material
change.   Nothing could as yet be milder or more strictly constitutional than the minister's domestic policy.   Not a single
act indicating an arbitrary temper or a jealousy of the people
could be imputed to him.   He had never applied to Parliament
for any extraordinary powers.   He had never used with harsh-
ness the ordinary powers entrusted by the constitution to the
executive government.   Not a single state prosecution which
would even now be called oppressive had been instituted by
him.   Indeed, the only oppressive state prosecution instituted
during the first eight years of his administration was that of
Stockdale, which is to be attributed, not to the government,
but to the chiefs of the opposition.   In office, Pitt had redeemed
the pledges which he had, at his entrance into public life, given
to the supporters of parliamentary reform.   He had, in 1785,
brought forward a judicious plan for the improvement of the
representative system, and had prevailed on the King, not only
to refrain from talking against that plan, but to recommend it

to the Houses in a speech from the throne.[1] This attempt
failed: but there can be little doubt that, if the French Revolution had not produced a violent reaction of public feeling, Pitt
would have performed, with little difficulty and no danger, that
great work which, at a later period, Lord Grey could accomplish only by means which for a time loosened the very foundations of the commonwealth. When the atrocities of the slave
trade were first brought under the consideration of Parliament,
no abolitionist was more zealous than Pitt. When sickness
prevented Wilberforce from appearing in public, his place was
most efficiently supplied by his friend the minister. A humane
bill, which mitigated the horrors of the middle passage, was, in
1788, carried by the eloquence and determined spirit of Pitt, in
spite of the opposition of some of his own colleagues; and it
ought always to be remembered to his honour that, in order to
carry that bill, he kept the Houses sitting, in spite of many
murmurs, long after the business of the government had been
done, and the Appropriation Act passed. In 1791 he cordially
concurred with Fox in maintaining the sound constitutional
doctrine, that an impeachment is not terminated by a dissolution. In the course of the same year the two great rivals contended side by side in a far more important cause. They are
fairly entitled to divide the high honour of having added to our
statute-book the inestimable law which places the liberty of the
press under the protection of juries. On one occasion, and one
alone, Pitt, during the first half of his long administration, acted
in a manner unworthy of an enlightened Whig. In the debate
on the Test Act, he stooped to gratify the master whom he
served, the university which he represented, and the great body
of clergymen and country gentlemen on whose support he rested,
by talking, with little heartiness, indeed, and with no asperity,
the language of a Tory. With this single exception, his conduct
from the end of 1783 to the middle of 1792 was that of an
honest friend of civil and religious liberty.

Nor did anything, during that period, indicate that he loved
war, or harboured any malevolent feeling against any neighbouring nation. Those French writers who have represented
him as a Hannibal sworn in childhood by his father to bear
eternal hatred to France, as having, by mysterious intrigues
and lavish bribes, instigated the leading Jacobins to commit

[1] The speech with which the King opened the session of 1785 concluded
with an assurance that His Majesty would heartily concur in every measure
which could tend to secure the true principles of the constitution. These
words were at the time understood to refer to Pitt's Reform Bill.

those excesses which dishonoured the Revolution, as having been the real author of the first coalition, know nothing of his character or of his history. So far was he from being a deadly enemy to France that his laudable attempts to bring about a closer connection with that country by means of a wise and liberal treaty of commerce brought on him the severe censure of the opposition. He was told in the House of Commons that he was a degenerate son, and that his partiality for the hereditary foes of our island was enough to make his great father's bones stir under the pavement of the Abbey.

And this man, whose name, if he had been so fortunate as to die in 1792, would now have been associated with peace, with freedom, with philanthropy, with temperate reform, with mild and constitutional administration, lived to associate his name with arbitrary government, with harsh laws harshly executed, with alien bills, with gagging bills, with suspensions of the Habeas Corpus Act, with cruel punishments inflicted on some political agitators, with unjustifiable prosecutions instituted against others, and with the most costly and most sanguinary wars of modern times. He lived to be held up to obloquy as the stern oppressor of England, and the indefatigable disturber of Europe. Poets, contrasting his earlier with his later years, likened him sometimes to the apostle who kissed in order to betray, and sometimes to the evil angels who kept not their first estate. A satirist of great genius introduced the fiends of Famine, Slaughter, and Fire, proclaiming that they had received their commission from One whose name was formed of four letters, and promising to give their employer ample proofs of gratitude. Famine would gnaw the multitude till they should rise up against him in madness. The demon of Slaughter would impel them to tear him from limb to limb. But Fire boasted that she alone could reward him as he deserved, and that she would cling round him to all eternity. By the French press and the French tribune every crime that disgraced and every calamity that afflicted France was ascribed to the monster Pitt and his guineas. While the Jacobins were dominant, it was he who had corrupted the Gironde, who had raised Lyons and Bordeaux against the Convention, who had suborned Paris to assassinate Lepelletier, and Cecilia Regnault to assassinate Robespierre. When the Thermidorian reaction came, all the atrocities of the Reign of Terror were imputed to him. Collot d'Herbois and Fouquier Tinville had been his pensioners. It was he who had hired the murderers of September, who had dictated the pamphlets of Marat and the Carmagnoles of Barère, who had paid Lebon to deluge Arras with blood, and Carrier to choke the Loire with corpses.

The truth is, that he liked neither war nor arbitrary government. He was a lover of peace and freedom, driven, by a stress against which it was hardly possible for any will or any intellect to struggle, out of the course to which his inclinations pointed, and for which his abilities and acquirements fitted him, and forced into a policy repugnant to his feelings and unsuited to his talents.

The charge of apostasy is grossly unjust. A man ought no more to be called an apostate because his opinions alter with the opinions of the great body of his contemporaries, than he ought to be called an oriental traveller because he is always going round from west to east with the globe and everything that is upon it. Between the spring of 1789 and the close of 1792, the public mind of England underwent a great change. If the change of Pitt's sentiments attracted peculiar notice, it was not because he changed more than his neighbours; for in fact he changed less than most of them; but because his position was far more conspicuous than theirs, because he was, till Bonaparte appeared, the individual who filled the greatest space in the eyes of the inhabitants of the civilised world. During a short time the nation, and Pitt, as one of the nation, looked with interest and approbation on the French Revolution. But soon vast confiscations, the violent sweeping away of ancient institutions, the domination of clubs, the barbarities of mobs maddened by famine and hatred, produced a reaction here. The court, the nobility, the gentry, the clergy, the manufacturers, the merchants, in short, nineteen-twentieths of those who had good roofs over their heads and good coats on their backs, became eager and intolerant Antijacobins. This feeling was at least as strong among the minister's adversaries as among his supporters. Fox in vain attempted to restrain his followers. All his genius, all his vast personal influence, could not prevent them from rising up against him in general mutiny. Burke set the example of revolt; and Burke was in no long time joined by Portland, Spencer, FitzWilliam, Loughborough, Carlisle, Malmesbury, Windham, Elliot. In the House of Commons, the followers of the great Whig statesman and orator diminished from about a hundred and sixty to fifty. In the House of Lords he had but ten or twelve adherents left. There can be no doubt that there would have been a similar mutiny on the ministerial benches, if

Pitt had obstinately resisted the general wish.   Pressed at once by his master and by his colleagues, by old friends and by old opponents, he abandoned, slowly and reluctantly, the policy which was dear to his heart.   He laboured hard to avert the European war.   When the European war broke out, he still flattered himself that it would not be necessary for this country to take either side.   In the spring of 1792 he congratulated the Parliament on the prospect of long and profound peace, and proved his sincerity by proposing large remissions of taxation. Down to the end of that year he continued to cherish the hope that England might be able to preserve neutrality.   But the passions which raged on both sides of the Channel were not to be restrained.   The republicans who ruled France were inflamed by a fanaticism resembling that of the Mussulmans, who, with the Koran in one hand and the sword in the other, went forth, conquering and converting, eastward to the Bay of Bengal, and westward to the Pillars of Hercules.   The higher and middle classes of England were animated by zeal not less fiery than that of the Crusaders who raised the cry of *Deus vult* at Clermont. The impulse which drove the two nations to a collision was not to be arrested by the abilities or by the authority of any single man.   As Pitt was in front of his fellows, and towered high above them, he seemed to lead them.   But in fact he was violently pushed on by them, and, had he held back but a little more than he did, would have been thrust out of their way or trampled under their feet.

He yielded to the current: and from that day his misfortunes began.   The truth is that there were only two consistent courses before him.   Since he did not choose to oppose himself, side by side with Fox, to the public feeling, he should have taken the advice of Burke, and should have availed himself of that feeling to the full extent.   If it was impossible to preserve peace, he should have adopted the only policy which could lead to victory. He should have proclaimed a Holy War for religion, morality, property, order, public law, and should have thus opposed to the Jacobins an energy equal to their own.   Unhappily he tried to find a middle path; and he found one which united all that was worst in both extremes.   He went to war: but he would not understand the peculiar character of that war.   He was obstinately blind to the plain fact, that he was contending against a state which was also a sect, and that the new quarrel between England and France was of quite a different kind from the old quarrels about colonies in America and fortresses in the

Netherlands. He had to combat frantic enthusiasm, boundless ambition, restless activity, the wildest and most audacious spirit of innovation; and he acted as if he had had to deal with the harlots and fops of the old Court of Versailles, with Madame De Pompadour and the Abbé de Bernis. It was pitiable to hear him, year after year, proving to an admiring audience that the wicked Republic was exhausted, that she could not hold out, that her credit was gone, that her assignats were not worth more than the paper of which they were made; as if credit was necessary to a government of which the principle was rapine, as if Alboin could not turn Italy into a desert till he had negotiated a loan at five per cent, as if the exchequer bills of Attila had been at par. It was impossible that a man who so completely mistook the nature of a contest could carry on that contest successfully. Great as Pitt's abilities were, his military administration was that of a driveller. He was at the head of a nation engaged in a struggle for life and death, of a nation eminently distinguished by all the physical and all the moral qualities which make excellent soldiers. The resources at his command were unlimited. The Parliament was even more ready to grant him men and money than he was to ask for them. In such an emergency, and with such means, such a statesman as Richelieu, as Louvois, as Chatham, as Wellesley, would have created in a few months one of the finest armies in the world, and would soon have discovered and brought forward generals worthy to command such an army. Germany might have been saved by another Blenheim; Flanders recovered by another Ramilies; another Poitiers might have delivered the Royalist and Catholic provinces of France from a yoke which they abhorred, and might have spread terror even to the barriers of Paris. But the fact is, that, after eight years of war, after a vast destruction of life, after an expenditure of wealth far exceeding the expenditure of the American war, of the Seven Years' War, of the war of the Austrian Succession, and of the war of the Spanish Succession united, the English army, under Pitt, was the laughing-stock of all Europe. It could not boast of one single brilliant exploit. It had never shown itself on the Continent but to be beaten, chased, forced to re-embark, or forced to capitulate. To take some sugar island in the West Indies, to scatter some mob of half naked Irish peasants, such were the most splendid victories won by the British troops under Pitt's auspices.

The English navy no mismanagement could ruin. But during a long period whatever mismanagement could do was done.

The Earl of Chatham, without a single qualification for high public trust, was made, by a fraternal partiality, First Lord of the Admiralty, and was kept in that great post during two years of a war in which the very existence of the state depended on the efficiency of the fleet.   He continued to doze away and trifle away the time which ought to have been devoted to the public service, till the whole mercantile body, though generally disposed to support the government, complained bitterly that our flag gave no protection to our trade.   Fortunately he was succeeded by George, Earl Spencer, one of those chiefs of the Whig party who, in the great schism caused by the French Revolution, had followed Burke.   Lord Spencer, though inferior to many of his colleagues as an orator, was decidedly the best administrator among them.   To him it was owing that a long and gloomy succession of days of fasting, and, most emphatically, of humiliation, was interrupted, twice in the short space of eleven months, by days of thanksgiving for great victories.

It may seem paradoxical to say that the incapacity which Pitt showed in all that related to the conduct of the war is, in some sense, the most decisive proof that he was a man of very extraordinary abilities.   Yet this is the simple truth.   For assuredly one-tenth part of his errors and disasters would have been fatal to the power and influence of any minister who had not possessed, in the highest degree, the talents of a parliamentary leader. While his schemes were confounded, while his predictions were falsified, while the coalitions which he had laboured to form were falling to pieces, while the expeditions which he had set forth at enormous cost were ending in rout and disgrace, while the enemy against whom he was feebly contending was subjugating Flanders and Brabant, the Electorate of Mentz and the Electorate of Treves, Holland, Piedmont, Liguria, Lombardy, his authority over the House of Commons was constantly becoming more and more absolute.   There was his empire.   There were his victories, his Lodi and his Arcola, his Rivoli and his Marengo.   If some great misfortune, a pitched battle lost by the allies, the annexation of a new department to the French Republic, a sanguinary insurrection in Ireland, a mutiny in the fleet, a panic in the city, a run on the bank, had spread dismay through the ranks of his majority, that dismay lasted only till he rose from the Treasury bench, drew up his haughty head, stretched his arm with commanding gesture, and poured forth, in deep and sonorous tones, the lofty language of inextinguishable hope and inflexible resolution.   Thus, through a long and calamitous period, every disaster that happened without the walls of Parliament was regularly followed by a triumph within them. At length he had no longer an opposition to encounter. Of the great party which had contended against him during the first eight years of his administration more than one half now marched under his standard, with his old competitor the Duke of Portland at their head; and the rest had, after many vain struggles, quitted the field in despair. Fox had retired to the shades of St. Anne's Hill, and had there found, in the society of friends whom no vicissitude could estrange from him, of a woman whom he tenderly loved, and of the illustrious dead of Athens, of Rome, and of Florence, ample compensation for all the misfortunes of his public life. Session followed session with scarcely a single division. In the eventful year 1799, the largest minority that could be mustered against the government was twenty-five.

In Pitt's domestic policy there was at this time assuredly no want of vigour. While he offered to French Jacobinism a resistance so feeble that it only encouraged the evil which he wished to suppress, he put down English Jacobinism with a strong hand. The Habeas Corpus Act was repeatedly suspended. Public meetings were placed under severe restraints. The government obtained from Parliament power to send out of the country aliens who were suspected of evil designs; and that power was not suffered to be idle. Writers who propounded doctrines adverse to monarchy and aristocracy were proscribed and punished without mercy. It was hardly safe for a republican to avow his political creed over his beefsteak and his bottle of port at a chop-house. The old laws of Scotland against sedition, laws which were considered by Englishmen as barbarous, and which a succession of governments had suffered to rust, were now furbished up and sharpened anew. Men of cultivated minds and polished manners were, for offences which at Westminster would have been treated as mere misdemeanours, sent to herd with felons at Botany Bay. Some reformers, whose opinions were extravagant, and whose language was intemperate, but who had never dreamed of subverting the government by physical force, were indicted for high treason, and were saved from the gallows only by the righteous verdicts of juries. This severity was at the time loudly applauded by alarmists whom fear had made cruel, but will be seen in a very different light by posterity. The truth is, that the Englishmen who wished for a revolution were, even in number, not formidable, and, in everything but number, a faction utterly contemptible, without arms, or funds, or plans, or organisation, or leader. There can be no doubt that Pitt, strong as he was in the support of the great body of the nation, might easily have repressed the turbulence of the discontented minority by firmly yet temperately enforcing the ordinary law. Whatever vigour he showed during this unfortunate part of his life was vigour out of place and season. He was all feebleness and languor in his conflict with the foreign enemy who was really to be dreaded, and reserved all his energy and resolution for the domestic enemy who might safely have been despised.

One part only of **Pitt's** conduct during the last eight years of the eighteenth century deserves high praise. He was the first English minister who formed great designs for the benefit of Ireland. The manner in which the Roman Catholic population of that unfortunate country had been kept down during many generations seemed to him unjust and cruel; and it was scarcely possible for a man of his abilities not to perceive that, in a contest against the Jacobins, the Roman Catholics were his natural allies. Had he been able to do all that he wished, it is probable that a wise and liberal policy would have averted the rebellion of 1798. But the difficulties which he encountered were great, perhaps insurmountable; and the Roman Catholics were, rather by his misfortune than by his fault, thrown into the hands of the Jacobins. There was a third great rising of the Irishry against the Englishry, a rising not less formidable than the risings of 1641 and 1689. The Englishry remained victorious, and it was necessary for Pitt, as it had been necessary for Oliver Cromwell and William of Orange before him, to consider how the victory should be used. It is only just to his memory to say that he formed a scheme of policy, so grand and so simple, so righteous and so humane, that it would alone entitle him to a high place among statesmen. He determined to make Ireland one kingdom with England, and, at the same time, to relieve the Roman Catholic laity from civil disabilities, and to grant a public maintenance to the Roman Catholic clergy. Had he been able to carry these noble designs into effect, the Union would have been a Union indeed. It would have been inseparably associated in the minds of the great majority of Irishmen with civil and religious freedom; and the old Parliament in College Green would have been regretted only by a small knot of discarded jobbers and oppressors, and would have been remembered by the body of the nation with the loathing and contempt due to the most tyrannical and the most corrupt

assembly that had ever sate in Europe.   But Pitt could execute
only one half of what he had projected.   He succeeded in obtaining the consent of the Parliaments of both kingdoms to the
Union; but that reconciliation of races and sects, without which
the Union could exist only in name, was not accomplished.   He
was well aware that he was likely to find difficulties in the closet.
But he flattered himself that, by cautious and dexterous management, those difficulties might be overcome.   Unhappily, there
were traitors and sycophants in high place who did not suffer
him to take his own time and his own way, but prematurely
disclosed his scheme to the king, and disclosed it in the manner
most likely to irritate and alarm a weak and diseased mind.   His
Majesty absurdly imagined that his coronation oath bound him
to refuse his assent to any bill for relieving Roman Catholics
from civil disabilities.   To argue with him was impossible.
Dundas tried to explain the matter, but was told to keep his
Scotch metaphysics to himself.   Pitt and Pitt's ablest colleagues
resigned their offices.   It was necessary that the King should
make a new arrangement.   But by this time his anger and
distress had brought back the malady which had, many years
before, incapacitated him for the discharge of his functions.   He
actually asssembled his family, read the Coronation oath to
them, and told them that, if he broke it, the Crown would
immediately pass to the House of Savoy.   It was not until after
an interregnum of several weeks that he regained the full use
of his small faculties, and that a ministry after his own heart
was at length formed.

The materials out of which he had to construct a government
were neither solid nor splendid.   To that party, weak in numbers,
but strong in every kind of talent, which was hostile to the
domestic and foreign policy of his late advisers, he could not
have recourse.   For that party, while it differed from his late
advisers on every point on which they had been honoured with
his approbation, cordially agreed with them as to the single
matter which had brought on them his displeasure.   All that
was left to him was to call up the rear ranks of the old ministry
to form the front rank of a new ministry.   In an age pre-
eminently fruitful of parliamentary talents, a cabinet was
formed containing hardly a single man who, in parliamentary
talents, could be considered as even of the second rate.   The
most important offices in the state were bestowed on decorous
and laborious mediocrity.   Henry Addington was at the head
of the Treasury.   He had been an early, indeed a hereditary,
friend of Pitt, and had by Pitt's influence been placed, while still

a young man, in the chair of the House of Commons. He was universally admitted to have been the best speaker that had sate in that chair since the retirement of Onslow. But nature had not bestowed on him very vigorous faculties; and the highly respectable situation which he had long occupied with honour had rather unfitted than fitted him for the discharge of his new duties. His business had been to bear himself evenly between contending factions. He had taken no part in the war of words; and he had always been addressed with marked deference by the great orators who thundered against each other from his right and from his left. It was not strange that when, for the first time, he had to encounter keen and vigorous antagonists, who dealt hard blows without the smallest ceremony, he should have been awkward and unready, or that the air of dignity and authority which he had acquired in his former post, and of which he had not divested himself, should have made his helplessness laughable and pitiable. Nevertheless, during many months, his power seemed to stand firm. He was a favourite with the King, whom he resembled in narrowness of mind, and to whom he was more obsequious than Pitt had ever been. The nation was put into high good humour by a peace with France. The enthusiasm with which the upper and middle classes had rushed into the war had spent itself. Jacobinism was no longer formidable. Everywhere there was a strong reaction against what was called the atheistical and anarchical philosophy of the eighteenth century. Bonaparte, now First Consul, was busied in constructing out of the ruins of old institutions a new ecclesiastical establishment and a new order of knighthood. That nothing less than the dominion of the whole civilised world would satisfy his selfish ambition was not yet suspected; nor did even wise men see any reason to doubt that he might be as safe a neighbour as any prince of the House of Bourbon had been. The treaty of Amiens was therefore hailed by the great body of the English people with extravagant joy. The popularity of the minister was for the moment immense. His want of parliamentary ability was, as yet, of little consequence: for he had scarcely any adversary to encounter. The old opposition, delighted by the peace, regarded him with favour. A new opposition had indeed been formed by some of the late ministers, and was led by Grenville in the House of Lords, and by Windham in the House of Commons. But the new opposition could scarcely muster ten votes, and was regarded with no favour by the country. On Pitt the ministers relied as on their firmest support. He had not, like some of his colleagues, retired in anger. He had expressed the greatest respect for the conscientious scruple which had taken possession of the royal mind; and he had promised his successors all the help in his power. In private his advice was at their service. In Parliament he took his seat on the bench behind them; and, in more than one debate, defended them with powers far superior to their own. The King perfectly understood the value of such assistance. On one occasion, at the palace, he took the old minister and the new minister aside. "If we three," he said, "keep together, all will go well."

But it was hardly possible, human nature being what it is, and, more especially, Pitt and Addington being what they were, that this union should be durable. Pitt, conscious of superior powers, imagined that the place which he had quitted was now occupied by a mere puppet which he had set up, which he was to govern while he suffered it to remain, and which he was to fling aside as soon as he wished to resume his old position. Nor was it long before he began to pine for the power which he had relinquished. He had been so early raised to supreme authority in the state, and had enjoyed that authority so long, that it had become necessary to him. In retirement his days passed heavily. He could not, like Fox, forget the pleasures and cares of ambition in the company of Euripides or Herodotus. Pride restrained him from intimating, even to his dearest friends, that he wished to be again minister. But he thought it strange, almost ungrateful, that his wish had not been divined, that it had not been anticipated, by one whom he regarded as his deputy.

Addington, on the other hand, was by no means inclined to descend from his high position. He was, indeed, under a delusion much resembling that of Abou Hassan in the Arabian tale. His brain was turned by his short and unreal Caliphate. He took his elevation quite seriously, attributed it to his own merit, and considered himself as one of the great triumvirate of English statesmen, as worthy to make a third with Pitt and Fox.

Such being the feelings of the late minister and of the present minister, a rupture was inevitable; and there was no want of persons bent on making that rupture speedy and violent. Some of these persons wounded Addington's pride by representing him as a lacquey, sent to keep a place on the Treasury bench till his master should find it convenient to come. Others took every opportunity of praising him at Pitt's expense. Pitt had waged a long, a bloody, a costly, an unsuccessful war. Addington had made peace. Pitt had suspended the constitutional liberties of Englishmen.   Under Addington those liberties were again enjoyed.   Pitt had wasted the public resources.   Addington was carefully nursing them.   It was sometimes but too evident that these compliments were not unpleasing to Addington.   Pitt became cold and reserved.   During many months he remained at a distance from London.   Meanwhile his most intimate friends, in spite of his declarations that he made no complaint, and that he had no wish for office, exerted themselves to effect a change of ministry.   His favourite disciple, George Canning, young, ardent, ambitious, with great powers and great virtues, but with a temper too restless and a wit too satirical for his own happiness, was indefatigable.   He spoke; he wrote; he intrigued; he tried to induce a large number of the supporters of the government to sign a round robin desiring a change; he made game of Addington and of Addington's relations in a succession of lively pasquinades.   The minister's partisans retorted with equal acrimony, if not with equal vivacity.   Pitt could keep out of the affray only by keeping out of politics altogether; and this it soon became impossible for him to do.   Had Napoleon, content with the first place among the sovereigns of the Continent, and with a military reputation surpassing that of Marlborough or of Turenne, devoted himself to the noble task of making France happy by mild administration and wise legislation, our country might have long continued to tolerate a government of fair intentions and feeble abilities.   Unhappily, the treaty of Amiens had scarcely been signed, when the restless ambition and the insupportable insolence of the First Consul convinced the great body of the English people that the peace, so eagerly welcomed, was only a precarious armistice.   As it became clearer and clearer that a war for the dignity, the independence, the very existence of the nation was at hand, men looked with increasing uneasiness on the weak and languid cabinet which would have to contend against an enemy who united more than the power of Lewis the Great to more than the genius of Frederick the Great. It is true that Addington might easily have been a better war minister than Pitt, and could not possibly have been a worse. But Pitt had cast a spell on the public mind.   The eloquence, the judgment, the calm and disdainful firmness which he had, during many years, displayed in Parliament, deluded the world into the belief that he must be eminently qualified to superintend every department of politics; and they imagined, even after the miserable failures of Dunkirk, of Quiberon, and of the Helder, that he was the only statesman who could cope with Bonaparte.

This feeling was nowhere stronger than among Addington's own colleagues. The pressure put on him was so strong that he could not help yielding to it; yet, even in yielding, he showed how far he was from knowing his own place. His first proposition was, that some insignificant nobleman should be First Lord of the Treasury and nominal head of the administration, and that the real power should be divided between Pitt and himself, who were to be secretaries of state. Pitt, as might have been expected, refused even to discuss such a scheme, and talked of it with bitter mirth. " Which secretaryship was offered to you? " his friend Wilberforce asked. " Really," said Pitt, " I had not the curiosity to inquire." Addington was frightened into bidding higher. He offered to resign the Treasury to Pitt, on condition that there should be no extensive change in the government. But Pitt would listen to no such terms. Then came a dispute such as often arises after negotiations orally conducted, even when the negotiators are men of strict honour. Pitt gave one account of what had passed; Addington gave another; and though the discrepancies were not such as necessarily implied any intentional violation of truth on either side, both were greatly exasperated.

Meanwhile the quarrel with the First Consul had come to a crisis. On the 16th of May 1803, the King sent a message calling on the House of Commons to support him in withstanding the ambitious and encroaching policy of France; and on the 22nd, the House took the message into consideration.

Pitt had now been living many months in retirement. There had been a general election since he had spoken in Parliament, and there were two hundred members who had never heard him. It was known that on this occasion he would be in his place, and curiosity was wound up to the highest point. Unfortunately, the shorthand writers were, in consequence of some mistake, shut out on that day from the gallery, so that the newspapers contained only a very meagre report of the proceedings. But several accounts of what passed are extant; and of those accounts the most interesting is contained in an unpublished letter written by a very young member, John William Ward, afterwards Earl of Dudley. When Pitt rose, he was received with loud cheering. At every pause in his speech there was a burst of applause. The peroration is said to have been one of the most animated and magnificent ever heard in Parliament. " Pitt's speech," Fox wrote a few days later, " was admired very much, and very justly. I think it was the best he ever made in that style." The debate was adjourned; and on the second night Fox replied in an oration which, as the most zealous Pittites were forced to acknowledge, left the palm of eloquence doubtful. Addington made a pitiable appearance between the two great rivals; and it was observed that Pitt, while exhorting the Commons to stand resolutely by the executive government against France, said not a word indicating esteem or friendship for the prime minister.

War was speedily declared. The First Consul threatened to invade England at the head of the conquerors of Belgium and Italy, and formed a great camp near the Straits of Dover. On the other side of those straits the whole population of our island was ready to rise up as one man in defence of the soil. At this conjuncture, as at some other great conjunctures in our history, the conjuncture of 1660, for example, and the conjuncture of 1688, there was a general disposition among honest and patriotic men to forget old quarrels, and to regard as a friend every person who was ready, in the existing emergency, to do his part towards the saving of the state. A coalition of all the first men in the country would, at that moment, have been as popular as the coalition of 1783 had been unpopular. Alone in the kingdom the King looked with perfect complacency on a cabinet in which no man superior to himself in genius was to be found, and was so far from being willing to admit all his ablest subjects to office that he was bent on excluding them all.

A few months passed before the different parties which agreed in regarding the government with dislike and contempt came to an understanding with each other. But in the spring of 1804 it became evident that the weakest of ministries would have to defend itself against the strongest of oppositions, an opposition made up of three oppositions, each of which would, separately, have been formidable from ability, and which, when united, were also formidable from number. The party which had opposed the peace, headed by Grenville and Windham, and the party which had opposed the renewal of the war, headed by Fox, concurred in thinking that the men now in power were incapable of either making a good peace or waging a vigorous war. Pitt had, in 1802, spoken for peace against the party of Grenville, and had, in 1803, spoken for war against the party of Fox. But of the capacity of the cabinet, and especially of its chief, for the conduct of great affairs, he thought as meanly as either Fox or Grenville. Questions were easily found on which all the enemies of the government could act cordially together. The unfortunate First Lord of the Treasury, who had, during the earlier months of his administration, been supported by Pitt on one side, and by Fox on the other, now had to answer Pitt, and to be answered by Fox. Two sharp debates, followed by close divisions, made him weary of his post. It was known, too, that the Upper House was even more hostile to him than the Lower, that the Scotch representative peers wavered, that there were signs of mutiny among the Bishops. In the cabinet itself there was discord, and, worse than discord, treachery. It was necessary to give way: the ministry was dissolved; and the task of forming a government was entrusted to Pitt.

Pitt was of opinion that there was now an opportunity, such as had never before offered itself, and such as might never offer itself again, of uniting in the public service, on honourable terms, all the eminent talents of the kingdom. The passions to which the French Revolution had given birth were extinct. The madness of the innovator and the madness of the alarmist had alike had their day. Jacobinism and Anti-jacobinism had gone out of fashion together. The most liberal statesman did not think that season propitious for schemes of parliamentary reform; and the most conservative statesman could not pretend that there was any occasion for gagging bills and suspensions of the Habeas Corpus Act. The great struggle for independence and national honour occupied all minds; and those who were agreed as to the duty of maintaining that struggle with vigour might well postpone to a more convenient time all disputes about matters comparatively unimportant. Strongly impressed by these considerations, Pitt wished to form a ministry including all the first men in the country. The Treasury he reserved for himself; and to Fox he proposed to assign a share of power little inferior to his own.

The plan was excellent: but the King would not hear of it. Dull, obstinate, unforgiving, and, at that time, half mad, he positively refused to admit Fox into his service. Anybody else, even men who had gone as far as Fox, or further than Fox, in what His Majesty considered as Jacobinism, Sheridan, Grey, Erskine, should be graciously received; but Fox never. During several hours Pitt laboured in vain to reason down this senseless antipathy. That he was perfectly sincere there can be no doubt; but it was not enough to be sincere; he should have been resolute. Had he declared himself determined not to take office without Fox, the royal obstinacy would have given way as it gave way a few months later, when opposed to the immutable resolution of Lord Grenville. In an evil hour Pitt yielded. He flattered himself with the hope that, though he consented to forego the aid of his illustrious rival, there would still remain

ample materials for the formation of an efficient ministry.   That
hope was cruelly disappointed.   Fox entreated his friends to
leave personal considerations out of the question, and declared
that he would support with the utmost cordiality, an efficient
and patriotic ministry from which he should be himself excluded.
Not only his friends, however, but Grenville and Grenville's
adherents, answered with one voice, that the question was not
personal, that a great constitutional principle was at stake, and
that they would not take office while a man eminently qualified
to render service to the commonwealth was placed under a ban
merely because he was disliked at Court.   All that was left to
Pitt was to construct a government out of the wreck of Addington's feeble administration.   The small circle of his personal
retainers furnished him with a very few useful assistants, particularly Dundas, who had been created Viscount Melville, Lord
Harrowby, and Canning.

Such was the inauspicious manner in which Pitt entered on
his second administration.   The whole history of that administration was of a piece with the commencement.   Almost every
month brought some new disaster or disgrace.   To the war with
France was soon added a war with Spain.   The opponents of
the minister were numerous, able, and active.   His most useful
coadjutors he soon lost.   Sickness deprived him of the help of
Lord Harrowby.   It was discovered that Lord Melville had been
guilty of highly culpable laxity in transactions relating to public
money.   He was censured by the House of Commons, driven
from office, ejected from the Privy Council, and impeached of
high crimes and misdemeanours.   The blow fell heavily on Pitt.
It gave him, he said in Parliament, a deep pang; and, as he
uttered the word pang, his lip quivered; his voice shook; he
paused; and his hearers thought that he was about to burst
into tears.   Such tears shed by Eldon would have moved
nothing but laughter.   Shed by the warm-hearted and open-
hearted Fox, they would have moved sympathy, but would have
caused no surprise.   But a tear from Pitt would have been
something portentous.   He suppressed his emotion, however,
and proceeded with his usual majestic self-possession.

His difficulties compelled him to resort to various expedients.
At one time Addington was persuaded to accept office with a
peerage; but he brought no additional strength to the government.   Though he went through the form of reconciliation it
was impossible for him to forget the past.   While he remained
in place he was jealous and punctilious; and he soon retired
again.   At another time Pitt renewed his efforts to overcome

his master's aversion to Fox; and it was rumoured that the King's obstinacy was gradually giving way. But, meanwhile, it was impossible for the minister to conceal from the public eye the decay of his health and the constant anxiety which gnawed at his heart. His sleep was broken. His food ceased to nourish him. All who passed him in the Park, all who had interviews with him in Downing Street, saw misery written in his face. The peculiar look which he wore during the last months of his life was often pathetically described by Wilberforce, who used to call it the Austerlitz look.

Still the vigour of Pitt's intellectual faculties, and the intrepid haughtiness of his spirit, remained unaltered. He had staked everything on a great venture. He had succeeded in forming another mighty coalition against the French ascendency. The united forces of Austria, Russia, and England might, he hoped, oppose an insurmountable barrier to the ambition of the common enemy. But the genius and energy of Napoleon prevailed. While the English troops were preparing to embark for Germany, while the Russian troops were slowly coming up from Poland, he, with rapidity unprecedented in modern war, moved a hundred thousand men from the shores of the ocean to the Black Forest, and compelled a great Austrian army to surrender at Ulm. To the first faint rumours of this calamity Pitt would give no credit. He was irritated by the alarms of those around him. "Do not believe a word of it," he said: "it is all a fiction." The next day he received a Dutch newspaper containing the capitulation. He knew no Dutch. It was Sunday; and the public offices were shut. He carried the paper to Lord Malmesbury, who had been minister in Holland; and Lord Malmesbury translated it. Pitt tried to bear up; but the shock was too great; and he went away with death in his face.

The news of the battle of Trafalgar arrived four days later, and seemed for a moment to revive him. Forty-eight hours after that most glorious and most mournful of victories had been announced to the country came the Lord Mayor's day; and Pitt dined at Guildhall. His popularity had declined. But on this occasion, the multitude, greatly excited by the recent tidings, welcomed him enthusiastically, took off his horses in Cheapside, and drew his carriage up King Street. When his health was drunk, he returned thanks in two or three of those stately sentences of which he had a boundless command. Several of those who heard him laid up his words in their hearts; for they were the last words that he ever uttered in public: " Let us hope that England, having saved herself by her energy, may save Europe by her example."

This was but a momentary rally. Austerlitz soon completed what Ulm had begun. Early in December Pitt had retired to Bath, in the hope that he might there gather strength for the approaching session. While he was languishing there on his sofa arrived the news that a decisive battle had been fought and lost in Moravia, that the coalition was dissolved, that the Continent was at the feet of France. He sank down under the blow. Ten days later, he was so emaciated that his most intimate friends hardly knew him. He came up from Bath by slow journeys, and, on the 11th of January 1806, reached his villa at Putney. Parliament was to meet on the 21st. On the 20th was to be the parliamentary dinner at the house of the First Lord of the Treasury in Downing Street; and the cards were already issued. But the days of the great minister were numbered. The only chance for his life, and that a very slight chance, was, that he should resign his office, and pass some months in profound repose. His colleagues paid him very short visits, and carefully avoided political conversation. But his spirit, long accustomed to dominion, could not, even in that extremity, relinquish hopes which everybody but himself perceived to be vain. On the day on which he was carried into his bedroom at Putney, the Marquess Wellesley, whom he had long loved, whom he had sent to govern India, and whose administration had been eminently able, energetic, and successful, arrived in London after an absence of eight years. The friends saw each other once more. There was an affectionate meeting, and a last parting. That it was a last parting Pitt did not seem to be aware. He fancied himself to be recovering, talked on various subjects cheerfully, and with an unclouded mind, and pronounced a warm and discerning eulogium on the Marquess's brother Arthur. " I never," he said, " met with any military man with whom it was so satisfactory to converse." The excitement and exertion of this interview were too much for the sick man. He fainted away; and Lord Wellesley left the house, convinced that the close was fast approaching.

And now members of Parliament were fast coming up to London. The chiefs of the opposition met for the purpose of considering the course to be taken on the first day of the session. It was easy to guess what would be the language of the King's speech, and of the address which would be moved in answer to that speech. An amendment condemning the policy of the government had been prepared, and was to have been proposed in the House of Commons by Lord Henry Petty, a young noble-man who had already won for himself that place in the esteem of his country which, after the lapse of more than half a century, he still retains. He was unwilling, however, to come forward as the accuser of one who was incapable of defending himself. Lord Grenville, who had been informed of Pitt's state by Lord Wellesley, and had been deeply affected by it, earnestly recommended forbearance; and Fox, with characteristic generosity and good nature, gave his voice against attacking his now helpless rival. "Sunt lacrymæ rerum," he said, "et mentem mortalia tangunt." On the first day, therefore, there was no debate. It was rumoured that evening that Pitt was better. But on the following morning his physicians pronounced that there were no hopes. The commanding faculties of which he had been too proud were beginning to fail. His old tutor and friend, the Bishop of Lincoln, informed him of his danger, and gave such religious advice and consolation as a confused and obscured mind could receive. Stories were told of devout sentiments fervently uttered by the dying man. But these stories found no credit with anybody who knew him. Wilberforce pronounced it impossible that they could be true; "Pitt," he added, "was a man who always said less than he thought on such topics." It was asserted in many after-dinner speeches, Grub Street elegies, and academic prize poems and prize declamations, that the great minister died exclaiming, "O my country!" This is a fable; but it is true that the last words which he uttered, while he knew what he said, were broken exclamations about the alarming state of public affairs. He ceased to breathe on the morning of the 23rd of January 1806, the twenty-fifth anniversary of the day on which he first took his seat in Parliament. He was in his forty-seventh year, and had been, during near nineteen years, First Lord of the Treasury, and undisputed chief of the administration. Since parliamentary government was established in England, no English statesman has held supreme power so long. Walpole, it is true, was First Lord of the Treasury during more than twenty years, but it was not till Walpole had been some time First Lord of the Treasury that he could be properly called Prime Minister.

It was moved in the House of Commons that Pitt should be honoured with a public funeral and a monument. The motion was opposed by Fox in a speech which deserves to be studied as a model of good taste and good feeling. The task was the most invidious that ever an orator undertook; but it was performed with a humanity and delicacy which were warmly acknowledged by the mourning friends of him who was gone.   The motion was carrried by 288 votes to 89.

The 22nd of February was fixed for the funeral.   The corpse having lain in state during two days in the Painted Chamber, was borne with great pomp to the northern transept of the Abbey.   A splendid train of princes, nobles, bishops, and privy councillors followed.   The grave of Pitt had been made near to the spot where his great father lay, near also to the spot where his great rival was soon to lie.   The sadness of the assistants was beyond that of ordinary mourners.   For he whom they were committing to the dust had died of sorrows and anxieties of which none of the survivors could be altogether without a share. Wilberforce, who carried the banner before the hearse, described the awful ceremony with deep feeling.   As the coffin descended into the earth, he said, the eagle face of Chatham from above seemed to look down with consternation into the dark house which was receiving all that remained of so much power and glory.

All parties in the House of Commons readily concurred in voting forty thousand pounds to satisfy the demands of Pitt's creditors.   Some of his admirers seemed to consider the magnitude of his embarrassments as a circumstance highly honourable to him; but men of sense will probably be of a different opinion.   It is far better, no doubt, that a great minister should carry his contempt of money to excess than that he should contaminate his hands with unlawful gain.   But it is neither right nor becoming in a man to whom the public has given an income more than sufficient for his comfort and dignity to bequeath to that public a great debt, the effect of mere negligence and profusion.   As first Lord of the Treasury and Chancellor of the Exchequer, Pitt never had less than six thousand a year, besides an excellent house.   In 1792 he was forced by his royal master's friendly importunity to accept for life the office of Warden of the Cinque Ports, with near four thousand a year more.   He had neither wife nor child; he had no needy relations: he had no expensive tastes; he had no long election bills.   Had he given but a quarter of an hour a week to the regulation of his household, he would have kept his expenditure within bounds.   Or, if he could not spare even a quarter of an hour a week for that purpose, he had numerous friends, excellent men of business, who would have been proud to act as his stewards.   One of those friends, the chief of a great commercial house in the city, made an attempt to put the establishment in Downing Street to rights; but in vain.   He found that the waste of the servant's hall was almost fabulous.

The quantity of butcher's meat charged in the bills was nine hundredweight a week. The consumption of poultry, of fish, of tea, was in proportion. The character of Pitt would have stood higher if, with the disinterestedness of Pericles and of De Witt, he had united their dignified frugality.

The memory of Pitt has been assailed, times innumerable, often justly, often unjustly; but it has suffered much less from his assailants than from his eulogists. For, during many years, his name was the rallying cry of a class of men with whom, at one of those terrible conjunctures which confound all ordinary distinctions, he was accidentally and temporarily connected, but to whom, on almost all great questions of principle, he was diametrically opposed. The haters of parliamentary reform called themselves Pittites, not choosing to remember that Pitt made three motions for parliamentary reform, and that, though he thought that such a reform could not safely be made while the passions excited by the French Revolution were raging, he never uttered a word indicating that he should not be prepared at a more convenient season to bring the question forward a fourth time. The toast of Protestant ascendency was drunk on Pitt's birthday by a set of Pittites who could not but be aware that Pitt had resigned his office because he could not carry Catholic emancipation. The defenders of the Test Act called themselves Pittites, though they could not be ignorant that Pitt had laid before George the Third unanswerable reasons for abolishing the Test Act. The enemies of free trade called themselves Pittites, though Pitt was far more deeply imbued with the doctrines of Adam Smith than either Fox or Grey. The very Negro-drivers invoked the name of Pitt, whose eloquence was never more conspicuously displayed than when he spoke of the wrongs of the Negro. This mythical Pitt, who resembles the genuine Pitt as little as the Charlemagne of Ariosto resembles the Charlemagne of Eginhard, has had his day. History will vindicate the real man from calumny disguised under the semblance of adulation, and will exhibit him as what he was, a minister of great talents, honest intentions, and liberal opinions, pre-eminently qualified, intellectually and morally, for the part of a parliamentary leader, and capable of administering with prudence and moderation the government of a prosperous and tranquil country, but unequal to surprising and terrible emergencies, and liable, in such emergencies to err grievously, both on the side of weakness and on the side of violence.

ON THE ROYAL SOCIETY OF LITERATURE

(JUNE 1823)

THIS is the age of societies. There is scarcely one Englishman in ten who has not belonged to some association for distributing books, or for prosecuting them; for sending invalids to the hospital, or beggars to the treadmill; for giving plate to the rich, or blankets to the poor. To be the most absurd institution among so many institutions is no small distinction; it seems, however, to belong indisputably to the Royal Society of Literature. At the first establishment of that ridiculous academy, every sensible man predicted that, in spite of regal patronage and episcopal management, it would do nothing, or do harm. And it will scarcely be denied that those expectations have hitherto been fulfilled.

I do not attack the founders of the association. Their characters are respectable; their motives, I am willing to believe, were laudable. But I feel, and it is the duty of every literary man to feel, a strong jealousy of their proceedings. Their society can be innocent only while it continues to be despicable. Should they ever possess the power to encourage merit, they must also possess the power to depress it. Which power will be more frequently exercised, let every one who has studied literary history, let every one who has studied human nature, declare.

Envy and faction insinuate themselves into all communities. They often disturb the peace, and pervert the decisions, of benevolent and scientific associations. But it is in literary academies that they exert the most extensive and pernicious influence. In the first place, the principles of literary criticism, though equally fixed with those on which the chemist and the surgeon proceed, are by no means equally recognised. Men are rarely able to assign a reason for their approbation or dislike on questions of taste; and therefore they willingly submit to any guide who boldly asserts his claim to superior discernment. It is more difficult to ascertain and establish the merits of a poem than the powers of a machine or the benefits of a new remedy. Hence it is in literature, that quackery is most easily puffed, and excellence most easily decried.

In some degree this argument applies to academies of the fine arts; and it is fully confirmed by all that I have ever heard of that institution which annually disfigures the walls of Somerset House with an acre of spoiled canvas. But a literary tribunal is incomparably more dangerous. Other societies, at least, have no tendency to call forth any opinions on those subjects which most agitate and inflame the minds of men. The sceptic and the zealot, the revolutionist and the placeman, meet on common ground in a gallery of paintings or a laboratory of science. They can praise or censure without reference to the differences which exist between them. In a literary body this can never be the case. Literature is, and always must be, inseparably blended with politics and theology; it is the great engine which moves the feelings of a people on the most momentous questions. It is, therefore, impossible that any society can be formed so impartial as to consider the literary character of an individual abstracted from the opinions which his writings inculcate. It is not to be hoped, perhaps it is not to be wished, that the feelings of the man should be so completely forgotten in the duties of the academician. The consequences are evident. The honours and censures of this Star Chamber of the Muses will be awarded according to the prejudices of the particular sect or faction which may at the time predominate. Whigs would canvass against a Southey, Tories against a Byron. Those who might at first protest against such conduct as unjust would soon adopt it on the plea of retaliation; and the general good of literature, for which the society was professedly instituted, would be forgotten in the stronger claims of political and religious partiality.

Yet even this is not the worst. Should the institution ever acquire any influence, it will afford most pernicious facilities to every malignant coward who may desire to blast a reputation which he envies. It will furnish a secure ambuscade, behind which the Maroons of literature may take a certain and deadly aim. The editorial *we* has often been fatal to rising genius; though all the world knows that it is only a form of speech, very often employed by a single needy blockhead. The academic *we* would have a far greater and more ruinous influence. Numbers, while they increase the effect, would diminish the shame, of injustice. The advantages of an open and those of an anonymous attack would be combined; and the authority of avowal would be united to the security of concealment. The serpents in Virgil, after they had destroyed Laocoon, found an asylum from the vengeance of the enraged people behind the shield of the statue of Minerva.   And, in the same manner, everything that is grovelling and venomous, everything that can hiss, and everything that can sting, would take sanctuary in the recesses of this new temple of wisdom.

The French academy was, of all such associations, the most widely and the most justly celebrated.   It was founded by the greatest of ministers: it was patronised by successive kings; it numbered in its lists most of the eminent French writers.   Yet what benefit has literature derived from its labours?   What is its history but an uninterrupted record of servile compliances, of paltry artifices, of deadly quarrels, or perfidious friendships?   Whether governed by the court, by the Sorbonne, or by the philosophers, it was always equally powerful for evil, and equally impotent for good.   I might speak of the attacks by which it attempted to depress the rising fame of Corneille; I might speak of the reluctance with which it gave its tardy confirmation to the applauses which the whole civilised world had bestowed on the genius of Voltaire.   I might prove by overwhelming evidence that, to the latest period of its existence, even under the superintendence of the all-accomplished D'Alembert, it continued to be a scene of the fiercest animosities and the basest intrigues.   I might cite Piron's epigrams, and Marmontel's memoirs, and Montesquieu's letters.   But I hasten on to another topic.

One of the modes by which our society proposes to encourage merit is the distribution of prizes.   The munificence of the king has enabled it to offer an annual premium of a hundred guineas for the best essay in prose, and another of fifty guineas for the best poem, which may be transmitted to it.   This is very laughable.   In the first place the judges may err.   Those imperfections of human intellect to which, as the articles of the church tell us, even general councils are subject, may possibly be found even in the Royal Society of Literature.   The French academy, as I have already said, was the most illustrious assembly of the kind, and numbered among its associates men much more distinguished than ever will assemble at Mr. Hatchard's to rummage the box of the English Society.   Yet this famous body gave a poetical prize, for which Voltaire was a candidate, to a fellow who wrote some verses about *the frozen and the burning pole*.

Yet, granting that the prizes were always awarded to the best composition, that composition, I say without hesitation, will always be bad.   A prize poem is like a prize sheep.   The object of the competitor for the agricultural premium is to produce an animal fit, not to be eaten, but to be weighed. Accordingly he pampers his victim into morbid and unnatural fatness; and, when it is in such a state that it would be sent away in disgust from any table, he offers it to the judges. The object of the poetical candidate, in like manner, is to produce, not a good poem, but a poem of that exact degree of frigidity or bombast which may appear to his censors to be correct or sublime. Compositions thus constructed will always be worthless. The few excellences which they may contain will have an exotic aspect and flavour. In general, prize sheep are good for nothing but to make tallow candles, and prize poems are good for nothing but to light them.

The first subject proposed by the society to the poets of England was Dartmoor. I thought that they intended a covert sarcasm at their own projects. Their institution was a literary Dartmoor scheme; a plan for forcing into cultivation the waste lands of intellect, for raising poetical produce, by means of bounties, from soil too meagre to have yielded any returns in the natural course of things. The plan for the cultivation of Dartmoor has, I hear, been abandoned. I hope that this may be an omen of the fate of the society.

In truth, this seems by no means improbable. They have been offering for several years the rewards which the king placed at their disposal, and have not, as far as I can learn, been able to find in their box one composition which they have deemed worthy of publication. At least no publication has taken place. The associates may perhaps be astonished at this. But I will attempt to explain it, after the manner of ancient times, by means of an apologue.

About four hundred years after the Deluge, King Gomer Chephoraod reigned in Babylon. He united all the characteristics of an excellent sovereign. He made good laws, won great battles, and white-washed long streets. He was, in consequence, idolised by his people, and panegyrised by many poets and orators. A book was then a serious undertaking. Neither paper nor any similar material had been invented. Authors were therefore under the necessity of inscribing their compositions on massive bricks. Some of these Babylonian records are still preserved in European museums; but the language in which they are written has never been deciphered. Gomer Chephoraod was so popular that the clay of all the plains round the Euphrates could scarcely furnish brick-kilns enough for his eulogists. It is recorded in particular that Pharonezzar, the Assyrian Pindar, published a bridge and four walls in his praise.

One day the king was going in state from his palace to the temple of Belus. During this procession it was lawful for any Babylonian to offer any petition or suggestion to his sovereign. As the chariot passed before a vintner's shop, a large company, apparently half-drunk, sallied forth into the street, and one of them thus addressed the king:—

"Gomer Chephoraod, live for ever! It appears to thy servants that of all the productions of the earth good wine is the best, and bad wine is the worst. Good wine makes the heart cheerful, the eyes bright, the speech ready. Bad wine confuses the head, disorders the stomach, makes us quarrelsome at night, and sick the next morning. Now therefore let my lord the king take order that thy servants may drink good wine."

" And how is this to be done? " said the good-natured prince.

" O king," said his monitor, " this is most easy. Let the king make a decree, and seal it with his royal signet: and let it be proclaimed that the king will give ten she-asses, and ten slaves, and ten changes of raiment, every year, unto the man who shall make ten measures of the best wine. And whosoever wishes for the she-asses, and the slaves, and the raiment, let him send the ten measures of wine to thy servants, and we will drink thereof and judge. So shall there be much good wine in Assyria."

The project pleased Gomer Chephoraod. " Be it so," said he. The people shouted. The petitioners prostrated themselves in gratitude. The same night heralds were despatched to bear the intelligence to the remotest districts of Assyria.

After a due interval the wines began to come in; and the examiners assembled to adjudge the prize. The first vessel was unsealed. Its odour was such that the judges, without tasting it, pronounced unanimous condemnation. The next was opened: it had a villainous taste of clay. The third was sour and vapid. They proceeded from one cask of execrable liquor to another, till at length, in absolute nausea, they gave up the investigation.

The next morning they all assembled at the gate of the king, with pale faces and aching heads. They owned that they could not recommend any competitor as worthy of the rewards. They swore that the wine was little better than poison, and entreated permission to resign the office of deciding between such detestable potions.

" In the name of Belus, how can this have happened? " said the king.

Merolchazzar, the high-priest, muttered something about the anger of the gods at the toleration shown to a sect of impious heretics who ate pigeons broiled, " whereas," said he, " our religion commands us to eat them roasted. Now therefore, O king," continued this respectable divine, " give command to thy men of war, and let them smite the disobedient people with the sword, them, and their wives, and their children, and let their houses, and their flocks, and their herds, be given to thy servants the priests. Then shall the land yield its increase, and the fruits of the earth shall be no more blasted by the vengeance of Heaven."

" Nay," said the king, " the ground lies under no general curse from Heaven. The season has been singularly good. The wine which thou didst thyself drink at the banquet a few nights ago, O venerable Merolchazzar, was of this year's vintage. Dost thou not remember how thou didst praise it? It was the same night that thou wast inspired by Belus and didst reel to and fro, and discourse sacred mysteries. These things are too hard for me. I comprehend them not. The only wine which is bad is that which is sent to my judges. Who can expound this to us? "

The king scratched his head. Upon which all the courtiers scratched their heads.

He then ordered proclamation to be made that a purple robe and a golden chain should be given to the man who could solve this difficulty.

An old philosopher, who had been observed to smile rather disdainfully when the prize had first been instituted, came forward and spoke thus—

" Gomer Chephoraod, live for ever! Marvel not at that which has happened. It was no miracle, but a natural event. How could it be otherwise? It is true that much good wine has been made this year. But who would send it in for thy rewards? Thou knowest Ascobaruch who hath the great vineyards in the north, and Cohahiroth who sendeth wine every year from the south over the Persian Gulf. Their wines are so delicious that ten measures thereof are sold for an hundred talents of silver. Thinkest thou that they will exchange them for thy slaves and thine asses? What would thy prize profit any who have vineyards in rich soils? "

" Who then," said one of the judges, " are the wretches who sent us this poison? "

" Blame them not," said the sage, " seeing that you have been the authors of the evil.   They are men whose lands are poor, and have never yielded them any returns equal to the prizes which the king proposed.   Wherefore, knowing that the lords of the fruitful vineyards would not enter into competition with them they planted vines, some on rocks, and some in light sandy soil, and some in deep clay.   Hence their wines are bad.   For no culture or reward will make barren land bear good vines.   Know therefore, assuredly, that your prizes have increased the quantity of bad but not of good wine."

There was a long silence.   At length the king spoke.   " Give him the purple robe and the chain of gold.   Throw the wines into the Euphrates; and proclaim that the Royal Society of Wines is dissolved."

SCENES FROM " ATHENIAN REVELS "

(JANUARY 1824)

A DRAMA

I

SCENE—*A Street in Athens*

Enter CALLIDEMUS *and* SPEUSIPPUS

Callidemus. So, you young reprobate! You must be a man of wit, forsooth, and a man of quality! You must spend as if you were as rich as Nicias, and prate as if you were as wise as Pericles! You must dangle after sophists and pretty women! And I must pay for all! I must sup on thyme and onions, while you are swallowing thrushes and hares! I must drink water, that you may play the cottabus [1] with Chian wine! I must wander about as ragged as Pauson,[2] that you may be as fine as Alcibiades! I must lie on bare boards, with a stone [3] for

---

[1] This game consisted in projecting wine out of cups; it was a diversion extremely fashionable at Athenian entertainments.

[2] Pauson was an Athenian painter, whose name was synonymous with beggary. See Aristophanes: *Plutus*, 602. From his poverty, I am inclined to suppose that he painted historical pictures.

[3] See Aristophanes: *Plutus*, 542.

my pillow, and a rotten mat for my coverlid, by the light of a wretched winking lamp, while you are marching in state, with as many torches as one sees at the feast of Ceres, to thunder with your hatchet [1] at the doors of half the Ionian ladies in Peiræus.[2]

Speusippus. Why, thou unreasonable old man! Thou most shameless of fathers!—

Callidemus. Ungrateful wretch; dare you talk so? Are you not afraid of the thunders of Jupiter?

Speusippus. Jupiter thunder! nonsense! Anaxagoras says, that thunder is only an explosion produced by—

Callidemus. He does! Would that it had fallen on his head for his pains!

Speusippus. Nay: talk rationally.

Callidemus. Rationally! You audacious young sophist! I will talk rationally. Do you know that I am your father? What quibble can you make upon that?

Speusippus. Do I know that you are my father? Let us take the question to pieces, as Melesigenes, would say. First, then, we must inquire what is knowledge? Secondly, what is a father? Now, knowledge, as Socrates said the other day to Theætetus [3]—

Callidemus. Socrates! what! the ragged flat-nosed old dotard, who walks about all day barefoot, and filches cloaks, and dissects gnats, and shoes [4] fleas with wax?

Speusippus. All fiction! All trumped up by Aristophanes!

Callidemus. By Pallas, if he is in the habit of putting shoes on his fleas, he is kinder to them than to himself. But listen to me, boy; if you go on in this way, you will be ruined. There is an argument for you. Go to your Socrates and your Melesigenes, and tell them to refute that. Ruined! Do you hear?

Speusippus. Ruined!

Callidemus. Ay, by Jupiter! Is such a show as you make to be supported on nothing? During all the last war, I made not an obol from my farm; the Peloponnesian locusts came almost as regularly as the Pleiades — corn burnt, olives stripped, fruit trees cut down, wells stopped up—and, just when peace came, and I hoped that all would turn out well, you must begin to spend as if you had all the mines of Thasus at command.

---

[1] See Theocritus: *Idyll* ii. 128.
[2] This was the most disreputable part of Athens. See Aristophanes: *Pax,* 165.
[3] See Plato's *Theætetus.*   [4] See Aristophanes: *Nubes,* 150.

Speusippus. Now, by Neptune, who delights in horses—

Callidemus. If Neptune delights in horses, he does not resemble me.   You must ride at the Panathenæa on a horse fit for the great king: four acres of my best vines went for that folly.   You must retrench, or you will have nothing to eat.   Does not Anaxagoras mention, among his other discoveries, that when a man has nothing to eat he dies?

Speusippus. You are deceived.   My friends—

Callidemus. Oh, yes! your friends will notice you, doubtless, when you are squeezing through the crowd, on a winter's day, to warm yourself at the fire of the baths; or when you are fighting with beggars and beggars' dogs for the scraps of a sacrifice; or when you are glad to earn three wretched obols [1] by listening all day to lying speeches and crying children.

Speusippus. There are other means of support.

Callidemus. What! I suppose you will wander from house to house, like that wretched buffoon Philippus,[2] and beg everybody who has asked a supper-party to be so kind as to feed you and laugh at you; or you will turn sycophant; you will get a bunch of grapes, or a pair of shoes, now and then, by frightening some rich coward with a mock prosecution.   Well! that is a task for which your studies under the sophists may have fitted you.

Speusippus.   You are wide of the mark.

Callidemus. Then what, in the name of Juno, is your scheme? Do you intend to join Orestes,[3] and rob on the highway?   Take care; beware of the eleven;[4] beware of the hemlock.   It may be very pleasant to live at other people's expense; but not very pleasant, I should think, to hear the pestle give its last bang against the mortar, when the cold dose is ready.   Pah!—

Speusippus. Hemlock?   Orestes! folly!   I aim at nobler objects.   What say you to politics, the general assembly?

Callidemus. You an orator! oh no! no!   Cleon was worth twenty such fools as you.   You have succeeded, I grant, to his impudence, for which, if there be justice in Tartarus, he is now soaking up to the eyes in his own tan-pickle.   But the Paphlagonian had parts.

Speusippus. And you mean to imply—

Callidemus. Not I.   You are a Pericles in embryo, doubtless. Well: and when are you to make your first speech?   O Pallas!

---

[1] The stipend of an Athenian juryman.

[2] Xenophon: *Convivium*.

[3] A celebrated highwayman of Attica.   See Aristophanes: *Aves*, 711; and in several other passages.

[4] The police officers of Athens.

Speusippus. I thought of speaking, the other day, on the Sicilian expedition; but Nicias [1] got up before me.

Callidemus. Nicias, poor honest man, might just as well have sate still; his speaking did but little good. The loss of your oration is, doubtless, an irreparable public calamity.

Speusippus. Why, not so; I intend to introduce it at the next assembly; it will suit any subject.

Callidemus. That is to say, it will suit none. But pray, if it be not too presumptuous a request, indulge me with a specimen.

Speusippus. Well; suppose the agora crowded; an important subject under discussion; an ambassador from Argos, or from the great king; the tributes from the islands; an impeachment; in short, anything you please. The crier makes proclamation. " Any citizen above fifty years old may speak —any citizen not disqualified may speak." Then I rise: a great murmur of curiosity while I am mounting the stand.

Callidemus. Of curiosity! yes, and of something else too. You will infallibly be dragged down by main force, like poor Glaucon [2] last year.

Speusippus. Never fear. I shall begin in this style:—
" When I consider, Athenians, the importance of our city; when I consider the extent of its power, the wisdom of its laws, the elegance of its decorations; when I consider by what names and by what exploits its annals are adorned; when I think on Harmodius and Aristogiton, on Themistocles and Miltiades, on Cimon and Pericles; when I contemplate our pre-eminence in arts and letters; when I observe so many flourishing states and islands compelled to own the dominion, and purchase the protection of the City of the Violet Crown " [3]—

Callidemus. I shall choke with rage. Oh, all ye gods and goddesses, what sacrilege, what perjury have I ever committed, that I should be singled out from among all the citizens of Athens to be the father of this fool?

Speusippus. What now? By Bacchus, old man, I would not advise you to give way to such fits of passion in the streets. If Aristophanes were to see you, you would infallibly be in a comedy next spring.

Callidemus. You have more reason to fear Aristophanes than any fool living. Oh, that he could but hear you trying to

---

[1] See Thucydides, vi. 8.
[2] See Xenophon: *Memorabilia*, iii.
[3] A favourite epithet of Athens. See Aristophanes: *Acharn.* 637.

imitate the slang of Straton [1] and the lisp of Alcibiades! [2]   You
would be an inexhaustible subject.   You would console him for
the loss of Cleon.

Speusippus. No, no.   I may perhaps figure at the dramatic
representations before long; but in a very different way.

Callidemus. What do you mean?

Speusippus. What say you to a tragedy?

Callidemus. A tragedy of yours?

Speusippus. Even so.

Callidemus. Oh Hercules! Oh Bacchus! This is too much.
Here is an universal genius; sophist, orator, poet. To what a
three-headed monster have I given birth! a perfect Cerberus of
intellect! And pray what may your piece be about? Or will
your tragedy, like your speech, serve equally for any subject?

Speusippus. I thought of several plots; Œdipus, Eteocles and
Polynices, the war of Troy, the murder of Agamemnon.

Callidemus. And what have you chosen?

Speusippus. You know there is a law which permits any
modern poet to retouch a play of Æschylus, and bring it forward as his own composition. And, as there is an absurd
prejudice, among the vulgar, in favour of his extravagant
pieces, I have selected one of them, and altered it.

Callidemus. Which of them?

Speusippus. Oh! that mass of barbarous absurdities, the
Prometheus. But I have framed it anew upon the model of
Euripides. By Bacchus, I shall make Sophocles and Agathon
look about them. You would not know the play again.

Callidemus. By Jupiter, I believe not.

Speusippus. I have omitted the whole of the absurd dialogue
between Vulcan and Strength, at the beginning.

Callidemus. That may be, on the whole, an improvement.
The play will then open with that grand soliloquy of Prometheus,
when he is chained to the rock.

> Oh! ye eternal heavens! ye rushing winds!
> Ye fountains of great streams! Ye ocean waves,
> That in ten thousand sparkling dimples wreathe
> Your azure smiles! All-generating earth!
> All-seeing sun! On you, on you, I call. [3]

Well, I allow that will be striking; I did not think you
capable of that idea. Why do you laugh?

Speusippus. Do you seriously suppose that one who has

---

[1] See Aristophanes: *Equites*, 1375.   [2] See Aristophanes: *Vespæ*, 44.
[3] See Æschylus: *Prometheus*, 88.

studied the plays of that great man, Euripides, would ever begin a tragedy in such a ranting style?

Callidemus. What, does not your play open with the speech of Prometheus?

Speusippus. No doubt.

Callidemus. Then what, in the name of Bacchus, do you make him say?

Speusippus. You shall hear; and, if it be not in the very style of Euripides, call me a fool.

Callidemus. That is a liberty which I shall venture to take, whether it be or no.   But go on.

Speusippus. Prometheus begins thus:—

> Cœlus begat Saturn and Briareus
> Cottus and Creius and Iapetus,
> Gyges and Hyperion, Phœbe, Tethys,
> Thea and Rhea and Mnemosyne.
> Then Saturn wedded Rhea, and begat
> Pluto and Neptune, Jupiter and Juno.

Callidemus. Very beautiful, and very natural; and, as you say, very like Euripides.

Speusippus. You are sneering. Really, father, you do not understand these things. You had not those advantages in your youth—

Callidemus. Which I have been fool enough to let you have. No; in my early days, lying had not been dignified into a science, nor politics degraded into a trade. I wrestled, and read Homer's battles, instead of dressing my hair, and reciting lectures in verse out of Euripides. But I have some notion of what a play should be; I have seen Phrynichus, and lived with Æschylus. I saw the representation of the Persians.

Speusippus. A wretched play; it may amuse the fools who row the triremes; but it is utterly unworthy to be read by any man of taste.

Callidemus. If you had seen it acted; the whole theatre frantic with joy, stamping, shouting, laughing, crying. There was Cynægeirus, the brother of Æschylus, who lost both his arms at Marathon, beating the stumps against his sides with rapture. When the crowd remarked him—but where are you going?

Speusippus. To sup with Alcibiades; he sails with the expedition for Sicily in a few days; this is his farewell entertainment.

Callidemus. So much the better; I should say, so much the worse. That cursed Sicilian expedition! And you were one of the young fools [1] who stood clapping and shouting while he was gulling the rabble, and who drowned poor Nicias's voice with your uproar. Look to it; a day of reckoning will come. As to Alcibiades himself—

Speusippus. What can you say against him? His enemies themselves acknowledge his merit.

Callidemus. They acknowledge that he is clever, and handsome, and that he was crowned at the Olympic games. And what other merits do his friends claim for him? A precious assembly you will meet at his house, no doubt.

Speusippus. The first men in Athens, probably.

Callidemus. Whom do you mean by the first men in Athens?

Speusippus. Callicles.[2]

Callidemus. A sacrilegious, impious, unfeeling ruffian!

Speusippus. Hippomachus.

Callidemus. A fool, who can talk of nothing but his travels through Persia and Egypt. Go, go. The gods forbid that I should detain you from such choice society! [*Exeunt severally.*

II

SCENE—*A Hall in the house of* ALCIBIADES

ALCIBIADES, SPEUSIPPUS, CALLICLES, HIPPOMACHUS, CHARICLEA, *and others, seated round a table, feasting*

Alcibiades. Bring larger cups. This shall be our gayest revel. It is probably the last—for some of us at least.

Speusippus. At all events, it will be long before you taste such wine again, Alcibiades.

Callicles. Nay, there is excellent wine in Sicily. When I was there with Eurymedon's squadron, I had many a long carouse. You never saw finer grapes than those of Ætna.

Hippomachus. The Greeks do not understand the art of making wine. Your Persian is the man. So rich, so fragrant, so sparkling! I will tell you what the Satrap of Caria said to me about that when I supped with him.

Alcibiades. Nay, sweet Hippomachus; not a word to-night about satraps, or the great king, or the walls of Babylon, or the Pyramids, or the mummies. Chariclea, why do you look so sad?

---

[1] See Thucydides, vi. 13.
[2] Callicles plays a conspicuous part in the Gorgias of Plato.

Chariclea. Can I be cheerful when you are going to leave me, Alcibiades?

Alcibiades. My life, my sweet soul, it is but for a short time. In a year we conquer Sicily. In another, we humble Carthage.[1] I will bring back such robes, such necklaces, elephants' teeth by thousands, ay, and the elephants themselves, if you wish to see them. Nay, smile, my Chariclea, or I shall talk nonsense to no purpose.

Hippomachus. The largest elephant that I ever saw was in the grounds of Teribazus, near Susa. I wish that I had measured him.

Alcibiades. I wish that he had trod upon you. Come, come, Chariclea, we shall soon return, and then—

Chariclea. Yes; then indeed.

Alcibiades. Yes, then—

> Then for revels; then for dances,
> Tender whispers, melting glances.
> Peasants, pluck your richest fruits:
> Minstrels, sound your sweetest flutes:
> Come in laughing crowds to greet us,
> Dark-eyed daughters of Miletus;
> Bring the myrtles, bring the dice,
> Floods of Chian, hills of spice.

Speusippus. Whose lines are those, Alcibiades?

Alcibiades. My own. Think you, because I do not shut myself up to meditate, and drink water, and eat herbs, that I cannot write verses? By Apollo, if I did not spend my days in politics, and my nights in revelry, I should have made Sophocles tremble. But now I never go beyond a little song like this, and never invoke any muse but Chariclea. But come, Speusippus, sing. You are a professed poet. Let us have some of your verses.

Speusippus. My verses! How can you talk so? I a professed poet!

Alcibiades. Oh, content you, sweet Speusippus. We all know your designs upon the tragic honours. Come, sing. A chorus of your new play.

Speusippus. Nay, nay—

Hippomachus. When a guest who is asked to sing at a Persian banquet refuses—

Speusippus. In the name of Bacchus—

Alcibiades. I am absolute. Sing.

Speusippus. Well, then, I will sing you a chorus, which, I think, is a tolerable imitation of Euripides.

[1] See Thucydides, vi. 90.

Chariclea. Of Euripides? Not a word.

Alcibiades. Why so, sweet Chariclea?

Chariclea. Would you have me betray my sex? Would you have me forget his Phædras and Sthenobœas? No: if I ever suffer any lines of that woman-hater, or his imitators, to be sung in my presence, may I sell herbs [1] like his mother, and wear rags like his Telephus.[2]

Alcibiades. Then, sweet Chariclea, since you have silenced Speusippus, you shall sing yourself.

Chariclea. What shall I sing?

Alcibiades. Nay, choose for yourself.

Chariclea. Then I will sing an old Ionian hymn, which is chanted every spring at the feast of Venus, near Miletus. I used to sing it in my own country when I was a child; and—ah, Alcibiades!

Alcibiades. Dear Chariclea, you shall sing something else. This distresses you.

Chariclea. No: hand me the lyre: no matter. You will hear the song to disadvantage. But if it were sung as I have heard it sung: if this were a beautiful morning in spring, and if we were standing on a woody promontory, with the sea, and the white sails, and the blue Cyclades beneath us, and the portico of a temple peeping through the trees on a huge peak above our heads, and thousands of people, with myrtles in their hands, thronging up the winding path, their gay dresses and garlands disappearing and emerging by turns as they passed round the angles of the rock, then perhaps—

Alcibiades. Now, by Venus herself, sweet lady, where you are we shall lack neither sun, nor flowers, nor spring, nor temple, nor goddess.

Chariclea. (*Sings*)

> Let this sunny hour be given,
>   Venus, unto love and mirth:
> Smiles like thine are in the heaven;
>   Bloom like thine is on the earth;
> And the tinkling of the fountains,
>   And the murmurs of the sea,
> And the echoes from the mountains,
>   Speak of youth, and hope, and thee.

---

[1] The mother of Euripides was a herb-woman. This was a favourite topic of Aristophanes.

[2] The hero of one of the lost plays of Euripides, who appears to have been brought upon the stage in the garb of a beggar. See Aristophanes: *Acharn.* 430; and in other places.

By whate'er of soft expression
  Thou hast taught to lovers' eyes,
Faint denial, slow confession,
  Glowing cheeks and stifled sighs;
By the pleasure and the pain,
  By the follies and the wiles,
Pouting fondness, sweet disdain,
  Happy tears and mournful smiles;

Come with music floating o'er thee;
  Come with violets springing round:
Let the Graces dance before thee,
  All their golden zones unbound;
Now in sport their faces hiding,
  Now, with slender fingers fair,
From their laughing eyes dividing
  The long curls of rose-crowned hair.

Alcibiades. Sweetly sung; but mournfully, Chariclea; for which I would chide you, but that I am sad myself. More wine there. I wish to all the gods that I had fairly sailed from Athens.

Chariclea. And from me, Alcibiades?

Alcibiades. Yes, from you, dear lady. The days which immediately precede separation are the most melancholy of our lives.

Chariclea. Except those which immediately follow it.

Alcibiades. No; when I cease to see you, other objects may compel my attention; but can I be near you without thinking how lovely you are, and how soon I must leave you?

Hippomachus. Ay; travelling soon puts such thoughts out of men's heads.

Callicles. A battle is the best remedy for them.

Chariclea. A battle, I should think, might supply their place with others as unpleasant.

Callicles. No. The preparations are rather disagreeable to a novice. But as soon as the fighting begins, by Jupiter, it is a noble time; men trampling, shields clashing, spears breaking, and the pœan roaring louder than all.

Chariclea. But what if you are killed?

Callicles. What indeed? You must ask Speusippus that question. He is a philosopher.

Alcibiades. Yes, and the greatest of philosophers, if he can answer it.

Speusippus. Pythagoras is of opinion—

Hippomachus. Pythagoras stole that and all his other opinions from Asia and Egypt. The transmigration of the soul and the vegetable diet as derived from India. I met a Brachman in Sogdiana—

Callicles. All nonsense!

Chariclea. What think you, Alcibiades?

Alcibiades. I think that, if the doctrine be true, your spirit will be transfused into one of the doves who carry [1] ambrosia to the gods or verses to the mistresses of poets. Do you remember Anacreon's lines. How should you like such an office?

Chariclea. If I were to be your dove, Alcibiades, and you would treat me as Anacreon treated his, and let me nestle in your breast and drink from your cup, I would submit even to carry your love-letters to other ladies.

Callicles. What, in the name of Jupiter, is the use of all these speculations about death? Socrates once [2] lectured me upon it the best part of a day. I have hated the sight of him ever since. Such things may suit an old sophist when he is fasting; but in the midst of wine and music—

Hippomachus. I differ from you. The enlightened Egyptians bring skeletons into their banquets, in order to remind their guests to make the most of their life while they have it.

Callicles. I want neither skeleton nor sophist to teach me that lesson. More wine, I pray you, and less wisdom. If you must believe something which you never can know, why not be contented with the long stories about the other world which are told us when we are initiated at the Eleusinian mysteries? [3]

Chariclea. And what are those stories?

Alcibiades. Are not you initiated, Chariclea?

Chariclea. No; my mother was a Lydian, a barbarian; and therefore—

Alcibiades. I understand. Now the curse of Venus on the fools who made so hateful a law! Speusippus, does not your friend Euripides [4] say

> The land where thou art prosperous is thy country?

Surely we ought to say to every lady

> The land where thou art pretty is thy country.

Besides, to exclude foreign beauties from the chorus of the

---

[1] Homer's *Odyssey*, xii. 63.

[2] See the close of Plato's *Gorgias*.

[3] The scene which follows is founded upon history. Thucydides tells us, in his sixth book, that about this time Alcibiades was suspected of having assisted at a mock celebration of these famous mysteries. It was the opinion of the vulgar among the Athenians that extraordinary privileges were granted in the other world to all who had been initiated.

[4] The right of Euripides to this line is somewhat disputable. See Aristophanes: *Plutus*, 1152.

initiated in the Elysian fields is less cruel to them than to ourselves.   Chariclea, you shall be initiated.

Chariclea. When?

Alcibiades. Now.

Chariclea. Where?

Alcibiades. Here.

Chariclea. Delightful!

Speusippus. But there must be an interval of a year between
the purification and the initiation.

Alcibiades. We will suppose all that.

Speusippus. And nine days of rigid mortification of the
senses.

Alcibiades. We will suppose that too. I am sure it was
supposed, with as little reason, when I was initiated.

Speusippus. But you are sworn to secrecy.

Alcibiades. You a sophist, and talk of oaths! You a pupil of
Euripides, and forget his maxims!

My lips have sworn it; but my mind is free.[1]

Speusippus. But, Alcibiades—

Alcibiades. What! Are you afraid of Ceres and Proserpine?

Speusippus. No—but—but—I—that is I—but it is best to be
safe—I mean—Suppose there should be something in it.

Alcibiades. Now, by Mercury, I shall die with laughing. O
Speusippus, Speusippus! Go back to your old father. Dig
vineyards, and judge causes, and be a respectable citizen. But
never, while you live, again dream of being a philosopher.

Speusippus. Nay, I was only—

Alcibiades. A pupil of Gorgias and Melesigenes afraid of
Tartarus! In what region of the infernal world do you expect
your domicile to be fixed?   Shall you roll a stone like Sisyphus?
Hard exercise, Speusippus!

Speusippus. In the name of all the gods—

Alcibiades. Or shall you sit starved and thirsty in the midst
of fruit and wine like Tantalus? Poor fellow? I think I see
your face as you are springing up to the branches and missing
your aim. Oh Bacchus! Oh Mercury!

Speusippus. Alcibiades!

Alcibiades. Or perhaps you will be food for a vulture, like the
huge fellow who was rude to Latona.

Speusippus. Alcibiades!

Alcibiades. Never fear. Minos will not be so cruel. Your

---

[1] See Euripides: *Hippolytus*, 6o8. For the jesuitical morality of this
line Euripides is bitterly attacked by the comic poet.

eloquence will triumph over all accusations. The Furies will skulk away like disappointed sycophants. Only address the judges of hell in the speech which you were prevented from speaking last assembly. " When I consider "—is not that the beginning of it? Come, man, do not be angry. Why do you pace up and down with such long steps? You are not in Tartarus yet. You seem to think that you are already stalking like poor Achilles,

With stride

Majestic through the plain of Asphodel.[1]

Speusippus. How can you talk so, when you know that I believe all that foolery as little as you do?

Alcibiades. Then march. You shall be the crier.[2] Callicles, you shall carry the torch. Why do you stare?

Callicles. I do not much like the frolic.

Alcibiades. Nay, surely you are not taken with a fit of piety. If all be true that is told of you, you have as little reason to think the gods vindictive as any man breathing. If you be not belied, a certain golden goblet which I have seen at your house was once in the temple of Juno at Corcyra. And men say that there was a priestess at Tarentum—

Callicles. A fig for the gods! I was thinking about the Archons. You will have an accusation laid against you to-morrow. It is not very pleasant to be tried before the king.[3]

Alcibiades. Never fear: there is not a sycophant in Attica who would dare to breathe a word against me, for the golden [4] plane-tree of the great king.

Hippomachus. That plane-tree—

Alcibiades. Never mind the plane-tree. Come, Callicles, you were not as timid when you plundered the merchantman off Cape Malea. Take up the torch and move. Hippomachus, tell one of the slaves to bring a sow.[5]

Callicles. And what part are you to play?

Alcibiades. I shall be hierophant. Herald, to your office. Torchbearer, advance with the lights. Come forward, fair novice. We will celebrate the rite within. (*Exeunt.*)

[1] See Homer's *Odyssey*, xi. 538.

[2] The crier and torchbearer were important functionaries at the celebration of the Eleusinian mysteries.

[3] The name of king was given in the Athenian democracy to the magistrate who exercised those spiritual functions which in the monarchical times had belonged to the sovereign. His court took cognisance of offences against the religion of the state.

[4] See Herodotus, viii. 28.

[5] A sow was sacrificed to Ceres at the admission to the greater mysteries.

LAYS OF ANCIENT ROME

LAYS OF ANCIENT ROME

INTRODUCTION

THAT what is called the history of the Kings and early Consuls of Rome is to a great extent fabulous, few scholars have, since the time of Beaufort, ventured to deny.   It is certain that, more than three hundred and sixty years after the date ordinarily assigned for the foundation of the city, the public records were, with scarcely an exception, destroyed by the Gauls.   It is certain that the oldest annals of the commonwealth were compiled more than a century and a half after this destruction of the records.   It is certain, therefore, that the great Latin writers of the Augustan age did not possess those materials, without which a trustworthy account of the infancy of the republic could not possibly be framed.   Those writers own, indeed, that the chronicles to which they had access were filled with battles that were never fought, and Consuls that were never inaugurated; and we have abundant proof that, in these chronicles, events of the greatest importance, such as the issue of the war with Porsena, and the issue of the war with Brennus, were grossly misrepresented.   Under these circumstances a wise man will look with great suspicion on the legend which has come down to us.   He will perhaps be inclined to regard the princes who are said to have founded the civil and religious institutions of Rome, the son of Mars, and the husband of Egeria, as mere mythological personages, of the same class with Perseus and Ixion.   As he draws nearer and nearer to the confines of authentic history, he will become less and less hard of belief.   He will admit that the most important parts of the narrative have some foundation in truth.   But he will distrust almost all the details, not only because they seldom rest on any solid evidence, but also because he will constantly detect in them, even when they are within the limits of physical possibility, that peculiar character, more easily understood than defined, which distinguishes the creations of the imagination from the realities of the world in which we live.

The early history of Rome is indeed far more poetical than anything else in Latin literature. The loves of the Vestal and the God of War, the cradle laid among the reeds of Tiber, the fig-tree, the she-wolf, the shepherd's cabin, the recognition, the fratricide, the rape of the Sabines, the death of Tarpeia, the fall of Hostus Hostilius, the struggle of Mettus Curtius through the marsh, the women rushing with torn raiment and dishevelled hair between their fathers and their husbands, the nightly meetings of Numa and the Nymph by the well in the sacred grove, the fight of the three Romans and the three Albans, the purchase of the Sibylline books, the crime of Tullia, the simulated madness of Brutus, the ambiguous reply of the Delphian oracle to the Tarquins, the wrongs of Lucretia, the heroic actions of Horatius Cocles, of Scævola, and of Clœlia, the battle of Regillus, won by the aid of Castor and Pollux, the defence of Cremera, the touching story of Coriolanus, the still more touching story of Virginia, the wild legend about the draining of the Alban lake, the combat between Valerius Corvus and the gigantic Gaul, are among the many instances which will at once suggest themselves to every reader.

In the narrative of Livy, who was a man of fine imagination, these stories retain much of their genuine character. Nor could even the tasteless Dionysius distort and mutilate them into mere prose. The poetry shines, in spite of him, through the dreary pedantry of his eleven books. It is discernible in the most tedious and in the most superficial modern works on the early times of Rome. It enlivens the dulness of the Universal History, and gives a charm to the most meagre abridgements of Goldsmith.

Even in the age of Plutarch there were discerning men who rejected the popular account of the foundation of Rome, because that account appeared to them to have the air, not of a history, but of a romance or a drama. Plutarch, who was displeased at their incredulity, had nothing better to say in reply to their arguments than that chance sometimes turns poet, and produces trains of events not to be distinguished from the most elaborate plots which are constructed by art. But though the existence of a poetical element in the early history of the Great City was detected so many ages ago, the first critic who distinctly saw from what source that poetical element had been derived was James Perizonius, one of the most acute and learned antiquaries of the seventeenth century. His theory, which, in his own days, attracted little or no notice, was revived in the present generation by Niebuhr, a man who would have been the first writer of his time, if his talent for communicating truths had borne any proportion to his talent for investigating them. That theory has been adopted by several eminent scholars of our own country, particularly by the Bishop of St. David's, by Professor Malden, and by the lamented Arnold. It appears to be now generally received by men conversant with classical antiquity; and indeed it rests on such strong proofs, both internal and external, that it will not be easily subverted. A popular exposition of this theory, and of the evidence by which it is supported, may not be without interest even for readers who are unacquainted with the ancient languages.

The Latin literature which has come down to us is of later date than the commencement of the Second Punic War, and consists almost exclusively of works fashioned on Greek models. The Latin metres, heroic, elegiac, lyric, and dramatic, are of Greek origin. The best Latin epic poetry is the feeble echo of the *Iliad* and *Odyssey*. The best Latin eclogues are imitations of Theocritus. The plan of the most finished didactic poem in the Latin tongue was taken from Hesiod. The Latin tragedies are bad copies of the masterpieces of Sophocles and Euripides. The Latin comedies are free translations from Demophilus, Menander, and Appollodorus. The Latin philosophy was borrowed, without alteration, from the Portico and the Academy; and the great Latin orators constantly proposed to themselves as patterns the speeches of Demosthenes and Lysias.

But there was an earlier Latin literature, a literature truly Latin, which has wholly perished, which had, indeed, almost wholly perished long before those whom we are in the habit of regarding as the greatest Latin writers were born. That literature abounded with metrical romances, such as are found in every country where there is much curiosity and intelligence, but little reading and writing. All human beings, not utterly savage, long for some information about past times, and are delighted by narratives which present pictures to the eye of the mind. But it is only in very enlightened communities that books are readily accessible. Metrical composition, therefore, which, in a highly civilised nation, is a mere luxury, is, in nations imperfectly civilised, almost a necessary of life, and is valued less on account of the pleasure which it gives to the ear, than on account of the help which it gives to the memory. A man who can invent or embellish an interesting story, and put it into a form which others may easily retain in their recollection, will always be highly esteemed by a people eager for amusement and information, but destitute of libraries. Such is the origin of ballad-poetry, a species of composition which scarcely ever fails to spring up and flourish in every society, at a certain point in the progress towards refinement. Tacitus informs us that songs were the only memorials of the past which the ancient Germans possessed. We learn from Lucan and from Ammianus Marcellinus that the brave actions of the ancient Gauls were commemorated in the verses of Bards. During many ages, and through many revolutions, minstrelsy retained its influence over both the Teutonic and the Celtic race. The vengeance exacted by the spouse of Attila for the murder of Siegfried was celebrated in rhymes, of which Germany is still justly proud. The exploits of Athelstane were commemorated by the Anglo-Saxons, and those of Canute by the Danes, in rude poems, of which a few fragments have come down to us. The chants of the Welsh harpers preserved, through ages of darkness, a faint and doubtful memory of Arthur. In the Highlands of Scotland may still be gleaned some relics of the old songs about Cuthullin and Fingal. The long struggle of the Servians against the Ottoman power was recorded in lays full of martial spirit. We learn from Herrera that, when a Peruvian Inca died, men of skill were appointed to celebrate him in verses, which all the people learned by heart, and sang in public on days of festival. The feats of Kurroglou, the great free-booter of Turkistan, recounted in ballads composed by himself, are known in every village of Northern Persia. Captain Beechey heard the bards of the Sandwich Islands recite the heroic achievements of Tamehameha, the most illustrious of their kings. Mungo Park found in the heart of Africa a class of singing men, the only annalists of their rude tribes, and heard them tell the story of the victory which Damel, the negro prince of the Jaloffs, won over Abdulkader, the Mussulman tyrant of Foota Torra. This species of poetry attained a high degree of excellence among the Castilians, before they began to copy Tuscan patterns. It attained a still higher degree of excellence among the English and the Lowland Scotch, during the fourteenth, fifteenth, and sixteenth centuries. But it reached its full perfection in ancient Greece; for there can be no doubt that the great Homeric poems are generally ballads, though widely distinguished from all other ballads, and indeed from almost all other human compositions, by transcendent sublimity and beauty.

As it is agreeable to general experience that, at a certain stage in the progress of society, ballad-poetry should flourish, so is it also agreeable to general experience that, at a subsequent stage in the progress of society, ballad-poetry should be undervalued and neglected. Knowledge advances: manners change: great foreign models of composition are studied and imitated. The phraseology of the old minstrels becomes obsolete. Their versification, which, having received its laws only from the ear, abounds in irregularities, seems licentious and uncouth. Their simplicity appears beggarly when compared with the quaint forms and gaudy colouring of such artists as Cowley and Gongora. The ancient lays, unjustly despised by the learned and polite, linger for a time in the memory of the vulgar, and are at length too often irretrievably lost. We cannot wonder that the ballads of Rome should have altogether disappeared, when we remember how very narrowly, in spite of the invention of printing, those of our own country and those of Spain escaped the same fate. There is indeed little doubt that oblivion covers many English songs equal to any that were published by Bishop Percy, and many Spanish songs as good as the best of those which have been so happily translated by Mr. Lockhart. Eighty years ago England possessed only one tattered copy of Childe Waters and Sir Cauline, and Spain only one tattered copy of the noble poem of the Cid. The snuff of a candle, or a mischievous dog, might in a moment have deprived the world for ever of any of those fine compositions. Sir Walter Scott, who united to the fire of a great poet the minute curiosity and patient diligence of a great antiquary, was but just in time to save the precious relics of the Minstrelsy of the Border. In Germany, the lay of the Nibelungs had been long utterly forgotten, when, in the eighteenth century, it was, for the first time, printed from a manuscript in the old library of a noble family. In truth, the only people who, through their whole passage from simplicity to the highest civilisation, never for a moment ceased to love and admire their old ballads, were the Greeks.

That the early Romans should have had ballad-poetry, and that this poetry should have perished, is therefore not strange. It would, on the contrary, have been strange if these things had not come to pass; and we should be justified in pronouncing them highly probable, even if we had no direct evidence on the subject. But we have direct evidence of unquestionable authority.

Ennius, who flourished in the time of the Second Punic War, was regarded in the Augustan age as the father of Latin poetry.

He was, in truth, the father of the second school of Latin poetry, the only school of which the works have descended to us.   But from Ennius himself we learn that there were poets who stood to him in the same relation in which the author of the romance of Count Alarcos stood to Garcilaso, or the author of the " Lytell Geste of Robyn Hode " to Lord Surrey.   Ennius speaks of verses which the Fauns and the Bards were wont to chant in the old time, when none had yet studied the graces of speech, when none had yet climbed the peaks sacred to the Goddesses of Grecian song.   "Where," Cicero mournfully asks, " are those old verses now? "

Contemporary with Ennius was Quintus Fabius Pictor, the earliest of the Roman annalists.   His account of the infancy and youth of Romulus and Remus has been preserved by Dionysius, and contains a very remarkable reference to the ancient Latin poetry.   Fabius says that, in his time, his countrymen were still in the habit of singing ballads about the Twins.   " Even in the hut of Faustulus,"—so these old lays appear to have run,— " the children of Rhea and Mars were, in port and in spirit, not like unto swineherds or cowherds, but such that men might well guess them to be of the blood of Kings and Gods."

Cato the Censor, who also lived in the days of the Second Punic War, mentioned this lost literature in his lost work on the antiquities of his country.   Many ages, he said, before his time, there were ballads in praise of illustrious men; and these ballads it was the fashion for the guests at banquets to sing in turn while the piper played.   " Would," exclaims Cicero, " that we still had the old ballads of which Cato speaks! "

Valerius Maximus gives us exactly similar information, without mentioning his authority, and observes that the ancient Roman ballads were probably of more benefit to the young than all the lectures of the Athenian schools, and that to the influence of the national poetry were to be ascribed the virtues of such men as Camillus and Fabricius.

Varro, whose authority on all questions connected with the antiquities of his country is entitled to the greatest respect, tells us that at banquets it was once the fashion for boys to sing, sometimes with and sometimes without instrumental music, ancient ballads in praise of men of former times.   These young performers, he observes, were of unblemished character, a circumstance which he probably mentioned because, among the Greeks, and indeed in his time among the Romans also, the morals of singing boys were in no high repute.

The testimony of Horace, though given incidentally, confirms the statements of Cato, Velerius Maximus, and Varro.   The poet predicts that, under the peaceful administration of Augustus, the Romans will, over their full goblets, sing to the pipe, after the fashion of their fathers, the deeds of brave captains, and the ancient legends touching the origin of the city.

The proposition, then, that Rome had ballad-poetry is not merely in itself highly probable, but is fully proved by direct evidence of the greatest weight.

This proposition being established, it becomes easy to understand why the early history of the city is unlike almost every thing else in Latin literature, native where almost every thing else is borrowed, imaginative where almost every thing else is prosaic.   We can scarcely hesitate to pronounce that the magnificent, pathetic, and truly national legends, which present so striking a contrast to all that surrounds them, are broken and defaced fragments of that early poetry which, even in the age of Cato the Censor, had become antiquated, and of which Tully had never heard a line.

That this poetry should have been suffered to perish will not appear strange when we consider how complete was the triumph of the Greek genius over the public mind of Italy. It is probable that, at an early period, Homer and Herodotus furnished some hints to the Latin minstrels:[1] but it was not till after the war with Pyrrhus that the poetry of Rome began to put off its old Ausonian character.   The transformation was soon consummated.   The conquered, says Horace, led captive the conquerors.   It was precisely at the time at which the Roman people rose to unrivalled political ascendency that they stooped to pass under the intellectual yoke.   It was precisely at the time at which the sceptre departed from Greece that the empire of her language and of her arts became universal and despotic.   The revolution indeed was not effected without a struggle.   Nævius seems to have been the last of the ancient line of poets.   Ennius was the founder of a new dynasty. Nævius celebrated the First Punic War in Saturnian verse, the old national verse of Italy.   Ennius sang the Second Punic War in numbers borrowed from the *Iliad*.   The elder poet, in the epitaph which he wrote for himself, and which is a fine specimen of the early Roman diction and versification, plaintively boasted that the Latin language had died with him. Thus what to Horace appeared to be the first faint dawn of

[1] *See* the Preface to the " Lay of the Battle of Regillus."

Roman literature appeared to Nævius to be its hopeless setting. In truth, one literature was setting, and another dawning.

The victory of the foreign taste was decisive: and indeed we can hardly blame the Romans for turning away with contempt from the rude lays which had delighted their fathers, and giving their whole admiration to the immortal productions of Greece. The national romances, neglected by the great and the refined whose education had been finished at Rhodes or Athens, continued, it may be supposed, during some generations, to delight the vulgar.   While Virgil, in hexameters of exquisite modulation, described the sports of rustics, those rustics were still singing their wild Saturnian ballads.[1] It is not improbable that, at the time when Cicero lamented the irreparable loss of the poems mentioned by Cato, a search among the nooks of the Apennines, as active as the search which Sir Walter Scott made among the descendants of the moss-troopers of Liddesdale, might have brought to light many fine remains of ancient minstrelsy.   No such search was made.   The Latin ballads perished for ever. Yet discerning critics have thought that they could still perceive in the early history of Rome numerous fragments of this lost poetry, as the traveller on classic ground sometimes finds, built into the heavy wall of a fort or convent, a pillar rich with acanthus leaves, or a frieze where the Amazons and Bacchanals seem to live.   The theatres and temples of the Greek and the Roman were degraded into the quarries of the Turk and the Goth.   Even so did the ancient Saturnian poetry become the quarry in which a crowd of orators and annalists found the materials for their prose.

It is not difficult to trace the process by which the old songs were transmuted into the form which they now wear.   Funeral panegyric and chronicle appear to have been the intermediate links which connected the lost ballads with the histories now extant.   From a very early period it was the usage that an oration should be pronounced over the remains of a noble Roman.   The orator, as we learn from Polybius, was expected, on such an occasion, to recapitulate all the services which the ancestors of the deceased had, from the earliest time, rendered to the commonwealth.   There can be little doubt that the speaker on whom this duty was imposed would make use of all the stories suited to his purpose which were to be found in the popular lays.   There can be as little doubt that the family of an eminent man would preserve a copy of the speech which

[1] *See* Servius, in Georg. ii. 385.

had been pronounced over his corpse. The compilers of the early chronicles would have recourse to these speeches; and the great historians of a later period would have recourse to the chronicles.

It may be worth while to select a particular story, and to trace its probable progress through these stages. The description of the migration of the Fabian house to Cremera is one of the finest of the many fine passages which lie thick in the earlier books of Livy. The Consul, clad in his military garb, stands in the vestibule of his house, marshalling his clan, three hundred and six fighting men, all of the same proud patrician blood, all worthy to be attended by the fasces, and to command the legions. A sad and anxious retinue of friends accompanies the adventurers through the streets; but the voice of lamentation is drowned by the shouts of admiring thousands. As the procession passes the Capitol, prayers and vows are poured forth, but in vain. The devoted band, leaving Janus on the right, marches to its doom through the Gate of Evil Luck. After achieving high deeds of valour against overwhelming numbers, all perish save one child, the stock from which the great Fabian race was destined again to spring, for the safety and glory of the commonwealth. That this fine romance, the details of which are so full of poetical truth, and so utterly destitute of all show of historical truth, came originally from some lay which had often been sung with great applause at banquets, is in the highest degree probable. Nor is it difficult to imagine a mode in which the transmission might have taken place.

The celebrated Quintus Fabius Maximus, who died about twenty years before the First Punic War, and more than forty years before Ennius was born, is said to have been interred with extraordinary pomp. In the eulogy pronounced over his body all the great exploits of his ancestors were doubtless recounted and exaggerated. If there were then extant songs which gave a vivid and touching description of an event, the saddest and the most glorious in the long history of the Fabian house, nothing could be more natural than that the panegyrist should borrow from such songs their finest touches, in order to adorn his speech. A few generations later the songs would perhaps be forgotten, or remembered only by shepherds and vine-dressers. But the speech would certainly be preserved in the archives of the Fabian nobles. Fabius Pictor would be well acquainted with a document so interesting to his personal

feelings, and would insert large extracts from it in his rude
chronicle.   That chronicle, as we know, was the oldest to which
Livy had access.   Livy would at a glance distinguish the bold
strokes of the forgotten poet from the dull and feeble narrative
by which they were surrounded, would retouch them with a
delicate and powerful pencil, and would make them immortal.

That this might happen at Rome can scarcely be doubted;
for something very like this has happened in several countries,
and, among others, in our own.   Perhaps the theory of Perizonius
cannot be better illustrated than by showing that what he supposes to have taken place in ancient times has, beyond all
doubt, taken place in modern times.

" History," says Hume, with the utmost gravity, " has preserved some instances of Edgar's amours, from which, as from
a specimen, we may form a conjecture of the rest."   He then
tells very agreeably the stories of Elfleda and Elfrida, two stories
which have a most suspicious air of romance, and which, indeed,
greatly resemble, in their general character, some of the legends
of early Rome.   He cites, as his authority for these two tales,
the chronicle of William of Malmesbury, who lived in the time
of King Stephen.   The great majority of readers suppose that
the device by which Elfleda was substituted for her young
mistress, the artifice by which Athelwold obtained the hand of
Elfrida, the detection of that artifice, the hunting party, and the
vengeance of the amorous king, are things about which there is
no more doubt than about the execution of Anne Boleyn, or the
slitting of Sir John Coventry's nose.   But when we turn to
William of Malmesbury, we find that Hume, in his eagerness
to relate these pleasant fables, has overlooked one very important
circumstance.   William does indeed tell both the stories; but
he gives us distinct notice that he does not warrant their
truth, and that they rest on no better authority than that of
ballads.

Such is the way in which these two well-known tales have
been handed down.   They originally appeared in a poetical
form.   They found their way from ballads into an old chronicle.
The ballads perished; the chronicle remained.   A great historian, some centuries after the ballads had been altogether
forgotten, consulted the chronicle.   He was struck by the lively
colouring of these ancient fictions: he transferred them to his
pages; and thus we find inserted, as unquestionable facts, in
a narrative which is likely to last as long as the English tongue,
the inventions of some minstrel whose works were probably

never committed to writing, whose name is buried in oblivion, and whose dialect has become obsolete. It must, then, be admitted to be possible, or rather highly probable, that the stories of Romulus and Remus, and of the Horatii and Curiatii, may have had a similar origin.

Castilian literature will furnish us with another parallel case. Mariana, the classical historian of Spain, tells the story of the ill-starred marriage which the King Don Alonso brought about between the heirs of Carrion and the two daughters of the Cid. The Cid bestowed a princely dower on his sons-in-law. But the young men were base and proud, cowardly and cruel. They were tried in danger, and found wanting. They fled before the Moors, and once, when a lion broke out of his den, they ran and crouched in an unseemly hiding-place. They knew that they were despised, and took counsel how they might be avenged. They parted from their father-in-law with many signs of love, and set forth on a journey with Doña Elvira and Doña Sol. In a solitary place the bridegrooms seized their brides, stripped them, scourged them, and departed, leaving them for dead. But one of the house of Bivar, suspecting foul play, had followed the travellers in disguise. The ladies were brought back safe to the house of their father. Complaint was made to the king. It was adjudged by the Cortes that the dower given by the Cid should be returned, and that the heirs of Carrion together with one of their kindred should do battle against three knights of the party of the Cid. The guilty youths would have declined the combat; but all their shifts were vain. They were vanquished in the lists, and for ever disgraced, while their injured wives were sought in marriage by great princes.

Some Spanish writers have laboured to show, by an examination of dates and circumstances, that this story is untrue. Such confutation was surely not needed; for the narrative is on the face of it a romance. How it found its way into Mariana's history is quite clear. He acknowledges his obligations to the ancient chronicles; and had doubtless before him the " Cronica del famoso Cavallero Cid Ruy Diez Campeador," which had been printed as early as the year 1552. He little suspected that all the most striking passages in this chronicle were copied from a poem of the twelfth century, a poem of which the language and versification had long been obsolete, but which glowed with no common portion of the fire of the *Iliad*. Yet such was the fact. More than a century and a half after the death of

Mariana, this venerable ballad, of which one imperfect copy on parchment, four hundred years old, had been preserved at Bivar, was for the first time printed. Then it was found that every interesting circumstance of the story of the heirs of Carrion was derived by the eloquent Jesuit from a song of which he had never heard, and which was composed by a minstrel whose very name had long been forgotten.

Such, or nearly such, appears to have been the process by which the lost ballad-poetry of Rome was transformed into history. To reverse that process, to transform some portions of early Roman history back into the poetry out of which they were made, is the object of this work.

In the following poems the author speaks, not in his own person, but in the persons of ancient minstrels who know only what a Roman citizen, born three or four hundred years before the Christian æra, may be supposed to have known, and who are in nowise above the passions and prejudices of their age and nation. To these imaginary poets must be ascribed some blunders which are so obvious that it is unnecessary to point them out. The real blunder would have been to represent these old poets as deeply versed in general history, and studious of chronological accuracy. To them must also be attributed the illiberal sneers at the Greeks, the furious party-spirit, the contempt for the arts of peace, the love of war for its own sake, the ungenerous exultation over the vanquished, which the reader will sometimes observe. To portray a Roman of the age of Camillus or Curius as superior to national antipathies, as mourning over the devastation and slaughter by which empire and triumphs were to be won, as looking on human suffering with the sympathy of Howard, or as treating conquered enemies with the delicacy of the Black Prince, would be to violate all dramatic propriety. The old Romans had some great virtues, fortitude, temperance, veracity, spirit to resist oppression, respect for legitimate authority, fidelity in the observing of contracts, disinterestedness, ardent patriotism; but Christian charity and chivalrous generosity were alike unknown to them.

It would have been obviously improper to mimic the manner of any particular age or country. Something has been borrowed, however, from our own old ballads, and more from Sir Walter Scott, the great restorer of our ballad-poetry. To the *Iliad* still greater obligations are due; and those obligations have been contracted with the less hesitation, because there is reason to believe that some of the old Latin minstrels really had recourse to that inexhaustible store of poetical images.

It would have been easy to swell this little volume to a very considerable bulk, by appending notes filled with quotations; but to a learned reader such notes are not necessary; for an unlearned reader they would have little interest; and the judgment passed both by the learned and by the unlearned on a work of the imagination will always depend much more on the general character and spirit of such a work than on minute details.

HORATIUS

THERE can be little doubt that among those parts of early Roman history which had a poetical origin was the legend of Horatius Cocles. We have several versions of the story, and these versions differ from each other in points of no small importance. Polybius, there is reason to believe, heard the tale recited over the remains of some Consul or Prætor descended from the old Horatian patricians; for he introduces it as a specimen of the narratives with which the Romans were in the habit of embellishing their funeral oratory. It is remarkable that, according to him, Horatius defended the bridge alone, and perished in the waters. According to the chronicles which Livy and Dionysius followed, Horatius had two companions, swam safe to shore, and was loaded with honours and rewards.

These discrepancies are easily explained. Our own literature, indeed, will furnish an exact parallel to what may have taken place at Rome. It is highly probable that the memory of the war of Porsena was preserved by compositions much resembling the two ballads which stand first in the *Relics of Ancient English Poetry*. In both those ballads the English, commanded by the Percy, fight with the Scots, commanded by the Douglas. In one of the ballads the Douglas is killed by a nameless English archer, and the Percy by a Scottish spearman: in the other, the Percy slays the Douglas in single combat, and is himself made prisoner. In the former, Sir Hugh Montgomery is shot through the heart by a Northumbrian bowman: in the latter he is taken, and exchanged for the Percy. Yet both the ballads relate to the same event, and that an event which probably took place within the memory of persons who were alive when both the ballads were made. One of the minstrels says:

> " Old men that knowen the grounde well yenoughe
> Call it the battell of Otterburn:
> At Otterburn began this spurne
> Upon a monnyn day.
> Ther was the dougghte Doglas slean:
> The Perse never went away."

The other poet sums up the event in the following lines:

> " Thys fraye bygan at Otterborne
> Bytwene the nyghte and the day:
> Ther the Dowglas lost hys lyfe,
> And the Percy was lede away."

It is by no means unlikely that there were two old Roman lays about the defence of the bridge; and that, while the story which Livy has transmitted to us was preferred by the multitude, the

"

other, which ascribed the whole glory to Horatius alone, may have been the favourite with the Horatian house.

The following ballad is supposed to have been made about a hundred and twenty years after the war which it celebrates, and just before the taking of Rome by the Gauls. The author seems to have been an honest citizen, proud of the military glory of his country, sick of the disputes of factions, and much given to pining after good old times which had never really existed. The allusion, however, to the partial manner in which the public lands were allotted could proceed only from a plebeian; and the allusion to the fraudulent sale of spoils marks the date of the poem, and shows that the poet shared in the general discontent with which the proceedings of Camillus, after the taking of Veii, were regarded.

The penultimate syllable of the name Porsena has been shortened in spite of the authority of Niebuhr, who pronounces, without assigning any ground for his opinion, that Martial was guilty of a decided blunder in the line,

> " Hanc spectare manum Porsena non potuit."

It is not easy to understand how any modern scholar, whatever his attainments may be,—and those of Niebuhr were undoubtedly immense,—can venture to pronounce that Martial did not know the quantity of a word which he must have uttered and heard uttered a hundred times before he left school. Niebuhr seems also to have forgotten that Martial has fellow-culprits to keep him in countenance. Horace has committed the same decided blunder; for he gives us, as a pure iambic line,

> " Minacis aut Etrusca Porsenæ manus."

Silius Italicus has repeatedly offended in the same way, as when he says,

> " Cernitur effugiens ardentem Porsena dextiam: "

and again,

> " Clusinum vulgus, cum, Porsena magne, jubebas."

A modern writer may be content to err in such company.

Niebuhr's supposition that each of the three defenders of the bridge was the representative of one of the three patrician tribes is both ingenious and probable, and has been adopted in the following poem.

1. LARS PORSENA of Clusium
   By the Nine Gods he swore
That the great house of Tarquin
   Should suffer wrong no more.
By the Nine Gods he swore it,
   And named a trysting day,
And bade his messengers ride forth,
East and west and south and north,
   To summon his array.

II. East and west and south and north
    The messengers ride fast,
And tower and town and cottage
    Have heard the trumpet's blast.
Shame on the false Etruscan
    Who lingers in his home,
When Porsena of Clusium
    Is on the march for Rome.

III. The horsemen and the footmen
    Are pouring in amain,
From many a stately market-place;
    From many a fruitful plain;
From many a lonely hamlet,
    Which, hid by beech and pine,
Like an eagle's nest, hangs on the crest
    Of purple Apennine;

IV. From lordly Volaterræ,
    Where scowls the far-famed hold
Piled by the hands of giants
    For godlike kings of old;
From seagirt Populonia,
    Whose sentinels descry
Sardinia's snowy mountain-tops
    Fringing the southern sky;

V. From the proud mart of Pisæ,
    Queen of the western waves,
Where ride Massilia's triremes
    Heavy with fair-haired slaves;
From where sweet Clanis wanders
    Through corn and vines and flowers;
From where Cortona lifts to heaven
    Her diadem of towers.

VI. Tall are the oaks whose acorns
    Drop in dark Auser's rill;
Fat are the stags that champ the boughs
    Of the Ciminian hill;
Beyond all streams Clitumnus
    Is to the herdsman dear;
Best of all pools the fowler loves
    The great Volsinian mere.

VII. But now no stroke of woodman
    Is heard by Auser's rill;
No hunter tracks the stag's green path
    Up the Ciminian hill;
Unwatched along Clitumnus
    Grazes the milk-white steer;
Unharmed the water fowl may dip
    In the Volsinian mere.

VIII. The harvests of Arretium,
    This year, old men shall reap;
This year, young boys in Umbro
    Shall plunge the struggling sheep;
And in the vats of Luna,
    This year, the must shall foam
Round the white feet of laughing girls
    Whose sires have marched to Rome.

IX. There be thirty chosen prophets,
    The wisest of the land,
Who alway by Lars Porsena
    Both morn and evening stand:
Evening and morn the Thirty
    Have turned the verses o'er,
Traced from the right on linen white
    By mighty seers of yore.

X. And with one voice the Thirty
    Have their glad answer given:
" Go forth, go forth, Lars Porsena;
    Go forth, beloved of Heaven;
Go, and return in glory
    To Clusium's royal dome;
And hang round Nurscia's altars
    The golden shields of Rome."

XI. And now hath every city
    Sent up her tale of men;
The foot are fourscore thousand,
    The horse are thousands ten.
Before the gates of Sutrium
    Is met the great array.
A proud man was Lars Porsena
    Upon the trysting day.

XII. For all the Etruscan armies
    Were ranged beneath his eye,
And many a banished Roman,
    And many a stout ally;
And with a mighty following
    To join the muster came
The Tusculan Mamilius,
    Prince of the Latian name.

XIII. But by the yellow Tiber
    Was tumult and affright:
From all the spacious champaign
    To Rome men took their flight.
A mile around the city,
    The throng stopped up the ways;
A fearful sight it was to see
    Through two long nights and days

XIV. For aged folks on crutches,
    And women great with child,
And mothers sobbing over babes
    That clung to them and smiled,
And sick men borne in litters
    High on the necks of slaves,
And troops of sun-burned husbandmen
    With reaping-hooks and staves,

XV. And droves of mules and asses
    Laden with skins of wine,
And endless flocks of goats and sheep,
    And endless herds of kine,
And endless trains of waggons
    That creaked beneath the weight
Of corn-sacks and of household goods,
    Choked every roaring gate.

XVI. Now, from the rock Tarpeian,
    Could the wan burghers spy
The line of blazing villages
    Red in the midnight sky.
The Fathers of the City,
    They sat all night and day,
For every hour some horseman came
    With tidings of dismay.

xvii. To eastward and to westward
    Have spread the Tuscan bands;
Nor house, nor fence, nor dovecot
    In Crustumerium stands.
Verbenna down to Ostia
    Hath wasted all the plain;
Astur hath stormed Janiculum,
    And the stout guards are slain.

xviii. I wis, in all the Senate,
    There was no heart so bold,
But sore it ached, and fast it beat,
    When that ill news was told.
Forthwith up rose the Consul,
    Up rose the Fathers all;
In haste they girded up their gowns,
    And hied them to the wall.

xix. They held a council standing
    Before the River-Gate;
Short time was there, ye well may guess,
    For musing or debate.
Out spake the Consul roundly:
    " The bridge must straight go down;
For, since Janiculum is lost,
    Nought else can save the town."

xx. Just then a scout came flying,
    All wild with haste and fear:
" To arms! to arms! Sir Consul:
    Lars Porsena is here."
On the low hills to westward
    The Consul fixed his eye,
And saw the swarthy storm of dust
    Rise fast along the sky.

xxi. And nearer fast and nearer
    Doth the red whirlwind come;
And louder still and still more loud,
From underneath that rolling cloud,
Is heard the trumpet's war-note proud,
    The trampling, and the hum.
And plainly and more plainly
    Now through the gloom appears,

Far to left and far to right,
In broken gleams of dark-blue light,
The long array of helmets bright,
   The long array of spears.

XXII. And plainly and more plainly,
   Above that glimmering line,
Now might ye see the banners
   Of twelve fair cities shine;
But the banner of proud Clusium
   Was highest of them all,
The terror of the Umbrian,
   The terror of the Gaul.

XXIII. And plainly and more plainly
   Now might the burghers know,
By port and vest, by horse and crest,
   Each warlike Lucumo.
There Cilnius of Arretium
   On his fleet roan was seen;
And Astur of the four-fold shield,
Girt with the brand none else may wield,
Tolumnius with the belt of gold,
And dark Verbenna from the hold
   By reedy Thrasymene.

XXIV. Fast by the royal standard,
   O'erlooking all the war,
Lars Porsena of Clusium
   Sat in his ivory car.
By the right wheel rode Mamilius,
   Prince of the Latian name;
And by the left false Sextus,
   That wrought the deed of shame.

XXV. But when the face of Sextus
   Was seen among the foes,
A yell that rent the firmament
   From all the town arose.
On the house-tops was no woman
   But spat towards him and hissed,
No child but screamed out curses,
   And shook its little fist.

XXVI. But the Consul's brow was sad,
  And the Consul's speech was low,
And darkly looked he at the wall,
  And darkly at the foe.
" Their van will be upon us
  Before the bridge goes down;
And if they once may win the bridge,
  What hope to save the town? "

XXVII. Then out spake brave Horatius,
  The Captain of the Gate:
" To every man upon this earth
  Death cometh soon or late.
And how can man die better
  Than facing fearful odds,
For the ashes of his fathers,
  And the temples of his Gods,

XXVIII. " And for the tender mother
  Who dandled him to rest,
And for the wife who nurses
  His baby at her breast,
And for the holy maidens
  Who feed the eternal flame,
To save them from false Sextus
  That wrought the deed of shame?

XXIX. " Hew down the bridge, Sir Consul,
  With all the speed ye may;
I, with two more to help me,
  Will hold the foe in play.
In yon strait path a thousand
  May well be stopped by three.
Now who will stand on either hand,
  And keep the bridge with me? "

XXX. Then out spake Spurius Lartius;
  A Ramnian proud was he:
" Lo, I will stand at thy right hand,
  And keep the bridge with thee."
And out spake strong Herminius;
  Of Titian blood was he:
" I will abide on thy left side,
  And keep the bridge with thee."

XXXI. " Horatius," quoth the Consul,
    " As thou sayest, so let it be."
And straight against that great array
    Forth went the dauntless Three.
For Romans in Rome's quarrel
    Spared neither land nor gold,
Nor son nor wife, nor limb nor life,
    In the brave days of old.

XXXII. Then none was for a party;
    Then all were for the state;
Then the great man helped the poor,
    And the poor man loved the great:
Then lands were fairly portioned:
    Then spoils were fairly sold:
The Romans were like brothers
    In the brave days of old.

XXXIII. Now Roman is to Roman
    More hateful than a foe,
And the Tribunes beard the high,
    And the Fathers grind the low.
As we wax hot in faction,
    In battle we wax cold:
Wherefore men fight not as they fought
    In the brave days of old.

XXXIV. Now while the Three were tightening
    Their harness on their backs,
The Consul was the foremost man
    To take in hand an axe:
And Fathers mixed with Commons
    Seized hatchet, bar, and crow,
And smote upon the planks above,
    And loosed the props below.

XXXV. Meanwhile the Tuscan army,
    Right glorious to behold,
Came flashing back the noonday light,
Rank behind rank, like surges bright
    Of a broad sea of gold.
Four hundred trumpets sounded
    A peal of warlike glee,

As that great host, with measured tread,
And spears advanced, and ensigns spread,
Rolled slowly towards the bridge's head,
   Where stood the dauntless Three.

XXXVI. The Three stood calm and silent,
   And looked upon the foes,
And a great shout of laughter
   From all the vanguard rose:
And forth three chiefs came spurring
   Before that deep array;
To earth they sprang, their swords they drew,
And lifted high their shields, and flew
   To win the narrow way;

XXXVII. Aunus from green Tifernum,
   Lord of the Hill of Vines;
And Seius, whose eight hundred slaves
   Sicken in Ilva's mines;
And Picus, long to Clusium
   Vassal in peace and war,
Who led to fight his Umbrian powers
From that grey crag where, girt with towers,
The fortress of Nequinum lowers
   O'er the pale waves of Nar.

XXXVIII. Stout Lartius hurled down Aunus
   Into the stream beneath:
Herminius struck at Seius,
   And clove him to the teeth:
At Picus brave Horatius
   Darted one fiery thrust;
And the proud Umbrian's gilded arms
   Clashed in the bloody dust.

XXXIX. Then Ocnus of Falerii
   Rushed on the Roman Three,
And Lausulus of Urgo,
   The rover of the sea;
And Aruns of Volsinium,
   Who slew the great wild boar,
The great wild boar that had his den
Amidst the reeds of Cosa's fen,
And wasted fields, and slaughtered men,
   Along Albinia's shore.

XL. Herminius smote down Aruns:
    Lartius laid Ocnus low:
Right to the heart of Lausulus
    Horatius sent a blow.
" Lie there," he cried, " fell pirate!
    No more, aghast and pale,
From Ostia's walls the crowd shall mark
The track of thy destroying bark.
No more Campania's hinds shall fly
To woods and caverns when they spy
    Thy thrice accursed sail."

XLI. But now no sound of laughter
    Was heard among the foes.
A wild and wrathful clamour
    From all the vanguard rose.
Six spears' lengths from the entrance
    Halted that deep array,
And for a space no man came forth
    To win the narrow way.

XLII. But hark! the cry is Astur:
    And lo! the ranks divide;
And the great Lord of Luna
    Comes with his stately stride.
Upon his ample shoulders
    Clangs loud the four-fold shield,
And in his hand he shakes the brand
    Which none but he can wield.

XLIII. He smiled on those bold Romans
    A smile serene and high;
He eyed the flinching Tuscans,
    And scorn was in his eye.
Quoth he, " The she-wolf's litter
    Stand savagely at bay:
But will you dare to follow,
    If Astur clears the way?"

XLIV. Then, whirling up his broadsword
    With both hands to the height,
He rushed against Horatius,
    And smote with all his might.

With shield and blade Horatius
  Right deftly turned the blow.
The blow, though turned, came yet too nigh;
It missed his helm, but gashed his thigh:
The Tuscans raised a joyful cry
  To see the red blood flow.

XLV. He reeled, and on Herminius
  He leaned one breathing-space;
Then, like a wild cat mad with wounds,
  Sprang right at Astur's face.
Through teeth, and skull, and helmet
  So fierce a thrust he sped,
The good sword stood a hand-breadth out
  Behind the Tuscan's head.

XLVI. And the great Lord of Luna
  Fell at that deadly stroke,
As falls on Mount Alvernus
  A thunder-smitten oak.
Far o'er the crashing forest
  The giant arms lie spread;
And the pale augurs, muttering low,
  Gaze on the blasted head.

XLVII. On Astur's throat Horatius
  Right firmly pressed his heel,
And thrice and four times tugged amain,
  Ere he wrenched out the steel.
" And see," he cried, " the welcome,
  Fair guests, that waits you here!
What noble Lucumo comes next
  To taste our Roman cheer? "

XLVIII. But at his haughty challenge
  A sullen murmur ran,
Mingled of wrath, and shame, and dread,
  Along that glittering van.
There lacked not men of prowess,
  Nor men of lordly race;
For all Etruria's noblest
  Were round the fatal place.

XLIX. But all Etruria's noblest
    Felt their hearts sink to see
On the earth the bloody corpses,
    In the path the dauntless Three:
And, from the ghastly entrance
    Where those bold Romans stood,
All shrank, like boys who unaware,
Ranging the woods to start a hare,
Come to the mouth of the dark lair
Where, growling low, a fierce old bear
    Lies amidst bones and blood.

L. Was none who would be foremost
    To lead such dire attack:
But those behind cried " Forward!"
    And those before cried " Back!"
And backward now and forward
    Wavers the deep array;
And on the tossing sea of steel,
To and fro the standards reel;
And the victorious trumpet-peal
    Dies fitfully away.

LI. Yet one man for one moment
    Strode out before the crowd;
Well known was he to all the Three,
    And they gave him greeting loud.
" Now welcome, welcome, Sextus!
    Now welcome to thy home!
Why dost thou stay, and turn away?
Here lies the road to Rome."

LII. Thrice looked he at the city;
    Thrice looked he at the dead;
And thrice came on in fury,
    And thrice turned back in dread:
And, white with fear and hatred,
    Scowled at the narrow way
Where, wallowing in a pool of blood,
    The bravest Tuscans lay.

LIII. But meanwhile axe and lever
    Have manfully been plied;

And now the bridge hangs tottering
  Above the boiling tide.
" Come back, come back, Horatius ! "
  Loud cried the Fathers all.
" Back, Lartius ! back, Herminius !
  Back, ere the ruin fall ! "

LIV. Back darted Spurius Lartius ;
  Herminius darted back :
And, as they passed, beneath their feet
  They felt the timbers crack.
But when they turned their faces,
  And on the farther shore
Saw brave Horatius stand alone,
  They would have crossed once more.

LV. But with a crash like thunder
  Fell every loosen'd beam,
And, like a dam, the mighty wreck
  Lay right athwart the stream :
And a long shout of triumph
  Rose from the walls of Rome,
As to the highest turret-tops
  Was splashed the yellow foam.

LVI. And, like a horse unbroken
  When first he feels the rein,
The furious river struggled hard,
  And tossed his tawny mane,
And burst the curb, and bounded,
  Rejoicing to be free,
And whirling down, in fierce career,
Battlement, and plank, and pier,
  Rushed headlong to the sea.

LVII. Alone stood brave Horatius,
  But constant still in mind ;
Thrice thirty thousand foes before,
  And the broad flood behind.
" Down with him ! " cried false Sextus,
  With a smile on his pale face.
" Now yield thee," cried Lars Porsena,
  " Now yield thee to our grace."

LVIII. Round turned he, as not deigning
    Those craven ranks to see;
Nought spake he to Lars Porsena,
    To Sextus nought spake he;
But he saw on Palatinus
    The white porch of his home;
And he spake to the noble river
    That rolls by the towers of Rome.

LIX. " Oh, Tiber! father Tiber!
    To whom the Romans pray,
A Roman's life, a Roman's arms,
    Take thou in charge this day!"
So he spake, and speaking sheathed
    The good sword by his side,
And with his harness on his back,
    Plunged headlong in the tide.

LX. No sound of joy or sorrow
    Was heard from either bank;
But friends and foes in dumb surprise,
    With parted lips and straining eyes,
    Stood gazing where he sank;
And when above the surges
    They saw his crest appear,
All Rome sent forth a rapturous cry,
And even the ranks of Tuscany
    Could scarce forbear to cheer.

LXI. But fiercely ran the current,
    Swollen high by months of rain:
And fast his blood was flowing;
    And he was sore in pain,
And heavy with his armour,
    And spent with changing blows:
And oft they thought him sinking,
    But still again he rose.

LXII. Never, I ween, did swimmer,
    In such an evil case,
Struggle through such a raging flood
    Safe to the landing place:

But his limbs were borne up bravely
　By the brave heart within,
And our good father Tiber
　Bare bravely up his chin.

LXIII. " Curse on him!" quoth false Sextus;
　　　" Will not the villain drown?
But for this stay, ere close of day
　　We should have sacked the town!"
" Heaven help him!" quoth Lars Porsena,
　　" And bring him safe to shore;
For such a gallant feat of arms
　　Was never seen before."

LXIV. And now he feels the bottom;
　　　Now on dry earth he stands;
Now round him throng the Fathers
　　To press his gory hands;
And now, with shouts and clapping,
　　And noise of weeping loud,
He enters through the River-Gate,
　　Borne by the joyous crowd.

LXV. They gave him of the corn-land,
　　　That was of public right,
As much as two strong oxen
　　Could plough from morn till night;
And they made a molten image,
　　And set it up on high,
And there it stands unto this day
　　To witness if I lie.

LXVI. It stands in the Comitium,
　　　Plain for all folks to see;
Horatius in his harness,
　　Halting upon one knee:
And underneath is written,
　　In letters all of gold,
How valiantly he kept the bridge
　　In the brave days of old.

LXVII. And still his name sounds stirring
　　　Unto the men of Rome,

As the trumpet-blast that cries to them
  To charge the Volscian home;
And wives still pray to Juno
  For boys with hearts as bold
As his who kept the bridge so well
  In the brave days of old.

LXVIII. And in the nights of winter,
  When the cold north winds blow,
And the long howling of the wolves
  Is heard amidst the snow;
When round the lonely cottage
  Roars loud the tempest's din,
And the good logs of Algidus
  Roar louder yet within;

LXIX. When the oldest cask is opened,
  And the largest lamp is lit;
When the chestnuts glow in the embers,
  And the kid turns on the spit;
When young and old in circle
  Around the firebrands close;
When the girls are weaving baskets,
  And the lads are shaping bows;

LXX. When the goodman mends his armour,
  And trims his helmet's plume;
When the goodwife's shuttle merrily
  Goes flashing through the loom;
With weeping and with laughter
  Still is the story told,
How well Horatius kept the bridge
  In the brave days of old.

THE BATTLE OF THE LAKE REGILLUS

THE following poem is supposed to have been produced about
ninety years after the lay of Horatius. Some persons mentioned in
the lay of Horatius make their appearance again, and some appel-
lations and epithets used in the lay of Horatius have been purposely
repeated: for, in the age of ballad-poetry, it scarcely ever fails to
happen, that certain phrases come to be appropriated to certain
men and things, and are regularly applied to those men and things
by every minstrel. Thus we find, both in the Homeric poems and
in Hesiod, βίη Ἡρακληείη, περικλύτος Ἀμφιγυήεις, διάκτορος Ἀργειφόντης,
ἑπτάπυλος Θήθη, Ἑλένης ἕνεκ' ἠϋκόμοιο. Thus, too, in our own national
songs, Douglas is almost always the doughty Douglas: England is
merry England: all the gold is red; and all the ladies are gay.

The principal distinction between the lay of Horatius and the lay
of the Lake Regillus is that the former is meant to be purely Roman,
while the latter, though national in its general spirit, has a slight
tincture of Greek learning and of Greek superstition. The story of
the Tarquins, as it has come down to us, appears to have been compiled from the works of several popular poets; and one, at least, of
those poets appears to have visited the Greek colonies in Italy, if
not Greece itself, and to have had some acquaintance with the
works of Homer and Herodotus. Many of the most striking
adventures of the house of Tarquin, before Lucretia makes her
appearance, have a Greek character. The Tarquins themselves
are represented as Corinthian nobles of the great house of the
Bacchiadæ, driven from their country by the tyranny of that
Cypselus, the tale of whose strange escape Herodotus has related
with incomparable simplicity and liveliness. Livy and Dionysius
tell us that, when Tarquin the Proud was asked what was the best
mode of governing a conquered city, he replied only by beating
down with his staff all the tallest poppies in his garden. This is
exactly what Herodotus, in the passage to which reference has
already been made, relates of the counsel given to Periander, the
son of Cypselus. The stratagem by which the town of Gabii is
brought under the power of the Tarquins is, again, obviously copied
from Herodotus. The embassy of the young Tarquins to the oracle
at Delphi is just such a story as would be told by a poet whose head
was full of the Greek mythology; and the ambiguous answer returned by Apollo is in the exact style of the prophecies which,
according to Herodotus, lured Crœsus to destruction. Then the
character of the narrative changes. From the first mention of
Lucretia to the retreat of Porsena nothing seems to be borrowed

from foreign sources.   The villany of Sextus, the suicide of his victim, the revolution, the death of the sons of Brutus, the defence of the bridge, Mucius burning his hand, Clœlia swimming through Tiber, seem to be all strictly Roman.   But when we have done with the Tuscan war, and enter upon the war with the Latines, we are again struck by the Greek air of the story.   The Battle of the Lake Regillus is in all respects a Homeric battle, except that the combatants ride astride on their horses, instead of driving chariots. The mass of fighting men is hardly mentioned.   The leaders single each other out, and engage hand to hand.   The great object of the warriors on both sides is, as in the *Iliad*, to obtain possession of the spoils and bodies of the slain; and several circumstances are related which forcibly remind us of the great slaughter round the corpses of Sarpedon and Patroclus.

But there is one circumstance which deserves especial notice. Both the war of Troy and the war of Regillus were caused by the licentious passions of young princes, who were therefore peculiarly bound not to be sparing of their own persons in the day of battle. Now the conduct of Sextus at Regillus, as described by Livy, so exactly resembles that of Paris, as described at the beginning of the third book of the *Iliad*, that it is difficult to believe the resemblance accidental.   Paris appears before the Trojan ranks, defying the bravest Greek to encounter him:

> Τρωσὶν μὲν προμάχιζεν 'Αλέξανδρος θεοειδὴς,
> . . . . . 'Αργειων προκαλίζετο πάντας ἀρίστους,
> ἀντίβιον μαχέσασθαι ἐν αἰνῇ δηιοτῆτι.

Livy introduces Sextus in a similar manner: " Ferocem juvenem Tarquinium, ostentantem se in prima exsulum acie."   Menelaus rushes to meet Paris.   A Roman noble, eager for vengeance, spurs his horse towards Sextus.   Both the guilty princes are instantly terror-stricken:

> Τὸν δ' ὡς οὖν ἐνόησεν 'Αλέξανδρος θεοειδὴς
> ἐν προμάχοισι φανέντα, κατεπλήγη φίλον ἦτορ ·
> ἂψ δ' ἐτάρων εἰς ἔθνος ἐχάζετο κῆρ' ἀλεείνων.

" Tarquinius," says Livy, " retro in agmen suorum infenso cessit hosti."   If this be a fortuitous coincidence, it is one of the most extraordinary in literature.

In the following poem, therefore, images and incidents have been borrowed, not merely without scruple, but on principle, from the incomparable battle-pieces of Homer.

The popular belief at Rome, from an early period, seems to have been that the event of the great day of Regillus was decided by supernatural agency.   Castor and Pollux, it was said, had fought, armed and mounted, at the head of the legions of the commonwealth, and had afterwards carried the news of the victory with incredible speed to the city.   The well in the Forum at which they had alighted was pointed out.   Near the well rose their ancient temple.   A great festival was kept to their honour on the Ides of Quintilis, supposed to be the anniversary of the battle; and on that day sumptuous sacrifices were offered to them at the public charge.   One spot on the margin of Lake Regillus was regarded during many ages with superstitious awe.   A mark, resembling in shape a horse's hoof, was discernible in the volcanic rock; and this mark was believed to have been made by one of the celestial chargers.

How the legend originated cannot now be ascertained: but we may easily imagine several ways in which it might have originated; nor is it at all necessary to suppose, with Julius Frontinus, that two young men were dressed up by the Dictator to personate the sons of Leda.   It is probable that Livy is correct when he says that the Roman general, in the hour of peril, vowed a temple to Castor.   If so, nothing could be more natural than that the multitude should ascribe the victory to the favour of the Twin Gods.   When such was the prevailing sentiment, any man who chose to declare that, in the midst of the confusion and slaughter, he had seen two god-like forms on white horses scattering the Latines, would find ready credence.   We know, indeed, that, in modern times, a very similar story actually found credence among a people much more civilised than the Romans of the fifth century before Christ.   A chaplain of Cortes, writing about thirty years after the conquest of Mexico, in an age of printing presses, libraries, universities, scholars, logicians, jurists, and statesmen, had the face to assert that, in one engagement against the Indians, Saint James had appeared on a grey horse at the head of the Castilian adventurers.   Many of those adventurers were living when this lie was printed.   One of them, honest Bernal Diaz, wrote an account of the expedition.   He had the evidence of his own senses against the legend; but he seems to have distrusted even the evidence of his own senses.   He says that he was in the battle, and that he saw a grey horse with a man on his back, but that the man was, to his thinking, Francesco de Morla, and not the ever-blessed apostle Saint James.   " Nevertheless," Bernal adds, " it may be that the person on the grey horse was the glorious apostle Saint James, and that I, sinner that I am, was un-worthy to see him."   The Romans of the age of Cincinnatus were probably quite as credulous as the Spanish subjects of Charles the Fifth.   It is therefore conceivable that the appearance of Castor and Pollux may have become an article of faith before the genera-tion which had fought at Regillus had passed away.   Nor could any thing be more natural than that the poets of the next age should embellish this story, and make the celestial horsemen bear the tidings of victory to Rome.

Many years after the temple of the Twin Gods had been built in the Forum, an important addition was made to the ceremonial by which the state annually testified its gratitude for their protection. Quintus Fabius and Publius Decius were elected Censors at a momentous crisis.   It had become absolutely necessary that the classification of the citizens should be revised.   On that classifica-tion depended the distribution of political power.   Party-spirit ran high; and the republic seemed to be in danger of falling under the dominion either of a narrow oligarchy or of an ignorant and head-strong rabble.   Under such circumstances, the most illustrious patrician and the most illustrious plebeian of the age were intrusted with the office of arbitrating between the angry factions; and they performed their arduous task to the satisfaction of all honest and reasonable men.

One of their reforms was a remodelling of the equestrian order; and, having effected this reform, they determined to give to their work a sanction derived from religion. In the chivalrous societies of modern times, societies which have much more than may at first sight appear in common with the equestrian order of Rome, it has been usual to invoke the special protection of some Saint, and to observe his day with peculiar solemnity. Thus the Companions of the Garter wear the image of Saint George depending from their collars, and meet, on great occasions, in Saint George's Chapel. Thus, when Lewis the Fourteenth instituted a new order of chivalry for the rewarding of military merit, he commended it to the favour of his own glorified ancestor and patron, and decreed that all the members of the fraternity should meet at the royal palace on the feast of Saint Lewis, should attend the king to chapel, should hear mass, and should subsequently hold their great annual assembly. There is a considerable resemblance between this rule of the order of Saint Lewis and the rule which Fabius and Decius made respecting the Roman knights. It was ordained that a grand muster and inspection of the equestrian body should be part of the ceremonial performed, on the anniversary of the battle of Regillus, in honour of Castor and Pollux, the two equestrian Gods. All the knights, clad in purple and crowned with olive, were to meet at a temple of Mars in the suburbs. Thence they were to ride in state to the Forum, where the temple of the Twins stood. This pageant was, during several centuries, considered as one of the most splendid sights of Rome. In the time of Dionysius the cavalcade sometimes consisted of five thousand horsemen, all persons of fair repute and easy fortune.

There can be no doubt that the Censors who instituted this august ceremony acted in concert with the Pontiffs to whom, by the constitution of Rome, the superintendence of the public worship belonged; and it is probable that those high religious functionaries were, as usual, fortunate enough to find in their books or traditions some warrant for the innovation.

The following poem is supposed to have been made for this great occasion. Songs, we know, were chanted at the religious festivals of Rome from an early period, indeed from so early a period, that some of the sacred verses were popularly ascribed to Numa, and were utterly unintelligible in the age of Augustus. In the Second Punic War a great feast was held in honour of Juno, and a song was sung in her praise. This song was extant when Livy wrote; and, though exceedingly rugged and uncouth, seemed to him not wholly destitute of merit. A song, as we learn from Horace, was part of the established ritual at the great Secular Jubilee. It is therefore likely that the Censors and Pontiffs, when they had resolved to add a grand procession of knights to the other solemnities annually performed on the Ides of Quintilis, would call in the aid of a poet. Such a poet would naturally take for his subject the battle of Regillus, the appearance of the Twin Gods, and the institution of their festival. He would find abundant materials in the ballads of his predecessors;

and he would make free use of the scanty stock of Greek learning
which he had himself acquired.   He would probably introduce some
wise and holy Pontiff enjoining the magnificent ceremonial which,
after a long interval, had at length been adopted.   If the poem
succeeded, many persons would commit it to memory.   Parts of it
would be sung to the pipe at banquets.   It would be peculiarly
interesting to the great Posthumian House, which numbered among
its many images that of the Dictator Aulus, the hero of Regillus.
The orator who, in the following generation, pronounced the
funeral panegyric over the remains of Lucius Posthumius Megellus,
thrice Consul, would borrow largely from the lay; and thus some
passages, much disfigured, would probably find their way into the
chronicles which were afterwards in the hands of Dionysius and
Livy.

Antiquaries differ widely as to the situation of the field of battle.
The opinion of those who suppose that the armies met near Cornu-
felle, between Frascati and the Monte Porzio, is at least plausible,
and has been followed in the poem.

As to the details of the battle, it has not been thought desirable
to adhere minutely to the accounts which have come down to us.
Those accounts, indeed, differ widely from each other, and, in all
probability, differ as widely from the ancient poem from which
they were originally derived.

It is unnecessary to point out the obvious imitations of the *Iliad*,
which have been purposely introduced.

    1. Ho, trumpets, sound a war-note!
       Ho, lictors, clear the way!
    The Knights will ride, in all their pride,
       Along the streets to-day.
    To-day the doors and windows
       Are hung with garlands all,
    From Castor in the Forum,
       To Mars without the wall.
    Each Knight is robed in purple,
       With olive each is crowned;
    A gallant war-horse under each
       Paws haughtily the ground.
    While flows the Yellow River,
       While stands the Sacred Hill,
    The proud Ides of Quintilis
       Shall have such honour still.
    Gay are the Martian Kalends:
       December's Nones are gay:
    But the proud Ides, when the squadron rides,
       Shall be Rome's whitest day.

II. Unto the Great Twin Brethren
       We keep this solemn feast.
     Swift, swift, the Great Twin Brethren
       Came spurring from the east.
     They came o'er wild Parthenius
       Tossing in waves of pine,
     O'er Cirrha's dome, o'er Adria's foam,
       O'er purple Apennine,
     From where with flutes and dances
       Their ancient mansion rings,
     In lordly Lacedæmon,
       The City of two kings,
     To where, by Lake Regillus,
       Under the Porcian height,
     All in the lands of Tusculum,
       Was fought the glorious fight.

III. Now on the place of slaughter
       Are cots and sheepfolds seen,
     And rows of vines, and fields of wheat,
       And apple-orchards green!
     The swine crush the big acorns
       That fall from Corne's oaks.
     Upon the turf by the Fair Fount
       The reaper's pottage smokes.
     The fisher baits his angle;
       The hunter twangs his bow;
     Little they think on those strong limbs
       That moulder deep below.
     Little they think how sternly
       That day the trumpets pealed;
     How in the slippery swamp of blood
       Warrior and war-horse reeled;
     How wolves came with fierce gallop,
       And crows on eager wings,
     To tear the flesh of captains,
       And peck the eyes of kings;
     How thick the dead lay scattered
       Under the Porcian height;
     How through the gates of Tusculum
       Raved the wild stream of flight;
     And how the Lake Regillus
       Bubbled with crimson foam,

What time the Thirty Cities
  Came forth to war with Rome.

iv. But, Roman, when thou standest
      Upon that holy ground,
    Look thou with heed on the dark rock
      That girds the dark lake round.
    So shalt thou see a hoof-mark
      Stamped deep into the flint:
    It was no hoof of mortal steed
      That made so strange a dint:
    There to the Great Twin Brethren
      Vow thou thy vows, and pray
    That they, in tempest and in fight,
      Will keep thy head alway.

v. Since last the Great Twin Brethren
      Of mortal eyes were seen,
    Have years gone by an hundred
      And fourscore and thirteen.
    That summer a Virginius
      Was Consul first in place;
    The second was stout Aulus,
      Of the Posthumian race.
    The Herald of the Latines
      From Gabii came in state:
    The Herald of the Latines
      Passed through Rome's Eastern Gate:
    The Herald of the Latines
      Did in our Forum stand;
    And there he did his office,
      A sceptre in his hand.

vi. " Hear, Senators and people
      Of the good town of Rome:
    The Thirty Cities charge you
      To bring the Tarquins home:
    And if ye still be stubborn,
      To work the Tarquins wrong,
    The Thirty Cities warn you,
      Look that your walls be strong."

vii. Then spake the Consul Aulus,
      He spake a bitter jest:

" Once the jays sent a message
  Unto the eagle's nest:—
Now yield thou up thine eyrie
  Unto the carrion-kite,
Or come forth valiantly, and face
  The jays in deadly fight.—
Forth looked in wrath the eagle;
  And carrion-kite and jay,
Soon as they saw his beak and claw,
  Fled screaming far away."

VIII. The Herald of the Latines
  Hath hied him back in state:
The Fathers of the City
  Are met in high debate.
Then spake the elder Consul,
  An ancient man and wise:
" Now hearken, Conscript Fathers,
  To that which I advise.
In seasons of great peril
  'Tis good that one bear sway;
Then choose we a Dictator,
  Whom all men shall obey.
Camerium knows how deeply
  The sword of Aulus bites;
And all our city calls him
  The man of seventy fights.
Then let him be Dictator
  For six months and no more,
And have a Master of the Knights,
  And axes twenty-four."

IX. So Aulus was Dictator,
  The man of seventy fights;
He made Æbutius Elva
  His Master of the Knights.
On the third morn thereafter,
  At dawning of the day,
Did Aulus and Æbutius
  Set forth with their array.
Sempronius Atratinus
  Was left in charge at home
With boys, and with grey-headed men,
  To keep the walls of Rome.

Hard by the Lake Regillus
  Our camp was pitched at night:
Eastward a mile the Latines lay,
  Under the Porcian height.
Far over hill and valley
  Their mighty host was spread;
And with their thousand watch-fires
  The midnight sky was red.

x. Up rose the golden morning
  Over the Porcian height,
The proud Ides of Quintilis
  Marked evermore with white.
Nor without secret trouble
  Our bravest saw the foes;
For girt by threescore thousand spears,
  The thirty standards rose.
From every warlike city
  That boasts the Latian name,
Foredoomed to dogs and vultures,
  That gallant army came;
From Setia's purple vineyards,
  From Norba's ancient wall,
From the white streets of Tusculum,
  The proudest town of all;
From where the Witch's Fortress
  O'erhangs the dark-blue seas;
From the still glassy lake that sleeps
  Beneath Aricia's trees—
Those trees in whose dim shadow
  The ghastly priest doth reign,
The priest who slew the slayer,
  And shall himself be slain;
From the drear banks of Ufens,
  Where flights of marsh-fowl play,
And buffaloes lie wallowing
  Through the hot summer's day;
From the gigantic watch-towers,
  No work of earthly men,
Whence Cora's sentinels o'erlook
  The never-ending fen;
From the Laurentian jungle,
  The wild hog's reedy home;

From the green steeps whence Anio leaps
  In floods of snow-white foam.

XI. Aricia, Cora, Norba,
  Velitræ, with the might
Of Setia and of Tusculum,
  Were marshalled on the right:
The leader was Mamilius,
  Prince of the Latian name;
Upon his head a helmet
  Of red gold shone like flame:
High on a gallant charger
  Of dark-grey hue he rode;
Over his gilded armour
  A vest of purple flowed,
Woven in the land of sunrise
  By Syria's dark-browed daughters,
And by the sails of Carthage brought
  Far o'er the southern waters.

XII. Lavinium and Laurentum
  Had on the left their post,
With all the banners of the marsh,
  And banners of the coast.
Their leader was false Sextus,
  That wrought the deed of shame:
With restless pace and haggard face
  To his last field he came.
Men said he saw strange visions
  Which none beside might see;
And that strange sounds were in his ears
  Which none might hear but he.
A woman fair and stately,
  But pale as are the dead,
Oft through the watches of the night
  Sat spinning by his bed.
And as she plied the distaff,
  In a sweet voice and low,
She sang of great old houses,
  And fights fought long ago.
So spun she, and so sang she,
  Until the east was grey,
Then pointed to her bleeding breast,
  And shrieked, and fled away.

XIII. But in the centre thickest
    Were ranged the shields of foes.
And from the centre loudest
    The cry of battle rose.
There Tibur marched and Pedum
    Beneath proud Tarquin's rule,
And Ferentinum of the rock,
    And Gabii of the pool.
There rode the Volscian succours:
    There, in a dark stern ring,
The Roman exiles gathered close
    Around the ancient king.
Though white as Mount Soracte,
    When winter nights are long,
His beard flowed down o'er mail and belt,
    His heart and hand were strong:
Under his hoary eyebrows
    Still flashed forth quenchless rage:
And, if the lance shook in his gripe,
    'Twas more with hate than age.
Close as his side was Titus
    On an Apulian steed,
Titus, the youngest Tarquin,
    Too good for such a breed.

XIV. Now on each side the leaders
    Gave signal for the charge;
And on each side the footmen
    Strode on with lance and targe;
And on each side the horsemen
    Struck their spurs deep in gore
And front to front the armies
    Met with a mighty roar:
And under that great battle
    The earth with blood was red;
And, like the Pomptine fog at morn,
    The dust hung overhead;
And louder still and louder
    Rose from the darkened field
The braying of the war-horns,
    The clang of sword and shield,
The rush of squadrons sweeping
    Like whirlwinds o'er the plain,

The shouting of the slayers,
  And screeching of the slain.

xv. False Sextus rode out foremost:
  His look was high and bold;
His corslet was of bison's hide,
  Plated with steel and gold.
As glares the famished eagle
  From the Digentian rock
On a choice lamb that bounds alone
  Before Bandusia's flock,
Herminius glared on Sextus,
  And came with eagle speed,
Herminius on black Auster,
  Brave champion on brave steed;
In his right hand the broadsword
  That kept the bridge so well,
And on his helm the crown he won
  When proud Fidenæ fell.
Woe to the maid whose lover
  Shall cross his path to-day!
False Sextus saw, and trembled,
  And turned, and fled away.
As turns, as flies, the woodman
  In the Calabrian brake,
When through the reeds gleams the round eye
  Of that fell speckled snake;
So turned, so fled, false Sextus,
  And hid him in the rear.
Behind the dark Lavinian ranks,
  Bristling with crest and spear.

xvi. But far to north Æbutius,
  The Master of the Knights,
Gave Tubero of Norba
  To feed the Porcian kites.
Next under those red horse-hoofs
  Flaccus of Setia lay;
Better had he been pruning
  Among his elms that day,
Mamilius saw the slaughter,
  And tossed his golden crest,
And towards the Master of the Knights
  Through the thick battle pressed.

Æbutius smote Mamilius
  So fiercely on the shield
That the great Lord of Tusculum
  Well nigh rolled on the field.
Mamilius smote Æbutius,
  With a good aim and true,
Just where the neck and shoulder join,
  And pierced him through and through;
And brave Æbutius Elva
  Fell swooning to the ground:
But a thick wall of bucklers
  Encompassed him around.
His clients from the battle
  Bare him some little space,
And filled a helm from the dark lake,
  And bathed his brow and face;
And when at last he opened
  His swimming eyes to light,
Men say, the earliest word he spake
  Was, " Friends, how goes the fight? "

XVII. But meanwhile in the centre
  Great deeds of arms were wrought;
There Aulus the Dictator
  And there Valerius fought.
Aulus with his good broadsword
  A bloody passage cleared
To where, amidst the thickest foes,
  He saw the long white beard.
Flat lighted that good broadsword
  Upon proud Tarquin's head.
He dropped the lance: he dropped the reins:
  He fell as fall the dead.
Down Aulus springs to slay him,
  With eyes like coals of fire;
But faster Titus hath sprung down,
  And hath bestrode his sire.
Latian captains, Roman knights,
  Fast down to earth they spring,
And hand to hand they fight on foot
  Around the ancient king.
First Titus gave tall Cæso
  A death wound in the face:

Tall Cæso was the bravest man
  Of the brave Fabian race:
Aulus slew Rex of Gabii,
  The priest of Juno's shrine:
Valerius smote down Julius,
  Of Rome's great Julian line;
Julius, who left his mansion
  High on the Velian hill,
And through all turns of weal and woe
  Followed proud Tarquin still.
Now right across proud Tarquin
  A corpse was Julius laid;
And Titus groaned with rage and grief,
  And at Valerius made.   -
Valerius struck at Titus,
  And lopped off half his crest;
But Titus stabbed Valerius
  A span deep in the breast,
Like a mast snapped by the tempest,
  Valerius reeled and fell.
Ah! woe is me for the good house
  That loves the people well!
Then shouted loud the Latines;
  And with one rush they bore
The struggling Romans backward
  Three lances' length and more:
And up they took proud Tarquin,
  And laid him on a shield,
And four strong yeomen bare him,
  Still senseless, from the field.

XVIII. But fiercer grew the fighting,
  Around Valerius dead;
For Titus dragged him by the foot,
  And Aulus by the head.
" On, Latines, on!" quoth Titus,
  " See how the rebels fly!"
" Romans, stand firm!" quoth Aulus,
  " And win this fight or die!
They must not give Valerius
  To raven and to kite;
For aye Valerius loathed the wrong,
  And aye upheld the right:

And for your wives and babies
  In the front rank he fell.
Now play the men for the good house
  That loves the people well!"

xix. Then tenfold round the body
  The roar of battle rose,
Like the roar of a burning forest,
  When a strong north wind blows.
Now backward, and now forward,
  Rocked furiously the fray,
Till none could see Valerius,
  And none wist where he lay.
For shivered arms and ensigns
  Were heaped there in a mound,
And corpses stiff, and dying men
  That writhed and gnawed the ground;
And wounded horses kicking,
  And snorting purple foam:
Right well did such a couch befit
  A Consular of Rome.

xx. But north looked the Dictator;
  North looked he long and hard;
And spake to Caius Cossus,
  The Captain of his Guard;
" Caius, of all the Romans
  Thou hast the keenest sight;
Say, what through yonder storm of dust
  Comes from the Latian right?"

xxi. Then answered Caius Cossus:
  " I see an evil sight;
The banner of proud Tusculum
  Comes from the Latian right;
I see the plumed horsemen;
  And far before the rest
I see the dark-grey charger,
  I see the purple vest;
I see the golden helmet
  That shines far off like flame;
So ever rides Mamilius,
  Prince of the Latian name."

XXII 　" Now hearken, Caius Cossus:
　　　　Spring on thy horse's back;
　　　Ride as the wolves of Apennine
　　　　Were all upon thy track;
　　　Haste to our southward battle:
　　　　And never draw thy rein
　　　Until thou find Herminius,
　　　　And bid him come amain."

XXIII. So Aulus spake, and turned him
　　　　Again to that fierce strife;
　　　And Caius Cossus mounted,
　　　　And rode for death and life.
　　　Loud clanged beneath his horse-hoofs
　　　　The helmets of the dead,
　　　And many a curdling pool of blood
　　　　Splashed him from heel to head.
　　　So came he far to southward,
　　　　Where fought the Roman host,
　　　Against the banners of the marsh
　　　　And banners of the coast.
　　　Like corn before the sickle
　　　　The stout Lavinians fell,
　　　Beneath the edge of the true sword
　　　　That kept the bridge so well.

XXIV. " Herminius! Aulus greets thee;
　　　　He bids thee come with speed,
　　　To help our central battle;
　　　　For sore is there our need.
　　　There wars the youngest Tarquin,
　　　　And there the Crest of Flame,
　　　The Tusculan Mamilius,
　　　　Prince of the Latian name.
　　　Valerius hath fallen fighting
　　　　In front of our array;
　　　And Aulus of the seventy fields
　　　　Alone upholds the day."

XXV. Herminius beat his bosom:
　　　　But never a word he spake.
　　　He clapped his hand on Auster's mane:
　　　　He gave the reins a shake,

> Away, away, went Auster,
>   Like an arrow from the bow:
> Black Auster was the fleetest steed
>   From Aufidus to Po.

XXVI. Right glad were all the Romans
>   Who, in that hour of dread,
>   Against great odds bare up the war
>   Around Valerius dead,
>   When from the south the cheering
>   Rose with a mighty swell;
>   " Herminius comes, Herminius,
>   Who kept the bridge so well! "

XXVII. Mamilius spied Herminius,
>   And dashed across the way.
>   " Herminius! I have sought thee
>   Through many a bloody day.
>   One of us two, Herminius,
>   Shall never more go home.
>   I will lay on for Tusculum,
>   And lay thou on for Rome! "

XXVIII. All round them paused the battle,
>   While met in mortal fray
>   The Roman and the Tusculan,
>   The horses black and grey.
>   Herminius smote Mamilius
>   Through breast-plate and through breast,
>   And fast flowed out the purple blood
>   Over the purple vest.
>   Mamilius smote Herminius
>   Through head-piece and through head;
>   And side by side those chiefs of pride
>   Together fell down dead.
>   Down fell they dead together
>   In a great lake of gore;
>   And still stood all who saw them fall
>   While men might count a score.

XXIX. Fast, fast, with heels wild spurning,
>   The dark-grey charger fled:
>   He burst through ranks of fighting men;
>   He sprang o'er heaps of dead.

His bridle far out-streaming,
  His flanks all blood and foam,
He sought the southern mountains,
  The mountains of his home.
The pass was steep and rugged,
  The wolves they howled and whined;
But he ran like a whirlwind up the pass,
  And he left the wolves behind.
Through many a startled hamlet
  Thundered his flying feet;
He rushed through the gate of Tusculum,
  He rushed up the long white street;
He rushed by tower and temple,
  And paused not from his race
Till he stood before his master's door
  In the stately market-place.
And straightway round him gathered
  A pale and trembling crowd,
And when they knew him, cries of rage
  Brake forth, and wailing loud:
And women rent their tresses
  For their great prince's fall;
And old men girt on their old swords,
  And went to man the wall.

xxx. But, like a graven image,
  Black Auster kept his place,
And ever wistfully he looked
  Into his master's face.
The raven-mane that daily,
  With pats and fond caresses,
The young Herminia washed and combed,
  And twined in even tresses,
And decked with coloured ribands
  From her own gay attire,
Hung sadly o'er her father's corpse
  In carnage and in mire.
Forth with a shout sprang Titus,
  And seized black Auster's rein.
Then Aulus sware a fearful oath,
  And ran at him amain.
" The furies of thy brother
  With me and mine abide,

      If one of your accursed house
        Upon black Auster ride!"
      As on an Alpine watch-tower
        From heaven comes down the flame,
      Full on the neck of Titus
        The blade of Aulus came:
      And out the red blood spouted,
        In a wide arch and tall,
      As spouts a fountain in the court
        Of some rich Capuan's hall.
      The knees of all the Latines
        Were loosened with dismay,
      When dead, on dead Herminius,
        The bravest Tarquin lay.

XXXI. And Aulus the Dictator
        Stroked Auster's raven mane,
      With heed he looked unto the girths,
        With heed unto the rein.
      " Now bear me well, black Auster,
        Into yon thick array;
      And thou and I will have revenge
        For thy good lord this day."

XXXII. So spake he; and was buckling
        Tighter black Auster's band,
      When he was aware of a princely pair
        That rode at his right hand.
      So like they were, no mortal
        Might one from other know:
      White as snow their armour was:
        Their steeds were white as snow.
      Never on earthly anvil
        Did such rare armour gleam;
      And never did such gallant steeds
        Drink of an earthly stream.

XXXIII. And all who saw them trembled,
        And pale grew every cheek;
      And Aulus the Dictator
        Scarce gathered voice to speak.
      " Say by what name men call you?
        What city is your home?

And wherefore ride ye in such guise
  Before the ranks of Rome? ”

xxxiv. “ By many names men call us;
    In many lands we dwell:
  Well Samothracia knows us;
    Cyrene knows us well.
  Our house in gay Tarentum
    Is hung each morn with flowers:
  High o’er the masts of Syracuse
    Our marble portal towers;
  But by the proud Eurotas
    Is our dear native home;
  And for the right we come to fight
    Before the ranks of Rome.”

xxxv. So answered those strange horsemen,
    And each couched low his spear;
  And forthwith all the ranks of Rome
    Were bold, and of good cheer:
  And on the thirty armies
    Came wonder and affright,
  And Ardea wavered on the left,
    And Cora on the right.
  “ Rome to the charge! ” cried Aulus;
    “ The foe begins to yield!
  Charge for the hearth of Vesta!
    Charge for the Golden Shield!
  Let no man stop to plunder,
    But slay, and slay, and slay;
  The Gods who live for ever
    Are on our side to-day.”

xxxvi. Then the fierce trumpet-flourish
    From earth to heaven arose,
  The kites know well the long stern swell
    That bids the Romans close.
  Then the good sword of Aulus
    Was lifted up to slay:
  Then, like a crag down Apennine,
    Rushed Auster through the fray.
  But under those strange horsemen
    Still thicker lay the slain;

And after those strange horses
  Black Auster toiled in vain.
Behind them Rome's long battle
  Came rolling on the foe,
Ensigns dancing wild above,
  Blades all in line below.
So comes the Po in flood-time
  Upon the Celtic plain:
So comes the squall, blacker than night,
  Upon the Adrian main.
Now, by our Sire Quirinus,
  It was a goodly sight
To see the thirty standards
  Swept down the tide of flight.
So flies the spray of Adria
  When the black squall doth blow;
So corn-sheaves in the flood-time
  Spin down the whirling Po.
False Sextus to the mountains
  Turned first his horse's head;
And fast fled Ferentinum,
  And fast Lanuvium fled.
The horsemen of Nomentum
  Spurred hard out of the fray;
The footmen of Velitræ
  Threw shield and spear away.
And underfoot was trampled,
  Amidst the mud and gore,
The banner of proud Tusculum,
  That never stooped before:
And down went Flavius Faustus,
  Who led his stately ranks
From where the apple blossoms wave
  On Anio's echoing banks,
And Tullus of Arpinum,
  Chief of the Volscian aids,
And Metius with the long fair curls,
  The love of Anxur's maids,
And the white head of Vulso,
  The great Arician seer,
And Nepos of Laurentum,
  The hunter of the deer;
And in the back false Sextus

Felt the good Roman steel,
And wriggling in the dust he died,
  Like a worm beneath the wheel:
And fliers and pursuers
  Were mingled in a mass;
And far away the battle
  Went roaring through the pass.

XXXVII. Sempronius Atratinus
  Sate in the Eastern Gate,
Beside him were three Fathers,
  Each in his chair of state;
Fabius, whose nine stout grandsons
  That day were in the field,
And Manlius, eldest of the Twelve
  Who keep the Golden Shield;
And Sergius, the High Pontiff,
  For wisdom far renowned;
In all Etruria's colleges
  Was no such Pontiff found.
And all around the portal,
  And high above the wall,
Stood a great throng of people,
  But sad and silent all;
Young lads, and stooping elders
  That might not bear the mail,
Matrons with lips that quivered,
  And maids with faces pale,
Since the first gleam of daylight,
  Sempronius had not ceased
To listen for the rushing
  Of horse-hoofs from the east.
The mist of eve was rising,
  The sun was hastening down,
When he was aware of a princely pair
  Fast pricking towards the town.
So like they were, man never
  Saw twins so like before;
Red with gore their armour was,
  Their steeds were red with gore.

XXXVIII. " Hail to the great Asylum!
  Hail to the hill-tops seven!

Hail to the fire that burns for aye,
  And the shield that fell from heaven!
This day, by Lake Regillus,
  Under the Porcian height,
All in the lands of Tusculum
  Was fought a glorious fight.
To-morrow your Dictator
  Shall bring in triumph home
The spoils of thirty cities
  To deck the shrines of Rome!"

xxxix. Then burst from that great concourse
  A shout that shook the towers,
And some ran north, and some ran south,
  Crying, " The day is ours! "
But on rode these strange horsemen,
  With slow and lordly pace;
And none who saw their bearing
  Durst ask their name or race.
On rode they to the Forum,
  While laurel-boughs and flowers,
From house-tops and from windows,
  Fell on their crests in showers.
When they drew nigh to Vesta,
  They vaulted down amain,
And washed their horses in the well
  That springs by Vesta's fane.
And straight again they mounted,
  And rode to Vesta's door;
Then, like a blast, away they passed,
  And no man saw them more.

xl. And all the people trembled,
  And pale grew every cheek;
And Sergius the High Pontiff
  Alone found voice to speak:
" The gods who live for ever
  Have fought for Rome to-day!
These be the Great Twin Brethren
  To whom the Dorians pray.
Back comes the Chief in triumph,
  Who, in the hour of fight,
Hath seen the Great Twin Brethren
  In harness on his right.

Safe comes the ship to haven,
  Through billows and through gales,
If once the Great Twin Brethren
  Sit shining on the sails.
Wherefore they washed their horses
  In Vesta's holy well,
Wherefore they rode to Vesta's door,
  I know, but may not tell.
Here, hard by Vesta's temple,
  Build we a stately dome
Unto the Great Twin Brethren
  Who fought so well for Rome.
And when the months returning
  Bring back this day of fight,
The proud Ides of Quintilis,
  Marked evermore with white,
Unto the Great Twin Brethren
  Let all the people throng,
With chaplets and with offerings,
  With music and with song;
And let the doors and windows
  Be hung with garlands all,
And let the Knights be summoned
  To Mars without the wall:
Thence let them ride in purple
  With joyous trumpet-sound,
Each mounted on his war-horse,
  And each with olive crowned;
And pass in solemn order
  Before the sacred dome,
Where dwell the Great Twin Brethren
  Who fought so well for Rome."

VIRGINIA

FRAGMENTS OF A LAY SUNG IN THE FORUM ON THE DAY WHEREON
LUCIUS SEXTIUS SEXTINUS LATERANUS AND CAIUS LICINIUS
CALVUS STOLO WERE ELECTED TRIBUNES OF THE COMMONS
THE FIFTH TIME, IN THE YEAR OF THE CITY CCCLXXXII.

A COLLECTION consisting exclusively of war-songs would give an imperfect, or rather an erroneous, notion of the spirit of the old Latin ballads. The Patricians, during more than a century after the expulsion of the Kings, held all the high military commands. A Plebeian, even though, like Lucius Siccius, he were distinguished by his valour and knowledge of war, could serve only in subordinate posts. A minstrel, therefore, who wished to celebrate the early triumphs of his country, could hardly take any but Patricians for his heroes. The warriors who are mentioned in the two preceding lays, Horatius, Lartius, Herminius, Aulus Posthumius, Æbutius Elva, Sempronius Atratinus, Valerius Poplicola, were all members of the dominant order; and a poet who was singing their praises, whatever his own political opinions might be, would naturally abstain from insulting the class to which they belonged, and from reflecting on the system which had placed such men at the head of the legions of the Commonwealth.

But there was a class of compositions in which the great families were by no means so courteously treated. No parts of early Roman history are richer with poetical colouring than those which relate to the long contest between the privileged houses and the commonalty. The population of Rome was, from a very early period, divided into hereditary castes, which, indeed, readily united to repel foreign enemies, but which regarded each other, during many years, with bitter animosity. Between those castes there was a barrier hardly less strong than that which, at Venice, parted the members of the Great Council from their countrymen. In some respects, indeed, the line which separated an Icilius or a Duilius from a Posthumius or a Fabius was even more deeply marked than that which separated the rower of a gondola from a Contarini or a Morosini. At Venice the distinction was merely civil. At Rome it was both civil and religious. Among the grievances under which the Plebeians suffered, three were felt as peculiarly severe. They were excluded from the highest magistracies; they were excluded from all share in the public lands; and they were ground down to the dust by partial and barbarous legislation touching pecuniary contracts. The ruling class in Rome was a monied class; and it made and administered the laws with a view solely to its own interest. Thus the relation between lender and borrower was mixed up with the relation between sovereign and subject. The great men held a large portion of the community in dependence by means of advances at enormous usury. The law of debt, framed by creditors, and for the protection of creditors, was the most horrible that has ever been known among men. The liberty, and even the life, of the insolvent were at the mercy of the Patrician money-lenders. Children often became slaves in consequence of the misfortunes of their parents. The debtor was imprisoned, not in a public gaol under the care of impartial public functionaries, but in a private workhouse belonging to the creditor. Frightful stories were told respecting these dungeons. It was said that torture and brutal violation were common; that tight stocks, heavy chains, scanty measures of food, were used to punish wretches guilty of nothing but poverty; and that brave soldiers, whose breasts were covered with honourable scars, were often marked still more deeply on the back by the scourges of high-born usurers.

The Plebeians were, however, not wholly without constitutional rights. From an early period they had been admitted to some share of political power. They were enrolled each in his century, and were allowed a share, considerable though not proportioned to their numerical strength, in the disposal of those high dignities from which they were themselves excluded. Thus their position bore some resemblance to that of the Irish Catholics during the interval between the year 1792 and the year 1829. The Plebeians had also the privilege of annually appointing officers, named Tribunes, who had no active share in the government of the Commonwealth, but who, by degrees, acquired a power formidable even to the ablest and most resolute Consuls and Dictators. The person of the Tribune was inviolable; and, though he could directly effect little, he could obstruct everything.

During more than a century after the institution of the Tribuneship, the Commons struggled manfully for the removal of the grievances under which they laboured; and, in spite of many checks and reverses, succeeded in wringing concession after concession from the stubborn aristocracy. At length in the year of the city 378, both parties mustered their whole strength for their last and most desperate conflict. The popular and active Tribune, Caius Licinius, proposed the three memorable laws which are called by his name, and which were intended to redress the three great evils of which the Plebeians complained. He was supported, with eminent ability and firmness, by his colleague, Lucius Sextius. The struggle appears to have been the fiercest that ever in any community terminated without an appeal to arms. If such a contest had raged in any Greek city, the streets would have run with blood. But, even in the paroxysms of faction, the Roman retained his gravity, his respect for law, and his tenderness for the lives of his fellow-citizens. Year after year Licinius and Sextius were re-elected Tribunes. Year after year, if the narrative which has come down to us is to be trusted, they continued to exert, to the full extent, their power of stopping the whole machine of government. No curule magistrates could be chosen; no military muster could be held. We know too little of the state of Rome in those days to be able to conjecture how, during that long anarchy, the peace was kept, and ordinary justice administered between man and man. The animosity of both parties rose to the greatest height. The excitement, we may well suppose, would have been peculiarly intense at the annual election of Tribunes. On such occasions there can be little doubt that the great families did all that could be done, by threats and caresses, to break the union of the Plebeians. That union, however, proved indissoluble. At length the good cause triumphed. The Licinian laws were carried. Lucius Sextius was the first Plebeian Consul, Caius Licinius the third.

The results of this great change were singularly happy and glorious. Two centuries of prosperity, harmony, and victory followed the reconciliation of the orders. Men who remembered Rome engaged in waging petty wars almost within sight of the Capitol lived to see her the mistress of Italy. While the disabilities of the Plebeians continued, she was scarcely able to maintain her ground against the Volscians and Hernicans. When those disabilities were removed, she rapidly became more than a match for Carthage and Macedon.

During the great Licinian contest the Plebeian poets were, doubtless, not silent. Even in modern times songs have been by no means without influence on public affairs; and we may therefore infer that, in a society where printing was unknown, and where books were rare, a pathetic or humorous party-ballad must have produced effects such as we can but faintly conceive. It is certain that satirical poems were common at Rome from a very early period. The rustics, who lived at a distance from the seat of government, and took little part in the strife of factions, gave vent to their petty local animosities in coarse Fescennine verse. The lampoons of the city were doubtless of a higher order; and their sting was early felt by the nobility. For in the Twelve Tables, long before the time of the Licinian laws, a severe punishment was denounced against the citizen who should compose or recite verses reflecting on another. Satire is, indeed, the only sort of composition in which the Latin poets, whose works have come down to us, were not mere imitators of foreign models; and it is therefore the only sort of composition in which they have never been rivalled. It was not, like their tragedy, their comedy, their epic and lyric poetry, a hothouse plant which, in return for assiduous and skilful culture, gave only scanty and sickly fruits. It was hardy and full of sap; and in all the various juices which it yielded might be distinguished the flavour of the Ausonian soil. "Satire," said Quinctilian, with just pride, "is all our own." Satire sprang, in truth, naturally from the constitution of the Roman government and from the spirit of the Roman people; and, though at length subjected to metrical rules derived from Greece, retained to the last an essentially Roman character. Lucilius was the earliest satirist whose works were held in esteem under the Cæsars. But many years before Lucilius was born, Nævius had been flung into a dungeon, and guarded there with circumstances of unusual rigour, on account of the bitter lines in which he had attacked the great Cæcilian family. The genius and spirit of the Roman satirists survived the liberty of their country, and were not extinguished by the cruel despotism of the Julian and

Flavian Emperors. The great poet who told the story of Domitian's turbot, was the legitimate successor of those forgotten minstrels whose songs animated the factions of the infant Republic.

Those minstrels, as Niebuhr has remarked, appear to have generally taken the popular side. We can hardly be mistaken in supposing that, at the great crisis of the civil conflict, they employed themselves in versifying all the most powerful and virulent speeches of the Tribunes, and in heaping abuse on the leaders of the aristocracy. Every personal defect, every domestic scandal, every tradition dishonourable to a noble house, would be sought out, brought into notice, and exaggerated. The illustrious head of the aristocratical party, Marcus Furius Camillus, might perhaps be, in some measure, protected by his venerable age and by the memory of his great services to the State. But Appius Claudius Crassus enjoyed no such immunity. He was descended from a long line of ancestors distinguished by their haughty demeanour, and by the inflexibility with which they had withstood all the demands of the Plebeian order. While the political conduct and the deportment of the Claudian nobles drew upon them the fiercest public hatred, they were accused of wanting, if any credit is due to the early history of Rome, a class of qualities which, in a military Commonwealth, is sufficient to cover a multitude of offences. The chiefs of the family appear to have been eloquent, versed in civil business, and learned after the fashion of their age; but in war they were not distinguished by skill or valour. Some of them, as if conscious where their weakness lay, had, when filling the highest magistracies, taken internal administration as their department of public business, and left the military command to their colleagues. One of them had been intrusted with an army, and had failed ignominiously. None of them had been honoured with a triumph. None of them had achieved any martial exploit, such as those by which Lucius Quinctius Cincinnatus, Titus Quinctius Capitolinus, Aulus Cornelius Cossus, and, above all, the great Camillus, had extorted the reluctant esteem of the multitude. During the Licinian conflict, Appius Claudius Crassus signalised himself by the ability and severity with which he harangued against the two great agitators. He would naturally, therefore, be the favourite mark of the Plebeian satirists; nor would they have been at a loss to find a point on what he was open to attack.

His grandfather, called, like himself, Appius Claudius, had left a name as much detested as that of Sextus Tarquinius. This elder Appius had been Consul more than seventy years before the introduction of the Licinian laws. By availing himself of a singular crisis in public feeling, he had obtained the consent of the Commons to the abolition of the Tribuneship, and had been the chief of that Council of Ten to which the whole direction of the State had been committed. In a few months his administration had become universally odious. It had been swept away by an irresistible outbreak of popular fury; and its memory was still held in abhorrence by the whole city. The immediate cause of the downfall of this execrable government was said to have been an attempt made by Appius Claudius upon the chastity of a beautiful young girl of humble birth. The story ran that the Decemvir, unable to succeed by bribes and solicitations, resorted to an outrageous act of tyranny. A vile dependent of the Claudian house laid claim to the damsel as his slave. The cause was brought before the tribunal of Appius. The wicked magistrate, in defiance of the clearest proofs, gave judgment for the claimant. But the girl's father, a brave soldier, saved her from servitude and dishonour by stabbing her to the heart in the sight of the whole Forum. That blow was the signal for a general explosion. Camp and city rose at once; the Ten were pulled down; the Tribuneship was re-established; and Appius escaped the hands of the executioner only by a voluntary death.

It can hardly be doubted that a story so admirably adapted to the purposes both of the poet and of the demagogue would be eagerly seized upon by minstrels burning with hatred against the Patrician order, against the Claudian house, and especially against the grandson and namesake of the infamous Decemvir.

In order that the reader may judge fairly of these fragments of the lay of Virginia, he must imagine himself a Plebeian who has just voted for the re-election of Sextius and Licinius. All the power of the Patricians has been exerted to throw out the two great champions of the Commons. Every Posthumius, Æmilius, and Cornelius has used his influence to the utmost. Debtors have been let out of the workhouses on condition of voting against the men of the people; clients have been posted to hiss and interrupt the favourite candidates: Appius Claudius Crassus has spoken with more than his usual eloquence and asperity: all has been in vain; Licinius and Sextius have a fifth time carried all the tribes: work is suspended: the booths are closed: the Plebeians bear on their shoulders the two champions of liberty through the Forum. Just at this moment it is announced that a popular poet, a zealous adherent of the Tribunes, has made a new song which will cut the Claudian nobles to the heart. The crowd gathers round him, and calls on him to recite it. He takes his stand on the spot where, according to tradition, Virginia, more than seventy years ago, was seized by the pander of Appius, and he begins his story.

YE good men of the Commons, with loving hearts and true,
Who stand by the bold Tribunes that still have stood by you,
Come, make a circle round me, and mark my tale with care,
A tale of what Rome once hath borne, of what Rome yet may
      bear.
This is no Grecian fable, of fountains running wine,
Of maids with snaky tresses, or sailors turned to swine.
Here, in this very Forum, under the noonday sun,
In sight of all the people, the bloody deed was done.
Old men still creep among us who saw that fearful day,
Just seventy years and seven ago, when the wicked Ten bare
      sway.

Of all the wicked Ten still the names are held accursed,
And of all the wicked Ten Appius Claudius was the worst.
He stalked along the Forum like King Tarquin in his pride:
Twelve axes waited on him, six marching on a side;
The townsmen shrank to right and left, and eyed askance with
     fear
His lowering brow, his curling mouth which alway seemed to
     sneer:
That brow of hate, that mouth of scorn, marks all the kindred
     still;
For never was there Claudius yet but wished the Commons ill:
Nor lacks he fit attendance; for close behind his heels,
With outstretched chin and crouching pace, the client Marcus
     steals,
His loins girt up to run with speed, be the errand what it may,
And the smile flickering on his cheek, for aught his lord may say.
Such varlets pimp and jest for hire among the lying Greeks:
Such varlets still are paid to hoot when brave Licinius speaks.
Where'er ye shed the honey, the buzzing flies will crowd;
Where'er ye fling the carrion, the raven's croak is loud;
Where'er down Tiber garbage floats, the greedy pike ye see;
And wheresoe'er such lord is found, such client still will be.

Just then, as through one cloudless chink in a black stormy sky
Shines out the dewy morning-star, a fair young girl came by.
With her small tablets in her hand, and her satchel on her arm,
Home she went bounding from the school, nor dreamed of shame
     or harm;
And past those dreaded axes she innocently ran,
With bright, frank brow that had not learned to blush at gaze
     of man;
And up the Sacred Street she turned, and, as she danced along,
She warbled gaily to herself lines of the good old song,
How for a sport the princes came spurring from the camp,
And found Lucrece, combing the fleece, under the midnight
     lamp.
The maiden sang as sings the lark, when up he darts his flight,
From his nest in the green April corn, to meet the morning light;
And Appius heard her sweet young voice, and saw her sweet
     young face,
And loved her with the accursed love of his accursed race,
And all along the Forum, and up the Sacred Street,
His vulture eye pursued the trip of those small glancing feet.

   .   .   .   .

Over the Alban mountains the light of morning broke;
From all the roofs of the Seven Hills curled the thin wreaths of
        smoke:
The city-gates were opened; the Forum all alive,
With buyers and with sellers was humming like a hive:
Blithely on brass and timber the craftsman's stroke was ringing,
And blithely o'er her panniers the market-girl was singing,
And blithely young Virginia came smiling from her home:
Ah! woe for young Virginia, the sweetest maid in Rome!
With her small tablets in her hand, and her satchel on her arm,
Forth she went bounding to the school, nor dreamed of shame or
        harm.
She crossed the Forum shining with stalls in alleys gay,
And just had reached the very spot whereon I stand this day,
When up the varlet Marcus came; not such as when erewhile
He crouched behind his patron's heels with the true client smile:
He came with lowering forehead, swollen features, and clenched
        fist,
And strode across Virginia's path, and caught her by the wrist.
Hard strove the frightened maiden, and screamed with look
        aghast;
And at her scream from right and left the folk came running fast;
The money-changer Crispus, with his thin silver hairs,
And Hanno from the stately booth glittering with Punic wares,
And the strong smith Muræna, grasping a half-forged brand,
And Volero the flesher, his cleaver in his hand.
All came in wrath and wonder; for all knew that fair child;
And, as she passed them twice a day, all kissed their hands and
        smiled;
And the strong smith Muræna gave Marcus such a blow,
The caitiff reeled three paces back, and let the maiden go.
Yet glared he fiercely round him, and growled in harsh, fell tone,
" She's mine, and I will have her: I seek but for mine own:
She is my slave, born in my house, and stolen away and sold,
The year of the sore sickness, ere she was twelve hours old.
'Twas in the sad September, the month of wail and fright,
Two augurs were borne forth that morn; the Consul died ere
        night.
I wait on Appius Claudius, I waited on his sire:
Let him who works the client wrong beware the patron's ire! "

    So spake the varlet Marcus; and dread and silence came
On all the people at the sound of the great Claudian name.

For then there was no Tribune to speak the word of might,
Which makes the rich man tremble, and guards the poor man's
    right.
There was no brave Licinius, no honest Sextius then;
But all the city, in great fear, obeyed the wicked Ten.
Yet ere the varlet Marcus again might seize the maid,
Who clung tight to Muræna's skirt, and sobbed, and shrieked for
    aid,
Forth through the throng of gazers the young Icilius pressed,
And stamped his foot, and rent his gown, and smote upon his
    breast,
And sprang upon that column, by many a minstrel sung,
Whereon three mouldering helmets, three rusting swords, are
    hung,
And beckoned to the people, and in bold voice and clear
Poured thick and fast the burning words which tyrants quake
    to hear.

" Now, by your children's cradles, now by your fathers' graves,
Be men to-day, Quirites, or be for ever slaves!
For this did Servius give us laws?   For this did Lucrece bleed?
For this was the great vengeance wrought on Tarquin's evil seed?
For this did those false sons make red the axes of their sire?
For this did Scævola's right hand hiss in the Tuscan fire?
Shall the vile fox-earth awe the race that stormed the lion's den?
Shall we, who could not brook one lord, crouch to the wicked Ten?
Oh for that ancient spirit which curbed the Senate's will!
Oh for the tents which in old time whitened the Sacred Hill!
In those brave days our fathers stood firmly side by side;
They faced the Marcian fury; they tamed the Fabian pride:
They drove the fiercest Quinctius an outcast forth from Rome;
They sent the haughtiest Claudius with shivered fasces home.
But what their care bequeathed us our madness flung away:
All the ripe fruit of threescore years was blighted in a day.
Exult, ye proud Patricians!   The hard-fought fight is o'er.
We strove for honours—'twas in vain: for freedom—'tis no
    more.
No crier to the polling summons the eager throng;
No tribune breathes the word of might that guards the weak
    from wrong.
Our very hearts, that were so high, sink down beneath your will.
Riches, and lands, and power, and state—ye have them:—keep
    them still.

Still keep' the holy fillets; still keep the purple gown,
The axes, and the curule chair, the car, and laurel crown:
Still press us for your cohorts, and, when the fight is done,
Still fill your garners from the soil which our good swords have
        won.
Still, like a spreading ulcer, which leechcraft may not cure,
Let your foul usance eat away the substance of the poor.
Still let your haggard debtors bear all their fathers bore;
Still let your dens of torment be noisome as of yore;
No fire when Tiber freezes; no air in dog-star heat;
And store of rods for free-born backs, and holes for free-born feet.
Heap heavier still the fetters; bar closer still the grate;
Patient as sheep we yield us up unto your cruel hate.
But, by the Shades beneath us, and by the Gods above,
Add not unto your cruel hate your yet more cruel love!
Have ye not graceful ladies, whose spotless lineage springs
From Consuls, and High Pontiffs, and ancient Alban kings?
Ladies, who deign not on our paths to set their tender feet,
Who from their cars look down with scorn upon the wondering
        street,
Who in Corinthian mirrors their own proud smiles behold,
And breathe of Capuan odours, and shine with Spanish gold?
Then leave the poor Plebeian his single tie to life—
The sweet, sweet love of daughter, of sister, and of wife,
The gentle speech, the balm for all that his vexed soul endures,
The kiss, in which he half forgets even such a yoke as yours.
Still let the maiden's beauty swell the father's breast with pride;
Still let the bridegroom's arms infold an unpolluted bride.
Spare us the inexpiable wrong, the unutterable shame,
That turns the coward's heart to steel, the sluggard's blood to
        flame,
Lest, when our latest hope is fled, ye taste of our despair,
And learn by proof, in some wild hour, how much the wretched
        dare."

  .   .   .   .
    .   .   .   .

  Straightway Virginius led the maid a little space aside,
To where the reeking shambles stood, piled up with horn and
        hide,
Close to yon low dark archway, where, in a crimson flood,
Leaps down to the great sewer the gurgling stream of blood.
Hard by, a flesher on a block had laid his whittle down:
Virginius caught the whittle up, and hid it in his gown.

And then his eyes grew very dim, and his throat began to swell,
And in a hoarse, changed voice he spake, " Farewell, sweet
       child! Farewell!
Oh! how I loved my darling! Though stern I sometimes be,
To thee, thou know'st, I was not so. Who could be so to thee?
And how my darling loved me! How glad she was to hear
My footsteps on the threshold when I came back last year!
And how she danced with pleasure to see my civic crown,
And took my sword, and hung it up, and brought me forth my
       gown!
Now, all those things are over—yes, all thy pretty ways,
Thy needlework, thy prattle, thy snatches of old lays;
And none will grieve when I go forth, or smile when I return,
Or watch beside the old man's bed, or weep upon his urn.
The house that was the happiest within the Roman walls,
The house that envied not the wealth of Capua's marble halls,
Now, for the brightness of thy smile, must have eternal gloom,
And for the music of thy voice, the silence of the tomb.
The time is come. See how he points his eager hand this way!
See how his eyes gloat on thy grief, like a kite's upon the prey!
With all his wit, he little deems, that, spurned, betrayed, bereft,
Thy father hath in his despair one fearful refuge left.
He little deems that in this hand I clutch what still can save
Thy gentle youth from taunts and blows, the portion of the
       slave;
Yea, and from nameless evil, that passeth taunt and blow—
Foul outrage which thou knowest not, which thou shalt never
       know.
Then clasp me round the neck once more, and give me one more
       kiss;
And now mine own dear little girl, there is no way but this."
With that he lifted high the steel, and smote her in the side,
And in her blood she sank to earth, and with one sob she died.

Then, for a little moment, all people held their breath;
And through the crowded Forum was stillness as of death;
And in another moment brake forth from one and all
A cry as if the Volscians were coming o'er the wall.
Some with averted faces shrieking fled home amain;
Some ran to call a leech; and some ran to lift the slain:
Some felt her lips and little wrist, if life might there be found;
And some tore up their garments fast, and strove to stanch the
       wound.

In vain they ran, and felt, and stanched; for never truer blow
That good right arm had dealt in fight against a Volscian foe.

    When Appius Claudius saw that deed, he shuddered and sank
        down,
And hid his face some little space with the corner of his gown,
Till, with white lips and bloodshot eyes, Virginius tottered nigh,
And stood before the judgment-seat, and held the knife on high.
"Oh! dwellers in the nether gloom, avengers of the slain,
By this dear blood I cry to you, do right between us twain;
And even as Appius Claudius hath dealt by me and mine,
Deal you by Appius Claudius and all the Claudian line!"
So spake the slayer of his child, and turned, and went his way;
But first he cast one haggard glance to where the body lay,
And writhed, and groaned a fearful groan, and then, with stead-
        fast feet,
Strode right across the market-place unto the Sacred Street.

    Then up sprang Appius Claudius: "Stop him; alive or dead!
Ten thousand pounds of copper to the man who brings his
        head."
He looked upon his clients; but none would work his will.
He looked upon his lictors; but they trembled, and stood still.
And, as Virginius through the press his way in silence cleft,
Ever the mighty multitude fell back to right and left.
And he hath passed in safety unto his woeful home,
And there ta'en horse to tell the camp what deeds are done in
        Rome.

    By this the flood of people was swollen from every side,
And streets and porches round were filled with that o'erflowing
        tide;
And close around the body gathered a little train
Of them that were the nearest and dearest to the slain.
They brought a bier, and hung it with many a cypress crown,
And gently they uplifted her, and gently laid her down.
The face of Appius Claudius wore the Claudian scowl and sneer,
And in the Claudian note he cried, "What doth this rabble
        here?
Have they no crafts to mind at home, that hitherward they
        stray?
Ho! lictors, clear the market-place, and fetch the corpse
        away!"

The voice of grief and fury till then had not been loud;
But a deep sullen murmur wandered among the crowd,
Like the moaning noise that goes before the whirlwind on the
        deep,
Or the growl of a fierce watch-dog but half-aroused from sleep.
But when the lictors at that word, tall yeomen all and strong,
Each with his axe and sheaf of twigs, went down into the
        throng,
Those old men say, who saw that day of sorrow and of sin,
That in the Roman Forum was never such a din.
The wailing, hooting, cursing, the howls of grief and hate,
Were heard beyond the Pincian Hill, beyond the Latin Gate.
But close around the body, where stood the little train
Of them that were the nearest and dearest to the slain,
No cries were there, but teeth set fast, low whispers and black
        frowns,
And breaking up of benches, and girding up of gowns.
'Twas well the lictors might not pierce to where the maiden lay,
Else surely had they been all twelve torn limb from limb that day.
Right glad they were to struggle back, blood streaming from
        their heads,
With axes all in splinters, and raiment all in shreds.
Then Appius Claudius gnawed his lip, and the blood left his
        cheek;
And thrice he beckoned with his hand, and thrice he strove to
        speak;
And thrice the tossing Forum set up a frightful yell;
" See, see, thou dog! what thou hast done; and hide thy shame
        in hell!
Thou that wouldst make our maidens slaves must first make
        slaves of men.
Tribunes! Hurrah for Tribunes! Down with the wicked Ten! "
And straightway, thick as hailstones, came whizzing through
        the air
Pebbles, and bricks, and potsherds, all round the curule chair:
And upon Appius Claudius great fear and trembling came;
For never was a Claudius yet brave against aught but shame.
Though the great houses love us not, we own, to do them right,
That the great houses, all save one, have borne them well in
        fight.
Still Caius of Corioli, his triumphs and his wrongs,
His vengeance and his mercy, live in our camp-fire songs.
Beneath the yoke of Furius oft have Gaul and Tuscan bowed;

And Rome may bear the pride of him of whom herself is proud.
But evermore a Claudius shrinks from a stricken field,
And changes colour like a maid at sight of sword and shield.
The Claudian triumphs all were won within the city towers;
The Claudian yoke was never pressed on any necks but ours
A Cossus, like a wild cat, springs ever at the face;
A Fabius rushes like a boar against the shouting chase;
But the vile Claudian litter, raging with currish spite,
Still yelps and snaps at those who run, still runs from those who
     smite.
So now 'twas seen of Appius.   When stones began to fly,
He shook, and crouched, and wrung his hands, and smote upon
     his thigh.
" Kind clients, honest lictors, stand by me in this fray!
Must I be torn in pieces?   Home, home, the nearest way! "
While yet he spake, and looked around with a bewildered stare,
Four sturdy lictors put their necks beneath the curule chair;
And fourscore clients on the left, and fourscore on the right,
Arrayed themselves with swords and staves, and loins girt up
     for fight.
But, though without or staff or sword, so furious was the throng,
That scarce the train with might and main could bring their lord
     along.
Twelve times the crowd made at him; five times they seized his
     gown:
Small chance was his to rise again, if once they got him down:
And sharper came the pelting; and evermore the yell—
" Tribunes! we will have Tribunes! "—rose with a louder swell:
And the chair tossed as tosses a bark with tattered sail
When raves the Adriatic beneath an eastern gale,
When the Calabrian sea-marks are lost in clouds of spume,
And the great Thunder-Cape has donned his veil of inky gloom.
One stone hit Appius in the mouth, and one beneath the ear;
And ere he reached Mount Palatine, he swooned with pain and
     fear,
His cursed head, that he was wont to hold so high with pride,
Now, like a drunken man's, hung down, and swayed from side
     to side;
And when his stout retainers had brought him to his door,
His face and neck were all one cake of filth and clotted gore.
As Appius Claudius was that day, so may his grandson be!
God send Rome one such other sight, and send me there to see!

   .   .   .   .

THE PROPHECY OF CAPYS

A LAY SUNG AT THE BANQUET IN THE CAPITOL, ON THE DAY WHEREON MANIUS CURIUS DENTATUS, A SECOND TIME CONSUL, TRIUMPHED OVER KING PYRRHUS AND THE TARENTINES, IN THE YEAR OF THE CITY CCCCLXXIX

IT can hardly be necessary to remind any reader that according to the popular tradition, Romulus, after he had slain his grand-uncle Amulius, and restored his grandfather Numitor, determined to quit Alba, the hereditary domain of the Sylvian princes, and to found a new city.   The Gods, it was added, vouchsafed the clearest signs of the favour with which they regarded the enterprise, and of the high destinies reserved for the young colony.

This event was likely to be a favourite theme of the old Latin minstrels.   They would naturally attribute the project of Romulus to some divine intimation of the power and prosperity which it was decreed that his city should attain.   They would probably introduce seers foretelling the victories of unborn Consuls and Dictators, and the last great victory would generally occupy the most conspicuous place in the prediction.   There is nothing strange in the supposition that the poet who was employed to celebrate the first great triumph of the Romans over the Greeks might throw his song of exultation into this form.

The occasion was one likely to excite the strongest feelings of national pride.   A great outrage had been followed by a great retribution.   Seven years before this time, Lucius Posthumius Megellus, who sprang from one of the noblest houses of Rome, and had been thrice Consul, was sent ambassador to Tarentum, with charge to demand reparation for grievous injuries.   The Tarentines gave him audience in their theatre, where he addressed them in such Greek as he could command, which, we may well believe, was not exactly such as Cineas would have spoken.   An exquisite sense of the ridiculous belonged to the Greek character; and closely connected with this faculty was a strong propensity to flippancy and impertinence.   When Posthumius placed an accent wrong, his hearers burst into a laugh.   When he remonstrated, they hooted him, and called him barbarian; and at length hissed him off the stage as if he had been a bad actor.   As the grave Roman retired, a buffoon who, from his constant drunkenness, was nicknamed the Pint-pot, came up with gestures of the grossest indecency, and bespattered the senatorial gown with filth.   Posthumius turned round to the multitude, and held up the gown, as if appealing to the universal law of nations.   The sight only increased the insolence of the Tarentines.   They clapped their hands, and set up a shout of laughter which shook the theatre.   " Men of Tarentum," said Posthumius, " it will take not a little blood to wash this gown."

Rome, in consequence of this insult, declared war against the Tarentines. The Tarentines sought for allies beyond the Ionian Sea. Pyrrhus, king of Epirus, came to their help with a large army; and, for the first time, the two great nations of antiquity were fairly matched against each other.

The fame of Greece in arms, as well as in arts, was then at the height. Half a century earlier, the career of Alexander had excited the admiration and terror of all nations from the Ganges to the Pillars of Hercules. Royal houses, founded by Macedonian captains, still reigned at Antioch and Alexandria. That barbarian warriors, led by barbarian chiefs, should win a pitched battle against Greek valour guided by Greek science, seemed as incredible as it would now seem that the Burmese or the Siamese should, in the open plain, put to flight an equal number of the best English troops. The Tarentines were convinced that their countrymen were irresistible in war; and this conviction had emboldened them to treat with the grossest indignity one whom they regarded as the representative of an inferior race. Of the Greek generals then living Pyrrhus was indisputably the first. Among the troops who were trained in the Greek discipline his Epirotes ranked high. His expedition to Italy was a turning-point in the history of the world. He found there a people who, far inferior to the Athenians and Corinthians in the fine arts, in the speculative sciences, and in all the refinements of life, were the best soldiers on the face of the earth. Their arms, their gradations of rank, their order of battle, their method of intrenchment, were all of Latian origin, and had all been gradually brought near to perfection, not by the study of foreign models, but by the genius and experience of many generations of great native commanders. The first words which broke from the king, when his practised eye had surveyed the Roman encampment, were full of meaning:—" These barbarians," he said, " have nothing barbarous in their military arrangements." He was at first victorious; for his own talents were superior to those of the captains who were opposed to him; and the Romans were not prepared for the onset of the elephants of the East, which were then for the first time seen in Italy—moving mountains, with long snakes for hands. But the victories of the Epirotes were fiercely disputed, dearly purchased, and altogether unprofitable. At length, Manius Curius Dentatus, who had in his first Consulship won two triumphs, was again placed at the head of the Roman Commonwealth, and sent to encounter the invaders. A great battle was fought near Beneventum. Pyrrhus was completely defeated. He repassed the sea; and the world learned, with amazement, that a people had been discovered, who, in fair fighting, were superior to the best troops that had been drilled on the system of Parmenio and Antigonus.

The conquerors had a good right to exult in their success; for their glory was all their own. They had not learned from their enemy how to conquer him. It was with their own national arms, and in their own national battle-array, that they had overcome weapons and tactics long believed to be invincible. The pilum and the broadsword had vanquished the Macedonian spear. The legion had broken the Macedonian phalanx. Even the elephants, when the surprise produced by their first appearance was over, could cause no disorder in the steady yet flexible battalions of Rome.

It is said by Florus, and may easily be believed, that the triumph far surpassed in magnificence any that Rome had previously seen. The only spoils which Papirius Cursor and Fabius Maximus could exhibit were flocks and herds, waggons of rude structure, and heaps of spears and helmets. But now, for the first time, the riches of Asia and the arts of Greece adorned a Roman pageant. Plate, fine stuffs, costly furniture, rare animals, exquisite paintings and sculptures, formed part of the procession. At the banquet would be assembled a crowd of warriors and statesmen, among whom Manius Curius Dentatus would take the highest room. Caius Fabricius Luscinus, then, after two Consulships and two triumphs, Censor of the Commonwealth, would doubtless occupy a place of honour at the board. In situations less conspicuous probably lay some of those who were, a few years later, the terror of Carthage, Caius Duilius, the founder of the maritime greatness of his country; Marcus Atilius Regulus, who owed to defeat a renown far higher than that which he had derived from his victories; and Caius Lutatius Catulus, who, while suffering from a grievous wound, fought the great battle of the Ægates, and brought the First Punic War to a triumphant close. It is impossible to recount the names of these eminent citizens, without reflecting that they were all, without exception, Plebeians, and would, but for the ever-memorable struggle maintained by Caius Licinius and Lucius Sextius, have been doomed to hide in obscurity, or to waste in civil broils, the capacity and energy which prevailed against Pyrrhus and Hamilcar.

On such a day we may suppose that the patriotic enthusiasm of a Latin poet would vent itself in reiterated shouts of *Io triumphe*, such as were uttered by Horace on a far less exciting occasion, and in boasts resembling those which Virgil put into the mouth of Anchises. The superiority of some foreign nations, and especially of the Greeks, in the lazy arts of peace, would be admitted with disdainful candour; but pre-eminence in all the qualities which fit a people to subdue and govern mankind would be claimed for the Romans.

The following lay belongs to the latest age of Latin ballad-poetry. Nævius and Livius Andronicus were probably among the children whose mothers held them up to see the chariot of Curius go by. The minstrel who sang on that day might possibly have lived to read the first hexameters of Ennius, and to see the first comedies of Plautus. His poem, as might be expected, shows a much wider acquaintance with the geography, manners, and productions of remote nations, than would have been found in compositions of the age of Camillus. But he troubles himself little about dates, and having heard travellers talk with admiration of the Colossus of Rhodes, and of the structures and gardens with which the Macedonian kings of Syria had embellished their residence on the banks of the Orontes, he has never thought of inquiring whether these things existed in the age of Romulus.

I. Now slain is King Amulius,
   Of the great Sylvian line,
Who reigned in Alba Longa,
   On the throne of Aventine.
Slain is the Pontiff Camers,
   Who spake the words of doom:
" The children to the Tiber,
   The mother to the tomb."

II. In Alba's lake no fisher
   His net to-day is flinging:
On the dark rind of Alba's oaks
   To-day no axe is ringing:
The yoke hangs o'er the manger:
   The scythe lies in the hay:
Through all the Alban villages
   No work is done to-day.

III. And every Alban burgher
   Hath donned his whitest gown;
And every head in Alba
   Weareth a poplar crown;
And every Alban door-post
   With boughs and flowers is gay;
For to-day the dead are living;
   The lost are found to-day.

IV. They were doomed by a bloody king:
   They were doomed by a lying priest:
They were cast on the raging flood:
   They were tracked by the raging beast:
Raging beast and raging flood
   Alike have spared the prey;
And to-day the dead are living:
   The lost are found to-day.

V. The troubled river knew them,
   And smoothed his yellow foam
And gently rocked the cradle
   That bore the fate of Rome.
The ravening she-wolf knew them,
   And licked them o'er and o'er,

And gave them of her own fierce milk,
  Rich with raw flesh and gore.
Twenty winters, twenty springs,
  Since then have rolled away;
And to-day the dead are living:
  The lost are found to-day.

VI. Blithe it was to see the twins,
    Right goodly youths and tall,
Marching from Alba Longa
  To their old grandsire's hall.
Along their path fresh garlands
  Are hung from tree to tree:
Before them stride the pipers,
  Piping a note of glee.

VII. On the right goes Romulus,
    With arms to the elbows red,
And in his hand a broadsword,
  And on the blade a head—
A head in an iron helmet,
  With horse-hair hanging down,
A shaggy head, a swarthy head,
  Fixed in a ghastly frown—
The head of King Amulius
  Of the great Sylvian line,
Who reigned in Alba Longa,
  On the throne of Aventine.

VIII. On the left side goes Remus,
    With wrists and fingers red,
And in his hand a boar-spear,
  And on the point a head—
A wrinkled head and aged,
  With silver beard and hair,
And holy fillets round it,
  Such as the pontiffs wear—
The head of ancient Camers,
  Who spake the words of doom:
" The children to the Tiber;
  The mother to the tomb."

IX. Two and two behind the twins
    Their trusty comrades go,

Four and forty valiant men,
   With club, and axe, and bow.
On each side every hamlet
   Pours forth its joyous crowd,
Shouting lads and baying dogs,
   And children laughing loud,
And old men weeping fondly
   As Rhea's boys go by,
And maids who shriek to see the heads,
   Yet, shrieking, press more nigh.

x. So they marched along the lake;
   They marched by fold and stall,
By corn-field and by vineyard,
   Unto the old man's hall.

xi. In the hall-gate sate Capys,
   Capys, the sightless seer;
From head to foot he trembled
   As Romulus drew near.
And up stood stiff his thin white hair,
   And his blind eyes flashed fire:
" Hail! foster child of the wonderous nurse!
   Hail! son of the wonderous sire!

xii. " But thou—what dost thou here
   In the old man's peaceful hall?
What doth the eagle in the coop,
   The bison in the stall?
Our corn fills many a garner;
   Our vines clasp many a tree;
Our flocks are white on many a hill;
   But these are not for thee.

xiii. " For thee no treasure ripens
   In the Tartessian mine:
For thee no ship brings precious bales
   Across the Libyan brine:
Thou shalt not drink from amber;
   Thou shalt not rest on down;
Arabia shall not steep thy locks,
   Nor Sidon tinge thy gown.

XIV. " Leave gold and myrrh and jewels,
    Rich table and soft bed,
To them who of man's seed are born,
    Whom woman's milk have fed.
Thou wast not made for lucre,
    For pleasure, nor for rest;
Thou, that art sprung from the War-god's loins,
    And hast tugged at the she-wolf's breast.

XV. " From sunrise unto sunset
    All earth shall hear thy fame:
A glorious city thou shalt build,
    And name it by thy name:
And there, unquenched through ages,
    Like Vesta's sacred fire,
Shall live the spirit of thy nurse,
    The spirit of thy sire.

XVI. " The ox toils through the furrow,
    Obedient to the goad;
The patient ass, up flinty paths,
    Plods with his weary load:
With whine and bound the spaniel
    His master's whistle hears;
And the sheep yields her patiently
    To the loud clashing shears.

XVII. " But thy nurse will hear no master,
    Thy nurse will bear no load;
And woe to them that shear her,
    And woe to them that goad!
When all the pack, loud baying,
    Her bloody lair surrounds,
She dies in silence, biting hard,
    Amidst the dying hounds.

XVIII. " Pomona loves the orchard;
    And Liber loves the vine;
And Pales loves the straw-built shed
    Warm with the breath of kine;
And Venus loves the whispers
    Of plighted youth and maid,
In April's ivory moonlight
    Beneath the chestnut shade.

xix. "But thy father loves the clashing
    Of broadsword and of shield:
He loves to drink the steam that reeks
    From the fresh battle-field:
He smiles a smile more dreadful
    Than his own dreadful frown,
When he sees the thick black cloud of smoke
    Go up from the conquered town.

xx. "And such as is the War-god,
    The author of thy line,
And such as she who suckled thee,
    Even such be thou and thine.
Leave to the soft Campanian
    His baths and his perfumes;
Leave to the sordid race of Tyre
    Their dyeing-vats and looms:
Leave to the sons of Carthage
    The rudder and the oar:
Leave to the Greek his marble Nymphs
    And scrolls of wordy lore.

xxi. "Thine, Roman, is the pilum:
    Roman, the sword is thine,
The even trench, the bristling mound,
    The legion's ordered line;
And thine the wheels of triumph,
    Which with their laurelled train
Move slowly up the shouting streets
    To Jove's eternal fane.

xxii. "Beneath thy yoke the Volscian
    Shall vail his lofty brow:
Soft Capua's curled revellers
    Before thy chairs shall bow:
The Lucumoes of Arnus
    Shall quake thy rods to see;
And the proud Samnite's heart of steel
    Shall yield to only thee.

xxiii. "The Gaul shall come against thee
    From the land of snow and night:
Thou shalt give his fair-haired armies
    To the raven and the kite.

XXIV. " The Greek shall come against thee,
    The conqueror of the East.
Beside him stalks to battle
    The huge earth-shaking beast,
The beast on whom the castle
    With all its guards doth stand,
The beast who hath between his eyes
    The serpent for a hand.
First march the bold Epirotes,
    Wedged close with shield and spear;
And the ranks of false Tarentum
    Are glittering in the rear.

XXV. " The ranks of false Tarentum
    Like hunted sheep shall fly:
In vain the bold Epirotes
    Shall round their standards die:
And Apennine's grey vultures
    Shall have a noble feast
On the fat and the eyes
    Of the huge earth-shaking beast.

XXVI. " Hurrah! for the good weapons
    That keep the War-god's land.
Hurrah! for Rome's stout pilum
    In a stout Roman hand.
Hurrah! for Rome's short broadsword,
    That through the thick array
Of levelled spears and serried shields
    Hews deep its gory way.

XXVII. " Hurrah! for the great triumph
    That stretches many a mile.
Hurrah! for the wan captives
    That pass in endless file.
Ho! bold Epirotes, whither
    Hath the Red King ta'en flight?
Ho! dogs of false Tarentum,
    Is not the gown washed white?

XXVIII. " Hurrah! for the great triumph
    That stretches many a mile.
Hurrah! for the rich dye of Tyre,
    And the fine web of Nile,

The helmets gay with plumage
 Torn from the pheasant's wings,
The belts set thick with starry gems
 That shone on Indian kings,
The urns of massy silver,
 The goblets rough with gold,
The many-coloured tablets bright
 With loves and wars of old,
The stone that breathes and struggles,
 The brass that seems to speak;—
Such cunning they who dwell on high
 Have given unto the Greek.

xxix. " Hurrah! for Manius Curius,
 The bravest son of Rome,
Thrice in utmost need sent forth,
 Thrice drawn in triumph home.
Weave, weave, for Manius Curius
 The third embroidered gown:
Make ready the third lofty car,
 And twine the third green crown
And yoke the steeds of Rosea
 With necks like a bended bow;
And deck the bull, Mevania's bull,
 The bull as white as snow.

xxx. " Blest and thrice blest the Roman
 Who sees Rome's brightest day,
Who sees that long victorious pomp
 Wind down the Sacred Way,
And through the bellowing Forum,
 And round the Suppliant's Grove,
Up to the everlasting gates
 Of Capitolian Jove.

xxxi. " Then where, o'er two bright havens,
 The towers of Corinth frown;
Where the gigantic King of Day
 On his own Rhodes looks down;
Where soft Orontes murmurs
 Beneath the laurel shades;
Where Nile reflects the endless length
 Of dark-red colonnades;

Where in the still deep water,
  Sheltered from waves and blasts,
Bristles the dusky forest
  Of Byrsa's thousand masts;
Where fur-clad hunters wander
  Amidst the northern ice;
Where through the sand of morning-land
  The camel bears the spice;
Where Atlas flings his shadow
  Far o'er the western foam,
Shall be great fear on all who hear
  The mighty name of Rome."

IVRY

A Song of the Huguenots

Now glory to the Lord of Hosts, from whom all glories are!
And glory to our Sovereign Liege, King Henry of Navarre!
Now let there be the merry sound of music and of dance,
Through thy corn-fields green, and sunny vines, oh pleasant
      land of France!
And thou, Rochelle, our own Rochelle, proud city of the waters,
Again let rapture light the eyes of all thy mourning daughters.
As thou wert constant in our ills, be joyous in our joy,
For cold, and stiff, and still are they who wrought thy walls
      annoy.
Hurrah! Hurrah! a single field hath turned the chance of war,
Hurrah! Hurrah! for Ivry, and Henry of Navarre.

Oh! how our hearts were beating, when, at the dawn of day,
We saw the army of the League drawn out in long array;
With all its priest-led citizens, and all its rebel peers,
And Appenzel's stout infantry, and Egmont's Flemish spears.
There rode the brood of false Lorraine, the curses of our land;
And dark Mayenne was in the midst, a truncheon in his hand:
And, as we looked on them, we thought of Seine's enpurpled
      flood,
And good Coligni's hoary hair all dabbled with his blood;
And we cried unto the living God, who rules the fate of war,
To fight for his own holy name, and Henry of Navarre.

The King is come to marshal us, in all his armour drest,
And he has bound a snow-white plume upon his gallant crest.
He looked upon his people, and a tear was in his eye;
He looked upon the traitors, and his glance was stern and high.
Right graciously he smiled on us, as rolled from wing to wing,
Down all our line, a deafening shout, " God save our Lord the
      King."

" An if my standard-bearer fall, as fall full well he may,
For never saw I promise yet of such a bloody fray,

Press where ye see my white plume shine, amidst the ranks of
      war,
And be your oriflamme to-day the helmet of Navarre."

Hurrah! the foes are moving. Hark to the mingled din,
Of fife, and steed, and trump, and drum, and roaring culverin.
The fiery Duke is pricking fast across Saint André's plain,
With all the hireling chivalry of Guelders and Almayne.
Now by the lips of those ye love, fair gentlemen of France,
Charge for the golden lilies,—upon them with the lance.
A thousand spurs are striking deep, a thousand spears in rest,
A thousand knights are pressing close behind the snow-white
      crest;
And in they burst, and on they rushed, while, like a guiding
      star,
Amidst the thickest carnage blazed the helmet of Navarre.

Now, God be praised, the day is ours. Mayenne hath turned
      his rein.
D'Aumale hath cried for quarter. The Flemish count is slain.
Their ranks are breaking like thin clouds before a Biscay gale;
The field is heaped with bleeding steeds, and flags, and cloven
      mail.
And then we thought on vengeance, and, all along our van,
" Remember Saint Bartholomew," was passed from man to
      man.
But out spake gentle Henry, " No Frenchman is my foe:
Down, down, with every foreigner, but let your brethren go."
Oh! was there ever such a knight, in friendship or in war,
As our Sovereign Lord, King Henry, the soldier of Navarre?

Right well fought all the Frenchmen who fought for France
      to-day;
And many a lordly banner God gave them for a prey.
But we of the religion have borne us best in fight;
And the good Lord of Rosny hath ta'en the cornet white.
Our own true Maximilian the cornet white hath ta'en,
The cornet white with crosses black, the flag of false Lorraine.
Up with it high; unfurl it wide; that all the host may know
How God hath humbled the proud house which wrought his
      church such woe.
Then on the ground, while trumpets sound their loudest point
      of war,
Fling the red shreds, a footcloth meet for Henry of Navarre.

Ho! maidens of Vienna; Ho! matrons of Lucerne;
Weep, weep, and rend your hair for those who never shall return.
Ho! Philip, send, for charity, thy Mexican pistoles,
That Antwerp monks may sing a mass for thy poor spearmen's
    souls.
Ho! gallant nobles of the League, look that your arms be bright;
Ho! burghers of Saint Genevieve, keep watch and ward to-
    night.
For our God hath crushed the tyrant, our God hath raised the
    slave,
And mocked the counsel of the wise, and the valour of the brave.
Then glory to his holy name, from whom all glories are;
And glory to our Sovereign Lord, King Henry of Navarre.

THE ARMADA

Attend, all ye who list to hear our noble England's praise;
I tell of the thrice famous deeds she wrought in ancient days,
When that great fleet invincible against her bore in vain
The richest spoils of Mexico, the stoutest hearts of Spain.

It was about the lovely close of a warm summer day,
There came a gallant merchant-ship full sail to Plymouth Bay;
Her crew hath seen Castile's black fleet, beyond Aurigny's isle,
At earliest twilight, on the waves lie heaving many a mile.
At sunrise she escaped their van, by God's especial grace;
And the tall Pinta, till the noon, had held her close in chase.
Forthwith a guard at every gun was placed along the wall;
The beacon blazed upon the roof of Edgecumbe's lofty hall;
Many a light fishing-bark put out to pry along the coast,
And with loose rein and bloody spur rode inland many a post.
With his white hair unbonneted, the stout old sheriff comes;
Behind him march the halberdiers; before him sound the drums;
His yeomen round the market cross make clear an ample space;
For there behoves him to set up the standard of Her Grace.
And haughtily the trumpets peal, and gaily dance the bells,
As slow upon the labouring wind the royal blazon swells.
Look how the Lion of the sea lifts up his ancient crown,
And underneath his deadly paw treads the gay lilies down.
So stalked he when he turned to flight, on that famed Picard
          field,
Bohemia's plume, and Genoa's bow, and Cæsar's eagle shield.
So glared he when at Agincourt in wrath he turned to bay,
And crushed and torn beneath his claws the princely hunters lay.
Ho! strike the flagstaff deep, sir Knight: ho! scatter flowers,
          fair maids:
Ho! gunners, fire a loud salute: ho! gallants, draw your blades:
Thou sun, shine on her joyously; ye breezes, waft her wide;
Our glorious SEMPER EADEM, the banner of our pride.
   The freshening breeze of eve unfurled that banner's massy fold;

The parting gleam of sunshine kissed that haughty scroll of gold;
Night sank upon the dusky beach, and on the purple sea,
Such night in England ne'er had been, nor e'er again shall be.
From Eddystone to Berwick bounds, from Lynn to Milford Bay,
That time of slumber was as bright and busy as the day;
For swift to east and swift to west the ghastly war-flame spread,
High on Saint Michael's Mount it shone: it shone on Beachy
      Head.
Far on the deep the Spaniard saw, along each southern shire,
Cape beyond cape, in endless range, those twinkling points of
      fire.
The fisher left his skiff to rock on Tamar's glittering waves:
The rugged miners poured to war from Mendip's sunless caves:
O'er Longleat's towers, o'er Cranbourne's oaks, the fiery herald
      flew:
He roused the shepherds of Stonehenge, the rangers of Beaulieu.
Right sharp and quick the bells all night rang out from Bristol
      town,
And ere the day three hundred horse had met on Clifton down;
The sentinel on Whitehall gate looked forth into the night,
And saw o'erhanging Richmond Hill the streak of blood-red light.
Then bugle's note and cannon's roar the deathlike silence broke,
And with one start, and with one cry, the royal city woke.
At once on all her stately gates arose the answering fires;
At once the wild alarum clashed from all her reeling spires;
From all the batteries of the Tower pealed loud the voice of fear;
And all the thousand masts of Thames sent back a louder cheer:
And from the furthest wards was heard the rush of hurrying feet,
And the broad streams of pikes and flags rushed down each
      roaring street;
And broader still became the blaze, and louder still the din,
As fast from every village round the horse came spurring in:
And eastward straight from wild Blackheath the warlike errand
      went,
And roused in many an ancient hall the gallant squires of Kent.
Southward from Surrey's pleasant hills flew those bright couriers
      forth;
High on bleak Hampstead's swarthy moor they started for the
      north;
And on, and on, without a pause, untired they bounded still:
All night from tower to tower they sprang; they sprang from
      hill to hill:
Till the proud peak unfurled the flag o'er Darwin's rocky dales,

Till like volcanoes flared to heaven the stormy hills of Wales,
Till twelve fair counties saw the blaze on Malvern's lonely height,
Till streamed in crimson on the wind the Wrekin's crest of light,
Till broad and fierce the star came forth on Ely's stately fane,
And tower and hamlet rose in arms o'er all the boundless plain;
Till Belvoir's lordly terraces the sign to Lincoln sent,
And Lincoln sped the message on o'er the wide vale of Trent;
Till Skiddaw saw the fire that burned on Gaunt's embattled pile,
And the red glare on Skiddaw roused the burghers of Carlisle.

   .   .   .   .

1832.

MISCELLANEOUS POEMS

MISCELLANEOUS POEMS

EPITAPH ON HENRY MARTYN

(1812)

Here Martyn lies.   In Manhood's early bloom
The Christian Hero finds a Pagan tomb.
Religion, sorrowing o'er her favourite son,
Points to the glorious trophies that he won.
Eternal trophies! not with carnage red,
Not stained with tears by hapless captives shed,
But trophies of the Cross! for that dear name,
Through every form of danger, death, and shame,
Onward he journeyed to a happier shore,
Where danger, death, and shame assault no more.

LINES TO THE MEMORY OF PITT

(1813)

Oh Britain! dear Isle, when the annals of story
  Shall tell of the deeds that thy children have done,
When the strains of each poet shall sing of their glory,
  And the triumphs their skill and their valour have won.

When the olive and palm in thy chaplet are blended,
  When thy arts, and thy fame, and thy commerce increase,
When thy arms through the uttermost coasts are extended,
  And thy war is triumphant, and happy thy peace;

When the ocean, whose waves like a rampart flow round thee,
  Conveying thy mandates to every shore,
And the empire of nature no longer can bound thee,
  And the world be the scene of thy conquests no more:

Remember the man who in sorrow and danger,
　When thy glory was set, and thy spirit was low,
When thy hopes were o'erturned by the arms of the stranger,
　And thy banners displayed in the halls of the foe,

Stood forth in the tempest of doubt and disaster,
　Unaided, and single, the danger to brave.
Asserted thy claims, and the rights of his master,
　Preserved thee to conquer, and saved thee to save.

A RADICAL WAR SONG

(1820)

Awake, arise, the hour is come,
　For rows and revolutions;
There's no receipt like pike and drum
　For crazy constitutions.
Close, close the shop!　Break, break the loom,
　Desert your hearths and furrows,
And throng in arms to seal the doom
　Of England's rotten boroughs.

We'll stretch that tort'ring Castlereagh
　On his own Dublin rack, sir;
We'll drown the King in Eau de vie,
　The Laureate in his sack, sir,
Old Eldon and his sordid hag
　In molten gold we'll smother,
And stifle in his own green bag
　The Doctor and his brother.

In chains we'll hang in fair Guildhall
　The City's famed Recorder,
And next on proud St. Stephen's fall,
　Though Wynne should squeak to order.
In vain our tyrants then shall try
　To 'scape our martial law, sir;
In vain the trembling Speaker cry
　That " Strangers must withdraw," sir.

Copley to hang offends no text;
 A rat is not a man, sir:
With schedules, and with tax bills next
 We'll bury pious Van, sir.
The slaves who loved the Income Tax,
 We'll crush by scores, like mites, sir,
And him, the wretch who freed the blacks,
 And more enslaved the whites, sir.

The peer shall dangle from his gate,
 The bishop from his steeple,
Till all recanting, own, the State
 Means nothing but the People.
We'll fix the church's revenues
 On Apostolic basis,
One coat, one scrip, one pair of shoes
 Shall pay their strange grimaces.

We'll strap the bar's deluding train
 In their own darling halter,
And with his big church bible brain
 The parson at the altar.
Hail glorious hour, when fair Reform
 Shall bless our longing nation,
And Hunt receive commands to form
 A new administration.

Carlisle shall sit enthroned, where sat
 Our Cranmer and our Secker;
And Watson show his snow-white hat
 In England's rich Exchequer.
The breast of Thistlewood shall wear
 Our Wellesley's star and sash, man:
And many a mausoleum fair
 Shall rise to honest Cashman.

Then, then beneath the nine-tailed cat
 Shall they who used it writhe, sir;
And curates lean, and rectors fat,
 Shall dig the ground they tithe, sir.
Down with your Bayleys, and your Bests,
 Your Giffords, and your Gurneys:
We'll clear the island of the pests,
 Which mortals name attorneys.

Down with your sheriffs, and your mayors,
    Your registrars, and proctors,
We'll live without the lawyer's cares,
    And die without the doctor's.
No discontented fair shall pout
    To see her spouse so stupid;
We'll tread the torch of Hymen out,
    And live content with Cupid.

Then, when the high-born and the great
    Are humbled to our level,
On all the wealth of Church and State,
    Like aldermen, we'll revel.
We'll live when hushed the battle's din,
    In smoking and in cards, sir,
In drinking unexcised gin,
    And wooing fair Poissardes, sir.

THE BATTLE OF MONCONTOUR

(1824)

Oh, weep for Moncontour! Oh! weep for the hour,
When the children of darkness and evil had power,
When the horsemen of Valois triumphantly trod
On the bosoms that bled for their rights and their God.

Oh, weep for Moncontour! Oh! weep for the slain,
Who for faith and for freedom lay slaughtered in vain;
Oh, weep for the living, who linger to bear
The renegade's shame, or the exile's despair.

One look, one last look, to our cots and our towers,
To the rows of our vines, and the beds of our flowers,
To the church where the bones of our fathers decayed,
Where we fondly had deemed that our own would be laid.

Alas! we must leave thee, dear desolate home,
To the spearmen of Uri, the shavelings of Rome,
To the serpent of Florence, the vulture of Spain,
To the pride of Anjou, and the guile of Lorraine.

Farewell to thy fountains, farewell to thy shades,
To the song of thy youths, and the dance of thy maids,
To the breath of thy gardens, the hum of thy bees,
And the long waving line of the blue Pyrenees.

Farewell, and for ever.   The priest and the slave
May rule in the halls of the free and the brave.
Our hearths we abandon; our lands we resign;
But, Father, we kneel to no altar but thine.

THE BATTLE OF NASEBY

By Obadiah Bind-their-kings-in-chains-and-their-nobles-
with-links-of-iron, Serjeant in Ireton's Regiment.
(1824)

Oh! wherefore come ye forth, in triumph from the North,
  With your hands, and your feet, and your raiment all red?
And wherefore doth your rout send forth a joyous shout?
  And whence be the grapes of the wine-press which ye tread?

Oh evil was the root, and bitter was the fruit,
  And crimson was the juice of the vintage that we trod;
For we trampled on the throng of the haughty and the strong,
  Who sate in the high places, and slew the saints of God.

It was about the noon of a glorious day of June,
  That we saw their banners dance, and their cuirasses shine,
And the Man of Blood was there, with his long essenced hair,
  And Astley, and Sir Marmaduke, and Rupert of the Rhine.

Like a servant of the Lord, with his Bible and his sword,
  The General rode along us to form us to the fight,
When a murmuring sound broke out, and swell'd into a shout,
  Among the godless horsemen upon the tyrant's right.

And hark! like the roar of the billows on the shore,
  The cry of battle rises along their charging line!
For God! for the Cause! for the Church! for the Laws!
  For Charles King of England and Rupert of the Rhine!

The furious German comes, with his clarions and his drums,
  His bravoes of Alsatia, and pages of Whitehall;
They are bursting on our flanks.   Grasp your pikes, close your
    ranks;
  For Rupert never comes but to conquer or to fall.

They are here! They rush on! We are broken! We are gone!
  Our left is borne before them like stubble on the blast.
O Lord, put forth thy might!   O Lord, defend the right!
  Stand back to back, in God's name, and fight it to the last.

Stout Skippon hath a wound; the centre hath given ground:
  Hark! hark!—What means the trampling of horsemen on our
    rear?
Whose banner do I see, boys?   'Tis he, thank God, 'tis he, boys,
  Bear up another minute: brave Oliver is here.

Their heads all stooping low, their points all in a row,
  Like a whirlwind on the trees, like a deluge on the dykes,
Our cuirassiers have burst on the ranks of the Accurst,
  And at a shock have scattered the forest of his pikes.

Fast, fast, the gallants ride, in some safe nook to hide
  Their coward heads, predestined to rot on Temple Bar;
And he—he turns, he flies:—shame on those cruel eyes
  That bore to look on torture, and dare not look on war.

Ho! comrades scour the plain; and, ere ye strip the slain,
  First give another stab to make your search secure,
Then shake from sleeves and pockets their broad-pieces and
    lockets,
  The tokens of the wanton, the plunder of the poor.

Fools! your doublets shone with gold, and your hearts were gay
    and bold,
  When you kissed your lily hands to your lemans to-day;
And to-morrow shall the fox, from her chambers in the rocks,
  Lead forth her tawny cubs to howl above the prey.

Where be your tongues that late mocked at heaven and hell and
    fate,
  And the fingers that once were so busy with your blades,
Your perfum'd satin clothes, your catches and your oaths,
  Your stage-plays and your sonnets, your diamonds and your
    spades?

Down, down, for ever down with the mitre and the crown,
  With the Belial of the Court and the Mammon of the Pope;
There is woe in Oxford halls: there is wail in Durham's Stalls:
  The Jesuit smites his bosom: the Bishop rends his cope.

And She of the seven hills shall mourn her children's ills,
  And tremble when she thinks on the edge of England's sword;
And the Kings of earth in fear shall shudder when they hear
  What the hand of God hath wrought for the Houses and the
  Word.

SERMON IN A CHURCHYARD

(1825)

Let pious Damon take his seat,
  With mincing step and languid smile,
And scatter from his 'kerchief sweet,
  Sabæan odours o'er the aisle;
And spread his little jewelled hand,
  And smile round all the parish beauties,
And pat his curls, and smooth his band,
  Meet prelude to his saintly duties.

Let the thronged audience press and stare,
  Let stifled maidens ply the fan,
Admire his doctrines, and his hair,
  And whisper, " What a good young man! "
While he explains what seems most clear,
  So clearly that it seems perplexed,
I'll stay and read my sermon here;
  And skulls, and bones, shall be the text.

Art thou the jilted dupe of fame?
  Dost thou with jealous anger pine
Whene'er she sounds some other name,
  With fonder emphasis than thine?
To thee I preach; draw near; attend!
  Look on these bones, thou fool, and see
Where all her scorns and favours end,
  What Byron is, and thou must be.

Dost thou revere, or praise, or trust
  Some clod like those that here we spurn;
Some thing that sprang like thee from dust,
  And shall like thee to dust return?
Dost thou rate statesmen, heroes, wits,
  At one sear leaf, or wandering feather?
Behold the black, damp, narrow pits,
  Where they and thou must lie together.

Dost thou beneath the smile or frown
  Of some vain woman bend thy knee?
Here take thy stand, and trample down
  Things that were once as fair as she.
Here rave of her ten thousand graces,
  Bosom, and lip, and eye, and chin,
While, as in scorn, the fleshless faces
  Of Hamiltons and Waldegraves grin.

Whate'er thy losses or thy gains,
  Whate'er thy projects or thy fears,
Whate'er the joys, whate'er the pains,
  That prompt thy baby smiles and tears;
Come to my school, and thou shalt learn,
  In one short hour of placid thought,
A stoicism, more deep, more stern,
  Than ever Zeno's porch hath taught.

The plots and feats of those that press
  To seize on titles, wealth, or power,
Shall seem to thee a game of chess,
  Devised to pass a tedious hour.
What matters it to him who fights
  For shows of unsubstantial good,
Whether his Kings, and Queens, and Knights,
  Be things of flesh, or things of wood?

We check, and take; exult, and fret;
  Our plans extend, our passions rise,
Till in our ardour we forget
  How worthless is the victor's prize.
Soon fades the spell, soon comes the night:
  Say will it not be then the same,
Whether we played the black or white,
  Whether we lost or won the game?

Dost thou among these hillocks stray,
  O'er some dear idol's tomb to moan?
Know that thy foot is on the clay
  Of hearts once wretched as thy own.
How many a father's anxious schemes,
  How many rapturous thoughts of lovers,
How many a mother's cherished dreams,
  The swelling turf before thee covers!

Here for the living, and the dead,
  The weepers and the friends they weep,
Hath been ordained the same cold bed,
  The same dark night, the same long sleep;
Why shouldest thou writhe, and sob, and rave
  O'er those with whom thou soon must be?
Death his own sting shall cure—the grave
  Shall vanquish its own victory.

Here learn that all the griefs and joys,
  Which now torment, which now beguile,
Are children's hurts, and children's toys,
  Scarce worthy of one bitter smile.
Here learn that pulpit, throne, and press,
  Sword, sceptre, lyre, alike are frail,
That science is a blind man's guess,
  And History a nurse's tale.

Here learn that glory and disgrace,
  Wisdom and folly, pass away,
That mirth hath its appointed space,
  That sorrow is but for a day;
That all we love, and all we hate,
  That all we hope, and all we fear,
Each mood of mind, each turn of fate,
  Must end in dust and silence here.

TRANSLATION FROM A. V. ARNAULT

Fables : Livre v. *Fable* 16

(1826)

Thou poor leaf, so sear and frail,
Sport of every wanton gale,
Whence, and whither, dost thou fly,
Through this bleak autumnal sky?
On a noble oak I grew,
Green, and broad, and fair to view;
But the Monarch of the shade
By the tempest low was laid.
From that time, I wander o'er
Wood, and valley, hill, and moor,
Wheresoe'er the wind is blowing,
Nothing caring, nothing knowing:
Thither go I, whither goes,
Glory's laurel, Beauty's rose.

————De ta tige détachée,
Pauvre feuille desséchée
Où vas-tu ?—Je n'en sais rien.
L'orage a frappé le chêne
Qui seul était mon soutien.
De son inconstante haleine,
Le zéphyr ou l'aquilon
Depuis ce jour me promène
De la forêt à la plaine,
De la montagne au vallon.
Je vais où le vent me mène,
Sans me plaindre ou m'effrayer,
Je vais où va toute chose,
Où va la feuille de rose
Et la feuille de laurier.

DIES IRÆ

(1826)

On that great, that awful day,
This vain world shall pass away.
Thus the sibyl sang of old,
Thus hath holy David told.
There shall be a deadly fear
When the Avenger shall appear,
And unveiled before his eye
All the works of man shall lie.
Hark! to the great trumpet's tones
Pealing o'er the place of bones:
Hark! it waketh from their bed
All the nations of the dead,—
In a countless throng to meet,
At the eternal judgment seat.
Nature sickens with dismay,
Death may not retain its prey;
And before the Maker stand
All the creatures of his hand.
The great book shall be unfurled,
Whereby God shall judge the world:
What was distant shall be near,
What was hidden shall be clear.
To what shelter shall I fly?
To what guardian shall I cry?
Oh, in that destroying hour,
Source of goodness, Source of power,
Show thou, of thine own free grace,
Help unto a helpless race.
Though I plead not at thy throne
Aught that I for thee have done,
Do not thou unmindful be,
Of what thou hast borne for me:
Of the wandering, of the scorn,
Of the scourge, and of the thorn.
Jesus, hast *thou* borne the pain,
And hath all been borne in vain?
Shall thy vengeance smite the head

For whose ransom thou hast bled?
Thou, whose dying blessing gave
Glory to a guilty slave:
Thou, who from the crew unclean
Didst release the Magdalene:
Shall not mercy vast and free,
Evermore be found in thee?
Father, turn on me thine eyes,
See my blushes, hear my cries;
Faint though be the cries I make,
Save me for thy mercy's sake,
From the worm, and from the fire,
From the torments of thine ire.
Fold me with the sheep that stand
Pure and safe at thy right hand.
Hear thy guilty child implore thee,
Rolling in the dust before thee.
Oh the horrors of that day!
When this frame of sinful clay,
Starting from its burial place,
Must behold thee face to face.
Hear and pity, hear and aid,
Spare the creatures thou hast made.
Mercy, mercy, save, forgive,
Oh, who shall look on thee and live?

THE MARRIAGE OF TIRZAH AND AHIRAD

(1827)

GENESIS VI. 3

It is the dead of night:
Yet more than noonday light
Beams far and wide from many a gorgeous hall.
Unnumbered harps are tinkling,
Unnumbered lamps are twinkling,
In the great city of the fourfold wall.
By the brazen castle's moat,
The sentry hums a livelier note.
The ship-boy chaunts a shriller lay
From the galleys in the bay.

Shout, and laugh, and hurrying feet
Sound from mart and square and street.
From the breezy laurel shades,
From the granite colonnades,
From the golden statue's base,
From the stately market-place,
Where, upreared by capitve hands,
The great Tower of Triumph stands,
All its pillars in a blaze
With the many-coloured rays,
Which lanthorns of ten thousand dyes
Shed on ten thousand panoplies.
But closest is the throng,
And loudest is the song,
In that sweet garden by the river side,
The abyss of myrtle bowers,
The wilderness of flowers,
Where Cain hath built the palace of his pride.
Such palace ne'er shall be again
Among the dwindling race of men.
From all its threescore gates the light
Of gold and steel afar was thrown;
Two hundred cubits rose in height
The outer wall of polished stone.
On the top was ample space
For a gallant chariot race,
Near either parapet a bed
Of the richest mould was spread,
Where amidst flowers of every scent and hue
Rich orange trees, and palms, and giant cedars grew.

In the mansion's public court
All is revel, song, and sport;
For there, till morn shall tint the east,
Menials and guards prolong the feast.
The boards with painted vessels shine;
The marble cisterns foam with wine.
A hundred dancing girls are there
With zoneless waists and streaming hair;
And countless eyes with ardour gaze,
And countless hands the measure beat,
As mix and part in amorous maze
Those floating arms and bounding feet.

But none of all the race of Cain,
    Save those whom he hath deigned to grace
With yellow robe and sapphire chain,
    May pass beyond that outer space.
    For now within the painted hall
    The Firstborn keeps high festival.
Before the glittering valves all night
    Their post the chosen captains hold.
Above the portal's stately height
    The legend flames in lamps of gold:
" In life united and in death
    May Tirzah and Ahirad be,
The bravest he of all the sons of Seth,
    Of all the house of Cain the loveliest she."

Through all the climates of the earth
This night is given to festal mirth.
The long continued war is ended.
The long divided lines are blended.
Ahirad's bow shall now no more
Make fat the wolves with kindred gore.
The vultures shall expect in vain
Their banquet from the sword of Cain.
Without a guard the herds and flocks
Along the frontier moors and rocks
    From eve to morn may roam;
Nor shriek, nor shout, nor reddened sky,
Shall warn the startled hind to fly
    From his beloved home.
Nor to the pier shall burghers crowd
    With straining necks and faces pale,
And think that in each flitting cloud
    They see a hostile sail.
The peasant without fear shall guide
Down smooth canal or river wide
    His painted bark of cane,
Fraught, for some proud bazaar's arcades,
With chestnuts from his native shades,
    And wine, and milk, and grain.
Search round the peopled globe to-night,
    Explore each continent and isle,
There is no door without a light,
    No face without a smile.

The noblest chiefs of either race,
  From north and south, from west and east,
Crowd to the painted hall to grace
  The pomp of that atoning feast.
  With widening eyes and labouring breath
  Stand the fair-haired sons of Seth,
  As bursts upon their dazzled sight
  The endless avenue of light,
  The bowers of tulip, rose, and palm,
  The thousand cressets fed with balm,
  The silken vests, the boards piled high
  With amber, gold, and ivory,
  The crystal founts whence sparkling flow
  The richest wines o'er beds of snow,
  The walls where blaze in living dyes
  The king's three hundred victories.
  The heralds point the fitting seat
  To every guest in order meet,
  And place the highest in degree
  Nearest th' imperial canopy.
  Beneath its broad and gorgeous fold,
  With naked swords and shields of gold,
Stood the seven princes of the tribes of Nod.
  Upon an ermine carpet lay
  Two tiger cubs in furious play,
Beneath the emerald throne where sat the signed of God.

  Over that ample forehead white
    The thousandth year returneth.
  Still, on its commanding height,
  With a fierce and blood-red light,
    The fiery token burneth.
  ·Wheresoe'er that mystic star
  Blazeth in the van of war,
    Back recoil before its ray
  Shield and banner, bow and spear,
    Maddened horses break away
  From the trembling charioteer.
  The fear of that stern king doth lie
  On all that live beneath the sky;
All shrink before the mark of his despair,
The seal of that great curse which he alone can bear.

Blazing in pearls and diamonds' sheen,
  Tirzah, the young Ahirad's bride,
Of humankind the destined queen,
  Sits by her great forefather's side.
The jetty curls, the forehead high,
  The swanlike neck, the eagle face,
The glowing cheek, the rich dark eye,
  Proclaim her of the elder race.
With flowing locks of auburn hue,
And features smooth, and eye of blue,
  Timid in love as brave in arms,
The gentle heir of Seth askance
Snatches a bashful ardent glance
  At her majestic charms;
Blest when across that brow high musing flashes
  A deeper tint of rose,
Thrice blest when from beneath the silken lashes
  Of her proud eye she throws
The smile of blended fondness and disdain
Which marks the daugthers of the house of Cain.

All hearts are light around the hall
Save his who is the lord of all.
The painted roofs, the attendant train,
The lights, the banquet, all are vain.
He sees them not.   His fancy strays
To other scenes and other days.
A cot by a lone forest's edge,
  A fountain murmuring through the trees,
A garden with a wildflower hedge,
  Whence sounds the music of the bees,
A little flock of sheep at rest
Upon a mountain's swarthy breast.
On his rude spade he seems to lean
  Beside the well remembered stone,
Rejoicing o'er the promised green
  Of the first harvest man hath sown.
  He sees his mother's tears;
  His father's voice he hears,
Kind as when first it praised his youthful skill.
  And soon a seraph-child,
  In boyish rapture wild,
With a light crook comes bounding from the hill,

Kisses his hands, and strokes his face,
And nestles close in his embrace.
In his adamantine eye
None might discern his agony;
But they who had grown hoary next his side,
    And read his stern dark face with deepest skill,
Could trace strange meanings in that lip of pride,
    Which for one moment quivered and was still.
No time for them to mark or him to feel
    Those inward stings; for clarion, flute, and lyre,
    And the rich voices of a countless quire,
Burst on the ear in one triumphant peal.
In breathless transport sits the admiring throng,
As sink and swell the notes of Jubal's lofty song.

" Sound the timbrel, strike the lyre,
Wake the trumpet's blast of fire,
    Till the gilded arches ring.
Empire, victory, and fame,
Be ascribed unto the name
    Of our father and our king.
Of the deeds which he hath done,
Of the spoils which he hath won,
    Let his grateful children sing.
When the deadly fight was fought,
When the great revenge was wrought,
When on the slaughtered victims lay
The minion stiff and cold as they,
Doomed to exile, sealed with flame,
From the west the wanderer came.
Six score years and six he strayed
A hunter through the forest shade.
The lion's shaggy jaws he tore,
To earth he smote the foaming boar,
He crushed the dragon's fiery crest,
And scaled the condor's dizzy nest;
Till hardy sons and daughters fair
Increased around his woodland lair.
Then his victorious bow unstrung
On the great bison's horn he hung.
Giraffe and elk he left to hold
    The wilderness of boughs in peace,
And trained his youth to pen the fold,

To press the cream, and weave the fleece.
As shrunk the streamlet in its bed,
As black and scant the herbage grew,
O'er endless plains his flocks he led
  Still to new brooks and pastures new.
So strayed he till the white pavilions
Of his camp were told by millions,
Till his children's households seven
Were numerous as the stars of heaven.
Then he bade us rove no more;
  And in the place that pleased him best,
On the great river's fertile shore,
  He fixed the city of his rest.
He taught us then to bind the sheaves,
  To strain the palm's delicious milk,
And from the dark green mulberry leaves
  To cull the filmy silk.
Then first from straw-built mansions roamed
  O'er flower-beds trim the skilful bees;
Then first the purple wine vats foamed
  Around the laughing peasant's knees;
And olive-yards, and orchards green
O'er all the hills of Nod were seen.

" Of our father and our king
Let his grateful children sing.
From him our race its being draws,
His are our arts, and his our laws.
Like himself he bade us be,
Proud, and brave, and fierce, and free,
True, through every turn of fate,
In our friendship and our hate.
Calm to watch, yet prompt to dare;
Quick to feel, yet firm to bear;
Only timid, only weak,
Before sweet woman's eye and cheek.
We will not serve, we will not know,
The God who is our father's foe.
In our proud cities to his name
No temples rise, no altars flame,
Our flocks of sheep, our groves of spice,
To him afford no sacrifice.
Enough that once the House of Cain

Hath courted with oblation vain
    The sullen power above.
Henceforth we bear the yoke no more;
The only gods whom we adore
    Are glory, vengeance, love.

" Of our father and our king
Let his grateful children sing.
What eye of living thing may brook
On his blazing brow to look?
What might of living thing may stand
Against the strength of his right hand?
First he led his armies forth
Against the Mammoths of the north,
What time they wasted in their pride
Pasture and vineyard far and wide.
Then the White River's icy flood
Was thawed with fire and dyed with blood,
And heard for many a league the sound
Of the pine forests blazing round,
And the death-howl and trampling din
Of the gigantic herd within.
From the surging sea of flame
Forth the tortured monsters came:
As of breakers on the shore
Was their onset and their roar;
As the cedar-trees of God
Stood the stately ranks of Nod.
One long night and one short day
The sword was lifted up to slay.
    Then marched the firstborn and his sons
O'er the white ashes of the wood,
And counted of that savage brood
    Nine times nine thousand skeletons.

" On the snow with carnage red
The wood is piled, the skins are spread.
A thousand fires illume the sky;
Round each a hundred warriors lie.
But, long ere half the night was spent,
Forth thundered from the golden tent
    The rousing voice of Cain.
A thousand trumps in answer rang

And fast to arms the warriors sprang
　　O'er all the frozen plain.
A herald from the wealthy bay
Hath come with tidings of dismay.
From the western ocean's coast
Seth hath led a countless host,
And vows to slay with fire and sword
All who call not on the Lord.
His archers hold the mountain forts;
His light armed ships blockade the ports;
　　His horsemen tread the harvest down.
On twelve proud bridges he hath passed
The river dark with many a mast,
And pitched his mighty camp at last
　　Before the imperial town.

" On the south and on the west,
Closely was the city prest.
Before us lay the hostile powers.
The breach was wide between the towers.
Pulse and meal within were sold
For a double weight of gold.
Our mighty father had gone forth
Two hundred marches to the north.
Yet in that extreme of ill
We stoutly kept his city still;
And swore beneath his royal wall,
Like his true sons to fight and fall.

" Hark, hark, to gong and horn,
Clarion, and fife, and drum,
The morn, the fortieth morn,
Fixed for the great assault is come.
Between the camp and city spreads
A waving sea of helmed heads.
From the royal car of Seth
Was hung the blood-red flag of death:
　At sight of that thrice-hallowed sign
Wide flew at once each banner's fold;
The captains clashed their arms of gold;
The war cry of Elohim rolled
　Far down their endless line.
On the northern hills afar

Pealed an answering note of war.
Soon the dust in whirlwinds driven,
Rushed across the northern heaven.
Beneath its shroud came thick and loud
The tramp as of a countless crowd;
And at intervals were seen
Lance and hauberk glancing sheen;
And at intervals were heard
Charger's neigh and battle word.

" Oh what a rapturous cry
From all the city's thousand spires arose,
    With what a look the hollow eye
Of the lean watchman glared upon the foes,
With what a yell of joy the mother pressed
The moaning baby to her withered breast;
When through the swarthy cloud that veiled the plain
Burst on his children's sight the flaming brow of Cain ! "

There paused perforce that noble song;
For from all the joyous throng,
Burst forth a rapturous shout which drowned
Singer's voice and trumpet's sound.
Thrice that stormy clamour fell,
Thrice rose again with mightier swell.
The last and loudest roar of all
Had died along the painted wall.
The crowd was hushed; the minstrel train
Prepared to strike the chords again;
When on each ear distinctly smote
A low and wild and wailing note.
It moans again.   In mute amaze
Menials, and guests, and harpers gaze.
They look above, beneath, around,
No shape doth own that mournful sound.
It comes not from the tuneful quire;
    It comes not from the feasting peers.
There is no tone of earthly lyre
    So soft, so sad, so full of tears.
Then a strange horror came on all
Who sate at that high festival.
The far famed harp, the harp of gold,
Dropped from Jubal's trembling hold.

Frantic with dismay the bride
Clung to her Ahirad's side.
And the corpse-like hue of dread
Ahirad's haughty face o'erspread.
Yet not even in that agony of awe
  Did the young leader of the fair-haired race
From Tirzah's shuddering grasp his hand withdraw,
  Or turn his eyes from Tirzah's livid face.
The tigers to their lord retreat,
And crouch and whine beneath his feet.
  Prone sink to earth the golden shielded seven.
All hearts are cowed save his alone
Who sits upon the emerald throne;
  For he hath heard Elohim speak from heaven.
Still thunders in his ear the peal;
Still blazes on his front the seal;
And on the soul of the proud king
No terror of created thing
From sky, or earth, or hell, hath power
Since that unutterable hour.
He rose to speak, but paused, and listening stood,
Not daunted, but in sad and curious mood,
  With knitted brow, and searching eye of fire.
A deathlike silence sank on all around,
And through the boundless space was heard no sound,
  Save the soft tones of that mysterious lyre.
Broken, faint, and low,
At first the numbers flow.
Louder, deeper, quicker, still
  Into one fierce peal they swell,
And the echoing palace fill
  With a strange funereal yell.
A voice comes forth.   But what, or where?
On the earth, or in the air?
Like the midnight winds that blow
Round a lone cottage in the snow,
With howling swell and sighing fall,
It wails along the trophied hall.
In such a wild and dreary moan
  The watches of the Seraphim
  Poured out all night their plaintive hymn
Before the eternal throne.
Then, when from many a heavenly eye

Drops as of earthly pity fell
For her who had aspired too high,
  For him who loved too well.
When, stunned by grief, the gentle pair
From the nuptial garden fair,
Linked in a sorrowful caress,
Strayed through the untrodden wilderness;
And close behind their footsteps came
The desolating sword of flame,
And drooped the cedared alley's pride,
And fountains shrank, and roses died.

" Rejoice, O Son of God, rejoice,"
Sang that melancholy voice,
" Rejoice, the maid is fair to see;
The bower is decked for her and thee;
The ivory lamps around it throw
A soft and pure and mellow glow.
Where'er the chastened lustre falls
On roof or cornice, floor or walls,
Woven of pink and rose appear
Such words as love delights to hear.
The breath of myrrh, the lute's soft sound,
Float through the moonlight galleries round.
O'er beds of violet and through groves of spice,
  Lead thy proud bride into the nuptial bower;
For thou hast bought her with a fearful price,
  And she hath dowered thee with a fearful dower.
The price is life.   The dower is death.
  Accursed loss!   Accursed gain!
For her thou givest the blessedness of Seth,
And to thine arms she brings the curse of Cain.
Round the dark curtains of the fiery throne
  Pauses awhile the voice of sacred song:
From all the angelic ranks goes forth a groan,
  ' How long, O Lord, how long? '
The still small voice makes answer, ' Wait and see,
Oh sons of glory, what the end shall be.'

" But in the outer darkness of the place
Where God hath shown his power without his grace,
Is laughter and the sound of glad acclaim,
  Loud as when, on wings of fire,

Fulfilled of his malign desire,
From Paradise the conquering serpent came.
The giant ruler of the morning star
  From off his fiery bed
  Lifts high his stately head,
Which Michael's sword hath marked with many a scar.
At his voice the pit of hell
Answers with a joyous yell,
And flings her dusky portals wide
For the bridegroom and the bride.

" But louder still shall be the din
In the halls of Death and Sin,
When the full measure runneth o'er,
When mercy can endure no more,
When he who vainly proffers grace,
Comes in his fury to deface
  The fair creation of his hand;
When from the heaven streams down amain
For forty days the sheeted rain;
And from his ancient barriers free,
With a deafening roar the sea
  Comes foaming up the land.
Mother, cast thy babe aside:
Bridegroom, quit thy virgin bride:
Brother, pass thy brother by:
'Tis for life, for life, ye fly.
Along the dear horizon raves
The swift advancing line of waves.
On: on: their frothy crests appear
Each moment nearer, and more near.
Urge the dromedary's speed;
Spur to death the reeling steed;
If perchance ye yet may gain
The mountains that o'erhang the plain.

" Oh thou haughty land of Nod,
Hear the sentence of thy God.
Thou hast said, ' Of all the hills
Whence, after autumn rains, the rills
  In silver trickle down,
The fairest is that mountain white
Which intercepts the morning light

From Cain's imperial town.
On its first and gentlest swell
Are pleasant halls where nobles dwell;
And marble porticoes are seen
Peeping through terraced gardens green.
Above are olives, palms, and vines;
And higher yet the dark-blue pines;
And highest on the summit shines
  The crest of everlasting ice.
Here let the God of Abel own
That human art hath wonders shown
  Beyond his boasted paradise.'

" Therefore on that proud mountain's crown
  Thy few surviving sons and daughters
Shall see their latest sun go down
  Upon a boundless waste of waters.
None salutes and none replies;
  None heaves a groan or breathes a prayer.
They crouch on earth with tearless eyes,
  And clenched hands, and bristling hair.
The rain pours on: no star illumes
  The blackness of the roaring sky.
And each successive billow booms
  Nigher still and still more nigh.
And now upon the howling blast
The wreaths of spray come thick and fast;
And a great billow by the tempest curled
  Falls with a thundering crash; and all is o'er.
And what is left of all this glorious world?
  A sky without a beam, a sea without a shore.

" Oh thou fair land, where from their starry home
Cherub and seraph oft delight to roam,
Thou city of the thousand towers,
  Thou palace of the golden stairs,
Ye gardens of perennial flowers,
  Ye moted gates, ye breezy squares;
Ye parks amidst whose branches high
Oft peers the squirrel's sparkling eye;
Ye vineyards, in whose trellised shade
Pipes many a youth to many a maid;
Ye ports where rides the gallant ship,
  Ye marts where wealthy burghers meet;

Ye dark green lanes which know the trip
  Of woman's conscious feet;
Ye grassy meads where, when the day is done,
  The shepherd pens his fold;
Ye purple moors on which the setting sun
  Leaves a rich fringe of gold;
Ye wintry deserts where the larches grow;
Ye mountains on whose everlasting snow
  No human foot hath trod;
Many a fathom shall ye sleep
Beneath the grey and endless deep,
  In the great day of the revenge of God."

THE COUNTRY CLERGYMAN'S TRIP TO CAMBRIDGE

An Election Ballad. (1827)

As I sate down to breakfast in state,
  At my living of Tithing-cum-Boring,
With Betty beside me to wait,
  Came a rap that almost beat the door in.
I laid down my basin of tea,
  And Betty ceased spreading the toast,
" As sure as a gun, sir," said she,
  " That must be the knock of the post."

A letter—and free—bring it here—
  I have no correspondent who franks.
No! Yes! Can it be? Why, my dear,
  'Tis our glorious, our Protestant Bankes.
" Dear sir, as I know you desire
  That the Church should receive due protection,
I humbly presume to require
  Your aid at the Cambridge election.

" It has lately been brought to my knowledge,
  That the Ministers fully design
To suppress each cathedral and college,
  And eject every learned divine.

To assist this detestable scheme
  Three nuncios from Rome are come over;
They left Calais on Monday by steam,
  And landed to dinner at Dover.

" An army of grim Cordeliers,
  Well furnished with relics and vermin,
Will follow, Lord Westmoreland fears,
  To effect what their chiefs may determine.
Lollard's bower, good authorities say,
  Is again fitting up for a prison;
And a wood-merchant told me to-day
  'Tis a wonder how faggots have risen.

" ͏   ance scheme of Canning contains
          ͏ Easter-offering tax;
And he means to devote all the gains
  To a bounty on thumb-screws and racks.
Your living, so neat and compact—
  Pray, don't let the news give you pain!—
Is promised, I know for a fact,
  To an olive-faced Padre from Spain."

I read and I felt my heart bleed,
  Sore wounded with horror and pity;
So I flew, with all possible speed,
  To our Protestant champion's committee.
True gentlemen, kind and well-bred!
  No fleering! no distance! no scorn!
They asked after my wife who is dead,
  And my children who never were born.

They then, like high-principled Tories,
  Called our Sovereign unjust and unsteady,
And assailed him with scandalous stories,
  Till the coach for the voters was ready.
That coach might be well called a casket
  Of learning and brotherly love:
There were parsons in boot and in basket;
  There were parsons below and above.

There were Sneaker and Griper, a pair
  Who stick to Lord Mulesby like leeches;

A smug chaplain of plausible air,
   Who writes my Lord Goslingham's speeches.
Dr. Buzz, who alone is a host,
   Who, with arguments weighty as lead,
Proves six times a week in the Post
   That flesh somehow differs from bread.

Dr. Nimrod, whose orthodox toes
   Are seldom withdrawn from the stirrup;
Dr. Humdrum, whose eloquence flows,
   Like droppings of sweet poppy syrup;
Dr. Rosygill puffing and fanning.
   And wiping away perspiration;
Dr. Humbug who proved Mr. Canning
   The beast in St. John's Revelation.

A layman can scarce form a notion
   Of our wonderful talk on the road;
Of the learning, the wit, and devotion,
   Which almost each syllable showed:
Why divided allegiance agrees
   So ill with our free constitution;
How Catholics swear as they please,
   In hope of the priest's absolution;

How the Bishop of Norwich had bartered
   His faith for a legate's commission;
How Lyndhurst afraid to be martyr'd,
   Had stooped to a base coalition;
How Papists are cased from compassion
   By bigotry, stronger than steel;
How burning would soon come in fashion,
   And how very bad it must feel.

We were all so much touched and excited
   By a subject so direly sublime,
That the rules of politeness were slighted,
   And we all of us talked at a time;
And in tones, which each moment grew louder,
   Told how we should dress for the show,
And where we should fasten the powder.
   And if we should bellow or no.

Thus from subject to subject we ran,
 And the journey passed pleasantly o'er,
Till at last Dr. Humdrum began;
 From that time I remember no more.
At Ware he commenced his prelection,
 In the dullest of clerical drones;
And when next I regained recollection
 We were rumbling o'er Trumpington stones.

SONG

(1827)

O stay, Madonna! stay;
 'Tis not the dawn of day
That marks the skies with yonder opal streak:
 The stars in silence shine;
 Then press thy lips to mine,
And rest upon my neck thy fervid cheek.

O sleep, Madonna! sleep;
 Leave me to watch and weep
O'er the sad memory of departed joys,
 O'er hope's extinguished beam,
 O'er fancy's vanished dream;
O'er all that nature gives and man destroys.

O wake, Madonna! wake;
 Even now the purple lake
Is dappled o'er with amber flakes of light;
 A glow is on the hill
 And every trickling rill
In golden threads leaps down from yonder height.

O fly, Madonna! fly,
 Lest day and envy spy
What only love and night may safely know:
 Fly, and tread softly, dear!
 Lest those who hate us hear
The sounds of thy light footsteps as they go.

POLITICAL GEORGICS

(MARCH 1828)

" Quid faciat lætas segetes," etc.

How cabinets are form'd, and how destroy'd,
How Tories are confirm'd, and Whigs decoy'd,
How in nice times a prudent man should vote,
At what conjuncture he should turn his coat,
The truths fallacious and the candid lies,
And all the lore of sleek majorities,
I sing, great Premier.   Oh, mysterious two,
Lords of our fate, the Doctor and the Jew,
If, by your care enriched, the aspiring clerk
Quits the close alley for the breezy park,
And Dolly's chops and Reid's entire resigns
For odorous fricassees and costly wines;
And you, great pair, through Windsor's shades who rove,
The Faun and Dryad of the conscious grove;
All, all inspire me, for of all I sing,
Doctor and Jew, and M——s and K——g.
Thou, to the maudlin muse of Rydal dear;
Thou more than Neptune, Lowther, lend thine ear.
At Neptune's voice the horse, with flowing mane
And pawing hoof, sprung from th' obedient plain;
But at thy word the yawning earth, in fright,
Engulf'd the victor steed from mortal sight.
Haste from thy woods, mine Arbuthnot, with speed,
Rich woods, where lean Scotch cattle love to feed:
Let Gaffer Gooch and Boodle's patriot band,
Fat from the leanness of a plundered land,
True Cincinnati, quit their patent ploughs,
Their new steam-harrows, and their premium sows;
Let all in bulky majesty appear,
Roll the dull eye, and yawn th' unmeaning cheer.
Ye veteran Swiss, of senatorial wars,
Who glory in your well-earned sticks and stars;
Ye diners-out from whom we guard our spoons;
Ye smug defaulters; ye obscene buffoons;

Come all, of every race and size and form,
Corruption's children, brethren of the worm;
From those gigantic monsters who devour
The pay of half a squadron in an hour,
To those foul reptiles, doomed to night and scorn,
Of filth and stench equivocally born;
From royal tigers down to toads and lice;
From Bathursts, Clintons, Fanes, to H—— and P——;
Thou last, by habit and by nature blest
With every gift which serves a courtier best,
The lap-dog spittle, the hyæna bile,
The maw of shark, the tear of crocodile,
Whate'er high station, undetermined yet,
Awaits thee in the longing Cabinet,—
Whether thou seat thee in the room of Peel,
Or from Lord Prig extort the privy Seal,
Or our Field-marshal-Treasurer fix on thee,
A legal admiral, to rule the sea,
Or Chancery-suits, beneath thy well known reign,
Turn to their nap of fifty years again;
(Already L——, prescient of his fate,
Yields half his woolsack to thy mightier weight;)
Oh! Eldon, in whatever sphere thou shine,
For opposition sure will ne'er be thine,
Though scowls apart the lonely pride of Grey,
Though Devonshire proudly flings his staff away,
Though Lansdowne, trampling on his broken chain,
Shine forth the Lansdowne of our hearts again,
Assist me thou; for well I deem, I see
An abstract of my ample theme in thee.
Thou, as thy glorious self hath justly said,
From earliest youth, wast pettifogger bred,
And, raised to power by fortune's fickle will,
Art head and heart a pettifogger still.
So, where once Fleet-ditch ran confessed, we view
A crowded mart and stately avenue;
But the black stream beneath runs on the same,
Still brawls in W——'s key,—still stinks like H——'s name.

THE DELIVERANCE OF VIENNA [1]

Translated from Vincenzio de Filicaia

" Le corde d'oro elette," etc.

The chords, the sacred chords of gold,
  Strike, O Muse, in measure bold;
And frame a sparkling wreath of joyous songs
For that great God to whom revenge belongs.
    Who shall resist his might,
    Who marshals for the fight
Earthquake and thunder, hurricane and flame?
    He smote the haughty race
    Of unbelieving Thrace,
And turned their rage to fear, their pride to shame.
    He looked in wrath from high,
     Upon their vast array;
    And in the twinkling of an eye,
    Tambour, and trump, and battle-cry,
    And steeds, and turbaned infantry,
     Passed like a dream away.
Such power defends the mansions of the just:

    But, like a city without walls,
    The grandeur of the mortal falls
Who glories in his strength, and makes not God his trust.
The proud blasphemers thought all earth their own;
  They deemed that soon the whirlwind of their ire
  Would sweep down tower and palace, dome and spire,
The Christian altars and the Augustan throne.
  And soon, they cried, shall Austria bow
  To the dust her lofty brow.
    The princedoms of Almayne
    Shall wear the Phrygian chain;
In humbler waves shall vassal Tiber roll;
    And Rome a slave forlorn,
    Her laurelled tresses shorn,
Shall feel our iron in her inmost soul.
    Who shall bid the torrent stay?
    Who shall bar the lightning's way?

[1] Published in the *Winter's Wreath*, Liverpool, 1828.

Who arrest the advancing van
Of the fiery Ottoman?

As the curling smoke-wreaths fly
When fresh breezes clear the sky,
Passed away each swelling boast
Of the misbelieving host.
From the Hebrus rolling far
Came the murky cloud of war,
And in shower and tempest dread
Burst on Austria's fenceless head.
    But not for vaunt or threat
    Didst Thou, O Lord, forget
The flock so dearly bought, and loved so well.

    Even in the very hour
    Of guilty pride and power
Full on the circumcised Thy vengeance fell.
Then the fields were heaped with dead,
Then the streams with gore were red,
And every bird of prey and every beast,
From wood and cavern thronged to Thy great feast.

What terror seized the fiends obscene of Nile:
    How wildly, in his place of doom beneath,
    Arabia's lying prophet gnashed his teeth,
And cursed his blighted hopes and wasted guile!
When, at the bidding of Thy sovereign might,
    Flew on their destined path
    Thy messengers of wrath,
Riding on storms and wrapped in deepest night.
    The Phthian mountains saw,
    And quaked with mystic awe:
The proud Sultana of the Straits bowed down
Her jewelled neck and her embattled crown.
The miscreants, as they raised their eyes
Glaring defiance on Thy skies,
Saw adverse winds and clouds display
The terrors of their black array;—
    Saw each portentous star
Whose fiery aspect turned of yore to flight
The iron chariots of the Canaanite
    Gird its bright harness for a deadlier war.

Beneath Thy withering look
   Their limbs with palsy shook;
Scattered on earth the crescent banners lay;
   Trembled with panic fear
   Sabre and targe and spear,
Through the proud armies of the rising day.
  Faint was each heart, unnerved each hand;
  And, if they strove to charge or stand,
   Their efforts were as vain
  As his who, scared in feverish sleep
  By evil dreams, essays to leap,
   Then backward falls again.
  With a crash of wild dismay,
  Their ten thousand ranks gave way;
  Fast they broke, and fast they fled;
  Trampled, mangled, dying, dead,
  Horse and horsemen mingled lay;
  Till the mountains of the slain
  Raised the valleys to the plain.
Be all the glory to Thy name divine!
The swords were ours; the arm, O Lord, was Thine.
Therefore to Thee, beneath whose footstool wait
The powers which erring man calls Chance and Fate,
   To Thee who hast laid low
   The pride of Europe's foe,
And taught Byzantium's sullen lords to fear,
   I pour my spirit out
   In a triumphant shout,
And call all ages and all lands to hear.
  Thou who evermore endurest,
  Loftiest, mightiest, wisest, purest,
  Thou whose will destroys or saves,
  Dread of tyrants, hope of slaves,
  The wreath of glory is from Thee,
  And the red sword of victory.

There where exulting Danube's flood
Runs stained with Islam's noblest blood
  From that tremendous field,
There where in mosque the tyrants met,
And from the crier's minaret
  Unholy summons pealed,
Pure shrines and temples now shall be

Decked for a worship worthy Thee.
To Thee thy whole creation pays
With mystic sympathy its praise,
    The air, the earth, the seas:
The day shines forth with livelier beam;
There is a smile upon the stream,
    An anthem on the breeze.
Glory, they cry, to Him whose might
Hath turned the barbarous foe to flight,
Whose arm protects with power divine
The city of his favoured line.
The caves, the woods, the rocks, repeat the sound;
The everlasting hills roll the long echoes round.

But, if Thy rescued church may dare
Still to besiege Thy throne with prayer,
Sheathe not, we implore Thee, Lord,
Sheathe not Thy victorious sword.
Still Panonia pines away,
Vassal of a double sway:
Still Thy servants groan in chains,
Still the race which hates Thee reigns:
Part the living from the dead:
Join the members to the head:
Snatch Thine own sheep from yon fell monster's hold,
Let one kind shepherd rule one undivided fold.

He is the victor, only he
Who reaps the fruits of victory.
    We conquered once in vain,
When foamed the Ionian waves with gore,
And heaped Lepanto's stormy shore
    With wrecks and Moslem slain.
Yet wretched Cyprus never broke
The Syrian tyrant's iron yoke.
        Shall the twice vanquished foe
        Again repeat his blow?
Shall Europe's sword be hung to rust in peace?
        No—let the red-cross ranks
        Of the triumphant Franks
Bear swift deliverance to the shrines of Greece,
And in her inmost heart let Asia feel
The avenging plagues of Western fire and steel.

Oh God! for one short moment raise
The veil which hides those glorious days.
The flying foes I see Thee urge
Even to the river's headlong verge.

Close on their rear the loud uproar
Of fierce pursuit from Ister's shore
   Comes pealing on the wind;
The Rab's wild waters are before,
   The Christian sword behind.
Sons of perdition, speed your flight,
   No earthly spear is in the rest;
No earthly champion leads to fight
   The warriors of the West.
The Lord of Hosts asserts His old renown,
Scatters, and smites, and slays, and tramples down.
Fast, fast beyond what mortal tongue can say,
   Or mortal fancy dream,
He rushes on his prey:
   Till, with the terrors of the wondrous theme
Bewildered and appalled, I cease to sing,
And close my dazzled eye, and rest my wearied wing.

THE LAST BUCCANEER

(1839)

The winds were yelling, the waves were swelling,
   The sky was black and drear,
When the crew with eyes of flame brought the ship without a
      name
   Alongside the last Buccaneer.

" Whence flies your sloop full sail before so fierce a gale,
   When all others drive bare on the seas?
Say, come ye from the shore of the holy Salvador,
   Or the gulf of the rich Caribbees? "

" From a shore no search hath found, from a gulf no line can
      sound,
   Without rudder or needle we steer;

Above, below, our bark, dies the sea-fowl and the shark,
  As we fly by the last Buccaneer.

" To-night there shall be heard on the rocks of Cape de Verde,
  A loud crash, and a louder roar;
And to-morrow shall the deep, with a heavy moaning, sweep
  The corpses and wreck to the shore."

The stately ship of Clyde securely now may ride,
  In the breath of the citron shades;
And Severn's towering mast securely now flies fast,
  Through the sea of the balmy Trades.

From St. Jago's wealthy port, from Havannah's royal fort,
  The seaman goes forth without fear;
For since that stormy night not a mortal hath had sight
  Of the flag of the last Buccaneer.

EPITAPH ON A JACOBITE

(1845)

To my true king I offered free from stain
Courage and faith; vain faith, and courage vain.
For him, I threw lands, honours, wealth, away.
And one dear hope, that was more prized than they.
For him I languished in a foreign clime,
Grey-haired with sorrow in my manhood's prime;
Heard on Lavernia Scargill's whispering trees,
And pined by Arno for my lovelier Tees;
Beheld each night my home in fevered sleep,
Each morning started from the dream to weep;
Till God who saw me tried too sorely gave
The resting place I asked, an early grave,
Oh thou, whom chance leads to this nameless stone,
From that proud country which was once mine own,
By those cliffs I never more must see,
By that dear language which I spake like thee,
Forget all feuds, and shed one English tear
O'er English dust.   A broken heart lies here.

LINES WRITTEN IN AUGUST
(1847)

The day of tumult, strife, defeat, was o'er;
  Worn out with toil, and noise, and scorn, and spleen,
I slumbered, and in slumber saw once more,
  A room in an old mansion, long unseen.

That room, methought, was curtained from the light;
  Yet through the curtains shone the moon's cold ray
Full on a cradle, where, in linen white,
  Sleeping life's first soft sleep, an infant lay.

Pale flickered on the hearth the dying flame,
  And all was silent in that ancient hall,
Save when by fits on the low night-wind came
  The murmur of the distant waterfall.

And lo! the fairy queens who rule our birth
  Drew nigh to speak the new-born baby's doom:
With noiseless step, which left no trace on earth,
  From gloom they came, and vanished into gloom.

Not deigning on the boy a glance to cast
  Swept careless by the gorgeous Queen of Gain;
More scornful still, the Queen of Fashion passed,
  With mincing gait and sneer of cold disdain.

The Queen of Power tossed high her jewelled head,
  And o'er her shoulder threw a wrathful frown;
The Queen of Pleasure on the pillow shed
  Scarce one stray rose-leaf from her fragrant crown.

Still Fay in long procession followed Fay;
  And still the little couch remained unblest:
But, when those wayward sprites had passed away,
  Came One, the last, the mightiest, and the best.

Oh glorious lady, with the eyes of light
  And laurels clustering round thy lofty brow,
Who by the cradle's side didst watch that night,
  Warbling a sweet, strange music, who wast thou?

"Yes, darling; let them go;" so ran the strain:
  "Yes; let them go, gain, fashion, pleasure, power,

And all the busy elves to whose domain
  Belongs the nether sphere, the fleeting hour.

" Without one envious sigh, one anxious scheme,
  The nether sphere, the fleeting hour resign.
Mine is the world of thought, the world of dream,
  Mine all the past, and all the future mine.

" Fortune, that lays in sport the mighty low,
  Age, that to penance turns the joys of youth,
Shall leave untouched the gifts which I bestow,
  The sense of beauty and the thirst of truth.

" Of the fair brotherhood who share my grace,
  I, from thy natal day, pronounce thee free;
And, if for some I keep a nobler place,
  I keep for none a happier than for thee.

" There are who, while to vulgar eyes they seem
  Of all my bounties largely to partake,
Of me as of some rival's handmaid deem,
  And court me but for gain's, power's, fashion's sake.

" To such, though deep their lore, though wide their fame.
  Shall my great mysteries be all unknown:
But thou, through good and evil, praise and blame,
  Wilt not thou love me for myself alone?

" Yes; thou wilt love me with exceeding love;
  And I will tenfold all that love repay,
Still smiling, though the tender may reprove,
  Still faithful, though the trusted may betray.

" For aye mine emblem was, and aye shall be,
  The ever-during plant whose bough I wear,
Brightest and greenest then, when every tree
  That blossoms in the light of Time is bare.

" In the dark hour of shame, I deigned to stand
  Before the frowning peers at Bacon's side:
On a far shore I smoothed with tender hand,
  Through months of pain, the sleepless bed of Hyde:

" I brought the wise and brave of ancient days
  To cheer the cell where Raleigh pined alone:
I lighted Milton's darkness with the blaze
  Of the bright ranks that guard the eternal throne.

" And even so, my child, it is my pleasure
   That thou not then alone shouldst feel me nigh,
When, in domestic bliss and studious leisure,
   Thy weeks uncounted come, uncounted fly;

" Not then alone, when myriads, closely pressed
   Around thy car, the shout of triumph raise;
Nor when, in gilded drawing-rooms, thy breast
   Swells at the sweeter sound of woman's praise.

" No: when on restless night dawns cheerless morrow,
   When weary soul and wasting body pine,
Thine am I still, in danger, sickness, sorrow,
   In conflict, obloquy, want, exile, thine;

" Thine, where on mountain waves the snowbirds scream,
   Where more than Thule's winter barbs the breeze,
Where scarce, through lowering clouds, one sickly gleam
   Lights the drear May-day of Antarctic seas;

" Thine, when around thy litter's track all day
   White sandhills shall reflect the blinding glare;
Thine, when, through forests breathing death, thy way
   All night shall wind by many a tiger's lair;

" Thine most, when friends turn pale, when traitors fly,
   When, hard beset, thy spirit, justly proud,
For truth, peace, freedom, mercy, dares defy
   A sullen priesthood and a raving crowd.

" Amidst the din of all things fell and vile,
   Hate's yell, and envy's hiss, and folly's bray,
Remember me; and with an unforced smile
   See riches, baubles, flatterers, pass away.

" Yes: they will pass away; nor deem it strange:
   They come and go, as comes and goes the sea:
And let them come and go: thou, through all change,
   Fix thy firm gaze on virtue and on me."

COSIMO is an innovative publisher of books and publications that inspire, inform and engage readers worldwide. Our titles are drawn from a range of subjects including health, business, philosophy, history, science and sacred texts. We specialize in using print-on-demand technology (POD), making it possible to publish books for both general and specialized audiences and to keep books in print indefinitely. With POD technology new titles can reach their audiences faster and more efficiently than with traditional publishing.

> ➢ **Permanent Availability:** Our books & publications never go out-of-print.

> ➢ **Global Availability:** Our books are always available online at popular retailers and can be ordered from your favorite local bookstore.

COSIMO CLASSICS brings to life unique, rare, out-of-print classics representing subjects as diverse as *Alternative Health, Business and Economics, Eastern Philosophy, Personal Growth, Mythology, Philosophy, Sacred Texts, Science, Spirituality* and much more!

COSIMO-on-DEMAND publishes your books, publications and reports. If you are an Author, part of an Organization, or a Benefactor with a publishing project and would like to bring books back into print, publish new books fast and effectively, would like your publications, books, training guides, and conference reports to be made available to your members and wider audiences around the world, we can assist you with your publishing needs.

Visit our website at www.cosimobooks.com to learn more about Cosimo, browse our catalog, take part in surveys or campaigns, and sign-up for our newsletter.

And if you wish please drop us a line at info@cosimobooks.com. We look forward to hearing from you.